MUIRHEAD LIBRARY OF PHILOSOPHY

An admirable statement of the aims of the Library of Philosophy was provided by the first editor, the late Professor J. H. Muirhead, in his description of the original programme printed in Erdmann's *History of Philosophy* under the date 1890. This was slightly modified in subsequent volumes to take the form of the following statement:

'The Library of Philosophy was designed as a contribution to the History of Modern Philosophy under the heads: first of different Schools of Thought — Sensationalist, Realist, Idealist, Intuitivist; secondly of different Subjects—Psychology, Ethics, Aesthetics, Political Philosophy, Theology. While much had been done in England in tracing the course of evolution in nature, history, economics, morals and religion, little had been done in tracing the development of thought on these subjects. Yet "the evolution of opinion is part of the whole evolution".

By the co-operation of different writers in carrying out this plan it was hoped that a thoroughness and completeness of treatment, otherwise unattainable, might be secured. It was believed also that from writers mainly British and American fuller consideration of English Philosophy than it had hitherto received might be looked for. In the earlier series of books containing, among others, Bosanquet's *History of Aesthetic*, Pfleiderer's *Rational Theology since Kant*, Albee's *History of English Utilitarianism*, Bonar's *Philosophy and Political Economy*, Brett's *History of Psychology*, Ritchie's *Natural Rights*, these objects were to a large extent effected.

In the meantime original work of a high order was being produced both in England and America by such writers as Bradley, Stout, Bertrand Russell, Baldwin, Urban, Montague and others, and a new interest in foreign works, German, French and Italian, which had either become classical or were attracting public attention, had developed. The scope of the Library thus became extended into something more international, and it is entering on the fifth decade of its existence in the hope that it may contribute to that mutual understanding between countries which is so pressing a need of the present time.'

The need which Professor Muirhead stressed is no less pressing today, and few will deny that philosophy has much to do with enabling us to meet it, although no one, least of all Muirhead himself, would regard that as the sole, or even the main, object of philosophy. As Professor Muirhead continues to lend the distinction of his name to the Library of Philosophy it seemed not inappropriate to allow him to recall us to these aims in his own words. The emphasis on the history of thought also seemed to me very timely; and the number of important works promised for the Library in the near future augur well for the continued fulfilment, in this and in other ways, of the expectations of the original editor.   H. D. LEWIS

MUIRHEAD LIBRARY OF PHILOSOPHY

General Editor: H. D. Lewis
Professor of History and Philosophy of Religion in the University of London

Action by SIR MALCOLM KNOX

The Analysis of Mind by BERTRAND RUSSELL

Clarity is Not Enough by H. D. LEWIS

Coleridge as Philosopher by J. H. MUIRHEAD

The Commonplace Book of G. E. Moore edited by C. LEWY

Contemporary American Philosophy edited by G. P. ADAMS and W. P. MONTAGUE

Contemporary British Philosophy First and second series edited by J. H. MUIRHEAD

Contemporary British Philosophy third series edited by H. D. LEWIS

Contemporary Indian Philosophy edited by RADHAKRISHNAN and J. H. MUIRHEAD 2nd edition

The Discipline of the Cave by J. N. FINDLAY

Doctrine and Argument in Indian Philosophy by NINIAN SMART

Essays in Analysis by ALICE AMBROSE

Ethics by NICOLAI HARTMANN translated by STANTON COIT 3 vols

The Foundations of Metaphysics in Science by ERROL E. HARRIS

Freedom and History by H. D. LEWIS

The Good Will: A Study in the Coherence of Theory Goodness by H. J. PATON

Hegel: A Re-Examination by J. N. FINDLAY

Hegel's Science of Logic translated by W. H. JOHNSTON and L. G. STRUTHERS 2 vols

History of Æsthetic by B. BOSANQUET 2nd edition

History of English Utilitarianism by E. ALBEE

History of Psychology by G. S. BRETT edited by R. S. PETERS abridged one-volume edition 2nd edition

Human Knowledge by BERTRAND RUSSELL

A Hundred Years of British Philosophy by RUDOLF METZ translated by J. H. HARVEY, T. E. JESSOP, HENRY STURT

Ideas: A General Introduction to Pure Phenomenology by EDMUND HUSSERL translated by W. R. BOYCE GIBSON

Identity and Reality by EMILE MEYERSON

Imagination by E. J. FURLONG

Indian Philosophy by RADHAKRISHNAN 2 vols revised 2nd edition

MUIRHEAD LIBRARY OF PHILOSOPHY

Introduction to Mathematical Philosophy by BERTRAND RUSSELL 2nd edition

Kant's First Critique by H. W. CASSIRER

Kant's Metaphysic of Experience by H. J. PATON

Know Thyself by BERNADINO VARISCO translated by GUGLIELMO SALVADORI

Language and Reality by WILBUR MARSHALL URBAN

Lectures on Philosophy by G. E. MOORE edited by C. LEWY

Matter and Memory by HENRI BERGSON translated by N. M. PAUL and W. S. PALMER

Memory by BRIAN SMITH

The Modern Predicament by H. J. PATON

Natural Rights by D. G. RITCHIE 3rd edition

Nature, Mind and Modern Science by ERROL E. HARRIS

The Nature of Thought by BRAND BLANSHARD

Non-Linguistic Philosophy by A. C. EWING

On Selfhood and Godhood by C. A. CAMPBELL

Our Experience of God by H. D. LEWIS

Perception and our Knowledge of the External World by DON LOCKE

The Phenomenology of Mind by G. W. F. HEGEL translated by SIR JAMES BAILLIE revised 2nd edition

Philosophical Papers by G. E. MOORE

Philosophy and Illusion by MORRIS LAZEROWITZ

Philosophy and Political Economy by JAMES BONAR

Philosophy and Religion by AXEL HÄGERSTRÖM

Philosophy in America by MAX BLACK

Philosophy of Space and Time by MICHAEL WHITEMAN

Philosophy of Whitehead by W. MAYS

The Platonic Tradition in Anglo-Saxon Philosophy by JOHN H. MUIRHEAD

The Principal Upanishads by RADHAKRISHNAN

The Problems of Perception by R. J. HIRST

Reason and Goodness by BRAND BLANSHARD

The Relevance of Whitehead by IVOR LECLERC

The Science of Logic by G. W. F. HEGEL

Some Main Problems of Philosophy by G. E. MOORE

Studies in the Metaphysics of Bradley by SUSHIL KUMAR SAXENA

The Theological Frontier of Ethics by W. G. MACLAGAN

Time and Free Will by HENRI BERGSON translated by F. G. POGSON

The Transcendence of the Cave by J. N. FINDLAY

Values and Intentions by J. N. FINDLAY

The Ways of Knowing: or The Methods of Philosophy by W. P. MONTAGUE

The Muirhead Library of Philosophy
EDITED BY H. D. LEWIS

NATURE, MIND AND MODERN SCIENCE

NATURE, MIND AND MODERN SCIENCE

BY

ERROL E. HARRIS

Professor of Philosophy in the
University of the Witwatersrand

'. . . *it is ambition enough to be employed as an*
under-labourer in clearing the ground a little,
and removing some of the rubbish that lies in the
way to knowledge.'

JOHN LOCKE

LONDON : GEORGE ALLEN & UNWIN LTD
NEW YORK: HUMANITIES PRESS INC

FIRST PUBLISHED IN 1954
SECOND IMPRESSION 1968

BRITISH SBN 04 109002 0

PRINTED IN GREAT BRITAIN
BY PHOTOLITHOGRAPHY
UNWIN BROTHERS LIMITED
WOKING AND LONDON

PREFACE

WHEN philosophical speculation has taken a wrong turning and followed an old and long-abandoned track, which has led it into a *cul-de-sac*, the only proper course is for us to retrace our steps and return to the high road, there to take our bearings again and to re-determine the direction of progress for the future. Believing this to be the present situation, I have attempted to put modern developments in their historical perspective and assess their value accordingly. This has required a good deal of recapitulation of what, to the professional philosopher, are familiar arguments, but I wish my readers and critics to ask themselves not whether the arguments are familiar but whether they are sound, and, if they are, whether theories which conflict with them can justifiably be maintained. If they are not sound, their error should be properly exposed, and I know no work in which this has been done. On the contrary, too many contemporary philosophers are content to ignore sound arguments because they are familiar and to indulge in new analyses which are faulty and misleading and against which the old arguments should have warned them. Meanwhile a generation of students is growing up whose attention is devoted only to the new, unmindful of its defects, to whom the old is by no means familiar and who therefore allow it to go unheeded. This, I think, is sufficient reason for presenting to the public once again theories and criticisms which are not new, though whenever I have been able and thought it necessary I have tried to throw new light upon them. My main purpose, however, has been to make them throw light upon contemporary views which seem to have gained too easily widespread approbation.

There will no doubt be those who wish to discredit the criticisms offered in Chapters I and XVI on the ground that the views criticized have been abandoned and superseded. But the question is whether such new doctrines as may have been suggested have corrected the faults of their predecessors so as to render the criticism inapplicable. Moreover, the abandonment of old theories is, these days, often more professed than real, and seldom amounts to any genuine recantation.

That there are many gaps in the account which I have given of my subject I am only too well aware, and at least one friend has urged me to deal at length with further topics (*e.g.* the nature of value, the finite self, and so forth), but I feel that the book is already too long and have tolerated defect in preference to excess, hoping that I may make good the omissions in some later work.

But a preface is not so much the place for apologia as for acknowledgement. My thanks are especially due to Mr. G. R. G. Mure, who has encouraged me from the first and has assisted me throughout the long process of producing the book with suggestion and criticism, to Professor T. M. Knox, who read an earlier draft and offered many extremely useful and penetrating criticisms, and to Professor H. D. Lewis, who has drawn my attention to weaknesses which might otherwise have gone unnoticed and unremedied. I wish to record my gratitude to Rhodes University, South Africa, where, as le May Research Fellow, I was given the opportunity to carry out much of the work of which this book is the fruit, and to Professor A. J. Barratt for his friendly assistance. Dr. Arthur Bleksley and Dr. B. Balinsky have assisted me by reading the draft of Chapter XVII and drawing my attention to important contemporary scientific developments. I am grateful, further, to the editors of *The Philosophical Quarterly* and *Dialectica* for permission to republish the portions of Chapter I, Chapter VII and Chapter XVII which have previously appeared in their journals, to Messrs. Routledge & Kegan Paul Ltd. for permission to quote the passage on p. 301 from Professor Broad's *Scientific Thought*, and to Mrs. Helen Bosanquet for permission to quote the passage from Bernard Bosanquet's *Meeting of Extremes in Contemporary Philosophy* which appears on pp. 268-70. I am much indebted to Professor H. D. Lewis and to Mr. D. A. Rees for reading the proofs and particularly to Mr. Rees for the Index. Finally, I have to thank the Sir Halley Stewart Trustees for their generosity which has helped to make the publication of this book possible.

E. E. H.

HIGH WRAY
December 1952

CONTENTS

PAGE

PREFACE   xi

PART ONE: METHOD AND PLAN OF
         PROCEDURE

CHAP.

I. ARE THERE ETERNAL PROBLEMS IN PHILOSOPHY?   3
   I. The Denial of Eternal Problems   3
   II. Positivist Theories   6
   III. Historicism   29

II. THE PROBLEM OF KNOWLEDGE   43
   I. The Mind in the World and the World in the Mind   43
   II. Allied Problems   51
   III. Procedure to be Adopted   55

PART TWO: THE PROBLEM IN GREEK
         PHILOSOPHY

III. THE PROBLEM IN EMBRYO   63
   I. Matter, Life and Mind   63
   II. Influences determining the Greek Conception of
       the Soul   68
   III. Physical Philosophers   69
   IV. Pythagoras and the Pythagoreans   73
   V. The One   75
   VI. The Many   78
   VII. Νοῦς   82
   VIII. The Development of Pre-Socratic Thought   84

IV. THE PROBLEM EMERGENT   85
   I. The Sophists   85
   II. Socrates   86
   III. Plato   87

V. THE GREEK SOLUTION   101
   I. Body and Soul as Matter and Form   101
   II. Immanence and Transcendence   108
   III. Summary   111

PART THREE: RENAISSANCE CONCEPTIONS OF NATURE AND MIND

CHAP.   PAGE

VI. THE PROBLEM EXPLICIT   117

    I. Presuppositions of 17th-Century Science   117
    II. The Cartesian Dichotomy   120
    III. Locke's Empiricism   125

VII. SUBJECTIVE IDEALISM   140

    I. Berkeley's Abolition of the External World   140
    II. Modern Criticisms of Berkeley   142
    III. Shortcomings of Berkeley's Theory   160

VIII. THE COLLAPSE OF EMPIRICISM   164

    I. The 'Awful Warning'   164
    II. Hume's Inheritance from Locke and Berkeley   165
    III. Analysis or Denial?   168
    IV. The Eclipse of Reason   171
    V. Our Knowledge of an External World   174
    VI. The Elimination of the Mind   179
    VII. The Nemesis of Empiricism   180
    VIII. Reasons for the Collapse of Empiricism   181

IX. TRANSITION TO THE MODERN VIEW OF MIND   187

    I. Kant's Copernican Revolution   187
    II. False Disjunctions   189
    III. The Coherence Theory of Truth   197
    IV. Mind and Nature   198

PART FOUR: THE MODERN CONCEPTION OF NATURE AND MIND

X. THE CONCEPT OF EVOLUTION   203

Section A: Precursors of the Modern Outlook

XI. SPINOZA AND LEIBNIZ   208

    Spinoza:
    I. 17th-Century Characteristics   208
    II. Modern Characteristics   209
    III. The Virus of Renaissance Thought   217

CONTENTS

CHAP.

Leibniz: PAGE

IV. Opposition to Renaissance Presuppositions   218
V. The Theory of Monads   219
VI. Evolutionism in Leibniz' Theory   223
VII. Finite and Infinite   225

XII. HEGEL   228
I. Hegel's Modernity   228
II. Hegel's Theory of the Understanding   229
III. The Concrete Universal   233
IV. Dialectic   235
V. The Philosophy of Nature   241
VI. The Philosophy of Mind   246
VII. Conclusion   254

Section B: The Persistence of the Renaissance View

XIII. 'IDEALISM' AND 'REALISM'   256
I. The Idealism of F. H. Bradley   256
II. Reinterpretation of Bradley's Theory   260
III. Reaction against Idealism   264
IV. The 'Refutation' of Idealism   265
V. History Repeats Itself   272

XIV. MODERN EMPIRICISM: THE FIRST PHASE (RUSSELL)   274
I. The Analysis of Mind into Particulars   274
II. Facts and Propositions   278
III. Facts and Beliefs   281
IV. Perspectives   283
V. Causal Theory of Perception   286
VI. Failure of the Perspective Hypothesis   289
VII. Assessment of Russell's Theory   293
VIII. Comparison with Locke   295

XV. MODERN EMPIRICISM: THE SECOND PHASE
    (SENSE-DATA THEORIES)   298
I. Moore, Broad and Price   298
II. Perception   302
III. Realistic Hankerings   308
IV. Defects of the Theory   312
V. Positive Contribution   317

CHAP.

XVI. MODERN EMPIRICISM: THE THIRD PHASE
(LOGICAL POSITIVISM)   PAGE 319
  I. The Bourne of Empiricism   319
  II. Underlying Metaphysic   322
  III. The Verification Principle   328
  IV. Pseudo-Sciences?   343

Section C: Contemporary Science and Philosophy

XVII. MODERN SCIENCE   352
  I. Scientific Verification   352
  II. Biological Conceptions   355
  III. The Revolution in Physics   375

XVIII. PHILOSOPHIES OF EVOLUTION   393
  I. Bergson   393
  II. The Theory of Emergence   399
  III. Emergent Mind   405
  IV. Alexander's Theory of Knowledge   410

XIX. THE PHILOSOPHY OF ORGANISM   416
  I. Whitehead's Vacillation   416
  II. Creativity or Process   418
  III. The 'Mental Pole'   422
  IV. Eternal Objects   425
  V. The Phases of Concrescence   430
  VI. The Solution of Problems   432
  VII. Dualisms and their Resolution   436

XX. THE ROAD AHEAD   439
  I. Evolution   439
  II. The Philosophical Task   442
  III. The Place of the Human Mind   447
  IV. Science, Philosophy and Religion   450

INDEX   453

Part One

METHOD AND PLAN OF
PROCEDURE

Chapter I

ARE THERE ETERNAL PROBLEMS
IN PHILOSOPHY?[1]

I. THE DENIAL OF ETERNAL PROBLEMS

1. QUESTIONS concerning the ultimate nature of the real, the existence
of God and His relation to the world, the nature of truth, of goodness
and of beauty, and the spirit and destiny of man—all such questions, in
fact, as have traditionally been called the eternal problems of philosophy
—have, in recent years, been repudiated as pseudo-problems. So loudly
and triumphantly proclaimed have been the doctrines which assign
these eternal problems to the dustbin, that no writer can seriously contemplate discussing anything even apparently related to them before he
has examined the arguments which claim finally to sweep them out of
existence. Accordingly, as the central theme of the present work is to be
a philosophical problem, of the persistence of which the very form and
character of the work give evidence, before even a beginning can be
made, the question must be raised whether there are eternal problems,
and the reasons which have been given for denying their existence must
be examined.

The answer to the question is closely bound up with our notion of
truth. Many modern philosophers scout the idea of an eternal truth as
much as that of eternal problems, though they do not deny that certain
propositions (notably those of mathematics) are tenseless. And if truth
is not eternal, we need not expect the questions to which the truth is the
answer to be eternal either. But if there is a body of eternal truth, the
problems which beset the philosopher in his search for it will always
be relevant to the same objective and there will be a sense in which
they may be called eternal also. But in calling them so we may mean
one of two things: a problem may be eternally insoluble and so, like
the poor, always with us; or it may be logically related to an eternal
truth (its solution), so that even when solved it would still be characteristic of a necessary phase in the process of thought required for the
attainment of that truth. In the second meaning, even a mathematical
problem, like that of the Pythagoreans about the incommensurability
of the diagonal, would be eternal in so far as it must always be faced

---

[1] Part of this chapter has appeared under the title, 'Collingwood on Eternal
Problems', in the *Philosophical Quarterly*, I, no. 3 (April 1951).

and surmounted by the student of mathematics at some stage in his progress. But if philosophical problems are relative to ultimate truths, they will be eternal in both these senses, for knowledge of the ultimate implies omniscience, short of which the problem must remain unsolved; yet an ideal solution may be presumed and some progress may be made towards it even by finite minds.

There are two schools of thought voicing opinions that bear upon this matter. First there are those who reject eternal problems primarily for epistemological reasons. They might admit that certain questions have been persistently raised but would contend that they give expression to no genuine problem. The answers which from time to time have been offered, they maintain, are meaningless and the problems themselves do not permit of solution. But this does not give us the right to call them eternal in the sense that they remain eternally unsolved for they are not considered to be problems, properly speaking, at all, but are said to arise only as the result of the misuse of language. This view I propose for convenience to call 'positivist', although some of its adherents would reject the designation, except in a very restricted sense, as committing them to too much. It will not, however, mislead the reader or misrepresent the doctrine it is intended to indicate so long as it is used only provisionally as a label to distinguish this kind of objection to eternal problems from the other kind, which I intend to call 'historical'.

Those who deny the eternity of philosophical problems on historical grounds, hold that what appears in the same verbal form and is discussed in comparable terms in different historical periods is not always—in fact is never—exactly the same question, but in each period is a new one which has arisen under new conditions. The view is that philosophical problems and the theories which profess to give their solutions are always relative to the times and can be fairly judged only in their historical context. 'It may be well to inquire', writes Basil Willey,[1] 'not with Pilate "What is Truth?" but what was *felt to be* "truth" and "explanation" [in the period under review].' Explanation, he says, cannot be defined absolutely, 'one can only say that it is a statement which satisfies the demands of a particular time and place'.[2] Similarly, T. D. Weldon writes that 'to suppose that there is a "problem of causality" or "problem of the interrelation of mind and body" which presents itself unaltered to succeeding generations of human beings is mere moonshine. The verbal form of the question

---

[1] *Seventeenth-Century Background* (London, 1934), p. 2.
[2] *Ibid.* p. 3.

may be identical but that is all.'[1] But the most formidable and important proponent of this view is R. G. Collingwood, who writes in his autobiography: 'Was it really true, I asked myself, that the problems of philosophy were, even in the loosest sense of that word, eternal? Was it really true that different philosophies were different attempts to answer the same questions? I soon discovered that it was not true; it was merely a vulgar error, consequent on a kind of historical myopia which, deceived by superficial resemblances, failed to detect profound differences.'[2]

It should follow from all this that the historical treatment of a philosophical problem is valueless. For if the problem is not the same, except in verbal form, in the various periods when it is discussed, and if a problem of contemporary interest which is or may be similarly stated is nevertheless a different question, the answers proposed in the past can give no guidance and can throw no light upon the solution demanded in the present. Yet, oddly enough, the writers who are most emphatic about the impermanence of problems are usually those who insist most strongly upon historical treatment. Those I have quoted are examples of this curiously contradictory attitude, and in the philosophy of Collingwood it is so important that I shall discuss it at some length. For, though he is emphatic about the non-existence of eternal problems, he is at the same time tirelessly insistent that philosophy is an historical study and maintains that this very discovery of perpetual change in philosophical problems makes the history of philosophy philosophically important.[3]

The question whether there are eternal problems in philosophy is, therefore, an epistemological question even when it arises from historical considerations; for if succeeding generations of philosophers are called upon to meet the same problems, or problems which have persisted in some recognizable and identifiable form from the past, the study of the work of their predecessors will be of primary importance in their attempts both to understand and to answer the questions with which they are faced. But if there are no such problems, the nature and the method of philosophy will be different. It will be concerned with matters of only immediate interest and the philosopher will be like Professor Ayer's journeyman [4] working at rather special questions in a field of more or less exact science, where a problem once solved is

---

[1] *Introduction to Kant's Critique of Pure Reason* (Oxford, 1945), p. 2.
[2] *Autobiography* (Penguin Books, 1944), p. 44; cf. *Essay on Metaphysics* (Oxford, 1940), p. 72. [3] *Vide Autobiography*, p. 54, and *Metaphysics*, chs. vi and vii.
[4] *Vide* 'The Claims of Philosophy' in *Polemic*, No. 7 (March 1947).

finally disposed of. Or alternatively, philosophy will be altogether impossible and one can but persuade the would-be philosopher that the questions he wishes to raise are not really questions at all. The denial of eternal problems, therefore, raises the whole issue of philosophical method and the discussion of it may not be neglected.

II. POSITIVIST THEORIES

2. *Wittgensteinists*. The attitude of the modern positivists derives from the doctrine, stated in its most radical form by Wittgenstein, that there is no philosophical science or theory whatsoever. There are no eternal problems, they would say, because there are no philosophical problems at all. Those questions which are called philosophical have no sense, for philosophy is not a theory but an activity.[1] It is an activity of elucidation, the purpose of which is not to state propositions but to clarify them.[2]

Wittgenstein tells us (i) that the world consists of facts, (ii) that a fact is a combination of 'things' or 'objects', (iii) that things constitute the substance of the world and (iv) that if the world had no substance it would be impossible to say whether a proposition had sense[3] (for that would depend upon the truth—and so, presumably, upon the sense—of another proposition). A proposition he defines as a thought expressed in sensible form, and its perceptible sign is a projection of the thought, which, in turn, is a picture of the fact or facts which it represents. The sense of the proposition, therefore, is inseparably dependent upon the fact of which the thought is the picture, and the form of the proposition is said to be its structure, which it has in common with the fact. But while it depicts or expresses the fact which gives it sense, it cannot express its form—*that* it simply 'shows forth'. Accordingly, no proposition can be about itself and every proposition which has sense must be about a fact. Consequently, all sensible propositions are about facts and if they are true their sense, what they represent, agrees with reality. The totality of all true propositions, it is maintained, constitutes the complete body of natural science[4] and beyond this there are no true propositions. But if all the problems of science were to be solved the philosopher would still maintain that his eternal problems—the problems of life and

---

[1] Cf. Wittgenstein, *Tractatus Logico-Philosophicus*, 4·112.   [2] *Ibid.*

[3] Cf. *ibid.* 2·0211. I shall not venture an opinion as to the exact meaning of this section of the *Tractatus*, but it does seem to imply an inseparable connection between 'fact' and 'sense'.

[4] Cf. *ibid.* 4·11.

existence[1]—had been left untouched. Yet if this is so, the answers to such 'eternal' problems are non-existent, for all true propositions would already have been enunciated in the sciences, and where no possible answer exists, no possible question can be raised.[2] The question to which there is no answer is no question. Consequently, the sole task of the philosopher is to convince would-be philosophers that philosophical questions are not questions, and that what claim to be philosophical propositions are meaningless[3]—'to prevent people', as Professor Ayer has succinctly expressed it, 'from committing an intellectual nuisance'.

The cogency of this argument depends upon the assertion that the complete body of natural science exhausts the totality of true propositions. And that assertion is either a dogma lacking justification and so without claim to our credence, or it can be supported. Any such support must obviously appeal to some conceptions of the world, of truth and of the relation between scientific knowledge and its object; and this, indeed, is the sort of theory by which Wittgenstein himself supports it.[4] In short, the basis of the assertion is a theory expressed in propositions that do not fall within the domain of science, a theory which would normally be called philosophical. But if there are no true propositions which do not belong to the natural sciences, this philosophical theory must be either false or senseless and so must any proposition that follows from it; and the proposition that science contains all the true and sensible statements which can be made follows from it and so must itself be either senseless or false. It is, in fact, a metaphysical proposition and must stand or fall with metaphysics. On the other hand, if the philosophical doctrine is true, it is in standing contradiction to the conclusion derived from it. The theory and the conclusion destroy each other, for if either is true the other cannot stand and if either is false the other cannot be true.

Wittgenstein, himself, seems to be aware of this, though not of the consequences to which it ought to lead him, for he admits that his propositions are senseless and exhorts us to throw away the ladder upon which we have climbed.[5] An extraordinary metaphor! Upon what ladder have we climbed? One that has never existed? One that is pure illusion? Is this not to exhort Macbeth to use the dagger which he sees before him? If the propositions of the *Tractatus* are senseless, they provide no ladder upon which to climb. But if they are other than senseless, and if we can base arguments upon them, we must reject

---

[1] Cf. *ibid.* 6·52.   [2] Cf. *ibid.* 6·5.   [3] Cf. *ibid.* 6·54.
[4] *Vide Tractatus*, I, I·I et seq., 2·021, 2·023, 2·1 et seq.   [5] *Op. cit.* 6·54.

7

them because they lead to conclusions which contradict their own premises.

'Of what one cannot speak one must be silent', but the repudiation of philosophy is not silence, nor can it be passed by in silence. Consequently we *must* speak; we must examine theories like that which Wittgenstein puts before us and which lead to such disastrous conclusions; we must, in other words, investigate the nature of reality and truth and the relation of knowledge to its objects. The study of these 'eternal' problems, the existence of which the positivist denies, is forced upon us by his very claim to have dispensed with them.

After the publication of the *Tractatus*, as a result of discussions with members of the Vienna Circle and others, Wittgenstein somewhat modified his opinions. But his later views have not yet [1] been published, and it would be dangerous to attempt to comment upon what is in effect an esoteric doctrine. The effect of the change, so far as I can gather, is to admit the possibility of sensible philosophical propositions but not in the same 'language' as that of common sense or empirical science. Philosophy is possible only in a 'meta-language'. This, however, either means that, *qua* reflection upon science and common sense, metaphysics is possible and legitimate after all, in which case the metaphysics of the *Tractatus* may be judged on its merits, and as it issues in a conclusion which contradicts its premises it must then be rejected. Or else it means that all philosophical propositions are purely linguistic, a view that is derived from the metaphysical doctrine of the *Tractatus*. For if ordinary propositions are about facts, the only other subject-matter of discourse can be the signs and symbols by means of which the form of the facts is 'shown forth'. Such discourse would be legitimate for the philosopher and is conducted in a meta-language. But the metaphysical doctrine of the *Tractatus* is not expressed in purely linguistic propositions and it is therefore incompatible with this conclusion derived from it. The introduction of meta-languages, therefore, in no way saves the situation.

3. Small wonder then that adherents of this doctrine, when they seek to put into practice Wittgenstein's advice, find apparent success only when they avoid the issues of real philosophical importance. 'The correct method of philosophy', they have been told, 'would be this . . . whenever someone else wished to say anything metaphysical, to demonstrate to him that he had given no meaning to certain signs in his propositions.' The Cambridge Wittgensteinists, accordingly, set them-

---

[1] At the time of going to press.

selves to remove 'philosophical puzzlement' in others. If there are no problems, they ought not to be felt as problems, and if we feel puzzled by them our doubt and wonder must be abnormal, though (as Mr. John Wisdom constantly avers) they may also be illuminating. What is illuminated (if Mr. Wisdom is to be believed) is no more than certain features of linguistic usage, and as such illumination neither reveals nor solves any 'eternal' problems, it amounts as much to a denial of their existence as does the allegation of abnormality. However this may be, philosophical doubt is regarded by Wittgensteinists as abnormal and they seek to cure it by a so-called therapeutic method which has been likened to that of the psycho-analyst.[1] The assumption is that the philosopher wants to be 'cured' of his wonder. It does not occur to the therapists that philosophy might be, like Orlando's love, something of which we 'would not be cured'.

The procedure is to attempt, with the help of a profusion of examples and analogies, to describe to the patient, or better, get him to describe for himself, the kind of question he is really asking. The description is designed to show that the questions really concern linguistic usage—the meaning of the signs in our propositions—and that once we have set these clearly in their place upon the language map[2] the wonder will evaporate.

But the presupposition of this method, however different the technique, is still the doctrine of the *Tractatus*, the falsity of which infects the practice of the therapist. First, the distinction alleged between philosophical doubt and the common doubt of the scientist or the unphilosophical layman, has no scientific basis, nor are the reasons sound for which the former is regarded as abnormal. Secondly, as a result of this, the words 'doubt', 'puzzlement' and the like are used loosely and with constantly shifting meanings which serve only to obscure the issue. And, thirdly, the cases 'treated' and the examples and analogies used are irrelevant, for they are not concerned with the so-called 'eternal' problems of philosophy but are, in the main, the products of confused and unphilosophical thinking.

I shall try to support these contentions by reference mainly to the writings of Mr. John Wisdom, who is the most brilliant and outstanding exponent of the method. Philosophical doubt, he maintains, is queer, unnatural and peculiar because of its exceptional attitude to

[1] I am told that both the analogy and the doctrine behind it have now been given up, but as the changes of opinion occurring among the Wittgensteinists are seldom published, it is difficult to keep track of them.

[2] *Vide* John Wisdom, 'Other Minds' (I), *Mind*, XLIX, 196, p. 371 n., and cf. 'Philosophical Perplexity', *Arist. Soc. Proc.*, 1936-7, p. 87.

evidence.[1] It is not caused by lack of evidence, and it cannot be removed by the production of more. Of this peculiar attitude Wisdom distinguishes three main types, the sources of 'chronic', incurable doubt:[2]

(1) where there is an infinity of criteria for judging that S is P—all can never be present, yet no number short of infinity can confidently be said to be enough;

(2) where there is a conflict of criteria—*e.g.* 'Can you play chess without a queen?' 'Is a tomato a fruit or a vegetable?' and so on;

(3) where one hesitates to jump from the criteria (even the infinite all) to the conclusion.

In none of these cases can the doubt be removed by the discovery of new evidence—not in the first case, because however much evidence there is, it is never enough; not in the second, because however much there is, it does not help us to choose our criterion; and not in the third case, because however much there is, we still hesitate to conclude.

Mr. Wisdom resolves these doubts into requests[3]

(1) for a decision as to the use of the word 'know'—the question takes the form: How do we *know* that S is P? or, How much evidence do we need before we *know* that S is P?;

(2) for a decision as to the use of S, if we doubt whether a tomato is a vegetable or that we can play chess without a queen, we require a decision as to the use of 'tomato' and 'chess';

(3) for a decision as to the use of the phrase 'mean the same', does it *mean the same* to say that $S_1, S_2, S_3 \ldots S_\infty$ as to say that Σ?

(a) I shall begin with the matter of evidence. A philosophical problem is thought to be queer and peculiar because the answer cannot be provided by the discovery of fresh evidence.[4] What sort of evidence,

---

[1] Cf. 'Metaphysics and Verification', *Mind*, XLVII, 188, pp. 457 ff. and 'Other Minds' (I), *Mind*, XLIX, 196, p. 369 n.

[2] *Vide* 'Other Minds' (I), *Mind*, XLIX, 196, p. 370 n.

[3] *Ibid.* p. 372 n.

[4] Unless I misunderstand him, Wisdom seems to be saying this slightly differently when he says (in 'Philosophy, Anxiety and Novelty', *Mind*, LIII, 210, p. 171): 'It isn't that the philosopher doesn't know how one who makes, *e.g.* a mathematical statement, is going to proceed, so when he asks for a description of mathematicians he is not asking a question of fact'.

Cf. also Norman Malcolm, 'The Nature of Entailment', *Mind*, XLIX, 195, p. 334: 'Their disagreement is not due, therefore, to the fact that one has certain knowledge which the other does not have'.

And Morris Lazerowitz, 'The Existence of Universals', *Mind*, LV, 217, p. 9: 'But what would be a test for ascertaining whether a person has achieved acquaintance

then, is effective in answering non-philosophical questions? There can be little doubt that Wisdom and others who adopt the same tactics admit only the evidence of the senses. A few quotations will make this clear:

(i) 'Perhaps I am a bit puzzled at first about the "invisible". Why does he say "there's a leprechaun in my watch" if there is no such thing to be seen or felt when it is opened? However, as soon as he explains that his watch sings songs, etc., then I quite understand....'[1]

(ii) '... We can never know of the presence of an invisible current in a wire in the way we can know of the presence of petrol in a pipe.'[2]

(iii) 'Can't we come to see that though "He has a picture in his head" differs in meaning from "He acts just as if he had a picture in his head" this difference is so different from the difference between "He has a stone in his bladder" and "He acts as though he has a stone in his bladder", that though the latter difference prevents knowledge of the symptoms giving knowledge of the cause the former difference does not'[3] (presumably because in the latter case we need further *sensible* evidence and in the former case no more is possible).

Now, to what extent is sense-perception acceptable evidence and what is it that must be perceived in order to provide the evidence? Taking a simple everyday example, how does one know whether or not one has a credit at the bank? Is it possible to go and look? If so what does one see?—not the actual money. A book-entry?—but how does that provide assurance? A note from the manager?—but is that not a kind of hearsay evidence? Why are we willing to take his word? Is it not that we presume a system of banking and book-keeping and an organization in which certain persons play definite parts, and on the basis of that system and that organization we *infer* from certain observations to the fact of which we want to be assured? The evidence is evidence only on the presumption of the system and what we actually perceive is only a small, and by no means the most important,

with a universal? ... Philosophers do not explicitly tell us. ... Their omission ... is important because, by putting them in a position comparable with that of an explorer who claims to have discovered a strange, new land but has brought back nothing which could serve as evidence for his claim, some philosophers get the idea that the theory of universals is false while others think it is unverifiable and therefore non-sensical.'

[1] 'Other Minds' (I), p. 382.   [2] *Ibid.* p. 398.

[3] 'Other Minds' (II), *Mind*, L, 197, pp. 19-20. (The argument throughout this series of papers seems to be that if you have all the *sensible* evidence you can possibly get, you know as much as you possibly can.) Cf. also G. A. Paul, 'Is there a Problem about Sense-data?', *Arist. Soc. Proc.* Suppl. Vol. XV (1936), pp. 61 ff., where he compares the use of 'sense-data' with that of 'fovea' in anatomy and points to the evidence afforded by dissecting eyes.

part of the evidence, which includes much to which we infer and still more that we tacitly assume.

How does a scientist assure himself that electrons are being given off from an electrode, or that bombardment of atomic nuclei by slow neutrons results in fission? What must he see? Certainly not the electrons themselves—certainly not the division of the nucleus on impact with the neutron. For these things are invisible. So far as he depends on sense-perception, it is the perception of something quite other than that which he seeks to verify. Again, though the chemist sees the blue colour of a copper-sulphate solution, how does he assure himself that the liquid does contain copper-sulphate? Or though he sees the crystals themselves how does he know what they are? Only by applying tests in which what he sees and feels is something quite other than either the crystals or their colour.

'No,' it might be countered, 'not *quite* other. What is observed is something deducible logically from what has to be ascertained. If there are electrons (the scientist reasons), such-and-such effects will be visible on a fluorescent screen: if fission occurs, vapour trails of such-and-such a kind will be observed in the Wilson cloud-chamber. Hence when the expected observations are made, they can be taken as signs of the fact to be established.' Now, however, the claim of perceptual evidence to sufficiency has been given up. The logical deduction is an essential factor in the discovery of the facts and if we ever doubt that S is P, the production of sensible evidence may well be inefficacious in removing the doubt, for what we doubt may be the validity of the inference involved in determining the evidence and in accepting it as relevant. For evidence is never pure sense-perception; it always includes inference from and thought about sense-perception, and the sensuous factor is so inextricably mingled with the inferential that no clear-cut division can be made between them. For all the advances of modern positivistic techniques, we shall do well not to forget that 'perception without conception is blind'.

It is simply false that the doubt of the scientist is always due to lack of sensible data. For at least a century the problem of the aberration of the perihelion of Mercury perplexed astronomers, and the improvement of the means of observation—larger telescopes, more accurate instruments of measurement and more efficient methods of calculation—only intensified the problem. What, with less accurate methods, might have been attributed to experimental error became a discrepancy impossible to explain away as the precision of new instruments developed. The increase of evidence only exacerbated the difficulty and it was not until the whole system of presuppositions of the science was revised that the problem was solved by the substitution of the Einsteinian for the Newtonian hypothesis. Yet this was no pseudo-problem. The doubts of the astronomers, incurable by 'evidence' though they were, were not pathological or queer—and there is no temptation to call them philosophical.

If then there are problems of this kind that are not philosophical, how can we use the inefficacy of evidence as a criterion for philosophical problems? We cannot go on to maintain that philosophical doubt is different because it will not give way even to a revision of our basic presuppositions, for that is exactly what philosophers seek. Their proper task is to examine the presuppositions commonly made by the layman and by the scientist and to reveal the source of the contradictions so often traceable to latent assumptions.

The three species of doubt described by Wisdom are common to both science and philosophy, to say nothing of unscientific thinking.

(i) Every scientific statement is known by the scientist to be infinitely corrigible, and if he does not normally express doubt about it on that account, it is because he is prepared to accept it provisionally until he requires something more accurate.

(ii) Every scientist is faced by conflicting criteria: Is light undulatory or corpuscular? Is the chromosome fibre an aperiodic crystal or is it amorphous?[1] Is *Peripatus* an annelid or an arthropod? Is the larval reproduction of the liverfluke parthenogenetic or asexual? These conflicts cannot be resolved by any decision about mere linguistic usage. The linguistic usage is fixed by the science concerned and we cannot modify it to include or to exclude the awkward cases without ceasing to be scientific.

(iii) Nor, as we have seen, is science exempt from those problems in which, however much evidence we may have, it does not enable us to reach the conclusion to which our theory tends.

We are, therefore, left with no criterion for distinguishing philosophical doubt. In fact, Wisdom's distinction between 'philosophical' and 'natural' doubt[2] can be traced back to Wittgenstein's self-destructive epistemology which confines sensible propositions to natural science on the grounds that only such as present the existence (and non-existence) of facts[3] can be meaningful and that none can present what they have in common with the facts—the so-called

---

[1] *Vide* Schroedinger, *What is Life?* (Cambridge, 1944), pp. 3 and 59 f.
[2] *Vide* 'Other Minds' (I), p. 369.
[3] '. . . *stellt das Bestehen und Nichtbestehen der Sachverhalte dar*' (*Tractatus*, 4·1).

logical form.[1] Consequently philosophical propositions are said to have no sense and 'philosophical doubt' to be doubt about nothing real. So also the attempt to identify it by reference to the 'evidence' which should resolve it is tainted with the same metaphysical pre-supposition—that science is about perceptible (picturable)[2] facts, whereas philosophy cannot be.

(b) The failure of this criterion, though of course unnoticed by Wisdom, results in a loose and shifting application of the word 'doubt'. We might well ask at the outset what sort of doubt 'natural doubt' might be if all it is due to is lack of evidence. If I doubt that X committed the murder, this is not simply because I lack evidence that he did, but either because I think a different interpretation may be put upon the evidence already produced, or because there is other evidence (though inconclusive) which shakes the inference to his guilt. We doubt only when we have reason to believe that the *wrong inference* is being drawn from the available evidence, so that some statement asserted as true may actually be false. If the evidence is clear but insufficient in extent to enable us to draw any conclusive inference, we do not doubt, we are simply undecided and suspend judgement. Of course, if we make our intention clear, we may use 'doubt' to mean 'suspended judgement' (or indecision) and at times it is so used, but we must then distinguish clearly between this use of the word and that in which it means 'disbelief'.

Now Wisdom uses it sometimes as equivalent to 'belief', sometimes to 'disbelief'; sometimes as equivalent to 'uncertainty', sometimes to 'indecision', and at least once he distinguishes between 'doubt' and 'indecision' without explaining the difference.

(i) When he asks 'What sort of doubt is this?'[3] Wisdom states that philosophical doubt cannot, like normal doubt, be 'put to use'. How then do we put doubt to use? From what he says it would seem to be by expecting something to happen—I doubt that Smith believes So-and-so, therefore I expect him to behave in such-and-such a way. But this is just how doubt never can be put to use. If I doubt, I don't know what to expect, and the only way I can put my uncertainty to use is to investigate further. The value of doubt is that it is a spur to research; he who never doubts makes little progress in knowledge. It is to this use that Descartes puts his doubt; he makes it a stepping-stone to the knowledge, *cogito ergo sum*. But if we speak of 'putting to use' in this way, what we mean by 'doubt' is 'uncertainty' based on

---

[1] *Tractatus*, 4·12. [2] *Ibid.* 2·1 *et seq.*
[3] 'Other Minds' (I), p. 374.

(partial) ignorance. Wisdom's use, however, is opposite to this, for he makes doubt lead to expectation whereas what normally leads to expectation is knowledge. But that surely cannot be what he intends 'doubt' to mean.

(ii) The footnote to the passage to which I have referred [1] confuses the matter still further. There he proposes to say, 'I doubt whether you doubt whether Smith believes flowers feel'. This is, of course, colloquial but that does not excuse the confusion. If I say, 'I doubt whether he will come' or 'I doubt if you could complete the course in one year', I usually mean 'I don't believe that . . .', and it seems pretty plain that this is the meaning of the first 'doubt' in Wisdom's sentence.

(iii) But at its second occurrence it plainly does not mean this, it means 'are uncertain'.

(iv) Yet, later in the same passage there occurs the sentence: 'This will be the case if your doubt arises because Smith's *doubt* [my italics] is philosophical and peculiar and queer'. Hitherto he has spoken of 'Smith's *belief*'; are we to take it now that 'doubt' is synonymous with 'belief'?

(v) Later (*op. cit.* p. 387) we are told that a conflict doubt, after treatment, 'becomes a cheerful indecision' and that *for that reason* it is not a doubt at all, or at best a very peculiar sort of doubt. Real, or 'natural' doubt seems thus to be limited to indecision or suspended judgement—for Wisdom cannot mean to imply that it is decision. What then becomes of the doubt normally arising from suspicion of a wrong inference from the evidence—the only sort that properly deserves the name and the sort which scientists, jurymen, stock-brokers and detectives, as well as philosophers, daily experience? Must we believe that this is always 'peculiar' and 'queer'? If so, Mr. Wisdom is like the man in his own example who asks 'Aren't we all mad, really—if you come to think of it?'[2]

In fine, Wisdom's attempt to stigmatize philosophical doubt as pathological leads him into a welter of confusion where the babel of conflicting voices drowns the fading echo of his master's cry: '*Alles was sich aussprechen lässt, lässt sich klar aussprechen*'.

(c) It is hardly surprising, therefore, if the questions with which the Wittgensteinists concern themselves prove, in the main, not to be eternal problems of traditional philosophy even when they appear at first sight to be like them. When Norman Malcolm[3] deals with necessary propositions, he does not discuss in any form the problem of

---

[1] *Ibid.* p. 375 n.　　　[2] *Ibid.* p. 395.
[3] *Vide* 'Are Necessary Propositions Really Verbal?', *Mind*, XLIX, 194.

necessary connection which Hume and Kant faced, but describes the way in which we use certain words and phrases and argues that statements about it *justify* our use of certain other statements in making inferences and doing calculations. In all this, however, he begs his question, which is *whether* necessary propositions are really verbal— for if they are not, there is no such justification. When he deals with entailment,[1] first he avoids the main issue and side-tracks the discussion into one of Wisdom's subdivisions of philosophical doubt— namely, doubt as to the use of 'mean the same'; and then, forsaking the therapeutic method, he plunges into metaphysics and produces, with the help of biassed examples and special pleading, a theory of something that is not properly speaking entailment at all.[2]

Wisdom, on 'Metaphysics and Verification',[3] has nothing to offer on the really interesting logical questions involved in the nature of verification and their bearing on the positivist repudiation of metaphysics. He devotes himself mainly to showing that metaphysicians habitually ask for the impossible when they object to the sort of procedure in which certain positivists delight. But he draws his examples from a very restricted circle of philosophers, doing scant justice even to them; and sweeping generalizations from the conduct of these few metaphysicians to that of metaphysicians as a class are hardly warranted. His examples of metaphysical puzzles, moreover, are not genuine philosophical problems. In the paper referred to they all take the form 'Can X-propositions be analysed (or translated) into non-X propositions?' But metaphysicians are not primarily interested in the translation of sentences; they are much more concerned with what the sentences are about. Nor are they concerned with such questions as whether you can find a perfect pulley in which W does not exactly balance $\frac{1}{2}$W, or 'What is a cow as opposed to a buffalo?', or 'Does a dog go round a cow if she keeps her horns always towards him?'

[1] 'The Nature of Entailment', *Mind*, XLIX, 195.

[2] I cannot here discuss Malcolm's view in detail. He holds that entailment between two contingent propositions is always due to their both expressing the same fact. I should ask, first, how much or how little fact goes to make *one* fact and at what point have we two different but related facts? And I should then put forward the following example to be explained according to Malcolm's doctrine:

Proposition 1: There is a certain measurable aberration in the orbit of the planet Uranus.

Proposition 2: There is a planet Neptune, beyond Uranus, the position of which can be ascertained.

    (a) Do these propositions express one fact or two?

    (b) Is there entailment between them?

    (c) If not, how did Adams and Leverrier get from the first to the second?

[3] *Mind*, XLVII, 188.

These are not philosophical questions but rather the products of confused and adolescent thinking.

The title of the series of papers on other minds suggests a real philosophical problem, but the interminable discussions which ensue never touch it. The real problem about other minds is a variant of the general problem of knowledge [1] and arises from the assumption that minds are finite entities, like bodies, in a world which is a collection of such finites. It is the question how, in such a world, any finite mind could have knowledge of the other finites, in fact of anything except itself. But Wisdom exerts himself only on the subject of people who profess to doubt the reliability, as evidence for psychological states, of the observable facts of outward behaviour. This is a matter which should concern the psychologist in his attempt to decide whether or not to become a behaviourist, but it is largely irrelevant to the 'eternal' problem of knowledge, for which knowledge of the 'outward' behaviour and that of the 'inner' states of others is all equally problematic.

My conclusion, therefore, is that the Wittgensteinists provide us with no acceptable reason for denying the existence of eternal problems. Can their philosophical kindred, the followers of Rudolf Carnap, do better?

4. *Carnapians.* Carnap rejects Wittgenstein's philosophical nihilism while he retains his anti-metaphysical attitude. He recognizes the age-old contradiction involved in scepticism which Wittgenstein admits in words but neglects in practice. 'Instead of keeping silent', complains Carnap, 'he writes a whole philosophical book.' [2] There are some philosophical propositions which Carnap will permit; some which have sense, namely, those which make assertions about linguistic expressions; but they are purely formal in the sense that they are not concerned with extra-linguistic objects and make no reference at all to the sense or meaning of the verbal expressions with which they deal.[3] Such propositions he calls 'syntactical' because they belong to the logical syntax of the language to which they refer, and this syntactical study of language is, he thinks, 'an exact method of philosophy'. There is here a large measure of agreement with Wittgenstein and disagreement only in the refusal to advocate complete philosophical silence. The traditional philosophy with its metaphysics, ethics, epistemology, nature-philosophy and the rest is still rejected. There

---

[1] *Vide* pp. 51-3, below.
[2] *Philosophy and Logical Syntax* (London, 1935), p. 38.　　　[3] *Ibid.* p. 39.

are for Carnap, no more than for Wittgenstein, any eternal questions. Only the natural sciences (all of which are in a sense held to be reducible to physics) and the logical syntax of their languages are regarded as worthy of serious study.

By means of a simple expedient Carnap appears to have avoided the self-contradiction of Wittgenstein's metaphysics which first enunciates a theory of the world and then on the basis of that theory asserts its meaninglessness. He avoids committing himself explicitly to any metaphysical doctrine by beginning from the dogmatic assertion that only verifiable propositions have sense and then denying the possibility of verification to metaphysical propositions. But the dogmatic assertion is itself a product of Wittgenstein's metaphysic and tacitly presupposes a certain type of epistemology. One cannot, as positivists habitually do,[1] evade this issue by refusing explicitly to commit oneself to a theory which is nevertheless logically implied in one's own teaching. Carnap is involved in contradiction, equally with Wittgenstein, when he rejects the possibility of a philosophical theory of knowledge, for his own doctrine assumes one in its insistence on verifiability as the test of meaning. Moreover, it is the same as that assumed by Wisdom and others of this ilk—that the truth resides in sense-perception, which alone provides evidence and by reference to which alone propositions can be verified. For a proposition is held to be verifiable (a) directly, when it describes an immediate, present sensory experience, and (b) indirectly, when we can deduce from it (together with other propositions which have already been verified) a proposition which is directly verifiable. Hence only immediate sensory experience enables us to verify and that alone can in the last resort provide a proposition with meaning.

Carnap's explanation of the fact that for some twenty centuries philosophers have persistently indulged in nonsense-mongering is that pseudo-problems are very prone to arise when we state syntactical sentences in a 'quasi-syntactical' form (one which makes them seem to be non-syntactical). The so-called eternal problems of philosophy, therefore, are the fruits of speaking in what he calls the 'material mode'—a manner of speech beset with gins and pitfalls.

Now, that this doctrine of pseudo-problems is specious I shall endeavour to show by revealing the fallacy in the argument by which Carnap supports it. He divides sentences into two types: (i) those about the objects of a given science or sphere of discourse, which he calls real-object-sentences, and (ii) those about linguistic expressions,

[1] Cf. B. A. Farrell, 'Appraisal of Therapeutic Positivism', *Mind*, LV, 217, p. 37.

which he calls syntactical sentences. Among the latter he distinguishes purely syntactical and pseudo-object sentences, or what he also calls quasi-syntactical sentences framed in the material mode. His technical explanation of this subdivision is briefly this: if a sentence ascribes to an object a quality to which a parallel syntactical quality can be found, it is a quasi-syntactical sentence in the material mode. If it ascribes a syntactical quality to a word or linguistic expression by which the object is designated, it is a syntactical sentence in the formal mode.[1] The quality ascribed to the object in a pseudo-object sentence is related to the syntactical quality which is its counterpart as follows: 'A syntactical quality Q_2 is called parallel to the quality Q_1 if it is the case that when, and only when, an object possesses the quality Q_1 does a designation of this object possess the quality Q_2'.[2] Examples of this classification are:

I. Object-sentences.	II. Pseudo-object sentences = quasi-syntactical sentences. Material mode of speech.	III. Syntactical sentences. Formal mode of speech.
1a. The rose is red.	1b. The rose is a thing. $Q_1(a)$	1c. The word 'rose' is a thing-word. Q_2 ('a')[3]
2a. The evening-star and the earth are about equal in size.	2b. The evening-star and the morning-star are identical.	2c. The words 'evening star' and 'morning-star' are synonymous.[3]
3a. Babylon was a big town.	3b. Babylon was treated of in yesterday's lecture.	3c. The word 'Babylon' occurred in yesterday's lecture.[4]

The sentences in the third column are said to be 'translations' of those in the second from the material into the formal mode of speech while those in the first column are real-object-sentences which cannot be so translated for there are no parallel syntactical qualities to those they ascribe to their objects.

Why are the statements in column II of this table regarded as *pseudo*-object statements? What is there about them which is false and how are they misleading? Carnap says that though they appear to be

---

[1] *Vide Logical Syntax of Language* (London, 1937), pp. 237-9 and 284-8 and *Philosophy and Logical Syntax*, pp. 58 ff.

[2] *Philosophy and Logical Syntax*, p. 63; cf. also *Logical Syntax of Language*, pp. 234 and 287.   [3] *Philosophy and Logical Syntax*, p. 61.

[4] *Logical Syntax of Language*, p. 286.

about the objects, rose, Babylon and evening-star, really they are not, but are simply a way of ascribing a syntactical (or linguistic) property to the words which designate these objects. So he calls them 'quasi-syntactical' and classes them with metaphors as a 'transposed mode of speech'—that is, 'one in which, in order to assert something about an object a, something corresponding is asserted about an object b which stands in a certain relation to the object a'.[1] But we have been told that the syntactical quality which is being asserted of the designation belongs to it *if, and only if*, the parallel quality belongs to the object designated. In other words we can never assert Q_2 of 'a', unless we know beforehand that Q_1 belongs to a, and so unless we can assert Q_1 (a). The so-called pseudo-object sentence makes a statement which is logically prior to the syntactical statement, for which it is supposed to be a substitute, and expresses a fact which is the condition of the formal statement's truth. It should follow, therefore, that the syntactical sentence is the pseudo-statement. *It* is the transposed mode of speech, for it asserts something about the object a by asserting something corresponding about b which stands in a certain relation to a (is its designation). If the object-statement is 'pseudo', it should be in some way misleading, somehow either false or senseless. If it is misleading, the syntactical statement must be to that extent false, and if it is senseless, the syntactical proposition cannot be asserted. If 'the rose is a thing' is not about the rose—*i.e.* if it does not attribute thing-hood to the rose—we cannot say of the word 'rose' that it is a 'thing-word'. In fact, 'thing-word' is meaningless unless it means 'a word which designates a thing'. Consequently, sentence 1c in the table is really pseudo-linguistic for it appears to be only about a word whereas really it is about a thing or 'object'. The genuine 'object-sentence' is 1b.

The second and third examples in the table are most apt illustrations of this *hysteron proteron*. The sentence 2c is simply false. The words 'evening-star' and 'morning-star' are as little synonymous as are the words 'evening' and 'morning'. We can see this at once in the following sentences: 'When he returned the evening-star was already bright in the darkening sky' and 'Not until the morning-star had faded into the dawn did the vigil end'. Moreover, if an astronomer, observing the planet Venus first at evening and again in the morning, were to imagine that he was observing two different planets, and if subsequent evidence revealed to him his mistake, he might well state his discovery in the words of sentence 2b. But in so doing he would be

[1] *Logical Syntax of Language*, p. 308.

making no assertion about the synonymity of the ancient designations. He would be stating a fact about the planet Venus. And this would be no pseudo-statement such as we get immediately by so-called 'translation into the formal mode', for the assertion that 'evening-star' and 'morning-star' are synonymous is either a disguised method of telling us that the designations refer to the same object, or else—if taken literally at its face value—it is false.

The third of Carnap's examples seems hardly serious. Yet he clearly intends that it should be so regarded. There is no equivalence (or 'equipollence') between 3b and 3c. The *word* 'Babylon' might occur in any lecture, whether it was about that city or not. 3c might be true of a lecture on the Book of Revelation or of one on Mr. Ralph Hodgson's poetry, but 3b would be true only if the lecture dealt with Babylon itself. And Carnap's allegation, that the sentence makes an assertion, not about the city, but only about its name, entirely overlooks the fact that if the name were ascribed to any other city the statement would be false. 'For our knowledge of the properties of the town of Babylon', he says, 'it does not matter whether $\mathfrak{S}_1$ [3b in my table] is true or false.'[1] Certainly it does. If the sentence is false, we should take it to be true only if our knowledge of the properties of the town were seriously defective, for we should then imagine a lecture to be about Babylon, which in fact was about something quite different.[2] At any rate the statement implies a knowledge of the properties of the city by anyone who makes it and a trust in such knowledge on the part of anyone who believes him.

There is nothing pseudo about these statements in the material mode and consequently the dangers which that manner of speaking is supposed to involve are figments of Dr. Carnap's imagination—in fact, his anxiety about pseudo-problems more nearly resembles a pathological condition than any of the philosophical doubts which worry Mr. Wisdom. These dangers are the pitfalls among which philosophers are said to flounder. They result from imagining that the objects of pseudo-object sentences are extra-linguistic and from disregard of the relativity to language of quasi-syntactical sentences. In

---

[1] *Logical Syntax of Language*, pp. 285-6.
[2] Suppose that on consulting the prospectus of a course on Ancient History, I learn that Professor X will deliver a lecture on Babylon at 9.30 A.M. tomorrow. That statement makes two assertions: (i) about the occurrence of the lecture and (ii) about the subject-matter. With (i) I am not here concerned, but if (ii) is false and the lecture is actually about Nineveh, either I shall be misled when I hear it into thinking that Babylon was situated on the Tigris, or, if I discover that the lecture is not about Babylon and that the prospectus was wrong, I can do so only because of my knowledge of the properties of that city.

the first case, pseudo-problems arise in connection with these pseudo extra-linguistic objects and, in the second case, disputes arise about seeming incompatibilities which are really compatible as linguistic assertions. So philosophers, thinking that statements using universal words are object-sentences, raise such pseudo-questions as 'Are numbers real or ideal?'[1] 'Are properties internal or external?'[2] and forgetting relativity to language, they quarrel about the definitions of material things as 'complexes of sense-data' on the one hand, or 'complexes of atoms' on the other.[3] Translation into the formal mode, it is alleged, removes all this confusion and with it the pseudo-problems disappear.

Now, in the light of what I have shown above about the priority of object-statements to syntactical statements, one who observes that 'Five is not a thing but a number' is stating a fact without the knowledge of which the syntactician could never be aware, that '"Five" is not a thing-word but a number-word'.[4] And he would be quite within his rights to raise the question: 'How, then, do we distinguish numbers from things?' and to go on to ask 'Is a number something real or something purely ideal?' Nor does the translation into the formal mode obviate such questions. How is a 'thing-word' to be distinguished from a 'number-word'? Does the latter designate anything real or only something ideal?

Further, translation into the formal mode does not settle philosophical disputes. If one philosopher argues (a) that numbers are classes of classes and another (b) that they are a special kind of primitive object,[5] the translations into the formal mode leave the dispute just where it was—even when the relativity to language is specified. The translations given are: (a) 'Numerical expressions are class-expressions of the second level'. (b) 'Numerical expressions are expressions of the zero level.' Now these formal statements are said to be (i) both wrong, if they are intended to hold for all languages—but this may be just what the disputants are disputing—or (ii) both right, if they are intended to hold each for at least one language—but the dispute would then continue as to which language was the correct one for Arithmetic—or (iii) they may be intended as proposals for a new language of science, in which case the only question that arises is, which is the more appropriate for certain purposes—and here there is endless material for dispute.

<hr />

[1] Cf. *Philosophy and Logical Syntax*, p. 79.
[2] *Logical Syntax of Language*, p. 304.   [3] *Ibid.* p. 301.
[4] *Ibid.* p. 286.   [5] *Ibid.* p. 300.

But it is in any case disputable whether, as Carnap asserts, 'it is possible to construct a language of arithmetic either in such a way that (a) is true or in such a way that (b) is true'.[1] For that presumes that the nature of numbers is a matter of linguistic convention—a highly doubtful and controversial point.

In like manner, what Carnap describes as the controversy between positivism and realism fails to dissolve on the translation into the formal mode of the rival assertions: (a) 'A *thing* is a complex of sense-data', and (b) 'A thing is a complex of atoms'. The translations suggested [2] are:

(a) 'Every sentence in which a thing-designation occurs is equipollent to a class of sentences in which no thing-designations but sense-data designations occur.'

(b) 'Every sentence in which a thing-designation occurs is equipollent to a sentence in which space-time co-ordinates and certain descriptive functors (of physics) occur.'

Such translation is supposed to reveal that each of the disputants is proposing an alternative rule for converting 'thing-sentences' into other equipollent sentences. These alternatives, we are told, are obviously not incompatible. But each of the parties to the dispute is contending that the rule put forward by the other is unsound: in the one case, that 'thing-sentences' are *not* equipollent to 'a class of sentences in which no thing-designations but sense-data designations occur'; and in the other case, that they are *not* equipollent to sentences 'in which certain space-time co-ordinates and certain descriptive functors (of physics) occur'. And the dispute continues.

The same is true of the other examples which Carnap provides and, whether these are eternal questions or not, if eternal questions arise in this way, Carnap's arguments have not abolished them.

Moreover, he is not guiltless of sophism and logomachy. He demonstrates that sentences about meaning are specially dangerous when expressed in the material mode and in one case, at least, a false statement may be derived from a true one. The example is, 'This letter is about Mr. Miller's son',[3] and the proof runs as follows. 'Instead of "this letter" we will write "b"; instead of "b is about a" we will write "H (b, a)" and instead of "the son of a" we will write "Son' a" (descriptional in Russell's symbolism . . .).' The sentence above now becomes 'H (b, Son' Miller)' ($\mathfrak{S}_1$). 'According to a well-known

---

[1] *Ibid.* (I have substituted letters for the numbers to make them fit the present context.)

[2] *Vide ibid.* p. 301.   [3] *Ibid.* pp. 290 f.

theorem in Logistics . . . from a sentence $\mathfrak{Pr}$ ($\mathfrak{Arg}$) in which a description occurs as argument, a sentence is derivable which asserts that there exists something which has the descriptional property. Accordingly from $\mathfrak{S}_1$ would be derivable "($\exists x$) . (Son (x Miller))" ($\mathfrak{S}_2$); or, in words: "a son of Mr. Miller exists". This, however, is a false sentence.'

This proof contains an elementary error. The predicate of $\mathfrak{S}_1$ is a two-termed predicate and 'Son' Miller' is only one of the arguments. The entire argument is 'b, son' Miller', which is not a description and, consequently, the proof is invalid. In fact, the form of the expression 'H (b, a)' is deceptive; it is not the simple form '$\mathfrak{Pr}$ ($\mathfrak{Arg}$)' but really the form 'a R b'. 'H' is not the predicate nor 'a' the argument, accordingly, the expression '($\exists x$) . (Son (x Miller))' cannot be derived from it. To operate Carnap's proof a different symbolism would have to be used, and the sentence $\mathfrak{S}_1$ would have to be written 'ϕa' where 'a' = 'this letter' and 'ϕ' = 'is about the son of Mr. Miller'. Then it is obviously possible to derive the expression '($\exists x$) . ϕx', and that, of course, is true. The alleged danger of the material mode consequently reveals itself to be chimerical.

In the same way a statement alleged to be about external and internal properties is shown to lead to contradiction by means of a sophistical argument.[1] The statement in Carnap's words is: 'A property of an object c is called an *essential* (or: *internal*) property of c, if it is inconceivable that c should not possess it (or: if c necessarily possesses it); otherwise it is an *inessential* (or: *external*) property'. c is then taken as the father of Charles and being related to Charles is said to be an essential property by the definition, while being a landowner is inessential. 'On the other hand,' Carnap continues, 'being a landowner is an essential property of the owner of this piece of land.' It is then sprung upon us that the father of Charles is the owner of this piece of land and we are convicted of self-contradiction in alleging that being a landowner is at once an essential property and an inessential property of that versatile gentleman.

But, alas, the owner of this piece of land is not c and so cannot be the father of Charles. Or, if it is c, the symbol is ambiguous and we have been tricked.[2]

---

[1] *Vide ibid.* p. 304.

[2] Strictly speaking Carnap should have argued thus: Let x be Mr. Brown. Let c be the father of Charles. Let d be the owner of this piece of land. If x is identical with c and with d, being related to Charles (an essential property of c) is an essential property of x, and being a landowner (an essential property of d) is an essential property of x. There is no contradiction.

Let us then take the lesson to heart. The real danger lies in the formal mode of speech with its pseudo-syntactical statements and in the use of a fascinating but misleading symbolism. Carnap's boasted precision is often a snare and a delusion, and though we need not be unduly alarmed when he warns us of the dangers of the material mode of speech, we must be on our guard against the deceptive sleight of hand by which translations into the formal mode can make real problems seem to disappear.

5. Those who have been misled by this verbal conjuring continue to shun the depths of the metaphysical forest and to pursue the pseudo-problems of linguistics through the thickets of the semantical undergrowth. Professor A. J. Ayer is one of these. He adopts the Wittgensteinist-Carnapian position that metaphysical propositions are unverifiable and therefore senseless and he describes the history of philosophy as a 'parade of pontiffs' who attempt 'to give a complete and definite account of "ultimate" reality',[1] whereas the modern journeymen philosophers are at pains to show that this 'ultimate' reality is a fiction. They do not try to build systems but busy themselves with a set of special problems all of which are in a broad sense semantic.[2] These, he feels, form the legitimate task of the philosopher, while what have been called the eternal problems of philosophy cannot fruitfully be discussed because there is no true answer to them.

But, like Wisdom and his associates, the sort of problem which Ayer rejects is not the sort typical of any reputable philosophy: 'What is the purpose (or the meaning) of life?' 'How ought men to live?' which he takes to be unanswerable pseudo-questions,[3] are not the kind with which any competent philosopher (in his capacity of philosopher) would formulate. The first is too vague to be clearly understood, and while philosophers have sought to make human experience intelligible as a whole, none of any reputation has claimed to reveal 'the meaning of life' (unless the phrase is taken to refer to the clarification of biological conceptions). No considerable philosopher claims to decide, by means of his philosophy, what in any particular set of circumstances men ought to do. On the contrary, moral philosophy proper never sets out to formulate even general moral rules, though not all moral philosophers have refrained from doing so. It is concerned with the theory of morality, not with exhortation.

We may thus agree with Ayer that such problems as he rejects are

---

[1] 'The Claims of Philosophy', *Polemic*, no. 7, March 1947, p. 20.   [2] *Ibid.*
[3] *Ibid.*; cf. also *Language, Truth and Logic* (2nd ed., London, 1946), pp. 35-6.

not the proper problems of philosophy. And those which he admits, 'the problem of perception, the problem of knowledge of other minds, the question of the significance of moral judgements',[1] and so on, are among those with which philosophers have concerned themselves for generations, but not until recently have they been regarded as purely semantic. Ayer's contention that they are so requires defence, and for such defence one must turn to his book, *Language, Truth and Logic*.

Here we find the view expressed that philosophy is concerned only 'with the provision of definitions and the study of their formal consequences'.[2] But both the explanation of this view and the examples given fail to show that philosophy (even as conceived by Ayer) is concerned purely with linguistics. First, let us examine the examples given to illustrate the misleading factual appearance of certain linguistic statements (here we have the echo of Carnap's pseudo-object sentences). 'A thing cannot be in two places at once' is not an empirical proposition, says Ayer, but is linguistic because 'it simply records the fact that, as a result of certain verbal conventions, the proposition that two sense-contents occur in the same visual or tactual sense-field is incompatible with the proposition that they belong to the same material thing.'[3] Now, quite apart from the fact that this last statement is certainly untrue (for two 'sense-contents' occurring in the same visual sense-field frequently do belong to the same material thing— even when the percipient is not inebriated), and apart from the paradox of saying that a statement is not empirical because it records the *fact* that . . . etc., both the propositions concerned are empirical and only on factual grounds can we say whether or not they are compatible.

How do I know whether and when two sense-contents belong to the same material thing? According to Ayer [4] by finding out whether the symbols that stand for them belong to a group which can be used in sentences to replace a sentence containing the symbol for the material thing. This is a complicated business, but how can I succeed with it

---

[1] 'The Claims of Philosophy', *loc. cit.*

[2] *Op. cit.* 2nd ed., p. 57. The view is modified in the introduction but not so far as to affect my argument in what follows.

[3] *Ibid.* p. 58. The term 'sense-content' is ambiguous. If it is used, as Ayer sometimes implies, synonymously with 'sense-datum', my following argument stands. If, however, it is used as Ayer uses it in his paper 'On Particulars and Universals' (*Arist. Soc. Proc.* XXXIV, 1933–4) to mean the entire visual or tactual appearance of any one thing at any one time, then to say that two sense-contents belonging to the same thing cannot occur in the same visual or tactual field is the same as to say that no two successive sense-contents can occur at the same time. That *is* tautological, but only as the result of a very arbitrary verbal convention—one may almost say 'invention'—and it is not at all what we commonly mean when we say that a thing cannot be in two places at once.   [4] *Ibid.* pp. 63 f.

unless I know the mutual relations of the sense-contents and their relation to the material thing? Ayer would possibly say that the latter relation does not exist and that the sense-contents *are* the material thing, or—if that smacks too much of metaphysics—that to speak of the material thing is a way of speaking about the sense-contents. Even so, it is all-important to know which sense-contents I am speaking about in any given case and that cannot be determined, as Ayer seems to allege, by linguistic convention. Possibly people may agree that every time they use (*e.g.*) the word 'table' they will be understood to refer to a group of sense-contents; but we cannot by means of this convention determine which sense-contents will be members of any particular group. Suppose that I come into my study in the twilight and I experience a sense-content in the form of an indefinitely shaped black patch in the middle of the rectangular brown patch that I habitually associate with the phrase 'my table'. What verbal convention will enable me to decide whether this new sense-content is in future to be included among the group to which I refer when I use that phrase, or among the group to which I refer when I use the word 'kitten'? I cannot, for my part, imagine. But I have a fair notion of the sort of empirical investigation which would enable me to decide whether someone had spilt the ink or the kitten had chosen the table as a place for his siesta. Accordingly, a proposition asserting or denying that two sense-contents belong to the same material thing is an empirical proposition; its truth or falsity can be established only by empirical investigation; and if it is incompatible with the obviously empirical proposition that the sense-contents occur in the same sense-field, the reason must be factual, or there can be none at all. In the example I have given above the propositions would not be incompatible, but they would be if, for instance, the sense-contents were visual and belonged respectively to the upper and to the under sides of the table-top. Then their incompatibility would be due solely to that fact and to no linguistic convention whatsoever.

Ayer's second example of a linguistic proposition that appears to be factual is: 'Relations are not particulars, but universals'.[1] This, he says, looks like the same sort of statement as 'Armenians are not Mohammedans, but Christians', but actually it is 'not a proposition about "things" at all', it simply 'records the fact that relation-symbols belong by definition to the class of symbols for characters, and not to the class of symbols for things'. Does this mean that the misleading proposition really states that relation-symbols are not symbols for

[1] *Ibid.* pp. 58 f.

relations, nor for things, but for a sort of characters? If so it gives us a curious piece of information, because, if relation-symbols are not symbols for relations, why are they so-called? Possibly, however, the proposition is not meant to deny that they refer to relations but really means 'Relations are not things but characters'. But then we have a proposition which is about 'things' of some sort, just like the one about Armenians, though not about things of the same sort. Ayer goes on to point out that from the original proposition the question arises 'What is a universal?' and that this has traditionally been mistaken for a question about 'certain real objects', whereas it is really a request for a definition of a certain term. And if the question raised were 'What is a relation?' or 'What is a character?' we should, I take it, be in no better case. So also, we are told, 'What is a material thing?' is a request, not for the description of the nature of a material object, but for the definition of the phrase. Now, anybody who could define the phrase 'material thing' without any sort of reference to the nature of a material object would certainly be a very accomplished person, but his definition, when achieved, would be entirely worthless, for unless such reference were made, the definition would not help us in the least to understand the meaning or the usage of the phrase. And in like manner it would be impossible usefully to define 'relations' or 'universals' without reference to the 'designata' of those terms (to use a jargon dear to the hearts of Carnapians) and no such reference can intelligently be made without some conception of the nature of the designata.[1]

Turning next to Ayer's explanation of philosophical analysis we find as an example of what he calls 'definitions in use' a reference to Russell's theory of definite descriptions, according to which phrases of the form the 'so-and-so' are defined by translation: *e.g.* 'The author of *Waverley* was Scotch' (*sic*) becomes 'One person, and one only, wrote *Waverley* and that person was Scotch'. The criticisms of this example to which Ayer defers in his introduction do not seem to bear upon (or in fact to reveal any awareness of) the fact that what is given is in no sense a definition of anything, nor is it primarily, as Ayer claims, an elucidation of 'the use of a certain class of expression in ordinary speech'. It is simply an example of two alternative statements about the same fact (in this instance, the fact that Scott wrote *Waverley*). Now our ability to describe a fact in different ways does not make our

[1] C. W. Morris (*Foundations of the Theory of Signs* in the *International Encyclopaedia of Unified Science*, I, no. 2) asserts that a sign may have a *designatum* without having an object of reference (*denotatum*). But whether or not the terms 'universal', 'relation', etc., have *denotata* is not here in question. To be terms at all they must refer to something and they cannot be defined in ignorance of what they refer to.

statements purely verbal (not even the statement that the alternative descriptions refer to the same fact). Indeed, unless they refer to philological or grammatical facts, statements of this kind are not, properly speaking, linguistic at all.

The contortions undergone by Carnapians in their efforts to escape from metaphysics will not avail, for however much we substitute linguistic terms for the things and ideas that they signify, we cannot avoid dealing with those things and ideas themselves, indirect though our reference to them must become.

ἦ, οἴει, τίς τι συνίησίν τινος ὄνομα, ὃ μὴ οἶδεν τί ἐστιν; [1]

We may conclude, therefore, that the purely linguistic character of philosophical questions has not been established, and the case for eternal problems remains *sub judice*.

III. HISTORICISM

6. Of the historical school, I shall deal only with Collingwood. He is quite clear that the question about eternal problems is one of method, and in his view it is only when the method of philosophy is misconceived that we are misled into believing in the existence of eternal problems. His first account of the matter is stated in his *Autobiography*, where he condemns the methods of those whom he calls 'realists'. They imagine, he says, that all philosophers in all ages have raised the same questions and it is simply their answers which have differed, so that it would be sensible and relevant to ask which of two answers to a given question was the right one. To do this one must find out first whether the proposed answer is self-consistent, for should it contradict itself it will have proved to be false. The method of philosophy, in consequence, would consist mainly of the analysis of propositions into other propositions in order to detect whether or not they contradict one another. To this process the history of philosophy would be secondary. If the object is to discover the 'right' answer to an 'eternal' question, it is not of immediate importance to know what answers others have given in the past, and our interest in other philosophers will be limited to ascertaining whether their answers are 'right'. To do so it will obviously be necessary to find out what those answers are and that is the work of the historian of philosophy, but it is useful only as a guide leading us by examples of other men's trial and error towards the goal which we seek—the 'right' answer.

[1] Plato, *Theaetetus*, 147 B.

Now all this, Collingwood maintains, is fundamentally mistaken and is based upon a false logic which commits the error of thinking that truth and falsehood belong to propositions as such—an error not confined to 'realists' but shared with them by 'idealists' and symbolic logicians.[1] Collingwood believes that it is impossible to determine whether or not a proposition is true without knowing what question it is meant to answer and the discovery of that requires historical investigation. We have no right to assume or to jump to the conclusion that a given philosopher's theories are intended as answers to a stock set of eternal questions without valid evidence that these actually were the questions he had in his mind. But we can only acquire the evidence by means of historical research. It follows, therefore, that the work of the historian of philosophy is an integral part of the work of evaluating the theories of the philosopher under consideration. More than this, when we know the question to which a theory is the answer, whether it is the right answer or not depends simply upon whether it 'enables us to get ahead with the process of questioning and answering',[2] not (it would seem) on conformity to any absolute standard of eternal truth.

When we turn to Collingwood's second account of the matter in the *Essay on Metaphysics*, we see why this is so and we learn, further, that the historian's work is not only essential to the philosopher's quest but that it is the whole of it—at least, so far as it is the quest of the metaphysician. For metaphysics, according to Collingwood, is the science of 'absolute presuppositions' and its method is to analyse the thought of the natural scientist with the object of unearthing these presuppositions and determining whether or not they are absolute. If they prove to be the answers to prior questions, they are only relative and it is legitimate to ask concerning them whether they are right or wrong. But if they are absolute, they are themselves prior to all questions and to ask whether or not they are true is nonsensical.

The subject-matter of metaphysics, accordingly, is described as a certain class of historical facts and the preliminary training of the metaphysician should be historical, for the proper method of metaphysics is the historical method [3]—not the out-dated and inefficient method of 'scissors and paste' history, but that of scientific historical research, by which evidence is sifted, marshalled and systematized and the facts are determined, not merely on hearsay or authority, but by direct scientific investigation.

---

[1] *Vide Autobiography*, p. 27.
[2] *Ibid.* p. 30.   [3] *Metaphysics*, pp. 61 f.

Consequently, though metaphysics is a systematic study, it is not the study of a closed system. Its task is not system-building.[1] The metaphysician should not and cannot aim at completeness; he is not faced with a repertory of problems which are *the* problems of metaphysics and of which the answer to one determines the answer to the rest, and he cannot, therefore, adopt a deductive or quasi-mathematical procedure similar to that attempted by Spinoza.[2] It will follow also that there are no 'schools' associated with eminent philosophers whose adherents are constantly at loggerheads about the 'truth' or 'falsehood' of their masters' doctrines. For the masters are not maintaining any doctrine except the historical one that such-and-such absolute presuppositions are made by the scientists of their time.[3]

When the metaphysician realizes that this is really what he is doing and when he studies the metaphysical results obtained by his predecessors in past ages, he will soon become aware that there are no eternal problems; that the questions raised in one generation are not the same, despite superficial likenesses, as those of the next. They change continually and continuously and so far as they are alike their sameness is not that of a 'universal' and their differences those between instances of the universal. The sameness is that of an historical process and the difference that 'between one thing which in the course of that process has turned into something else, and the other thing into which it has turned'.[4]

The contradiction, which I earlier attributed to the historicists, implied in their denial of eternal problems concurrently with their insistence upon the importance of the history of philosophy, seems here to have been avoided. Eternal problems are certainly denied, and just as it would be futile, therefore, to try to discover their solutions, so, Collingwood would as certainly have held, it would be futile to seek to trace the history of past attempts to solve them. His emphasis on the importance of the history of philosophy has different grounds. Yet they are grounds which, as I hope to show presently, only re-establish the contradiction.

(i) If the metaphysician is to display the presuppositions of the science of a particular period he will find evidence in the work of the metaphysicians of that period, who were engaged on the work of unearthing those very presuppositions. But his attitude towards such evidence will not be simply to take it at its face value. He will have to check it, by himself examining and analysing the propositions of the

---

[1] *Ibid.* pp. 64 f.   [2] *Ibid.* p. 67.
[3] *Ibid.* pp. 68-9.   [4] *Autobiography*, p. 45.

co-temporary science, to discover whether the co-temporary meta-physician has successfully revealed its absolute presuppositions—for *his* analysis may have been faulty.

(ii) But the historian-metaphysician's interest in doing this is directed primarily towards the absolute presuppositions of science themselves, and only secondarily towards the account given of them by the philosophers of the day; and it is so directed because his real object is to trace, from one period to the next, the processes of change in the 'constellations' of absolute presuppositions which are at the basis of scientific thought. In doing so, as has been said, he will discover the impermanence of problems and the stupidity of imagining that they can be eternal, but his attention will also be directed to the more fascinating, more difficult and more important question 'Why do they change?' In answer to this question, Collingwood declares, no reason can be given which makes sense, except an historical reason. There are stresses and strains in the intellectual systems of every age which render their presuppositions (in Collingwood's terminology) 'con-supponible' only under pressure, and as those strains increase so the constellations break down and must be replaced by others. But what is abandoned does not altogether disappear; it persists in suspension (as it were), or as Collingwood says, 'incapsulated in a context of present thoughts which, by contradicting it, confine it to a plane different from theirs'.[1]

The essential aim of the true metaphysicians' study, therefore, is to discover the strains which give rise to the changes—it is what one might call (borrowing a word from Bernard Bosanquet) the 'morphology' of the absolute presuppositions of knowledge.

7. This view of the nature of metaphysics is not lightly to be brushed aside, but in the last analysis it will not survive criticism. In the first place, the doctrine of absolute presuppositions as expounded by Collingwood is, I think, unsound. That all philosophy is concerned with the uncovering of latent presuppositions is hardly to be disputed, and that some body of these might be described as absolute in the sense that they are ultimate—that unless they are presupposed no science, no inference, no thinking in short, would be possible—this too cannot in the end be denied. It is true also that these presuppositions are not the same in every historical period any more than the conceptions of the natural sciences remain the same, as those sciences progress and develop. But the account which Collingwood gives of such absolute

---

[1] *Autobiography*, p. 78. Cf. also pp. 67-8.

presuppositions, of their relations to one another and to the questions which arise from them, is, in my opinion, faulty, though he himself, as I hope to show presently, provides the means of correcting the error.

Collingwood states his case in such a way as to suggest that absolute presuppositions are something quite contingent—something which, on analysis of the propositions of science, we just find to be so-and-so. The stresses and strains to which they are said to be subject are never explained. What is their source? In what sort of tension do they result? It would seem not to be due to logical inconsistency, for Collingwood says that absolute presuppositions cannot be deduced one from another (though they must be 'consupponible'—whatever that may mean) and if this is so it will likewise be impossible to deduce the contradictory of any one of them from any other. The strains remain a mystery and the 'unstable equilibrium' in which they result is a metaphor to which no literal meaning is given. Consequently, when the historian-meta-physician discovers the absolute presuppositions of science in success-ive periods and traces the series of their changes, he has no means of explaining that series. For it is not sufficient to say that the changes are due to internal strains if it is not known what sort of strains to look for. Yet we are told that no sensible answer can be made to the question 'Why do absolute presuppositions change?' except an historical answer and we now see that historical answer there is none.

The history which is metaphysics should, if we follow this account of it, be a purely descriptive study stating the presuppositions of science in each successive period baldly side by side, and all Colling-wood's impassioned protests that history 'is concerned not with "events" but with "processes"' come to naught, for the process has been reduced to a mere series of events. Such a study would be devoid of philosophical interest and would bear little resemblance to the work of the great metaphysicians of the past whom Collingwood claims as examples of the method he is advocating.

The contradiction thus remains between the rejection of eternal problems and the insistence upon the historical method. For if the problems are not the same from one period to the next, the historical method can enlighten us very little. It can tell us what they have been in the past; it can give us a chronological list of the presuppositions made in succeeding ages; but if it cannot explain their continuity it can throw no light upon the present in which our immediate interest lies. On the other hand, if the historical method is of real value; if the past remains 'incapsulated' in the present so that the present cannot be properly understood without it; if the historical process is really

33

continuous and the historian can really explain the changes involved in it, then there must be an identity running throughout its course which will justify our inclination to call the problems of one age the same problems as those of another—there will be *some* sense in which problems are eternal.

The contradiction is the result of the unsatisfactory account we have been given of absolute presuppositions and to this we must first turn our attention. If absolute presuppositions are to give rise to questions they must have some implications, and if they are to be 'consupponible' the implications of one must, at least in part, be identical with those of another (to say that they must be mutually consistent means no more nor less than this). Consequently, absolute presuppositions must be in some way mutually implicated. Collingwood denies this because, he says, they would then be relative and not absolute, but, as we shall presently see, the disjunction is based upon a fallacy. Once it is realized that to be consupponible is to have compatible implications, it becomes clear that the source of internal strains in any constellation of absolute presuppositions will be some logical incompatibility and we should have to examine the implications of the presuppositions in order to discover this, so we should be led to the investigation of a matter which Collingwood always passes over in silence. He tells us that the logical efficacy of a supposition is that it causes questions to arise,[1] but just how questions arise and what makes suppositions give rise to them he never inquires. What is the relation between absolute presuppositions and the science that they underlie and are said to render possible? Questions such as these demand nothing less than a logic of science and, in the light of *that*, the study of the morphology of absolute presuppositions would become a philosophical history of thought on the lines of Hegel's history of philosophy, demonstrating that it is throughout a dialectical process—whether or not the principle of the dialectic were Hegelian. A good deal of what Collingwood has written seems to support such a conception both of metaphysics and of history, but if this conception is to be taken seriously, his repudiation of eternal problems in philosophy cannot stand.

The questions involved in the study of absolute presuppositions are, therefore, not all of them historical and, though what I have called the morphology of absolute presuppositions is certainly in one aspect an historical study, it follows a method which, if universal in history (as Collingwood seems at times to be implying), would make history a philosophical study rather than *vice versa*.

[1] *Essay on Metaphysics*, p. 27.

8. It is astonishing that Collingwood, in the *Essay on Metaphysics*, should so far have obfuscated what seven years earlier he had so lucidly explained.[1] For in his *Essay on Philosophical Method* he gives a profound and convincing account of the relation of philosophy to its history [2] and provides by implication an admirable answer to the question of eternal problems. In the earlier work Collingwood points out that the distinguishing feature of philosophical thinking, which marks it off from the natural sciences, is the principle which he calls 'the overlap of classes'. In science, a universal concept or genus is specified into mutually exclusive classes or species, whereas in philosophy the universal is such that the species overlap. 'The overlap', he writes, 'is not exceptional, it is normal; and it is not negligible in extent, it may reach formidable dimensions.' By numerous and convincing examples he shows that this is the case, and the principle proves to be fundamental, explaining all the features of philosophical method subsequently discussed. Neglect of the principle leads to what he calls the fallacy of false disjunction and its alternative applications, the fallacy of precarious margins and the fallacy of identified coincidents. Those who fail to recognize the overlap of classes imagine that the instances of a philosophical universal can be rigidly divided into separate groups corresponding to the division of the universal into species, whereas any instance, owing to the overlap, may belong to two (or more) such groups at once. The proposition that it belongs either to one or to another of two species is, therefore, a false disjunction. If, on the other hand, observing the overlap, we seek to identify two species altogether, we fail to make a necessary distinction and falsely identify what are only coincident. The attempt to steer a middle course, to ignore the area of overlap as one of ambiguity and to confine our attention to that part of the subject-matter in which the overlap is not apparent, would be to ignore those instances which are philosophically most important and so to commit the error of attending only to precariously marginal examples.

But if philosophical species overlap, the classes of presupposition distinguished in the *Essay on Metaphysics* should likewise display this propensity. And this is just what we find when we examine their character more closely. An absolute presupposition is logically prior to every question and every proposition of the science in which it is

---

[1] Though it must not be forgotten that his later works were written hurriedly in a tragic race against death from an ailment which, as it advanced, affected his brain. (Cf. Professor Knox's preface to *The Idea of History*.)

[2] *Vide* especially *Philosophical Method* (Oxford, 1933), ch. ix, 3.

presupposed. It is not the answer to any question raised in that science and so it cannot be scientifically 'justified'. A relative presupposition, on the other hand, is the answer to a prior question and it is therefore possible to justify it as the right answer or to reject it as wrong. But when they are raised to what Collingwood calls 'the philosophical phase',[1] it becomes apparent that absolute presuppositions are no more than the basal hypotheses of the sciences, and the philosopher's task is not only to discover what they are, but, as Plato maintained, to cancel or remove them by revealing their merely hypothetical character in the light of a more comprehensive and fundamental conception which is not a mere hypothesis but is capable of maintaining and justifying itself.[2] The presuppositions which are absolute for science prove to be relative when viewed philosophically. Using Kantian instead of Platonic language we may say that they are empirically absolute but transcendentally relative. Empirically (or scientifically) it does not make sense to question their validity, but transcendentally they can be *deduced*, an account ($\lambda\acute{o}\gamma o\varsigma$) can be given of them in a theory the subject-matter of which is not hypothetical but is categorical,[3] a philosophical theory making no assumptions [4] and following a method whereby we can at once establish our starting-point by reasoning and check the principles of the reasoning by experience, a method not strictly deduction nor strictly induction but having something in common with both.[5]

Collingwood's contention in the later essay that metaphysics is the science of absolute presuppositions may, therefore, be correct, but his description of its aim and method certainly is not; for it does not confine itself to determining what those presuppositions are. The scientist himself is able, often enough, to do as much as that (and Collingwood holds that the more scientific he is the more clearly will he be aware of what he presupposes). The metaphysician's object is to go further and to criticize those presuppositions—a task which, in his later work, Collingwood declares to be impossible. Yet the very process of discovery is already the beginning of criticism. What Collingwood calls 'metaphysical analysis',[6] the process of discovering what question is presupposed as prior to a given proposition and again what that

[1] Cf. *Philosophical Method*, p. 33 and *passim*.
[2] Cf. *Republic*, 511 B and 533 C. Collingwood, in *Metaphysics*, emphatically rejects this interpretation of Plato (*vide* ch. xv), apparently failing to see that it is in keeping with and, in fact, required by his own doctrine in *Philosophical Method*.
[3] *Vide Philosophical Method*, ch. vi.
[4] *Op. cit.* ch. viii, § 2, directly contradicted in *Metaphysics*, p. 63 and ch. xv.
[5] *Philosophical Method*, ch. viii, §§ 3 and 4.   [6] *Metaphysics*, pp. 40-1.

36

question presupposes, is, as I shall try to explain, a method of criticism. It is a process of developing the implications of a proposition and displaying its connections with others in some systematic body of knowledge the structure of which becomes apparent as we proceed. Collingwood is, therefore, right to insist on its continuity with scientific analysis. But this process cannot go on *in vacuo*. Only on the basis of a total experience, in the light of which the given proposition from which we begin has meaning and significance, and only by reference to that, can we develop its implications and so discover what it presupposes. And what comes to light as we do so is the systematic structure of that experience itself. Yet, as the system grows, so experience develops and is modified. What was before confused and obscure becomes, by the operation of thought upon it, definite and articulated (and let us not forget that thought is no mere 'armchair' occupation but may, on occasion, require considerable practical activity by way of observation and experiment); so that what was before 'known' only vaguely and 'in dim forecast' becomes known precisely and in its explicit relations to the rest of experience. The process by which initial confusions are clarified and consequent contradictions removed may properly be called criticism; and it is just this process, by which the systematic structure of experience is elucidated, that reveals what in our thinking is derived from what presuppositions. It is, moreover, this process that, in an unselfconscious manner, is going on throughout the development of a science; but when we come to reflect upon it, when it becomes self-conscious or (as Collingwood says) raised to its philosophical phase, it becomes the philosophical method—the critical method elaborated (though not originated) by Kant.

The metaphysician, therefore, discovers the absolute presuppositions of science (its '*a priori* principles') by reflection upon the nature of the experience which the science investigates. The form of his argument (as in Kant's first *Critique*) is 'If our experience is to be such as it is and if such-and-such propositions are to be made in science, then such-and-such presuppositions (*e.g.* that all perceptible things have extensive magnitude, or that all change is supported by a permanent substratum) are necessarily implied'. But the principles he discloses, though *a priori* for the scientist (absolutely presupposed by him), are so only because of the admitted nature of experience. Experience, as we have it, is prior to the absolute presuppositions and is presupposed in them. If our experience were other than it is, the *a priori* elements in science would be different. Accordingly, the presuppositions which are absolute for science are for philosophy relative to experience. They are the defining characteristics of experience or, as Hegel expressed it, provisional definitions of the Absolute.

It follows that as science advances and as knowledge grows, the nature of our experience is modified. The manner in which we interpret it at one stage, at a later stage will not serve, and absolute presuppositions change. These changes, exhibited in the course of scientific progress, are the changes incident upon and inherent in the development of knowledge. The series of changes, like the development, is continuous—it is an historical process—and the continuity running through it is as important as the differences which display themselves *seriatim* within it.

Collingwood, therefore, is right to maintain that metaphysics is an historical study, but the important point is the nature of the historical process, which turns out to be a critical (or, as I called it before, a dialectical) process, and the historical method adopted, accordingly, may not be simply descriptive but must also be dialectical. This may be what Collingwood means to suggest when he rejects the methods of scissors-and-paste history, but, if it is, he has not made himself very clear, for the scientific historian, sifting and weighing his evidence, may still content himself, when he has drawn his conclusions, with a description of facts and events. But for the metaphysician description, however necessary, is not enough (and we may question whether it is enough even for the historian). The dynamic of the process of historical change must be investigated and analysed, and this dynamic is the dialectical principle running through the process. History and metaphysics, as branches of knowledge, overlap.

Seven years after the *Essay on Philosophical Method* Collingwood had so far forgotten what he had written [1] as to distinguish rigidly between history and metaphysics, apparently forgetting that these are specifications of the philosophical concept, knowledge, and then, discovering that they overlap, he identified them entirely, committing the fallacy of false disjunction issuing in the false identification of coincidents, to which he had himself earlier drawn attention. He failed to see that though both the specific forms may be exemplified in the same instances, yet they remain two. The Aristotelian formula (which he quotes) applies here as elsewhere in philosophy, ἔστι μὲν τὸ αὐτὸ τὸ δὲ εἶναι αὐτοῖς οὐ τὸ αὐτό. Consequently, he is led into further confusion

---

[1] We cannot say 'rejected', for in his autobiography, published only one year before the *Essay on Metaphysics*, he refers to the earlier work as 'my best book in matter, and in style . . . my only book, for it is the only one I ever had time to finish as well as I knew how'.

from which his own earlier warnings might have saved him. Let us therefore return to his exposition in the earlier work.

9. The specification of the philosophical universal into overlapping classes is further explained by showing that it always takes the form of an ascending scale. The overlapping classes cannot be mere differences in kind, for that is the characteristic of non-philosophical species; nor can they be mere differences in degree, for even such differences are mutually exclusive. But if these two sorts of difference are combined (if they overlap), we have a generic concept specified into a scale of forms such that each embodies a variable element in a specific degree, the distinction between the species occurring at critical points on the scale of gradations. But it further transpires that the variable element and the generic essence are the same thing—the principle of overlap applies here as elsewhere—and the scale is one throughout which the generic essence is successively displayed by the specific forms in continuously increasing fulness. Moreover, the specific forms prove to be both opposites and distincts, so that the scale consists of a gradation of forms, each embodying the generic essence more fully than the last, each distinct from every other and each the opposite of its predecessor in the scale; just as the feelings of heat and cold are not only distinct feelings but also opposite feelings and at the same time gradations in a scale of feelings of temperature; or as goodness and badness are at once distinct and opposite moral conditions and gradations in a scale of moral worth.

Now a scale of forms of this kind is a development, and if it occurs in time it is an historical process. When, therefore, we compare the philosophical theories of different generations, as Collingwood does in Chapter VII of the *Autobiography* (pp. 44 ff.), and we find that, while they have a certain sameness, they differ both as to the questions raised and the answers offered, and when we discover, as Collingwood does, that these differences and this sameness are those of an historical process, should we not realize that the theories are phases in a scale of forms which is the specification of a philosophical universal? This, indeed, is exactly what Collingwood himself maintains in Chapter IX of the *Essay on Philosophical Method* [1] where the history of philosophy is given as an example of such a scale. What, then, are we to make of his assertion in the *Autobiography* [2] that the sameness of and difference between two philosophical theories are *not* 'the sameness of a "universal"' . . . and the difference between two instances of that universal'

[1] § 3, ¶ 13.   [2] P. 45.

but *are* 'the sameness of an historical process and . . . the difference between one thing which in the course of that process has turned into something else, and the other thing into which it has turned'? Again the principle of the overlap of classes has been forgotten and the teaching that the philosophical universal specifies itself into a scale of forms.

But if we accept the earlier statement of Collingwood's theory, we find good reason for saying that the problems with which philosophers deal are in every age the same, as well as for saying (as he does in his later works) that they are not. Philosophies differ, it is true, in degree and in kind; they are also opposed to one another, so as to give rise to argument and dispute, but they are nevertheless the specifications of one and the same philosophical universal and so their differences and oppositions are only the normal characteristics of the phases in a scale of forms.[1] What is still more significant is the fact that such a scale is always an ascending scale. The phases embody progressively more and more fully the generic essence, and such a progression implies a completion, a summit to the ascent, an acme—that which throughout the scale is, in ever-increasing degrees, becoming more fully itself. The generic essence in such a universal is that which, throughout the gamut of gradations, informs the particulars and makes them *its* particulars and yet does so in varying degrees, so that none of them except the last fully typifies the universal. When these phases or gradations, then, are the successive notions of a philosophical problem and its solution, each of them indeed will differ from the last, will even in a sense be in opposition to it, yet each will be a fuller and a truer account of that eternal problem and that eternal truth which all are attempting to express with varying degrees of success. The eternal problems are relative to the philosophical universals which in the history of philosophy are specified in a scale of forms, and accordingly the method of philosophy is at once historical and dialectical. It must trace the scale of forms throughout its length in order to achieve its goal (a goal of which the best achievements of the human intellect fall far short), but the method it adopts must nevertheless always be critical and even, to a certain extent, eristic.

The metaphysician, accordingly, *must* be a system-builder; but his system being a philosophical system will display itself as a scale of forms. And it will be one that, among its various methods of self-manifestation,[2] expresses itself in an historical process the course of

---

[1] This is the real reason why philosophers inevitably and perpetually disagree.

[2] Cf. *Philosophical Method*, ch. ix, 3. The other modes of self-manifestation of the system are (i) as a body of philosophical sciences, (ii) as the philosophical doctrines of

which the metaphysician must study. He will, therefore, also be an historian tracing the series of differing and opposing doctrines in which the universal he is seeking to characterize has, in the past, revealed its specifications.

Thus the implication of contradiction in the doctrine of the *Essay on Metaphysics* is avoided in the *Philosophical Method* and the contradiction itself can be resolved by the application of the principles there expounded. And, for all that he says in the later work, these principles surely must be regarded as fundamental to Collingwood's whole position, for he is emphatic in his assertion that there is a continuity of development in historical changes, and when he maintains that metaphysics is an historical study he insists at the same time that its essential interest lies in the manner of and the reasons for the changes in absolute presuppositions from one period to the next. He insists, also, that the understanding of the past is indispensable to the proper understanding of the present, whether we are dealing with absolute presuppositions or with other historical matters. And to admit all this is to admit, after all, that there is a sense—not loose or indefinite, but precise—in which the problems of philosophy are eternal; not the sense in which any historical fact can be called eternal because it has happened once and for all,[1] but that in which it is true to say (with Kant) that only the permanent can change. The new form which a problem takes is only a new *form*, but the problem is still the same. Its form is new because new material relevant to it has come to hand, because new evidence has been discovered and new interpretations have been made. All this has certainly modified it, but it has not sheerly changed; it has developed and grown, which it could not have done if it had been replaced by an utterly different question. We cannot, therefore, refuse to call philosophical problems eternal, at least in *this* sense, for if the resemblances between those of one generation and those of another were purely superficial and deceptive, we should have to believe that these resemblances had deceived the philosophers themselves who raised the questions and must consequently have falsified their attempted solutions. They must have mistaken one problem for another entirely different and so have been ignorant of the questions they were trying to answer. For, clearly, the philosophers of the past believed themselves to be discussing the same problems as had been tackled by their predecessors and they built upon foundations which their predecessors had laid.

a single age and (iii) as the philosophy of a single man. All of these are overlapping classes and so all are mutually intervolved.

[1] *Vide Autobiography*, p. 49.

The denial of eternal problems, in *this* sense, then, would make non-sense of the whole history of philosophy and would render contemporary thought completely unintelligible.

To support this conclusion we may call Collingwood himself as witness, for, writing of the history of philosophical thought, he says:

> 'It is a genuine history in so far as the events contained in it lead each to the next: so far, that is, as each philosopher has learnt his philosophy through studying the work of his predecessors. For in that case each is trying to do what his predecessors did—to philosophize; but to do it better by doing it differently; assimilating whatever seems true, rejecting whatever seems false, and thus producing a new philosophy which is at the same time an improved version of the old. His successor in turn stands in this same relation to himself, and thus the entire history of thought is the history of a single sustained attempt to solve a single permanent problem, each phase advancing the problem by the extent of all the work done on it in the interval, and summing up the fruits of this work in the shape of a unique presentation of the problem.'[1]

The existence of perennial problems in philosophy has thus been demonstrated and also the proper method of philosophical procedure has been laid down. It is a method both historical and critical; in part an examination of the work of past philosophers, and in part, through criticism of their theories, an attempt to develop one more suited to modern needs. But my object in this essay is not to write a history of philosophy. It is to study a particular problem in the light both of its past development and of contemporary discussion. I shall proceed immediately to state the problem in the form which first occurs in reflection and shall not be daunted by the derisive chatter of those who would dismiss it as a pseudo-problem to be explained away as ungrammatical talk. I have already exposed the rottenness of the foundation on which they seek to build and as my thesis develops it will appear that they inhabit a ruin long forsaken by men and haunted only by the ghosts of their philosophical ancestors.

[1] *Philosophical Method*, pp. 194-5.

Chapter II

THE PROBLEM OF KNOWLEDGE

I. THE MIND IN THE WORLD AND THE WORLD IN THE MIND

1. THE dual character of Man: his membership in the universe on the one hand, and his capacity to know it on the other, has, for many centuries, provided philosophers with their principal and most difficult problem. The human mind is the apparent possession of a finite creature. It seems to be somehow attached to an animal organism with a material body which is one entity among innumerable others in a world of finite things. Yet the mind has a character which seems quite incompatible with these facts of its existence, for there is nothing in the universe which is not at least a possible object of its knowledge, and while, in one sense, it appears to be confined to a single finite entity among a multitude of others, in another sense it claims to be able to possess and comprehend in knowledge the whole of the universe. Furthermore, it sets out to explain in theory its own relation to its objects and so complicates the position still further.

The problem is that of the relation of mind to its objects, and the way in which we deal with it is fundamental to our entire *Weltanschauung*. That man is a finite creature in a world of innumerable finites is obvious, and that he is a creature produced by the processes of nature and evolved through long periods of time from other less complex natural entities is nowadays a generally accepted fact. But also, man *knows* all this. He is conscious of the world in which he is but one member, he is aware of the objects around him which together constitute his world and of his own relation to them, and from this awareness he has been able to elaborate a knowledge of that world, a system of sciences, both comprehensive and exact. How is it possible that a quantitatively insignificant part of a vast system should be able somehow to grasp within itself the whole of that system, as well as the relation between itself and the whole which accounts for this accomplishment? How is it possible that a mere product of nature should be capable somehow of laying hold upon the entire system of nature and in some sense of comprehending within itself what lies so far beyond its own apparent limits? Not the least paradoxical feature of this situation is the fact that it is through the very elaboration of man's knowledge of the world that his own diminutive membership of it becomes apparent.

The position is epitomized in the epigram:

The mind is in the world and the world is in the mind.

Though there is a sense in which each of these statements compels our assent, it seems hardly possible to maintain them together unless either 'world' or 'mind' is given a different meaning in each. Yet as will presently appear, when we attempt to assign to those words different senses which will make the two statements seem more compatible, we find that the meanings we adopt cannot consistently be maintained.

In one sense, of course, the human mind does not comprehend the *whole* of the universe; its knowledge is confessedly imperfect and fragmentary. Moreover we are frequently the victims of error, and much which has no place in the world of actuality may be included within our consciousness. But neither of these facts removes the problem, for sufficient of nature is known to make evident our own memberships of a world which extends infinitely beyond ourselves. Enough is known to inform us of the processes by which nature has brought the human race to birth. The knowledge of nature that we have makes us acutely aware of our own relative minuteness, yet the very possession of this knowledge contradicts that awareness and reverses the judgement of our own insignificance which scientists are often so ready to pronounce.

Moreover, there is another sense, in which our knowledge does embrace the whole world. However limited and fragmentary a man's knowledge of the world may be it always provides him with what has been called a 'world-picture'—a cosmology of some sort—and, even though very imperfect and rudimentary, this is a conception of the universe as a whole. And in this 'world-picture' he is himself always but one small item, so that it immediately becomes pertinent to ask: How can any cosmology account for the fact that it has been conceived by what is represented within it as only one very subordinate detail?

Collingwood was only partly right to discredit as 'philosophically foolish' the idea that the Copernican astronomy diminished the importance of man in the scheme of things.[1] Admittedly the degree of this diminution is not material to the philosophical problem, for in any astronomy the importance of the human animal is almost negligible and Collingwood is quite right to protest against the historical error of attributing the discovery of this fact to Copernicus. But when he

[1] *The Idea of Nature* (Oxford, 1945), p. 96.

alleges that the philosophical problem of the relation between man and the universe is not affected by the relative amount of space they occupy he is wrong. If the part is in any sense subordinate to the whole, it does affect the problem. For the crux of the whole problem is just how so infinitesmal a part of so stupendous a whole can become possessed of the knowledge of the whole. The study of the vast expanse of the heavens, the immense aeons of astronomical time involved in the histories of the galaxies and the precariousness of the conditions indispensable to the emergence of life, cannot fail (as Sir James Jeans has so rightly emphasized [1]—despite the strictures of the late Professor Stebbing [2]) to impress upon us the relative smallness, brevity and insecurity of our own existence, and the paradox lies in just this, that the possession of this knowledge contradicts the apparent insignificance which it reveals. To say, therefore, that simply because human beings are quite small inhabitants on a minor planet of a medium-sized star they are unimportant, is certainly foolish, but that these facts are irrelevant to the philosophical problem of relating man to the universe is far from true.

2. The problem is commonly so little recognized that the bare statement of it may at first seem captious. In everyday life, a relation between consciousness and its objects is universally assumed which *prima facie* dissolves the difficulty. So universal is this assumption that we are hardly aware of making it, and even philosophers, whose business it is to reveal hidden presuppositions and to criticize them, are often content to take this one for granted, or to adopt it explicitly, unmindful of the contradictions which it entails and which vitiate the whole of their subsequent thinking.

The assumption is that consciousness is a reflection of a world external to the mind and that knowledge is a sort of picture or representation of the world built up by the mind out of the materials which its consciousness provides. When made explicit, it becomes what has been called [3] the representative theory of knowledge, and if it could be maintained our problem would disappear, for there is no difficulty in conceiving that even a small part of a great system may contain within itself some sort of replica or reflection of the system as a whole. The unphilosophical person usually assumes some such relation between

[1] *The Mysterious Universe* (Penguin Books), pp. 13 ff.
[2] *Vide Philosophy and the Physicists* (Penguin Books), pp. 15 ff.
[3] Cf. Sinclair, *Introduction to Philosophy* (Oxford, 1945), pp. 31 ff., also Joachim, *Logical Studies* (Oxford, 1948), pp. 219-41.

45

consciousness and its objects (complicated, no doubt, by the existence in the mind of some knowledge of itself), yet we shall presently see that it is just this view of the matter which on examination raises the problem in its sharpest form.

If, in everyday life, we ever reflect upon the nature of knowledge, we usually tend to think of a mind much on the analogy of a camera, our senses corresponding to the lens, through which images of objects outside are transmitted (in the case of a mind the process is complicated by the existence of several 'lenses', each transmitting images of a different kind which are somehow combined within). Our consciousness is thought of as constituted by these images, which may be retained in the mind as the photographs taken by a camera are retained on the film. (We may ignore, for the purposes of the analogy, the fact that in photography the images are negatives.) To make the analogy more exact the camera must be able to project the whole hemisphere of the heavens at once and complexities in the recording machinery must be added to correspond to the mental processes involved in memory, imagination and the like. These processes are sometimes thought of as a kind of internal photography, as if the camera were able by its own interior mechanism to rephotograph its own photographs. Moreover, in this internal photography we must imagine it possible for new combinations to be made and we must impute to the camera the capacity to compare, to analyse, to select and to recombine the images, in order to build up new and more intricate pictures of the world without, which are not directly obtainable through the lens. Further complications arise in connection with what we call 'abstract' or 'general ideas' and they are often conceived as the result of superimposing the original impressions one upon another, in the manner of a composite photograph. Again, just as a camera will sometimes produce distorted images which are not good likenesses of the objects before the lens, so the mind is regarded as occasionally forming images of external things which do not exactly copy them. Such 'ideas' are called errors, while those which are exact copies are said to be 'true'. But more especially are misrepresentations of the external reality liable to be made in the course of analysis, selection and recombination. Truth, therefore, is understood as the correspondence of the images, whether original or factitious, with the actualities of the external world.

This is more or less the conception which the ordinary man might form of mind and its knowledge. He would see no more difficulty in the statement that the mind is a finite entity in the world and yet the world is experienced by the mind than if this statement were made of the camera in the analogy. The camera is one thing in a world of things and yet it can form within it the images of all the other things; they are depicted on the photographic plate.

One has only to attempt clearly to state this conception of the mind to become immediately aware of the immense difficulties which it involves.[1] But the inadequacy of the analogue never dawns upon common sense. It is seldom realized that no sort of reflection can produce anything else than a dead image which may be an object of *our* consciousness but is not itself the consciousness of anything. A photograph has no meaning for itself, represents nothing to itself, but only to the mind which perceives it together with its likeness to the original. It is really nothing like the consciousness of an object, and is an image of anything only for a consciousness. As a simile the comparison between a mind and a camera may serve certain purposes, but there is nothing whatever in the nature of a photographic projection which can answer to the living, intelligent self-illumination of conscious apprehension in a mind.

The common consciousness, however, neglects this divergence of the analogue, by means of which it thinks of the mind, from the true and even obvious nature of consciousness. What is most obvious and universal in experience is most frequently overlooked, probably because it is too familiar to evoke special comment. Accordingly, speculation usually begins with a notion of mind not unlike the camera in the analogy.[2] As a result difficulties are soon encountered which wreck the theory.

Only the images which pass through the lens of the camera can be recorded and by no means can the photographic plate lay hold of and possess the actual objects it reflects. The archetypes of its images are inevitably beyond its reach. Similarly, it soon becomes apparent that, on a theory which likens the mind to a recording instrument of this kind, only 'ideas' can be known and these are the sole indication of any external reality. But if the mind's knowledge is confined to what appears in its own consciousness (its own ideas), it cannot possibly know how those ideas are produced; it cannot reach out beyond itself to its supposed objects and form an idea of the relation between itself and them. For the knowledge of such a relation requires the knowledge of both its terms, and the only knowledge of objects which the

---

[1] See the whole discussion in Joachim, *Logical Studies*, pp. 110 ff.

[2] Cf. Locke's conception of the mind as 'white paper void of all characters' on which 'the busy and boundless fancy of Man' paints, and his other metaphors, quoted below, p. 127.

mind can possess is *ex hypothesi* comprised in its furniture of ideas, which constitutes only one term of the relation. This is equally true whether the relation is one of resemblance or of causation and the argument is fatal to both representative and causal theories of perception which frequently go hand in hand. We thus arrive at the curious position in which, if the theory were true, the mind could never form it, and if the mind can and does claim truth for such a theory, then the theory must, in the nature of the case, be false, for it follows from it that no mind could ever know it.

It is obvious, likewise, that the criterion of truth which common sense attempts to uphold, namely, correspondence of the idea with its object, falls to the ground in the general ruin of the theory. For if only one term of the relation is known to the mind, it has no means of judging whether it corresponds to the other or not.

3. Two possible objections may be raised to this argument. The first is that the testimony of others can provide me with the knowledge of the relation which I seek. It may be said, though (according to the theory) it is impossible for my mind to have any direct knowledge of the objects of which its consciousness provides only the replicas, it is possible for others to observe them and their effects upon my mind, and then to communicate to me the observed relation between the external things on the one hand, and my consciousness on the other. Clearly this cannot be. For, in the first place, no other mind has access to my consciousness, for just as my knowledge is confined to my own presentations, so my presentations are confined and private to my mind. There is no way, therefore, in which another mind can become aware of the effects of external things upon my consciousness. Neither, in the second place, would other minds have access to external things, for on the theory we are assuming, they, like my own, would be confined to the presentations in their own private experiences.

This defence of the representative theory is often supported by an attempt to argue from the analogy of one's own experience to the existence and nature of the experience of others, and then to maintain that the observed relation between material things and other people gives us the model for that between those things and our own minds.[1] If, for instance, I hear a man shout, 'Look out', and immediately afterwards see a motor-car rushing towards me, I presume that the man saw the motor-car also, because had I been in his position I should have shouted a warning to anyone in danger of being run over. All this

---

[1] Cf. Bertrand Russell's arguments in *The Analysis of Matter*, ch. xx.

THE PROBLEM OF KNOWLEDGE

is of course true, but how is it to be explained on a representative theory? According to that, my perception of the man and his shout followed by that of the car are all internal to my mind and I have no means of knowing that there is any real man or car corresponding to them. If I leap aside to avoid the car, that can only mean that I have certain other experiences of the behaviour of what I call my body (which is itself only a set of ideas in my mind), and the connection of these experiences with the earlier ones could be explicable only by the laws of association. If I say that I should have shouted in such-and-such circumstances, I can mean only that certain experiences in my mind (seeing a motor-car) are habitually followed by certain others (feelings of impulse, sensations of laryngial movement, the hearing of a shout, etc.). I should have no grounds whatever for attributing similar experiences to what is but one, or a set, of my own. The relation between the objects, which I experience, and the bodies and behaviour of other people, which I experience likewise, is not at all analogous to the relation between all these and my mind which experiences them. On the hypothesis assumed it could never occur to me that these things had a separate existence external to my consciousness, so that they could be related to my mind as they are related to one another in my experience of them. And if it could, I should already have what I sought and should not need to reason from the analogy of my own experience to other people's, and then back from theirs to the relation of my own mind to external things. Once I know (or assume) that things and minds are mutually external, I know (or assume) that the relation between my mind and the things which it knows is the same as that between other minds and those same things. To allege, therefore, that our experience of the behaviour of others could inform us of the relation between our own minds and the things of the material world, while maintaining at the same time a representative theory of knowledge, is both to beg the question and to contradict oneself.

The second possible objection to the argument against the representative theory is that, though a mind may be circumscribed in the manner alleged, it may yet *presume* the existence of something beyond it which is correlative to the consciousness which it experiences, and may thus quite easily form a theory such as we are considering of its own relation to an outside world. And though in such circumstances we should never know whether or not the theory were true, it might well be so. But if it were true, that would not (as has been maintained) prevent our forming it, nor would our forming it be evidence of its falsity.

C

But what sort of correlation is this that we are supposed to be presuming? The world we know through the medium of our consciousness is all we have. If we now imagine another world corresponding to it, we are simply imagining a duplicate of the contents of our consciousness and labelling it 'external'. And this newly imagined 'external world', because imagined, is still part of the content of our consciousness and demands a new correlate external to it. Or if it is denied that we imagine a double to our experienced world, and asserted that we merely assume 'something' unknown to us which is the external source of our experience, we are postulating no intelligible correlate and no intelligible relation.

Moreover, our problem is to understand how one member of an infinitely various world can contain within itself the knowledge of a multitude of others; and the world presumed as 'external' to our minds, if it is alleged to be unknown and unknowable, cannot be the world of which we *know* ourselves to be members. That has vanished. It has somehow got inside our minds and our membership of it has become an enigma. To say that we presume a world just like that we know (or differing from it we know not how), of which we are finite members, is to render our membership meaningless. For membership is a definitely known relation both to the whole and to the other members, and what is being postulated is an unknown and unknowable relation which illuminates the matter in no way whatsoever.

Finally, this presumption of an unknown 'external' world cannot remove the difficulty attaching to the criterion of truth which the representative theory requires, for there can be no intelligible correspondence between an unknown something and that of which we are aware; and if any sort of correspondence were possible, it is obvious that on this hypothesis it could not be known. But if it is not known, it cannot enable us to distinguish between truth and falsehood, and if we could not distinguish, we could not know that there was a distinction, and the very conception of knowledge would consequently dissolve away. To know, we must be able to distinguish between appearance and reality, and that we could never do if the criterion of truth were inaccessible to us.

The representative theory of knowledge is quite indefensible and once its untenability is fully appreciated much unhelpful thinking can be avoided—all, in fact, which leads us back to such a theory. We can use this as a criterion in criticizing philosophical systems. Do they entail a representative theory of knowledge? If so they cannot be true, for, as we have seen, that theory is self-annihilating and any by which it is entailed will likewise be false. On the other hand, the immense difficulty of the problem before us is now more apparent, for what looked like an easy and obvious way out is now closed to us. The courses which philosophers have taken who realized its pitfalls have been more heroic but they have not always been more successful. Before we go on to examine them, however, we must notice three variations of the problem of relating the mind to nature which may seem at first to be separate questions from the problem of knowledge but which are actually the same problem becoming apparent in different connections.

II. ALLIED PROBLEMS

4. (i) The first of these is that arising from the difficulty of conceiving the mutual relations of finite minds. My consciousness of the world includes the awareness of other beminded creatures like myself. In fact without them and the intercommunication which we enjoy through speech and writing, my knowledge of the world could not be what it is. Their minds, like mine, are finite and they too reach beyond themselves in an endeavour to know our common world, which is the object of their consciousness, as it is of mine. Yet though I know this multiplicity of minds, any attempt to understand how they are to be distinguished from and related to one another meets at once with obstacles.

The difficulty may be stated thus: My knowledge of the world includes other persons who, like myself, are taken to be finite members of the world and, like myself, are yet taken to comprehend in their experience the world of which we are all members. So far as I experience a world, other minds are items or factors in it; yet each of them is believed to contain a world within itself of which I am one finite member. Not only, then, does my experience embrace a world of which I am supposed to be no more than one finite member, but also it includes in that world numerous other supposed finite entities each of which claims to comprehend a world and in each of which I figure as one entity. How can we be thus *mutually* related as part and whole? The easy-going explanation offered by the representative theory, we have seen, is in the end no explanation. If each mind were a reflection of the world, we could easily relate them (it would seem) as reflections of it from differing view-points. But in that case each would be confined to its own view-point and could know nothing of the others and so nothing of their differences and correlations. No mirror can reflect from one point of view what another reflects from a different point of view, so none can reflect the relationship of its own images to those of any other. No camera can photograph the images projected in another camera, so none can portray the interrelations between its own point of view and that of others.

But if we cannot resort to a theory of representation, what alternative have we? Difference of point of view is strictly a spatial relation, and neither the relation between a mind and its objects nor that between different minds can be spatial. For to know the positions and mutual relations of objects in space, the whole spatial system must be before the knowing mind, which cannot therefore be tied down to any one position relative to the positions of other objects, without ceasing to be aware of its own relations to them. And if the other objects are minds, no more can they be confined each to one point of view. The mind can never be made one term of a known relation, for knowledge brings both terms necessarily within the mind. On the other hand, if the phrase 'difference of view-point' is used only metaphorically, it sheds no light upon the mutual relations of minds, for then it can mean only that their experiences differ, but it gives no clue as to how they differ.

If we say that each mind has knowledge of a different part or section of the world and that their divergence lies in the possession by one of knowledge that others have not got, a further difficulty arises, for none of us can know of this difference except by mutual comparison of our knowledge, and such comparison is possible only when we know all of the things to be compared. But when we know all, we each know what in the others' knowledge we are supposed to lack. Knowing it, we no longer lack it, and thus the alleged differences between us disappear. This is no mere sophism. Knowledge is common property and if I begin by admitting that I am ignorant of much that others have learnt, by that admission itself I claim, in a measure, the knowledge which I disavow. Moreover, *potentially*, I have that knowledge. For it is at the disposal of all mankind (at any rate, so far as men are able to communicate with one another). In one sense it is true that human knowledge never is and never was the sole possession of one individual nor has there ever been one man who could claim it all. Yet every educated man is in some measure aware of it all and his 'world-picture' is the product of contemporary knowledge, most of which has been acquired by the researches of others. The way, moreover, in which he becomes possessed of what he has not himself directly discovered (and this is the point I wish to stress) is by comparison with others; by consultation with them upon those fields which his own direct experience has not covered; and thus by acquiring what he has hitherto lacked, he cancels

THE PROBLEM OF KNOWLEDGE

out the differences between himself and others. So the paradox develops that because the limitations of the human mind impose on it the necessity to specialize, human knowledge becomes (it seems, inevitably) distributed among a multitude; yet to be a body of *knowledge*, properly so called, it must all belong to one mind and the very fact of its division and distribution cannot otherwise be known.

5. (ii) The second variation of the problem is that arising from the relation between the human body and its mind. That this is really another manifestation of the problem of knowledge can be seen when it is noticed that our possession of knowledge raises a difficulty mainly because the human mind is so intimately related to a material body. It is the body that is so obviously and undeniably an infinitesimal fraction of the physical universe. It is the mind which comprehends that universe in knowing it. If we were not compelled to associate the two, the problem (if any arose) would be different. If the mind in question were a universal mind, associated not with any particular part of the world but rather with the world as a whole, our task of understanding the relation between them might at least be easier.[1] But such a mind would not be human.

My body is something which I regard as peculiarly my own; it is something the consciousness of which in some manner accompanies my awareness of everything else, and without which my knowledge would be utterly different from what it is. It is the body which provides the mechanism of the camera, according to the analogy by which the mind has just been represented. The sense-organs are the 'lenses' through which the images of things seem to enter the mind, and certainly if all the channels of sense were somehow to be stopped, it is clear that we could never acquire the sort of knowledge that we now enjoy. The nervous system and the brain are commonly taken to provide the mechanism of those other activities of the mind, in which it differs from and surpasses the capacity of a mere camera, by which it revives, selects, compares and recombines the images. And here we are faced with a double problem: first, it is not known and is hardly conceivable how the functioning of the nerves and brain should produce the effects in consciousness which are commonly attributed to them, and, secondly, it is as little understandable how the mind should acquire and, as it needs them, should in its memory be able to revive perceptions of material things, without the instrumentality of the

[1] Cf., however, the problem of the relation between the attributes of substance in the philosophy of Spinoza.

53

physical organism. And this mysterious yet seemingly indispensable conjunction of the mind with a material body is what gives rise to our main problem, for the wide-embracing knowledge of nature which belongs to the mind seems so obviously to come to us through the instrumentality of a bodily organism which is a mere product of nature. Our difficulty in attaching the knowledge of nature to one of its own products is thus precisely the problem of relating the mind to its body.

6. (iii) The third variation in which our problem may appear can be made clear by reference to the second. The obvious imperfections and limitations of the human mind result (at least in all the more obvious ways) from its association with the body. Yet the very nature of consciousness and the knowledge of the world which it gives to us, is to transcend the limits to which the body is subject. Consciousness is essentially a reaching out beyond the material boundaries of the body and our perpetual striving to perfect our knowledge is a continual launching forth into a further and still further 'beyond', by the contrivance of new methods of discovery and new instruments of research the great majority of which are simply the means of overcoming limitations imposed upon us by the material circumstances of our existence. If our knowledge could be perfected it would comprehend the universe, as a whole and in detail. Yet within this whole our own finite human existence would remain a factor, and unless it did so the knowledge of the universe of which we are a part could not be perfect. Yet here again we have a paradox. How can a finite and imperfect fragment aspire so to transcend its own limits as to cancel its fragmentary and imperfect character, which yet must be maintained in order that its knowledge should not be defective?

Again to know of limitations is at once to have transcended them, and to know fully the nature of those limitations implies a knowledge of the standard by which we judge of limits. Our consciousness of our own imperfections is in itself an incipient knowledge of perfection. On the one hand the conditions of our finite existence create an inevitable and unbridgeable gulf between us and that infinity to which our knowledge constantly aspires; on the other, such knowledge as we have and the progress (however little) which we make towards its perfection, reveals to us an infinity 'in vague forecast conceived', in the light of which alone our own limitations can be adequately known. How are we, then, to understand the revelation (however inchoate) of an infinite reality and an aspiration towards fuller knowledge of it in a merely finite being? (If a captious critic should exclaim 'Ah, but not *merely* finite', we must ask 'How then at once both finite and not finite?') In short, our problem displays another aspect and resolves itself into that of understanding the relation between finite minds and the infinite.

The problem as a whole may be summed up by observing that the human mind has both a particular and a universal character. As a product of nature it appears to be a function (or a part?) of a particular entity. But it is also the subject of knowledge which is objective to all minds and universal in its scope. These two aspects of the human mind seem incompatible, yet somehow it has them both. How they may be reconciled is perhaps the most important and difficult problem in the whole field of philosophical speculation, and it is not solved if either aspect is neglected or denied. We shall find that theories which stress either at the expense of the other break down, and that no satisfactory theory of knowledge is possible which fails to do justice to both.

III. PROCEDURE TO BE ADOPTED

7. It is not my intention to discuss exhaustively all these forms of the problem of knowledge. My main concern will be the relation of the mind to nature, which it knows in science and of which it seems itself to be a product. But it is well to realize beforehand that the question has various forms and aspects, which, as the discussion proceeds, are liable to make themselves apparent. Moreover, in an historical treatment, it will be necessary to discuss theories some of which have given prominence to one form of the problem and others to another. And we must realize that these seemingly different questions, of the relation between finite minds, of the relation between the mind and the body and of the relation between the finite mind and the infinite, are, so far from being irrelevant to the main discussion, actually aspects of the problem of knowledge which is its theme, and that light shed upon any one of them is likely to illuminate the others also.

It is clear that any examination of these questions must be closely concerned both with the conception of nature which results from scientific discoveries and is set out in cosmological theory, and with the conception of mind evolved by philosophers. These conceptions have changed and developed in the course of time and to trace their development adequately would require a full-scale history both of science and of philosophy. But the scope of this essay is not so large and my intention is simply to select theories typical of the main periods of western thought and to examine them as phases in the development of the notions of nature and of mind.

I shall first consider briefly the ideas of nature and mind as they appear in the philosophy of the ancient Greeks and shall observe that, even if we accept Collingwood's contention that the Greek idea of nature was that of a vast living creature, 'saturated or permeated by mind',[1] we cannot accept his further contention that for them 'the problem of the relation between dead matter and living matter, and the problem of the relation between matter and mind, did not exist'.[2] These two problems are not unrelated, and I think there is definite evidence that the Greeks were aware of both and that they were not unconcerned to find their solution.

It seems to me, however, that the most characteristic feature of the Greek conception of nature, and one most important for the problem of the relation to it of the human mind, is that, apart from their idea of nature as a living organism, they regarded it as the realm of perpetual change. This is what raised for them the problem of knowledge, for they thought that to know something was to apprehend its determinate character—that which it really is—and it seemed to them impossible to know determinately what is constantly changing. The knowable, they thought, was the eternal and unchanging, and natural things and events, therefore, could not be knowable unless, and except in so far as, they partook of that which is eternal. It is clear at once that the position of the human mind is problematical, for it is in close dependence upon and association with a natural, changing entity, the body, and at the same time it is cognizant of the eternal (knowable) realities. The attempts of the Greek philosophers to reconcile these conflicting aspects of human nature were never wholly successful. For them, in the main, the eternal reality and the perpetually changing realm of nature tended to fall apart. Aristotle came nearest to uniting them, though in the end even he fell short of a complete reconciliation; and the position as the Greeks left it was broadly that the intelligible, eternal world is the true reality of which the changeable world of nature is somehow (with varying degrees of success) imitative. In the soul of man, likewise, they distinguished two parts: (i) the sensory and emotional part, which they regarded as mortal, and which was akin (or belonged) to the world of change; and (ii) the intellectual part, which they regarded as immortal and as akin to (though one must hesitate to say one of) the eternal realities. So far as it was at all possible, therefore, for man to know the changing world of nature (in the strict sense of the word 'know') it was only by means of the intellect and only by reference to the eternal verities. The world of sense thus tended to

[1] *The Idea of Nature*, p. 3. [2] *Ibid.* p. 111.

56

be viewed as one of misleading appearances, or even illusions, the relation of which to the eternal realities was never (at any rate before Aristotle) satisfactorily explained.

When we come to the beginnings of modern science at the Renaissance, we find a revulsion against these ideas which is reflected in the philosophy of the time. Stress is now laid on the changing events of the natural world which are revealed to man in sense-perception. The sensuous revelation of these events is held to be the original and only source of human knowledge of nature, which is raised to scientific form only through the observation of particulars and the abstraction from them of general laws determining the course of their occurrence. Two kinds of knowledge, in consequence, come to be distinguished: sensuous knowledge of direct acquaintance, and abstract or scientific knowledge of the general laws governing the course of natural events, the latter strictly derivative from the former. This notion of knowledge is the result of the second conception of nature with which I shall be concerned—a conception antithetical to that ascribed by Collingwood to the Greeks. So far from being alive and 'permeated by mind', nature for the Renaissance thinker was purely material and mechanical, its changes determined entirely *a tergo* by efficient causation. Mind has thus no place in nature, which is viewed as wholly corporeal, but is something set over against corporeal nature as its knower (and, in the case of God, as its creator). Divorced in this manner from the object of its knowledge, the human mind receives its knowledge of the world from without as something given, and its relation to the natural body becomes inexplicable, for the body belongs to the corporeal world from which mind is excluded.

In the modern conception of nature, which is the third that I shall consider, there is a union of the two earlier ideas. For modern thought, nature is a continuous process of evolution in which the human organism comes into existence as a development from earlier material forms. The purely physical now appears as an early phase in a development of which the later phases are the forms of life, and here in the higher manifestations we find mind and consciousness. As a phase in such a development, what had hitherto been regarded as sheerly mechanical can no longer be so regarded, for from the sheerly mechanical nothing whatever can develop or evolve. The process of nature is, of course, a process of change, but it is not for that reason thought to be unknowable, and the theory of knowledge consequent upon the modern conception of nature makes the relation of the mind to its objects, as well as to the human body, intelligible, by seeing in the evolutionary

C*

process the self-evolution of a consciousness in which human know-ledge is a late stage. The process of change is, therefore, a knowable and intelligible process just because it is, throughout, the process of coming to be of what is essentially and entirely intelligible—namely, mind. Though this theory of knowledge has been stated in various forms, none of them have been quite adequate to modern requirements owing to their infection, in some way or other, with obsolete Renais-sance ideas, and it will be my endeavour, in the conclusion of this study, to suggest how it might be restated without contamination by survivals of this kind.

Those who are steeped in the doctrines of modern empiricism will, no doubt, immediately reject so 'idealistic' a view both of nature and of mind (failing to notice that it satisfies the legitimate demands of a realistic philosophy as much as those of idealism) and they will claim that it is quite out of harmony with the deliverances of modern science. But what I shall set myself to demonstrate in the chapters which follow is that a new statement of a theory akin to what has been called 'ideal-ism' can better satisfy the requirements of contemporary science than can any merely empirical realism, and that, on the contrary, empiricism is appropriate only to the scientific conceptions which prevailed in the 17th and 18th centuries, and is now (despite noisy and persistent survivals) more obsolete than Newtonian physics. Like Newtonian physics, it has an honourable place in the history of thought, and like Newtonian physics it has contributed valuable elements to contem-porary doctrine; but sheer and naked empiricism, without radical qualification, has implications for the nature of mind and matter which have long been abandoned by science. What science requires today is an interpretation of mind and nature which satisfies the demands both of realism and of idealism—a theory to which neither of these names will exclusively apply, and yet to which both may be applied so far as they are names of specific philosophical concepts which consequently tend to overlap.

Finally, it is to be observed that, in the history of the idea of nature, we have three conceptions which are dialectically related. They are at once distinct, mutually opposite and continuously connected as gradations or phases in the development of a theory. Consequently they constitute a scale of forms such as is required in the explication of every philosophical concept, and in the elaboration of them we shall be following the characteristic method of philosophy described in the opening chapter.

In outlining the conceptions of nature typical of the three main historical periods, I have, on the whole, followed Collingwood. But he does not in his statement of any of them make fully explicit the consequences of the idea of nature for the co-temporary theory of knowledge. It is this that I shall attempt to do in the sequel, and I shall try, as I do so, to develop the modern view beyond the account which Collingwood gives of it, and to show that the conception of natural evolution itself rests upon more ultimate presuppositions. Collingwood seems himself to have felt that there were ulterior implications, but he never made them clear. At the end of *The Idea of Nature*, after he has expounded the modern idea as that of a process of evolution, he declares that 'no one can answer the question what nature is unless he knows what history is';[1] and as he also held the view that history is the self-knowledge of mind, the inference would seem to be that the process of nature itself is intelligible only in the light of that self-knowledge.

[1] *Op. cit.* p. 177.

Part Two

THE PROBLEM IN GREEK PHILOSOPHY

Chapter III

THE PROBLEM IN EMBRYO

I. MATTER, LIFE AND MIND

1. 'FOR the early Greeks quite simply, and with some qualification for all Greeks whatever, nature was a vast living organism', writes Collingwood [1]—an organism with not only a soul and life of its own, but having mind and rationality by virtue of which its movements and the arrangement of its parts were systematically organized. The life and intelligence of finite living creatures inhabiting the world was to be explained, he asserts, as specialized local organizations of the all-pervading vitality and rationality, 'participating', each in its own degree, in the life and mind of the cosmos. There may be some who would contest this view, and it does seem a little strange that if it were true of 'all Greeks whatever' Aristotle should remark: 'When one man said that reason was present—as in animals, so throughout nature—as the cause of order and of all arrangement, he seemed like a sober man in contrast to the random talk of his predecessors'.[2] Nevertheless, there is much evidence in favour of Collingwood's thesis, and for the discussion of the problem in which I am directly interested here, no good purpose will be served by calling it in question. But, when he goes on to say that the problems of relating living to non-living matter and matter to mind did not exist for the Greeks because of their conception of nature as a beminded organism, objections may be raised both on logical and on historical grounds.

The mind is apparently related to matter in two different ways. First, material things are presented to it as objects of its knowledge and, secondly, it is held to inhabit a material body the organs of which are instrumental to its knowing. In the last chapter I tried to show that the problem of understanding both these relations was really in the end the same, for it is the instrumentality of the body which is supposed to relate the external objects to the knowing mind, and if the nature of this instrumentality were clearly intelligible, the relation of knowing would be also. So scholarly a writer as Collingwood could hardly have meant to deny that, for the Greeks, the problem of knowledge did not exist. That, indeed, would have been to fly in the face of the facts. But

[1] *Idea of Nature*, p. 111. Cf. also pp. 3-4.
[2] *Metaphysics*, A, 984 b 15.

if the two ways in which mind and matter are to be related are as closely connected as I maintain, it is unlikely that the problem of knowledge would have troubled the Greek philosophers unless the difficulty of relating matter to mind had also had some place in their thought.

2. The conception of the universe as a living organism 'permeated and saturated' by vitality and mind is one of a body, or system of bodies, imbued with vitality and rationality in every part. It is no doubt conceivable that consciousness might be one of the properties of body, but it is not that property in virtue of which it is corporeal. Accordingly, any attempt to explain the universe as an organism permeated by mind at once involves the necessity to explain the relation between those properties which make it corporeal and those which make it live and conscious. Moreover the consciousness of one part of the corporeal whole must somehow be related to that of the other parts. And if the mind of the whole is taken to be a distinct consciousness, its relation to its beminded parts also requires to be made intelligible. The problems arise because, however we try to conceive the material universe, the peculiar attributes of consciousness, whether sensory, emotive or cognitive, are quite other than those of corporeality, which are intimately bound up with the fact that bodies are extended in space and time in a way in which consciousness is not. To say that the corporeal universe is permeated and saturated by mind, in fact, is to imply that the relation between mind and body is a spatial relation, and that is incompatible with the very nature of consciousness which is the very essence of mind.[1] Consequently, even though the universe were regarded as a vast beminded organism, the problem of relating its body (*qua* matter) to its mind (*qua* consciousness) would not be avoided.

Similar difficulties arise in the case of vitality as in the case of consciousness, for if the whole universe is alive and every part of it (however small) is also alive, all movement will be vital movement. Now either that which moves is distinct from that which is moved or they are the same. If they are different the distinction as well as the relation between them must be explained and the vital principle must be identified with the active term of the relation. What then will be the passive term? It cannot be that which is *alive* so far as that means 'vitally active'. Nothing which is merely passive is so in virtue of its vitality, and so far as it is *merely* passive it must be regarded as non-living. The task of explaining the relation between the vitality which moves and that which it moves is, then, precisely that of explaining the relation between

[1] Cf. Aristotle, *De Anima*, 407 a 2–b 13.

the living and the non-living, between vitality and that which it vitalizes. On the other hand, it is impossible altogether to identify the mover and the moved, for then every movement would be self-motivated and it would be impossible for one movement to cause any other, or to be caused by anything other than itself. In that case, co-ordination of movement would be possible only by means of some sort of pre-established harmony (for accidental co-ordination is not properly co-ordination at all), and, without it, the movements in the members of no living organism could ever be controlled by the life of the whole—neither of the universe as one organism, nor of the lesser organisms within it. Their organic character would, in fact, be dissipated, for with the disappearance of co-ordination 'organism' becomes a meaningless term. The vitalization of any organism implies control of the movements of its bodily parts and co-ordination of their functions, and this again implies the relation of activity and passivity, either mutually between the parts, or between some sort of vitalizing entelechy and its body, and the problem of explaining this relation cannot be escaped.

Both the problems which Collingwood excludes from Greek speculation do, therefore, arise from the conception of the universe as a living organism, for there must be in such an organism a principle of vitality and rationality which is quite different from its corporeal nature, and the relation of the vital and rational nature to the corporeal nature remains to be explained. Either the principles of vitality and rationality must be regarded as themselves material substances of a certain sort intermixed with others, which will then be neither alive nor conscious; and in that case we must explain how such intermingling can account for the phenomena of life and consciousness in animate nature. Or else vitality and rationality are immaterial principles, in which case their 'permeation' and 'saturation' of matter are mere metaphors which defy interpretation. They give us no clue to the nature of life or of consciousness; nor do they explain how the mind which permeates is aware of that which it permeates or of its own permeation. They in no way illuminate the intimate relation assumed between that which is both spatial and corporeal and that which is neither. The Greek conception of nature, therefore, does not eliminate these problems; nor is it true that they were left unrecognized or unconsidered by Greek philosophers; nor yet that, because of their view of nature, those philosophers were easily able to solve and dispose of them.

In Greek philosophy these problems are combined in the problem

65

of relating the soul to the body, whether of the cosmos as a whole or of its animate members. In the thought of the earlier Greek thinkers they were only beginning to take shape and the awareness of them was by no means clear, so that hardly before Plato and certainly not before Democritus do we find anything like a definite statement of them. But that the early philosophers were even dimly aware of them is sufficient to prove that they did exist for the Greeks and the more explicit discussions which we find in Plato and Aristotle do so conclusively.

3. The word ψυχή in Greek philosophy always means, not only that which vitalizes the organism—that which is alive, sensitive and the source of spontaneous movement in the living thing—but also that which perceives, thinks and knows, or is at least capable of thought and knowledge. In Greek philosophy, therefore, any discussion of the relation of soul to body, or of soul to what is other than soul, is concerned with either or both of the questions of relating mind to body or life to non-living matter. It is true that in Homer ψυχή is used to signify the shade or ghost of the dead, and that this is thought of as devoid of feeling or consciousness. But Jaeger argues[1] that this sense of the word is derivative and secondary and that the primary meaning in Homer (when the word is used in connection with living persons) is 'life'. Even then, however, its meaning is not intended to include consciousness, for which the term θυμός is used, or some other word denoting a bodily organ and implying a purely physiological function. But Jaeger points out that already in Homer there is a tendency for the phenomena of life and of consciousness to be brought under a single concept, as the use of the expression ψυχὴ καὶ θυμός indicates. By the 6th century, he maintains, the word ψυχή alone had come to express this composite idea, and the Orphic conception of the soul is one in which the Homeric notion has been quite superseded and in which the separation of life from consciousness cannot be made.[2] This was necessarily the case, for the Orphic soul was a divine and immortal being which came from the Gods and was held to be entombed in successive bodies until its purification was complete, and such an idea is quite incompatible either with the notion of an insensate shade or of an unconscious *élan vital*. Certainly the philosophers, from the 6th century onward, always used the term ψυχή to include both the principle of life in

[1] *Vide The Theology of the Early Greek Philosophers* (Oxford, 1947), ch. v, esp. pp. 76 ff.
[2] Cf. Jaeger, *op. cit.* p. 83; E. Rohde, *Psyche* (London, 1925), pp. 345 f.; Burnet, *Early Greek Philosophy* (4th ed., London, 1945), pp. 81 f., and *Thales to Plato* (London, 1950), p. 31.

living things and the subject of consciousness and knowledge;[1] and all that is necessary to refute Collingwood's denial of the existence in Greek philosophy of the problems with which we are concerned, is to show that the problem of the relation of the soul to the body did exist.

That is a task which involves no great difficulty, for little more is needed than to point to the first three chapters of Aristotle's *De Anima* where it is clearly stated, not only that Aristotle's own treatise is to include the discussion of the relation of body and soul,[2] but also that theories of that relation had been put forward by almost all the outstanding figures among his predecessors. But it is not sufficient simply to display the fact that the problem was considered and discussed by the Greeks; we must also examine the solutions which were offered in order to discover whether the Greek conception of nature was such as to enable the philosophers to solve and dispose of the question at issue. And here too Aristotle provides an answer, for not only does he mention the theories of his predecessors but he rejects them as unsatisfactory. They suggest, he says, that the soul moves the body by a sort of mechanical causation (as Daedalus, in the story, made the wooden Aphrodite move by pouring in quicksilver)[3] whereas 'in general the soul does not seem to move the animal in this way but, as it were, by choice and a process of thinking'.[4] If we accept the testimony of Aristotle, therefore, we must conclude both that the relation of body to soul was a live question among the Greeks and that they failed, at any rate before Aristotle (who includes Plato in his criticism[5]), to reach a satisfactory answer. And confirmation of Aristotle's judgement is certainly to be found in the theories of the earlier philosophers themselves.

---

[1] Aristotle remarks that Anaxagoras distinguished soul (ψυχή) from mind (νοῦς) (*De Anima*, 404 b 1-3), though he admits that he treated them both as one nature and that he attributed the power of knowing and that of moving both to one principle (*ibid.* 405 a 14-19). But Aristotle's reason for saying that Anaxagoras made the distinction is simply that he held νοῦς to be in all animate things in spite of the fact that, in the sense of intelligence, it does not belong to all animals nor even to all men. But the distinction is Aristotle's rather than Anaxagoras', who held both that νοῦς was intelligence and that it governed all things which have soul (besides the vortical movement of the world). Aristotle's own classification of soul, as nutritive, sensitive and rational, is no obstacle to my argument, because (i) even if not all soul is intelligent, all intelligence does belong to soul; (ii) the problem of relating living to non-living matter, one which Collingwood excluded from Greek thought, concerns the lower forms of soul no less than the higher; and (iii) Aristotle's own doctrine unites the different kinds of soul as a single scale of forms in which the lower is proximate matter to the next above it, so that νοῦς is the form which is being progressively actualized throughout the series.

[2] *De Anima*, 403 a–b.
[3] *Ibid.* 406 b 15-25.
[4] *Ibid.* 406 b 24-5.
[5] *Ibid.* 406 b 26 *et seq.*

II. INFLUENCES DETERMINING THE GREEK CONCEPTION
OF THE SOUL

4. Two main ingredients seem to have gone to the making of the philosophical theory of the soul in Ancient Greece. The first is the doctrine of the Orphic religion that the soul is a divine being inhabiting, temporarily and in succession, each of a great number of animal bodies until such time as its original offence against the divine nature shall have been expiated and it is reunited with God. The second is the conception of the nature of the world developed in the teachings of the Ionian philosophers of the early 6th century B.C. The influence of these two factors can be seen in the work of almost every Greek philosopher from Pythagoras onward, and their union at once raises the problem of relating the soul, with all the activities of mind, to the body as a material entity, and explains the kind of solution attempted by the pre-Socratics.

The Orphic doctrine is traced back by Erwin Rohde[1] to the myth of the dismemberment of the god Dionysus-Zagreus by the evil and earthborn Titans, who, having devoured his body, were destroyed by the lightning-stroke of Zeus, and from whose ashes the race of mankind arose. The myth was treated by the Orphics as symbolic, the Titans representing the powers of evil in the world and the god the element of good. Man, depicted as springing from a combination of these two (for the Titans had consumed the body of the god), has within him a fragment of the divine imprisoned by that which is earthly and evil. 'The distinction between the Titanic and Dionysiac elements in man', writes Rohde, 'is an allegorical expression of the popular distinction between body and soul.'[2] It is the soul which is held to be the divine fragment of the god and the body is the earthly tegument in which it is imprisoned as the result of the original crime committed against his divinity. The constant yearning of the soul is for reunion with the Godhead which it can achieve only by a long process of self-purification, and until that process is completed it is destined to continue in 'the Wheel of Birth', freed from one body at its natural death only to be blown by the wind into another. According to this doctrine the relation between the soul and the body is conceived as wholly external. Neither has anything in common with the other and their inter-connection is left entirely unexplained. One is simply incarcerated in the other by the decree of Necessity to be released eventually only as a result of its own inner purification. Nevertheless, so far as this doctrine is taken

---

[1] *Psyche*, ch. x, § 3.   [2] *Op. cit.* pp. 341-2.

as a basis for speculation it sets the problem to the philosopher of explaining the vital and mental functionings of living things in terms of soul and body, and of arriving at a rational conception of their inter-communion.

5. The conception of the universe evolved by the Ionian natural philosophers was one in which the various forms taken by things and the various processes of change which occur in the world were explained as the differentiation of one basal material substance. From this ultimate material soul and mind are not distinguished. Their characteristics are included among its properties, and we get, in consequence, a materialistic psychology. The question of the relation of soul to body thus becomes that of the relation of the original substance to its various modifications; for it is only in its pure form that the properties of soul are attributed to it and they are, in varying degrees, lost by its modifications. That this sort of idea was entertained by the Milesian philosophers, Thales, Anaximander and Anaximenes, is difficult to establish, as such meagre relics of their work remain to us; but evidence is not entirely lacking, and the theories of their successors which show definite signs of their influence do include notions of soul and mind which represent them as material substances, either elementary in all forms of matter or separate and different from other forms.

It is characteristic, therefore, of the pre-Socratic philosophers that they accept the opposition between soul and body and try to explain it in terms of the mutual relations of material substances. The soul is thought of as a purified or attenuated form of matter, inspired into, mixed with, or permeating other forms; so that while the distinction between soul and body is recognized, that between mind and matter is not yet made.

III. PHYSICAL PHILOSOPHERS

6. This characteristic is to be observed in the single remaining fragment of Anaximenes: 'Just as our soul, being air, holds us together, so do breath ($\pi\nu\epsilon\hat{u}\mu\alpha$) and air encompass the whole world'. The soul is identified with air, which Anaximenes believed to be the primary substance of all things, and the relation of the soul to the body is here used as an analogy on which to explain the relation of the visible, physical world to the immanent cause and principle of its being. The significance of the statement that our soul 'holds us together' is, almost certainly, that it is the soul which makes the body a single organism

and unites its parts into a living whole. The recognition of a relation between body and soul and of the need to give some account of it, if not explicit, is at least implied, and the analogy with the cosmos gives presage of a solution. The use of the word πνεῦμα is important, for from the earliest times the word for the soul was etymologically connected with that for the breath of life,[1] and Anaximenes in this fragment obviously intends to identify the air which encompasses the world with the life-breath (πνεῦμα) and the soul of the living being. It is hardly credible that he should have divorced from this the attributes of consciousness and thought and Jaeger asserts that he 'is obviously thinking of mental and not merely physiological phenomena'.[2] Moreover, Diogenes of Apollonia, who revived Anaximenes' theory a century later, explicitly attributes thought and consciousness to air. Accordingly, the primary matter of all things is at the same time the principle of life and mind, and as Anaximenes holds that every form of matter is a modification of air by condensation or rarefaction, this principle of life and mind is immanent in and fundamental to all reality. The solution of the problem of relating the soul to the body, therefore, which is adumbrated in the doctrine of Anaximenes, is that both are manifestations of the same ultimate principle of being, the former in its purest and most essential form.

But to say that the soul is air is no real explanation of the phenomena either of life or of mind. Even though Anaximenes may have been (and Diogenes certainly was) thinking of mental and not merely of physical characteristics when he identified the soul with air, there is nothing in the nature of air as we know it which makes our conscious awareness of objects, our capacity for thinking, or even our vital processes intelligible. For the only properties of air of which we are cognizant are physical and spatio-temporal, and these, as I have said above, are totally different from and (*prima facie* at least) incompatible with those of consciousness and thought. An awareness of the problem, vague and dim though it be, is thus traceable in the thought of Anaximenes, and in that of Diogenes an even fuller awareness of it, but, though their conception of the world seems to have been exactly what Collingwood regards as typical of the Greeks, they are very far from reaching anything like a satisfactory conclusion. Nevertheless, there is some sign that even Anaximenes may have been struggling towards a clearer conception of the problem. There is a statement falsely attri-

---

[1] Observe the connection between ψυχή and ἀποψύχω, in Greek, and cf. in Latin the use of the words *anima* (cf. ἄνεμος), *spiritus*, etc.

[2] Jaeger, *op. cit.* p. 36.

buted to him by Olympiodorus[1] that 'air is near to the incorporeal' and there may well have been something in his theories which made it plausible to attribute some such view to him. It is, however, not unlikely that the actual author of the remark was a Pythagorean (possibly even Pythagoras himself), for we know that the Pythagoreans identified air with the void.

7. In the same way Heraclitus' identification of soul with the dry and fiery element, as opposed to the moist and the solid, indicates the beginning of a distinction between soul and body without that between matter and mind. But the relation between body and soul is much more interestingly conceived by Heraclitus than by his predecessors. He develops an idea inchoate in Anaximander's doctrine of 'the boundless' from which the 'opposites' separate out constituting by their different combinations the variety of things in the world. Anaximander alleged that all things returned to 'the boundless' making 'reparation' to one another for their 'injustice'.[2] 'Justice', by implication, is the uniform mixture of opposites in the oneness of the $\mathring{a}\pi\epsilon\iota\rho\sigma\nu$. Similarly, Heraclitus declares that the opposites are one and the same.

'The transformations of fire', he says, 'are first sea; of sea half is earth and half fiery storm-cloud.'[3] 'Water', he tells us, 'comes from earth; and from water soul.'[4] Soul is fire, so these two processes of transformation constitute what he calls 'the way down' and 'the way up', and they are, he maintains, one and the same.[5] He also tells us that the dry soul is the wisest and best (Fr. 74) and that it is death to souls to become water (Fr. 68). The human being, it appears, is made up of all three forms, fire, water and earth, the last two forming the body and the first constituting the soul;[6] a theory of their relation is therefore at hand. Like the world, so man, 'is an ever-living fire, with measures of it kindling, and measures going out';[7] the soul is the fiery exhalation of the body (the way up) and the body the extinguished 'measures' of the soul (the way down).

In all this, apart from the substitution of fire for air, there is little essential difference from the position suggested by Anaximenes, and in a passage, quoted by Burnet[8] from Sextus Empiricus, an interpretation is given of Heraclitus' theory of the body-mind relation which assimilates it closely to the sort of doctrine generally attributed by the Ancients to Anaximenes. But though Heraclitus does not ask the

[1] Diels, *Fragmente der Vorsokratiker*, 3, B 3.   [2] *Ibid.* 2, 9.
[3] Fr. 21, according to Bywater's numbering.   [4] Fr. 68 (Bywater).
[5] Fr. 69 (Bywater).   [6] Cf. Burnet, *E.G.Ph.* p. 151.
[7] Fr. 20.   [8] *E.G.Ph.* p. 152.

critical question how the nature of fire, even if kept pure and dry, can account for our experience of knowing, how it can explain that relationship between the knower and the known which enables the finite mind to possess within itself the spectacle of the surrounding world, he does provide some better means, though still very obscure, of finding an answer.

8. The key to the difficulty lies in his very first utterance: 'It is wise to hearken, not to me, but to my Word, and to confess that all things are one' (Fr. 1). This λόγος, he tells us further, is 'the common' which we should follow (Fr. 92) if we are to understand all things (cf. Fr. 91 b). It is wisdom, which is one thing set apart, and is the knowledge of 'the thought by which all things are steered through all things' (Frs. 18 and 19). It can hardly be anything other than this to which he refers when he says that the waking (as opposed to those who are asleep) have one common world; for, as Jaeger contends,[1] he means by 'waking' a state of intellectual enlightenment, as opposed to the condition of those who do not comprehend the Logos and 'know not what they do when awake, even as they forget what they do in sleep' (Fr. 2). They do not 'follow the common' but 'live as if they had a wisdom of their own' (Fr. 92). The true object of knowledge, we must conclude, is not the world of common sense (for those who live as if they had a wisdom of their own are described as 'the many'), which is deceptive and leads to contrary opinions, but the real world which is the same for all who attain to wisdom and understanding, and 'confess that all things are one'. There may be a sense in which the interpretation of some commentators is justifiable that by this 'one' Heraclitus means the universal principle of fire. He does indeed tell us that the world which is the same for all is just that (Fr. 20). But this is not inconsistent with Burnet's view[2] that, when he speaks of the Logos and the one thing necessary for wisdom, he is referring to that principle which he regarded as his own special discovery: that 'that which is at variance with itself agrees with itself; it is an attunement of opposite tensions' (Fr. 45). This is the thought which steers all things through all things, and this alone enables us to understand the nature and the metamorphoses of the fire which constitutes the common world. For if we ask how fire, by being kept pure and dry, is able to know its own transformations into water and earth, in which its thought and consciousness become submerged and extinguished, the reply is that opposites are

[1] *The Theology of the Early Greek Philosophers*, pp. 112 f.
[2] *Thales to Plato*, p. 62.

one and the way up and the way down are the same. In short, the conclusion to which Heraclitus points is that subject and object are, in the end, the same, and the mind knows the world because the world is no more nor less than the generation of mind, as it is itself generated out of mind.

Obscure though this may be, it holds in germ a conception of the world and knowledge, which becomes more explicit in the later dialogues of Plato and in the philosophy of Aristotle, where the solution of our problem begins to become apparent and to a new form of which, enriched by the intervening centuries of thought and the discoveries of modern science, we might with profit turn again even at the present time for enlightenment and the dissipation of many difficulties.

IV. PYTHAGORAS AND THE PYTHAGOREANS

9. Chronologically the philosophy of Heraclitus is later than that of Pythagoras, but I have dealt with it first because of its affinity to that of the Milesians and the relative absence from Heraclitus' thought of the influence of Orphicism. He does, it is true, speak of immortality; but it is an immortality very different from that which the Orphics contemplated and is little more than the cycle and exchange of the fiery metamorphoses [1] as applied to the soul. In the Pythagorean philosophy, however, the Orphic and the Ionian influences appear side by side without any apparent attempt to reconcile their implications. The religious side of Pythagoras' teaching is obviously deeply in debt to the Orphic creed. The soul is conceived as immortal and divine; the doctrines of transmigration and the 'wheel of birth' are adopted; the necessity for purification as the condition of the soul's release from imprisonment in successive bodies is emphasized, and there are numerous minor evidences of similarity between the beliefs and practices of the Pythagoreans and those of the Orphic sect.[2] But the Pythagorean teaching makes an important advance on earlier religious beliefs in its conception of catharsis. The methods of purification of the

---

[1] Cf. Frs. 67-8 and 78. It seems to me that Burnet's interpretation of Heraclitus' views on immortality is more coherent and consistent with the general tenor of his philosophy, as revealed in the fragments, than that given by Dr. Kathleen Freeman. Cf. Burnet, *E.G.Ph.* pp. 153-5, and Freeman, *Companion to the Pre-Socratic Philosophers* (Blackwell, Oxford, 1946), pp. 126-7.

[2] While not denying that Pythagoras and his followers were influenced by the Orphics, Burnet asserts that the mystical side of his doctrine derived from Apolonian rather than the Dionysiac and Orphic sources (*vide Thales to Plato*, p. 40). I do not, however, wish to press the question of origin, my interest being primarily in the content of the doctrines.

soul current among the earlier religions, by which it was to be freed from its confinement in the body, apart from various abstinences and taboos (many of which were practised by the 'akousmatics' in the Pythagorean Order), included ceremonies and orgiastic rites of a very primitive character. Pythagoras, however, seems to have introduced a new conception of purification as that which results from the activity of the intellect rather than from the inducement of ecstatic emotional conditions; and the distinction of the three kinds of life, theoretic, practical and apolaustic, on the analogy of the classes of persons who attended the Olympic games, with its obvious preference for the first (the theoretic), indicates the direction in which the Pythagorean teaching moved. Science and philosophy, with particular stress on mathematics, came to be regarded as the true purification of the soul, a view which implies that the truest and most characteristic of the soul's activities are those of the intellect. The suggestion is, pretty obviously, that desire and action are activities of soul less pure than knowledge because more closely involved with bodily functions, and the process of purification, therefore, is one in which the soul turns constantly more towards and concentrates its activity ever more fully in thinking and knowing.

It is clear that a doctrine of this kind has involved some reflection upon the relation of the soul to the body and implies an idea of it somewhat in advance of that entertained by the Orphics. Rohde seems to have overlooked this characteristic of the Pythagorean teaching when he says that it conceived the soul as having no real relationship with the body, as absolutely distinct from 'nature' and opposed to it, thrust into the world of nature which is foreign to it, preserving its individuality intact and self-enclosed, and escaping only to undergo new incarnations.[1] This is almost exactly what one would imagine the Orphic conception to have been and it is quite probable that the less scientific of Pythagoras' followers, the akousmatics, who were later disowned by the mathematicians of the Order, held fast to a view of this kind. Nevertheless, it must have been modified by the new view of catharsis which is apparent in Pythagorean thought, and though the implications of this view were not fully developed, it is significant that those who applied themselves to the scientific side of the Pythagorean teaching and who, at a later date, repudiated the religious practices, produced a doctrine of the soul in accordance with the theory that the essence of all things is number—the special contribution to Greek philosophy of the Pythagorean school.

[1] *Psyche*, pp. 375 f.

10. The importance of this contribution can hardly be exaggerated. Burnet has drawn attention to the connection between the designation of numbers as 'figures' (εἴδη, σχήματα) and the later development of the theory of 'forms' in the work of Socrates and his successors. The great contribution of Pythagoras to philosophy,[1] he says, is that he supplemented the idea of 'matter', already reached by the Milesians, by the correlative conception of 'form'. Collingwood, in a brilliant piece of imaginative reconstruction, has suggested the probable reasoning which led to this result. The logical implication of the Ionian theories, he argues, was that the basal material of the universe must be qualitatively indeterminate.[2] That being the case, not even Anaximenes' notion of condensation and rarefaction will serve to explain the qualitative differences of things in the world; for what is qualitatively indeterminate is indistinguishable from the space that it occupies and rarefaction and condensation depend solely upon the quantity of matter occupying a given space. Pythagoras, however, seems to have observed that geometrical figures have a qualitative difference which is not dependent upon any material content but is purely formal, and he suggested, therefore, that the qualitative differences of material things are ultimately due to geometrical or (as he did not distinguish numbers from figures) numerical structure.

The theory of the soul which eventually arose out of this was propounded by Philolaus, who taught that it was a harmony or ratio of the elements which made up the body—its numerical character, so to speak—and this is not only a definite theory of the relation of the soul to the body, but also an important step towards the Aristotelian view of their relation as form and matter, which is the nearest to providing a solution of the problem that we find in Greek thought. But a numerical ratio, although it is a product of thought, is not that which thinks, and the Pythagorean doctrine leaves us still far from our goal.

V. THE ONE

11. The antithesis of form to matter and its correlation with that of soul and body is, however, a late development even as foreshadowed in the philosophy of the Pythagorean Order; and though the doctrine that all things are in essence numbers is the source of the conception, it implies an idea of the immaterial which we do not find in any explicit form before we come to Socrates. Meanwhile, another antithesis came

---

[1] *Vide Thales to Plato*, p. 44, and cf. pp. 52 and 56.
[2] Collingwood, *Idea of Nature*, p. 51.

to be recognized and its implications developed, the connection of which with the opposition of matter to form was worked out only later, by Plato and Aristotle. The implication of the Ionian theories was that the multitude of different kinds and appearances of things in the world was to be explained as the differentiation of one elemental stuff (water, or air, or fire, or something distinct from all of these), and so contrast was emphasized between the one underlying substance and its many manifestations. The distinction of the One from the Many and the relation between them became henceforth one of the major preoccupations of Greek speculation. Attention was more particularly drawn to the opposition by the flat denial, by Parmenides of Elea, of the reality of one of its terms. For him, the appearance of multiplicity in the world was sheer illusion. The One alone is real, unchanging, undifferentiated and unmoved.

From one who denies the existence of anything but the single, uniformly continuous sphere of the All, we can hardly expect a theory of the relation of finite beings to others or to the infinite in any form whatsoever. The relation of the finite mind to its body as well as to the objects of its knowledge simply disappears in the all-embracing uniformity of the One Being. Nevertheless, the fragments of Parmenides do provide us with some evidence relevant to our investigation and his philosophy contains at least two important ideas, significant for the development of the theory of knowledge.

12. Parmenides' poem is divided into two main sections setting out respectively what he calls 'The Way of Truth' and 'The Way of Belief', in the second of which he says 'there is no truth at all'.[1] Nevertheless, he expounds these false 'opinions of mortals' so that no human doctrine may ever get the better of him.[2] Despite the differing opinions on the matter, it seems most unlikely that Parmenides is expounding his own views in this part of the poem; but whether he is, as some say, giving an account of 'appearances' as opposed to the 'reality' with which the first section deals, or whether he is stating the contemporary Pythagorean view, which he once held and is now renouncing (as Burnet maintains), what is important for my purpose is that 'The Way of Belief' contains a theory of the relation of the soul to the body and gives evidence of the fact that this matter was not neglected in Greek speculation. 'Just as thought stands at any time to the mixture of its erring organs', he writes, 'so does it come to men; for that which thinks is the same, namely, the substance ($\phi\acute{v}\sigma\iota\varsigma$) of the limbs,

[1] Diels, Fr. 1, 30. [2] Fr. 8, 61.

in each and every man; for their thought is that of which there is more in them.'[1] There does seem to be some connection between this and the notion that the soul is the harmony or ratio of the elements constituting the body, but in the way it is stated by Parmenides little help can be derived from it in the effort to understand how the human mind can grasp, in knowledge, the nature of the world in which it finds itself; for the mixture of the substances which go to make the body in no way renders the nature of thought or of consciousness intelligible.

13. More light, however, is thrown upon the relation of thought to its object in 'The Way of Truth', for there we learn that 'it is the same thing that can be thought and that can be' (Fr. 5), that 'it needs must be that what can be spoken and thought *is*' (Fr. 6), and that 'the thing which can be thought and that for which the thought exists is the same' (Fr. 8, 34). By 'what can be thought' Parmenides clearly means here what is logically necessary as distinct from what is imagined or opined on the evidence of the senses, for his whole argument about Being is a logical deduction from the proposition that what is not cannot be.[2] This, in effect, is an assertion of the doctrine that the real is the rational, and it follows that to know the truth we have only to think aright, only to follow our reason. Finite minds, bodies, the extended world of finite things around us are all revealed by reason as sheer non-entities —illogicalities which just cannot be thought; though how we should ever have come to imagine their existence is left unexplained. Further, it would seem to follow that we, who think, can be no other than 'that which is', for there can be nothing else. To think and to be thought must be one and the same; mind and object are identical and any appearance to the contrary is the result of error and illusion. The occurrence of such error is clearly admitted by Parmenides, but its possibility remains unexplained and inexplicable in his doctrine of Being.

The first contribution of the Eleatic philosophy, then, is the suggestion that knowledge is possible because what is conceivable and what is real are one and the same; but though this suggestion proved later to be of the utmost value and importance, it is not efficacious in Parmenides' philosophy owing to his failure to explain by its means the appearances to the contrary. For him, therefore, it is an evasion rather than a solution of the real problem of human knowledge.

The second contribution is the emphasis upon one very necessary half-truth in metaphysics, the neglect of which is as fatal as that of the

[1] Fr. 16 (Burnet's translation).   [2] Cf. Frs. 6 and 8.

opposite half-truth. The variety and multiplicity of things can never adequately be explained except as the differentiation of a universal. The search for the universal might, in fact, be regarded as the proper definition of explanation. The same is true of any adequate theory of change and becoming: it is only as the manifestation of what is permanent and unchanging that either can be made intelligible.[1] In emphasizing the oneness of the real and its permanence, therefore, Parmenides is laying one of the necessary foundation stones of metaphysical theory; but his neglect of the other and his denial of change and multiplicity is the source of his failure. It is only in the reconciliation of these two opposite aspects of reality that the problem of human knowledge finds its solution, and this is especially true for Greek philosophy, in which the permanent and universal alone were regarded as ultimately knowable while the knower was at least in part, or at least in part appeared to be, a changing individual existent. For the notion that only the One and the Unchanging can be known Parmenides was primarily responsible, and if this is only half of the truth it is at least as vital and as fundamental as the other half—that what we are constantly seeking to understand is the many changing appearances of the experienced world.

VI. THE MANY

14. The pluralists who follow Parmenides in the history of Greek thought attempted to supply what, in his philosophy, was left out. They accept the principle that what is cannot be generated or destroyed and they therefore deny absolute coming to be and passing away. But that which is, is not for them a unity, but is in various ways multiple. Empedocles divides it into the four elements, earth, water, air and fire; for Anaxagoras it consists of infinitesimal 'seeds', of which all varieties are in all things, and for the atomists, Leucippus and Democritus, it is the innumerable atoms, varying in shape and size. In one way or another the differences between things result, for all these thinkers, from the mixing and separation of what they take to be the primary elements; and in the course of this process the human organism, along with the other finite existences, comes into being. The explanation of its capacity to think and to know is a problem for all these philosophers and one which they by no means neglect.

The explanation of perception put forward by Empedocles is a physiological one, derived from the study of medical science. 'It is

[1] Cf. Aristotle, *Metaphysics*, 1012 b 28: ἔτι ἀνάγκη τὸ ὂν μεταβάλλειν.

impossible', says Burnet, 'to understand the history of philosophy from this point onwards without keeping the history of medicine constantly in view';[1] and it is clear that any attempt to account for perception and thought physiologically reveals an awareness that the relation between mental and bodily functioning presents a problem, though it reveals, also, a failure to appreciate its implications to the full.

Empedocles explains perception as the entry through 'pores' or passages in the sense-organs[2] of 'effluences' from outer objects.[3] These are composed, like all else, of the elements and are apprehended, or known, by means of the like elements in us, on the principle (which from now on becomes prominent in Greek philosophy) that 'like knows like'. According to Theophrastus,[4] Empedocles 'gives a precisely similar account of thought and ignorance'. The organ of thinking, he held, was the heart 'dwelling in the sea of blood that runs in opposite directions, where chiefly is what men call thought; for the blood round the heart is the thought of men' (Diels, 21, B 105, Burnet's translation). The blood, being the finest mixture and closest combination of the elements, is that in us which is best fitted and best able to think and know.

Though we have here the germ of a theory of our knowledge of the world it is far from promising, for it would be at best a causal theory of knowledge, which shares with the representative theory all its characteristic difficulties. The effluences are clearly not the things themselves from which they flow and they must somehow convey into the mind the knowledge of those things. All that the mind receives, however, are the effluences. How, then, does it know the source from which they come? The principle that like knows like does not help, for it implies the knowledge of both terms of the comparison and, *ex hypothesi*, the mind possesses only one. Moreover, the same objections are valid against the view that blood is the agent of thought as against those which identify it with fire or air or water. In fact all that Empedocles has done is to combine the elements in that which thinks, whereas his predecessors attributed thought to only one of them.

15. But if Empedocles' account of perception and thought seems to make them no more than bodily functions, he also taught that the soul was immortal and divine in origin and that it had been expelled from

---

[1] *E.G.Ph.* p. 201, n. 4.
[2] A theory derived from Alcmaion of Croton.
[3] For the full statement of the theory see Theophrastus' account of Empedocles' doctrine: Ritter and Preller, *Historia Philosophiae Graecae*, §§ 177 B and 178, quoted by Burnet, *E.G.Ph.* pp. 246-8.   [4] *Loc. cit.*

the abode of divine bliss to be tossed from one element to another, inhabiting successive bodies, until it had expiated some original sin.[1] This is obviously an Orphic doctrine and it appears side by side with his physical theories with no apparent attempt at co-ordination. There are, however, suggestive passages in the fragments which make it possible to conceive a connection between them, though it is very much a matter of conjecture.

The part played in Empedocles' system by Love and Strife provides us with the key. Under the influence of Love, the elements are combined into one uniform mixture and the cosmos becomes a sphere of almost undifferentiated matter, similar to that envisaged by Parmenides. This Empedocles calls 'the God' and he gives it the name of Sphairos.[2] Saturated with Love, the God is an absolute unity, without limbs or bodily parts, 'spherical and equal on all sides', 'rejoicing in his circular solitude'.[3] So he describes Sphairos in the poem *On Nature* and he uses almost the same words to describe God in the *Catharmoi*,[4] adding that 'he is only a sacred and unutterable mind flashing through the whole world with rapid thoughts' (B 134). It is, therefore, presumable that in both cases he is referring to the same divinity. On the re-entry of Strife into the cosmos, however, 'all the limbs of the God in turn quake' and his unity is broken up, the elements separating out to form by various stages the things of the world known to us, and finally to destroy them by complete dissipation until they are recreated by Love in the gradual recovery of her dominion in the cosmos. Human beings are among the finites thus created and destroyed and, accordingly, are to some extent the product of Strife, though it is Love which (if only temporarily) holds them together as organic wholes and maintains the combination of elements in them

---

[1] Cf. Diels, 21, B 115.

[2] It is true that he speaks of other gods; but, probably due to the literary tradition of the Homeric and Hesiodic theogonies, it is common throughout Greek philosophy for thinkers to assert the existence of numerous deities while they attribute the essential character of Godhead only to one. Anaximander spoke of the innumerable worlds as 'gods', but attributed the divine characteristics *par excellence* to the Boundless; Heraclitus speaks of gods and of immortals in the plural, yet it is clear that he regarded one God as the supreme deity (cf. Frs. 96-9); likewise in Plato and Aristotle we read of a plurality of divinities, yet there can be no doubt that both these philosophers believed in the existence of one Supreme Being.   [3] Cf. Diels, 21, B 27-9.

[4] Diels, 21, B 29:

> οὐ γὰρ ἀπὸ νώτοιο δύο κλάδοι ἀίσσονται,
> οὐ πόδες, οὐ θοὰ γοῦν(α), οὐ μήδεα γεννήεντα . . .

B 134:

> οὐδὲ γὰρ ἀνδρομέηι κεφαλῆι κατὰ γυῖα κέκασται,
> οὐ μὲν ἀπαὶ νώτοιο δύο κλάδοι ἀίσσονται,
> οὐ πόδες, οὐ θοὰ γοῦν(α), οὐ μήδεα λαχνήεντα . . .

(*e.g.* in the blood) by which they perceive and know. Now, in the *Catharmoi*, Empedocles gives as the reason for the soul's expulsion from the realm of the blessed that it had 'followed Strife'. 'One of these [daemons]', he writes, 'I now am, an exile and a wanderer from the Gods, for I put my trust in furious Strife.'[1] We should infer that to follow Love, which is also called Joy (Γηθοσύνη—B 17), would reconcile the soul once more to the Gods, and this might be taken along with what is said in the poem *On Nature* to mean that the exile of the soul from bliss is the effect of Strife, which separates it out from the unity of Sphairos and assigns it to a joyless realm of discord and warring opposites (cf. B 121-3); whereas its reconciliation to and atonement with the Divine would be its mergence in Sphairos under the influence of Love.[2]

The generation of bodies is thus the work of Strife, while the soul is the residual product of Love, which, when wholly triumphant in Sphairos, is an 'unutterable mind'. The diremption of the whole by Strife creates finite things—both minds and bodies—but the minds are no more (nor less) than the cohesion of the bodily parts (or elements) under the persisting influence of Love. In its finite and fragmentary character, the soul is a product of Strife, by putting its trust in which it has become an exile from Heaven; but it is its own internal cohesion alone (its service of Love) that constitutes it a mind or soul, that gives it its intellectual powers and its measure of divinity, as well as its perpetual yearning and striving for complete reunion with the divine totality. This *nisus* to the whole is its immortality. The notion of trans-migration is not necessarily inconsistent with such an interpretation, for Empedocles describes a stage in the process in which creatures are born 'with faces and breasts looking in different directions', oxen with the faces of men, men with the heads of oxen and hermaphroditic beasts of both sexes at once (B 61). It is not inconceivable that, in this confused mingling and re-sorting of bodily parts, what is now a man might once have been 'a boy and a girl, a bush and a bird and a dumb fish in the sea' (B 117). May we not, then, agree with Jaeger[3] that the soul, according to Empedocles, undergoes the same cycle of dis-solution, or estrangement from the God, and reunion and reconcilia-tion with the divine as do the elements in the cosmic process of nature? If so, the account of the physical universe given in the work *On Nature*

---

[1] Diels, 21, B 115.
[2] Aristotle maintains that the logical implication of Empedocles' teaching is an identification of love with good and strife with evil. *Vide Metaphysics*, 985 a 4-10.
[3] *Vide The Theology of the Early Greek Philosophers*, p. 145.

is simply the obverse of that of the soul's peregrinations and tribulations expressed in poetic language and imagery in the *Catharmoi*.

Though this interpretation of Empedocles does little to mitigate the difficulties of a causal theory of perception, it does suggest that the human mind is a part of that divine whole—a pulse in its life—which is 'an unutterable mind flashing throughout the world with rapid thoughts'.

16. The theory of Empedocles is followed in several respects by the atomists of the late 5th century. Democritus, developing Leucippus, maintained that the soul, like everything else, consisted of atoms and that sensation was the reception through the passages of the senses of atoms from without, the impact of which upon the soul's atoms produces awareness. He even speaks of bodies shedding 'images' of themselves, so that his account is explicitly representational. But the contradiction involved in a representational theory is avoided by Democritus' denial that sensation is a source of true knowledge. Its deliverances are as illusory for him as they are for Parmenides. 'By use', he says, 'there is sweet, by use there is bitter; by use there is warm and by use there is cold; by use there is colour:—but in truth there are atoms and the void.'[1] True knowledge is produced by the direct action of the external atoms on those of the soul, which is held to permeate the body in every direction and so to come into immediate contact with the outer world. Knowledge of the real nature of the world is thus accessible to us independently of the senses; but the manner in which it is imparted is no less mechanical and seems open to no less objection than the sensory process.[2] It is, in fact, again a causal process which can as little account for knowledge as can a process of representation, for the relation of cause and effect is in like case with that of resemblance. Nor is impact between the atoms of the soul and those surrounding the body any explanation of the generation of consciousness; still less can it provide a theory of truth, without which knowledge is a meaningless term.

VII. ΝΟΥΣ

17. Among the pre-Socratics, Anaxagoras alone comes near to recognizing the immateriality of mind, and even he is only groping in

[1] Diels, 55, B 125.
[2] This explanation of true knowledge in Democritus' theory is rejected by Cyril Bailey (*The Greek Atomists and Epicurus*, p. 183), but the alternative he suggests would succumb to the same criticism besides involving all the difficulties attendant upon the theory of primary and secondary qualities.

the direction of that conception. He still speaks of mind as if it were a fluid substance—'the thinnest of all things', but he nevertheless thinks of it as different from all other material things in a way which seems to indicate that he was beginning to realize its peculiar character. Genuinely material things are, according to Anaxagoras, infinitely mixed: 'all things', he says, 'are in all things, nor is it possible for them to be apart, but all things have a portion in all'.[1] This being so, if mind were like the rest (*i.e.* a material thing), it too would be in all things. But mind is only in those things which have soul and is, therefore, unmixed, for, had it been mixed, it would have been in all (46, B 11, 12). It alone, in fact, is 'altogether separate and distinct', and on account of its unmixed purity it is able to have knowledge of and power over all else and is the source, not only of the original movement of the vortex which produces the world, but also of all order and arrangement within it (Diels, 46, B 12).

It seems clear that in making mind pure and separate Anaxagoras was trying to distinguish it from other things in such a way as to imply its immateriality, and when he calls it 'the thinnest of all things' he is only struggling to express the idea, dawning at last in Greek philosophy, that it really is incorporeal.

Its presence in living things, which after all are bodies, has thus to be explained. It cannot be *mixed* with the substances which constitute the body. They are what Aristotle later called ὁμοιομερῆ, and are each and all a mixture of all the opposites [2] which constitute matter. It must, then, remain separate within the living body while governing its vital movement. Further, we are told that it is always the same,[3] and Burnet [4] infers that differences in intelligence (and presumably of vital functioning also) are due entirely to differences in anatomical structure.

The relation to the body of the mind thus comes to be conceived much as the Orphics and Pythagoreans conceived that of the soul. Mind is a different substance having no real intimacy with the body, separate and aloof, but somehow occupying it and governing its vital movements. But also 'it had power over the whole revolution' which produced the world and separated out the different kinds of material things; moreover, it *knows* all things—how they are mixed and how they have been separated—and it has set all things in order (cf. B 12). Knowledge, therefore, being an attribute of mind, is in all the souls which it governs, and our knowledge is thus the immanence in us of that mind which knows all things.

---

[1] Diels, 46, B 6.   [2] Cf. Burnet, *E.G.Ph.* p. 263.
[3] Diels, 46, B 12.   [4] *E.G.Ph.* p. 272.

We have reached, at this point, a theory of body-mind relationship in which the mind is all but conceived as incorporeal and in which knowledge is taken to be its special attribute. The suggestion is also strong that this power of knowing is what gives mind the capacity to govern all things and to set them in order. But to say that mind is what knows and that it is by virtue of mind that we know is to explain little, for it tells us nothing of *how* mind knows. To assert, further, that it also governs and organizes the physical universe is a momentous claim and one full of fruitful possibilities. But Anaxagoras, as Aristotle and the Socrates of the *Phaedo* both complain, never worked out the theory in full and did not demonstrate how mind could be a cause of movement and a principle of order in the world of nature.

VIII. THE DEVELOPMENT OF PRE-SOCRATIC THOUGHT

18. The early period of Greek philosophy is, as it were, the gestation period of philosophical problems which emerge later into the clear light of day. Some of them (like that with which this study is mainly concerned) become fully explicit only in modern times; but even at this early stage the problem of relating the mind to nature can be detected struggling to be born. It appears first in the effort to explain thought and consciousness in terms of the one material substance which is thought to be the original matter of all things. A difference is recognized between that which thinks and that which does not. The first is identified with soul and with the pure form of the original substance, and the second with its derivative adulterations. Next, soul and body are completely separated (partly as a result of religious influences), but the soul is not clearly distinguished from matter and is still conceived as a material thing differing either in degree or kind from other things. Finally, soul and mind are explicitly brought together by Anaxagoras and are so distinguished from the rest of the material universe as to suggest a fundamental difference between mind and matter.

Thus, despite Collingwood's contention, the distinction between matter and mind and the consequent question of their mutual relation actually develop out of a conception of nature in which originally the two are confused together and the whole cosmos is thought of as alive and intelligent. With Socrates the problem comes openly to light, and the philosophies of Plato and Aristotle are concerned with it in a manner which not only leaves no doubt of their awareness of it but also throws no little light upon its solution.

Chapter IV

THE PROBLEM EMERGENT

I. THE SOPHISTS

1. The results of physical speculation at this stage seemed, at least to common sense, entirely fantastic, and a reaction against physical philosophy set in of which the mouthpiece was the group of itinerant teachers called Sophists. With their teaching, the problem of knowledge became explicit in Greek thought.

The Eleatic doctrine had rejected the deliverances of sense-perception and the dialectic of Zeno claimed to prove that the common conceptions of plurality and motion were riddled with contradictions. On the other hand, the pluralists and atomists had produced a picture of the universe entirely foreign to common experience. A different account of the world was given and 'knowledge' seemed to take a different form as each new thinker came into prominence, so that the view began to find favour that of truth itself there could be no absolute or objective measure. This view found expression in the work of Protagoras, who declared that 'Of all things the measure is man, of those that are that they are, of those that are not that they are not'. In other words, appearance to us is all, with the implications that the world of reality has no independent existence (for if it had there would be a more certain measure of the existence and non-existence of things than man) and that no opinion is more true (or false) than any other.

Such a doctrine leads directly to scepticism, for if no opinion is more true than another, there is no distinction between truth and falsity and, in consequence, neither are applicable terms. It is all one to admit every opinion as true and to admit none, for in either case what is being denied is the existence of a stable criterion. These sceptical implications were developed by Protagoras' contemporary, Gorgias, who denied the possibility both of knowledge and of existence.[1] The answer to both is the same: that the doctrine destroys itself; and the argument which Plato used in the *Theaetetus* against Protagoras is equally effective against Gorgias.[2]

---

[1] *Vide* Sextus Empiricus, *Adversus Dogmaticos*, I, 65 ff.
[2] *Theaetetus*, 171 B–C.

NATURE, MIND AND MODERN SCIENCE

II. SOCRATES

2. Scepticism is the challenge that brings the problem of knowledge to the fore. Just as Descartes' method of doubt was the beginning of modern epistemology, so the scepticism of the Sophists raised the problem for the Greeks, and at once champions appeared who were ready to meet the challenge. Democritus opposed them with the weapons of physical science, but Socrates abjured physics and turned to logical and metaphysical speculation. Both these philosophers distinguish between true and apparent knowledge and identify the latter with sense-perception; but while Democritus (as we saw) gives a mechanical account even of true knowledge, Socrates teaches that the real objects of knowledge are immaterial and purely intelligible, and that the soul which knows them is akin to them—a purely spiritual entity, whose perfection and essential nature lies in the cultivation of wisdom and virtue, qualities which he found to be identical with each other.

Burnet maintains that Socrates was the first Greek philosopher to combine the Orphic with the Ionian conception of the soul [1]—the first to combine the idea of the soul as the normal waking consciousness, with that of a divine and spiritual being distinct from the body and from all material existence. In effect, then, he was the first to recognize that the distinction of body from soul involved that of matter from mind.

So much at least one may say without great danger of controversy, for it is generally agreed by scholars that Socrates taught (whether or not he ever systematized it in a metaphysical theory) a doctrine of the soul as a spiritual being contrasted with and opposed to the body. Such a view is implicit even in Maier's thesis that he was no more than a moral teacher with a special dialectical method of his own, for it is upon this doctrine of the soul that his moral teaching is admitted to rest: 'I go about doing nothing else but urging you, young and old alike, not to care for your bodies or for money rather than or even as much as for your soul and its perfection'.[2] Maier himself admits that this position was characteristically Socratic.

It is not my intention, however, to enter into discussion of the much debated Socratic problem. Burnet's arguments have always seemed to me to be the most convincing and his conclusions the most helpful and enlightening in the study of Plato. But I shall not here commit myself

[1] *Vide* 'The Socratic Doctrine of the Soul' in the *Proceedings of the British Academy* 1915–16. [2] Plato, *Apology*, 30 A.

86

to any view of the distinction between the philosophies of Socrates and Plato and shall so far as possible refer to the doctrines contained in the body of Plato's writings by his name alone, venturing to distinguish the Socratic from the Platonic only where failure to do so would result in contradiction.

III. PLATO

3. There can be no doubt that Plato, like Socrates, held the soul to be the subject at least of the ordinary waking consciousness and regarded its most characteristic function as knowing and its most peculiar excellence as wisdom. This is made explicit almost in so many words in the *Philebus*.[1] Moreover, the soul is held to be distinct from the body and to use it as an instrument. It is immortal and akin to all that is eternal and divine, prior to matter and (so far at least as human beings are concerned) housed in the body only temporarily. Yet, during their association, body and soul are mutually compounded [2] and affect each other intimately. Their exact relationship, however, remains a problem and one the solution of which Plato never attempts to give in any precise form, for whenever he describes the soul and its connection with the body he does so by means of myth, a course to which he always resorts when he holds that the subject of discussion is one about which we are incapable of absolute knowledge. This in itself is a sign that the relation of body and mind was, for Plato, problematical, and as soul is invariably understood to be the principle of life as well as of mind,[3] the problem of relating the living to the non-living is similarly posited.[4]

Further, this question of the nature of the soul and its relation to the body is never separable, in the work of Plato, from the problem of knowledge, which seems, if we are to believe Aristotle, to have been his primary consideration. Aristotle tells us that Plato, having first learned from the Heraclitean, Cratylus, that the world of physical nature was one of perpetual flux, so that nothing in it was so much as nameable with any degree of accuracy, then came under the influence of Socrates, who, in dealing with ethical matters, sought the universal and concentrated upon definition. He was also undoubtedly influenced by

---

[1] 30 C: Σοφία μὴν καὶ νοῦς ἄνευ ψυχῆς οὐκ ἄν ποτε γενοίσθην.

[2] Cf. *Phaedrus*, 246 C.

[3] Cf. *Phaedo*, 105 C; *Laws*, 895 C, and *Sophist*, 249 A.

[4] For Plato, the only thing really alive, in the strict sense, is soul. The arguments for immortality in the *Phaedo* (esp. 71 D—72 D) bring this out very clearly. To speak of 'living matter' should then be a contradiction in terms. Matter, as such, must always be non-living. The relation of soul to body and that of living to non-living matter are thus one and the same.

Pythagoreanism and saw that in the sphere of mathematics, harmonics and the like what was scientifically knowable was an intelligible entity, a number or numerical ratio (usually called by some such name as σχῆμα, λόγος or εἶδος). It would naturally follow (i) that what enables us to name things and to classify them is that which Socrates sought—a universal essence—and (ii) that it is this intelligible element in our experience, as opposed to the changing and passing deliverances of sense, which makes scientific knowledge possible. Accordingly, Plato postulated the existence of intelligible essences which are eternal and unchanging [1] and which he called forms, maintaining that scientific knowledge is and can be of these alone. On the one hand, it is clear from his treatment of them in his later dialogues that he conceived these forms as interrelated and intercommunicating among themselves, as forming a complete system. Some commentators identify this system with the Form of the Good, and certainly Plato did hold that the order and arrangement of forms was determined by the Good. On the other hand, he held them to exist quite apart from the continuous processes and transformations which we roughly identify as 'things' in the sensible world, and often seems to imply that the forms themselves are never in the things, for it is not through our perception of the natural world that we become aware of them—they are not given in sense. But we do recognize some sort of similarity or approximation to forms in the particular objects of sense, and we could do so only if we had prior knowledge of the forms themselves. Such prior knowledge Plato explains by means of the soul's immortality and its kinship to the divine. The forms, he says, have been seen by the soul in a previous life, and we are now reminded of them by our sensuous experience of things in the physical world. So we recall the universal principles which are essential to any sort of knowledge and which (qua universal) are never given by and cannot be derived from sense.

Here we have the transcendent and unchanging Being of Parmenides side by side with the Heraclitean flux. But whereas Being for Parmenides is one and undifferentiated and is material, for Plato it is a differentiated system of purely intelligible forms; and whereas Parmenides failed to explain the illusions of sense in terms of Being, the realms of Being and Becoming are not, for Plato, merely juxta-

---

[1] Mr. G. R. G. Mure has drawn my attention to the importance of making it clear that by 'unchanging', as applied to the eternal realities, neither Plato nor Aristotle meant 'static'. Rest as well as motion is a property of things in the sensible world and both are opposed to eternity. For Aristotle, the absolutely immutable is pure activity (ἐνέργεια) and, as will later appear, Plato did not exclude life and the activity of thinking from absolute being.

posed; he does quite definitely set himself to explain the sensible world by relating it to the eternal world of forms, though we shall have to consider anon how far his successive attempts to forge a link between them are in the end successful.

It is, however, clear that, according to Plato, human knowledge is possible only because the soul is immortal and has been able in a previous existence to become acquainted with the forms. In us its vision is blurred and confused by its connection with the body and by the impact, through that, of other bodies upon it.[1] But these bodies are not, properly speaking, knowable. Of them we have nothing better than more or less reliable opinion, which is reliable only so far as we recognize the forms in the passing phenomena of sense and only to the extent that we recognize them accurately and clearly.

In Plato as elsewhere, therefore, we find the problems outlined in Chapter II inseparably connected. The explanation of human knowledge is dependent upon the doctrine of the nature of the soul and of its relation to the human body. The answers to three questions are required: (i) What is the relation of the soul to the body? (ii) What is that of the soul to the forms? and (iii) What is that of the forms to the particular events and groups of events which pass for 'things' in the material world of becoming? But these questions are never satisfactorily answered by Plato, though his teaching points the way along which a solution may be discoverable.

4. (i) The reality which is to be known consists of (a) the forms—the eternal essences—and (b) the flux of material processes. Of these the first are supposed to be known by the soul directly, and the second produces, through our body which is a part of it, effects of various kinds upon the soul, both sensory and emotional. These effects, however, seem only to be deleterious and never to produce knowledge, which the soul acquires best when completely free from them.[2] Its association with the body seems to cause division in the soul, which in its purity is simple and uncompounded,[3] and to produce a 'lower' part (or parts) experiencing bodily feelings, as opposed to the higher part whose activity is purely intellectual. The former is sometimes described as the mortal part of the soul, as opposed to its immortal part [4] and sometimes as a kind of disfigurement of the pure soul [5] which, if it becomes too great, drags the soul perpetually to earth and keeps it

---

[1] Cf. *Phaedo*, 65 *et seq.*, and *Timaeus*, 43 A—44 C.
[2] Cf. *Phaedo*, 66 D–E, 79 D.   [3] Cf. *Republic*, X, 611 B.
[4] Cf. *Timaeus*, 69 C–E.   [5] Cf. *Republic*, X, 611 C–D.

always in association with bodies,[1] but which, if the effects of the body are minimized and disregarded in the soul's concentration upon the pursuit of virtue and wisdom, may be shed at death. Plato constantly wavers between these two accounts of the soul in his attempts to describe its conjunction with the body. Sometimes, in keeping with the notion that the soul has parts, he speaks of it as the subject of the whole of the experience of the organism, treating the body as no more than a dead material covering,[2] so that the soul experiences in itself physical reactions and sensations such as itching, prickling, sweating and heat, almost as though it had a body of its own distinct from the physical body.[3] At other times, consonant with the view that the body disfigures the pure soul, he speaks as if the passions and sensations were purely bodily affections and were experienced by the soul, as it were, only at second hand, almost as if the body had an inferior form of soul of its own.[4] But whenever he deals with these matters Plato speaks metaphorically, using the language of myth, and his statements cannot be too closely pressed. Consequently, his exact meaning remains obscure and the relation of the soul to the physical world with which its point of contact is the body is never clearly explained.

It is always doubtful, therefore, whether sense-perception (the perception by the soul of the effects in the body of external causes) is merely a physiological process creating confusion in the mind, or really a source of knowledge, if only of an inferior kind. If it conveys to the soul the knowledge of the fluid nature of the material world, it must be admitted as one means, at least, of our knowing; and this Plato seems to suggest when he says that in our perception of material things we recognize a certain likeness to the forms which 'reminds' us of our pre-existent knowledge—for, unless we do perceive the material things which have this resemblance to the forms, our previous knowledge could not be re-awakened. In the *Republic*, accordingly, we find εἰκασία and πίστις ranked as forms of knowledge, albeit the lowest.[5] Yet the account which he gives of sensation in the *Theaetetus* and the *Timaeus* leaves the external world inaccessible to us by direct perception, and, indeed, in the *Theaetetus* it is explicitly denied that perception can be knowledge. The first suggestion is to be found in the earlier dialogues [6] while the second appears only in the later. Might it not be, therefore, that the first is the Socratic doctrine and the second the view of Plato himself?

---

[1] *Phaedo*, 81 B–D, 83 D–E; *Phaedrus*, 248 C.   [2] *Ibid.* 250 C.
[3] *Ibid.* 251 B–C, 254 C.   [4] Cf. *Phaedo*, 83.
[5] *Republic*, VI, 509 D–510 A.   [6] *Meno, Phaedo, Republic* and *Phaedrus*.

According to the account in the *Theaetetus*, what we perceive
through the senses is an effect produced by the interaction of the two
processes, one in the sense-organ and one in the outer world.[1] In the
Timaeus[2] it is the effect on the bodily organ of some process without.
The perception of an effect, however, is not the perception of the cause,
and sensation, if this account of it is to be accepted, cannot tell us
anything about the outer world and very little about the body itself.
Plato does not explicitly draw this conclusion and he denies that perception can be knowledge for another reason, namely, that its deliverances are unstable and that it is itself a flux. But he does make it clear
that this is not the flux of the external world (which perception is
supposed to reveal to us) but one produced by the interaction of two
natural processes, one of which is in the human body. I do not think,
therefore, that we can say, as Collingwood does,[3] that Plato held
sense-perception to be the source of all such knowledge as is possible
of the physical world (though this might be true of Socrates), and if he
did think so, his theory of sensation is by no means compatible with the
view.

If we take the earlier (Socratic?) view, we find that what is stressed is
not so much the constant flux of the physical world as the resemblance
of material things (in some way) to the forms, and whatever knowledge
perception affords us is dependent upon our 'recollection' of these.
If, however, we take the later view, we may still hold that the deliverances of sense, though they do not directly give us knowledge of the
world of nature, may put us in mind of the forms. And if the processes
of the natural world are themselves directly related to the forms in
some way, our knowledge of the latter, once clarified and systematized,
might include a knowledge of the former also—or at any rate might
enable us to interpret the deliverances of sense in such a way as to
reveal the truth about them. We must turn, then, to the examination of
that relation between the soul and the forms which makes its knowledge
of them possible in its previous existence and that between the forms
and the processes in the world of becoming.

5. (ii) We are explicitly told by Plato on several occasions that the
soul is not itself a form, though it is more akin to the eternal realities
than anything else in the natural world. Its knowledge of the forms is
thus to be explained in terms of a relation connecting two things which
are not to be identified.

---

[1] *Theaetetus*, 156 c et seq.   [2] 65 c et seq.
[3] *Idea of Nature*, p. 70.

We must bear in mind, however, that there are other kinds of soul besides those of human beings: there is the soul of God, the creator and efficient cause of the physical world; there is the world-soul, which contains within itself the souls of lesser living things,[1] and there are the souls of the created gods. We are primarily concerned with the human soul but we shall find, as has already been predicted in Chapter II, that some consideration of its relation to the other kinds will be forced upon us by our investigation into the nature and conditions of human knowledge.

Before proceeding to that, however, a word of explanation is needed of the difference between the soul of God and that of the cosmos, on the one hand, and the particular created souls on the other, which are contained as parts within the world-soul. These latter are the souls of the created gods, of men and of animals and I shall call them 'finite', meaning to convey by that term that they are subject to certain limitations to which the former are not. One could not, however, properly call either Plato's God or his cosmos 'infinite' unless it were simply by way of contrast with the imperfections of humanity. Nevertheless, God is an eternal being. He is, it is true, a soul and not a form, but He is not in time, which belongs only to the created world of nature. His knowledge of the forms is complete and perfect and He is himself perfectly good. His perfection and his knowledge are, therefore, unexcelled and to that extent we may think of Him as infinite, while both the created gods and men, in their finiteness, fall, in varying degrees, short of His perfection. The cosmos, also, has a certain perfection of its own. It is a complete and (of its kind) perfect totality, in which the created gods and men are but parts and are, it seems, spatially contained.[2] It is undying, although created, and its body is everlasting. This characteristic is shared by the created gods but not by men whose souls are implanted in short-lived bodies that are mere fragmentary material parts of the physical world. Though the cosmos excludes God and the realm of eternal realities and cannot therefore properly be called infinite, there is a sense in which, by comparison with the shortcomings of the human creature, the word might be applied to it.

The imperfections of the human soul are, however, always connected in Plato's thought with its association with the body, apart from which, as we shall see, it becomes free from them. It is never clear whether, or to what extent, similar disadvantages are suffered by the souls of the created gods or even by that of the cosmos itself in consequence of their association with bodies. It would seem that they are

[1] Cf. *Timaeus*, 30 D.   [2] Cf. *Ibid.* 36 E, 39 E—40 A and 42 D.

not, and probably for the reason that their bodies are not the transitory and fragmentary things to which our souls are attached. The 'finiteness' of the human soul, therefore, seems largely, if not wholly, to be due to the imperfections of its body, and the nature of its knowledge when unfettered by the body should be the same as that of the created gods and of the cosmos itself.[1]

Plato constantly avers that the soul knows the forms by direct cognizance;[2] but, with one exception, he nowhere explains the manner of this cognition in other than mythical language. The interpretation of his doctrine is, therefore, far from easy. He almost invariably speaks of the soul as having 'seen' the forms before it was born into an earthly body. In the *Phaedrus* he describes how the souls of the gods parade on the outer surface of the heavens to view the realities of the eternal world, and how the souls of men struggle to control the horses which draw their chariots sufficiently to raise their heads above the surface and to catch a fleeting glimpse of the galaxy of forms. Again, in the *Republic* he speaks of education as turning 'the eye of the soul' towards the light and uses the parable of the cave to describe how the soul is freed from the underworld of shadows to emerge into the light of the sun and behold the realities themselves. But all this is metaphor and it cannot be taken literally, for the 'eye' of the soul is very different from the bodily eye and its vision is not the vision of the physical world. The forms, we are emphatically told, are invisible, and our apprehension of them cannot be similar to sense-perception from which Plato rigidly distinguishes it and with which it is sharply contrasted.

If we were to take the metaphor in its natural sense, we should have to believe that by some sort of non-sensuous vision images or reflections of the forms were conveyed into the soul, and this would be as unsatisfactory a conception of the matter as it is clearly not what Plato intended. It would be unsatisfactory because it would require a conception of the soul as a sort of picture-gallery in which the subjects of the pictures would be the forms—the eternal world, as it were, in miniature—and it would lead to a representative theory of knowledge with all its attendant difficulties. It is plain that Plato never intended anything of this sort. He never speaks of the soul as if it were, or possessed, a representation in miniature of the eternal world; and if he ever speaks of images or copies of the forms, it is with reference only to the objects of the material world, in which the forms are in some sense

---

[1] The souls of animals need not be considered in this connection, because, as such, they do not know the forms. (*Vide Phaedrus*, 249 B.)

[2] *Meno*, 81 C; *Phaedrus*, 247 D, 248 A; *Repub.* 516 A–B; *Theaet.* 185 D–E.

held to be exemplified. If the soul itself is a copy at all, it is of one form only—that of life,[1] and if it contains images of anything else, they are of the physical things percepts of which are 'imprinted on it', as on a wax tablet, by means of the bodily sense-organs.[2] But even this idea Plato puts forward only as an analogy and he does not intend it to be taken as a literal description. That the soul's knowledge of the forms is visual, in anything more than a metaphorical sense, is therefore a suggestion which must at once be rejected. But some interpretation of the metaphor must be sought that will render it intelligible.

One such interpretation might be that the soul apprehends the forms by some kind of intellectual intuition, in a flash of conceptual insight. But intellectual intuition is a very mysterious thing and no rational account has ever been given of it. Examples produced in the attempt to explain it, moreover, are usually spurious.[3] Moreover, even if this interpretation be accepted, we must still consider what it is which becomes the soul's possession when it apprehends the forms. Not the forms themselves, for they remain sacrosanct, each in its eternal oneness and separation, and they cannot so divide themselves as to enter, in their own essential substance, into all the innumerable souls of gods and men who intuit them. Such a notion would lead to the same difficulties as the doctrine of the participation in the forms of material things (a theory presently to be examined). If, then, it is not the forms themselves that the soul possesses, it must be some representation of them, and we are back with the very conception that the notion of intellectual intuition was intended to avoid. Alternatively, it might be argued that in intellectual intuition the mind (or pure soul) becomes identified with its object. But, if that is so, each soul *in propria persona* would actually become the system of forms and all souls would unite in one transcendent intelligence. This conception might well enable us to understand the nature of the mind of God, but it leaves the separation from His soul of the world-soul and the finite souls of men and the created gods wholly inexplicable and unintelligible. For the necessary implication of the Platonic doctrine is that the soul, when completely purified, is able to 'view' the realm of the eternal world in its entirety. Failure to do so in any degree is always explained in terms of its attachment to the body. Even the black horse of the *Phaedrus*, though ostensibly it represents a part of the soul itself, is obviously intended to represent that part which is corrupted and tainted by the

---

[1] Cf. *Phaedo*, 104-5, and Burnet's interpretation, *Thales to Plato*, p. 166; also *Timaeus*, 30 B–C.
[2] *Theaetetus*, 191 C *et seq.*   [3] *Vide* Joachim, *Logical Studies*, pp. 152 ff.

body and its immersion in sensuality. We are expressly told in the *Republic* that the soul in her truest nature is uncompounded and that she seems to be composite only because we see her 'marred by communion with the body', damaged and scarred by its incrustation and misshapen by the impact of physical processes through its mediation. In her purity, in pure reason and φιλοσοφία, accordingly, liberated from the cramping disfigurement of corporeal associations, nothing will stand between her and the forms which she contemplates, and she must know them all. If, therefore, intellectual intuition is an identity of subject and object, the omniscient soul is one with the eternal reality and there cannot be a multiplicity of such souls. But if that is so, how can soul be imparted at all either to the cosmos or to finite creatures?

By whichever of these interpretations we understand the metaphor of vision Plato's theory collapses, and the problem of human learning raised in the *Meno* remains in principle unsolved, for the very foundation of that recollection, which is there called in to solve it, is incapable of explanation.

There may, however, be another interpretation the clue to which is to be found in Spinoza's remark that 'demonstrations (and these alone) are the eyes with which the mind sees things'.[1] If we follow this clue we must conclude that the soul's vision of the forms is a process of reasoning; and Plato's identification of the highest kind of knowledge with dialectic suggests that this may be his meaning. But if it is, the whole conception of the forms and of their relation to the visible world will have to be modified in a way which would take us beyond anything to be found in Plato. Apart from the metaphors already discussed, Plato tells us very little even about dialectic. He says that the dialectician uses the unquestioned hypotheses of the sciences as *mere* hypotheses and goes beyond them to the first principle of all things,[2] and that dialectic alone goes straight to this principle, cancelling the hypotheses [3] presumably by criticism. Though Plato himself does not say so, the method may perhaps be illustrated in his own dialogues in two different ways. (a) In the Socratic arguments of the earlier dialogues a definition of an ethical concept is tendered provisionally as an hypothesis; it is then criticized until it is shown to contradict itself and is corrected so as to avoid the contradiction and to reconcile its conflicting moments. The new definition thus reached is then submitted to the same process until something still more satisfactory is found.[4]

---

[1] Quoted by Joachim in *Logical Studies*, p. 54. The correct reference is *Ethics*, V, xxiii, *Schol.*   [2] *Repub.* 511 B.   [3] *Repub.* 533 C.
[4] Cf. G. R. G. Mure, *Aristotle* (London, 1932), pp. 28-30.

But the earlier dialogues end, as a rule, inconclusively, and the goal of the dialectical movement is never reached. (b) In the later dialogues, especially the *Parmenides* and the *Sophist*, a method is again demonstrated of criticizing hypotheses. In the latter part of the *Parmenides* the consequences of pairs of contrary hypotheses are analysed, demonstrating that each turns into the other, so that each, if taken alone and in abstraction, contradicts itself. In the *Sophist* it is argued that the definition of anything implies the negation of its other—a statement of what it is not—so that contraries are mutually implicated and definitive. From this it follows that certain concepts (forms?), such as Being, Not-being, Same, Other, Rest and Motion, exclude and imply each other in definite ways, suggesting (though Plato does not go so far as to draw the conclusion) that they are mutually derivative. All this points to a process of thought in which provisional hypotheses or definitions, when their consequences are developed, first cancel each other out by their opposition, then, by their opposition, define each other and enable the contradiction to be resolved and transcended in a new concept. As the definition of a thing is the statement of its essence or form, it would seem to follow that the dialectical process is one in which forms are generated one from another by their mutual implications.

If the soul's knowledge of the forms is a process of this sort, however, it is not an immediate intuitive vision of a truth set over against the knowing mind, but the activity of the soul itself, which generates the forms by its own motion, so that the soul (or mind) itself, in the course of the process, is developing and progressing towards that goal of omniscience which is the intelligible world and the mind of God in one. But such a theory can hardly be attributed to Plato [1] so far as he denies generation in the eternal world and separates the forms from God and both of these from the human soul. To distinguish all these from one another may well be necessary, but the distinctions cannot be made absolute if the implications are developed of the view that knowledge of the forms is a discursive process of the soul's own thinking.

We may conclude, then, that so far as his explicit statements go, Plato fails to answer satisfactorily the question how the soul, in its

[1] He comes near to it in his account of the Form of the Good as αἰτία both of being and of truth. But 'being' here does not include 'becoming'. The Form of the Good is the cause of the essence of things in the same way as the sun is the cause of their existence (cf. *Repub.* VI, 509 B). But Plato does not make the Form the cause also of becoming as it should in some sense be if the soul (which is not a form) is able to develop towards omniscience in the manner required by the above account of dialectic. Nevertheless, Plato's attempts to relate the forms to the physical world do foreshadow a conclusion, never actually reached in the dialogues, in which the union of being with becoming is implied. (See below, pp. 99-100.)

direct perception of the forms, is related to them. But what he does tell us points to an answer which, if we accepted it and developed its implications, would transform the whole of his theory.

6. (iii) A similar result, and one closely connected with the foregoing conclusion, emerges from an examination of the third question— namely, that of the relation of the forms to the physical world of nature. This question has been discussed by all Plato's critics and commentators from Aristotle onward. I need not, therefore, go into it at any great length and shall do no more than sketch, in the briefest outline, the alternative answers and the criticisms which prove them to be unsatisfactory, devoting most of my attention to the indications given by Plato of the direction in which the true answer is to be found.

Plato offers two explanations of the relation between forms and sensible things, neither of which satisfied him completely but each of which represents an effort to express a more profound conception implicit in his latest writings. The relation is sometimes alleged to be that of participation and sometimes that of imitation. The first, as Collingwood has pointed out, implies immanence and the second transcendence, yet what the theory requires is both, as Plato himself seems to have been aware.

If we take the relation to be that of participation, so that the thing 'partakes of' the form, we must conceive the form either to be multiple (entering as a whole into each particular instance) or else to be divisible into parts. But to regard it as a multiplicity of identical forms (one in each instance) destroys its universal character and reduces it to a mere heap of indistinguishable particulars;[1] and to regard it as divisible not only destroys its essential unity but renders it incapable of explaining the sensible things; for it is the form as a whole that gives the sensible thing its specific character, not a mere part or segment of the form.[2] It is just this unitary or universal element in the form that is required to make the differences of the many sensibles intelligible. Further, if the things participate in the form because of their common character, there must be some similar community between them as a class and the form itself, and that would have to be explained by a further form in which both would participate. This participation again would entail yet another form, and the relationship would involve an infinite regress.[3]

On the other hand, if we take the relation to be that of imitation, a similar infinite regress is forced upon us, because the 'likeness' of a to

---

[1] Cf. *Parmenides*, 131 A–B.
[2] *Ibid.* C–E.   [3] Cf. *ibid.* 132 A–B.

97

A implies an identical element present in both which makes them similar, and this third term must again be related to each of the other two, and so on *ad infinitum*.[1] Moreover, likeness accounts only for what is common to all the instances and is the same in each. It is the same also in the form. Thus the sensible things become assimilated to the form in a way which leaves their differences (both from it and from one another) unexplained and inexplicable. But the relationship that we are seeking must be one which explains the multiplicity of the sensible things as well as their identity, their difference from the form as well as their participation in it; and this the relation of resemblance cannot do. Further, the notion that the world of becoming imitates the world of forms implies that they are separate and apart from one another. The forms *themselves* are not in the things at all, but utterly transcend them. If that be so, however, they cannot serve as principles to explain the mutual affinities of the things and the very relationship of likeness between the material and the eternal worlds becomes impossible.[2]

That Plato was fully aware of these difficulties is apparent from his detailed and brilliant treatment of them in the *Parmenides*; and this, to my mind, is evidence enough that the theory of forms as expounded in the earlier dialogues is not so much Platonic as Socratic. But in his later works Plato seems to suggest another method of bridging the gulf between the eternal and the material worlds which may bring us nearer to our goal.

There is a sense of 'imitation' that does imply both immanence and transcendence. The ideal which the artist envisages and to which he tries to make his work, as nearly as he can, approximate, is at once immanent in that work (for it makes it what it is) and transcendent beyond it (as an ideal not yet achieved). It is clearly this sort of relationship that Plato has in his mind, for he is always talking of approximations to the forms and certainly conceived the material things as 'attempts' in varying degrees successful, to embody an ideal essence as perfectly and completely as possible. Burnet has argued that this view is adumbrated in the *Phaedo*, where Socrates maintains that things become beautiful to the extent that they participate in absolute beauty,[3] and Collingwood asserts that this was Plato's mature conception of the forms.[4] Ultimately, it seems, the form must be conceived as final cause. But though this idea is easily acceptable in the case of human art, if we apply it also to the processes of nature, we make them

---

[1] Cf. *Parmenides*, 132 E.   [2] Cf. *ibid.* 133 ff.
[3] *Vide Thales to Plato*, pp. 164-5.
[4] *Vide The Idea of Nature*, pp. 70-2.

all, without exception, teleological, and we are then obliged to explain by what urge or *nisus* the process is impelled towards its end. Can the form supply this internal dynamic? According to the letter of Plato's doctrine we must answer, No. But, though it is not the form which supplies it, yet Plato did believe that there was a dynamic, an original cause of all movement and becoming, and that this cause was soul. Now soul is cognizant of the eternal verities and, if we examine the nature of its causation, we may be able, by its means, to close the gap between the forms and the natural world, and to find a way to the solution of the problems both of knowledge and of body and soul at the same time.

In the *Sophist* [1] Plato asserts, through the mouth of the Eleatic stranger, that knowledge is an activity, and also that it is unthinkable that the most perfect being should be static and dead, devoid of life and mind.[2] True being, it appears from what he says here, is not simply intelligible but also intelligence. And having life and mind, it must have soul as well.[3] This is a departure from the doctrine that the world of forms is unchanging and eternally the same, indicating once more the line of distinction between the Socratic and Platonic.

In the *Laws* [4] the doctrine already stated in the *Phaedrus*[5] is reaffirmed and expanded: that the soul is self-moving and is therefore the only thing that could possibly be the original cause of physical motion. What is moved by external impulsion, he argues, can never be an original cause of motion, and as soul alone moves itself, it must be the original cause of all movement and becoming in the realm of nature. According to the description in the *Timaeus*, the soul is spread out and interwoven with the body of the cosmos throughout its volume, and its circular motion is imparted to physical nature in this way. Aristotle rightly criticizes this conception as materialistic,[6] pointing out that the proper movement of the mind is not in space but is the process of thinking. But if, with Taylor, we regard the *Timaeus* as expounding Pythagorean rather than Platonic doctrine (though Plato was undoubtedly sympathetic to it), and if we realize once again that it is not intended to be more than an elaborate myth, it is possible to understand Plato to mean by his statement in the *Laws* that the soul's movement is not mechanical and is nevertheless the cause of physical motion. We have already observed that both for Socrates and Plato the soul is essentially incorporeal, immortal and akin to the eternal and divine. Its characteristic activity is knowledge and its proper movement

---

[1] 248 E.   [2] *Ibid.* 249 A.   [3] *Ibid.*
[4] Bk. X, 896 A–B.   [5] 245 D–E.   [6] *De Anima*, I, iii, 406 b 26 *et seq.*

is acknowledged to be that of thought—the movement of dialectic. And the dialectical process, when we investigated its nature, proved to be a process of self-development in which the forms were generated. Though Plato never goes as far as this in any explicit statement, the passage in the *Sophist*, referred to above, does indicate that some such idea may have been dawning in his mind. If the soul's self-movement is, moreover, the original cause of all natural motion, its causation cannot be regarded as external and must be immanent. It should follow, therefore, that the soul's movement is reflected in all the processes of nature, which should all be, at least in some sense, dialectical processes.

Plato does not develop the consequences of this doctrine, but, if we were to do so, we should conclude that the soul's knowledge of the forms in dialectic is, after all, a union of subject and object, a movement in which the forms are generated by the mind's own thinking. And we should then have to maintain that this process is immanent in, and thus the ultimate cause of, all movement in nature. The generation of the animal organism being one of the natural processes in which the dialectical movement is manifested, the mind of man might then turn out to be simply that immanent movement of the soul brought to consciousness in him through the processes of nature of which his body is a part.

But in Plato we have only the merest intimations of any such theory, and even Aristotle, who explicates it much further, does not develop it completely. In a brief preliminary statement such as I have given here, it may even seem too obscure and too fantastic to carry conviction. Yet we shall find ourselves forced to return, again and again in this study, to a doctrine of this kind, and it is one in which the solution of our problem ultimately lies.

Chapter V

THE GREEK SOLUTION

I. BODY AND SOUL AS MATTER AND FORM

1. THAT the forms in Plato's theory were not and could not be efficient causes was one of the objections brought against it by Aristotle. But Plato did make the soul an efficient cause, and we have seen that if the soul's self-movement proves to be a process in which subject and object are identified, its efficient causation might at the same time be that of the forms, and that this conception might be the key to the problems of human knowledge. By developing a conception of process in which form is the efficient (as well as the final) cause of movement, and by making the soul a phase in the process, Aristotle brings us as near to a solution of those problems as we get in Greek philosophy, and it was not until the real significance of his thought was recognized and developed by Hegel in modern times that substantial advance was made beyond the point that he had reached.

Although latterly Plato seemed inclined to admit some form of life, activity and movement in the realm of true being, his attitude is in the main that which is typical of Greek thought generally, that only what is unchanging can properly be known and that absolute being, because it is eternal, is also absolutely knowable (as nothing else is).[1] The world of change he never regards as knowable in the full sense of the word, and such indications as we have in the *Sophist* of his later view is never reconciled with his doctrine that the world of becoming (because it is constantly in motion) can be no more than the subject of opinion in varying degrees dubious. Aristotle, however, refused to separate, as with a knife, the sensible from the intelligible, and sought in the realm of change that in the light of which it could be understood. He took his cue from Plato and found this intelligible element to be form, but not form separate and apart from that which it informed. The intelligible element is for him embodied in the thing which is changing. It is one ingredient in a composite entity of which the other, the non-intelligible element, is matter. But matter is a purely relative term and only relatively unintelligible, for whatever in the concrete we identify as matter at one particular level reveals itself at a lower level as already composite of both matter and form.

[1] Cf. *Repub.* 477 A.

2. To Aristotle, therefore, the universe presents itself as a scale of forms, in which each serves the next above it as its proximate matter. In this scale, the living organism, like all else, is a concrete of form and matter. The organs are so formed as to subserve the purposes of life and their matter is a combination of the physical elements. But they themselves are but matter vitalized, and what distinguishes the total organism from the non-organic is its vital principle—the soul—and that, therefore, is its form. What the soul vitalizes is the body, which is, accordingly, its matter, and the relation of body and soul is explained in these terms. There can be no question, therefore, whether Aristotle recognized the distinction between living and non-living matter and between matter and mind. Still less can it be doubted that he recognized the existence of a problem in understanding their relation to each other, or that he attempted to solve it.

These problems of relating body to soul and living to non-living matter emerge quite explicitly in the *De Anima*, where it is made abundantly clear that Aristotle thought of the soul as incorporeal and realized the difficulty of understanding its connection with a corporeal entity. It moves the living creature not by physical propulsion but 'by choice and a process of thought'.[1] As opposed to spatial movement (φορά), 'the movement of the soul is thinking (νόησις)',[2] and this thinking cannot pertain to a corporeal entity by reason of its corporeality, for it is clear that many bodies are altogether devoid of consciousness.[3] It is something connected with a body of a particular kind, but it is not itself a body in any sense at all.[4] Yet the affections of the soul can be physiologically as well as psychologically described, and to define soul in such a way as to explain this duality is part of the problem to which Aristotle addresses himself.[5] Further, he says that soul is the cause of existence in living things, for their existence is life,[6] meaning that the being or existence of a *living* thing is not the body *qua* body, but is that which enlivens it. Soul is thus at once distinguished from body and identified with life, so that the question of relating living to non-living matter is immediately raised. It is, however, no sooner raised than solved, for Aristotle, in the same passage, is explaining how soul, as the form of the body (which is its proximate matter), is the efficient, the formal and the final cause of the living thing, and from this fundamental conception of the relation of body and soul the whole of Aristotle's subsequent theory of sense-perception and of

[1] *De Anima*, 406 b 25.
[2] *Ibid.* 407 a 20.
[3] *Ibid.* 410 a 27–b 5.
[4] *Ibid.* 414 a 20-5.
[5] *Ibid.* 403 a and b.
[6] *Ibid.* 415 b 13.

knowledge develops. The mutual implications of the problems of matter and life, body and soul and of the nature of human knowledge become, accordingly, evident once again.

3. The contention that the soul and the body are related as form and matter does, however, lead to what, at least *prima facie*, is a difficulty and an inconsistency in Aristotle's theory. The notions of matter and form are inseparable in his thought from those of potentiality and actuality—form being the actuality of which matter is the potentiality. Now the soul, while it is the form of the body, itself takes several forms which constitute a series. The most rudimentary is the nutritive and reproductive soul of plant life, the next is the sensitive and appetitive soul of animals, and finally there is the rational soul of man. In each of the three kinds of soul in this series the higher presupposes and is subserved by the lower, so that while nutrition and reproduction may exist without sensation and appetite, the last two cannot be without the first two, and while all of these may exist without thought, thought arises only by supervention upon the lower functions.[1] It would not be wrong, therefore, to say that thought is that for the sake of which the lower functions exist, and that it is the realization of their potentiality— the form of which they are the proximate matter. In thought, therefore, the whole potentiality of the soul is realized, and, as the soul is the form of the body, thought is also the realization of the potentiality of the body as a material thing.

On the other hand, the act of sensing is, according to Aristotle, not simply the realization of the potentiality of a proximate matter, but of a capacity (ἕξις) already formed in the soul and actualized instantaneously in the sensing. And it is also the realization of a potentiality which is ostensibly not in the living body or its soul at all—namely, that of the material thing which stimulates the sense. The sensed quality is the (sensible) form of the thing sensed, which the soul receives without its matter [2] and which, before it is sensed, exists only in potentiality. As Mure has very aptly expressed it, the actual, though not the potential, *esse* of the perceptible is *percipi*; [3] and the potentiality is realized only in the sensing. This sensible form is retained in the soul, or rather it is further actualized, as φάντασμα in imagination, and finally its intelligible form is actualized in thought. But at this stage the mind and the object are one, 'for in the case of things without matter,

[1] Cf. Mure, *Aristotle*, p. 97.
[2] Cf. *De Anima*, 424 a 17-19.
[3] *Introduction to Hegel* (Oxford, 1940), p. 20. Cf. Aristotle, *Metaphysics*, 1047 a 5.

that which thinks and that which is thought are the same, for speculative knowledge and its objects are identical'.[1] Consequently, the soul is 'in a sense all things that are',[2] because all things are either sensible or thinkable.

The soul is thus, on the one hand, the form of the body and, on the other, the form of all things. How can this be? Does it not commit us to the impossibility of identifying the part with the whole? For the human body is only a minute part of the physical world and its form can hardly be identical with that of the entire cosmos.

It is no answer to say that the human being is the microcosm and the world the macrocosm, because that would mean that the forms received by the soul were not the actualizations of the objects known, but were some sort of replica or copy in miniature of forms which existed elsewhere. Such a notion is quite contrary to Aristotle's express statements and would leave us once more with a representative theory of knowledge, which (except by implication, in some of his weaker moments [3]) he does not accept. We must therefore conclude that Aristotle means in sober earnest that the human soul, which is but the form of the human body, is in its knowledge identical with the whole world of nature: so much as it actually knows, it actually is; and what it does not yet know, it is potentially. This position, if it is not hopelessly paradoxical, does seem to set us a conundrum difficult of solution.

Aristotle's theory of sensation does assume the existence of two material things in physical relation as the condition of the occurrence of sensing. The object sensed, though until it is perceived it is only potential, nevertheless exists and is assumed to be 'compresent' (the word is borrowed from S. Alexander) with the sense-organ. It is certainly not created by the act of sensing, but its form, *qua* unsensed, is not actualized. The sense-organ, moreover, is a *sine qua non* of sensation; yet it too is in itself a material entity the form of which can only be actualized if it is perceived. This fact Aristotle seems altogether to overlook.[4] Nevertheless, as an organ of the living body, the sense-organ is part of the matter, of which the form is the soul, and that is no more nor less than the activities of life and mind. The contents of the soul, therefore, its feelings, sensations, imaginings and the rest, are, in appropriate correlations, the forms of the various organs and are the actualizations of the essential nature of those organs—that for the sake of which the organs are. The sensum, accordingly, actualizes the form

---

[1] *De Anima*, 430 a 4-5.   [2] *Ibid.* 431 b 21.   [3] Cf. *De Interpretatione*, i-vi
[4] Cf. Mure, *Introduction to Hegel*, p. 20, to which I am indebted for the above and for much of what follows.

of the sense-organ in one way and that of the object in another, yet it is a single entity and it is the form of both. 'The actualization (ἐνέργεια) of the objects sensed and of the sense are one and the same, though their being (τὸ εἶναι) is not the same.'[1]

If we adhere strictly to this position, the difficulty is insuperable because the object and the organ are separate material existents and as such they do and must have different forms. The form of the object (say, a red triangle) is the sensed quality that it is seen to possess, and the form of the organ (the eye) is certainly different (it is neither red nor triangular). On the other hand, as perceived by the eye of another percipient, the sense-organ has an appropriate form which is peculiar to itself. It might be argued that this form is only the proximate matter to the sense-faculty (vision) in the soul. But if that is so, it is certainly not the case with the red triangle. That is not the proximate matter to the sense-faculty, but only to the sensum. If it were edible it might become proximate matter to the tissue of the body as organic matter, but it is inevitably at a stage (at least) lower in the scale of forms than the sense-organ.

There is, in consequence, a hiatus between the sensum and the sense-faculty. As the form to which the organ is proximate matter, the sense-faculty is one stage higher than the quality of any object which is sensed, and an ambiguity is discovered in the word 'sensation' which undermines the theory. As the exercise of a disposition or faculty in the soul, sensation may be regarded as the activity (or actualization of the potentiality) of the organ; but as a quality sensed, it is the 'activity' only of a lower phase in the *scala naturae*. In attempting to bring together and to identify these two is Aristotle simply committing a blunder, or is the hiatus between sensum and sense-faculty really bridgeable?

4. The solution is outlined by Mure in the discussion of Aristotle in his *Introduction to Hegel*.[2] Our common mistake, he points out, is to imagine the living, sentient creature as inhabiting 'an alien and indifferent physical universe by a sort of precarious squatter's right', to think of animate and inanimate being as juxtaposed patches in this world, mutually related on the same level of physical existence in space and time. The physical interpretation of the world, however, is appropriate to the *whole* at a certain level of abstraction, and the animate and sentient patches, which we tend to import into the hypothetical conception of the world which physics envisages, belong to

---

[1] *De Anima*, 425 b 26.   [2] Pp. 22 ff.

altogether different and more concrete phases of interpretation. This confusion, from which Aristotle is not entirely free, is what leads to our difficulty.

Instead of conceiving the condition of consciousness as the compresence of juxtaposed physical entities on the same level, we must substitute the conception of different levels of development each of which embraces both subject and object. The conception is a difficult one and is never really made explicit by Aristotle, but we can derive it from his teaching by going somewhat beyond the letter, while doing no violence to the spirit.

Physical matter—the four elements—can be combined in various ways and each compound which results is a composite of matter and form. Yet each again may become matter out of which the tissue of living things is formed and this again is matter to the animal as one organism. The animal, however, is what it is only in virtue of its life, and that is its soul, its actuality or ἐντελέχεια. Further, the activities of the soul are themselves a graded series in which the lower functions come to fruition in the higher activities of consciousness. If now we regard the proximate matter of consciousness as its object, that of sense would be the sense-organ *in its organic relation to the rest of the body and its environment*. We do not see simply the eye. But what we do see is the organic product of the system constituted by the eye in its setting in the body, nourished by the digestive system through the blood, sensitized by the nervous system, actuating the cortex of the brain and stimulated to activity by the incoming light.[1] And by this product the entire system is brought to fruition and 'realized'. The sensum is its end or final cause. But the sensum fails us if any one of the organic conditions fails and for that reason the object sensed is as much a part of the organic situation as is the body itself. Vision, in consequence, *is* the form at once of the body and of the visible world, for they are not to be conceived as separate entities existing apart, but as having become, in the sensation, one organic totality.

The form so actualized is then further developed in imagination and thought, with their concomitant activities of appetite and action. Each stage of this development is related to the next above, as elsewhere in the *scala universi*, as matter to form, so that knowledge is no less than the whole world actualizing itself at the level of consciousness.[2] In the

---

[1] I have, of course, gone beyond Aristotle's physiology in attempting to restate his case.

[2] Cf. Mure, *Introduction to Hegel*, p. 39: 'Aristotle's doctrine justifies no realist conception of the natural world as possessing its character in independence of, and

human mind it is the form at once of the human body and of nature, to which that body is organically related in its living activity. Man's consciousness is the emergent product of that total relationship, not merely one term of a relation between his body and the outer world. It is the world's consciousness actualized in and through him.

The Platonic world-soul and that of the individual tend thus to coalesce. The world-soul becomes actual in and through humanity. But this implies transcendence of the merely singular percipient, as indeed does the very fact of perception. For if, in perception, subject and object are actualized in one, the singular subject is already transcended; and so far as different percipients perceive the same objects, the difference between them is overcome. The perceptum is, in fact, never a barely particular sense-datum (and, as we shall see later,[1] if it were it could not be material for knowledge) but is always to some extent universal. In Aristotle's terminology, it is not only a 'this' but also 'such', and in the apprehension of its universal character, the singular subject of consciousness is immediately transcended; for as 'such' it is the same for all percipients, and its actualization in their consciousness unites not only subject and object but the separate percipients also. Moreover, at the final stage the form actualized is purely intelligible and its activity is reason, which in its efficient form is, for Aristotle, the characteristic activity of God. In fact, God is the pure activity of reason, νόησις νοήσεως, with no residue of potentiality —pure form without matter—and, in isolated flashes of intellection, the human mind becomes one with Him. The ultimate reality of the world should, therefore, be God, who would be revealed as the world came to final consciousness of itself through the hierarchy of substantial forms which is nature and among which man's mind is a relatively highly developed phase.

There is in this interpretation of Aristotle considerable anticipation of the modern view of nature, but it seems to be justified by what he has written. Aristotle is, indeed, one of the great figures in the history of philosophy whose thought, though inevitably a product of a period, rises above the special view-points of the time and comes nearer to grasping the eternal truth which is the goal of the whole historical development. At any time, therefore, profit is to be derived and illumination to be gained by the study of his works.

indifference to, mind. Nature is even more than the essential *correlate* of a highly developed form of mind: it is something which is only actual as the *object and content* of mind. Nature and mind are not merely concurrent in their development: their single actualization has its seat in mind.'

[1] Pp. 179, 181, 289-92, 314, 331 ff.

II. IMMANENCE AND TRANSCENDENCE

But, as Mure remarks (*loc. cit.*), 'Aristotle is, of course, not in full possession of this thought'. There are a number of difficulties and ambiguities in his teaching which must make us hesitate to impute to him the whole theory as it is here outlined. In particular, his doctrine seems to come to grief when we examine the position of efficient reason in the human mind, and again when we try to understand the relation of God to the world.

5. (a) Aristotle speaks of active reason as being *in* the human soul [1] and as acting upon passive reason as upon a plastic material. He also maintains that it is in a man what is most truly himself.[2] Yet elsewhere [3] he seems to imply that it is something almost alien to the mortal human animal, coming to him, as it were, from without and remaining immortal at his death. The human soul is the form of the body and is therefore perishable with the body. But efficient reason is independent of the body. It is the activity of God, eternal and imperishable, and so far as it pertains to the soul of man at all, it is separable from its other faculties and functions and survives their decay. It is, moreover, quite impersonal in its activity, and in his sublimest moments of thought man apparently actualizes something quite beyond his singular and separate personality.

These two seemingly conflicting ideas of human individuality are not necessarily irreconcilable, for that which truly is the substance of anything is its form, and its formal cause is also its final cause, and that again, for all finite entities, is an end beyond the process of their becoming. Accordingly, what any finite entity really is is that which it is coming to be, while nevertheless it is *not yet* that. Man, then, may well be a finite separate and mortal creature in one aspect, though his true nature may only be realized in that aspiration beyond the finite which governs all the functionings of his soul. But, on the other hand, if the active reason which realizes itself through the human mind is severed from the rest of the soul's functionings, it cannot relate in man to the lower activities of his soul as it should do if it is to be their real consummation. If it is implicit in them they must be 'sublated' in it, and if it is utterly separable and self-sufficient they cannot be. It is reason which gives its form to sensation and without it sensation is not

---

[1] *De Anima*, 430 a 10-15; *vide* also Ross, *Aristotle* (3rd ed., London, 1937), pp. 149-150.   [2] *Nicomachean Ethics*, 1178 a 1-7.   [3] *De Anima*, III, v.

even an image or reflection of an object, it would be a mere modification of an unintelligent and unintelligible 'consciousness'—less even than an 'appearance', for to what could it appear? It could represent no object because the object would have none but a potential existence unless and until it could be actualized in thought. Apart from such actualization the object either has no reality at all or one contained entirely in itself and inaccessible to the human mind. Without active reason, in short, there can be neither consciousness nor object. As Aristotle himself asserts, 'without this nothing knows'.[1] The severance of efficient reason from the human soul would, therefore, render the problem of knowledge insoluble and, if insistence upon it is unqualified, Aristotle's theory cannot achieve its end.

6. (b) God, as we have seen, should be the consummation of the process whose phases constitute the world of nature. As such He should be the immanent cause of the process—the *forma informans* of nature. So by Aristotle He is intended to be. He is the efficient cause of all movement in the world: directly of the movement of the outer heaven and indirectly of the movements of the spheres and all other motion caused by them. He is also the final cause of the entire development, and His self-conscious activity is, in the end, what gives each phase its significance. But He causes movement without Himself being moved, as the object of desire; and, as pure activity without matter, He is a thinking which is its own object, 'substance eternal, without motion, and separate from sensible things'.[2] Consequently, He stands apart from the processes of nature and transcends them utterly. Aristotle explicitly states that God is both immanent and transcendent, asserting that the highest good is contained in the universe both as the order of its parts and as something 'separate and by itself'.[3] But, again, he never quite succeeds in making its twofold character intelligible. Transcendence and immanence are, after all, at least *prima facie* contradictory characters, and if they are to pertain to the same reality they must be intelligibly reconciled. But, in Aristotle's theory, their reconciliation is not achieved.

---

[1] *De Anima,* 430 a 25: ἄνευ τούτου οὐθὲν νοεῖ. The Greek is ambiguous. Ross gives the following alternative renderings: (i) 'and without the passive reason the active reason knows nothing'; (ii) 'and without the active reason the passive reason knows nothing'; (iii) 'and without the passive reason nothing knows'; (iv) 'and without the active reason nothing knows'. (*Aristotle*, p. 152.) They all imply, however, that knowledge depends on the active reason, even if the passive reason is also a *condicio sine qua non*. And they all imply that a severance between active and passive reason, if absolute, would destroy knowledge.
[2] *Metaph.* 1073 a 4. [3] *Metaph.* Λ, x, 1075 a 11 ff.

As God is perfect and self-sufficient, without unrealized potentiality, He is pure form without matter. The processes of nature, therefore, cannot relate to Him as proximate matter and He is indifferent to the lesser creatures in whom He excites love and aspiration. Yet if they are not His proximate matter, how can He be their final form and their ultimate reality? The object of His thought can only be a perfect object, and it is thus Himself alone, as pure timeless activity. But this means that the sublunary world cannot be an object of His consciousness. Further, His efficient causation *is only* final causation:[1] He moves only as the object of desire. But movement actuated by desire implies an efficient cause distinct from the object of the desire as something working on (or in) the body moved. The movement of the outer heaven, if it is the expression of desire and love, implies the possession by the heaven of a soul (which is not the soul of God), and this soul must be the efficient cause of the movement. God cannot be its efficient cause unless His activity is something else besides νόησις νοήσεως. He must be, in some sense, its creator, as well as the aim of its endeavour. If He is not this, He can as little exercise efficient causation as could the Platonic forms. Accordingly, a chasm opens between Aristotle's God and the *scala naturae* of which He ought to be the crown; and, in consequence, similar gaps appear in the system of nature itself.[2]

The form characterizing any matter in the sublunary world is only provisional. It is a proximate form, as its matter is only proximate matter susceptible at a lower level of its own analysis into matter and form. The significance of any provisional form lies beyond itself in a higher form which it subserves. But if this higher form cannot be embodied in a proximate matter, no more can the lower; for it is only from such embodiment of the higher form within it that the lower derives its formal character. Consequently, the severance of God from the world of nature breaks the chain in every link.

Efficient reason (the activity of God) is the activity which actualizes passive reason, and this again is the form of sense. Without it sense becomes an unintelligible succession of particular sensa which cannot serve as the form of any object. But without sensible form there can be no object for appetite and so no living movement. Yet this again is the form which the nutrition and propagation of plant life subserve, and if it is removed, nutrition and self-propagation appear as mere chemical processes and life degenerates into non-living matter. As God draws away into His own ethereal perfection, so the lower orders shrink back

---

[1] Cf. Ross, *Aristotle*, p. 181.
[2] Cf. Mure, *Introduction to Hegel*, pp. 44 and 49 ff., and *Aristotle*, pp. 173 ff.

into themselves and take on an independent reality, each apart from the next above. For if the form is not immanent in its proximate matter, it cannot *actualize* it, and it must then be actual, if at all, in some other than a teleological sense. Accordingly, either the stages of the *scala naturae* must stand, each separable from the next, as a series of mutually independent stages externally related, or else they all disintegrate into primary matter, which is ultimately formless and unintelligible. The first alternative is a notion full of conflict and contradiction and the system collapses finally into the second.

Nor can Aristotle escape the dilemma of immanence and transcendence, for the final actualization which forms the summit of the *scala universi* must be a total actuality (or activity) wholly without matter. Until that is reached the potentiality of the lower orders has not been realized to the full. The consummation implicit in the natural processes can be no less than an absolutely perfect being. Yet the realization of such perfection seems inevitably to require its severance from the imperfect approximations which constitute the sensible world. Despite his progress beyond Plato, therefore, Plato's problem reappears unsolved in Aristotle and we must conclude that his theory, while bringing us near to a solution of our problem, still fails to achieve it. Its coherence depends in the last resort upon the reconciliation in the conception of God of immanence with transcendence, and this, despite his best efforts, Aristotle is unable to achieve. He leaves us, in consequence, with the notion of a God who is only transcendent, influencing nature, as it were, only from afar.

III. SUMMARY

7. The movement of the heavens was what led the Greeks to regard the whole world as a living creature, for it seemed to them that what moves of its own accord must be alive. Hylozoism is thus only the obverse of the view that nature is the realm of constant change and movement. From this view, we have seen, arose the belief that natural entities were unknowable, because what is never for one moment the same cannot intelligibly be identified. It seemed to follow that what is knowable must be permanent and the existence of knowledge must imply that of an eternal, unalterable realm of intelligible objects and this, moreover, must be what is truly real, for, as Parmenides argued, what is conceivable must be. Out of hylozoism, which Collingwood stresses, therefore, arose the antithesis between the perpetual flux of the sensible world and the eternal realm of intelligible reality. The

central problem of Greek philosophy, in consequence, was the explanation of becoming, and with this the whole question of human knowledge is involved.

8. The human mind seemed somehow to participate in both being and becoming, and knowledge could be explained only by reconciling the opposing terms of the antithesis. But this the Greeks were never able to do satisfactorily. To the very end the intelligible reality stood aloof from the process of becoming and not even Aristotle's analysis was finally effective as a means of uniting them. Nevertheless, throughout the development of Greek philosophy, we find flashes of insight which penetrate far beyond the actual explicit statements of Greek theorizing. In so early a conception even as that of Anaximander, in which change is conceived as the reparation which things make to one another for their injustice, the idea is apparent that becoming is explicable only in terms of the union of opposites. Heraclitus carries the conception further in his identification of the upward and the downward paths and his declaration that 'war is the father of all things' inasmuch as 'what is at variance with itself agrees with itself' like the attunement of opposite tensions. Again in Plato the notion has developed further that contradiction is but a means to definition and a source of further advance; but inevitably after Parmenides' identification of thought and being, the process for Plato has become a dialectical process—a process of thought—and this is imported into the material world by the self-motivation of soul. The process of becoming begins thus to merge with being through the mediation of the process of knowing. Finally, in Aristotle, becoming is change from one contrary to its correlative other and is explained as the realization of a potentiality in which every phase is a coalescence of matter and form. The intelligible is thus introduced into the very substance of the changeable, and what proves in the end to be the actuality implicit in the entire series of forms and the final realization of all potentialities is no less than the pure activity of thinking which is the essence of knowledge.

9. But the effort, stupendous though it is, is not finally successful and the impression left by Greek thought is still an emphasis upon the intelligible and eternal as the real and a derogation of the alterable and moving world of nature as in some sense unreal. Possibly we shall have to admit in the end that this contrast is an expression of the true nature of things and is never wholly avoidable in sound theory. Be that as it may, the Greeks never quite succeeded in explaining becoming in

terms of being and the reaction which came at the Renaissance[1] completely reversed the emphasis. The exaggerated other-worldliness which grew up in the Middle Ages was, perhaps, a more direct cause of this reaction than the effect of Greek philosophy itself; yet even the Mediaeval attitude was to some extent an outgrowth from Greek thought, so far, at any rate, as it resulted from the influence of Neo-Platonism. It was, however, the product of several factors,[2] and the influence of such writers as Tertullian, Jerome and Augustine turned the Mediaeval mind away from natural science, stigmatized human nature as depraved, and condemned the sublunary world as utterly corrupted under the sway of Satan.

The Renaissance thinkers, in reaction against this, devoted their attention primarily to the world of change. It was not the incorruptibility of the heavens that interested Galileo, but the generation of new stars. The study of nature by observation and experiment took precedence over the explanation of phenomena by *a priori* reasoning. The deliverances of the senses were given priority over the demands of the intellect and reality was identified with the perceptible, all universal conceptions being regarded as attenuated abstractions from the rich variety of sensuous experience. Where Plato spoke of the sensible world as a poor imitation of the intelligible forms, Hume made 'ideas' the paler copies of sense-impressions. To the character and effects of this revolution in attitude I shall next devote my attention.

[1] This is not, of course, strictly correct. If the Renaissance is the name we give to the revival of interest in Greek culture which occurred in the 15th century, the reaction to which I refer here is as much against Renaissance thinking as against Greek. But inaccurate though it be, I shall continue to use the name for the thought of the 17th and 18th centuries, as it indicates a convenient demarcation of periods and because, as applied to the beginnings of modern science, it is not misleading.

[2] For an admirable account of these see C. E. Raven, *The Gospel and the Church*, ch. iii.

RENAISSANCE CONCEPTIONS OF

Part Three

RENAISSANCE CONCEPTIONS OF NATURE AND MIND

Chapter VI

THE PROBLEM EXPLICIT

I. PRESUPPOSITIONS OF 17TH-CENTURY SCIENCE

1. THE thought of the 17th century is characterized by its reaction against Aristotle—not the Aristotle of antiquity, but Aristotle as seen through the eyes of the mediaeval scholastics. This hostility to an Aristotelianism that was often a travesty of the work of the Greek philosopher himself is a mark of what has come to be called empiricism, the attitude of the new science which had come into being with the Renaissance, and one which persists to the present day (though with far less justification) among a certain school of thinkers. Philosophical empiricism emerges (with some qualification) in the writings of Francis Bacon, is explicit in the work of Hobbes and comes to its maturity in the philosophy of Locke, Berkeley and Hume. But not every reaction against mediaevalism is to be regarded as empirical in character. The philosophy of Descartes, for instance, was a typical product of the age and a direct reaction against scholasticism, yet in some respects it was the direct antithesis of empiricism. This antithesis, we shall see, has been exaggerated; but it is true, nevertheless, that Descartes's philosophy was continuous with, and may not unjustly be regarded as a development from mediaeval thought,[1] which can hardly be said of the work of the British empiricists who made a clean break with the Middle Ages. Hobbes is well aware that 'the philosophy-schools, through all the universities of Christendom, grounded upon certain texts of Aristotle, teach another doctrine', and Locke complains that 'the imputation of Novelty is a terrible charge amongst those who judge of men's heads, as they do of their perukes, by the fashion'.

In this Part I shall devote attention more especially to the empiricism of the 17th and 18th centuries, not because the other forms of cotemporary philosophy were unimportant—on the contrary, perhaps the most important of all is that of Spinoza—but because the empirical philosophers present the problem I mainly wish to consider in its most obvious form and approach it from a standpoint similar to that of common sense, to which I have already drawn attention. Accordingly, by tracing the development of the empirical doctrine we shall be able

---

[1] Cf. Boyce Gibson, *The Philosophy of Descartes* (London, 1932), p. 4: 'Descartes's conception of philosophy ... is still that of Thomas Aquinas'.

both to understand more clearly the nature of the problem and to appreciate more fully the merits and the difficulties of some of the attempts which have been made at its solution. There is, moreover, another reason why the study of the 17th and 18th century Empiricists is important at the present time. Much contemporary philosophy is based, tacitly or openly, upon a metaphysical position closely akin to that adopted by Locke, with apparent disregard of its most serious difficulties and inadequate appreciation of their consequences as developed in the philosophy of Berkeley and of Hume. The conclusions to which they bring us, therefore, must be borne in mind in any consideration of the value of contemporary theories. The interpretation and criticism of these philosophers current at the beginning of this century is now generally discounted, but it will be my object to show that it was substantially correct, and when we come to consider modern theories of similar temper we shall find that the same criticisms are fatal to them. In this and the two following chapters, accordingly, I shall be traversing what to many readers will be familiar ground.

2. The revolution in scientific method and outlook, which took place at the Renaissance and which culminated in the view of nature presented in Newton's *Principia*, had a double aspect. (i) In the first place, the scholastic notions of essence and final causes were abandoned and the explanation of phenomena was sought in efficient causation and the assessment of quantitative change. As Joseph Glanvil remarked, the doctrines of Aristotle gave place to 'the more excellent Hypotheses of Democritus and Epicurus' and nature came to be regarded as consisting entirely of material bodies, changing their mutual disposition in obedience to calculable forces (cf. the *vis insita* and *vis impressa* of Newton). 'The universe', Hobbes declared, 'that is, the whole mass of all things that are, is corporeal, that is to say, body, and hath dimensions of magnitude, namely length, breadth, and depth; also, every part of body is likewise body, and hath the like dimensions, and consequently every part of the universe is body and that which is not body is no part of the universe.'[1] Changes were to be explained solely in terms of matter and motion and mechanical accounts of natural phenomena, expressed in quantitative terms, came to be regarded as the only proper form of scientific explanation. Measurement was the means of investigation and mathematics the supreme instrument of scientific discovery.

And what of the mind? Was that to be explained also in terms of

[1] *Leviathan*, ch. xlvi.

matter and motion? Some thinkers, notably Gassendi and Hobbes, adopted the view that it was, strangely oblivious of the difficulties in which any such view must immediately become involved. Sensible qualities, Hobbes asserts, are in the object nothing but motions of matter. 'Neither in us', he continues, 'are they anything else, but diverse motions; for motion produceth nothing but motion. But their appearance to us is fancy, the same waking as dreaming.' It never occurs to him that the 'appearance to us' remains, on his principles, totally inexplicable. Others, however, were aware of this difficulty and preferred to regard the mind as something entirely different from matter and not as part of the material world at all. While Hobbes denied altogether the existence of 'that which is not body', Descartes postulated a thinking substance besides that which is extended. The dichotomy of mind and matter became characteristic of the age and has troubled philosophy in some form ever since; for, as the peculiar properties of the thinking mind in man are its knowledge of the world of material things and its close association with one of the bodies which belong to that world, this alienation of mind and the material world each from the other poses, in their acutest form, the problems of accounting for that knowledge and of explaining that association.

3. (ii) In the second place, it became clear that the discovery of efficient causes and the assessment of quantitative change could be made only by means of observation and experiment and by no mere argument from first principles. The world of nature, as we have seen, was conceived as something set over against the knowing mind and related to it, so to speak, *ab extra*—something which the mind viewed from the outside and must explore by external observation, as an astronomer explores the surface of the moon through a telescope. This was the only fruitful method for discovering its structure and the interaction of its parts, the details of which could not be explicated from any general principles that the mind might possess *ab initio* (or 'innately'), but could be revealed only empirically, through experience which comes from without, and which was assumed to come only as a result of causal action upon the mind by external things. What comes to us in experience, however, comes (or at any rate seems *prima facie* to come) through the senses, and the second presupposition of the new science thus came to be what has since been called the principle of empiricism: that there can be no genuine knowledge of the world which has not been given in sense or derived from sense-experience, or, in other words, that there can be no genuine universal principles in

knowledge which have not been generalized or abstracted from sense-given particulars (including, among these, what are given by 'internal' sense, in the mind's introspection of its own activities). This principle, be it noted, results from the first presupposition of Renaissance science, that nature is something purely corporeal, entirely devoid of mind, so that the natural objects about which the mind is concerned are set apart from it and knowledge of them comes to it from without, as it approaches them, so to speak, from a distance. This is, at least historically, the origin of the empirical principle, and I shall try to show at a later stage[1] that, whenever it is maintained, a dualism between physical nature and the knowing mind is assumed.

The metaphysic of Descartes sets out the first of these two presuppositions of Renaissance science, and the epistemology of Locke is the theoretical expression of the second. The opposition between these two philosophers is therefore not so radical as has traditionally been supposed, for their theories are in certain respects mutually implicated and they both develop (each in his particular manner) the underlying assumptions of the scientific revolution of their age. But there is a manifest contradiction in maintaining *both* the existence of an utter separation between the mind and the material world, *and* that material things by a process of physical causation produce sensations in our minds. For the second hypothesis subverts the first and provides a connection between matter and mind which the first denies. It is, however, not an intelligible connection, for it still leaves inexplicable the relation of a physical cause to a psychical effect. Consequently, the assertion that knowledge of the material world comes to us solely from external things through the channels of sense is based upon the mutually contradictory assumptions (i) that mind and matter are two totally different and separate things, the connection between which cannot be explained, and (ii) that material objects have a causal relationship to the mind. Descartes, who is no empiricist, avoids this contradiction, though, as we shall see, only at some considerable cost; but Locke embraces it without the slightest qualm.

II. THE CARTESIAN DICHOTOMY

4. In the philosophy of Descartes the cleavage between the mind and external objects is effected immediately by his method of radical and evacuating doubt, which enables him to suspend belief in the existence of everything represented in consciousness as an

[1] *Vide* pp. 126, 277 ff., 299, 308 ff., 322 ff., 399, 410 ff.

object [1] while it compels him to assert the existence and the activity of his own mind. The 'notion of thought', he writes,[2] 'precedes that of all corporeal things and is the most certain; since we still doubt whether there are any things in the world, while we already perceive that we think'. He thus makes his famous assertion, '*cogito ergo sum*', the means of distinguishing mind from body, and establishes the dualism from the outset.

On its positive side Descartes's first argument is intended to prove the existence of nothing but cognitive awareness [3] as the essence of the mind or thinking thing, and this pure cognition, he repeatedly asserts, might conceivably exist entirely alone. The element of subjectivism that haunts modern philosophy in a variety of forms is thus introduced at its very beginning. For there can be no question, up to this point, of any relation between the mind (*res cogitans*) and anything other than itself. As yet Descartes has taken everything that is presented in consciousness to be no more than an elaborate phantasmagoria in which he finds no criterion for distinguishing reality from illusion, waking from dream. The search for this criterion is the root from which the whole of his philosophy grows; the effort to discover a test for truth, without which the whole of our experience, he thinks, is no better than a bewildering fantasy conjured up in the mind by some malicious demon.

Having satisfied himself that the reason for the certainty of his conviction of his own existence is the clearness and distinctness with which he apprehends the nexus between thinking and being, he adopts as his criterion of truth clearness and distinctness in ideas. What exactly he means by this he never, himself, makes very clear or distinct by definition, and when he does attempt to do so [4] he suggests that clearness of ideas is similar to clearness of visual perception; but it is evident from his use and application of the formula that what he really means is the precise apprehension of logical necessity. With the aid of this criterion, Descartes sets himself to prove the existence of God and among the arguments which he uses by far the most important is the Ontological Proof, though in his philosophy it appears to be little more than an ingenious and somewhat sophistical device enabling him to call

---

[1] Cf. *Meditations on First Philosophy*, I, and *Principles of Philosophy*, Pt. I, i-v.

[2] *Principles*, I, viii; cf. also *Method*, Pt. IV and *Medit*. II.

[3] *Vide* Gassendi's objection (*Objections*, V) to the second Meditation and Descartes's reply: '. . . motion and sensibility I refer for the most part also to the body, and ascribe nothing that belongs to them to the soul, save only as much as consists in thinking'. (English Edition, Haldane and Ross, Vol. II, pp. 137 ff. and 207.)

[4] *Principles*, I, xlv.

in a *deus ex machina* to bridge the gulf between mind and matter, which, as we shall shortly see, is otherwise impassable. But the Onto-logical Proof is ultimately vital for the whole theory of knowledge and the inspiration is sound which prompts Descartes to use it as he does. Spinoza made it the foundation of his entire system and at a much later date it came to be interpreted as fundamental both to knowledge and to being.

5. It is not until he has proved the existence of God as a perfect being that Descartes proceeds to reconsider the question of the existence of a material world.[1] He observes that in the past he had habitually assumed that the ideas which he received through the senses, because of their vivacity and the fact that they were presented without his consent or co-operation, were caused by things other than his own mind; and having no knowledge of any such things except through the medium of the ideas themselves, he had imagined them to be similar to the ideas. He enumerates also the apparent reasons for which he had assumed a close connection between his mind and his body, provided by his experience of physical appetites, the feelings of pleasure and pain and his habitual localization in the parts of his body of various sensations. But all these considerations he had rejected as insufficient justification for the beliefs they had led him to form, not only because other elements in his experience conflicted with them, but also because the content of consciousness contains no internal evidence of resemblance to, correspondence with or representation of anything beyond itself.[2] Having, however, proved the existence both of himself as a thinking thing and of God as a perfect being, he is prepared to reconsider the existence of a corporeal world and he reflects that the passive faculty which he possesses of receiving and cognizing the ideas of sensible things implies, either in himself or in some other thing, an active faculty of producing those ideas. Such a faculty, however, does not involve thinking, nor does it operate with his co-operation, but frequently against his will; it cannot, therefore, be in himself, but must be in some other substance, 'in which all the reality which is objectively in the ideas that are produced . . . is formally or eminently contained'.

[1] *Vide Medit.* VI.
[2] Cf. *ibid.* III: 'But there was yet another thing which I affirmed, and which, owing to the habit which I had formed of believing it, I thought I perceived very clearly, although in truth I did not perceive it at all, to wit, that there were objects outside of me from which these ideas proceeded, and to which they were entirely similar. And it was in this that I erred, or, if perchance my judgement was correct, this was not due to any knowledge arising from my perception.' (Haldane and Ross, Vol. I, p. 158.)

This substance must be either body (a corporeal nature) containing formally, or really, all that is 'objectively' in the ideas, or it must be God Himself or another of His creatures 'more noble than body' in which that reality is contained eminently.[1] To adopt the latter alternative would be tantamount to reducing all perception of material things to an illusion deliberately produced by God, and that would detract from God's goodness, for He, being perfect, is incapable of practising deception. Descartes concludes, accordingly, that corporeal things exist, though not exactly as we perceive them by the senses. At least, he holds, everything in them is real which can be clearly and distinctly conceived, 'that is to say, all things which, speaking generally, are comprehended in the object of pure mathematics'; in fact, the essential nature of bodies consists entirely in extension, as that of mind consists entirely of thought.

It is only the mathematical properties that exist 'formally' in the bodies themselves. Those qualities which we perceive by the senses, such as colour, sound, scent and the like, are not in them but are only the ways in which we perceive them—they are the result of 'the intimate union which exists between body and mind' in us.[2] But, though these qualities are not in the bodies themselves, there is that in them which excites the sensations in us. We have here the doctrine of primary and secondary qualities, adopted from Galileo and taken over later by Locke, which is the direct consequence of the co-temporary conception of nature as mechanical. The essential reality of material things is taken to be comprised in their purely mathematical properties, while the sensible qualities, as we perceive them, are regarded as entirely mind-dependent.

The world of reality is thus presented in the philosophy of Descartes as consisting of God and two created substances: that which thinks and that which is extended. Consciousness is totally confined to the mind, and the material world, as extended substance, so far as its formal reality is concerned, is totally excluded from it. The knowledge which the mind has of the world is, accordingly, representative. Material things are represented 'objectively' in our ideas, which exist as 'modes of thought',[3] while the 'formal' reality of bodies is vested solely in

---

[1] *Ibid.* VI (Haldane and Ross, Vol. I, p. 191). The reality which is said to be 'objectively' in ideas is what they present to the mind—their ideal content. It is 'formally' in things so far as they are in themselves what they are presented to be in ideas; and it is 'eminently' in that which, as cause, has power to produce the formal or objective reality in its effect. Cf. Spinoza, *Renati Descartes Principiorum Philosophiae, more geometrico demonstratae*, Part I, Defs. III and IV.

[2] *Vide Principles*, Pt. II, iii.

[3] *Medit.* III (Haldane and Ross, Vol. I, p. 161).

extended substance. Descartes, however, is not unaware of the difficulties involved in a representative theory of knowledge and he seeks to avoid them by appealing to faith in God's veracity, apart from which we should have no knowledge (properly speaking) of an external world at all, but only a dreamlike presentation in ideas of a world the formal reality, or actuality, of which (as opposed to its 'objective' reality—its reality simply as experienced ideally) would be wholly unknown. For Descartes, we may say, our knowledge of ourselves is immediate and indubitable, but our knowledge of the external world is a divine revelation.

6. Part of this revelation is the fact that the thinking thing which is the human mind (or soul, as Descartes chiefly calls it) inhabits a body which belongs to the material world. Descartes has little difficulty in describing how this body is acted upon by others and how it is affected by such action, but to explain how these effects are transmitted to the soul is another matter.

We must observe first that the soul's function is purely that of thinking.[1] Sensation and imagination, as we have already seen, belong 'for the most part' to the body, and though the term, thought, is used by Descartes to cover what he calls both actions and passions, it is clear from what he says of these that he regards them as purely cognitive, so far, that is to say, as they pertain to the soul. What we should call emotion and conation Descartes regards as, strictly speaking, a feature of the bodily movement they produce, the perception of them alone belonging to the soul.[2]

The soul is thus a purely thinking thing, simple, indivisible and unextended. How are we to conceive its conjunction with a body which is extended and has parts? Descartes says that it is joined to the body as a whole, for the body is a complete and organic totality which becomes defective (though the soul does not) if any limb or organ is destroyed, and all parts of it equally are related to the soul.[3] Yet he believes that the pineal gland [4] in the centre of the brain is the principal seat of the soul because it is there that all the nerve paths from all our double organs of sense, as from the two cerebral hemispheres themselves, may be brought together. Nevertheless, it remains a mystery how a non-corporeal, unextended entity can be united with a material organ like a gland, or how its thoughts can stimulate glandular action and set in motion the animal spirits which Descartes believed, by their

[1] *The Passions of the Soul*, Pt. I, xvii.
[2] *Ibid.* xxxviii and xl.   [3] *Ibid.* xxx.   [4] *Ibid.* xxxi.

passage through the nerves, to be instrumental in stimulating muscular movement.[1] And, in whatever manner external bodies might affect the sense-organs and whatever impulses they might promote in the animal spirits and communicate through the nerves to the brain and pineal gland, it is still impossible to understand how mere matter in motion can produce a thought in an unextended (non-spatial), thinking substance. Small wonder that Joseph Glanvil, an adherent of the Cartesian philosophy, should write: 'How the purer spirit is united to this Clod, is a knot too hard for fallen Humanity to unty'.

Others of the school solved the problem by yet another appeal to God's goodness. They denied all interaction between soul and body and explained their concomitant variations solely by the intervention of God on each occasion. As human knowledge proved to be a divine revelation, so human action is seen as a perpetually repeated miracle.

To resort to the intervention of Providence, however, is no philosophical solution of any problem but is rather a confession of its insolubility. Nevertheless, the Cartesian philosophy has left a mark upon modern thought which has persisted to the present day. In starting from the subjective aspect of experience and insisting first upon the ineluctable existence of the thinking *ego*, Descartes created a cleavage between the mind and the objects of its knowledge which determined the character of metaphysical speculation for the next two centuries and left a legacy to future generations which is not yet exhausted. But the real growing point of his doctrine was not his conception of the two created substances, but rather his proof of the existence of God; and Spinoza, by making this, instead of the *ego*, his starting-point and by making the human mind a mode of the divine, was able to go far towards a resolution of the Cartesian dualism and to point a way for future development. But his work was neglected for almost two hundred years after his death and had little influence on the course of development which it is my purpose, in this Part, to review. Discussion of his system, therefore, may be deferred until we reach those conceptions of nature in which the 17th-century opposition of matter to mind was largely overcome and which Spinoza, in many ways, anticipated.

III. LOCKE'S EMPIRICISM

7. John Locke rushed in where Descartes feared to tread. Descartes never fell into the error of thinking that a representative theory of

[1] Cf. *Method*, Pt. V and *Passions*, Pt. I, x *et seq.*

knowledge could stand in its own right; it was for this reason that he called in the Deity to bridge the gap between our perceptions and the things of the external world which they are held to represent. And the idea of God is one which Descartes finds originally (or innately) in his mind as something prior (at least, logically) to all others of less perfect beings. If, however, the innateness of ideas such as this is abandoned we are thrown back upon adventitious ideas, from which alone our experience can be built up. Our knowledge, in other words, will consist entirely of what comes to us in the course of experience, and it is upon this assumption that Locke bases his philosophy and on this basis that he tries to erect a theory of knowledge in part causal and in part representative. His failure with its consequences, as developed by his immediate successors, is a lesson too little regarded by contemporary writers and, for that reason alone, it is important to examine his position.

Locke accepted the current scientific presupposition which sepa-rated the material world from the mind and he sought to explain the acquisition of knowledge by 'the historical plain method' of tracing the process by which it is built up out of its simplest elements, which come to us (so he thought) through the senses from external objects. The assumption that 'ideas' are the effects upon our minds, through the mediation of our bodily organisms, of things existing independently of our thought is the hall-mark of empiricism, and though Locke was not the first to make it, he was the first to develop *in extenso* the theory of knowledge which it demands.

The denial of the existence of innate ideas springs directly from the adoption of this empiricist standpoint; for if we seek the origin of ideas in experience we can always find a point in the immaturity of mind where there is no evidence of the existence of a given idea. Thus, because in children and savages he can find no traces of ideas alleged to be innate by his opponents (whoever he imagined them to be), and because at no stage of mental development does he find these ideas universally admitted by mankind, Locke refuses to countenance the existence of innate ideas. Against whom he is arguing in the first Book of the *Essay Concerning Human Understanding* is not very clear (for if it be Descartes he must sadly have misunderstood his doctrine), nor does it particularly matter; for even if nobody had ever maintained that some of our ideas are innate, it would have been necessary for Locke to deny it in order to justify his own starting-point. And deny it he does at great length, not content merely with the empirical arguments men-tioned above, but showing also that universal assent, even were it discoverable, and self-evidence, even if it were conceded, are them-selves no criteria of the innateness of ideas. The fact is, he maintains, that we come to know general (or any other) truths only after we have made acquaintance with the particulars, and the particulars are acquired only in the course of experience.

To begin with, therefore, we must presume the mind to be com-pletely empty and blank, 'white paper, void of all characters, without any ideas', and it is experience alone that can 'furnish' it with contents. Locke uses several metaphors to describe the mind and its means of ac-quiring experience. It is an 'empty cabinet'[1] furnished with the particu-lar ideas let in by the senses, or a mirror which cannot refuse to reflect, cannot 'alter, or obliterate the images or ideas which the objects set before it do therein produce',[2] or a 'dark room' to which the only windows by which light is let in are external and internal sensation.[3] His conception of the mind and its knowledge is thus substantially the same as that which is commonly assumed by unphilosophical persons, and in fact by all of us in the practical affairs of every day. The examination and criticism of Locke's theory, therefore, is of great importance, for it is at the same time the examination of that assumption which commonly enables us to ignore [4] the problem of our finite existence in a universe which extends infinitely beyond us and of which we nevertheless know so much as to enable us to form dim prophetic visions of the whole.

Locke's own statement of the theory is confused, rambling, repeti-tive and inconsistent, but these defects are, at least in part, the natural result of an attempt to state intelligibly and to maintain plausibly a doctrine which is inherently self-contradictory. I shall not follow the detail nor the digressions of Locke's exposition but shall attempt to set out only the more essential features of his position as briefly as is possible without misrepresentation.

8. The mind, originally empty and blank, receives, in the first place, simple ideas of two kinds: those of sensation and those of reflection; and although Locke asserts in his Introduction that his purpose is not to 'meddle with physical considerations of the mind', he does from time to time make statements about the physical causation of our sensations which, when pieced together, enable us to gather his belief as to their origin. Simple ideas of sensation, he says, are furnished by 'external objects' or bodies, which produce the ideas in us by mechanical action upon our organism, 'by impulse, the only way which we can conceive

[1] *Essay*, I, i, 15.   [2] *Ibid*. II, i, 25.
[3] *Ibid*. II, xi, 17.   [4] See above, p. 45.

bodies to operate in'.[1] They either communicate to us some motion or transmit to us some insensible moving[2] particles, which, through the organs of sense, are conveyed by the 'nerves or animal spirits ... to the brains or the seat of sensation, there to produce in our minds the particular ideas we have of them' (i.e. of the external objects).[3] Just what relation there is between the brain and the mind, Locke does not profess to know and he frequently speaks of them indiscriminately, as if the brain itself were the thing which thinks; and just how the physical impulse transmitted to the brain produces an idea in consciousness he never attempts to explain. Possibly it is to this that he refers when he declines to 'meddle with physical considerations' or to inquire 'by what motions of our spirits or alteration of our bodies we come to have any *sensations* by our organs, or any *ideas* in our understandings'.[4] Yet this link between the physical transmission of the impulse from the object and the idea which is our consciousness of the object is all-important, and without it no description of a process of physical transmission can help us (or Locke); for a physical effect can as little explain or substitute for the conscious awareness of an object as the vibration rate of a plucked string can explain the quality of a musical tone or could substitute for it in the mind of a deaf man. However this may be, those ideas which Locke calls simple ideas of sensation he takes to have been produced in our minds by the action upon us of external objects.

The examples he gives are '*yellow, white, heat, cold, soft, hard, bitter, sweet,* and all those which we call sensible qualities', speaking as if the ideas in the mind were themselves the qualities of the external objects which produce them; and though he frequently speaks of them thus ambiguously, we shall presently see that this can hardly be what he means. At other times he writes of qualities as if they were universals (solidity, power, existence, unity, and the like), but this again is not his intention. For him they are each and all of them particulars, as are 'all things that exist'.[5]

'In the things themselves', Locke tells us, 'the qualities that affect our senses are ... so united and blended, that there is no separation, no distance between them.'[6] A piece of wax is soft, warm, white and cylindrical, and these, its qualities, are united in it so that they cannot be separated; but we perceive its whiteness by vision, its softness and

<hr/>

[1] *Essay*, II, viii, 11. [2] Cf. *ibid.* IV, ii, 11. [3] *Ibid.* II, viii, 12. [4] *Ibid.* Introd. 2.
[5] Cf. *ibid.* III, iii, 1 and 6, and IV, xvii, 8: 'Every man's reasoning and knowledge is only about the ideas existing in his own mind, which are truly, every one of them, particular existences'. [6] *Ibid.* II, ii, 1.

temperature by touch and its shape by both. In our minds the ideas are distinct and separable, as well as simple and unmixed, 'the coldness and hardness which a man feels in a piece of ice being as distinct ideas in the mind as the smell and whiteness of a lily; or the taste of sugar, and smell of a rose'.

The second source of our simple ideas is the reflection of the mind upon its own operation 'as it is employed about the ideas it has got'. Such reflection produces ideas which are, for the mind, 'as capable to be the objects of its contemplation as any of those it received from foreign things',[1] but being wholly internal to the mind and, having nothing directly to do with external things, it is not strictly speaking sensation. 'Yet', says Locke, 'it is very like it, and might properly enough be called *internal sense*.'[2]

Such simple ideas are the first beginnings of knowledge. It is when a man first has any sensation that he first begins to have any ideas;[3] and though they do not in themselves constitute knowledge, they are the materials out of which all the knowledge of which we are capable is constituted. They comprise 'our whole stock of ideas' and we have nothing in our minds which cannot be traced back to one of these two sources.[4] 'All those sublime thoughts which tower above the clouds, and reach as high as heaven itself, take their rise and footing here: in all that great extent wherein the mind wanders, in those remote speculations it may seem to be elevated with, it stirs not one jot beyond those ideas which *sense* or *reflection* have offered for its contemplation.'[5]

In the receipt of simple ideas, both those of sensation and those of reflection, the mind is wholly passive. 'The understanding can no more refuse to have, nor alter when they are imprinted, nor blot them out and make new ones itself, than a mirror can refuse, alter, or obliterate the images or ideas which the objects set before it do therein produce.' But, though it can neither make nor destroy them, it can repeat, compare, unite and separate them, producing an almost infinite variety of permutations and combinations.[6] Passive in the receipt of simple ideas, the mind is active in such operations and its products are of three kinds: (i) complex ideas, that is, combinations of simple ones; (ii) relations, the comparison of ideas, either simple or complex, by bringing them together; and (iii) abstraction, the making of general ideas by separation from all others that normally accompany them.[7]

---

[1] *Ibid.* II, vi.   [2] *Ibid.* II, i, 4.
[3] *Ibid.* II, i, 23.   [4] *Ibid.* II, i, 5.
[5] *Ibid.* II, i, 24; cf. II, vii, 10.   [6] *Ibid.* II, ii, 2.
[7] Locke says, 'accompany them in their real existence'—an instance of his tendency to speak of ideas as if they were qualities or even things. *Vide* II, xii, 1.

Here we have the furnishings of the mind entire, from which all our knowledge is composed and to which it is severely limited.[1] But the nature of ideas is described by Locke with bewildering ambiguity. On the one hand, he asserts that they come to us from without and are imprinted on the understanding through the instrumentality of the bodily sense-organs by external objects; and if we adhere to this account of them, we are faced with the impenetrable mystery of the transformation of physical impulses into conscious awareness. On the other hand, he insists that they are nothing at all except 'actual perceptions in the mind which cease to be anything when there is no perception of them'.[2] 'Whatsoever the mind perceives *in itself*', he says, 'or is the immediate object of perception, thought, or understanding, that I call *idea*';[3] and their being imprinted on the understanding is nothing but the making them to be perceived.[4] According to this account of ideas they are wholly internal to the mind and there is nothing in them to suggest in any way the manner of their causation. Whichever alternative we prefer, however, that the mind can know only its own ideas Locke never tires of reiterating and it is, indeed, a position to which he is committed both by his starting-point and, paradoxically enough, even by his account of the manner in which simple ideas of sensation are produced in our minds from external objects, for he has insisted that before the understanding receives these impressions it contains nothing whatsoever and that the only way in which it can acquire ideas is the one which he has described. The devastating effect of this limitation of knowledge to ideas is obvious immediately, not only upon what he has already maintained, but also upon any theory he is subsequently to put forward of the status of our knowledge and the truth of our ideas.

9. The augury of impending disaster is also to be seen in two other features of Locke's doctrine. These are his account of primary and secondary qualities and his theory of substance. He begins the first by distinguishing our ideas as they are 'perceptions in our minds' and 'as they are modifications of matter in the bodies that cause such perceptions in us'.[5] What the mind perceives in itself as an immediate object he calls idea; what in the bodies are powers to produce ideas in us he calls qualities, and these he divides into two classes. (i) The primary qualities, solidity, extension, figure and mobility, are 'utterly inseparable from the body in what state soever it be' ('the body' here

---

[1] Cf. *Essay*, II, i, 2; xxiii, 28-9, and IV, iii, 2.
[2] *Ibid.* II, x, 2.   [3] *Ibid.* II, viii, 8.
[4] Cf. *ibid.* I, i, 5.   [5] *Ibid.* II, viii, 7.

being that which produces the idea in us and not our own bodily organism). (ii) The secondary qualities, such as colours, sounds, tastes and the like, are produced in our minds by the bulk, figure, texture and motion of the insensible parts of the bodies to which we attribute them. Our ideas of the former, he says, are resemblances of the qualities 'and their patterns do really exist in the bodies themselves', while those of the latter resemble nothing really existing in the bodies and are utterly different in aspect from the bulk, figure and motion of the insensible particles that produce them—'It being no more impossible to conceive that God should annex such ideas to such motions, with which they have no similitude, than that he should annex the ideas of pain to the motion of a piece of steel dividing our flesh, with which that idea hath no resemblance'.[1] In fact, it is somewhat misleading and inappropriate to attribute secondary qualities to bodies at all, and Locke admits that he calls them qualities only 'to comply with the common way of speaking', for they are simply powers to produce effects in us [2] on a par with powers to produce effects in other bodies, like that of fire to produce a new colour or consistency in wax. We tend to regard the ideas as qualities of the bodies producing them because the ideas 'contain nothing at all in them of bulk, figure and motion' and we are not directly aware of their causes, 'which appear not, to our senses, to operate in their production';[3] but we do not so regard the operation of one body on another where we can perceive both cause and effect (though it is in principle the same as that operation upon our bodies, by others, which produces the ideas of secondary qualities). Here we can observe the difference between the cause and the effect, which in the case of our ideas we cannot.

It never occurs to Locke that this inability to compare our ideas with their causes affects the whole of his doctrine. For what, in external objects, does not appear to our senses is not to be found among our ideas, and beyond our ideas our knowledge cannot go. How, then, do we ever infer from our ideas to their causes, be they bulk, figure and motion of *insensible* parts or the bodies themselves taken as wholes? We are told in a later chapter (Bk. II, xxiii, 11) that 'had we senses acute enough to discern the minute particles of bodies, and the real constitution on which their sensible qualities depend . . . they would produce quite different ideas in us'. Would they then be ideas of

---

[1] *Ibid.* II, viii, 13.
[2] *Ibid.* II, viii, 10. Locke here seems to forget that he has just *defined* 'quality' as 'the power to produce any idea in our mind'. (*Ibid.* 8.)
[3] *Ibid.* II, viii, 25.

secondary qualities? It would seem not, for (Locke proceeds) 'that which is now the yellow colour of gold, would then disappear, and instead we should see an admirable texture of parts, of a certain size and figure'—but, presumably, of no colour at all; yet we should *see* it! Locke never seems to reflect that once the sensible 'ideas' of secondary qualities *disappear*, we are left with nothing, and that the primary qualities which exist really in the bodies themselves are, without the secondary, beyond our reach. Yet the secondary are not properly the qualities of bodies at all; they are 'resemblances' of nothing really in them. So it seems that those ideas which represent external reality most nearly are accessible to us only by the mediation of those which are in a sense illusory, which do not represent external reality at all, except so far as we (gratuitously) assume that they are the effects of causes which we can never perceive. Though the doctrine of primary and secondary qualities had been current, as a presupposition of science, at least since Galileo, it was only after Locke had stated the theory of knowledge which it implied that its untenability became obvious and it was, as Collingwood has it, 'ready to collapse at the first touch of Berkeley's finger'.[1]

10. Our idea of substance reveals still further the difficulty, on Locke's theory, of our knowing anything of the external world. The mind observes that certain simple ideas 'go constantly together' and so, presuming that they 'belong to one thing' and 'are united in one subject', it calls them by a single name. But being unable to imagine how simple ideas can subsist by themselves, we customarily suppose 'some *substratum* wherein they do subsist' and our idea of this is what we call substance. It is to be noticed that Locke speaks of the 'simple ideas' and not the qualities of the thing, and alleges that it is these which we cannot imagine to subsist by themselves. He gives no reason why we cannot so imagine them, and later Hume found no difficulty in conceiving them exactly in this way.[2] But what this substance is, which we suppose as the substratum of the ideas or qualities, we have no means of knowing. It is but something—we know not what.[3] The groups of simple ideas which go constantly together, each accompanied by a confused idea of an unknown something in which they are supposed to inhere, constitute our complex ideas of particular substances;

[1] *Idea of Nature*, p. 102.
[2] Cf. *Treatise of Human Nature*, Bk. I, Pt. IV, Sect. v: 'If . . . the definition of substance is *something which may exist by itself* . . . I should observe that this definition agrees to everything, that can possibly be conceiv'd' (Selby-Bigge, p. 233).
[3] Cf. *Essay*, II, xxiii, 2 *et seq.*

and when we form a general idea of substance, it is nothing else than that vague notion of an unspecified something, 'the supposed, but unknown, support of those qualities we find existing'. Strictly speaking, in short, we have no idea of substance; all we know of bodies is the sensible qualities which we perceive, and these leave us 'as far from the idea of the substance of body, as if we knew nothing at all'.[1] Yet it is surely the idea of substance that should correspond most nearly to the reality of things; for secondary qualities are but powers depending on the real and primary qualities of the insensible parts, and the primary qualities inhere in the substance and are 'utterly inseparable' from it; and secondary qualities are only ideas in our minds resembling nothing actually in the things, whereas the primary conform to patterns really existing in the bodies themselves. But the ideas of secondary qualities are all that we ever *perceive*. The primaries are known to us only by the intervention of the secondaries and that in which the primaries inhere is something that we do not know at all. Nor could it be otherwise if knowledge comes to us as Locke alleges—and yet, unless it could be otherwise, he should not so allege. From this point it is but a short step to Berkeley's denial of the existence of any corporeal substance whatsoever.

The account which Locke has given, in the first two books of the *Essay*, of the materials of knowledge and the way in which they are acquired, leaves the thinking subject in possession only of simple sensations (external and internal) and what can be derived from them by combination, comparison and abstraction. It is clear that for such a subject the imputation to bodies of their secondary qualities must be purely inferential—for, as Locke tells us, their causes (the bulk, figure and motion of insensible particles) 'appear not, to our senses, to operate in their production'. It is clear, likewise, that, for such a subject, the resemblance of the primary qualities to their patterns in the bodies themselves, can only be an inference; and finally, from these two inferences, it can but be by further inference that the knower will conclude to the inherence of qualities *in re substante*. But as the knowing mind began empty and blank and was furnished with simple ideas without its active co-operation, it can know nothing of the process by which those ideas are alleged to have been produced in it from external objects, nothing of bodies beyond itself or of its own corporeal apparatus for conveying impulses from them by nerves and animal spirits to the brain; of none of these things is the mind ever directly aware in sensation. The inferences to them, consequently, could never be made

[1] *Ibid.* 16.

by a knower provided as Locke describes, for the premises of the inferences would be inaccessible to him.

11. From this unpromising position Locke proceeds to the explanation of knowledge and truth, and the failure of his theory, obvious on the face of it, is hardly surprising. He begins by reaffirming what throughout the *Essay* he untiringly repeats, that knowledge is limited to our own ideas. 'Since the mind in all its thoughts and reasonings, hath no other immediate object but its own ideas, which it alone does or can contemplate, it is evident that our knowledge is only conversant about them.'[1] Accordingly he defines knowledge, in conformity with this restriction, as 'the perception of the connexion of and agreement, or disagreement and repugnancy of any of our ideas'. 'In this alone', he says, 'it consists.' He then enumerates four species of agreement and disagreement between ideas: (i) identity or diversity; (ii) relation; (iii) co-existence or necessary connection, and (iv) real existence. Truth he defines as 'the joining or separating of signs as the Things signified by them do agree or disagree one with another'.[2] This joining and separating of signs is what we call proposition' and of this he distinguishes two species: mental and verbal. His treatment of the latter is a complication of his theory so full of confusion that it is scarcely intelligible.[3] Fortunately, it is not necessary for us to consider it here and we may confine ourselves to 'mental' proposition which consists in the putting together or separating of ideas 'by the mind perceiving or judging their agreement or disagreement'. Between this and knowledge, as he has defined that, there is obviously no difference, and truth as applied to both will consist in the agreement of the ideas with the things which they represent.

No sooner has Locke elaborated his definition of knowledge into its four species than he destroys at least three-quarters of its validity by admitting that the first three species are, as knowledge, 'of no more use than the reveries of a crazy brain; and the truths built thereon of no more weight than the discourses of a man who sees things clearly in a dream, and with great assurance utters them'.[4] The only sort of knowledge worthy of the name transpires to be 'a *conformity* between our ideas and the reality of things', and this is what we should expect, for knowledge and truth cannot be separated. But such conformity is either not an agreement between our ideas and is not confined to them,

---

[1] *Essay*, IV, i, 1; cf. also iii, 1.   [2] *Ibid.* IV, v, 2.
[3] For discussion of it see Joachim, *Logical Studies*, pp. 194-203.
[4] *Essay*, IV, iv, 2.

or else it concerns ideas between which no conformity or agreement can ever be found; for by Locke's own contention 'the cause of any sensation and the sensation itself in all simple ideas of one sense, are two ideas; and two ideas so different and distant one from another that no two can be more so'.[1] We have already seen the discrepancy between the primary qualities and the secondary which they are said to cause, and Locke confesses that reason cannot 'show how bodies *by their bulk, figure and motion*, should produce in the mind the ideas of blue or yellow, etc.'[2] So far, therefore, as things and ideas are considered both to belong to the furniture of the mind they can never agree together. But though Locke speaks at times as if the things which cause our ideas were also ideas, it is plain from other passages that it is not the agreement of these ideas with others that he has in mind when he speaks of the conformity of things to ideas. He is fully aware that what has to be provided is a criterion by which to judge of the agreement of ideas with what are not ideas at all, and though he admits that this 'seems not to want difficulty', yet he thinks it not impossible.

In the final analysis, Locke's criterion is no more than that simple ideas of sense, being passively received and unalterable by us, do give us assurance that they are 'the product of things operating on the mind in a natural way'. This, I say, is the only criterion he offers, for though he alleges two other sources of real knowledge, they both depend on this. Our complex ideas of modes, he says, 'being archetypes of the mind's own making cannot want any conformity necessary to real knowledge'; and, so long as we do not attempt to combine in them mutually contradictory ideas, whenever anything in the world does conform to them, they must necessarily be true. But plainly, we can know whether anything in the world ever does conform to them only by the mediation of simple ideas of sense. Again, in the case of complex ideas of substance, the reality of our knowledge consists in this alone, that in them we combine only such simple ideas 'as have been discovered to co-exist in nature'—yet how discovered, except through simple ideas of sense as intermediaries? We may, therefore, confine ourselves to the examination of this one touchstone of real knowledge, and ask how well founded is Locke's assurance that simple ideas of sense have real conformity to external things.

12. The criterion which Descartes rejected, that our sense-perceptions come to us without our co-operation and despite our will, Locke accepts without more ado. Descartes's scruples he contemptuously

---

[1] *Ibid.* III, iv, 10. [2] *Ibid.* II, viii, 25.

waves aside, for it is undoubtedly the Second Meditation which he has in mind when he writes: 'If anyone say, a dream may do the same thing, and all these ideas may be produced in us without any external objects; he may please to dream that I make him this answer: That it is no great matter whether I remove his scruple or no: where all is but dream, reasoning and arguments are of no use, truth and knowledge nothing'.[1] But this, as Descartes saw, is the very crux of the matter. Unless we can definitely distinguish at least between dream and waking, unless we have a means at least of knowing the perception of present objects from the floating imagery of phantasy, truth of fact and knowledge about the external world in no sense exist. Yet we have already seen that Locke's simple ideas of sense have in them no mark of their origin, that their causes 'appear not to our senses', and despite Locke's assurance that we are all 'invincibly conscious'[2] of a different perception when we look on the sun by day and think of it by night, it is notoriously the case that there is no means of distinguishing between sense and imagi-nation, dream and waking, in the immediate experience we have of them, which will not fail us in the last resort.[3] If we are to follow Locke, we must believe that we know our simple ideas of sense from what is merely imaginary as those that come direct from external objects, 'by that perception and consciousness we have of the *actual entrance* of ideas from them [external objects]'.[4] But this actual entrance is the process of transmission, through the nerves and animal spirits, of the motion of insensible particles to produce a modification in the brain, and of all this, in perceiving what we take to be external objects, we never have the slightest inkling—there is no perception nor conscious-ness of it. For the understanding as Locke describes it, in fact, white paper, devoid of all characters, or a dark room illuminated only by the windows of sense, simple ideas of sensation, *so far as they involve perception of their actual entrance from external things*, are utterly impossible, for the very existence of external things is *ex hypothesi* unknown. If on the other hand we give up the qualification and accept ideas simply as they are immediately perceived, we have no basis whatsoever for any inference to their causes or any knowledge of external things.

Thus with the destruction of its sole foundation, Locke's whole edifice of knowledge by ideas descends in ruins about our ears; for once deprived of the criterion of reality allegedly afforded by simple

---

[1] *Essay*, IV, ii, 14.   [2] *Ibid.*
[3] Cf. Joachim, *Logical Studies*, pp. 121 ff.
[4] *Essay*, IV, ii, 14, my italics.

ideas, the other supposed sources of the knowledge of external objects
fail us likewise. Complex ideas of substances can but be 'put together
at the pleasure of our thoughts', for no 'real pattern' is provided anywhere in our experience, and what 'co-exist in nature' we have no
means of knowing. They are then no different in status from complex
ideas of modes, archetypes of the mind's own making, and though
these may be the subject 'of demonstrative knowledge', which in one
place Locke couples with intuition [1] as knowledge *par excellence* in that
it is certain, while the perception of particular things existing without
us is said to pass by the name of knowledge, as if only by a misuse of
the term; yet elsewhere he tells us that all this which terminates in our
own ideas is as little knowledge as a crazy reverie or an idle dream.
And, indeed, it can as well be said of every fictitious and fantastic
notion that it is an archetype of the mind's own making; our ideas of
harpies or of centaurs [2] are certainly in no worse case. How then are
we to distinguish the real from the imaginary, the true from the false?

In fact, we are here involved in such a situation that either we must
revise our conception of knowledge altogether, particularly in its
reference to the world of bodies, or we must deny that the term has any
intelligible meaning. For nothing which Locke has offered us can be a
valid test of truth, nor can he satisfactorily explain how we come by the
knowledge of a world in which we ourselves are finite members. Yet he
is entirely oblivious of his own failure and has not the least misgiving.
'Wherever', he says, 'we perceive the agreement or disagreement of any
of our ideas there is certain knowledge; and wherever we are sure that
those ideas agree with the reality of things, there is certain real knowledge. Of which agreement of our ideas with the reality of things,
having here given the marks, I think, I have shown *wherein it is that
certainty, real certainty, consists*' (IV, iv, 18).

With the collapse of Locke's theory goes the assumption from
which he begins, that knowledge is built up from sensations derived
from objects external to the mind. That, as we have seen, is the presupposition of empiricism, the assumption made by the founders of
modern science in the 16th and 17th centuries, and the one which we
all commonly make (if ever we think about it at all) in the practical
affairs of our daily lives. Yet it is the assumption of a relation between
the mind and the world which, if pressed, makes knowledge of the
world a sheer impossibility; for any consciousness which was so built
up from sensations would exclude all knowledge of external objects.

The inherent contradiction of Locke's position is that between the

[1] *Ibid.*   [2] Cf. *ibid.* IV, iv, 1.

two main presuppositions of Renaissance science; the conception of dichotomy between the mind and the material world, on the one hand, and on the other, the empiricist presupposition (resulting from it) that knowledge of the world is derived from the particulars given in sense. If the material world is absolutely devoid of mind and stands over against the knowing subject as an external object, it is natural to suppose that knowledge of it can reach us only in this way. Yet on the other hand, if the mind is utterly separate from the corporeal world, whatever knowledge it might have could be generated only *a priori* from ideas, which are its peculiar possession. That such knowledge is the truth about a corporeal world could then be only a matter of faith, or a divine revelation, and the relation of the human mind to the human body must remain a mystery. Alternatively, if knowledge is to come through the action of external things upon our organs of sense, the mind must have some intelligible relation to material things and must somehow be able to transcend its merely adventitious presentations and embrace at once the external object, the process resulting from its action upon the physical organism, and the effects in consciousness which they are supposed to produce. Neither the relation nor the transcendence is compatible with the rigid separation of the material world from the mind, and so the empiricist principle which seems to follow from that separation is involved in an intractable contradiction.

No sooner had the implications of Locke's doctrine been fully appreciated than it was superseded in the work of his successors. The criticism of his position is embodied in the philosophies of Berkeley and of Hume and again in that of Kant; and once this criticism had been made and the untenability of the empirical hypothesis had become obvious, it is difficult to see how it could again have come to find favour among serious philosophers. Nevertheless it has persisted among certain schools until the present day. Bertrand Russell, indeed, has commended Locke for his willingness to sacrifice logic in order to avoid the pronouncement of paradoxes. 'To a logician', he writes, 'this is irritating; to a practical man it is a proof of sound judgement.'[1] What subtle distinction Russell intends between logic and sound judgement, I do not understand, nor yet how paradox can be avoided by the sacrifice of consistency; but it takes no great philosophical acumen to discern that the light of criticism reveals paradox in almost every chapter of the *Essay Concerning Human Understanding*. One of the soundest of modern philosophers, referring to Locke's account of 'the

[1] *A History of Western Philosophy* (London, 1946), p. 630.

"first beginnings and materials" of our knowledge' as 'an outworn position', has said: 'Now these assumptions have been exposed over and over again by philosophical criticism. The general situation in which Locke has planted himself is no longer held by any *careful* thinker.'[1] Whether the contemporary doctrines which do, in fact, adopt and build upon a position in close accord with that of Locke, have been propounded by those who deserve to be described as 'careful thinkers', the reader must be left to judge hereafter for himself.

[1] Joachim, *Logical Studies*, p. 113. The italics are mine.

Chapter VII

SUBJECTIVE IDEALISM

I. BERKELEY'S ABOLITION OF THE EXTERNAL WORLD

1. The hopeless contradictoriness of the position as Locke left it made a new attempt at a theory of knowledge imperative. The conflict lay between the notion, on the one hand, that our knowledge of the world can come to us only in experience and, on the other, the assertion that that experience is limited to our own ideas (and so irremediably cut off from the world we are to know). Locke's dark room illuminated only by the windows of sense, proves to be something like Plato's cave in which we perceive only the shadows cast on its interior walls. There seemed only one way of escape from the contradiction and that was to deny the existence of any external world, and to identify all reality with ideas and the minds that perceive them. Certain matters seemed to have been established beyond possibility of doubt. First, Descartes had placed the existence of the knowing mind in an unassailable position. Secondly, Locke had made it obvious and undeniable that whatever was known must be part of the 'furniture' of the mind and had shown that our knowledge of corporeal substances was limited to that of their sensible qualities. The existence of spirits and ideas was thus secure, but that of 'things', of bodies, of matter as such—unthinking, extended substance—had been left extremely doubtful. Descartes had persuaded himself of it only by an appeal to the veracity of God; but need God be accused of deception even if there were no such thing as material substance?—for in which of our perceptions does it appear to us? Berkeley argues, on the contrary, that it is unnecessary for God to create archetypes in an unthinking substance as the causes of our ideas, when He is able to produce the ideas themselves immediately in our minds; and the sufficient guarantee of their truth is that they are produced in us by God. He sets himself, accordingly, to show that the whole and only reality that an idea can have is to be perceived, and that the postulation of any other sort of being similar or corresponding to ideas is neither necessary nor intelligible.

2. For Berkeley it is impossible that an idea should exist otherwise than in the mind that thinks or perceives it. This, he claims, is readily admitted by everyone in the case of our thoughts, passions and ideas

formed by our imagination, and can be no less true of 'ideas imprinted on the sense'. 'Their *esse* is *percipi*;[1] nor is it possible they should have any existence out of the minds or thinking things which perceive them.'[2]

The belief in matter existing independently of any mind is not, Berkeley thinks, so much a vulgar prejudice as the fallacious result of theoretical refinement. For what the average man means by matter is what he can see and feel [3]—in short, a cluster of ideas. But, by the help of the false doctrine that there exist abstract ideas, philosophers have persuaded themselves that they can separate from our perceptions of bodies all the sensible qualities, and that something then remains which is real and independent of our perceiving. So they persist in the demand for an unknown and unknowable somewhat which they call corporeal substance. Berkeley, however, rejects the view that ideas can be abstract, for every idea, as Locke taught, is particular, though we may sometimes use one such particular to stand as a sign for a group which possess a common property. Locke, it is true, with his wonted inconsistency, allowed of abstract ideas but Berkeley has no difficulty in disposing of his doctrine.[4] He then has no difficulty in disposing, likewise, of the distinction between primary and secondary qualities and of corporeal substance, and we are left with active, thinking beings (or spirits) and ideas (the passive and immediate objects of their perception) the existence of which is inconceivable without some mind. Thus 'all the choir of heaven and furniture of earth, in a word all those bodies which compose the mighty frame of the world, have not any subsistence without a mind . . . their *being* is to be perceived or known . . . consequently, so long as they are not actually perceived by me, or do not exist in my mind, or that of any other created spirit, they must either have no existence at all, or else subsist in the mind of some Eternal Spirit'.[5]

A common misunderstanding of Berkeley's philosophy issues in the belief that he denied the existence of the world of sensible objects. It is from this that Dr. Johnson's famous refutation springs. But Berkeley himself protested loudly against the accusation and maintained that he had established the existence of the sensible world the more firmly

[1] The meaning of 'perceive' in the philosophy of the 17th and 18th centuries does not necessarily imply sensuous presentation; it is much more nearly 'to cognize'. Cf. the meaning of '*cogitare*' in Descartes's philosophy.

[2] *Principles of Human Knowledge*, I, 3; Fraser's ed. (Oxford, 1901), Vol. I, p. 259. Cf. *Dialogues between Hylas and Philonous*, I, Fraser, Vol. I, p. 406.

[3] Cf. *Commonplace Book*, 'I side in all things with the mob' (Fraser, Vol. I, p. 8).

[4] *Vide Principles of Human Knowledge*, Introd. 11 *et seq.*

[5] *Principles of Human Knowledge*, I, 6.

by accepting what we do or can perceive by sense as constituting its reality. Those who assert that these perceptions are 'a false imaginary glare' and seek the reality beyond the mind are, he declares, the real sceptics;[1] for they doubt the evidence of their senses and are forced to confess that the substance to which they attribute reality is beyond their ken. But for him the world is as real as anything can be just because it consists entirely of ideas.

'The distinction between realities and chimeras' he states, 'retains its full force.' The realities are those ideas imprinted in our minds by God according to 'the set rules, or established methods' which come to be called the laws of nature.[2] They have 'a steadiness order and coherence' superior to those which we voluntarily excite at random, and it is by this order and regularity that we distinguish the real from the imaginary and the true from the false.[3] The spectacle of the universe is direct evidence of God's existence and His goodness,[4] and our scientific knowledge of natural phenomena is the discovery of His wisdom.

This brief summary of Berkeley's position will suffice for my present purpose. His own exposition is so clear and coherent that it needs no commentator to make it intelligible. His philosophy is chiefly remarkable for the fact that, within an empiricist framework, he produces an idealistic metaphysic. It is seldom, if ever, realized by empiricists, with their zeal for the reality of the external world, that the very basis of empiricism commits them inevitably to subjectivism, and it is this fact that Berkeley's philosophy demonstrates. Starting as he does from the position which Locke left him, his reasoning is irrefutable: yet it is curious to see how those who sympathize with Locke's realism squirm and wriggle to avoid the conclusions of Berkeley. It may be instructive, therefore, to consider the attempts made by some modern empiricists to refute Berkeley's central tenet: that the *esse* of perceptibles is *percipi*.

II. MODERN CRITICISMS OF BERKELEY

I shall deal only with the criticisms of three authors: (i) Bertrand Russell's judgement of Berkeley in his *History of Western Philosophy*, (ii) G. E. Moore's well-known 'Refutation of Idealism', which is supposed to be fatal to Berkeley's doctrine in particular and other idealisms in general, and (iii) the implied criticism of Berkeley to be

---

[1] *Dialogues between Hylas and Philonous*, II, Fraser, pp. 422 ff.
[2] *Principles*, I, 30; cf. also *Hylas and Philonous*, II, *loc. cit.*
[3] *Principles*, I, 33.   [4] *Ibid.* I, 146 ff.

found in Professor H. H. Price's discussion of the philosophy of Hume. None of these critics deny or show any inclination to reject Locke's contentions that our ideas are caused by external things, that ideas so derived are the original source of our knowledge of the world and that our own ideas are the sole medium of our knowledge. Yet, so long as these assertions stand, Berkeley's position is unassailable and the arguments brought against him leave his theory unscathed.

3. Russell divides his criticism into two parts. First he deals with what he refers to as Berkeley's logical arguments, and then with what he calls his empirical arguments, holding it a fault to mix both varieties. I shall deal with his criticisms in that order; but first it must be observed that the whole of Russell's treatment of Berkeley's position is vitiated by a misunderstanding which appears in almost his first expository statement. He asserts that Berkeley thinks he is proving that all reality is mental,[1] and this, to say the least, is very misleading as an interpretation of Berkeley; for 'mental' is a term implying antithesis to 'physical', and Berkeley never denied reality to physical nature,[2] nor did he attempt to identify physical objects with the operations of the mind, which (had he used the term) he would have regarded as mental. On the contrary, he carefully distinguishes between 'ideas imprinted on the senses' and 'such as are perceived by attending to the passions and operations of the mind', and these again from those formed by the help of memory and imagination.[3] Nowhere does he attempt to reduce the first of these three classes of ideas to either of the other two. It is not, therefore, Berkeley's reasoning that 'suffers from the absence of any definition of the word "mental"', as Russell avers, but rather his own criticism, because what Berkeley contends for is not the mental but the *ideal* character of all reality, meaning by that term its presence to and apprehension by a cognizant subject. He is maintaining that, unless a passive object is known, it is nothing, for its *esse* is *percipi* (the subject itself, being active, is never an object [4] and its *esse* is not *percipi* but *percipere*). Mental events, if they are passions, will, of course, be in like case with physical, but the disjunction of material and mental which Russell says Berkeley regarded as exhaustive,[5] is not the basis of Berkeley's argument (though it is the source of Locke's theory on which Berkeley's follows). Berkeley himself admits the distinction only

---

[1] *Vide History of Western Philosophy*, p. 674. The error is shared by Russell with Professor C. D. Broad (*vide Mind and Its Place in Nature*, p. 624) and Professor G. E. Moore (*Philosophical Studies*, p. 6).
[2] Cf. *Principles* I, 34-6, and *Hylas and Philonous*, II. [3] *Vide Principles*, I, 1.
[4] *Ibid.* I, 89 and 142. [5] *Western Philosophy*, p. 677.

within the realm of ideas for beyond that there is nothing except spirits, who are not 'mental', but are active subjects of understanding and will.[1] He saw that Locke's assumption of 'external' things corresponding to ideas was untenable, but by abandoning the external things and accepting the ideas (the existence of which seemed undeniable) he is very far from reducing all reality to mentality. Any attempt to disprove that reality is mental, therefore, is irrelevant as a refutation of Berkeley who did not maintain that it was, and it will not be surprising if we find that Russell's arguments, aimed as they are at the wrong target, fall beside the mark.

(i) *Logical Arguments*. (a) Berkeley writes in the *Dialogues between Hylas and Philonous*, 'that any immediate object of the senses . . . should exist in an unthinking substance, or exterior to *all* minds, is in itself an evident contradiction'.[2] Here, according to Russell, is a fallacy analogous to asserting that Mr. A must have an uncle because all nephews of necessity have uncles, without showing that Mr. A is a nephew. But Berkeley makes no such mistake. So far from neglecting to show that sensible qualities are immediate objects of sense, that is how he defines them.[3] We cannot discover by analysis of Mr. A, says Russell, that he is a nephew, and (though the sort of analysis required is not specified) that may well be so. But that sensible qualities are immediate objects of sense is surely an analytic proposition. Russell, however, like Locke, wishes to make sensible qualities both sensations and the properties of self-existent external things. But, according to Locke, sensible qualities are all, without exception, simple ideas of sensation, and he provides no vestige of evidence that these have any external causes. Russell is unwilling to abandon Locke's position, though he is fully aware of the contradiction which it involves.[4]

There is no analogy between Russell's example of the nephew and Berkeley's reasoning and, consequently, the rest of the argument is a little difficult to follow. 'So, if anything is an object of the senses,' Russell continues, 'some mind is concerned with it; but it does not follow that the same thing could not have existed without being an object of the senses.' Is it possible that the founder of modern scientific philosophy has fallen into an elementary logical error,—an error so obvious, indeed, that one is almost ashamed to point it out? Are we not involved here in the fallacy of denying the antecedent? And whether we are or not, it is clearly the case that if something is *not* an object of the

---

[1] Cf. *Principles*, I, 27.   [2] Fraser, Vol. I, p. 406.
[3] *Vide Hylas and Philonous*, I, Fraser, Vol. I, p. 383: 'sensible things are those only which are immediately perceived by sense'.   [4] *Vide Western Philosophy*, p. 636.

senses, it cannot *by definition* be 'the same thing'. Even if the definition is not invoked against him Russell's argument fares no better, for we can obviously have no means of knowing whether anything unsensed is the same as an object of the senses, nor whether it can exist unless it is an object for *some* mind. In fact, the main purpose of the argument between Hylas and Philonous in this dialogue is just to demonstrate this very point—the impossibility of knowing what sort of existence sensible objects could have without their being immediately perceived. Russell, of course, is using the word 'object' ambiguously to mean (a) the content of an experience and (b) the cause of the experience. But if, with Locke, we assume the latter to be external to the mind, we leave ourselves with no means of knowing its existence nor any pretext for assuming it. It is just for this reason that Berkeley denies the existence of any causes of ideas other than the will of God and the activity of the mind itself in perception and imagination.

(b) Of course the existence of what is sensed may, when it is not being sensed, become an object of thought or imagination, but this is no refutation of Berkeley, for such an object is still apprehended by a mind, as Berkeley himself points out.[1] But Russell tilts against this argument also. In the person of Hylas he replies: 'When I say that I can conceive a house which no one perceives, what I really mean is that I can understand the proposition "there is a house which no one perceives", or better still "there is a house which no one either perceives or conceives" '.[2] The proposition, he maintains, is composed entirely of intelligible words correctly put together and, whether it is true or false, it certainly cannot be shown to be self-contradictory. But how can anyone understand the proposition without conceiving the existence of a house? And as soon as we do that, the very act of propounding the proposition contradicts its sense. To propound it is to make it false; to claim that it is true is to confess that it cannot be intelligibly entertained. Is this or is it not self-contradiction? It is hard to believe that so distinguished a philosopher as Russell seriously means what he has written and that he is not capable of seeing that the proposition, if genuinely asserted, means, and can only mean, 'I judge (or believe or think) that there is a house which no one either perceives or conceives'.[3]

---

[1] *Vide Hylas and Philonous*, I (Fraser, Vol. I, p. 411), and *Principles*, I, 23.

[2] *Western Philosophy*, p. 678.

[3] Even Locke maintained that words 'stand for nothing but *the ideas in the mind of him that uses them*' (*Essay*, III, ii, 2), and compare Russell's own theory of language in *The Analysis of Mind* (London, 1922), p. 191, 'The essence of language lies . . . in the employment of fixed associations . . . in order that something now sensible—a spoken word, a gesture, or what not—may call up the "idea" of something else'.

F

(c) He supports his case, further, by the example from Mathematics of the infinite number of possible multiplications of two integers. Some of these, he says, must never have been thought of. One is tempted to ask how then the mathematician knows that they are infinite in number; and whether knowing the principle of generation of a series is not in some way to think of all its members. It could hardly be the part of one who claims to know the solutions of Zeno's paradoxes to reply that we cannot think of all the members of an infinite series. Indeed we cannot enumerate them in a finite time, but we can surely think of them and reason about them [1] as easily as we can think and reason about the shape of a chiliagon or the root of minus one. But if there are some which never have been thought of, we must ask what sort of existence they possess, and no good answer is readily forthcoming.

(d) Russell's example of the pebbles similarly falls short of his objective. It does not follow, he maintains, that all pebbles must be perceived because we can form the empirical concept, 'pebble'. The empirical concept, however, has been formed only from the experience of such pebbles as have been, and can apply only to such as are, perceived. Russell should be the first to maintain (if we are to believe what he says elsewhere [2]) that the very next example we may meet might fail to satisfy the empirical concept formed from prior experience. It should not, therefore, be possible, as Russell holds, to construct statements by means of empirical concepts 'about classes some or all of whose members are not experienced'. But in any case, by this argument Berkeley's withers are not wrung for *he* claims that God always and everywhere perceives all pebbles.

(e) Finally, Russell reduces Berkeley's logical arguments to the following syllogism:

> Sensible objects must be sensible: [3]
> A is a sensible object,
> Therefore A must be sensible.

And he contends that it is valid only if A *must* be a sensible object; but that is what the syllogism proves and is not a condition of its validity. The argument, he says, does not prove that, from the properties of A

---

[1] Cf. *Our Knowledge of the External World* (London, 1926), p. 187.
[2] *Ibid.* p. 44.
[3] Had Russell stated the major premise as 'Sensible objects must be sensed', though the syllogism (*mutatis mutandis*) would still be valid, the truth of the major might reasonably be questioned. As the point is raised in the sequel we may defer its discussion.

other than its being sensible, it can be deduced that A is sensible. For my own part I am ready to dispense with the syllogism, and cannot doubt that Berkeley never felt the need of it, in order to prove so palpable a tautology. But, as to the *other properties* of A, if they are not sensible, they are surely irrelevant, and we may even wonder by what private revelation Russell discovered there were any such; Berkeley certainly does not claim to know of any and that is why he so insistently avers that a sensible object is always and only the immediate experience of a cognizant subject. But if these other properties are sensible, then Russell's conclusion contradicts itself. 'So far as logic is concerned', Russell proceeds, 'there is no reason why there should not be colours where there is no eye or brain.' Berkeley would undoubtedly agree. Eyes and brains are for him sensible objects which exist only as ideas and we might even say that they could not exist where there are no colours (at least, so far as they are experienced visually). But what logic requires is that, as colours are immediate objects of sense, they can exist only for a subject which experiences such objects; for the definition and meaning of 'immediate object of sense' entails that it is directly experienced.

Let us glance now at the refutation of the empirical arguments.

(ii) *Empirical Arguments.* (a) To Berkeley's argument for the subjectivity of sensations, from the fact that they are pleasant or painful, Russell objects on the ground that he uses the word 'pain' (and, presumably, 'pleasure' likewise) ambiguously to mean either the quality of a sensation or the sensation that has that quality. We should say (for instance) not that 'the most vehement and intense heat is a very great pain' but that it *causes* pain. 'We say a broken leg is painful without implying that the leg is in the mind.' [1] It is difficult to see just what this means. If the pain is only the quality of the sensation of heat, what on earth does it mean to say that heat *causes* pain? It should follow rather that Berkeley's argument is strengthened, for the quality of the sensation is what is sensed. On the other hand if we take a pain to be a separate sensation, 'heat causes pain' means only that one sensation causes another and Berkeley's argument is not affected. Indeed, this is exactly Berkeley's point. We know of the existence of heat (or, for that matter, of broken legs) only by experiencing sensations and have no right or reason to regard only some of these as ideal and others not. It is Russell who seems to be using words ambiguously when he says that heat causes pain, for one may suspect that he is thinking of heat (1) as either a sensation or a sense-datum and (2) as a physical condition in an

[1] *Western Philosophy*, p. 679.

'external' body, which may be an object of scientific conception but is never in any way given in sense.

(b) The example of conflicting sensations of heat and cold on immersing both hands in lukewarm water, when one hand has been warmed and the other chilled, is perfectly legitimate for Berkeley, and again Russell appears not to have appreciated the point of the argument. Hylas' contention is that the heat is in the 'external' thing, and Philonous is demonstrating that whatever is alleged to be 'in the external thing' is unknown to us, while what we do experience is two contradictory qualities which obviously cannot belong to the same thing. Neither of these qualities, be it noted, is a relation of comparison. We do not feel 'warmer' in one hand and 'colder' in the other, but have a definite and specific sensation in each which is utterly incompatible with the other. Any comparison we make is inferential and is made only in later reflection. It is not true, therefore, as Russell alleges, that 'what we *perceive* [1] in that experiment is not hot and cold but hotter and colder'; and we have no other means of discovering the temperature of the water that does not involve sense-perception.[2] Russell says that 'there is nothing to prove that these (sensed qualities) are subjective', but is not that just what is proved by the fact that they conflict? What Berkeley is trying to show, however, is that there is nothing to prove that they are 'external', and it cannot be denied that he succeeds.

(c) Of the rest of Russell's arguments only one need be mentioned which is important. When he comes to Berkeley's treatment of primary qualities, though he allows the force of the reasoning, he qualifies his concession in an inadmissible way. 'Such arguments', he writes, 'must, I think, be allowed to prove the subjectivity of perceived space. But this subjectivity is physical: it is equally true of a camera, and therefore does not prove that shape is "mental".'[3] I shall not comment again on the misunderstanding of Berkeley implied in the use of the word 'mental'. The matter with which I want to concern myself is the camera. No camera experiences any appearances of the sizes and positions of objects whatsoever, so far as we can ascertain. All that we can discover about it is that, when *we* inspect the photograph, the spatial relations intrinsic to the image are analogous to what *we* experience directly on looking at the objects, and we can construct a theory to

[1] My italics.
[2] A thermometer reading involves sense-perception, and from this we only infer the temperature, we do not perceive it directly. Even so, what we infer is something we never really sense, viz. a physical condition which is a matter of theory, an object of thought and not of sense.   [3] *Western Philosophy*, p. 680.

account for the correspondence. The 'subjectivity' which Russell claims to be 'physical' is thus not the sort of subjectivity that Berkeley is talking about when he asserts that our perceptions are only 'in a mind'. Certainly the photographic image is subjective[1] *to us*, when we perceive it; but this is not Russell's 'physical' subjectivity. That is the manner of projection of the image inside the camera which is 'subjective' to the camera only in so far as *we* conceive it so. Moreover, the physical existence without the mind of such things as cameras as well as of the objects reflected within them, is exactly what is under investigation and to use it as an instance against Berkeley at all is to beg the question.

Had arguments such as these been put forward by anyone less eminent than Bertrand Russell it is hardly likely that they would have been taken seriously, and I have treated them here at such length only because one cannot neglect views which are liable to gain authority from their association with so celebrated a name.

4. The second criticism of Berkeley which I shall discuss is G. E. Moore's famous 'Refutation of Idealism'.[2] This was not, of course, directed solely against Berkeley but claimed to be a refutation of all idealism, for Moore says that he is attacking a single proposition on which all idealist arguments depend for their plausibility, and that proposition is Berkeley's principle that *esse* is *percipi*. To what extent Professor Moore's statements are true about idealist philosophers in general is not my present concern. I shall consider primarily how far his criticism is damaging to Berkeley. But if he is right in saying that all idealist arguments rest on the proposition, *esse* is *percipi*, and if his disproof of that were shown to be unsound, the whole position of idealism would be affected. One thing that Moore asserts of idealism in general is, however, not true of Berkeley (whatever may be the case with other philosophers): that he used this proposition as a premise from which to conclude that *esse* is *percipere*. In his system the statement does not cover the whole of human knowledge[3] but applies only to ideas or unthinking things.[4] The basis for asserting the existence of spirits is the argument of Descartes which, like Locke, Berkeley accepts;[5] and that, in effect, is that *percipere* is *esse*. Berkeley would no more have maintained universally, either that *esse* is *percipi* or that it is

---

[1] I should not deny that there is a sense in which it is also objective, but that is not relevant here.
[2] *Philosophical Studies*, I (London, 1922).   [3] *Vide Principles*, I, 86.
[4] *Ibid.* 88.   [5] *Ibid.* 139.

percipere, than would Descartes himself, but whereas for Descartes the being of thinking substances consisted in their thinking and of non-thinking substances in their being extended, for Berkeley the existence of the latter was wholly included in their being perceived.

Moore proceeds to distinguish three possible meanings of the copula in the crucial proposition.

(a) It may mean that 'esse' signifies neither more nor less than 'percipi', in which case the statement would be a pure tautology. Moore rejects this possibility as clearly not the intention of the philosophers who assert the proposition.

(b) 'Esse' may not be identical with 'percipi' but may include the latter as a part, in which case 'to be real' would mean to be experienced and something else besides. This other constituent Moore calls *x*.

(c) The third possibility is that what is meant by 'esse' not only includes as a part what is meant by 'percipi' but that there is a necessary connection between *percipi* and *x* (that in reality which is not *percipi*). This last meaning of the proposition is the only one, Moore holds, which is important and the only one which will give the idealist what he wants, because if the connection between *x* and *percipi* were contingent all other arguments for the ideality (or spirituality) of the real would lose their plausibility.

We may at once agree that '*esse* is *percipi*' was not intended by those who asserted it as a pure tautology. But if there is some difference between 'esse' and 'percipi' there is no necessity that it should take the form Moore suggests. Is it not even more probable that 'percipi' is intended to be the wider term and that it absorbs 'esse' without remainder while it connotes more than is meant by bare existence? This possibility Moore does not even consider; yet to be perceived is potentially to be an element in judgement and inference, it is potentially to be a moment in feeling and emotion and the starting-point of action, which is much more than merely to exist. But to have any kind of existence (so the idealist philosopher contends) the object must be perceived in some way or other, whether it be by sense, by imagination or in conception; and this is certainly Berkeley's position, for he argues long and vehemently against the view that there is any residue in things beyond their being perceived. That *esse* includes *x* as well as *percipi* is what the greater part of his reasoning is directed to disprove and the onus is on his opponents to show where he has failed.

Let us, however, pursue the course of Moore's argument and see what follows if we distinguish within existence an *x* besides its being perceived. Moore supports this distinction by an analysis of sensation which has become famous. In the sensation of blue he distinguishes (a) what it has in common with other sensations, and this he calls consciousness (but is unable to say further what it is[1]), and (b) what differentiates it from, say, the sensation of green, and this he calls the object of the sensation. The idealist mistake, he says, is to identify one of these with the combination of the two—or the part with the whole. For, when I say that the sensation of blue exists in my mind, (i) I certainly do not mean that blue exists without consciousness and must, therefore, mean either (ii) that the consciousness exists alone or (iii) that both consciousness and its object, blue, exist together. Now Berkeley and the idealists tell us that to say 'blue exists' is *the same thing* as to say 'the sensation of blue exists' and this is a contradiction because it either identifies the part with the whole (object with consciousness-cum-object), or it identifies one of the parts with the other (object with consciousness).

This peculiar relation of consciousness and object, Moore asserts, is equally involved in every experience and is alone what gives us reason to call it a mental fact,[2] and so he concludes that in all cases of awareness 'the object, when we are aware of it, is precisely what it would be, if we were not aware of it'.[3] The awareness of a sensation thus resolves itself into three factors: (i) that part of *esse* which was earlier called x, and which now apparently turns out to be the object; (ii) that part of *esse* which is *percipi*, and (iii) consciousness, which, not being itself perceived, presumably cannot be identified with *percipi*.

We have been told that it was a contradiction to identify 'blue exists' with 'the sensation of blue exists' and we see now that this is because blue exists whether the sensation exists or not. But the existence of blue is its *esse* and that was assumed to contain both x and *percipi*; yet, if it does, it cannot possibly be precisely the same when we are not as when we are aware of it, for when we are not aware of it there is no *percipi*. On the other hand, if *esse* is to be confined to x and to exclude *percipi* altogether, the same duality reappears in it and it can be subjected to the same sort of analysis as the sensation of blue.

x is now the existence of blue (its *esse*) and the proposition 'blue exists' which may not be identified with 'the sensation of blue exists' may be identified with 'x exists'. But we must now distinguish within x that which it has in common with all other objects, which I propose

[1] The nearest that he gets to it in this essay is to say: 'The element ... which I have called "consciousness" really is consciousness'. And that helps us very little. He says it is something distinct and unique, utterly different from its object and related to it in a unique and peculiar way. And that helps us little more.
[2] *Op. cit.* p. 29.   [3] *Ibid.*

(quite arbitrarily) to call its 'being', and that which distinguishes it from other objects, which I shall call its 'quality'. Now when we say '*x* exists' we cannot mean that the quality exists without the being and must mean either that the being exists without the quality (in which case it is not blue), or that both being and quality exist together. But in that case to say ' "*x* exists" is the same as "blue exists" ' is a contradiction, for either it identifies the part (the quality) with the whole (quality + being), or it identifies one part with the other (quality with being).

Moore's method of analysis is applicable to any qualitied existent and can be used to reveal an alleged contradiction in the conception of it; and every entity we can distinguish is the subject of qualities. To try to analyse out that which barely exists is to embark upon the fruitless and futile search for Locke's unknowable substance, and it is just this search in which Moore is here engaged.

His analysis of sensation, in fact, is bogus. First he gives us an undefined *x* plus *percipi* (the 'being perceived' of something), and then we get an undefined 'consciousness' uniquely related to a clearly conceived object, such as blue. A little attention reveals that the 'being perceived' in one case and the 'object' in the other is really the whole of the experience with which we are dealing and that, despite Moore's protestations, neither 'consciousness' nor *x* contributes anything to it at all. As soon as we try to tell ourselves what *x* is, it turns out to be sensed, or imagined, or conceived blue (its *percipi*); and, similarly, as soon as we try to get a conceivable notion of consciousness it becomes the consciousness *of the object*, blue. The same sort of confusion (along with some others) is involved in, and the same sort of criticism applies to, Moore's treatment in this essay of the sensation and its 'content', but I think I have given sufficient space to his argument already and will not pursue the matter further.

The effort to maintain the existence of unexperienced sensibles is bound to fail, for however one seeks to express the view one is involved in a contradiction of terms, and it is usually when they pronounce just this contradiction that protagonists of the theory declare most emphatically that their statements contain none. 'For a patch of colour', writes Professor Moore in another paper,[1] 'even if it were not actually experienced, would be an entity *of the same sort* as some which are experienced . . . and there is no contradiction in supposing that there are patches of colour, which yet are not experienced; since by calling a thing a patch of colour we merely make a statement about its intrinsic

[1] 'The Status of Sense Data', *Philosophical Studies*, V, p. 169.

quality and in no way assert that it has to anything else any of the relations which may be meant by saying that it is experienced.' But this supposition that there are patches of colour which are not experienced is flatly contradictory and Moore's statement disguises the fact only by abstracting what he calls its 'intrinsic quality' from the actual experience and then postulating certain relations in addition which are supposed to be necessary to its being experienced. Whatever these relations are supposed to be, clearly there could be no 'intrinsic quality' *of the same sort* without them. For the position which Moore is striving to maintain is in effect the position of Locke: that there exist entities independent of our perception which we come to know only when they come into external relation with us. This external relation is, for Locke, a causal relation through which effects are produced upon our sense-organs, so that our experience of external things is mediated by the conditions of sensation (physical and physiological). The qualities experienced are therefore, of necessity, 'secondary' qualities which are mind-dependent and different from—not possibly 'of the same sort' as—the 'powers' in the things to produce the sensory effects in us. Berkeley showed that no exception from this condition could be made in favour of primary qualities, so that Locke's hypothesis (which is implicit in Moore's view) leads inevitably to the conclusion that all qualities as we experience them must be mind-dependent—*i.e.* mediated by the conditions of experiencing. Accordingly, no unexperienced entity can be of the same sort, and to allege that it could is to contradict oneself. Moore does not specify the kind of relation which he assumes as the condition of experiencing, but unless he intends some mysterious doctrine of pre-established harmony, it must involve mediation of some kind; and a patch of colour, if reference to the conditions of sensation is omitted, is simply an immediate object of sense—Berkeley's definition (as we saw when discussing Russell's criticism) of sensible quality. The assertion that such an object may exist unexperienced is thus obviously a contradiction in terms.

'Colour' and 'immediate object of visual experience' are, therefore, synonymous. (To say 'possible object' would in this case be merely quibbling, for it is not something which might in certain circumstances become such an object, but something which could not possibly be anything else than such an object.) Moore seems to deny this by postulating an 'experiencing', or a 'consciousness', the relation to which *ab extra* of a quality or object constitutes 'the experience of' that quality or object. But he can tell us nothing significant about either the consciousness or the relation. We have only his word for it (which of

F*

course we must accept) that in his own experience he can distinguish them. But this cannot help us, for if we ask (and this is what we must know if we are to understand him) what the object or quality is without the consciousness or experiencing, all he can tell us is that it is *the same* (or of the *same sort*) as the object or quality in relation to the consciousness—the same (or of the same sort) as it is when experienced. And this he cannot possibly know and has not a vestige of right to assume. A patch of colour, therefore, even for Professor Moore, is identical with an object of visual experience, and what is not actually experienced is no such object and so cannot be a patch of colour. Consequently, it would be as contradictory to say that a patch of colour, even if it were not experienced, would be an entity of the same sort, as to say that a triangle, even if it were not a three-sided rectilinear figure, would be a figure of the same sort.

To conclude, the point which Berkeley is perpetually making reasserts itself, that we cannot by any means conceive what an experienced object may be *qua* unexperienced, and every attempt we make always leaves upon our hands only another concept, or some imagined counterpart of the presumed 'external' thing.

5. The third and most formidable criticism of Berkeley's main contention which I intend to discuss comes from the pen of Professor H. H. Price. It is a criticism of Berkeley only by implication, for Professor Price is directly concerned only with Hume; but he is criticizing a point in Hume's theory which has been taken over from Berkeley and is supported by a closely similar argument. The point, moreover, is precisely this, that the *esse* of sense-impressions is *percipi*, and it is not unlikely that Hume's consciousness that Berkeley had already set out the argument effectively and at length, was the reason for what Price describes as his 'brief and airy manner of stating it'. Accordingly, it may not be inappropriate to discuss, as applying to Berkeley, Price's criticism of this one feature of Hume's doctrine: namely, his conviction (as Price puts it) that there can be no unsensed *sensibilia*.[1]

The conviction is based, not on *a priori* reasoning (for Hume did not regard the separate or continued existence of 'sensible objects or perceptions' as self-contradictory) but is thought to follow from certain empirical considerations. We must observe immediately, however, that what Hume considered feasible was the separate and continued existence of 'sensible objects or *perceptions*'. His addition of the alternative designation indicates (as, I think, does the whole tenor of his doctrine)

[1] *Vide Hume's Theory of the External World* (Oxford, 1940), ch. iv, p. 105.

that by 'sensible objects' what he means is 'sensed objects',[1] and this is far from being the same as unsensed *sensibilia*. It certainly was not possible for Hume to maintain, as Berkeley did, that 'ideas' (or 'impressions') could exist only in the mind of some spirit; for Hume denied the existence of spirits, and of minds as anything more than 'a heap or collection of different perceptions'. As, for him, these perceptions had no necessary connection one with another, he held it perfectly possible for them to exist separately. But there is no evidence that he believed that they could exist *unperceived*. I am sure Hume would have thought the supposition of unperceived perceptions [2] contradictory, and that, I think, is what 'unsensed *sensibilia*' would mean for him. Price, however, apparently taking Hume's phrase 'sensible object' to be synonymous with '*sensibile*' and accepting Hume's statement that there is no absurdity in separating sensible objects from the mind, does not feel himself called upon to argue against the view that the notion of unsensed *sensibilia* is self-contradictory.

Even when he is criticizing Hume's empirical arguments against the 'independent existence of sensible perceptions', he does not claim to be able to *prove* the existence of unsensed *sensibilia*, but only to show that Hume has failed to disprove it. Nevertheless, in order to do this he is drawn into the description of alternative possibilities which involve tremendous difficulties and land us ultimately in the contradiction of claiming independent existence for that which we imagine or suppose.

Price maintains that Hume's arguments (and so Berkeley's where they are the same) from such facts as the occurrence of double vision when one eye-ball is pressed, the changes of perspectival appearances with bodily movements, variation in perceived colours and tastes during illness, and so on, do not provide evidence that all our sense-impressions 'are dependent on our organs, and the disposition of our nerves and animal spirits'. He criticizes them both in detail and in principle. (a) His criticisms of detail are as follows: (i) Perspectival distortions give no evidence of the dependence of sense-impressions on the percipient's sense-organs or nervous system but only of relativity to certain positions in space. But if we are not to beg the question at issue (an error Price is usually very careful to avoid) by assuming a spatio-temporal world of material objects existing independently of our perception, with all its implication of unsensed *sensibilia*—if we are not

---

[1] Cf. his use of 'unchangeable object' for 'unchanged' or 'unchanging object', *Treatise of Human Nature*, Bk. I, Pt. iv, Sect. ii (Selby-Bigge's edn.), p. 200, noted by Price as 'odd', *op. cit.* p. 39.

[2] Price (*op. cit.* p. 222) attributes this phrase to Hume, but I cannot discover that he ever uses it.

to assume all this, what can we mean by 'positions in space'? Clearly, we cannot mean positions in the visual field, for perspectival distortions are not relative to these. And if we mean positions in 'perceived space' as opposed to a hypothetical 'physical space', we must remember that perceived space is, to a very great extent, if not wholly, a construction, in part imaginative and in part logical, which is not given in sense.[1] The perspectival character of what is given in sense is certainly relative to the position in perceived space to which it is referred. An elliptical colour patch is taken to be 'really' elliptical if it is referred to a position in which the surface would be perpendicular to the line of sight and taken to be circular if referred to a position in which it would be at an angle. Likewise, a small image is taken to be 'really' much larger if referred to a distant object and *vice versa*. But all this depends on imaginative supplementation and inferential interpretation of sense-impressions, so that even if perspectival distortions imply nothing as to dependence upon the nerves and sense-organs of the percipient, the explanation of them as relative to positions in space does nothing to release them from dependence upon the percipient's thought and imagination.

When Price says, 'the flat and perspectively distorted shape which I see when I look at a distant mountain could still continue in existence . . . when I go away or shut my eyes',[2] does he mean that it could continue to exist in my imagination or that I must presume that I should see it again if I went back and looked? If he does he says nothing in favour of the existence, unsensed, of *sensibilia*. What is thought or imagined might be said to exist, and is certainly not sensed, but (*qua* thought or imagined) it is equally not a *sensibile*. But I do not think this is what he means. I believe that he is actually maintaining the possibility of existence of the flat, perspectively distorted shape, as I see it, when neither I nor anyone else sees or thinks about it at all. But this is quite unacceptable. The flat, perspectively distorted shape is neither the mountain itself nor its actual shape and it is alleged to exist in a place where there is no mountain nor anything else having that shape except a bare 'unsensed *sensibile*'—a pure *ens rationis*—and this, even if it be not excised from the world by the use of Occam's razor, is clearly not independent of mind for its existence. To assert the possibility of existence of the unsensed *sensibile* when nobody is thinking of

[1] Cf. Hume, *Treatise*, Bk. I, Pt. iv, Sect. ii, 'Even our sight informs us not of distance or outness (so to speak) immediately and without a certain reasoning and experience' (Selby-Bigge, p. 191); also Berkeley, *New Theory of Vision*; and Price, *Perception* (London, 1932), pp. 139-46.

[2] *Hume's Theory of the External World*, p. 107.

it is thus a self-contradiction: it is to allege the existence unthought of a pure product of thought.

When he goes on to say, 'but it would only exist *from a certain place*', this contradiction is underlined. To speak of something's existing without the mind is to imply that it is part of an independent spatio-temporal world; it is to say that it exists in some place and at some time. But it can mean nothing intelligible to say that it exists *from* some place (the italicized word obviously not being used in its Shakespearean sense of 'away from', or 'in some *other*' place). It can, of course, be *seen* from one place to exist in another, but then whatever it is that exists at the place from which it is seen depends for its existence on the seeing. This is true even if we admit the principles of relativity which destroy the conception of simple location. We may regard the place at which something exists as relative to an event at some other place and may be unable to specify where anything is absolutely, without being committed to the unintelligible phrase that it exists from a place. All that Price's phrase can mean, then, is that from the place where I see a flat and perspectively distorted shape, I or anyone else always would see it if we looked.[1] But neither can we determine the place nor what can be seen from it apart from what I or somebody else sees, thinks or imagines, and what exists there when *nobody* looks may be described by a physicist as a certain pattern of waves in the ether (or in some other appropriate way) but neither is this a flat, perspectively distorted shape, nor is it anything the existence of which (apart from the mind of the physicist) we have any right to assume in the present discussion without begging the question at issue.

(ii) Price goes on [2] to set out a theory according to which *sensibilia*, whether sensed or not, are generated in a continuous stream of momentary particulars and when the consecutive members of the series are sufficiently alike we (loosely) say that the particular *sensibile* persists. When the resemblance is gradually decreased we say that the *sensibile* is the same, though it has been somewhat modified; and when there is a marked and sudden difference we say that the *sensibile* has been annihilated and a new one has taken its place. Such generation may be supposed to go on 'autonomously' when no sense-organ, nervous system or brain is concerned in its generation and to be dependent upon these organic concomitants only when the *sensibilia* are sensed. However odd or distorted the sensed particulars may be, if they are sufficiently like those unsensed, autonomously produced, particulars

---

[1] This is what is meant by saying that an *aspect* exists from a certain point of view. No aspect exists which is not experienced.   [2] *Ibid.* pp. 111-13 and 126-9.

which precede and follow them, they may be regarded as continuous with them. So that though the distorted or illusory *sensibilia* may be dependent on the human organism, we may nevertheless be permitted to call them the same as the unsensed *sensibilia* which precede and which follow. The evidence from distortion, etc., adduced by Hume and Berkeley, therefore, is insufficient to disprove the existence of unsensed *sensibilia*.

Passing over the metaphysical difficulties involved in the continuity of a series of separate particulars, we must ask at once how we can have any criterion of likeness and difference as between the sensed and the unsensed portions of the series? How could they ever be compared? To speak of unsensed particulars, in a series, resembling those which are sensed is simply to imagine other members of the series similar to those we sense. But it is impossible to imagine them unimagined; and if it were possible, we could not then speak of resemblance, for they could resemble each other in nothing but sensed quality. If, therefore, resemblance is to be the qualification for membership of the same series, it is clear that no unsensed particulars can belong to a series containing sense-data; and no resemblance between sensed particulars can ever serve as evidence for the existence of unsensed particulars similar to them. Nor does it even give a pretext for assuming their existence as an hypothesis, for the hypothesis would not, strictly speaking, be intelligible. 'An idea', says Berkeley,[1] 'can be like nothing but an idea', and not even Professor Price's ingenuity can explain such resemblance and still leave unsensed *sensibilia* secure in their isolation from the knowing mind.

(iii) I need not discuss the cases in which Price admits that the *sensibilia* are dependent on the sense-organs and nervous system, except to point out that the hypothesis he suggests that even here the *sensibilia* might exist unsensed [2] is equally subject to the above criticism. But any reference to the body and its nervous system involves the difficulty of principle that Price himself points out and to that I shall pass at once.

(b) Berkeley and Hume are trying to prove by reference to physiological data that things do not exist external to the mind. But if their conclusion is sound their premises must be false, for if there are no external things, there are no physiological facts from which to reason. We must confess that both these philosophers do commit this error; but if we afford them the sort of charity which Price himself recommends,[3] if we attempt to interpret them in the spirit as well as barely in the letter, we can see what they were getting at and how they might have

---

[1] *Principles*, I, 8.   [2] *Op. cit.* pp. 114 f.   [3] *Op. cit.* pp. 3 f.

met this criticism. The existence of bodies, sense-organs and nerves, they would say, is commonly assumed but we have no indubitable knowledge of it.[1] All that we know directly are our sense-impression and ideas, and these are so variable and inconstant that no evidence whatsoever can be derived from them that they represent or resemble any persistent independent existences at all. In short, they have not any of the characteristics we commonly assume in permanently and inde-pendently existing things. Our belief in these must therefore be derived from some source within the mind itself and there is nothing to show that anything outside our own consciousness corresponds to it. Price himself almost suggests this answer;[2] but instead of stating the case in this way, he concludes that the causal connections implied in the argument for the dependence on the nervous system of sense-impres-sions cannot then be established. Of course it cannot. But if we realize this we can dispense with the argument altogether and maintain the non-existence of unsensed *sensibilia* on the strength of the very irregularity of occurrence of those which are sensed. What Price does not realize is that the 'constancy' and 'coherence' among our im-pressions, which Hume describes as the basis of the imaginative construction of an independently existing world, is itself undermined by the objection to deriving causal laws from unsupplemented sense-impressions. In his own words: 'The sense-impressions, if we take them just as they come, are far too few and fragmentary. We must fill up the gaps in them by postulating unsensed sensibilia if we are to be aware of any constant conjunctions. There are no constant conjunc-tions of pure and unsupplemented sense-impressions.'[3] But if this is the case, the character of coherence disappears altogether from among our sense-impressions, for no series will ever be repeated, even in part, sufficiently to provide the conditions of what Price calls 'gap-indiffer-ence'.[4] Of the series ABCDE, not only may A . . . DE and AB . . . E occur, but also ED . . . A and even DE . . . A (as when I observe a man approaching the porter's lodge, in the last stages of his progress across the quadrangle, and again, after an interruption, as he disappears up the hall stairs, in the last stages of his return). The various conjunc-tions of sense-impressions will be entirely random and the conditions of 'gap-indifference' will not obtain. Further, Price admits that 'coher-ence' is really prior to 'constancy', as without coherence mere resem-blance of separated particulars produces no sufficient basis for gap-indifference.[5] Apart from 'constancy' and 'coherence', however, and

---

[1] Cf. Descartes, *Medit.* I. [2] *Op. cit.* pp. 116-20.
[3] *Ibid.* p. 116. [4] *Ibid.* pp. 60-71. [5] *Ibid.* p. 67.

the gap-indifference that they induce, we have no pretext, according to the theories either of Hume or of Price, for postulating unsensed *sensibilia*. But to pursue the matter further would carry me too far from the discussion of Berkeley and enough has already been said to show that his doctrine does not succumb to criticisms such as those which I have examined.

Berkeley's theory emerges unscathed from the attacks of such critics as these because all of them, in one way or another, attempt to return to a position similar to that of Locke. The modern version of this position may briefly be stated as follows: Consciousness is the result of a relation between the mind and something else which is not mind—something one can hardly describe otherwise than as an 'external' object. Though, obviously, we never are conscious of any such object which does not in fact stand in this relation to a mind, and though there may not even happen to be any such, yet it is not only conceivable that the existence of the object is not dependent upon the relation, but if it were so dependent we could not properly be said to *know* the object. Now this position is just as untenable as is Locke's and for the same reason. If the object of consciousness is 'external' and exists independently of its relation to the mind, then it exists independently of consciousness, for that belongs wholly to the mind and depends for its existence wholly upon it. But in that case the object would be *excluded* from consciousness and could never be known at all, for as soon as it is included in consciousness it becomes something different which is mind-dependent. The error lies in regarding consciousness and object as two separate terms connected by a relation, whereas consciousness is constituted by the relation and includes both its terms. We never can assert a relation one term of which is unknowable, much less can we regard knowledge as resulting from such a relation. It is the recognition of this fact which is Berkeley's permanent contribution to philosophy, and the neglect of it is the cause of the failure of his modern critics.

III. SHORTCOMINGS OF BERKELEY'S THEORY

6. But the difficulties of Berkeley's position are none the less formidable and though his doctrine survives the attacks from realist quarters, there are other criticisms to which it is vulnerable and our very appreciation of his achievement makes us aware of the defect in his system which brings about its downfall and makes its supersession inevitable. The problem of relating the mind to nature he solved by making nature the creation of the mind—not the finite mind of any human being, but

the infinite mind of God, who communicates His ideas to men in the form of perceptions. But when we reflect more closely upon the relation of the finite mind of man to the infinite mind of God, and of our perceptions to whatever it is that exists in God's mind, we can find nothing that will serve the required purpose of making intelligible man's knowledge of a world of which his own mind is one finite member.

According to Berkeley, objects are known to us as ideas; but we have no ideas of spirits and are said to have 'notions' of them derived from our intuitions of the existence and operation of our own minds. By analogy from this, we infer to the existence of other finite minds from the perceptions we have of their effects in action.[1] So, likewise, from the 'Works of Nature', which in their harmony, order and beauty, we are conscious do not depend for their production on our own wills, we infer to the existence of an Infinite Spirit, who produces the ideas of them in us.[2] All the choir of heaven and furniture of earth consist of ideas, but the relations between ideas as well as the existence of spirits are known, not by ideas, but by notions.[3] To distinguish among these between the true and the false, the real and the imaginary, we must depend on the 'settled order' in which God produces the ideas of natural objects in our minds. Their objectivity consists solely in their existence in the eternal mind of God and the settled order in which He chooses to produce them in us. But the order is simply a matter of His choice, and when He wishes He does (on rare occasions) depart from it and produce a miracle 'to surprise and awe men into an acknowledgement of the Divine Being'. In this settled order, moreover, there is nothing necessary. We know it all by observation only and not by discovering any connection between our ideas.[4] How then do the ideas which constitute the entire spectacle of the natural world exist in the mind of God?

When I see a man, Berkeley tells us, I do not see 'that which lives, moves, perceives and thinks', but only 'a collection of ideas' which are his body and its movements, and from which I infer from the analogy of my own movements to the existence of his mind. But if these ideas are not to be delusory they must exist also in the mind of God and must be produced in me by Him. In God's mind, however, they cannot

---

[1] *Vide Principles*, I, 145.   [2] *Ibid.* I, 146.   [3] *Ibid.* I, 89.
[4] Cf. *ibid.* I, 31: 'That food nourishes, sleep refreshes, and fire warms us; that to sow in the seed-time is the way to reap in the harvest; and in general that to obtain such or such ends, such or such means are conducive—all this we know, not by discovering any *necessary connexion* between our ideas, but only by the observation of the *settled laws* of nature'.

be ideas of the man's body, for that, as such, does not exist, and the same is true of any other body as it is of the human frame. Bodies are only collections of ideas in *our* minds produced in them by God; but what can they be in God's mind? They cannot be perceptions passively received, for God is not passive and there is nothing, neither material substance nor yet another Infinite Spirit, which could produce such ideas in His mind. Thus, despite what Berkeley frequently says of them, they cannot be ideas at all like ours. In God, therefore, they can have no representative content and can be only acts of His will producing ideas in us which are particular and subjective to our minds. *Our* ideas cannot exist in the mind of God at all and we cannot rightly be said to perceive what is in His mind when we perceive what is true. As a source of objectivity, therefore, identity between our ideas and those of God will not serve and the criterion of truth must be sought elsewhere.

7. The only clue we have to the way in which God produces ideas in us is what we can observe of the settled order of nature. But, if our ideas are mere particulars they can constitute no order of any kind. For that they must, as Berkeley rightly holds, occur in accordance with settled laws. But if there is no necessary connection between them, the will of God by which they are produced must be an arbitrary will subject to no laws at all. Moreover, if our ideas are all purely particular, they cannot recur, nor can two of them even be similar unless there is some element of identity uniting them. But Berkeley provides no universal element and no connections, so that the repetitions of conjunctions between them, the observation of which is necessary to our perception of a settled order in their occurrence, would, on his principles, be impossible.

Further, such order as might be presumed is frequently interrupted by the interpolation of fortuitous ideas produced by the imagination, and not every such interpolation (to take dream as only one example) is dependent on the will. Again, the knowledge which I have of my own willing is not an idea, it is only a notion, and we are not told how notions rank as knowledge or how we can distinguish by means of them between true ideas and false. It is, in fact, difficult to see how my notions of my own mind and its operations can help me to distinguish its effects from those produced in it by God, for to do that is to discriminate among my ideas those which I myself produce and those which I do not. But the ideas which are supposed to be dependent on my will do not differ intrinsically from those which are not so dependent, and the fact that they accompany my acts of volition is no evidence of any connection between them and those acts. On the contrary, unless I know the content of the idea (what it is an idea of), I cannot will to have it, nor can I so much as know what it is that I am supposed to be willing. The actual experiencing of the idea, therefore, can never be dependent on the volition. All that can be said is that volition sometimes accompanies certain of my ideas, but so far from excluding these ideas from reality, I explicitly claim reality for those which are evidence of my own overt acts. The will, therefore, supplies us with no means of distinguishing between ideas that belong to the settled order of nature and ideas which are purely fantastic.

In short, we are reduced to an experience which is purely subjective, in which there are no valid principles of order and so no means of deciding what is produced in us by God and what is purely fortuitous. Our standards of objectivity have dissolved away and truth and error have become indistinguishable. But in going so far we have come more than half-way to the philosophy of Hume in which this development of Berkeley is made explicit.

Chapter VIII

THE COLLAPSE OF EMPIRICISM

1. THE 'AWFUL WARNING'

1. 'DURING the Absolute Idealist period, which ended early in the present century, Hume was the great bogeyman, and the duty of all self-respecting philosophers was to refute him. In our own days things are different.... People now read the *Treatise* not as an awful warning, but as a source of stimulus and illumination.' So writes Professor Price,[1] and for my own part I must agree that the *Treatise* has always been for me a source of stimulus and illumination, but what it chiefly illuminates is the catastrophic consequences of the Lockian empiricism, and it should therefore stand for all future philosophers as an awful warning. So far from attempting to refute Hume (which seems to me to be what Price persistently attempts to do), what they should realize is that he was (so far as he went) perfectly right, and, above all, that he was actually and professedly a thorough-going sceptic. Price and others have passed by the 'awful warning' by treating it as a sort of joke.

> 'Though he sometimes tries to shock us', says Price, 'by calling himself a sceptic, he is very far from holding that there is nothing much to choose between superstition and science, myth and history, delirium and sanity. Those who think that he wants to deny these distinctions (despite his own express words to the contrary) are so debauched with learning and High Seriousness that they cannot recognize irony when they meet it; and so unphilosophical that they cannot see the difference between rejecting a proposition, and rejecting those analyses of it with which they happen to be most familiar.'[2]

Let us turn for one moment to Hume's own express words:

> 'The *intense* view of these manifold contradictions and imperfections in human reason has so wrought upon me, and heated my brain, that I am ready to reject all belief and reasoning, and can look upon no opinion even as more probable or likely than another. Where am I, or what? From what causes do I derive my existence, and to what condition shall I return? Whose favour shall I court, and whose anger must I dread? What beings

[1] In 'The Permanent Significance of Hume's Philosophy', *Philosophy*, XV, No. 57 (January 1940).
[2] *Hume's Theory of the External World*, pp. 139 f.

164

surround me? and on whom have I any influence, or who have any influence on me? I am confounded with all these questions, and begin to fancy myself in the most deplorable condition imaginable, inviron'd with the deepest darkness, and utterly depriv'd of the use of every member and faculty.'[1]

This does not read like irony and we need no learned debauchery to take Hume at his word when he offers as the only cure for 'this philosophical melancholy and delirium' an 'indolent belief in the general maxims of the world', which is itself insufficient to rid him of an inclination to throw all his books and papers into the fire. The view that Hume is doing no more than offer alternative analyses of certain propositions is itself the result of wearing philosophical blinkers, which Price (in his weaker moments) borrows from Logical Positivism, but discussion of this point belongs more properly to what follows.

It would consume too much space to enter into a detailed account of Hume's theory. All that I shall try to do is to show that it professes to be and is one of unmitigated scepticism, both as it is stated and in what it implies, and that it derives both logically and historically from the position inherited from Locke and Berkeley.

II. HUME'S INHERITANCE FROM LOCKE AND BERKELEY

2. Locke had taught that all knowledge originates from simple ideas of sensation; these Hume calls 'impressions' and he distinguishes them from 'ideas' by the force and violence with which they 'strike upon the mind'. The ideas are faint images of these which are formed in thinking and between them they exhaust 'all the perceptions of the human mind'. This is Locke's starting-point and Hume, in accepting it, is far too astute a philosopher to suggest any source or cause of our impressions and so to step beyond the limit set upon our knowledge. Their causes, he maintains, are unknown. But, inasmuch as impressions are the originals of all our knowledge, Hume lays down the general principle 'that all our simple ideas in their first appearance are derived from simple impressions, which are correspondent to them and which they exactly represent'.[2] In order to understand any idea, therefore, it is necessary to trace it to its origin and examine the impression from which it is derived.[3]

---

[1] *Treatise*, Bk. I, Pt. iv, Sect. vii (Selby-Bigge, pp. 268 f.). The entire Section is relevant.
[2] *Ibid.* Bk. I, Pt. i, Sect. i (Selby-Bigge, p. 4).
[3] Cf. *ibid.* Bk. I, Pt. iii, Sect. ii (Selby-Bigge, pp. 74-5).

Locke's classification of ideas into those of sensation and reflection, and into simple and complex, is taken over intact and applied also to impressions; and from Berkeley Hume accepts and confirms in a way which he hopes 'will put it beyond all doubt and controversy' the doctrine that there are no abstract ideas and that 'general ideas are nothing but particular ones, annexed to a certain term, which gives them a more extensive signification, and makes them recall upon occasion other individuals, which are similar to them'. Locke, as we have already seen, had declared that every one of our ideas is a particular existence, and Hume, with his clear and incisive mind, proceeds at once to draw the consequence 'that whatever objects are different are distinguishable, and whatever objects are distinguishable are separable by thought and imagination',[1] and that the converse is likewise true. He goes even further and maintains that what is separable by thought or imagination may be considered as separately existent.[2] 'Every distinct perception, which enters into the composition of the mind,' he says, 'is a distinct existence.'[3]

3. With Berkeley, Hume rejects the idea of material substance as an 'unintelligible chimera'; and of the idea of external existence I shall quote what he says at more length, so that we may be in no doubt as to his opinion.

'Now since nothing is ever present to the mind but perceptions, and since all ideas are deriv'd from something antecedently present to the mind; it follows, that 'tis impossible for us so much as to conceive or form an idea of anything specifically different from ideas and impressions. Let us fix our attention out of ourselves as much as possible: Let us chace our imagination to the heavens, or to the utmost limits of the universe; we never really advance a step beyond ourselves, nor can conceive any kind of existence, but those perceptions, which have appear'd in that narrow compass. This is the universe of the imagination, nor have we any idea but what is there produc'd.'[4]

4. One more feature of Hume's inheritance from Locke and Berkeley need be mentioned. Professor Price has said[5] that it is a gross error to think that Hume denied the existence of necessary connections, and

---

[1] *Treatise*, Bk. I, Pt. i, Sect. vii (Selby-Bigge, p. 18).
[2] *Ibid.* Bk. I, Pt. iv, Sect. ii (Selby-Bigge, p. 207).
[3] *Ibid.* Bk. I, Pt. iv, Sect. vi (Selby-Bigge, p. 259).
[4] *Ibid.* Bk. I, Pt. ii, Sect. vi (Selby-Bigge, pp. 67 f.).
[5] 'The Permanent Significance of Hume's Philosophy', *Philosophy*, XV, No. 57, p. 17.

Professor Ayer that, so far from denying causation, Hume was concerned only to define it.[1] But why they should be so concerned about Hume's alleged denials and not at all about similar denials by Locke and Berkeley it is difficult to understand; unless it is that the perilous consequences of the denials only emerge in Hume's philosophy and, if taken seriously, they are as disastrous to 20th as to 18th century empiricism. Hume's attitude to causation and necessary connection is no more than the development, more consistent and more penetrating no doubt, of what had already been adumbrated in Locke and Berkeley. Locke writes,[2] '. . . to have the idea of cause and effect, it suffices to consider any simple idea or substance, as beginning to exist, by the operation of some other, without knowing the manner of that operation'. And he frequently contends that the various qualities that are constantly conjoined in a particular substance have mutually no essential connection: '. . . the simple ideas whereof our complex ideas of substances are made up are, for the most part, such as carry with them, in their own nature, no *visible* necessary connexion or inconsistency with any other simple ideas, whose co-existence with them we would inform ourselves about'[3] . . . 'it is impossible we should know which have a *necessary* union or inconsistency one with another'.[4] Berkeley is even more definite in his denial both of causation and of necessary connection. He maintains that passive and inert things (even if they be assumed) can exercise no causation, no activity or efficacy,[5] nor yet can passively received ideas: '. . . the connexion of ideas does not imply the relation of *cause* and *effect*, but only of a mark or *sign* of the *thing signified*. The fire which I see is not the cause of the pain I suffer upon my approaching it, but the mark that forewarns me of it . . .'[6] and so on. That food nourishes and fire warms, that seeds sown in seedtime may be reaped in harvest and that certain means conduce to certain ends, 'all this', Berkeley tells us, 'we know, not by discovering any *necessary connexion* between our ideas, but only by the observation of the *settled laws* of nature'.[7] Hume's theories of causation and necessary connection, therefore, were not entirely original, though they are no less credit to him for that reason; and whether they amount to the denial of the existence of the principles or merely a new definition of them, I shall consider presently. At least, it seems fairly plain that Berkeley made no scruple to deny them.

There are many more traces of the influence of Locke and Berkeley

[1] *Language, Truth and Logic*, 2nd ed., p. 54.   [2] *Essay*, II, xxvi, 2.
[3] *Ibid.* IV, iii, 10.   [4] *Ibid.* 11. Cf. also III, vi, 5-6, and IV, iii, 16.
[5] *Vide Principles*, I, 61.   [6] *Ibid.* I, 65.   [7] *Ibid.* I, 31.

in Hume's writing than I have mentioned; in fact, these three philosophers are so close in their mutual relations that it is difficult, in dealing with Berkeley or Hume, to impose a strict limit upon what is
derivative and distinguish it sharply from what is original. It is wiser,
perhaps, to realize that by philosophers of this stature the whole treatment of their subject is original, though no man's work is free from
debt both to his predecessors and to his contemporaries. Our question
is not what Hume invented for himself in his theory of knowledge, but
what sort of a theory he evolved out of the 'first beginnings and
materials' left to him by Locke and Berkeley.

III. ANALYSIS OR DENIAL?

5. Hume distinguishes seven kinds of philosophical relation and
divides them into two classes, those which do and those which do not
depend upon the ideas 'compared together'. Those which depend
upon the ideas are the foundations of exact science and, of those which
do not, only that of causation can serve as a principle of inference
beyond what is immediately present to the senses. He follows Locke in
confining intuition and demonstration to the relations which depend
upon the ideas, whereas our opinions about matter of fact, which,
according to Locke, pass under the name of knowledge, are acquired in
a different way.[1] I shall consider the question later to what extent
Hume is entitled to separate these two sorts of knowledge and whether
what is true of inference in the one case will not affect the nature of
inference in the other. It is sufficient, here, to note that causation
alone enables us to go beyond what is immediately present to the
senses, and to observe that if this fails to give us reliable knowledge,
all our conceptions of the world of material things are liable to
disintegrate.

Hume analyses the relation of cause and effect into contiguity,
succession and necessary connection and the last of these, he finds, is
neither a quality of the objects connected nor a recognizable relation
between them, nor can he find at the first attempt any impression from
which the idea has been derived. He then proceeds to examine the
nature of the inference from the impression or idea of the cause, in any
particular case, to the idea of the effect (or, when appropriate, from
effect to cause); and he finds that this cannot be demonstration, for
any two distinct ideas are separable and so can be thought of as existing

[1] Cf. Hume, *Treatise*, Bk. I, Pt. iii, Sect. i, and *Enquiry concerning Human Understanding*, Sect. iv, 20-1.

THE COLLAPSE OF EMPIRICISM

separately and there is no contradiction involved in the notion of a different predecessor or successor to any given idea or impression. The connection must, therefore, be learned from experience. We are able to make the inference from one to the other only because we find them constantly conjoined. But there we are met with the difficulty of inductive reasoning—How can we know that future occurrences will be similar to those of the past? Hume maintains that we cannot; neither can we demonstrate it, for it is never inconceivable that the conjunction should *not* recur, nor can we argue that it is even probable that the future should resemble the past, for we could only regard it as probable on the ground that our past experience bears it out. To argue from probability is thus a *petitio principii*. Reasoning from cause to effect, therefore, is neither *a priori* nor *a posteriori*, it is neither demonstrative nor empirical, in short, it is not reasoning at all.[1] The inference from the existence of one thing to that of another turns out to be based upon no rational principle but only upon a psychological law of imaginative association. 'Had ideas no more union in the fancy', says Hume, 'than objects seem to have to the understanding, we cou'd never draw any inferences from causes to effects, nor repose belief in any matter of fact.'

The inference from cause to effect or *vice versa*, we are later told, is the result of a habit of association formed by the imagination on the repeated experience of their conjunction, and the impression from which the idea of necessary connection is derived is the impression of reflection formed by introspection of the 'determination' of the mind by custom to imagine either the cause or the effect on experiencing the impression or idea of the other. There is no 'real' connection between them, or if there is it is something utterly unknown[2] and the transition of our imagination from one to the other is something entirely subjective. The constant repetition of the conjunction makes the transition easier and so imparts more force and liveliness from the impression to the associated idea and this heightened liveliness Hume finds to be the distinguishing feature of belief. Thus when we experience the impression of the cause (or the effect) we not only call up the idea of the effect (or cause) but also believe in its existence. It is not surprising, therefore, to find Hume deriving prejudice from the same source as reason,[3] for, as he says himself, 'all reasonings are nothing but the effects of

---

[1] Cf. *Treatise*, Bk. I, Pt. iii, Sect. vi: 'Reason can never shew us the connexion of one object with another, tho' aided by experience, and the observation of their constant conjunction in all past instances'. (Selby-Bigge, p. 92.)

[2] *Vide ibid.* p. 102.

[3] *Vide ibid.* Bk. I, Pt. iii, Sect. xiii (Selby-Bigge, pp. 146-7).

custom'[1] and any cause of greater vivacity in our ideas will have the same effect.

6. We may now consider whether what we have here is only a new analysis of necessary connection or a denial of it, whether Hume has merely defined causation or whether, in effect, he has abolished it. That he has analysed the conception of cause and effect is obvious, but the question still remains whether the factors into which he has analysed it do not exclude the one thing essential. Hume himself asserts that contiguity and succession are insufficient, by themselves, to constitute causation—'an object may be contiguous and prior to another without being considered as its cause'—and that necessary connection is 'of much greater importance'.[2] If then necessary connection does not exist neither does causation and the question resolves itself into whether Hume's account of necessary connection does or does not amount to its denial.

So far as objects are concerned the answer is clear and immediate. 'Necessity', says Hume, 'is something that exists in the mind, not in objects; nor is it possible for us ever to form the most distant idea of it, consider'd as a quality in bodies.'[3] 'All events', he says in the *Enquiry*,[4] 'seem entirely loose and separate. One event follows another; but we never can observe any tie between them. They seem *conjoined*, but never *connected*.' Between objects, therefore, necessary connection is denied. And these objects, we must remember, are not 'external' to the mind. We have already seen what Hume's view is of the idea of external existence and shall shortly find more evidence in favour of his rejecting that notion altogether. They are ideas and impressions between which we can find no necessary connection.

In what way, then, does necessity exist in the mind? Hume says that it is 'an internal impression of the mind, or a determination to carry our thoughts from one object to another',[5] an impression of reflection that 'belongs entirely to the soul'; it is a feeling of expectation or of habitual transition, what Price calls the feeling of 'of-course-ness'. But such a feeling is in itself no bond between the ideas conjoined. A law of imaginative association produces no necessary connection between the associated impressions, and even the principle of association remains a mystery. This is admitted by Hume himself. 'The uniting principle among our internal perceptions', he tells us, 'is as unintelligible as that among external objects, and is not known to us any other way than by

---

[1] *Treatise*, p. 149.   [2] *Ibid.* p. 77.   [3] *Ibid.* pp. 165 f.
[4] Selby-Bigge, p. 74.   [5] *Treatise, loc. cit.*

experience.'[1] But by experience, as we saw, we cannot come by any idea of necessary connection; surely, then, we may conclude that there is no such thing. Hume has analysed cause and effect into contiguity, succession and a feeling of expectation, and the connection between any of these is as loose as that between any two ideas or impressions of which we are capable. Apart from pure mathematics and logic, therefore, nowhere in our experience does any necessity exist, and we cannot be satisfied with the view that Hume has simply analysed the notion of necessary connection, for the account which he has given of it explains it away altogether. Nor can we accept the opinion that he was concerned only with defining causation, for, on his own admission, that does not exist without necessary connection.[2]

IV. THE ECLIPSE OF REASON

7. But if the sole principle of all our reasonings concerning matters of fact is reduced to a subjective feeling of expectedness, the distinction between superstition and science becomes so blurred as almost to disappear; and though Price contends that Hume is far from holding that there is nothing to choose between them, many of Hume's examples belie that opinion, as may be gathered from a perusal of those chapters of the *Treatise*[3] which deal with the effects of other relations than that of cause and effect in producing belief and with the influence of belief itself. Moreover, all judgement and inference is identified by Hume with belief,[4] and that is induced by anything which produces an increase in the vivacity of our ideas. Hume never gives us any clear criterion for distinguishing one sort of belief, as scientific, from any other sort; and if he holds a preference for one above another, it can, on his own showing, be no more than a prejudice. 'Thus', he says, 'all probable reasoning is nothing but a species of sensation. 'Tis not solely in poetry and music, we must follow our taste and sentiment, but likewise in philosophy. When I am convinc'd of any principle, 'tis only an idea, which strikes more strongly upon me. When I give the preference

---

[1] *Ibid.* p. 169. The distinction here between 'internal perceptions' and 'external objects' is intended to be parallel to that between impressions of reflection and those of sensation; it does not imply externality to the mind.

[2] Cf. Kant, *Kritik der reinen Vernunft*, B5: '... *ja in dem letzteren enthält selbst der Begriff einer Ursache so offenbar den Begriff einer Notwendigkeit der Verknüpfung mit einer Wirkung und einer strengen Allgemeinheit der Regel ... gänzlich verlorengehen würde, wenn man ihn, wie Hume tat, von einer öftern Beigesellung dessen was geschieht, mit dem, was vorhergeht, und einer daraus entspringenden Gewohnheit (mithin bloss subjektiven Notwendigkeit) Vorstellungen zu verknüpfen, ableiten wollte*'.

[3] Bk. I, Pt. iii, Sects. ix and x. [4] *Vide Treatise*, p. 96 n.

to one set of arguments above another, I do nothing but decide from my feeling concerning the superiority of their influence.'[1]

8. All that has been said so far concerns only 'probable reasoning' about matters of fact; but Hume maintains that all reasoning ultimately resolves itself into probability, that though the rules of the demonstrative sciences are certain and infallible, the weakness of our powers of reasoning causes us to err so that our calculations have always to be checked, and repeated checkings can at best be only means of increasing the probability of correctness in the conclusion. Yet as the same arguments affect our judgements concerning our own possibilities of error as well as those by which we check our original reasonings, our thinking progressively reduces the probability of the knowledge that is held to result from it. Consequently, by reasoning alone, our beliefs would be reduced by stages to nothing, if it were not that 'nature by an absolute and uncontrollable necessity has determined us to judge as well as to breathe and feel'.[2] The source and nature of this 'uncontrollable necessity' is not explained, but it is quite clear that Hume's attitude to ratiocination is entirely sceptical.

If we apply his principles just a little further, however, we find reason for being even more sceptical. Hume, unfortunately, tells us little about the character or principles of demonstrative reasoning. We gather that it is closely allied to intuition and, like that form of knowledge, is concerned only with the comparison of ideas and the relations between them which depend intrinsically upon them. In this he follows Locke, who held that we are able to intuit immediately certain relations between ideas which are held before the mind, and that demonstration consists, as it were, of a string of such intuitions by means of which two ideas are related together through intermediaries, the relations between every pair being perceived intuitively. So Hume tells us that 'the necessity, which makes two times two equal to four, or three angles of a triangle equal to two right ones, lies only in the act of the understanding, by which we consider and compare these ideas'.[3] The rejection of abstract ideas, however, entails the impossibility of our ever comparing anything but particulars; and, though an act of the understanding which compares them may reveal an agreement or resemblance between them, it can provide no basis for generalization from those which it compares, or for the assertion of any universal judgement. It can reveal no necessary connection between these particulars and any

---

[1] *Treatise*, p. 103.
[2] *Ibid*. Bk. I, Pt. iv, Sect. i (Selby-Bigge, p. 183).   [3] *Ibid*. p. 166.

others. That the angles of a particular triangle are found equal to two right angles is no proof that this is true of all triangles.

Again, Hume allows precision to the sciences of Algebra and Arithmetic[1] solely on the ground that the unit is a reliable standard of comparison of quantities. But here he departs from his own principles, for, it may be asked, from what impression do we get the idea of a unit? Any impression or idea of the larger objects of our acquaintance can be regarded equally well as one, as a fraction, or as a sum. A finger, for instance, is at once a unit, one-fifth of those contained in a hand, and three knuckle joints. We cannot separate these aspects by what Hume calls a distinction of reason[2] because that involves separate resemblances to other objects and (with one exception) all other objects are similarly ambiguous as regards number. The one exception and the only impression from which the idea of unity could arise is that of the *minimum sensibile*. But here again we are met by serious difficulty. The only idea that can be derived from an impression is a paler, but otherwise exact, copy of the impression itself. If, therefore, the idea of a unit is derived from that of a *minimum sensibile* it can only be a paler image of the *sensibile* itself, and no one would suggest that what the arithmetician does is to count and compare the numbers of his mental images of *minima sensibilia*. Hume himself asserts that this is impossible; 'this standard of equality', he declares, 'is entirely *useless*, and . . . it never is from such a comparison we determine objects to be equal or unequal with respect to each other'.[3] Where then do we find an infallible standard of comparison between particular ideas? Even if we could compare particulars accurately, as when we say that two fingers plus two more are equal to four fingers, how can we assume with any degree of certainty that this will be the case in all instances?—for there is no necessary connection between these impressions or ideas which we compare and any others that may subsequently arise. The necessity that belongs to mathematics, therefore, is no more secure than that which belongs to cause and effect, and it is difficult to see what can be the source of the certain and infallible rules which Hume attributes to the demonstrative sciences.

9. There remains the question of necessity in logic and with this Hume deals briefly but conclusively in a footnote.[4] Judgement and inference, he maintains, are the same as conception: they are, all of them, 'nothing but particular ways of conceiving our objects', whether

---

[1] *Ibid.* Bk. I, Pt. iii, Sect. i, p. 71.   [2] *Vide ibid.* p. 25.
[3] *Ibid.* p. 45.   [4] *Ibid.* p. 96.

we contemplate one, or several, or run from one to others. In some cases, however, we join belief to our contemplation of the suggested ideas and this is nothing more than an increase in their vivacity. All inference, accordingly, is of the same kind as that from cause to effect; in fact, Hume says that causal inference 'is not only a true species of reasoning, but *the strongest of all others*,[1] and more convincing than when we interpose another idea to connect the two extremes'. *A fortiori*, therefore, necessary connection can no more exist in logic than in probable reasoning about matters of fact, and all inference is equally affected, whether it be demonstrative or inductive.

V. OUR KNOWLEDGE OF AN EXTERNAL WORLD

With both deductive and inductive reasoning thus disposed of, there is only sense-perception left as a source of knowledge. Let us next consider Hume's opinion of its efficacy as an instrument and the value as knowledge of the conception we derive from it of the world in which we live.

10. Here we find that the situation is, if anything, even worse than in the case of pure reasoning, for here our reason and our senses come into conflict and all our attempts to reconcile them serve only to increase the confusion. Our belief in the existence of bodies is something which we hold simply because Nature has left us no choice. We believe by a sort of instinct that they exist and we cannot in any way maintain the truth of the belief.

The question, 'Whether there be body or not', Hume sets aside as impossible to answer.[2] He concerns himself only with the reasons which induce us to believe that there are bodies, and he concludes that all of them are bad reasons, that we have no valid reason at all, but in our habitual state of 'carelessness and inattention' our natural propensity to take for granted the existence of an external world reasserts itself.

Briefly, Hume's exposition proceeds as follows. The belief in the existence of bodies resolves itself into two distinct but mutually implicated propositions: (a) that our objects continue to exist when they are

[1] My italics.
[2] Price interprets Hume as meaning that it is psychologically impossible to doubt that there are bodies; he then criticizes him for doing so, and re-interprets his statement as saying that the question is meaningless (*vide Hume's Theory of the External World*, pp. 11-13). But, if we take what Hume says here along with what I quoted earlier from the *Treatise* (Bk. I, Pt. ii, Sect. vi, pp. 67 f.), it is clear that what he means is that the question is unanswerable, because we have no means of knowing anything except ideas and impressions. Consequently, ''tis vain to ask'.

not perceived, and (b) that their existence is distinct from and independent of our perception. For neither of these propositions can any evidence be given by the senses, for obviously the senses cannot operate 'even after they have ceas'd all manner of operation', and so cannot reveal any continued existence of their objects when they are not perceived; nor do they give any but single perceptions, and so cannot suggest any likeness to external archetypes existing independently of the mind. They cannot present objects as external to 'ourselves' because we cannot perceive 'ourselves' by sense, nor to our bodies because the external and independent existence of our bodies presents precisely the same problem as does that of all other bodies. Finally, our sensations do not appear as external to the mind (sounds, smells and tastes obviously do not and visual sensations not immediately) but are referred to external objects only as a result of inference and experience.

Equally reason is not the source of our belief in the continued and independent existence of objects. Not only do the vulgar believe without any knowledge of the arguments put forward by philosophers, but they believe what is contrary to those arguments. For they attribute continued and independent existence to the perceptions themselves, whereas the philosophers affirm that these are dependent on the mind while they postulate objects corresponding to them which are independent. Yet whether or not we distinguish the external and persistent objects from the perceptions, we have no grounds for inference from the latter to the existence of the former. We can infer to existence only by means of the relation of cause and effect, and the knowledge of that is acquired only from the experience of the constant conjunction of the objects; but as nothing but perceptions is ever present to the mind, we can experience conjunctions only between them and never between a perception and an unperceived object.

It is, therefore, solely due to the imagination that we come to think of continuously and independently existing bodies, for our perceptions are notoriously fragmentary and discontinuous and it is only by imaginative supplementation that we arrive at the notion of continuous existence. Such supplementation is induced by two characteristics observable in some of our impressions: namely, coherence and constancy. The first is an appearance of regular dependence upon one another and the second is the constant reappearance of similar perceptions. The first provides the foundation for a sort of argument from cause and effect, but it goes beyond this and attributes a regularity of conjunction to the objects beyond what is experienced. The second provides the imagination with a relationship between the disparate impressions (that of resemblance) which enables it to run easily from one to the other, and so it tends to identify the separate impressions and to attribute continued existence to them during the interval between the first and subsequent perceptions. This ascribed continuity is a fiction, but it is believed because the memory of the resemblance imparts vivacity to the imagined existence.

11. In all this, however, what is assumed to exist continuously is the impressions themselves, and the belief in their independent existence follows from it. Yet, even as far as we have gone we are entangled in errors and fallacies, and more and worse are to follow. Hume says that our identification of resembling impressions is a mistake and an illusion,[1] and the continuity which we attribute to similar but interrupted perceptions is a fiction which presently turns out to be a fallacy; for though it is conceivable that a perception may exist separate from the 'heap or collection of different perceptions' that we call a mind, it 'is contrary to the plainest experience'. Here Hume gives a summary statement of the arguments against the existence of unperceived objects to which reference has already been made, most of which are borrowed from Berkeley and all of which are akin to those that Berkeley presents.

Not only are we aware, therefore, that our perceptions are fragmentary and interrupted, but we have, also, strong reasons for believing that their objects cannot exist independently of being perceived. These considerations conflict with the natural propensity which is strong in us to imagine our perceptions as continuing to exist when we do not experience them. Neither can the reason overcome the tendency of the imagination, nor can the imagination altogether stifle the reason. Consequently, we devise the theory that the perceptions are separate from their objects and that, while the first are fleeting and intermittent, the second exist persistently and independently. We also attempt to connect them by relations of causation and resemblance. That the assumed causal relation can have no possible basis has already been shown, and the relation of resemblance is equally unfounded. In short, as Hume puts it, the theory 'is the monstrous offspring of two principles, which are contrary to each other, which are both at once embrac'd by the mind, and which are unable mutually to destroy each other'.[2]

According to Hume, then, our conception of the world of material bodies, including that of the thinker himself, is an elaborate figment of

[1] Cf. *Treatise*, pp. 200, 202, 204 and 209.
[2] *Ibid.* p. 215.

the imagination bolstered up and accredited by vicious arguments and hollow reasoning.

'I cannot conceive', he concludes, 'how such trivial qualities of the fancy, conducted by such false suppositions, can ever lead to any solid and rational system. They are the coherence and constancy of our perceptions, which produce the opinion of their continu'd existence; tho' these quali-ties of perceptions have no perceivable connexion with such an existence. The constancy of our perceptions has the most considerable effect, and yet is attended with the greatest difficulties. 'Tis a gross illusion to suppose, that our resembling perceptions are numerically the same; and 'tis this illusion, which leads us into the opinion, that these perceptions are uninterrupted, and are still existent, even when they are not present to the senses. This is the case with our popular system. And as to our philosophical one, 'tis liable to the same difficulties; and is over-and-above loaded with this absurdity, that it at once denies and establishes the vulgar supposition. Philosophers deny our resembling perceptions to be identi-cally the same, and uninterrupted; and yet have so great a propensity to believe them such, that they arbitrarily invent a new set of perceptions, to which they attribute these qualities. . . . What then can we look for from this confusion of groundless and extraordinary opinions but error and falsehood? And how can we justify to ourselves any belief we repose in them?'

For this desperate state of affairs 'carelessness and inattention alone can afford us any remedy'.[1]

12. This is what Hume actually says. What he ought to have said had he been a pupil of Professor Price may be found in that author's book entitled *Hume's Theory of the External World*. I should be the last to belittle Price's masterly explanation and expansion of Hume's account of coherence and constancy and of the imaginative supplementation of sense-given particulars that they are supposed to occasion. But his corrections of and improvements upon Hume's doctrine suffer, I think, from an oversight. It is an oversight of which Hume himself is guilty; but whereas it does not vitiate Hume's conclusion, the whole plausibility of Price's theory depends upon it.

Price's account of constancy and coherence and his theory of 'gap-indifferent' and 'succession-indifferent' series depend (like Hume's) on the presumption of the repeated occurrence of similars in sensation. It is the resemblance of the sensed portions of interrupted series, to

[1] *Ibid.* pp. 217-18.

portions of a series which is uninterruptedly sensed, that make 'gap-indifference' possible. This, again, is the basis of that spatial continuity and synthesis, in series of varying temporal orders, which makes them 'succession-indifferent'; for any such series (*e.g.* the succession of views of a house from the north-west corner to the south-west and so on back to the north-west) is bound to be interrupted by particulars (if only eye-blinks) which are not spatially continuous with the rest and cannot be synthesized. Moreover, any series which can be completely synthesized must end where it began, it must repeat at least one item, and such repetition depends on the identification of similar particulars.

But, if we confine ourselves strictly to sense-given particulars, without imaginative or interpretative supplementation—if, that is, we do not tacitly assume the system of the material world with which to correlate our particulars—we shall be hard put to discover any such recurring resemblances as we require. The order of occurrence of what is given in sense is always more or less arbitrary and largely depends on where we choose to begin the series. Any stretch we may choose will be irregular to an indefinite extent, for there are innumerable reasons why any given or expected order may be varied, interrupted, or even reversed. Price himself has given admirable examples of this variability,[1] though he does not seem to realize how far it undermines his theory. Let us take the simple example given by Hume of a survey of the furniture in a room. In terms of purely sense-given particulars, even this simple survey is a highly complex matter and involves a considerably variegated and constantly varying series. There is a white expanse (the wall), a vaguely striped and corrugated stretch of red light and shade (a curtain), numerous coloured patches of differing shape and hue (books in a bookcase), dark bars over a flickering red and yellow light (the fireplace), and so on, with almost infinite variety. With the fading light of the day and the changing fire-light, the quality of each and all of these particulars is constantly varying, and the order in which they are experienced is entirely fortuitous, depending upon any number of chance occurrences (the direction in which I turn my head, the way in which I focus my eyes, etc.). It may be interrupted in all manner of ways: by the movement of a cat or a porter, by chance displacement of objects, the wind wafting a curtain or blowing a sheet of paper across the line of vision. And never is the same particular repeated, while those that are recognizably similar may well belong to quite different objects (two books may have similar covers or the colour of the carpet at noon may resemble that of the ceiling at dusk).

[1] *Vide Hume's Theory of the External World,* pp. 116-20.

Where in all this change and confusion are we to find sufficient regularity in the repetition of similars to permit of gap-indifference and succession-indifference? As it is, I have been unable to describe the series of sense-given particulars without referring them to material objects existing in what Berkeley would have described as 'the settled order of nature'. It is only by the presupposition of such an order that Price can establish the gap-indifferent characteristics of sense-given series, and without it the succession of particulars cannot even be intelligibly described. This presupposition is what Price overlooks, and the fact that, without it, the recurrent similars which he requires are not forthcoming. But this order is what has to be derived from sense-given particulars and the whole argument is a *petitio principii*. Consequently, his reconstruction of Hume's position which follows rests upon a spurious foundation.

It is obvious from the examples that he uses that Hume makes the same presupposition, but had he not done so, his conclusion would only have been reinforced. Constancy and coherence would then have disintegrated and the imaginative construction of an external world would have been revealed as sheer fantasy without a shred of justification. It is, however, doubtful if we could stop there; for if our impressions are nothing but particulars and all our ideas are but copies of them, no imaginative construction could be made. The manifold of sense, as Kant saw, is as good as nothing, and the point is reached at which Hume's philosophy breaks down, demanding a new effort at reconstruction. To this I shall return anon, for I have not yet exhausted the range of Hume's scepticism.

VI. THE ELIMINATION OF THE MIND

13. If the world of material objects existing continuously and independently and of events related as causes and effects—if all this is no more than an elaborate fiction, with what reality are we left? Is there not still the mind which imagines and feigns as well as reasons and perceives? Hume is not prepared to admit even the existence of the mind. He can as little find an impression or idea of a thinking substance as one of material substance, and the search for *himself* leads him only to some particular perception or other in which no self is revealed at all. All that remains is 'a bundle or collection of different perceptions, which succeed each other with an inconceivable rapidity, and are in a perpetual flux and movement'.[1] To this bundle an identity is ascribed

[1] *Treatise*, p. 252.

and it is regarded as a mind only because the ease of transition from one perception to another simulates that between the successive phases of a persistent and unchanging object, and the fluid variety is accordingly mistaken for identity. The contradiction involved, however, does not go unnoticed, but we are so prone to fall into it that we 'justify to ourselves this absurdity', much as we did that of the continued existence of our perceptions, by the fiction of a simple and unchanging soul-substance in which all our varying perceptions inhere. The mind itself is a mere fiction resulting from a mistake and an absurdity. What, we may wonder, is guilty of the error and who the author of the fiction?

VII. THE NEMESIS OF EMPIRICISM

14. Hume has thus disposed of all reasoning, reduced perceptive judgements to the play of fancy and the external world to an imaginary structure full of confusion and self-contradiction, dissolved away the mind into a flux of perceptions and left us no criterion by which to choose 'between superstition and science, myth and history, delirium and sanity'. As if in answer to Professor Price, Hume writes in his conclusion to the first Book of the *Treatise*:

'Can I be sure, that in leaving all established opinions I am following truth; and by what criterion shall I distinguish her, even if fortune shou'd at last guide me on her foot-steps? After the most accurate and exact of my reasonings, I can give no reason why I should assent to it; and feel nothing but a *strong* propensity to consider objects *strongly* in that view, under which they appear to me. . . . Without this quality by which the mind enlivens some ideas beyond others (which seemingly is so trivial, and so little founded on reason) we cou'd never assent to any argument, nor carry our view beyond those few objects, which are present to our senses.' [1]

And even this criterion Hume finds to be 'inconstant and fallacious', leading us into one confusion after another and setting us in the dilemma of either having to assent to every whim of the fancy, whatever absurdities and errors it may involve, or of adhering strictly to the understanding which 'when it acts alone, and according to its most general principles, entirely subverts itself, and leaves not the lowest degree of evidence in any proposition, either in philosophy or common life'.[2] The only reason Hume can give for continuing his speculations into the field of morals is that he has an inclination to do so, if he should restrain which, he feels he should be a loser in point of pleasure—this, he says, is the origin of his philosophy.

[1] *Treatise*, p. 265.   [2] *Ibid.* pp. 267 f.

15. Yet if we accept the principles of Hume's system strictly and press them with relentless rigour they lead to even worse despair than he describes. For in a stream of bare particulars we are ultimately deprived of all relations. No bare particular can so much as resemble another unless both possess a universal character in virtue of which they can be compared. Succession itself implies a unity in and through differences which bare particulars exclude. Contiguity is impossible unless the contiguous particulars have some point in common, and that alone would transcend their pure particularity. Contrariety itself involves a common basis of comparison and distinction. It follows that unless our impressions and ideas are more than mere particulars they cannot even form a bundle or collection, they cannot follow each other in succession, there can be no smooth transition from one to another and we can have no means of knowing which of them is more or less vivacious.

But to say all this is not so much to 'refute' Hume as to underline the 'awful warning' which is the permanent value of his philosophy. That demonstrates conclusively the final bankruptcy of the empirical principle: the maxim that everything in our knowledge is derived from sense-given particulars. For if we are not furnished with more than these, no knowledge can emerge at all.

VIII. REASONS FOR THE COLLAPSE OF EMPIRICISM

16. The materialistic conception of nature which arose in the 17th century led, as we saw, either to the attempt to explain mind in terms of matter and motion, or to separate it utterly from material things. In either case the result is to regard the human mind as a finite, singular entity, and for the empiricist it is one among others in a world made up entirely of particular things. This is the characteristic assumption of empiricism and is the root-cause of its failure. The assumption is, of course, also that of 'common sense', and the importance of 17th and 18th century empiricism is that it displays once and for all its untenability. Such a conception of the mind arises, no doubt, from its evident conjunction with the body, of which the finite and singular character seems obvious; and accordingly, another (more or less tacit) assumption of the empiricist is that consciousness is the product of physiological processes. He is at once involved in the problems of explaining how consciousness can be the effect of a physical cause and how this effect can convey to the mind in which it occurs the knowledge of a world which is external to it. The result is the effort to maintain at

times a representative theory of perception, and when that gives trouble, to eke out its deficiencies with a causal theory. But always the same insuperable difficulty arises of attributing to the mind the knowledge of a relation between two terms one of which is inevitably beyond its reach. If the mind is conceived as something separate and singular, this difficulty is unavoidable, for the relation of subject and object then becomes of necessity a relation between singulars; yet only one of them enjoys knowledge, which must embrace both terms.

The impossibility of maintaining such a position leads the empiricist to modify his theory so as to remove the inaccessible source of sense-impressions, and he proceeds to deny the very presupposition in which his principle originated. The credibility of the proposition, that knowledge originates from and is ultimately based upon sense-data, is derived from the assumption that the mind and its objects are separate entities with causal connections between them. But once it becomes clear that if knowledge is an effect occurring in the mind it is wholly confined within the limits of one finite entity, the knowledge of the cause must be relinquished. Consciousness is then conceived as a series of appearances to a subject, without the assumption either of causes or of archetypes to which the appearances correspond. They are, in fact, appearances of nothing—*Schein* rather than *Erscheinung*—and the result is phenomenalism with a consequent descent into solipsism.

Having lapsed so far, however, the empiricist has more trouble with his original presupposition; for the finite singular which the mind was originally assumed to be has now become an all-embracing theatre in which a series of phenomena appears. But the mind itself is not a phenomenon; it never appears upon the stage, and the subsequent endeavour to characterize the theatre itself fails, because the only available terms in which it might be characterized are phenomenal. The mind as the subject of consciousness must then be relinquished also and the theory of knowledge becomes a theory of appearances which are appearances of nothing and to no one. Solipsism, in fine, has (as it inevitably must) lost the *ipse*, which alone seemed to remain.

But what now becomes of knowledge? There is no longer anything to be known and no longer a mind to know. The material world of nature, which was assumed to exist over against the mind as an object to be apprehended, was first translated into the ideal content of consciousness, and then the conscious subject which gave that content its being dissolved away, leaving a flurry of ghostly shadows observed by and belonging to no subject whatsoever. These shadows contain no substance and their flitting is subject to no principles which could unite them into a world. There is in them no semblance of knowledge and sceptical nihilism is the inexorable end.

17. There is yet a second train of consequences to the conception of the mind as a finite singular related to a world of other finites, which leads to similar catastrophic results. The only way in which 'ideas' of external things could be 'imprinted' on a mind of that kind is some sort of causation by the external singulars which are their objects, and this ensures that all ideas must be particular and separable. There is thus no possible source of any universal element in knowledge. Consequently, despite the best efforts of the empiricist to save them, the relations, which are the binding mortar of any experience of a world, dissolve away in his hands. The particulars which are the bricks fall apart, and the edifice of knowledge disintegrates. We have seen how Hume's dissolution of the concept of necessary connection in causality infects all connections between impressions and ideas, and if we are to insist on their particularity, not only must we assert that no connection can be necessary, but that no connection is even conceivable.[1]

The basis of every sort of connection (or relation) is a systematic structure which embraces the terms and makes both them and the relation between them what they are. Such a structure is a universal or whole, without which neither terms nor relations are intelligible. For the terms are what they are only in virtue of the way in which they stand to one another. A is A by virtue of its not being B, C or D, etc., and by virtue of its not being so in special and determinate ways. In other words, it is A because it has definite relations to B, C and D. Equally, of course, it is true that unless A were A its distinction from (and relation to) B, C and D would have no basis, for the correct conception of the matter is that of a system in which the relata mutually constitute one another and their interrelations are simply the ways in which they do this. The essence of this kind of systematic structure is the universal —a principle of order and interconnection giving each particular its place in the system and so implicit in each, but explicit only in the whole set of particulars that constitutes the system. Isolate the particulars as separate existences and each is nothing—or else each persists only by implying all that we have attempted to sever from it. What all this comes to is that unless an object of knowledge is a whole, it is

[1] Cf. Hume, Appendix to *Treatise* (Selby-Bigge, p. 636): 'In short there are two principles, which I cannot render consistent; nor is it in my power to renounce either of them, viz. *that all our distinct perceptions are distinct existences*, and *that the mind never perceives any real connexion among distinct existences*'.

uncognizable. The part can be known only as part of a whole—it is correlative to the whole to which it belongs and is nothing apart from that. Wholes can, of course, be analysed; but *ipso facto* every such analysis presupposes the whole within which it takes place: it presupposes a correlative synthesis.

The universal is always a principle of order or system—a 'concrete' universal (as it has been called by some writers). Those who take it to be a common property or class-concept are always misled by empiricist notions of the nature of the mind and the world. They are those who think of things as particular existences and of minds as singular entities with certain faculties or accomplishments, including one (called 'abstraction') of selecting similar characters among a number of different particulars and then of forming the concept of a quality or property common to them all which makes them members of a class. This common character or class-concept is then held to be a universal. But, obviously, it is only another particular. And, as no such abstraction can exist like the things from which it has been abstracted, attempts are made to explain it, first as a sort of idea in the mind, and then, since all 'ideas' are themselves 'particular existences', as no more than a feature of language, a way in which we express our thoughts. Modern thinkers along this line have gone even further and have renounced all belief in the existence of thinking, regarding language simply as a form of behaviour, and the universal as a kind of sign habitually used in a certain way. Of the fact that the habit itself implies a universal principle they seem entirely oblivious. The complete failure of such thinkers to give any coherent account of the relation between the mind and its objects, or of the nature of knowledge and truth, will appear in later chapters.

It is by neglect of the universal element in experience that empiricism fails. For empiricists invariably (and on their principles necessarily) explain away or deny altogether the universal element in knowledge, and the final result of their analysis is, in consequence, dust and ashes—a congeries of unconnected and mutually repellent atoms, none of which has the necessary character of an object of knowledge. But this is not what they started from. They began from experience as it comes to us, and that is the experience of a world. It is a world constituted of parts, of entities, of particular things; but they are always parts of wholes (if not complete yet demanding completion), entities in mutual relation, particular things conjoined in a systematic framework. It is the context and the background in every case which makes the particular significant, gives it its peculiar character and renders it intelligible. The context, in fact, invades the single entity so that the entity is a kind of nexus in, or focus of, an ordered system to which it is organic and into the fabric of which it is woven. We may sometimes gain clarity in the understanding of particular parts by isolating them and scrutinizing them in abstraction, by dissecting the particular out of the context in which it is enmeshed. But no such scrutiny will prove informative unless the context, which is temporarily overlooked, is all along presupposed, and except in the light of that presupposition.

The world of our experience is always and throughout of this texture; nor can we give any veridical account of it by attempting to cut it up into minimal, unanalysable bits and then to combine these irreducible minima without the sinews and ligaments which our dissection has severed and destroyed. But what is the source of this structural character? Whence comes this aspect of wholeness, this universal element in experience? It makes itself evident in every part and in every particular of our world, but it is to be identified with none of them. However much of the world we include in our purview, we never have the universal as such, and nothing less seems to answer to its character than a whole which goes beyond the limits of our finite knowledge. Yet if our experi ence does not comprehend this whole, how are we aware of it? The answer to this question can be attempted only at a later stage, but so much may provisionally be maintained: (i) that the world we know does, as a matter of fact, display, in its various departments, a holistic character which may not be overlooked in any attempt to understand it, and (ii) that this holistic tendency in nature finds its greatest satisfaction and its most typical example in the operation of the human mind. Thus we are led to suspect that the universal element in experience is the activity of thought itself—a conclusion to which the study of Plato and Aristotle has already brought us very near—and which appears in the philosophy of Kant (that we are next to consider) as the doctrine that without the synthesizing agency of the unitary subject there can be no experience at all.

No theory of knowledge can be adequate which fails, as empiricism must fail, to do justice to the universal; and just as no satisfactory account can be given of the relation between the mind and its object if the nature of the mind is misconceived (as it is when it is held to be a mere singular finite), so no satisfactory account of experience can be given if—in consequence of that first misconception—the nature of the object is misconceived also.

Human knowledge, however, displays also an aspect of finiteness, and we cannot deny altogether that its objects are particulars. Our problem, in fact, is to understand how this aspect of finiteness and particularity can be reconciled with that universality and potential infinity without which there could be no knowledge at all. Empiricism does not help us, for it confines its attention wholly to the first and begins by overlooking and ends by denying the existence of the second. Nor can it do otherwise on the basis of the presuppositions to which it is initially committed. Nevertheless, it has played an important role in the development of the theory of knowledge by insisting so uncompromisingly upon that aspect of experience which the Greeks could never fully explain—the never-ceasing and ever-changing process of finite appearances in and as which the world is presented to us. For, though no knowledge is possible unless what is presented does constitute a world, yet it is equally true that no such world can be made intelligible wholly in terms of conceptual abstracta. No 'dance of bloodless categories' exhausts its reality, and it is the great merit of empiricism that it sets its face so resolutely against any view which seems to empty experience of the rich variety of its content.

Chapter IX

TRANSITION TO THE MODERN VIEW OF MIND

I. KANT'S COPERNICAN REVOLUTION

1. THOUGH Hume said of his *Treatise* that it fell still-born from the press, and though it had long to wait before either its main problem or the essential point of its argument were properly appreciated, before the century was out it had spurred one of the greatest minds in the history of thought to initiate in metaphysics what he himself compared to the Copernican revolution in astronomy.[1] The warning of Hume's philosophy, which the modern empiricist brushes aside, Kant was prepared to take seriously. He saw that Hume's conclusion was the direct result of Locke's beginning, and he proposed, therefore, to reverse Locke's initial hypothesis and asserted that objects must conform to our knowledge rather than that our knowledge should conform to objects. For Kant, the very possibility of experience requires the presupposition of certain *a priori* principles in the mind which are not and cannot be derived from sense-given experience, which mould our consciousness of objects into the forms they have for us, and to which everything that we perceive must conform. This is a complete abandonment of the two main requirements of empiricism: the denial of 'innate' ideas and the assertion that all our knowledge is derived from sense-given particulars. Though Kant is most insistent that all our scientific knowledge begins and ends with experience, he insists also that it is not all *derived* from experience, and it is no misrepresentation of his teaching to say that from mere sense-given particulars alone no knowledge whatever is derived. 'Perception without concepts is blind' and if sensation does provide the material of knowledge, without the *a priori* forms of perception and the concepts of the understanding, it is as good as nothing.

2. A peculiarity of Kant's philosophy is his persistent endeavour to distinguish rigidly and to hold apart elements in experience which the whole force of his argument compels us to unite as inseparable condi-

---

[1] The *Treatise* was published in 1739–40 and Kant was roused 'from his dogmatic slumber' about, or soon after, 1772. Kemp Smith, following Vaihinger, maintains that Kant at that time probably became acquainted with the most important of Hume's arguments in the *Treatise* as they were quoted by Beattie. *Vide* Kemp Smith, *Commentary to Kant's Critique of Pure Reason* (London, 1930), pp. xxv–xxix.

tions of any experience whatsoever. The reason for this has been clearly set out by Lindsay :[1] that he constantly used the notions and the terminology of traditional doctrines which the revolution in his own thought was in process of superseding. 'No one nowadays', writes Lindsay, 'can possibly accept all that Kant says, because if he agrees with the main thing Kant has to say—if he understands the main principles of his teaching—he cannot put it in Kant's way, or accept some of the presuppositions which Kant carries into his thinking without really making them alive. The Kantian student is forced to say sooner or later that, whatever Kant may have said in this or that place, *this* is what he really meant—or to dismiss certain elements in Kant's teaching as pre-critical.' This peculiarity is an unfortunate source of misunderstanding, leading some thinkers to agree with and others to reject Kant's views for reasons which are not material to their real import. Consequently, on the one hand, we find him quoted with approval by modern empiricists to support a position he would never have countenanced and which his own work rendered obsolete, and, on the other hand, some who follow Hegel (but do not preserve the balance of Hegel's estimate of Kant) tend to criticize too severely Kant's failure to anticipate doctrines to which he more than any other philosopher led the way. Such criticisms, even so far as they are just, I do not intend to repeat, but I shall try to show that Kant, despite all his shortcomings, fully justifies his claim to have effected in metaphysics a Copernican revolution and that he rendered a return to the empiricism which preceded him impossible by anyone who properly understands his teaching. What Kant himself did not appreciate was that the revolution he effected was one in logic as much as in metaphysics, and accordingly his metaphysic halts half-way to the goal to which his theory points.

3. The empiricist asserts that all knowledge is derived from sense, and Kant appears to agree when he asserts that all knowledge *begins* with experience; but he contradicts the empirical principle when he maintains that not all knowledge is *derived* from experience, and his subsequent account of both the elements which, he says, go together to make our experience what it is (the knowledge of an objective world) makes it impossible to attribute even the beginnings of knowledge to bare sensation or even the least content of knowledge to pure *a priori* concepts. Anything worthy of the name of knowledge at all must be both at once and in one. Consequently, the distinctions from which

[1] *Vide* A. D. Lindsay, *Kant* (Oxford, 1936), p. 39.

Kant begins prove ultimately to be distinctions between complementary moments within knowledge which is a concrete of both, and not between separate or separable elements conjoined in a composite experience. He begins by distinguishing perception (*Anschauung*) from conception (*Begriffe*), what we passively receive (*die Rezeptivität der Eindrücke*) from what we spontaneously think (*Spontaneität der Begriffe*), the *a posteriori* from the *a priori*, and to these distinctions he relates the classification of judgements as analytic and synthetic. Yet some of the most cogent and important of his arguments in the *Critique of Pure Reason* cancel out these distinctions, making it progressively more and more clear that no judgement is purely analytic or purely synthetic but that all judgements are both, that no knowledge (properly speaking) is simply *a priori* or simply *a posteriori* but that all knowledge is both. In fact, Kant's philosophy displays *in extenso* that characteristic of the philosophical universal to which Collingwood draws attention: the overlap of its specific forms despite their mutual opposition.

4. Hume's assertion, that all our distinct perceptions are distinct existences between which we never perceive any real connection, makes any scientific knowledge impossible. For where no necessary connection can be found no universal laws or principles can be formulated and everything in experience must be contingent. Kant realized this and he saw too that the remedy lay in the re-introduction into experience of the universal (or *a priori*) element. The possibility of knowledge, he saw, depended upon the mind's capacity to synthesize the manifold given in sense, which, without such synthesis, could be for consciousness not even a chaotic manifold.[1] As Hume's argument clearly shows, no such synthesis is provided by sense; but (Kant sets himself to prove) it is necessarily implied in the apprehension of even the simplest object. He concludes, accordingly, that it is an *a priori* synthesis—one following universal rules of combination inherent in the faculty of apprehension itself. It is thus the source of that universal element which the empiricists omitted from their account of experience and which is the *condicio sine qua non* of all knowledge.

II. FALSE DISJUNCTIONS

5. As Kant's theory develops this universal element is seen to permeate experience in every detail. In perception it is present (if in no other way) as the *a priori* forms of intuition (*Anschauung*), space and

[1] Cf. *Kritik der reinen Vernunft*, A 99.

time. In the apprehension of objects, of whatever sort, it is present as the operation of the understanding in the application of the categories to the manifold of sense. And though Kant in the earlier portions of the *Critique of Pure Reason* speaks as if objects are *given* in sense and are passively received by the mind,[1] yet he proceeds to show with the utmost cogency that they cannot be so given and can be experienced at all only if and in so far as the understanding has been active in the apprehension of them.

Even in the Transcendental Aesthetic the assertion that objects are merely given in sense is by implication refuted. For it is there proved that the forms of space and time are prior to and are presupposed in any possible perception of spatial and temporal objects. It is not that sensation delivers to us such objects out of mutual relation and that the relations we impose upon them and between them are of necessity spatial and temporal, but that the objects themselves are structurally constituted by spatial and temporal determinations, without which they would not be objects of our perception at all. Yet such determinations, Kant shows, cannot be derived empirically from sensation.[2] Any spatial or temporal relationship presupposes the whole of space or time and these are not 'discursive concepts'[3] (empirical generalizations) but are presupposed *a priori* by all perceptions as the indispensable condition of their possibility. Nevertheless, Kant still maintains that space and time are themselves intuitions (or percepts), even though they are non-empirical, pure, *a priori* intuitions. He thus continues to assert that objects can be given to us in perception, as if that were possible apart from what is *thought* by means of conceptions. Yet the Aesthetic itself provides evidence that the pure perception of space and time (the forms of intuition) is not a matter of mere passive acceptance: 'As the form of intuition does not represent anything, except so far as something is posited in the mind, it can be nothing else than the way in which the mind is affected by *its own activity* (viz. that of positing of its representation), and so by itself'[4] (my italics).

But when we come to the Transcendental Analytic, the doctrine that objects can be merely given in perception breaks down altogether. If it can be shown, Kant says (as he presently intends to show), that the *a priori* concepts of the understanding are antecedent conditions under which alone anything can be thought as an object, then all empirical knowledge must conform to such concepts, 'because without thus pre-

---

[1] Cf. B 1, A 50, B 74.   [2] Cf. A 23 ff., B 38 ff.; A 30 ff., B 46 ff.
[3] Cf. A 24-5, B 39; A 31-2, B 47.
[4] B 67-8. Cf. Mure, *Introduction to Hegel*, p. 95, n. 2.

supposing them nothing is possible as *object of experience*'.[1] The categories, the nature and necessity of which he is about to expound, are the principles of objectivity which enable us to distinguish between what is mere fancy or delirium and what is fact. Unless we can so distinguish, there can be for us no experience of an objective world, and without the activity of the understanding applying these categories there can be no such distinction. Accordingly, Kant says that concepts must be recognized as the *a priori* conditions of the possibility of experience 'whether of the intuition which is found in it or the thought'.[2] But if this is so, no objects can be merely given in perception, for the very possibility of the perception of objects implies and presupposes the work of the understanding involved in distinguishing the merely subjective from the objective and universally valid.[3]

He then proceeds at length to show that the concepts of the understanding are such antecedent conditions of objectivity, and it follows that without them nothing can be given *as an object* in any way at all. The Deduction of the Categories establishes in principle the prior necessity of synthesis in all consciousness of objects, and the Analytic of Principles does so in detail, dealing with each of the categories in turn. In the Deduction (though he is not aware of it) Kant is really doing the work of the Aesthetic over again and doing it more thoroughly. He is demonstrating the essential conditions of any experience of objects, and he points out [4] that if consciousness were broken up into mutually separate and repellent states or representations (*Vorstellungen*), nothing like knowledge could ever result; because knowledge is always a whole of related and connected elements. The essential condition of the experience of objects is therefore synthesis. But inasmuch as our *Vorstellungen* occur successively, no such synthesis can simply be received *a posteriori* and must depend wholly upon the activity of the understanding. Kant even goes so far as to assert that such synthesis cannot be intuited (or perceived) and is not contained even in the pure forms of sensible intuition (space and time) but is always and only a spontaneous act of the understanding.[5] It does not, he says, lie in the object and cannot be first taken up through perception into the understanding, but is solely an accomplishment of the understanding itself. The original synthetic unity of apperception in the subject, which alone makes the unity of apprehension possible, is, therefore, said to be the most fundamental principle of all human

---

[1] A 93, B 126.   [2] A 94, B 126.
[3] Cf. Lindsay, *op. cit.* pp. 92-3.
[4] A 97.   [5] B 129-30.

knowledge.[1] If this is so, however, and if perception is regarded at all as a way of apprehending objects, it is clear that perception and conception can no longer be held apart but that they interpenetrate and are mutually inseparable; that perception itself is dependent upon and is shot through and through with the activity of thought.

When we pass to the Analytic of Principles we find the work of thought still more inextricably involved in the perception of objects in space and time. The exposition of these principles is, in fact, a further development of the ideas already emerging in the Aesthetic, the effect of which is to show that in the very forms of intuition the principles of the understanding are already implied. First, in his account of the mathematical categories, what Kant tells us is in effect that the sensible perception (intuition) of an object is made possible only by that same synthesizing activity as is involved in the mathematical conception of quantity. The opening passage of the proof of the 'Axioms of Intuition' is worth quoting at length:

'Appearances, in their formal aspect, contain an intuition in space and time, which conditions them, one and all, *a priori*. They cannot be apprehended, that is taken up into empirical consciousness, save through that synthesis of the manifold whereby the representations of a determinate space or time are generated, that is, through combination of the homogeneous manifold and consciousness of its synthetic unity. Consciousness of the synthetic unity of the manifold homogeneous in intuition in general, in so far as the representation of an object first becomes possible by means of it, is, however, the concept of a magnitude (*quantum*). Thus even the perception of an object, as appearance, is only possible through the same synthetic unity of the manifold of the given sensible intuition as that whereby the unity of the combination of the manifold homogeneous is thought in the concept of a *magnitude*.'[2]

This synthesis 'whereby the manifold homogeneous is thought in the conception of a magnitude' is nothing less than the pure mathematical idea of quantity, and it is here said to be the *same* synthesis as that involved in the apprehension of the sensible manifold as an object in space and time.

Next, in the proofs of the Analogies of Experience, we find that it is the character of time itself that necessitates a permanent substratum of all change, without which no time relations would be possible at all, and the relations of objects as they exist in time could not be determined as

[1] B 134-5. [2] B 202-3.

distinguishable from the succession of our subjective states.[1] The perpetual changes of temporal succession could not be apprehended even as successive differences unless they were united in some 'underlying ground' which is regarded as abiding and permanent. Without this underlying substrate, in consequence, the relations both of simultaneity and of succession would be inconceivable. Consequently, the very nature of time and the temporal character of our perceptions are dependent upon the conception of substance—a category, or principle of the pure understanding.

Further, the necessity which connects cause to effect is shown to be due to the fact that, unless we *think* the temporal order of two events as so determined, it is impossible to decide in what order they occur in the object at all. 'For time', Kant points out, 'cannot itself be perceived' (as an objective series) 'and in relation to it what precedes and what follows in the object cannot be empirically determined.'[2] The order of succession of our subjective representations does not give us the objective order of events. It is entirely contingent; and without necessary, universal rules determining the temporal connection of appearances we should have, Kant points out, only 'a play of representations relating to no object'. Consequently, the relation of objects in a time series, of *events* properly so called, would be impossible.[3] In other words, the experience of time, as an order of events, depends for its very existence upon our *thinking* the necessary connection in the sequence of their occurrence between events as cause and effect. What Kant realized and what Hume and the empiricists did not was that the necessity of the connection between cause and effect is a logical necessity—a necessity of thought—and the demonstration that it is not and cannot be perceived by means of the senses is therefore irrelevant.

In the same way, the proof of the third Analogy shows that the perception of objects as co-existing simultaneously in space is dependent upon and presupposes the conception of reciprocity, which must already be present by implication in any such perception.

Over and over again perception and conception are revealed as inseparably interdependent, not simply, as Kant says, because one supplies the matter and the other the form of experience, but because the very matter of experience is constituted by the form in which it is apprehended, and the very possibility of apprehension is dependent upon the operation of thought in accordance with specific *a priori* categories.

[1] Cf. B 220-1, and A 183, B 226.
[2] B 233. Cf. A 200, B 245.   [3] Cf. A 194, B 239.

This is one of the chief results of Kant's reasoning and from it consequences follow which are not only fatal to empiricism but also to the other distinctions, between the *a priori* and the *a posteriori* and between analytic and synthetic judgements, which Kant himself retains and which are still dear to the hearts of many contemporary philosophers.

6. Kant makes the explicit statement, and the Analytic demonstrates it with irresistible force, that *all* synthesis is *a priori* synthesis and is the work of the understanding.[1] In the Introduction to the first edition of the *Critique* he had said that the connecting link between subject and predicate in empirical (synthetic *a posteriori*) judgements was supplied by experience—'the complete experience of the object' (A 8). But the Analytic proves that this complete experience is itself the result of an *a priori* synthesis and that we can find in experience no combination not already put into it *a priori* by the understanding. Accordingly it becomes apparent that all synthetic judgements must be *a priori* and not even empirical synthesis is merely given. There can thus be no *a posteriori* synthetic judgements.

Further, Kant tells us (B 130) that all analysis presupposes synthesis and that nothing can be separated that has not previously been combined. It follows that every analytic judgement must be one which already contains a synthesis and there can be no purely analytic judgements. Though Kant does not observe the point, it is clear, likewise, that no synthesis can be made where there is no multiplicity to synthesize, so that every synthesis contains within it an implicit analysis. Every judgement, therefore, must be at once both analytic and synthetic.

Moreover, there is, in the last resort, nothing to synthesize except the intuited manifold, for the *a priori* concepts themselves are synthetic only because they are principles of combination of the representations which make up our consciousness. Kant claims to derive them all from the original synthetic unity of apperception, the source of which is the unitary subject of consciousness. But, as he asserts, 'it is only so far as I can unite a manifold of given representations *in one consciousness*, that I can represent to myself the identity of the consciousness in *these*

---

[1] B 129-30: '*Allein die Verbindung* (conjunctio) *eines Mannigfaltigen überhaupt, kann niemals durch Sinne in uns kommen, und kann also auch nicht in der reinen Form der sinnlichen Anschauung zugleich mit enthalten sein; denn sie ist ein Aktus der Spontaneität der Vorstellungskraft, und, da man diese, zum Unterschiede von der Sinnlichkeit, Verstand nennen muss, so ist alle Verbindung . . . eine Verstandeshandlung, die wir mit allgemeinen Benennung* Synthesis *belegen würden. . . .*'

representations' (B 133). In short, without diversity no unity is think-able. It follows that synthetic judgements, even though principles are involved in them which are *a priori* in the sense that they are not derived from sensation, cannot be purely *a priori*, for they must synthesize a manifold which can, in the last resort, only be empirical. And analytic judgements, in consequence, can never be wholly *a priori* either. The elements which they distinguish must be elements of an empirical manifold already combined by the synthesizing activity of the understanding. There can, therefore, be no absolute distinction between *a priori* and *a posteriori* knowledge. All knowledge and all the judgements it involves, are both *a priori* and *a posteriori*, both synthetic and analytic. In short, the universal and the particular in experience are interdependent, as I have endeavoured to suggest above.

7. This point may be approached from a slightly different angle. Kant establishes the *a priori* principles in knowledge by showing that they are the necessary presuppositions without which our experience could not be what it is. They are not deduced *in vacuo* but are dictated by the nature of experience: their deduction is precisely the argument by which they are shown to be the indispensable presuppositions of the sort of experience we have and the only sort we can have. They are, therefore, *a priori* only in the sense that they must be presupposed in order that any experience should be possible for us. They are logically prior to the experience of objects. But they are not independent of experience in the sense that we could know them as self-evident truths apart from any experience whatsoever (though Kant often speaks as if this were so). It still remains true that all knowledge *begins* with experience and it is only by reference to it that even the categories themselves can be brought to light. It is, however, not by reference simply to the particular deliverances of sense, but by reference to the universal character of experience—its character as a whole. We may say, therefore, that the categories are the formal principles of experience *as a whole*, which are implied and immanent in any and every particular experience whatever. They are its universal principles.

Accordingly,—and this is the whole force of Kant's argument—it is impossible to construct a world such as we know out of the particular deliverances of sense, except by presupposing the universal principles of objectivity and of the spatio-temporal relations of objects in that construction. The fundamental tenet of empiricism is thus subverted and no attempt to return to it is permissible until the Kantian argument has been disposed of. On the other hand, the universal principles of experience are not self-evident truths immediately intuited by pure reason and there can be no logic, such as was assumed by Descartes and the Rationalists, which proceeds from self-evident first principles, or axioms, intuited by pure thought, and reaches conclusions by purely analytic reasoning, each step of which is also taken to be self-evident. The only sort of logic permissible is what Kant called Transcendental Logic—that which bases the universal and necessary principles of judgement and reasoning on the character of experience as a whole.

This is the real revolution which Kant effected in philosophy—one which rendered even some of his own teaching obsolete. Henceforward it could not be maintained that knowledge was derived exclusively either from sensation or from pure reason, or even from both taken as separate and independent sources. Knowledge must be regarded as a whole in which the universal and the particular moments are mutually necessitating, and in which neither can be derived from a source which does not presuppose the other. The presuppositions of Renaissance science are here superseded, for the mind has been shown to be the source of the very laws which led the scientist to regard physical nature as mechanical and to exclude from it the knowing subject. The phenomena of nature themselves have been revealed as conditioned and constructed by the spontaneous activity of mind. After Kant wrote, the dichotomy of subject and object was no longer possible, and though Kant himself did not appreciate to the full the implications of his own doctrine, the revolution of philosophical attitude and method which it demands is nevertheless complete.

It is all the more important nowadays that attention should be drawn afresh to the fact and the character of this Kantian revolution because so much contemporary philosophical discussion ignores it. Modern empiricists assume quite openly what Kant proved to be impossible—that the objects of knowledge can be given by sensation. They have, as a result, gone back to the old distinctions between analytic and synthetic propositions, between *a priori* reasoning and *a posteriori*, as if Kant had never written. The old assumption that minds and things are separate entities able to affect each other externally has been revived, with its attendant belief that everything in knowledge originates from sense-data and must be traced back to sense-data if it is to be explained. On the other hand, the developments in philosophy which the Kantian revolution initiated have been summarily thrown overboard and the very mention of such names as Hegel, Bradley and Bosanquet (except as objects of opprobrium) has become, at any rate in much contemporary English philosophy, almost a taboo. The modern empiricists have not only neglected Hume's awful warning, they have entirely overlooked the critical problem of Kant and the reconstruction in philosophy which his treatment of it made possible.

III. THE COHERENCE THEORY OF TRUTH

8. The outcome of Kant's reasoning is a theory of knowledge and truth the foundation of which is coherence. Kant maintains[1] that truth consists in the agreement of knowledge with its object and that, though it is absurd to ask for a general test or criterion of the truth of any particular content of knowledge, it is possible to give a purely logical criterion which refers only to the form of knowledge. The test is 'the agreement of an [item of] knowledge with the general and formal laws of the understanding and reason as the *condicio sine qua non* and so the negative condition of all truth'. He shows, however, that the 'formal laws of the understanding' are themselves the *condiciones sine qua non* of any experience of objects, for the reason that they are the principles of synthesis which constitute the objects *qua* phenomena. In that case the agreement of knowledge with its object and its conformity to the formal principles of the understanding are one and the same thing. Our conclusion, however, cannot be that all experience must necessarily be true, but only the experience of objects, or, as we say, of facts, distinguished from mere imaginings, dreams, random fancies and the like. They can be and are so distinguished, Kant has shown, by being constructed according to rules, and these rules are necessarily interrelated, forming a coherent system which is the self-differentiation of the original unity of apperception in the activity of the knowing subject. Though Kant asserts that this is an analytic unity, it is clear that the whole of his doctrine would collapse if the statement were rigorously pressed, and he has to admit that the condition of its being known even as an analytic unity is the presupposition of its synthetic activity in combining the manifold of representations.[2] Despite his professions, therefore, Kant arrives at the rules or principles of objectivity, as little by pure analytical deduction as by comparison with sense-given data. On the contrary, he does so by consideration of the general character of our experience as a whole. Accordingly, this general character of our total experience is the foundation of the system of principles which at once determines the nature of objects and provides the criterion of truth.

[1] A 58-9, B 83-4.   [2] B 133.

Kant's advocacy of the coherence theory is apparent in many passages. His argument against Hume is that no knowledge is possible if our representations are mutually isolated and separate, because knowledge 'is a whole of representations mutually compared and connected'.[1] This is, of course, necessarily implied in the whole doctrine of synthesis developed in the Transcendental Deduction and its dependence on the original transcendental unity of apperception. Further, in distinguishing phenomena from noumena, he maintains that the understanding with its principles confers upon experience a unity, in relation to and in agreement with which all appearances must stand *a priori*.[2] These rules of the understanding, he says, 'are indeed the source of all truth (that is, of the agreement of our knowledge with objects), inasmuch as they contain in themselves the ground of the possibility of experience viewed as the sum of all knowledge wherein objects can be given to us'.[3] Finally, when explaining the regulative use of the Ideas of Reason he propounds the coherence theory quite unequivocally: 'The law of reason which requires us to seek unity is necessary, because without it we should have no reason at all, and without that no coherent use of the understanding (*zusammenhängenden Verstandesgebrauch*), and in the absence of this no adequate criterion of empirical truth. With this last in view, therefore, we must presuppose the systematic unity of Nature throughout as objectively valid and necessary.'[4]

This conception of truth as coherence is the necessary philosophical basis of the succeeding phase in the development of the theory of knowledge. The modern conception of nature and its implied relation to the mind cannot, in the end, stand without it. This has not always been understood even by those thinkers who have themselves been responsible for evolving the new ideas, for in many cases the influence of the Renaissance has been so persistent that it has blinded them (wholly or partially) to the advance which they have themselves effected.

IV. MIND AND NATURE

9. This is indeed the case with Kant whose thought was still immersed in the ideas of 17th and 18th century science. The Renaissance presupposition of the separation of mind from physical nature reappears in his philosophy in the doctrine of things-in-themselves, assumed as the unknown and unknowable source of our sensations. These unknowable 'external' things are the remnants of the unbe-

---

[1] A 97: '*ein Ganzes verglichener und verknüpfter Vorstellungen*'.
[2] A 237, B 296.   [3] *Ibid.*   [4] A 651, B 679.

minded material bodies which the 17th-century scientists held to be the sole constituents of nature. They are the archetypes of Locke's complex ideas of substances. Kant not only assumes their existence but he also considers them to be the ultimate realities of which our knowledge is only an appearance, and it is because he does so that he so persistently holds apart, despite his own account of knowledge, the two elements in experience—sense-perception (regarded as the effects upon the mind of things-in-themselves) and conception (which is the mind's spontaneous activity upon what is passively received in sense). It is this separation again which dictates the distinctions between *a priori* and *a posteriori* knowledge and between analytic and synthetic judgements; and an even more ominous consequence is his denial of objective validity to the Ideas of Reason and the consequent limitation of knowledge to phenomena. For Kant insists that neither the categories nor the forms of space and time apply to things-in-themselves, but that the objects they constitute for us are only appearances and are objective only as phenomena. Consequently, our knowledge, for all its phenomenal objectivity, is in the end only subjective and is never knowledge of reality as it is in itself.

10. As a result, Kant is unable to solve the problem of the mind's relation to nature. As a product of nature and an existent in the natural world, the mind is known as a phenomenon. As such it is the empirical self, whose life and activity all the laws of nature determine. But that is not the mind which knows. The knowing subject is not a phenomenon and is unknowable as an object of scientific speculation. It is, in fact, a thing-in-itself. But as Kant's theory develops and as the implications of his Copernican revolution make themselves (however dimly) felt, his conception of the *Ding an sich* changes and what was at first a bare external thing, foreign to the mind and no more than the presumed (but unknown) source of its sensations, is transformed into a noumenon —a product of pure thought or reason. In the end, after the implications of the reality and efficacy of the noumenal self have been worked out in the second *Critique*, Kant asserts in the third that the thing-in-itself must be something with the character of a mind, giving final significance to his remark in the *Critique of Pure Reason* that the ultimate (unknown) source of both perception and conception may be the same.

Nevertheless, the relation between the phenomenal self and the noumenal self remains wholly obscure and is, in Kant's philosophy, as unknowable as the relation of the *Ding an sich* to the sense-presentations of which it is supposed to be the source. The mind which knows nature is not the mind which belongs to nature. One is the phenomenal object of the other and they cannot intelligibly be identified. The problem remains unsolved, for the edifice of knowledge which Kant rescues from Hume's demolition is haunted by the ghost of Locke's substance. Nature (as with Berkeley) is a totally subjective appearance of a world the reality of which remains a mystery and our own membership of which an enigma.

Part Four

THE MODERN CONCEPTION OF
NATURE AND MIND

Chapter X

THE CONCEPT OF EVOLUTION

1. THE dominant idea in cosmology since the beginning of the 19th century has been that of evolution. Even in the astronomical theories of Kant and Laplace the conception was implicit, and with the growth in importance of biology and its kindred disciplines it became steadily more prominent until its triumphant capture of the scientific world in the middle of the century with the publication of Darwin's *Origin of Species*.

The application of the idea was, however, not long confined to biology. It soon influenced thought in almost every other department of knowledge—with the notable exception of the physical sciences, which for long remained the stronghold of mechanistic principles. Geology had contributed much to the confirmation of the hypothesis that living species evolved from one form to another, and in anthropology, a science of which certain branches border upon the zoological field, the notion of evolution was soon found to be applicable and illuminating. Hence it found easy access into the realms of political theory and philosophy and it soon became customary for thinkers to present their subject-matter as constituting an evolutionary process. The conception of nature which arose in consequence was that of a vast process of evolution in which matter generated life and the living species evolved one from another until man with his conscious mind and intellectual capacities eventually emerged: the highest product to date of the entire process, a creature capable of apprehending both the universe in which he lives and his own nature as a conscious, thinking being.

A proper consideration of the growth and the philosophical implications of the idea of evolution will occupy later chapters, but in order to draw attention to the anticipation of this idea in certain earlier systems, I shall here state, very briefly and dogmatically, the main tenets of the philosophical position to which it leads. If the reader feels that in doing so I am taking too much for granted, I must crave his patience until the matter is argued more in detail in Section C of this Part.

The conception is one of a process of continuous change; but change by itself is not enough to constitute evolution. For that, a recognizable direction of change is required and the presupposition of an end (however dimly prefigured) by reference to which that direction is determined. The whole process and every phase in it must be determined by the nature of the end, for each phase is what it is and can be assigned its place in the process only by virtue of its contribution towards the unfolding of that which is, all along, coming to be. The position may be (and has been) put by saying that each phase is (though in some sense also it is not) that which it is in process of becoming. Accordingly, the end pervades the entire process and in some sense is always present, though it displays itself constantly in new and different forms, each more adequate to its developed nature than the last. As a preliminary and provisional analysis of the conception this will serve my immediate purpose, but a more thorough examination of its implications must be undertaken at a later stage.

2. Such a conception is the combination and reconciliation of the ideas of permanence and change, which respectively predominated in the Greek and the Renaissance views of reality, and a new basis is provided for the theory of knowledge doing justice to both. In the evolutionary process the permanent is that which is developing throughout, which is immanent in all its phases and which emerges complete at the end. The changes are its various successive embodiments that constitute the process itself. The Greeks, as we saw, always insisted upon the importance of the first term in this antithesis, rather at the expense of the second, in their theory both of knowledge and of reality; while in the thought of the Renaissance the second was made the original from which the first was regarded as derivative and to which it was subsidiary. In the conception of evolution they become inseparable, neither being possible or intelligible without the other. We have seen this view beginning to emerge in Kant's thought; it was adumbrated in Plato and Aristotle and (as I shall presently show) it was by no means altogether absent in the thought of the 17th and 18th centuries. Nevertheless, the new conception of nature, just because it is a synthesis of the typical Greek and Renaissance ideas, brings a contrasting phase in the history of thought, the revolutionary effects of which may briefly be summarized thus:

(i) Renaissance science rejected the notions of final cause and teleology and sought to explain all phenomena by means of efficient causation. Nature was accordingly thought of as a mechanical system external to mind. The theory of evolution, on the other hand, reinstates the final cause as the ultimate source of explanation and so excludes mechanism as a principle of interpretation. A machine cannot evolve and what does evolve cannot in any phase of the process be purely mechanical. While mechanism postulates a moving force acting *a tergo*, evolution demands a *nisus* operating *a fronte*. The second, it is true, may manifest itself also in the form of an efficient cause, as it is shown to do in Aristotle's theory; but the first can never manifest itself in the form of the second.

(ii) Evolution implies an end which gives direction to the process of change and by reference to which the phases of the process constitute an order of ascending grades of value. It implies, therefore, that the principle of value is the ultimate principle of interpretation and truth in any theory of the universe. This can never be the case for a purely mechanistic outlook and it is therefore a position to which the Renaissance view is entirely antipathetic.

(iii) Empiricism, the typical product of Renaissance presuppositions, definitely excludes coherence either as a test of truth (which, for the Empiricist, is always some form of correspondence) or as characterizing the real (which, for the Empiricist, is always a congeries of discrete particulars). On the other hand, in any process of evolution, the permanent must be immanent in the successively appearing differences, the universal must in some way pervade, and express itself in and through, the particulars. The whole process must be conceived as one, the parts (or phases) so contributing to its unity that the whole is implicit in each one of them. The process, accordingly, can only be adequately explained and understood in terms of an absolutist theory, which makes the particulars intelligible solely in the light of the whole which they constitute, and which involves as a result a coherence theory of knowledge. It is true that absolutist-coherence theories have sometimes been propounded and more often interpreted so as to exclude the notion of evolution, but I hope to show that such interpretation is misunderstanding and that not only does evolution require an absolute, but the absolute cannot properly be conceived except as involving an evolutionary process.

(iv) In 17th-century thought a gulf was fixed between matter and mind, the nature of each being conceived as totally exclusive of and different from the other. The modern idea of nature involves the direct opposite of this position. As the final products of the evolutionary process are life and mind, and as these are its higher phases, we must presume that what is evolving throughout the process is more fully and adequately manifested in these forms than in forms which are prior to them and lower in the scale. The further the process advances the more dominant in the product are the characteristics of mind. We can but conclude, therefore, that the end towards which the development tends and with reference to which it is a development at all, is of the nature of a mind. This end, moreover, determines the universal character of the process and must be immanent in all its phases. However difficult it may be to demonstrate this in any particular case, it follows from the conception of nature as a continuous process of evolution eventually producing living and be-minded creatures that mind is immanent throughout its course and in every natural form.

(v) Consequently, the object of knowledge is itself imbued with mind, and subject and object cannot be so rigidly separated as they were in the 17th century. The distinction must still be made, but we are liable to find the distincta each infected (or 'contaminated') with the character of the other. At first sight this may not seem to affect the problem of knowledge, which presents the same difficulty whether the object is taken to be a person, or other living thing, or whether it is a stick or a stone; and to contend that the stick and the stone are in some way animate does not alter the situation. But this is so only if we persist in the attitude of the empiricist who thinks of the relationship between subject and object as one of 'compresence'. For the evolutionist subject and object must be related as phases in a process of becoming, in which the later phase is implicit in the earlier and the earlier sublated into the later, and this, we shall find, makes all the difference in the world to the understanding of the nature of knowledge.

The philosophical theory demanded by the modern outlook must, accordingly, maintain five main theses: (i) that mind is immanent in all things; (ii) that reality is a whole, self-sufficient and self-maintaining, and that coherence is the test of truth of any theory about it; (iii) that the subject and object of knowledge are ultimately one—the same thing viewed from opposite (and mutually complementary) stand-points; (iv) that events and phenomena can adequately be explained only teleologically, and (v) that the ultimate principle of interpretation is, in consequence, the principle of value.

3. The separation of the Renaissance from classical times by the intervening period of the Middle Ages sharpens the contrast between the conceptions which characterize Greek philosophy on the one hand and 17th-century thought on the other. But from Renaissance ideas to modern the development has been unbroken and no hard line can be drawn between the periods in which they have been expressed. Even in biology the hypothesis of evolution took over sixty years to estab-lish itself, and even then Renaissance presuppositions continued

strongly to influence both scientific and philosophic thought. The effect of the physical sciences on the new conception was not felt until comparatively recently, and their contribution to the modern revolution, though by no means the less important, was made at a much later date and from a somewhat different direction. On the other hand, the biological hypothesis was by no means the first sign of the coming change. The difficulties and contradictions involved in the philosophical position entailed by the presuppositions of Renaissance science were themselves a sufficient spur to the more synoptic minds to look for some better foundation for the rational explanation of the universe, and the essential elements of the modern conception are already apparent in the thought of at least two great thinkers of the earlier period. Spinoza and Leibniz both sought to heal the fissure between matter and mind which the 17th-century empiricism had cleft, and in doing so they both anticipated to a remarkable extent the ideas underlying the modern view. Moreover, when Kant, by his criticism, had made a return to empiricism impossible for any unbiassed thinker, Hegel succeeded, by a conscious effort to unite the thought of the Ancients with that of the 17th and 18th centuries, in laying the foundations of the type of philosophy adequate to the requirements of modern science. Hegel's theories were, however, far in advance of the scientific thought of his own day and, though he is not entirely free of its influence, he so far anticipated modern ideas that only now can we begin to estimate his importance correctly.

4. In the first section of this Part I shall try to show the extent to which modern conceptions were anticipated by these three great philosophers. In the next section I shall turn my attention to the work of more recent and of contemporary thinkers who (in different degrees) display the opposite tendency—a tendency to revert to the ideas of the 17th century. Thereafter, I shall give some account of modern scientific thought in order to bring to light its underlying assumptions and to indicate the sort of philosophical theory which they imply. I shall examine theories definitely embodying the modern view, though not always a full awareness of its implications, and shall conclude with an outline of the kind of philosophy demanded in the modern context and the solution it would provide of the problem from which I began.

Section A
Precursors of the Modern Outlook

Chapter XI

SPINOZA AND LEIBNIZ

*

1. In the consideration of any philosophy it is, of course, important to recognize its shortcomings as well as the measure of its adequacy, but in examining the work of the philosophers to which this chapter is devoted, my main concern is to demonstrate that they did anticipate the five essential features of the modern conception of nature enumerated on p. 206 above. The defects in their systems have been displayed often enough by other commentators and, as Collingwood has shown, they result in almost every instance from the (very natural) influence of the scientific ideas current at the time. The works of Spinoza and Leibniz are in many ways typical products of their age, but for this very reason it is all the more remarkable that they so far transcended the limitations which the prevailing preconceptions of science imposed on other thinkers of their day. Consequently, I shall at most indicate very briefly those features of their thought in which Renaissance presuppositions are reflected and shall largely confine my attention to those in which modern ideas are foreshadowed.

SPINOZA

I. 17TH-CENTURY CHARACTERISTICS

2. As a precursor of the modern conception of nature, Spinoza may seem at first sight a singularly unfortunate example to choose. The foundation of his system is the infinite and absolutely perfect being of God or substance, which, being complete and perfect in itself, is eternally one and unchanging. This, for Spinoza, is nature. How then can it possibly be 'a vast process of evolution' or anything like it? How can any such conception be at all admitted in what is not susceptible of change? As Spinoza held that substance included the whole of reality and that there was nothing whatever besides, it is surely obvious that

evolution must be totally excluded from nature and that he could not, without blatant contradiction, have admitted the conception at all. Moreover, he is emphatic and uncompromising in his condemnation of the notions of free will and teleology and scathing in his criticism of those who believe in final causes. Everything in the universe, he declares, is fixed and determined, flowing as it does by inexorable necessity from the divine nature.[1] For the same reason he maintains that judgements of good and evil are wholly relative to human desires and are not applicable to things as they are in nature.[2] It would therefore seem mere perversity to uphold his doctrine as one which makes value the ultimate principle of interpretation.

That Spinoza could somehow have transplanted himself out of the intellectual soil and climate of his time is hardly to be maintained, and these characteristics of his philosophy are clearly the product of co-temporary influences. But only a very superficial reading of his works could lead us to accept these views as expressing the full significance of his doctrine, and very different results emerge on a careful examination of his theory. It must be observed at once that his polemic against the notions of final cause, freedom and teleology are always aimed at abstract and unphilosophical forms of these ideas. His own system includes a theory of freedom much more satisfactory than any he attacks, it admits a form of development or progress at least in human affairs which has implications also for the world of nature, and he accepts a test of truth which in the end turns out likewise to be the only criterion of value.

II. MODERN CHARACTERISTICS

3. There are two respects at least, by no means insignificant, in which Spinoza does, undoubtedly, supply fundamental requirements of the modern conception.

(i) He does most emphatically assert that the real is one whole, self-maintaining and self-sufficient. God, or substance, or nature, is in his philosophy the permanent basis of all things, the cause of all change and of every occurrence. Without such a permanent basis development cannot be conceived, for unless there is some identical element running through the whole process, no succession of differences can in any way constitute a developing series. The question, however, remains whether Spinoza conceived this permanent basis in a way which is compatible with evolution. What is permanent in an evolutionary process is that

[1] *Vide Ethics*, I, prop. xvi and Appendix; IV, preface.   [2] *Ibid.*

which is evolving—the subject of developmental change. Can Spinoza's substance possibly be so conceived, or is it not rather what we might regard as the end of a development without the process which should have led to it (a process entirely excluded by Spinoza's theory)? We shall have to return to this question when we have considered other features of his system. Here it need only be noted that he does maintain an absolutist metaphysic and this issues, as we should expect, in a coherence theory of knowledge.

(ii) For Spinoza the highest form of knowledge is *scientia intuitiva*, defined as knowledge that 'advances from an adequate idea of the formal essence of certain attributes of God to the adequate knowledge of the essence of things'.[1] It is accordingly knowledge and truth in the fullest sense of the words. But 'an adequate idea of the formal essence of certain attributes of God' is an adequate idea of the totality which is substance or nature.[2] It is the knowledge of the whole. And that this supplies the ultimate criterion of all truth becomes apparent on consideration of Spinoza's theory of error. Falsity (or inadequacy) is, he maintains, nothing positive but only the privation of knowledge which mutilated and confused ideas involve. It is only by reference to what they leave out that they are recognized as false and can be corrected. The process of correction is, therefore, progressive supplementation increasing the amount of reality or 'perfection' comprehended by the idea. He identifies reality and perfection and defines perfection as completeness,[3] so that it is only by seeing things as they are in God that we can recognize the extent to which they are misconceived in *imaginatio*, the sole source of error. 'Truth', says Spinoza, 'is the criterion of itself and of the false, as light reveals itself and darkness.'[4] It is thus

---

[1] *Ethics*, II, prop. xl, *schol.* 2.

[2] An attribute is 'that which the intellect perceives of substance, as if constituting its essence'. Consequently, an adequate idea of an attribute is an adequate idea of what constitutes the essence of substance. In other words, it is knowledge of the nature of the whole. Spinoza, however, asserts that God has infinite attributes, and the adequate idea of one or of some few, it may be held, is far from being an adequate idea of them all. But in all the attributes, the modes are substantially the same. It is the same thing (*res*) which is expressed differently in each. An adequate idea of any attribute thus involves knowledge of God's nature as a whole. Moreover, God's intellect is identical with the attribute of thought and, in this, an adequate idea of every attribute must be contained. Thought is, moreover, common to men with God and to conceive *this* attribute adequately must be to know the absolute whole of substance. This may be a knowledge beyond the power of the finite intellect, but, even for that, it is, nevertheless, the final standard of truth. But if we are to take literally what Spinoza has written we must conclude that he did not regard even the most perfect knowledge as wholly beyond the capacity of man.

[3] *Vide Ethics*, II, def. vi, and IV, preface.

[4] *Ethics*, II, prop. xliii, *schol.*; cf. also II, props. xxxiii-xxxv, xl, *schol.* 2, xli-xlii.

abundantly clear that he holds a coherence theory of truth as well as an absolutist theory of reality.

4. Further, the identification of thought and things, so foreign to empiricism, is explicit in Spinoza. 'A mode of extension', he says, 'and the idea of that mode are one and the same thing expressed in two different ways.'[1] This is another of the presuppositions of the modern view, and we shall find that in Spinoza's doctrine it is the source of great illumination, even in spite of residual difficulties with respect to the mutual relation of the attributes in God. It is, of course, precisely relevant to our main problem and provides an explanation of the relation of the human mind to the body as well as to the objects of its knowledge. In fact, Spinoza has recognized that we are dealing here with one problem and not with two. The mind's relation to the body and its relation to its object is one and the same relation—as he puts it: 'The object of the idea constituting the human mind is a body, or certain mode of extension actually existing, *and nothing else*'[2]—and the mind is adapted to the perception of many things only in so far as and because the body is capable of being affected in many different ways.[3] This means that my awareness of my own body is not of the same sort as my perception of other bodies, for though every perception that I have is the perception, and that alone, of some affection or activity of my body, I am not directly aware of this. My perception of other bodies is solely through this awareness of the affects and actions of my own, yet my sense-organs, the inescapable media of my perceptions, are not immediately perceived as such—they are like the glass of the window through which I view a landscape. I come to recognize them as parts of a body which is my own, partly through their mutual revelation (each revealing the others as it does external objects), and partly by imaginative construction based on inference from what I perceive through them. Body and mind are thus substantially one and the same thing differing only in the attribute under which they are conceived. They do not interact, nor are ideas in the mind caused by events in the body, but the human mind is nothing else than the body's awareness of itself in its organic relations to its environment—relations ultimately involving all other bodies and the whole attribute of extension,[4] so that the mind is in the end nothing less than the consciousness of the world. This

---

[1] *Ethics*, II, prop. vii, *schol.*
[2] *Ethics*, II, prop. xiii. The italics are mine.
[3] *Vide Ethics*, II, prop. xiv. An admirable elucidation of this doctrine is given by Professor H. F. Hallett in his article 'On a Reputed Equivoque in Spinoza', *Review of Metaphysics*, III, 2, no. 10 (December 1949).   [4] Cf. *Ethics*, II, prop. xlv.

Spinoza expresses in his proposition that 'the order and connection of ideas is the same as the order and connection of things'[1] and develops in the Fifth Part of the *Ethics*,[2] where he shows that *scientia intuitiva* involves a knowledge of God (or nature), of the body and of the mind, *sub specie aeternitatis* and makes the mind co-eternal with its ultimate object.[3]

5. When we take into consideration Spinoza's theory of the human mind, its three kinds of knowledge and its capacity (or rather its continual effort) to progress from the less adequate to the more adequate, this doctrine of the identity of body with mind and of the order and connection of ideas with that of things has momentous consequences. Although not explicitly stated, it is clear (if only from the title of his unfinished *Tractatus de Intellectus Emendatione*) that Spinoza entertained the idea of development of the human mind and conceived the progress from *imaginatio*, through *ratio*, to *scientia intuitiva* as a process of intellectual growth. This is further apparent from the opening propositions of Part Five of the *Ethics*, which demonstrate how the affects resulting from ideas arising in *imaginatio* can be detached from the thought of their external cause and connected with adequate ideas conceived through *ratio*. It is apparent also from Prop. xxviii of Part Five, in which it is asserted that the desire for the third kind of knowledge (*scientia intuitiva*) can arise only out of the second and not from *imaginatio*. The progress is from confused and partial ideas of things as separate singulars, coming to be, enduring and passing away in time, to adequate ideas of common properties enabling the mind to conceive things *sub specie aeternitatis* as necessarily proceeding from the eternal and infinite essence of God, and so to attain the highest kind of knowledge through an adequate idea of His attributes.

But if the order and connection of things is the same as that of ideas, and if in the mind (which is a complex mode of the attribute of thought) we can trace a process of development, ought we not to be able to do so likewise in the order and connection of things? This development would primarily occur in the body which is the mind's counterpart in extension, and Spinoza tells us that the extent of the mind's achievements is in accordance with the aptitude of the body for doing and suffering many things.[4] But he also tells us that every body is in some

---

[1] *Ethics*, II, prop. vii. [2] Props. xxx–xxxi and *schol.*
[3] The similarity of Spinoza's solution of the problem and that of Aristotle is remarkable. Cf. the discussion of the latter on pp. 103 ff. above.
[4] *Ethics*, II, prop. xiv, and V, prop. xxxix.

degree animate[1] and that bodies form a hierarchy[2] according to the complexity of their structure and the arrangement and interaction of their parts. The simplest bodies are distinguished only by motion and rest and velocity; more complex bodies are formed by the juxtaposition and cohesion of a number of simple bodies; more complex still are those which consist of a number of different kinds of complex bodies so held together and related that they communicate to one another motion and rest in constant proportions. The human body is of the most complex kind. It is clearly implied that the more complicated the body the more will it be adapted to do and to suffer many things, and as every body is be-minded the minds of the simplest will be extremely rudimentary while those of the most complex are capable, as we have seen, of increasing their capacity so as to attain the highest knowledge and ultimately immortality itself.

Here then we have, if not explicitly a process of development, at least a definite scale of forms in which the highest do constitute phases in an evolutionary process.[3] And if we take all this together with Spinoza's assertion that 'each thing, so far as it is in itself, strives to persevere in its own being'[4] and with what he regards as following from that, we do find no small indication that the scale of forms as a whole should be conceived as a process of evolution. For the *conatus* is no mere inertia keeping the thing fixed and unchanging within prescribed limits. It is an urge in the thing resisting invasion and destruction by the contrary efforts of other things and impelling its subject towards a perfection of being implicit in its own essence. For the true nature of every finite entity is what it is in the infinite being of God (is its place in the whole), and what it is in itself—its essence—is identical with its *conatus in suo esse perseverare*.[5] In thought this can only be the effort of the thing to become conscious of itself—intelligible to itself—and such intelligibility depends entirely on the recognition of its interrelations with other things defining its place in the whole. It follows that the *conatus* must in every case be a *nisus* to the whole, for the being of anything, what it is in itself, is its implication of all the rest. Hence its striving to persist in its own being can be nothing else than an effort to comprehend its other. If this were not so it would be difficult to see how Spinoza could assert, as he does, that the human mind is

---

[1] *Ethics*, II, prop. xiii, *schol.*
[2] *Ibid.* Axioms, Defs. and *Lemmata* following prop. xiii.
[3] That the conception of such a scale of forms is Spinoza's deliberate intention is borne out by what he says elsewhere. *Vide Epistles* 19 and 23 and Joachim's comment, *The Ethics of Spinoza*, Bk. I, ch. iv, § 1.
[4] *Ethics*, III, prop. vi. [5] *Ethics*, III, prop. vii.

conscious of its own *conatus* as desire and will—as an effort to increase its power of action.[1] This active drive in the human being is the same *conatus* as that by which every other thing endeavours to persevere in its being, and it would be natural to conclude that, just as the human being strives to increase its power of action, so does every other being (as it might do by uniting its body with others to become more complex and ascend in the scale of forms).

Spinoza does not work out in detail the consequences which seem in this way to flow from his doctrine, but they do afford evidence that his system permits of an evolutionary process within the totality of substance or nature. Nor is such evolution excluded (but may even be implied) by the fixed necessity with which 'an infinite number of things in infinite ways' are said to flow from God's essence. For the endless succession of finite modes, each related to the next as transitive cause, is as necessary an effect of God's nature as are the infinite modes which are eternal.[2] The processes of time and change and the causal series they involve are in God and follow from God's essence as well as His infinite attributes and their infinite modes; and this being so, processes of development in time are not excluded.

There is, it is true, much in the *Ethics* which suggests that the representation of things as finite singulars, coming to be and passing away in time, is no more than the confused and inadequate deliverance of *imaginatio*, with its constant tendency to abstract arbitrarily from its context what is in actuality nothing apart from its place in the whole. *Sub specie aeternitatis* everything is eternally in God, and His infinite essence cannot be split up into finite pieces, however endless their succession. All are absorbed into His unity, which is seamlessly one. But this, very largely, is a position forced upon Spinoza by the abstract method he adopts under the influence of the Renaissance belief in the omnicompetence of mathematical reasoning, and it is not the whole doctrine he is striving to propound, for he does not maintain that the modal affections of substance are merely illusory. They are actual modes in and through which God's nature expresses itself,[3] and they each have an 'essence' the idea of which is eternally in God's mind.[4] In their determination of one another to action, moreover, God determines them.[5] Just how their finite character is compatible with their being produced by the infinitely perfect divine nature Spinoza

---

[1] Cf. *Ethics*, III, prop. ix and *schol.*; prop. xii and *dem.*; and IV, prop. xxxviii.
[2] *Ethics*, I, prop. xxviii and *schol.*
[3] Cf. *Ethics*, I, prop. xv, and prop. xxix, *dem.* and *schol.*
[4] Cf. *Ethics*, V, prop. xxii.   [5] *Ethics*, I, prop. xxvii.

never makes wholly intelligible;[1] but, as Joachim avers,[2] to expect that he should do this in detail is to expect more than is reasonable. In general, we must admit, he does provide a principle of explanation which enables us to conceive the articulated system of nature as a scale of degrees of reality or perfection, even though, perhaps, he fails to reconcile this aspect of God's nature in a thoroughly intelligible manner with His unity.

Moreover, if we can admit the existence in God of succession and change as well as of modes varying in degree of perfection, we can admit the occurrence, within the eternal totality of substance, of evolutionary change among finite modes from lower degrees of perfection to higher degrees. And though in Spinoza's thought the conception remains undeveloped and obscure, we have already noted, and shall further maintain at a later stage, that the idea of absolute wholeness and that of developmental change are mutually complementary—they are concepts which overlap—and each requires the other for its intelligibility.

6. The hierarchical structure within the attributes of extension and thought, the doctrine of the *conatus* and the admission of development in human nature, all taken together, leave us no alternative but to conclude that, despite his polemics, the ultimate explanation of things in Spinoza's system is teleological. It is only another way of saying this to maintain, as he does, that their ultimate explanation is in the infinite perfection of God. If we trace the development of the human mind, we discover that its *conatus* impels it finally towards the understanding and love of God which is nothing short of union with His infinite nature. As this is the final end of our endeavour, so it is the final end of the endeavour of all things. For, as we have observed, the effort in each thing to be itself is, on the side of thought, the effort to be self-intelligible, which is, in the end, just that effort to understand and to become one with the divine essence which is the final perfection of man. Accordingly, the explanation of all things can ultimately be given only in terms of their *nisus* to the whole, and is therefore teleological.

That the end for man is, according to Spinoza, the union of his mind

---

[1] The problem of the relation of the finite to the infinite modes of substance comes in here. It is no mean difficulty, but I have not discussed it because (i) it is to a great extent a technical question peculiar to Spinoza, and (ii) the presence of difficulties in Spinoza's theory is not enough to dispose of my main contention that his system involves a scale of degrees of perfection and admits of, if it does not definitely require, the existence of an evolutionary process.

[2] *Op. cit.* p. 108.

with the infinite intellect of God is quite clearly demonstrable. We are told in the *Ethics* (IV, prop. iv, *dem*.) that the *conatus* is the actual power of God; and in man it is his constant effort towards self-preservation. This is the basis and the only foundation of virtue, because virtue is nothing other than our capacity to act, and action proceeds from desire, which *is* our *conatus* as we are conscious of it, and that again is identical with our essence—the being which we strive to preserve.[1] But action is possible only if we are determined to it by adequate ideas (inadequate ideas being the source only of passions, and their only source).[2] Virtue, then, is action in accordance with reason, in which man is free (though freedom, here, does not mean freedom from all determination but freedom from the tyranny of the passions). Accordingly, the only thing that is really conducive to our good is what perfects the understanding[3] and the highest good we can attain is the knowledge of God in whom all things have their being and through whom alone they can be or be conceived.[4] This knowledge of God is *ipso facto* that intellectual love of God which ought above all else to occupy the mind,[5] the attainment of which is its highest endeavour[6] and which fills it with perfect peace and satisfaction.[7] But this intellectual love of God is one and the same thing as God's own love for Himself and men;[8] as indeed it must be, for the knowledge of God is an adequate conception of His attributes and that is no more nor less than the attribute of thought itself[9] which is the mind of God. The more fully man understands God, therefore (the better, that is to say, he understands things by the third kind of knowledge), the more completely is his mind at one with the mind of God Himself. Man's highest virtue and greatest perfection is to be one with the eternal mind.

This is the 'model of human nature' by reference to which Spinoza gives meaning to the terms 'good' and 'bad', 'perfect' and 'imperfect', and in so doing he does nothing inconsistent with his emphatic assertion that the degree of a thing's perfection is the amount of reality which it possesses. For God possesses and is all reality and man is most perfect when most nearly one with God. The criterion of truth thus in the end becomes identified with the criterion of goodness.

[1] *Vide Ethics*, IV, props. xx *et seq.*
[2] *Ethics*, III, prop. i; IV, prop. xxiii.
[3] *Ethics*, IV, prop. xxvii and *dem.*, and Appendix iv.
[4] *Ethics*, I, prop. xv, and IV, prop. xxviii, and Appendix iv-v.
[5] *Ethics*, V, prop. xvi.
[6] *Ethics*, V, props. xxv-xxvii.
[7] *Ethics*, V, prop. xxvii, *dem.*, prop. xxxiii, *schol.* and prop. xl, *cor.*
[8] *Ethics*, V, props. xxxv, xxxvi and *cor.*
[9] *Ethics*, I, def. iv; II, prop. i, and IV, Appendix iv.

The greatest good is the love of God and that is the same as the knowledge of God (who *is* substance and nature). Yet another requirement
of the modern conception of nature is, in this way, provided by the
philosophy of Spinoza.

7. It remains only to show that Spinoza held mind to be in some
sense immanent in all things; and this is, in fact, evident from what has
already been said. God's mind is identical in substance with every other
attribute and it is from His infinite nature that all things proceed. Of
all things, therefore, God is the immanent cause[1] and His intellect,
'in so far as it is conceived to constitute God's essence, is in truth the
cause of things, both of their essence and of their existence'.[2] God's
mind, therefore, is the source of all being and is immanent throughout
nature.

That God is pure thought, however (as in the philosophy of
Aristotle), is not Spinoza's view. For him, God is also an extended
thing and can be assigned an infinite number of other attributes. But
this in itself is a sign of modernity in Spinoza's thought, for the modern
view abjures the abstract conception of thought divorced from all
matter (or mind from body) as well as that of matter which excludes all
thought.[3] Substance, in the modern conception (provisionally to use a
word which does not belong to the modern idiom), is not pure form,
but form and matter in one; and that mind which, for the concept of
evolution, must be everywhere implicit, is not an attenuated, abstracted ghost, but the concrete whole of the real spiritualized by its
own self-consciousness. This is, perhaps, as good a definition of
Spinoza's God as can be given.

III. THE VIRUS OF RENAISSANCE THOUGHT

8. The position in Spinoza, however, is obscured by a difficulty
which he never succeeded in resolving—that of the relation in God
between the attributes. They are all substantially one and the same
thing, and their variety is, *prima facie*, due only to the intellect—the
way in which the intellect conceives the essence of substance. But (as
Joachim points out) so to explain the diversity would not be legitimate
for Spinoza, because it would reduce the attributes to mere appearance
and render the ultimate nature of God, in His oneness, unknowable.

[1] *Ethics*, I, prop. xviii.
[2] *Ethics*, I, prop. xvii, *schol.*
[3] Cf. Whitehead's rejection of 'vacuous actuality'.

H*

For Spinoza the attributes *are* the ultimate nature of God, with its innumerable facets or aspects; but he never explains on what principle God's unity can be so diversified, nor just how such diverse attributes can all be one and the same thing. This difficulty is critical in Spinoza's philosophy, because upon the substantial identity of the attributes depends the identity of *idea* and *ideatum*, of body and mind, and everything that follows from it. But he fails in the end to solve the problem, despite his amazing insight. He is still a product of the Renaissance, and its virus is at work in his thought, so that extension and thought still reveal themselves each as starkly other and their unity in substance is asserted as brute fact unexplained and inexplicable. Consequently, the solution of our problem which Spinoza offers does no more than push it back a stage to create this new difficulty of the unity of the attributes. Enlightening as Spinoza's theory is, it does not solve this ulterior problem and it cannot, therefore, give us all that we require. For this we must pass on to other thinkers, not gifted with greater minds but enjoying greater historical advantages.

LEIBNIZ

IV. OPPOSITION TO RENAISSANCE PRESUPPOSITIONS

9. Characteristics of Renaissance thinking are apparent in the work of Spinoza, despite the fact that attention to the deeper implications and the spirit of his teaching leads us to conclude that it does not properly belong to the period in which he lived. But the alignment of the philosophy of Leibniz with modern thought rather than with that of the 17th century is still more marked. He explicitly challenges the Renaissance assumptions, asserts the principles typical of the modern conception of nature and forms a bridge from the dualistic Cartesian metaphysic to the Kantian synthesis which opened the way for the development of new ideas.

The first and main object of his attack was the mechanistic conception of the physical world based on the assumption that all natural phenomena could be explained in terms of matter and motion. Descartes had declared that the essence of matter was extension, and motion is obviously a function of extension in space and time. But for Leibniz the very conception of extension presents a problem—one of those 'two famous labyrinths in which our reason often goes astray'.[1] Arguing from physical facts he proves that the essence of bodies cannot

[1] *Théodicée*, preface.

be mere extension[1] and, after reflection upon the nature of extended matter, he argues that mathematical points cannot form the units of material aggregates.[2] The explanation of physical phenomena, he declares, is ultimately metaphysical. It can be found only by returning to the notions of substantial forms and final causes that Renaissance science had discarded, and by regarding things as appearances of which the reality is something 'to be conceived after the manner of the notion we have of *souls*'.[3] Here immediately we have two of the modern requirements—the immanence in all things of mind (or soul) and the teleological conception of reality (final causes)—and, as might be expected, from the development of these two, the other main elements of the modern position emerge.

V. THE THEORY OF MONADS

10. In brief, Leibniz' theory is that reality is entirely constituted by immaterial monadic substances, each of which is a mind of a sort, of which no two are exactly alike (for indiscernibles are identical), and which form in consequence a continuous series. Their differences consist in the extent to which their 'perceptions' are clear or confused, and these perceptions are the 'expression' in each of what occurs in all the rest. Between them there are no actual (physical) relations, for every monad is 'windowless' and contains its whole nature within itself from which all predicates belonging to it as subject could (if we perceived it clearly and distinctly) be deduced. But there is a harmony, pre-established by God when He created them, between the monads; so that the perceptions of each express all the rest and each mirrors the entire universe. It does so, however, with varying degrees of clarity. In each monad certain of its perceptions are clearer than others, and monads differ in the extent of their clear perceptions. Accordingly, in each, its perceptions form a scale of varying degrees of clarity and confusion, and similarly the monads themselves constitute a series from those in which perception is most confused to those in which the greater part is clear and distinct. Only in some monads does this clarity of

---

[1] *Vide* H. W. B. Joseph, *Lectures on the Philosophy of Leibniz* (Oxford, 1949), pp. 27 ff.

[2] Cf. *Système nouveau de la nature*, § 3: 'I perceived after much meditation, that it is impossible to find *the principles of a real unity* in matter alone, or in that which is only passive, since it is nothing but a collection or aggregate of parts *ad infinitum*. Now a multiplicity can derive its reality only *from genuine units*, which come from elsewhere and are quite other than mathematical points of which it is certain that the continuum cannot be composed.'

[3] *Système nouveau, loc. cit.*; cf. *Lettre à Arnaud* (1686), Gerhardt, ii, 58.

perception amount to consciousness (or 'apperception', as Leibniz calls it), within which we may assume that there are also degrees of clarity. In consequence, we get a continuous series from the most rudimentary, unconscious minds up to the most highly developed and self-conscious. The mind in which all perceptions are perfectly clear is that of God—the 'Monad of monads'—who forms the end and consummation of the series.[1]

Like Spinoza, Leibniz holds that confused perception constitutes passivity in the mind and clear and distinct perception (Spinoza's 'adequate ideas') activity, so that God is *actus purus* (as both for Spinoza and for Aristotle), while all other monads contain a certain amount of mere potentiality proportional to their passivity or the confusion of their perceptions.[2] The variety among monads resulting from these differences is described by Leibniz as a difference of 'point of view' from which each mirrors the universe, and just how these points of view are determined is important for the understanding of Leibniz' theory of the relation between body and mind.

11. Bodies are for Leibniz only phenomena, though, as compared with dreams and other illusory perceptions, they are *phenomena bene fundata*. That is to say, they are perceptions of real entities, but they are confused perceptions representing what is in reality a number of non-material monads as material, spatial aggregates. Every such aggregate or body is thus a group of monads confusedly perceived. But no two of the monads in any such group are exactly alike and they always constitute some sort of a series, one of them being more highly developed than the rest. This is called the dominant monad of the group and is related to the rest as mind to body. It is active in respects in which the others are passive and this relationship is phenomenally represented as one of cause and effect, being not actually a physical relation but a logical one. For the cause (the relatively clear perception which is activity) is the ground or explanation of the effect (the passivity or relatively confused perception). Further, among the perceptions of the dominant monad, the monads which constitute its body are more clearly expressed than others which do not; and those which do not form part of the group are perceived by the dominant monad through its perception of their reflection in its subordinate monads. Consequently it is through the mediation of its body that the dominant monad mirrors the universe. We are told, further, that any aggregate

[1] Cf. *Monadology*, § 30: '. . . what is limited in us is in Him without limits'.
[2] Here again the debt to Aristotle is obvious.

body such as has been described is composed of similar smaller aggregates, each of which is similarly divisible and so on *ad infinitum*. The whole structure is organic, having organisms for its parts. In any such group the grade of development of the dominant monad will determine whether the body as which the group appears is 'non-living', 'alive', or 'conscious'; and, as in Spinoza the more complex the *res extensa* the more developed the corresponding *idea* or mind, so with Leibniz the grade of the dominant monad is higher as the group which forms its body is more complicatedly organic. It is the same thing, therefore, to say that the point of view of the monad is determined by the degree of its activity and passivity as to say that its point of view is its body, through the mediation of which it mirrors the universe.

There is certainly a serious difficulty in all this which Leibniz does nothing to remove. What sort of grouping is possible for spiritual entities such as monads? What is the real relationship that appears phenomenally as aggregation? To these questions Leibniz supplies no answer, and yet if the theory is to be properly intelligible, monads must have some kind of 'togetherness' which will enable us to distinguish one group from another. If the gradations of activity and passivity are the only relations between them, they are not enough to account for the kind of groupings that Leibniz assumes as the bases of phenomenal bodies.

Body as an aggregate conceived quantitatively and consisting of *partes extra partes* is called by Leibniz *materia secunda*. What he calls *materia prima* is the passive element (or moment) inevitably present in every monad (other than God), and, having regard to the single monad in itself, this *materia prima* is said to be its body. If the monad is dominant in a group, its passivity will be its confused perceptions of its subordinates, representing them as a material body. The two senses of 'body' (as opposed to 'mind') thus coalesce, their difference being only one of view-point. With regard simply to the single monad, its passivity is its body, but with regard to the group over which it dominates, its body is the subordinate monads confusedly expressed in its own perception. However confused this perception may be, it is less so than any in the subordinate monads themselves, and still less so than any 'expression' in the dominant monad of those extrinsic to its group. Though in the dominant monad it is passivity, relative to the subordinate members of the group it is activity. There is, no doubt, obscurity here, for we must ask what, in the dominant monad and, so to speak, for itself, constitutes its activity, since its perception of all other monads would seem to constitute its passivity if its perception of its own group (those which it reflects most clearly) is to be its *materia prima*. I am not sure what the answer to this question is, but it seems to lie in the other propensity of the monad, its appetition. That is an urge towards fuller explication of what in its perception is merely implicit. The activity of clarification is activity in the truest sense, and, as we shall presently discover, it is a mistake to regard the perceptions in the monad as merely static images. They are never simply passive, but at any level are in some degree active. This relativity or overlap of activity and passivity is, in fact, the key to the whole problem of the relation of body to mind. We must, strictly speaking, view them as respectively lower and higher grades in a series of entities which are in essence all spiritual, whether the relation is taken to be one between the subordinate and the dominating monads of a group or one between the more confused and the more distinct perceptions in a single monad. As in Aristotle's theory, sheer matter is an abstraction—an ideal limit of activity—for there is no sharp line separating confused from distinct perception, each perception being both in some degree—each being a union of opposites constituting a distinct intermediary grade in a series connecting the extremes.[1] The distinction of body from mind is thus purely relative, as everything is in some degree both. Pure matter (or body) without mind is an impossibility and pure mind without matter exists (for Leibniz as for Aristotle) only in God.

12. It needs no elaborate argument to show that the relation between mind and body and that between subject and object in consciousness are, for Leibniz, one and the same. The object of all perception is *really* the universe of monads and *apparently* the bodies constituting the physical world. But the latter are perceived from the point of view of the percipient monad, and that point of view is its body. Its objects, therefore, other than its own body, are perceived through the mediation of those monads which are its body (*i.e.* in so far as those monads perceive them) and its perception of them is thus identical with its perception of its own body. The physical counterpart of this argument[2] shows that every material thing reflects, through its causal interrelations with others, the entire physical universe; so that, in our perception of the body, we perceive all things. The position is in all essentials similar to that of Spinoza and is not very different from that of Aristotle (*vide* pp. 106-7 and 211-12 above).

[1] Cf. Collingwood's discussion of the scale of forms in *Philosophical Method*, ch. iii.   [2] *Vide Monadology*, 61, and *Lettre à Arnaud* (1687), Gerhardt, ii, 112.

VI. EVOLUTIONISM IN LEIBNIZ' THEORY

13. Neither the series of monads, however, nor that of perceptions within a monad is just a gamut of static grades. In each case it is a developing series. For Leibniz maintains that monads have appetition as well as perception. There is in them a *conatus* or tendency issuing in continuous change of perception which may be in either of two opposite directions. It may be 'development' from a lower to a higher grade in the scale of distinctness, or it may be 'envelopment'—passage from more distinct to more confused perception. As every monad is constantly changing in either of these two ways, so the 'body' of any dominant monad is in a state of perpetual flux. According to the general direction of the change, the total entity may develop from a 'dead' to a 'living' thing and from a lower to a higher grade of self-consciousness, or it may degenerate from conscious life to lower forms and even to the level of 'non-living' matter. But, we are told,[1] the general tendency of all monads is upward. 'In a confused way they all strive after the infinite, the whole'; and (we must presume) it is only when they fail to achieve greater distinctness of perception that monads degenerate.

14. Everything which we commonly regard as physical or material is thus an appearance of and is determined by what is in reality spiritual; and, as the activity of the spiritual entity is purposive, final causes are the ultimate determinants of all things and events. 'Efficient causes', writes Leibniz, 'are dependent upon final causes and spiritual things are in their nature prior to material things.'[2] Physical laws, though valid as far as they go, are not, he considers, completely intelligible in themselves but require the purposive activity of spiritual substances to explain them.[3]

The conception of evolution is thus explicit in Leibniz' philosophy and it is inseparable from the doctrine that reality is throughout spiritual—that matter is only a confused appearance of what is essentially mind. From this doctrine, moreover, it follows that the mind and its object are not two separate things in external relation but two different phases (or aspects) of the same thing (namely, the activity of the monad).

15. It follows, also, that knowledge constitutes a single system. As Leibniz puts it: from the nature of the subject all its possible predicates

---

[1] *Monadology*, 60.   [2] *Epistola ad Bierlingium* (1711), Gerhardt, vii, 501.
[3] Cf. *Lettre à Arnaud* (1686), Gerhardt, ii, 77.

follow of necessity. The subject is and can only be substance, that is, a monad; and its predicates are the properties or qualities of the monad. These, however, are all implicit in it, and its life and existence is no more than the continuous unfolding or explication of them. It is a unity of innumerable differences exhibited *seriatim* but always the manifestation of the same substance. The subject is the universal and its predicates are the particulars in and through which it displays its essential nature. The truth about it is the whole of it and the more clearly and distinctly the complex articulation of its unity can be brought to consciousness the more fully and truly is it known. So far as the conception of it fails of clarity, so far is it incomplete and merely implicit and for that reason it is constantly impelled towards the whole—that whole which is the complete explication of its diversity, in which it is held together in one coherent totality and which is the final truth about it.

Furthermore, the monad is the expression of the whole universe and its own unity can thus be no other than the unity of the universe *in toto*. Leibniz' teaching appears paradoxical in that it asserts that the universe is composed solely of monads each utterly separate and all mutually unrelated, and yet that each monad is wholly constituted by its expression from its own point of view of all the rest. In other words, monads constitute one another though they remain unrelated. He seems to be maintaining that the world is an irreducible multiplicity while at the same time he requires us to regard each item as inseparable from all the rest. We must, however, interpret him to mean by the windowlessness of monads no more than the absence of *spatial* and *physical* interrelation between them [1]—for how can spiritual entities be spatially and physically related? Their metaphysical or logical [2] interrelation is undeniable, and together they all constitute a single system—a graded and developing series from the most rudimentary, in which the whole is merely *implicit*, to the complete explication of the whole in the activity of God. It should, of course, follow that the life of the monad, as a development from the most confused to the most distinct perception, is identical with the development in the world from the most rudimentary monad to the most fully developed, for passage from one level of explication to the next is indistinguishable from the transition from a monad at one stage to another at the next higher stage, and even the differences of point of view are really no more than differences of degree of confusion or distinctness. In its own

[1] *Vide Monadology*, 51.
[2] Logical because metaphysical. What is constituted by other things cannot logically be independent of them.

private development, therefore, each monad must assume in turn every
point of view and the distinction between microcosm and macrocosm
tends to dissolve away; or rather, to appear only as a relative distinction
between different levels in the same developmental process. An unsolved
—in fact, by Leibniz, an unrecognized—problem obviously remains:
that of understanding the relation between the process of development
and its end (the relation, really, of the finite to the infinite). It is the
problem of understanding how the end of the process can at the same
time be the whole; how the process can be carried up into, or sublated
in the end.

VII. FINITE AND INFINITE

16. On this problem of relating the finite to the infinite—the process
to the end—Leibniz' theories concerning God and His relation to the
monads should naturally shed some light. But what he says in various
contexts on this subject is by no means clear-cut or straightforward.
God, we are told, is the sufficient reason for the occurrence of all
contingent events, the finite causes of which form an inexhaustible
regression *in infinitum.* Yet they are all summed up in God and
accounted for in His choice of the best from among the infinite number
of possible worlds which His intellect conceives. He chooses this
world as a whole and with all its defects (such as there are), because
the removal of such defects is not 'compossible' with the advantages
which make the world better than the rival possibilities. God chooses
this best of all possible worlds because His will is perfectly good and
He acts in accordance with an ideal of goodness. The efficient causes
of all things, therefore, are themselves dependent upon the perfect will
of God as their ultimate cause or sufficient reason; but that, as it aims at
the production of what is best, is a final rather than an efficient cause.
'I hold that it is just in this [final cause]', writes Leibniz, 'that the
principle of all existences and of all the laws of nature must be sought,
because God always proposes to Himself the best and the most perfect.'[1] The teleological character of Leibniz' system is thus reinforced
by a doctrine somewhat more obscure than that of the purposive
appetition in monads, but one in which value is quite clearly made the
ultimate principle of all explanation.

17. Again, in the *Monadology*, he says that God is the primary substance and that the created monads are produced 'so to speak, through
continual fulgurations of the Divinity from moment to moment'

[1] *Discours de métaphysique*, XIX.

(§ 47). Of these, all are mirrors of the universe, but the higher souls or minds are mirrors more especially of God.[1] The last point seems to follow simply from the difference in clarity of perception between monads which would naturally bring the more developed and conscious nearer to God, who, we have already observed, is the culmination of the developing series. Accordingly, God is 'not only the principle and the cause of all substances and of all existing things, but also the chief of all persons or intelligent substances, as the absolute monarch of the most perfect city or republic, such as is constituted by all the spirits together in the universe'.[2]

In order to make this doctrine intelligible we must interpret it somewhat freely. If God is the most perfect spirit, if He is *actus purus*, in whom everything is clear and distinct which in created spirits is obscure and confused, He must express the universe as an absolutely complete and articulated whole. But the universe is nothing besides the ordered series of monads and, if God is the expression of this, monads cannot have been created *subsequent* to His perfection. The fulgurations which give rise to finite spirits, if they are to be conceived at all consistently with Leibniz' principles, must be actual modes or phases of God's being—as in the doctrine of Spinoza. For, as Spinoza teaches, to maintain that the world was created subsequently to God's existence is to argue an imperfection in the prior being of God. But if God is the complete expression of the universe, He must reflect the whole process of development which is motivated by the appetition of the monads, and in Him the lower phases of the process, with all the passivity and obscurity incident upon them, must also somehow be expressed. The absolute conception of the process as a whole, however, which this expression of the universe implies, might then be represented as a series of fulgurations (or crises) expressing, each in its appropriate degree, the divine nature, and each for that reason (whatever its degree of perfection) presupposing the whole and necessary to it. However lowly the phase of the development, what it represents in some degree is always the end. But whether or to what extent this is Leibniz' intention is far from clear.

It should follow that the defects of the lower phases cannot be purely accidental, but must be necessary conditions of the ultimate consummation. The world, in short, must be 'the best of all possible worlds' because, whatever evils it includes, if it were otherwise it could not constitute just that process of development which issues in the ultimate perfection. But we must part company with Leibniz in his

[1] *Op. cit.* 83, and *Disc. de mét.* XXXVI.   [2] *Disc. de mét.* XXXV.

presumption that other possible worlds are conceivable. No world which, in its fullest development and articulation, was other than God —the absolutely perfect being—could in any way be possible; for its existence would make God's existence impossible, and that is the cause of *all* existence. For God to have 'created' any other world would thus have been for Him to contradict His own essence, and that even He is unable to conceive.

But, however we choose to interpret the doctrine, there can be no doubt of Leibniz' intention to give his system a teleological character, nor of the fact that his principles lead us necessarily to unite the criteria of goodness and truth. Moreover, his doctrine of monads entails both a coherence theory of knowledge and an absolutist theory of the universe. Even though he sometimes writes what seems to contradict the second of these positions, he cannot ultimately escape either of them; and in one place at least he seems clearly to recognize the implication of his doctrine. 'In strictness', he writes, 'the true infinite is found only in the *absolute*, which is prior to all composition and is not formed by the composition of parts.'[1] In short, his metaphysical theory is one of the universe as a development, and it implies, where it does not explicitly state, all the main requisites of the modern conception of nature.

[1] *Nouveaux Essais*, II, xvii.

Chapter XII

HEGEL

I. HEGEL'S MODERNITY

1. SPINOZA and Leibniz were unable to deal satisfactorily with certain important philosophical problems. Spinoza, as we have noticed, solved the problem of relating *idea* to *ideatum* only provisionally by holding them to be identical in substance and different only in attribute. The problem then became one of relating the attributes so that their differentiation of one substance became intelligible, and this Spinoza never succeeded in doing. It is the problem of finding and comprehending the principle of the differentiation of substance which produces the variety of the experienced world—or, better, the principle on which substance differentiates itself into that variety. As Spinoza left the unity of his God in the last resort blank and unrelated to the diversity of the attributes, so the same tendency to obliterate all differences in an abstract unity appears in the Leibnizian spiritualism, for the differences of view-point between the monads must vanish as they approach the goal of complete clarity and pure activity. In the Leibnizian God there should be no differences of view-point and so no reflection (or 'expression') of the universe of monads—yet what else is there for the mind of God to express? If God is not sheerly to transcend the process of development He must somehow include it, and how this is to be conceived Leibniz is never able to make clear.

Here again we have the problem of immanence and transcendence which finally defeated the Greeks. This failure of Spinoza to reconcile God's unity with the diversity of His attritbues and of Leibniz to reconcile God's activity with the passivity of the monads is the same in principle as Plato's failure to relate the forms to sensible things and Aristotle's to make God *forma informans* as well as *forma assistens* of the *scala universi*.

In the philosophy of Hegel, however, this problem becomes soluble and in the light of his solution it is possible to form some more intelligible view of the relation of the human mind to the world, as its object in knowledge, as well as to the natural organism, its body, through the instrumentality of which it becomes conscious. For once we understand how the infinite is immanent in the finite as well as transcendent beyond it we can understand how a finite entity such as the human organism can become the vehicle of a self-transcending consciousness.

2. That Hegel's theory embodies the five principles listed above as characteristic of the modern conception of nature needs no argument. The reader may even suspect that in enumerating them I have first derived them from Hegel and then transplanted them into the modern context. Such an impression is unavoidable unless I were first to examine in detail the presuppositions of contemporary science and then to treat Hegel out of his historical context as if he were an ultra-modern philosopher, or else to state the tenets of his philosophy baldly without reference to modern ideas and then, after eliciting the implications of modern science, to argue that the moderns have never advanced beyond Hegel. Neither of these alternatives is admissible, for, though I believe and shall try to show that some modern thinkers are far behind Hegel both in their handling of the problem of knowledge and in their interpretation of modern science, it is nevertheless true that Hegel, like Spinoza and Leibniz, was a product of his age, and though his philosophy is astonishingly prophetic, it nevertheless bears the mark of cotemporary influences. For the statement of a philosophical system appropriate to our own times we must look to Whitehead, and if we find in him Hegelian echoes (albeit inadvertent and unconscious) our surprise will be mitigated by the realization of the not less remarkable anticipation by Hegel of modern concepts. I have therefore sought to compromise between two evils by stating the principles presupposed by modern science dogmatically before showing that they are in fact implied by modern scientific theories, in order that I may emphasize the extent to which those principles are already at work in the thought of the three philosophers with which this section deals.

II. HEGEL'S THEORY OF THE UNDERSTANDING

3. The typical Renaissance separation of the mind from nature, and all the consequences that follow from it in the empiricist theory of knowledge, Hegel attributes to the understanding, the special province of which is 'sound common sense' and empirical science. The understanding is that level of thought which immediately succeeds upon sense-perception and which seeks to divide, define, classify and analyse the deliverances of sense, constructing a neatly arranged system of sharply distinguished and mutually exclusive classes of characters and

entities. 'Thought, as understanding,' he writes, 'sticks to fixity of characters and their distinctness from one another: every limited abstract it treats as having subsistence and being of its own.'[1] The understanding, in fact, is the source and playground of abstractions, as opposed on the one hand to feeling, in which all differences are merely implicitly contained, and on the other to reason, in which they become reconciled and united in their mutual opposition. Empiricism, along with the opposing forms of dogmatism, Hegel criticizes, therefore, as attempts to philosophize at the level of the understanding, which is appropriate only to empirical science. Even Kant errs, he thinks, for though the Critical Philosophy itself transcends the level of the understanding, Kant sought to set limits upon it dictated by the understanding. It is actually from Kant that Hegel adopts the term and its distinction from reason and, in Hegel's opinion, Kant defined the province of the understanding rightly in limiting it to the sphere of phenomena and the range of sense-perception, to which alone its categories are meant to apply. His error was to deny to reason the right which it claims to transcend that sphere and to determine its own supersensible objects by its own categories. That claim could not be made good, however, until the dichotomy between thought and sense, which is itself a product of the understanding, had been superseded. Reason would then be seen to concern itself, not so much with supersensible objects, as with objects reconstituted from the sensible by the activity of thought.[2]

It is typical of the understanding, accordingly, to separate subject from object, and (if we follow the Hegelian doctrine) the presupposition of that dichotomy is to be expected of empirical science, which never questions it and never should, for the function of science is no more nor less than that of the understanding itself. The scientist, therefore, makes no error in adopting an empirical attitude. It is the one appropriate to his science. The error arises only when the attempt is made to elevate this assumption of separation between subject and object into a metaphysical theory, for it is the duty of the metaphysician to think on the higher level of reason, and on that level the assumed separation leads to all kinds of difficulties and contradictions which require resolution and which the understanding can never resolve.

[1] *Encyclopädie der philosophischen Wissenschaften*, 80 (Wallace's translation).
[2] Even this is an inadequate statement of the position, for thought (it is maintained) does not work upon an alien object but is shown to be already at work in the objects of sense, and their reconstitution is no more than their own self-development due to that very activity of thought within them.

4. Here at once appear both Hegel's advance beyond the presuppositions of the Renaissance and his limitation by them. His advance consists in his ability to see Renaissance science in its place as a phase of a development which goes beyond it. But his limitation, natural and inevitable, is that for him that development is *only* a dialectical one. He could not have seen it as an historical development, for, as such, it had not yet taken place. Accordingly, he limits science *for all time* to the level of the understanding and elevates philosophy above it to the level of reason. But modern science has left behind it the presuppositions of the 17th and 18th centuries; it has transcended what Hegel called the level of the understanding and has been forced, by its own discoveries, to adopt an outlook which Hegel considered appropriate only to reason. Consequently, we find modern philosophers complaining of Hegel and his followers that they fail to do justice to the scientific outlook and belittle its achievements while they exalt as the ultimate truth a mystical philosophy without foundation in established fact. There is some justice in this criticism but also much misunderstanding. That Hegel fails to do justice to *modern* science is true, but it cannot be held against him as a fault, for he could not have had prevision of the character of future scientific advance. He did full justice to the science of his own day and was so much wiser than his co-temporaries as to see its limitations where they (and their successors for the next two generations) were infatuated by its successes and began to think it capable of omniscience. It was not until a century later that scientists themselves recognized and surpassed these limitations. Hegel's later followers were less perspicacious. They might have seen and recognized the trend of scientific advance beyond anything that Hegel could have anticipated, but they followed his leadership too closely to realize the revolutionary character of that advance. They believed, as Hegel had taught them, that science never could transcend the level of the understanding and so were blinded to the full significance of the scientific achievements of their own time. It was not until Collingwood drew attention to the presuppositions of modern cosmology that this significance was made clear and only now does it become apparent how Hegel's doctrine requires modification. Science and philosophy are not related as subordinate and superior levels of thought, but both levels distinguished by Hegel as understanding and reason are operative in both (with respect to philosophy Hegel admitted this [1]); and at the higher level the apparent conflict between the two disciplines is overcome. The reconciliation, however, is a levelling up and not a levelling

[1] Cf. *Encyclopädie*, 80, *Zusatz*.

down as is implied in the opinions of so many contemporary empiricists. This result is, of course, implicit in Hegel's theory, but at the time when he wrote it could not have been explicitly developed.

But neither Hegel nor his followers wished to belittle the achievements of science; nor did they seek to hypostatize a vague and nebulous metaphysic as the final and ultimate truth. That the rational interpretation of experience does not float loose from its empirical foundations, but rather consolidates and renders them intelligible, is precisely what they claim to demonstrate and what they repeatedly maintain. Accordingly common sense and science are for them of fundamental importance, as many passages in their works bear witness. Furthermore, they never claim that their philosophy is the final and ultimate truth, but only the furthest point which reason has so far reached. This is Hegel's explicit statement[1] and, after all, if one accepts a philosophy at all that is what one must take it to be.

5. The method of the understanding, according to Hegel, is to analyse and distinguish, for purposes of more exact study, elements and aspects of a whole, which in reality are inseparable from one another. This method is an indispensable moment in all thinking and though it is not the *differentia* of reason it is not excluded by reason and is by no means useless in philosophy. It is the first of three main forms in which thought works, of which the other two are dialectic and speculative reason and each of which predominates at a certain level. All of them are, however, present to some extent in all thinking, and it is only the understanding which would seek to separate them rigidly into water-tight compartments.[2] Where understanding predominates, matter and mind are mutually opposed and subject and object are held apart as separate and externally related in knowing; but at the level of speculative reason this opposition is seen to be the result of abstraction and only the dialectical aspect of a more concrete concept in which subject and object are one.

Accordingly, Hegel criticizes the Kantian doctrine of the thing-in-itself in all its forms. As a purely unknowable 'reality' external to consciousness it is nothing (as Kant himself admits[3]); yet even nothing, Hegel argues, is a category of thought and is identical with pure, empty, abstract being, which is not unknowable, but is indeed an idea holding the least possible content to be known. As Idea of Reason, the

---

[1] *Vide Geschichte der Philosophie*, III, iii, E: 'This then is the standpoint of the present day, and the series of spiritual forms is with it, for the present, concluded'.
[2] *Vide Enc.* 79. [3] Cf. *Kritik der reinen Vernunft*, A 104-5.

Kantian thing-in-itself is limited to a regulative influence upon our empirical knowledge and is supposed to have no constitutive value. This view Hegel rejects, for it results from the imposition of a limit upon knowledge which could be justified only by the demonstration that that limit had been passed. If we are to pronounce phenomena to be only appearances as compared with things-in-themselves, we must already know the superior reality. The limitation of the sphere of phenomenal knowledge must lie within and not beyond experience, and if it did not it could never be set. Nor should we have any grounds whatever for permitting the Ideas of Reason (which profess to represent the unconditioned) to regulate our knowledge of phenomena.

But in the philosophy of Kant the *Ding an sich*, and its limitation of knowledge to the relatively subjective realm of phenomena, are the last vestiges of Renaissance presuppositions, and by rejecting them Hegel has once and for all departed from the Renaissance point of view. For Kant's subjective idealism he substitutes what he calls absolute idealism, the central principle of which is the identity of the real with the rational in Absolute Mind, which sublates matter, unites subject and object and comprehends all reality, holding within its concrete unity all the phases of the dialectical process of which it is the culmination. Of that dialectical process it is the source as well as the immanent *nisus*, and in that dialectical process it manifests itself as all the multifarious forms of nature and mind. They are real and intelligible only as phases of the self-development of the Absolute, and the degree of their wholeness, or concreteness, is the measure at once of their truth and of their value.

It is obviously impossible to show how Hegel works all this out in detail and I shall attempt no more than the discussion of certain general characteristics of his system, assuming the reader's acquaintance with the detail of his exposition.

III. THE CONCRETE UNIVERSAL

6. Followers of Hegel, especially F. H. Bradley[1] and Bernard Bosanquet, have laid great stress upon the provisional (and almost spurious) character of the abstract universal of the understanding— the universal as presented in formal logic and as it is taken to be by the empirical scientist, namely, a common property or class-concept. In its place they put the 'concrete' universal, which is itself an individual because it is a concrete system of all its particulars. The particulars are

---

[1] Whose acceptance of Hegel's views was subject to severe reservations.

not simply indifferent instances of a common character, but each is a specific determination or embodiment of the universal essence, and its differences from the other embodiments of that essence are at least as important as its similarity to them. Moreover, the universal is not merely differentiated into the coherent system of its particulars, but it supplies the very principle of differentiation. In short, it is self-differentiating.

7. All this is true of the universal in Hegel's logic, but it is not a complete account of it. The conception of system may be formed at various levels of thinking and at each we shall have an example of universality, but they will not all be adequate to what Hegel calls 'the notion'—the universal *par excellence*. Bosanquet, in various contexts, gives different illustrations of universal systems, and I think it is clear that he is alive to the provisional and unsatisfactory character of some of them. For Bosanquet a concrete universal is 'a world',[1] or 'a system with different features or properties, such that without being all similar or repetitions of each other they present variations connected by law, and therefore the variation of one is an index to the variation of the others'.[2] But such a system may be exemplified in a geometrical construction, in a machine, in a chemical reaction, in a living organism, or in a scientific theory. These are all on different grades and are in varying degrees inadequate to the full nature of the Hegelian 'notion', which is fully realized only in self-conscious mind. Only self-consciousness can display the concrete system in its proper form: that is, as the totality constituted by the interplay of all its parts and rendering their differences each relevant to the systematic unity of the whole. To bring the differences to consciousness and make them aware of themselves, their place and function in the whole, is in the last resort the only way to make the systematic character explicit. But this can be done only in and as a self-conscious mind. To be a true whole is to be a whole of conscious experience and anything less can only be a part, or (according to the way in which we view the matter) an aspect, or a phase in the development or self-explication of the whole. The other examples of system are examples of universality only because mind is immanent in them. Just how it is so immanent we shall consider presently. What is to be observed at this point is that if we can make intelligible the notion of a concrete universal which is at once a unity and the principle of its own differentiation into a systematically related

---

[1] *Vide Principle of Individuality and Value*, ch. ii, § 2.
[2] *Implication and Linear Inference* (London, 1920), p. 8.

multiplicity, we can solve Spinoza's problem of the differentiation of God's oneness.

This Hegel does by propounding the doctrine inchoate in Spinoza that substance is only a provisional characterization of ultimate reality. That reality can be no less than the activity of thought which is both subject and object in one. In so doing he returns to the Aristotelian conception of God as the pure form or ἐνέργεια that is νόησις νοήσεως. But he goes beyond Aristotle in making this activity the very being of the scale of forms which is subordinate to its absolute fulfilment. The generation of the scale is precisely that activity of thought which consummates itself in the absolute self-consciousness of mind. The forms are all forms of thought—*Denkbestimmungen* or categories —and it is in and through them that the Absolute Mind realizes itself. They are its differentiations and they flow from it on the principle which is its own essence. Absolute Mind is, in short, self-differentiating and such as to account for both its own variety and its own unity. We can understand this only after we have examined the nature of that principle which is the essence of thought and which in its operation does at the same time unify and differentiate the Absolute—namely, dialectic.

IV. DIALECTIC

8. In the Absolute, unity and difference are reconciled, and in fact neither concept is intelligible without the other. We never do and never can conceive pure, abstract, blank unity as such, and when we think that we do we are always surreptitiously mediating the idea by contrast with the notion of diversity—of which, in its abstract purity, the same is true. Completely blank unity is, indeed, nothing. It is the same as Hegel's pure being which, in the beginning of his Logic, he identifies with nothing.[1] For, having no inner diversity, it has nothing to determine it to any definite character. It cannot be really one, for in it there is nothing to unite, and if the attempt is made to conceive it by reference to something outside itself it must be defined in terms of its difference from that. Then at once the idea of unity will be mediated by that of its opposite and the two will be combined in a more comprehensive and concrete concept.

The same reasoning applies *mutatis mutandis* to the abstract idea of pure difference. Two entities without any common basis of comparison cannot be compared and so cannot be thought as different. To be

[1] 'Identity is, in the first place, the repetition of what we had earlier as Being . . .' (*Enc.* 115, *Zusatz*).

different they must share some element of identity and without it each is simply one and self-identical excluding all difference. It is, therefore, unintelligible and so not even anything by itself. Neither the concept of identity nor that of difference—neither that of unity nor that of diversity—is anything thinkable without the other, and the more the understanding tries to hold them apart the more is it involved in confusion and self-contradiction.[1]

The result is the paradox that identity and difference are identical. As Hegel puts it: 'That which is different from Difference is Identity. Difference is therefore both itself and Identity: the two together constitute Difference . . . Difference is the whole and its own moment just as Identity is the whole and its moment'.[2] They are opposite concepts, yet both are contained in each. They thus provide an example (in fact, the archetype) of that identity of opposites which is the nerve of the Hegelian dialectic.[3] We must, however, guard against the error of reverting immediately to the very abstraction from which we are trying to free ourselves. When we say that identity and difference are identical, we are using the term 'identical' at the end of the sentence in a new sense. The concrete concept is both opposites at once. The identity of the moments, therefore, cannot be the abstract identity which is but one moment of the concrete notion formed by their synthesis. Either of the two opposites, if taken alone, is a pure abstraction and has significance only proleptically. Its only reality is its function as a moment in the more concrete union with its opposite, and its attempt to maintain itself can succeed only by calling into being that which it excludes but without which it cannot be what it is—*i.e.* cannot be a moment in the whole. What it is really, is just the function that it fulfils as a moment in the higher totality, and to make that explicit the complementary function of its opposite must be fulfilled along with it. This evocation of the other is what Hegel describes as the revulsion of one concept into its opposite and it is the effect necessarily produced by the immanence of the whole within each partial idea. For the intelligibility of the abstracted moment *is*, and only is, its union with its other, and if we try to find something intelligible in its isolated self we see only a constant oscillation between abstract opposites. 'The truth of' either of these is the concrete unity in which each interprets or mediates the other. But this unity is no mere fusion—no mere mergence into a uniform and undifferentiated oneness—but a true reconciliation of the

[1] Cf. Mure, *A Study of Hegel's Logic* (Oxford, 1950), p. 99.
[2] *Wissenschaft der Logik, Werke* (Berlin, 1834), IV, p. 38.
[3] Cf. Reyburn, *Hegel's Ethical Theory* (Oxford, 1921), p. 9.

opposition which makes allowance for—nay rather demands—their divergence.[1] In this concrete union the moments remain, not in their separateness, but still in their opposition, for it is their opposition that unites them.

The objection frequently brought against Hegel, that the identity of opposites undermines all rational discourse because it requires one to contradict oneself at every step, is based on an elementary misunderstanding. If I say that something is a unity, the critic objects, I am to mean that it is a diversity; if I say that two things are different I am to mean that they are the same. In each case the meaning of my statement is to be exactly what I do not intend to convey. The objector is committing the error to which attention has already been drawn. The Hegelian identification of opposites is not a confusion of them and it does not produce an *undifferentiated* unity, for in the identification the opposition is not lost. If the two moments were without qualification the same they could not be identified. The essential point is that you can only identify opposites, and the result is a concept higher and more concrete than either of its components, each of which, taken alone, is no more than an abstraction from the higher totality. But the abstraction is not something utterly meaningless. Taken in isolation and credited with the sort of truth and reality which rightly belongs only to the higher totality it is certainly a mere error; but the higher totality, by its very nature, demands the reality of the opposite moments within it, without which it could not be what it is. The fact that they may not be taken in isolation does not prevent their being distinguished as moments within the concrete. That indeed is most necessary and it is the legitimate function of the understanding to make the distinction. Hegel insists that the understanding is one of the essential moments in all thought.[2]

9. The first triad of the Hegelian logic is such identification of opposites: it is the identity of 'being' and 'nothing', the outcome of which is 'becoming'. The word 'becoming' in this context is, I think, significant as descriptive of the sort of unity which has been formed. Hegel meant the term to express the nature of the identity and of the movement which it initiates, rather than to serve as the name of a new category. More properly it is the name of the whole triad—the *minimum rationale*, as Mure calls it.[3] The new category resulting from the union

[1] Cf. *Enc.* 88 (4) and *Zusatz* and also *Wissenschaft der Logik*, I, i, Kap. I, C 1, *Anmerkung* 2. (*Werke*, III, pp. 88 f.)   [2] *Enc.* 79 (referred to above, p. 232, n. 2).
[3] *Vide A Study of Hegel's Logic*, p. 34.

of being and nothing is 'being determinate' (*Dasein*), but the word 'becoming' is descriptive of the whole dialectical process of logic.[1] The unity of the opposite concepts is not, we said, a blank uniformity but is the perpetual contradistinction of its component moments. It is the self-differentiating activity of thought, unable to rest in any empty self-identity but always (to use a metaphor) vibrating or oscillating between opposites which determine each other. Vibration and oscillation are only metaphors because the dialectical becoming is not in time and space but is prior to all spatio-temporal movement. Physical process which we commonly imagine when we talk of becoming is only one special case of the more fundamental principle of unity in difference.

The becoming which is the identity of opposites is the principle of all movement and all development. It is the dynamic which, we shall see presently, urges every partial and abstract form of reality beyond its own narrow limits towards greater completion and wholeness. It is the essence of the dialectic, of which Hegel says: 'it is the principle of all movement, all life and all effectiveness (*Betätigung*) in the actual world'.[2]

10. While the principle of movement is, so to say, the commerce or conversation of moments in a concrete unity, the moving force is the whole immanent in each moment. Every unity is an identity of opposites and so a dynamic unity, but it is so just because it (the concrete) is immanent in each of the opposite abstractions which are identified in it and which otherwise could not be so identified. Each taken by itself must call up the other in order to maintain itself—its true self, its membership in the higher totality. Accordingly, nothing (unless it is the Absolute) can maintain itself as it stands but must always, in its attempt to do so, go over into that which it lacks and which would, if united with it, constitute a more stable whole. Any finite thing is defined by what limits it, in other words, by what is other than it. It is its context and setting that gives meaning to a finite entity. The concrete universal is always, at the very least, a system in which the significance of the particular is derived from its place and function in the system. What

---

[1] Cf. *Wissenschaft der Logik*, *Werke*, III, p. 92. '*Da nunmehr diese Einheit von Sein und Nichts als erste Wahrheit ein für allemal zu Grunde liegt, und das Element von allem Folgenden ausmacht, so sind auszer dem Werden selbst, alle ferneren logischen Bestimmungen Dasein, Qualität, überhaupt alle Begriffe der Philosophie, Beispiele dieser Einheit.*'

[2] *Enc.* 81, *Zusatz* 1. He makes a similar remark in *Wissenschaft der Logik* in his discussion of Identity and Difference: 'This is to be considered the essential nature of Reflection and the precise original basis of all activity and self-movement'. (*Werke*, IV, pp. 38-9.)

the finite is in itself, therefore, can be expressed only in terms of what it is not—to maintain itself it must go over into its other. The need for definition is itself the generation of an opposition between the given fragment and what more must be given in order to make that intelligible as a fragment of the whole to which it belongs, and the reconciliation of this opposition is the fulfilment, the realization, of the 'truth' of the original finite. The need for completion is the way in which the whole implied in every partial factor makes its presence felt. Because the whole is implicit in each part, the part cannot remain at rest within itself but must supplement itself by union with that which, in abstraction, it excludes, yet which in union with it makes it what it really is.

This process is the activity of thought, but it is not simply the way in which we think about the real. Hegel insists that it is the very essence and nature of the real and that every movement and process in nature is a manifestation of it. Thought, he maintains, is immanent in all things, and our thinking is only a phase in a dialectical process which runs throughout nature and culminates beyond the finite limits of our minds.

The movement is not in space and time, yet because each union of opposites (prior to the Absolute itself) is always only a provisional whole, it issues in a succession of triads. The first synthesis, of being and nothing, gives rise to being-determinate, but that is itself finite and abstract and the dialectic of the whole working within it breaks it up into opposites to generate a new triad, whose synthesis is again only a provisional and temporary resting-place. The activity which is essentially an oscillation between abstract opposites—their dynamic communion in a synthetic totality—cannot remain simply in equilibrium (however dynamic), but must press on to further concretion while ever its product lacks anything short of the absolute whole; for any totality short of that must be unstable. The result of this instability can only be a succession of triads the order of which is determined by the principle which generates it; namely, the dialectic which forbids any partial entity (any term of the succession) to maintain itself by itself and urges it, in order to be what it really is, to call up what it excludes and to unite with it.

11. The source from which the 'other' is 'called up' is the Absolute. But this does not mean that the Absolute is, as it were, spread out in space, or that it exists like some storehouse beside the finite entity, from which it may draw material to supplement its own finiteness. The Absolute is a mind, and what is spread out in space is nature—a

manifestation of mind, it is true, but one whose very self-externality makes it inadequate to the nature of mind and impels it to evolve beyond the phase of mere self-externality. It is finite and must go over into its other and unite with it. The source from which this other proceeds, however, is in itself. It is the Absolute, but the Absolute immanent in the developing finite, that is the spring and origin of the dialectic.

The generation of opposites and their identification is, then, the immanence of the Absolute in its finite self-manifestations as the dialectical activity of thought. As the process advances, its phases become more comprehensive and its inner dynamic more complicated, for it carries the lower phases up with it into the higher, in each of which the whole process below is sublated (*aufgehoben*)—that is, cancelled and transcended, yet at the same time maintained as a moment in the realized whole. The higher phases imply and require the process which produces them as much as they are implied in it. Their immanence in the more abstract forms makes the development, for those forms, inevitable; and similarly the fact that the higher forms are the realization of the lower makes the process indispensable to the more concrete phases also. For this reason the Absolute is not merely the end of the development, is not something merely beyond the process nor something which might possibly stand alone without any process. The Absolute must manifest itself as and by means of such a development. All the finite forms are necessary to its wholeness and (although in the Absolute the succession is sublated) it must allow within its own unity for the entire process, or else its unity would be abstract and it could not be absolute.[1] For the process is the self-evolution of the end and only through it can the complete nature of the end be realized. Without development there could be no fulfilment nor, unless this were so, could any process be of significance.

It follows that criticisms of the Hegelian Absolute as 'a block universe' in which everything is given at once, or as 'the night in which all cows are black', are mere products of the understanding and entirely miss the point. They assume that the unity of the Absolute is not a concrete unity and fail to see that its wholeness can consist in and can be displayed as nothing short of the entire dialectical process generating

---

[1] Hegel's answer to the question 'If God is the All-sufficient, the Unwanting, how does He come to resolve Himself into something plainly different and other?' is 'The Divine Idea is precisely this: that it does so resolve itself, does posit this other out of itself and take it back into itself again, in order to be subjectivity and Spirit' (*Enc.* 247, *Zusatz*). The point is that unless it did this, if it remained simply at rest within itself, it would not be absolute—it would not be divine.

seriatim a scale of forms, a development impelled towards and sublated in the Absolute itself.

But not only is this the case. The converse is also true: that any evolutionary process is a dialectical process consisting essentially of the unfolding of phases or moments of a totality. What develops is something finite and incomplete, and that into which it develops is something more complete and so a stage nearer the absolute whole. But the reason why it develops is the working within it of the dialectical dynamic which is nothing less than the immanent whole revealing the finiteness of the inadequate form by contrast with and opposition to its other (the finite which it excludes) and urging it on to a higher synthesis. All process, according to Hegel, is of this sort, though at different levels it takes on different characters. All process, therefore, implies the Absolute, the existence of which must be postulated wherever evolution is presumed. A philosophy of evolution which is not absolutist should, therefore, if Hegel is right, prove unintelligible, exactly as an absolutist philosophy would do if it excluded evolution. Each would be an attempt to elevate to the status of self-subsistent reality an opposite abstraction.

V. THE PHILOSOPHY OF NATURE

12. For Hegel, the dialectical process is all-pervasive. As it is the immanence and self-manifestation of the Absolute in all things, it could not be otherwise; for the entire universe is no more nor less than the dialectical unfolding of the forms of the Absolute. The Logic is the doctrine of this dialectic and of the manner of its operation, but it is not the whole of Philosophy, for, as Hegel never wearies of declaring, the forms of thought are also the forms of the real. 'The truth', he says, 'is actual and must exist.'[1] Accordingly, though the Logic is *die selbstbewuszte Vernunft*, there is also *die seiende Vernunft*[2]—the reason in existence—which is nature.

13. The Philosophy of Nature, however, has been held suspect even by Hegel's own disciples, some of whom have alleged that it is inconsistent with his absolute idealism; and it is regarded as spurious by neo-idealists of the school of Croce and Gentile as well as by empiricists. Two objections in particular, one much more formidable than the other, warrant some discussion. I shall take first the one which is easier to meet.

---

[1] *Enc.* 38, *Zusatz.*   [2] Cf. *Enc.* 6.

(i) The radical empiricist maintains that the only genuine knowledge of nature comes from the natural sciences, upon the subject-matter of which philosophy has no right to pronounce. Hegel's philosophy of nature, he avers, is a preposterous and impossible attempt to deduce the whole scheme of nature *a priori*, founded upon a misconception of the function of logic and an exaggerated faith in its power to discover truth. Truth, the critic maintains, is to be had only by reference to the data of sense-perception, and the ludicrous attempt to discover it by pure thought furnishes only metaphysical propositions which are unverifiable and therefore meaningless.

This is, of course, a criticism based on the thinking of the understanding in which the presuppositions of the Renaissance are still at work. More than to any other philosopher, it is to Hegel that we owe our recognition of the artificiality and one-sidedness of so-called *a priori* deduction. If nothing else, Hegel's own criticism of the Kantian dualism of perception and conception puts him beyond the reach of any such cavil as the above. Only a careless and superficial reading of Hegel can lead to the opinion that the dialectic is a pure *a priori* deduction *ex nihilo*. As I have already asserted, at every stage the whole is presupposed—it is the source as well as the product of the process—and I hope presently to show even more fully that logic, in Hegel's philosophy, is anything but the mere spinning of ideas 'out of one's head' which have no connection with 'facts'. Nobody has protested more violently than Hegel himself against just this abstract and ridiculous view of reasoning. His own logic, in fact his entire philosophy, professes to be nothing else than the reflection upon experience as we have it. Sense-experience is but part of this and is that part which most needs interpretation. But when that interpretation has been accomplished, to refer it back to sense for 'verification' would be merely futile, and to regard it as something produced '*a priori*' out of our minds, if that means (as for the empiricist it seems to do) out of nothing, is merely ludicrous. The empiricist never does and never can regard 'our minds' as themselves the coming to consciousness of nature and of all the facts that science finds in it, but is committed to the view of the mind as a sort of mirror reflecting an external reality and of truth as the passively received image of the external thing. For Hegel, on the other hand, thought is the self-development of sense and as such is its truth and verification, and mind is the product of the self-development of nature where it is already implicit and embodied.

(ii) The more serious objection is one put forward by idealists themselves, who hold that the philosophy of nature is supererogatory when once you have denied the separation in reality between thought and things. Your logic and your metaphysic are then one and the same, as Hegel maintains, and when you have traced the development of the forms of thought, you have, by the same process, reviewed all the forms of existence. Nothing beyond logic, therefore, is necessary to complete the system.

I take this, in effect, to be the same objection as Croce has stated, in *What is Living and What is Dead in the Philosophy of Hegel*,[1] where he alleges that Hegel has revived the very dualism between nature and spirit that his philosophy is supposed to have abolished, and in a way which his logic is powerless to overcome. But Croce's interpretation includes several serious misunderstandings of Hegel's doctrine which undermine his criticism and of which the worst is his misconception of the sort of opposition and reconciliation involved in the dialectic. The parallel principle of the synthesis of distincts, which he recommends, is inadequate and unsound, for he asserts that each of the distincts is concrete and sufficient in itself, in which case it could have no *nisus* to further development, and no synthesis nor any further progress could result. Consequently, Croce quite fails to comprehend the relationship in Hegel's system between nature and spirit, and all that is needed to answer his criticism is to make this relationship clear.

14. Hegel regarded the universe as one continuous process of dialectical development, essentially a process of thought throughout its whole course. In every phase mind is immanent, and each succeeding phase is one of greater explicitness or concreteness. The lowest grades are not, however, forms of *consciousness*. That emerges only on a relatively high level. This important point is altogether overlooked by the majority of Hegel's opponents, and it is significant to note that a very similar position reappears in the philosophy of Whitehead. Thought, Hegel contends, is present and at work at levels far below that of consciousness—levels which constitute the grades or 'categories' of nature.

Nature is 'the idea' 'under the form of externality'[2] and the emergence of consciousness marks the stage at which mind becomes aware of nature as an external object. But because nature is itself mind, as Hegel says, 'in the form of other-being',[3] this consciousness is, (so to

---

[1] Chapter X. The objection, however, has been voiced by others as well. For a fuller discussion of the whole matter, see my article, 'The Philosophy of Nature in Hegel's System', in *The Review of Metaphysics*, III, 2, no. 10 (December 1949).
[2] Cf. *Enc.* 244 and 247.   [3] *Ibid.*

speak) inadvertently, self-consciousness. From this point every advance is an advance in self-consciousness, in which the self, as object, is the prior phase of its own development. The higher phases, we must always remember, are not simply supervenient upon the lower but maintain the lower sublated in themselves.

The emergence of consciousness, therefore, is the becoming aware by mind of the process prior to that point—that is, of the world of nature. It is not, of course, a sudden and total revelation, but a gradual process of development of consciousness: first as mere immediate feeling, then as sensation, then as cognition and eventually, in understanding, as the knowledge of an external world.[1] It is only after this, in the still higher stage of philosophical reflection upon its own experience, that the mind becomes aware of itself as the union of subject and object. This, however, brings us to an entirely new level in the development of self-consciousness, and, on this new level, the first product of critical reflection is the Logic and all its contents.

We may observe again at this point how misguided it is to imagine that the Logic is something that generates itself *in vacuo*. It is, far otherwise, the product of a vast process of evolution, not only in conscious experience, but even below that in nature itself. But at the lower levels of consciousness, even that of the understanding, mind and its object are not recognized to be the same thing in different manifestations, still less is nature regarded as the self-evolution of mind; and logic is the reflection upon only the cognitive phases of consciousness—those at which the mind can ordinarily be said to *know*. But in all these phases, prior to the philosophical level itself, nature is looked upon as an alien and external object (or other) confronting a knowing subject. Accordingly, the account of nature as the idea in the form of other-being, that is, as implicit (or, as Schelling said, 'petrified') mind, cannot be appropriate to any stage of knowledge—certainly not empirical science—prior to the consummation of the logic in the 'absolute idea' itself. Self-consciousness must, therefore, advance still further and the logic cannot be regarded as the whole of philosophy. The mind must go on to know itself as the spirit immanent in and developing out of nature. The discovery, made in the logic, that subject and object are identical is a turning-point in the development of self-consciousness, for hitherto thought has been aware of itself only as a 'subjective' activity, and now it becomes aware of itself as 'at the same time the real

---

[1] The detailed course of this development is described by Hegel in the *Philosophie des Geistes*, but I am not here attempting to give an accurate summary of the relevant sections.

essence of things',[1] as 'the idea which has being'.[2] Consequently, its next step is the development of this new phase of self-consciousness as the philosophy of nature, a task which could not possibly be undertaken by the natural sciences so far as they operate only at the level of the understanding.

The transition from the Logic to the *Naturphilosophie*, so much disputed by Schelling and others, is thus only the passage from one level of self-consciousness (that at which mind makes itself, as knowledge, its own object in logic) to the next higher level (that at which it makes itself, as immanent in nature, its own object in nature-philosophy). As emergent from nature in the form of conscious awareness, mind becomes its own object in the final phase—the *Philosophie des Geistes*, where nature and mind are united and reconciled in the consummating wholeness of absolute self-knowledge.

15. If in this way we can explain and justify Hegel's transition from logic to philosophy of nature and of mind, we must nevertheless face the fact that he himself is struggling throughout the *Naturphilosophie* with a difficulty which was forced upon him by his own advance beyond the view-point of co-temporary science. To render coherent the system I have outlined, it is necessary to regard nature literally as a process of evolution in which each form actually develops into and generates the next above it. Hegel could not maintain that it was so because in his day the theory of evolution was, at best, a very questionable biological hypothesis. It was not until nearly thirty years after his death that it was confidently accepted by scientific opinion. Consequently, Hegel asserts that the connection between the forms of nature is only dialectical. He rejects the suggestion that they can be naturally engendered one from another and attributes their continuity only to the idea implicit in them.[3] This immediately lands him in trouble and he has to explain the fixity of natural forms by saying that it is the mark of essential opposition between nature and the idea, which is resolved only in mind, and by postulating a 'weakness' in nature which hampers and

---

[1] *Enc.* 41, *Zusatz* 2. [2] *Enc.* 244, *Zusatz.*

[3] *Vide Enc.* 249, *Zusatz.* Cf. also 339, *Zusatz* 2. So faithful is he to the science of his day that he even admits the evidence for the history of the earth and gives a full account of the co-temporary geological discoveries, including those of fossilized remains of extinct flora and fauna. But he dismisses them all as interesting curiosities with no rational significance. The Earth's history is a mere fact to be accepted; its philosophic interest lies only in the system of co-existent and interrelated parts which has come into being. So he persists in his denial of temporal evolution and maintains the doctrine that in nature the phases of the dialectic co-exist side by side in mutual externality.

disorganizes the dialectic.[1] Nowhere, however, is this weakness made good, for it cannot be attributed to the mere abstraction of our conceiving, it cannot be overcome through natural development itself, nor yet can it be explained in terms of the perfection of the Absolute.

But Hegel cannot rest content with this fixity and disconnectedness in nature. He constantly allows himself to contradict it by saying that the *Naturphilosophie* traces the evolution of nature into spirit. 'God', he says, 'does not remain stony and dead; the stones cry out and raise themselves to spirit.'[2] And whenever he can he uses just those forms of natural development which are evident to common observation—forms of the development of living organisms—as illustrations of the movement of the dialectical process. The conflict in his philosophy is caused by his own vision. His insight showed him that if any intelligible account is to be given of man's relation to the world, nature must be mind in potentiality; yet science had provided no acceptable evidence of the fact that this could be so. Accordingly, Hegel denies the actual occurrence of an evolutionary process in nature, while he provides the philosophical principles on which such a process could be rendered intelligible. This could not be demonstrated in his own day, for the demonstration had to await the discoveries of modern biology and, still further, of modern physics.

VI. THE PHILOSOPHY OF MIND

16. *Body and Soul.* 'Mind (*Geist*) *came into being* as the truth of nature.' The distinction between matter and spirit must be made but they are not to be looked upon as two 'things' on the same level of development or 'reality'. It is only the understanding that so regards them and, in consequence, propounds to itself the insoluble problem of their interrelation—insoluble because, as so regarded, they are in absolute antithesis. But once it is realized that they are not *in pari materia* and are not co-ordinately related at all, once they are seen to be respectively lower and higher phases in a development, the problem becomes soluble. Body and mind, Hegel tells us, are not related as particular to particular, but as particular to universal.[3]

---

[1] *Vide Enc.* 250.

[2] *Enc.* 247, *Zusatz.* Even in explaining away the geological history of the Earth he compares it to the dream life of a sleeper now awakened and come to consciousness in man: '. . . *ein Leben, das, in sich selbst gährend, die Zeit an ihm selbst halte; der Erdgeist, der noch nicht zur Entgegensetzung gekommen,—die Bewegung und Träume eines Schlafenden, bis er erwacht und im Menschen sein Bewusztseyn erhalten'*. (*Enc.* 339, *Zusatz* 2.)   [3] *Enc.* 389, *Zusatz.*

This truth has in recent times sought expression in the behaviouristic attitude in psychology as well as in certain modern empiricist doctrines of mind.[1] It is expressed in the insistence that the mind is nothing over and above the manner in which the body behaves, whether in physiological, in practical or in linguistic activity. This doctrine is sound so far as it is certainly true that the mind is not another thing on a par with the body (a more tenuous material body, a wraith or a 'smoke'), but, as Aristotle recognized, it is no more (nor less) than the form of the body —the universal manifesting itself in the body's organic functioning[2] and the activity of its dispositions.

In nature this universal is displayed in the form of externality—*i.e.* self-externality—each part or 'moment' being external to the other. Matter in space and time is everywhere other than itself and no material body can be *simply* located anywhere.[3] But the whole process of development in nature is one of the progressive overcoming of this external otherness. The self-externality of separate bodies is first annulled in their physical interrelation. In chemical combination matter constitutes its unity by combining differents, each of which in separation is propertied only by its affinities to the others. In life the material entity has become an organic whole, the parts of which have no independent reality at all, but are what they are only in virtue of the whole. The living thing is organic, not merely by virtue of its structure (even a mechanical system might be so described), but because it is a complex of functions mutually related as ends and means. Its being or substance is its functioning [4] as an organic unity. Moreover, its functioning is not confined to the limits of its bodily parts but is a system of responses and reactions to its environment instrumental to its own purposes. These reactions and responses may, in fact, be described as the way in which the organism appropriates its world, masters its environment and makes it its own.[5] Self-externality has thus been overcome in the life of the organism, though its material manifestation is still subject to it.[6] Self-externality, however, is negation—as Spinoza

[1] Cf. Alexander, *Space, Time and Deity*, Bk. III, ch. i; Ayer, *Thinking and Meaning*; and Ryle, *The Concept of Mind*. Bosanquet states a similar view from quite a different standpoint in *Principle of Individuality and Value*, p. 193.

[2] Cf. Bosanquet, *Three Chapters on the Nature of Mind* (London, 1923), pp. 80-8, and *Principle*, Lect. V.

[3] Cf. the parallel drawn by Collingwood between Hegel and Whitehead on this point, *The Idea of Nature*, pp. 127-8.

[4] Cf. Aristotle, *De Anima*, 415 *b* 13.   [5] Cf. Hegel, *Enc.* 219, *Zusatz*.

[6] *Enc.* 389: '*In der Tat ist in der Idee des Lebens schon an sich das Auszersichsein der Natur aufgehoben, und der Begriff, die Substanz des Lebens, ist als Subjektivität, jedoch nur so, dass die Existenz oder Objektivität noch zugleich an jenes Auszersichsein verfallen ist*'.

declared: *omnis determinatio est negatio*. But in life the negation (the otherness) is negatived and taken up into the self of the organism, the life of which becomes a thorough unity of self and other—a reflection into self—which Hegel calls 'absolute negativity' (because it cancels or negates the negativity of externality), and this absolute negativity is the very form of mind, as being what it is in and for itself.

Viewed on the empirical level it can be cognized only as organic behaviour such as is studied, according to the level of its functioning, by biology, physiology and psychology. The empirical psychologist must, therefore, be a behaviourist; as Hegel says, he rejects any attempt at 'speculative' treatment. But the reflection-into-self or inwardness of which this observed behaviour is the outward expression and which is the reality or truth of the organic functioning (that alone which, in the end, makes it intelligible) is subjectivity,[1] and here the thought immanent and blindly at work in lower nature begins to come aware of itself. 'In the soul', writes Hegel, 'is the awakening of consciousness; consciousness sets itself up as reason, which is immediately awake to the knowledge of itself and which, through its activity, emancipates itself to objectivity and the awareness of its own concept.'[2]

The empirical psychologist treats consciousness (quite rightly) as 'the control of present behaviour with reference to future adjustment'.[3] But what it is that enables 'future adjustment' to control present behaviour is the universal—the systematic world—come to consciousness of itself in a mind. As such, the phases of its self-development are not the concern of the psychologist, who views them as various (less and more efficient) ways in which 'anticipation of the future' governs present behaviour. They are, however, the concern of the philosopher; and the radical empiricist in contemporary philosophy who denies their existence produces in consequence only an empty technique devoid of content, in lieu of a positive contribution to the body of philosophical knowledge.

The finite mind emerges at that point in the dialectical process where self-external matter, having overcome its outwardness in organic functioning, goes over into the inwardness of subjectivity and realizes itself as 'soul'. It is the proximate truth of the body, but the succeeding phases transcend what is finite in both body and soul and develop a still higher truth, which in them is only implicit or potential.

---

[1] Cf. *Enc.* 389: 'Subjectivity is the very substance and conception of life'.
[2] *Enc.* 387.
[3] B. H. Bode, 'Consciousness and Psychology' in *Creative Intelligence* (New York, 1917), p. 249.

17. *Subject and Object.* It has already been observed that the phases
in the development of mind are phases of self-consciousness, where the
object of each is the preceding phase.[1] The solution of the problem of
the relation between subject and object in our knowledge of the
'external' world can now be given in terms of this principle. The
totality of nature has become sublated in the organic unity of the living
animal, and the reflection-into-self which is its inner[2] aspect, as the
subjectivity which is characteristic of soul. Hegel elaborates Spinoza's
conception of the mind as the idea of the body into the doctrine that the
soul is the feeling of the affections of the living organism. This feeling
is at first and in itself merely one, immediate and undifferentiated. It is
the sublation in sensibility of physical influences upon and alterations
of the body. In later reflection it is specified according to the affected
organs and subdivided into the various 'senses', but at the merely
sentient level it is the sensing of the body as one feeling.[3] But as the
body is the sublated whole of nature, so the soul is that totality sublated
as feeling (*Empfindung*), and as such it is self-enclosed—a monad[4]—
containing all the material of what will later emerge as knowledge.

Consciousness, the next phase of mental development, has the
natural soul as its object, but its content, which was purely immediate
and undifferentiated feeling, is now projected as an object set over
against a conscious subject. Consciousness is the stage of self-reflection
and correlation, the proper dwelling-place of mediation. The awareness
of this object as a 'somewhat' opposed to the subject is sense-perception (*Wahrnehmung*). It is not, however, the developed awareness of
'external' objects in space and time, but a continuous flux of sensuous
qualia which form the material for such perception. It is the Kantian
manifold of sense on which the *a priori* forms are imposed, and before
it can become formed and moulded as a perceived world of objects it
must pass to the stage of 'intuition' (*Anschauung*) and beyond, bringing
us to the level of mind (*Geist*) which makes consciousness itself its
object.[5] For the sake of brevity, I shall omit here the intervening stages
and proceed at once to this higher level, where what in consciousness
was a mere projected 'somewhat' becomes the presentation of an
objectified world.

In intuition the alien object of consciousness is recognized by mind
as its own, controllable and specifiable by the activity of attention,

[1] Cf. *Enc.* 413 and 443.
[2] The word is not intended here to have any spatial reference, but only as a way of
expressing the essential difference between subjectivity and the self-externality of
things spatial. Subjectivity has all its moments identified in itself.
[3] *Enc.* 403.   [4] *Ibid.*   [5] *Enc.* 443.

which focusses selected elements within it, characterizing them as 'this-here-now' and setting them in a spatio-temporal context.[1] In such intuition the universal is still implicit, but it is henceforward explicated, through the mediation of recollection, imagination and memory, as 'presentation'. The process is that which Kant described as the synthesis of the imagination, through which the universal (or concept) is unfolded as image and presentation (*Vorstellung*) wherewith the sensuous intuition in turn is clothed and, as an element in a systematic world, becomes an object of thought or knowledge.

To borrow a phrase from Bradley, our world is an elaborate 'ideal construction' which is built up by memory, imagination and thought out of the materials of sense; and, by the 'experienced world' so constructed, our present perception of objects is always mediated and its significant character determined.[2] We learnt from Kant that such perception is nothing merely passively received, but is essentially a product of thinking; and thinking, for Hegel, is the explicit form of theoretical mind. Mind now knows its own determinations as the determinations of what is real—its own reason as 'the reason in being'. This is the description Hegel gives of 'reason' as the culminating phase of consciousness (*Enc.* 439); but that reason is the transition to mind[3] and the foreshadowing of its explicit self-consciousness in thinking. Hegel, himself, remarks that 'thought constantly recurs in these different parts of knowledge, because these parts are different only through the medium they are in and the form of the antithesis implied'.[4]

This is a brief and summary account of the way in which Hegel elaborates the doctrine that subject and object are related as higher and lower phases in the development of mind. The world which thus comes to be known is not, however, a mere artefact of a purely subjective consciousness (as Kant would have us believe). So to misinterpret the theory would be to return to the standpoint of the understanding. It is the explication, or coming to full awareness of itself, of that universal totality which is immanent in nature and implicit in the soul's immediacy, where nature is held sublated as feeling. Nature *is* thus the object of knowledge, mediated by the intervening phases of the self-development of mind.

[1] Cf. Mure, *Study of Hegel's Logic*, p. 9.
[2] To call in evidence witnesses of rather diverse outlooks, cf. Joachim, *Logical Studies*, pp. 85-102, and B. H. Bode, *op. cit.* p. 245.
[3] '*Die wissende Wahrheit ist der Geist*' (*loc. cit.*).
[4] *Enc.* 467.

18. *Self and Others*. In feeling there is no 'self', for subject and object have not yet been distinguished and are merged and absorbed into a unity of confusedly experienced variety. In consciousness the self emerges as that to which an object is presented, and with the development of consciousness the awareness of self comes into being. This stage of the process, consequently, culminates in self-consciousness. But in the first instance it is a consciousness of self as opposed to an object, and this opposition it is the *nisus* of the dialectic to overcome. At this stage, therefore, the dialectical drive takes the form of appetite or desire,[1] which is the urge of the self fully to possess and to be one with the object. Such an urge has both a theoretical and a practical aspect. On the practical side it is a felt want, the satisfaction of which is identified as the object, which the self, accordingly, claims and strives to possess and consume. On the theoretical side it is the urge to know the object in order to become master of it and so to have it under control. Science itself is the result of just such a desire. It is the outcome of practical needs, develops into a desire for knowledge for its own sake and issues, when the desire is realized, in the knowledge of nature which at the same time gives control over nature and the means of subordinating natural processes to human purposes.

It is evident that the working out of such purposes in the singular self will give rise to conflicts with other selves actuated by similar purposes; and so the self becomes cognizant of others like itself. But before we can deal with this stage of mind's development we must retrace our steps to consider how the awareness of other selves can emerge.

The content of feeling must include elements arising from the manifestation of life in singular organisms, for the content of feeling is the sublation of the totality of nature in which these manifestations are included. At the level of consciousness, the projection of the contents of feeling as 'external' objects will, therefore, include the objectification of living and conscious beings. Other selves are the organisms other than my own in and through which nature has come to consciousness. The concrete universal which is all along coming to self-consciousness is becoming more fully aware of its own self-differentiation, and that includes its manifestation in living forms and their development of (or into) finite minds.

In the first instance this knowledge of other selves is immediate; that is, they are known as ordinary objects (albeit as living).[2] But this, Hegel maintains, is inadequate to produce *certainty* of self. That

[1] Cf. *Enc.* 426 ff., and *Phänomenologie* (*Jubiläumsausgabe*), pp. 120-2.
[2] Cf. *Phänomenologie*, B, IV A, 2, p. 125.

requires reciprocal recognition of self-consciousness by the selves who are mutually subject and object. As in desire the self tries to make the object its own, so here each of the mutually cognizant selves strives to master and control the other, so that the first phase of their intercourse is conflict; but though this is primarily internecine strife, if it issues in the destruction of either combatant, it defeats its own end, because the victor can realize himself only in the possession of the vanquished as his own. The first resolution of the antagonism, therefore, is the subjection by one of the other in servitude. But this again is only a provisional solution, for repression of the other is *ipso facto* repression of self, and complete self-realization involves mutual recognition of selves on equal terms. Each must find himself realized in the other.

Accordingly, interrelation and interdependence of selves gives rise to the entire system of moral and political institutions which is the expression of mind in the objective phase of its development. In this system each personality reflects the whole, not by mere repetition of its content, but by concrete implication through the reciprocal interplay of mutually complementary functions.

What has been so far and what, through social intercourse, perpetually is being actualized is one universal—one mind—of which the 'finite' individuals are specific differentiations. The political community as a whole is a further stage of development of the 'notion', or universal. The universal, however, is actual only in its particulars and so here it is actual only in its members. There is no separate consciousness, or *esprit de corps*, besides theirs. But their consciousnesses or minds are not a mere plurality, for each is not a separate and enclosed entity. The social self is made up of its capacities in the various institutions to which it belongs, and no capacity is anything at all apart from the others into which it dovetails. The system is, accordingly, indivisibly one and the consciousness of it is also. It is differentiated into a plurality of functions and activities and these are actualized in physical organisms. But the 'mind' of each organism is something which goes beyond it and is (according to the level of its thinking) to a greater or lesser degree common to the members of the social whole. As minds they cannot be mutually separated by hard divisions.

The mutual knowledge of minds as individual persons is, therefore, a stage in the development of the 'notion'—the universal, or mind as such. This doctrine is not in conflict with what was said earlier: that the soul is a self-enclosed monad. The soul *is* the totality, but at the stage before that at which the distinction between selves emerges. At that later stage the fact does come to consciousness that there are many organisms and so many souls, or points at which consciousness emerges. But this multiplicity is far from being sheer multiplicity, for the very nature of organism puts it into organic relationship with other organisms. It is the world epitomized. The monadic character of soul, therefore (as it proved for Leibniz), is only one aspect of it. Its other aspect is its interpenetration with other souls; but that becomes explicit only in later development.

19. *Finite and Infinite.* The forms and institutions of moral and political life are the means of providing the objective conditions of freedom—that is, of the mind's self-realization in the higher spiritual activities of Art, Religion and Philosophy. It is here finally that its subjective and its objective, its theoretical and its practical, development find their joint consummation in the absolute realization of its concrete totality. The final phase of Mind Absolute is the supreme awareness of itself as the fruition of the entire process of development, in, through and out of nature. This awareness, however, is no momentary flash of intuition, for its content is no less than the whole gamut of the dialectical process as it is set out in the system of philosophical sciences. Of philosophy Hegel says, 'The real subject-matter is not exhausted in its purpose, but in working the matter out; nor is the mere result obtained the concrete whole itself, but the result along with the process of its coming to be'.[1] At this level of knowledge mind is no longer finite, but absolute—no longer a singular subject but the communion and atonement in the whole of all singular subjects. According to Hegel, the unity of subject and object in all three forms of Absolute Mind is God, self-fulfilled through the processes of nature and mind, which are real only as His own self-externalization and re-union with self. The Absolute in Hegel's philosophy corresponds (as will appear later) with what Whitehead calls 'the consequent nature of God'. It is God at once immanent in and transcendent above nature and finite mind.

Finite minds are characteristic only of certain phases of the process through which this Absolute realizes itself. It is thus in and through singular subjects that the Absolute is realized, but, on the one hand, they are never merely singular or merely finite, for the infinite is always implicit (always potentially) in them and it is in their very nature to transcend their own finiteness in order to find satisfaction. The real self of the finite mind lies in its infinite potentialities, not in its limitations, and the realization of this self is at once fulfilment and transcendence

[1] *Phän.* preface, p. 5.

of its finitude. On the other hand, the Absolute is not purely transcendent, because it is the sublation of the finite and because unless it were so it could not be absolute. As it is implicit (potential) in the finite, so the finite is implicit (sublated) in it. Immanence and transcendence are accordingly reconciled; the Absolute transcends the finite only in virtue of the realization of the potentiality which is its immanence in the finite.

VII. CONCLUSION

20. The philosophy of Hegel, by restating and reinterpreting our original problem, provides its solution. We asked, in the beginning, what was the relation between nature and the mind, and in stating the problem we alleged, first, that the mind was a quantitatively small part of a vast spatio-temporal whole, which we designated 'nature'. Such a conception, Hegel shows, is due to a confusion, and is inadequate. What is quantitatively a small part of nature is not mind but the material substances which subserve the life of the animal organism. We alleged, secondly, that the mind was a product of nature. This is a better conception, but is still unsatisfactory, for nature is not a separate agency producing natural objects out of a cornucopia like a conjurer out of a hat: it is not even right to think of it as a universal matrix from which natural objects crystallize out. Nature, we learn from Hegel, is a process or development, and the natural kinds are its phases. But the entire process is not exhausted in merely physical nature, nor in animate nature, nor even in both taken together. It goes beyond life to produce mind—beyond physical nature altogether. Thus mind is not a part of nature at all, but is what nature becomes when it achieves consciousness. The mind, in short, is the world come to consciousness. The apparent attachment of this consciousness to an animal organism is explained by showing that the animal organism is that phase of the process of nature at which it passes into mind, but even the relation of the organism to the rest of nature cannot be viewed as that of spatial and quantitative part to spatial and quantitative whole. The organism, it is true, is but one phase of a larger process, but it is the culminating phase of the natural process in which all the others are implicitly contained as sublated.

This, however, is but part of the restatement of the problem which makes the solution possible. The process of nature is itself only one section of the total continuous development which is, throughout, dialectical—which is the progressive explication of the concrete universal. This is completely explicated and wholly concrete only in its absolute form; that is, as Absolute Mind. The evolution of nature into mind, therefore, is a phase in the development of self-consciousness. The bringing of nature to consciousness thus makes nature the object which mind comes to know. The object of mind in knowledge is itself, in its lower phase of development. In other words, the mind comprehends nature in knowledge just because it is the product of nature, in the sense that it is what nature has become. Knowledge is the sublation of nature in mind.

21. That Hegel was able to go so far is the more remarkable that when he wrote science had not yet laid the foundation of a conception of nature as an evolutionary process, and just so far as he accepted the co-temporary scientific view of nature did he fall short of the promise of his philosophical insight. Because he restricted scientific knowledge to the level of the understanding, both he and his followers failed to contemplate the possibility of a dialectical progress in science itself which would raise its view-point above that level, and when, in the 20th century, science had made that advance, we find Whitehead, the philosopher who (with the possible exception of Collingwood) had most appreciated it, complaining that 'the idealistic school has swallowed the scientific scheme in its entirety as being the only rendering of the facts of nature, and has then explained it as being an idea in the ultimate mentality'.[1] What Whitehead really meant was that science had by now produced an entirely new rendering of the facts, the significance of which the idealistic school had altogether failed to appreciate.

Nevertheless, the conception of nature which has emerged as the result of modern scientific development implies a metaphysic which is Hegelian in its main essentials. The only philosophy which has so far been produced which interprets that development with anything like adequacy is Whitehead's, and so far as it is not also tainted with survivals of Renaissance thought, it displays Hegelian characteristics. Collingwood, had he lived, might have gone further, and he has left indications, to which I shall return in due course, of the path which philosophy ought to pursue. But those who have revolted completely against idealism and have set their faces firmly against anything with the least suggestion of Hegelianism have succeeded only in repeating, in modern guise and in a new technical jargon, the philosophical position appropriate to an age of scientific progress prior to Hegel's time— a position which in our own day is utterly outdated and has long been obsolete.

[1] *Science and the Modern World* (Cambridge, 1926), p. 79.

Section B
The Persistence of the Renaissance View

Chapter XIII
'IDEALISM' AND 'REALISM'
*

THE presuppositions of scientific thinking change slowly, but the recognition of the change by scientists and philosophers is a still slower process. Though ideas underlying modern science were anticipated in the doctrines of the greater philosophers of the 17th and 18th centuries, thinkers of the 19th and 20th, with few exceptions, lagged far behind the progress of science. By the selection of typical examples I shall in the following chapters review the main trends of modern philosophy and consider their bearing upon the problem of relating nature and mind, and I hope to show that their success or failure in dealing with this problem is commensurate with the degree in which they do or do not appreciate the nature and significance of contemporary scientific progress.

I. THE IDEALISM OF F. H. BRADLEY

1. The British idealism of the late 19th century, influenced as it was by Hegel's thought, was strong in its opposition to empiricism, and it did produce a philosophical doctrine in some respects agreeable to the modern outlook. But the idealistic position was still vitiated by remnants of Renaissance thinking and few members of the school were aware of the change which was taking place in the science of their own day. Their philosophy is for the most part an outgrowth from or modification of the position left by Kant and Hegel, and little attempt was made by any of them to relate it to the new scientific ideas.[1] Their view of nature remains that of the Renaissance, but, finding this view contradictory and unviable, they denied reality to nature and relegated it to the sphere of appearance, explaining it as an abstraction of scientific thought working on the level of the understanding.

---

[1] Bernard Bosanquet is, perhaps, an exception and he states the idealist position in a way more satisfactory to modern needs than any other writer of the school.

F. H. Bradley may be taken as the typical example of those who proceeded in this way. While admitting that the term 'nature' may be given different meanings, that which he explicitly assigns to it in his most important attempt to estimate its reality, is precisely that attached to it in 17th-century thought. 'Abstract from everything psychical', he writes, 'and then the remainder of existence will be Nature. It will be mere body or the extended, so far as that is not psychical, together with the properties immediately connected with or following from this extension.'[1] This is almost exactly how Hobbes defined the universe, and further it is consciously connected by Bradley with the doctrine of primary and secondary qualities.[2] Conceiving nature in this way, Bradley proceeds to prove its unreality, but he does not conclude that a new conception of nature is needed; he accepts the Renaissance view as the only one possible and so maintains that nature is only an appearance and that the reality must be sought elsewhere. 'The physical world', he says, 'is for each of us an abstraction from the entire reality',[3] and that entire reality is what he calls a complete and 'concrete' experience. Whose experience it is, as we shall presently see, remains in some doubt, and it is in part this uncertainty which led other philosophers to react against the Bradleian type of idealism and to deny that reality as such can be wholly reduced to any experience at all—not even God's.

2. Accordingly, Bradley deals with our problem of relating mind to nature by degrading to appearance both nature and the alleged natural product which we commonly call the human mind. The experience which is reality is to be identified with neither of them. The mind in the world, in other words, is something quite different from the mind in which the world is known, and the attempt to identify them is based upon a confusion. As a criticism of the common-sense view, there is some truth in this contention, but the way in which Bradley develops the position is unsatisfactory, and it is so because for him nature is never more than an abstraction, never more than an 'ideal construction' made by a mind within the concrete totality of its experience, and as a result the doctrine becomes involved in solipsistic entanglements.

What is ultimately real for Bradley is the Absolute and this is and can only be an absolutely complete and concrete experience. The relation to it of our finite minds is obscure, but all such conceptions as space and time, soul and body, the self, nature, and even goodness and truth

---

[1] *Appearance and Reality* (Oxford, 1930), p. 231.
[2] *Vide ibid.* p. 232.   [3] *Loc. cit.*

are, he thinks, abstractions from this whole. They are ideal constructions which we make from the elements of the whole so far as we
experience it. As abstractions (*i.e.* as they appear to us) they are not real
and if taken for more than abstractions they become illusions; but in the
Absolute they are all united and transformed in one concrete experience. How this is accomplished, however, we do not and cannot know,
for our minds are only finite and are incapable of comprehending the
Absolute.

The idea of a mind or self which is one finite entity among others in
a world of finites is one for which Bradley can find no definite or
satisfactory meaning. He shows that all the meanings we attempt to
attach to it are self-contradictory. For him, therefore, the self is only
an appearance, at best a group of ideas separated from the total mass of
'feeling' which makes up a whole experience. But this total experience
is not necessarily the Absolute, it may be no more than the experience
of a 'finite centre'—a notion to be explained anon.

3. The question naturally arises, if the mind is only an abstraction
from a more concrete whole of experience, if it is only 'an ideal construction' (as Bradley sometimes calls it) within a more comprehensive
whole, who or what makes the abstraction, what does the constructing?
Bradley holds the distinction between subject and object to be made
within an experience which includes both, but while this may well be
the case, we must recognize another meaning of 'subject' than that
which implies opposition to 'object'. The word may be taken to indicate the active principle of experiencing. It is not the abstraction but
that which abstracts. It is that *for* which what Bradley calls 'self',
'body', 'soul', etc., are separate entities held in relation.

Further, there seems some ground for thinking that unless this is so
the word 'appearance', as opposed to 'reality', can have no proper
meaning. What is only appearance is, one would imagine, the result of
the imperfect thought of a finite mind which is not itself an appearance.
Yet, if what has been said above is all that there is to Bradley's theory,
it would seem to make the mind one of the products of its own abstraction—one of its own phenomena. For we cannot, surely, maintain that
the abstraction is made by the Absolute and, if it is not, what else can be
the source of the 'appearance' unless it is that mind which itself *is* the
appearance?

4. In answer to this objection, it might be said that the minds which
are only appearance are not the minds which enjoy the experience,

even on Bradley's theory. The latter are 'finite centres', in and as which the Absolute (for reasons which we cannot discover) manifests itself. The abstraction is not to be attributed to the Absolute *in propria persona* but to the finite forms in which its experience is imparted to us.

We must remember that the experience of these finite centres is nothing merely subjective. 'This my world, of feeling and felt in one,' says Bradley, 'is not to be called "subjective" nor is it to be identified with my self. That would be a mistake at once fundamental and disastrous.'[1] All distinctions fall within this world. 'Self' and 'not-self' are ideal constructions secondarily abstracted from the 'felt mass' of immediate experience. Accordingly, what we have called the mind in the world, my self as opposed to your self, physical nature and the processes of evolution of which, science tells us, man is the product— all these are appearances in the experiences of finite centres. But if all distinctions are made within the one experience which I call 'mine' and which belongs to my finite centre, what is to be said of the distinctions between my finite centre and others? This is also made within my experience and the same difficulty breaks out here as arose in the case of 'my self'. For as 'self' and 'not-self' were found to be abstractions within one experience, so now my centre and other centres must likewise be pronounced abstractions and appearances. Thus the finite centre must either be reduced again to one of its own phenomena, or else it must be identified with the Absolute which is the concrete union of all finite centres. Both these alternatives are self-contradictory, and again the theory seems to have failed. If we regard experience as composed of appearances and ideal constructions in this way, there can be no doubt of the failure of a theory such as Bradley's. For if the mind and nature are pronounced to be appearances, some account must still be given of that to which they appear, and this we have seen the theory fails to do. Moreover, our common experience presents to us a world of objects in space and time, of suns and galactic systems, mountains and rivers, animals and men, all of which seem to have an existence distinct from our experience. And if all this is simply a texture of phantasy floating before the mind (be it of a finite centre or of the Absolute itself), if none of these objects have the sort of existence we take them to have and if we can put nothing more real in their place, then all our experience is not only appearance but is illusion.

[1] *Essays on Truth and Reality* (Oxford, 1914), p. 189.

II. REINTERPRETATION OF BRADLEY'S THEORY

5. But Bradley's philosophy need not be so interpreted. He constantly declares that appearance is not mere illusion but is appearance of the 'real'.[1] He says that appearances are real in varying degrees and he holds them to be appearance and not reality only so far as they are incomplete, so far as they are not the *whole* of reality. He maintains that only the real can appear, and if this is the case he clearly does not mean by 'appearance' something which merely floats before a mind.[2]

What Bradley does mean by the word is rather a manifestation of the real, a way in which the Absolute displays itself, not merely to a mind or subject but in and as some form of experience—much the same as what Hegel meant by *Erscheinung*. This interpretation of the term gives the theory a different aspect. That anything should appear is now seen to be a warrant of its reality (at least in some degree), and to say that it is not the whole of reality and is therefore only appearance, is not to reduce it to sheer error and illusion. Thus the world of our experience is not a mere phantasmagoria but is a series of appearances which can be graded according to their various degrees of reality. Nature, minds, selves and 'finite centres' are all ways in which the real manifests itself —to borrow a term from Spinoza, they are all 'modes' of the Absolute. This correction of our first interpretation of Bradley does not, however, save his doctrine altogether, for there are two features of his theory which leave his meaning obscure and render his position still subject to a criticism similar to that already made. The first is his insistence on 'feeling' as the basis of all experience, and the second is his belief that the complete interpretation and explanation of the appearances is beyond our knowledge.

There are, he thinks, three phases of experience (each of which is at the same time a degree of reality). The first is 'immediate experience' which he describes as a 'positive non-relational non-objective whole of feeling'.[3] This is the foundation of all knowledge and explicit thought and no reality can fall outside it—'the real, to be real, must be felt'.[4] We can never get rid of immediacy; it persists as an ever-present aspect of all forms of experience. The second phase is relational thinking, in which terms and relations, substances and adjectives come to be distinguished within and separated out of the 'felt mass' of the immediate. In the third phase all relations are transcended and all distinctions

[1] Cf. *Appearance and Reality*, pp. 114-15 and ch. xxiv.
[2] Cf. *ibid.* pp. 429-30.
[3] *Truth and Reality*, p. 189.　　　　[4] *Ibid.* p. 190, n. 1.

concretely united in one whole of experience which is at once immediate and beyond relational thought. The relations have all been absorbed and digested within it.

The sphere of appearance is the second of these phases. It is here we find the ideas of self, of space and time, of nature and, in fact, of everything that comprises our explicit knowledge of the world. These notions are incomplete and self-contradictory, their elements are incompatible and we cannot combine them into one self-consistent whole of experience as it is the aim of our thinking to do.

Such a concrete whole would form the third sphere of experience, but it is largely beyond our finite knowledge. Hence we cannot know in detail how the whole is unified nor how the appearances are, in the end, made complete. That they are so, Bradley says, is indubitable; to believe otherwise would be to contradict oneself.[1]

6. The first difficulty which arises is that of determining why we should postulate, as Bradley does, a multitude of finite centres of feeling. Such a multiplicity implies terms and relations and must *ex hypothesi* fall within the sphere of mediated experience. Here one would expect it to coincide with the notion of selves or souls. But Bradley distinctly says that 'my world of feeling and felt in one' is not to be identified with my self. Yet all the distinctions which come to be recognized in the second sphere of experience are explicated out of material which was in the sphere of feeling, and surely there can be nothing in the 'non-relational non-objective whole of feeling' which suggests a multiplicity of such wholes. What is there in the distinction between my world of feeling, or my centre, and yours which is different from the distinction between my self and your self? It is always distinction and, on Bradley's theory, it should have some ground in the differences felt, though not distinguished, in immediate experience. That would mean that the differences which lead to the distinction of my centre of feeling from other centres must all, in some sense, fall within my world of feeling. If this were not so, no one could develop the theory that there are a number of finite centres. But this leads to the very dilemma we are trying to avoid. It postulates a 'not-mine' and at the same time includes it in the 'mine' so that either my world of feeling must be all-inclusive, or else, if there are other centres of experience outside and beyond my felt world, it is impossible for me ever to come to know them. It has always seemed to me difficult to reconcile what Bradley says in the sixth of the *Essays on Truth and Reality*, especially what he says about

[1] *Vide Appearance and Reality*, ch. xi.

the inclusion of 'the unknown' in my experience [1] with the following statements in *Appearance and Reality*:[2] 'I deny that the felt reality is shut up and confined within *my* feeling. For the latter may, by addition, be extended beyond its own proper limits. It may remain positively itself, and yet be absorbed in what is larger. . . . There may be a further experience immediate and direct, something that *is* my private feeling and also much more. . . . There is a "more" of feeling, the extension of that which is "now mine". . . .' How can I, on Bradley's theory, speak of a 'beyond' into which 'my feeling' may be extended 'a further experience', which is 'much more' than merely mine, a 'more of feeling', and so on, unless this 'beyond' is itself to be included in my felt world? The only alternative seems to be to postulate something outside experience, in effect to rehabilitate Kant's *Ding-an-sich*. Accordingly the problem seems to reassert itself, in a form slightly different from that in which we first stated it but, for Bradley's theory, seemingly still unsolved.

The second difficulty is that when we ask what the appearances of nature and an external world of objects really mean—what sort of a reality we can take them to have—Bradley's reply can ultimately be only to refer us to the Absolute, where, we may be sure, all the appearances are explained. But *how* they are explained and what is their real significance he thinks we can never discover owing to the finiteness of our minds. That there is some explanation why the appearances do appear as they do, and that they are appearances of the real, Bradley is certain. But he holds that we cannot know the explanation—the 'how' and the 'why' we can never understand.

But this is, in effect, to abandon as insoluble the problem from which we set out. For we asked how we could intelligibly conceive the relation between the appearance of finite minds in a world which includes them among other finite things and the experience which embraces the whole of that world. The answer which we get from Bradley is that the first is an abstraction from the second, an abstraction not wholly false and meaningless but one the full significance and truth of which can be found only when it is united with all other abstractions in one concrete whole. Yet this whole, except in its general outlines, is beyond our knowledge. If we ask, further, why such abstractions should ever be made, the reply is that we must make the abstractions in our effort to understand our experience (otherwise we should be lost in the vague mass of the immediate). But the abstractions are self-contradictory, our intellect rejects them and in them our effort to

[1] *Op. cit.* p. 183. [2] Ch. xxi, p. 223.

understand has not reached its object. Yet we cannot discover how the contradictions may be overcome or the appearances rendered intelligible, for we can never know the full detail of the Absolute which alone could supply us with the explanation we are seeking. More than a general conception of the nature of reality, Bradley thinks, is beyond our finite capacity. Thus, in the last resort our problem remains, for us, insoluble.

This conclusion is hardly likely to satisfy many. Even those who sympathized most with Bradley's doctrine felt that if we can go so far we should be able to go further.[1] If our knowledge were utterly transcended by the Absolute it could in no way satisfy the demands of the intellect which can be met only by the Absolute. Again, if the Absolute transcends our minds so completely, what warrant has Bradley for his positive and confident assertions about the general nature of the ultimately real? Yet if the tendency of our thought is towards concrete wholeness and if we can go so far as to recognize the defects of our own first efforts at systematizing our experience, there seems reason to hope that we have not progressed entirely in the wrong direction and that our prescience of perfection has some real value.

7. Bradley's fundamental error lies in his view that nature is no more than an abstraction from an experience; and this again arises from his acceptance of the Renaissance conception as the only one possible. Accordingly, although he is prepared to concede a certain measure of reality to nature as one appearance of the real, the word 'reality' in his usage is itself tainted with subjectivism and nature remains an 'ideal construction', or as Whitehead puts it, 'an idea in the ultimate mentality'. Though Bradley regards nature as a feature of a certain level in the development of experience, he cannot think of it as the prior phase in an evolutionary process in which mind, or experience, is a later phase. To do that would be to abandon at once both the Renaissance conception and subjectivism. But Bradley embraces that conception and then attempts to sterilize it by dissolving it away in conscious experience.

Partly he has been misled by Hegel's logical doctrine and the relegation of science to the level of the abstract understanding, and partly he has misinterpreted Hegel to mean that nature itself is therefore only an appearance transcended in the Absolute Idea. Consequently, he ignores Hegel's philosophy of nature and concerns himself exclusively with the later phases of a long development, to the earlier process of which he cannot do proper justice. It appears in his system as no more

[1] Cf. Joachim, *Logical Studies*, pp. 287 ff.

than an ideal construction, an abstraction, or an 'appearance' in some vague sense of that word that is never satisfactorily elucidated.

III. REACTION AGAINST IDEALISM

8. Not all Bradley's idealistic *confrères* commit this error to quite the same extent. In particular, Bernard Bosanquet avoids it in the main, recognizing that mind 'does not come before us, in the animal world, except as something which arises, so to speak, on top of a vast evolution. . . .'[1] In this school of idealism he presents a philosophical position most nearly adequate to modern needs, agreeing in principle and in the more important respects with what is to be found in the doctrines of Whitehead.[2]

But the general impression created by the so-called British Hegelians was that created by Bradley, and it resulted in a reaction which carried some thinkers so far in the opposite direction as to take them, full against the current of modern progress, back to the positions of the 17th and 18th century empiricisms. The general title often given to this reaction was 'realism', but that name covers so many divergent doctrines that I shall avoid its use. It is, moreover, repudiated almost as strongly as is 'idealism' in much contemporary philosophy which has directly sprung from the reaction against the Hegelians. What we are witnessing today is, in the main, a complete reversion to an empirical philosophy which the progress of modern science has left far behind. To the doctrines in which this reversion is most evident I shall turn immediately; but some 'realist' theories, though still infected by the lingering taint of empiricism, are genuine efforts to give expression to modern ideas and the study of them will find a place in the third section of this Part.

9. The reaction against the Bradleian type of doctrine has taken several forms, but few, if any, of them are the result of a thorough understanding of the theory. The various 'refutations' of idealism to be found among the writings of the opposing school are all, in the main, irrelevant, and the best of the so-called 'realists' (that is, those who have propounded any positive doctrine) have reasserted the main essentials of the views they imagined themselves to be controverting in forms usually more confused and less tenable. But in most cases the unsatisfactory conception of mind, as something in which the material

[1] *The Nature of Mind*, p. 86; cf. also *Principle of Individuality and Value*, Lect. IV et seq. [2] Cf. Bosanquet, *Contemporary Philosophy* (London, 1924), p. 16.

reality of the external world is somehow dissolved or volatilized away, is replaced by an equally unsatisfactory conception of the physical world as something existing independently of mind and exclusive of consciousness—a resuscitation, in fact, of the Renaissance conception of nature. It is hardly surprising that a new empiricism has, in consequence, emerged and has followed a course of development not dissimilar to that of the empiricism of the 17th and 18th centuries.

The characteristics of this new empiricism are, in all essentials, the same as those outlined in Part III. The English writers of the school do, as a rule, profess to have returned to the general position of Locke or of Hume, though less eager to claim affinity with Berkeley. They all display more or less hostility to the classical tradition in philosophy, especially to anything which savours of Aristotelianism; they all assume a cleavage between physical nature and man's consciousness of it and several of them adopt, as a result, some form of the doctrine of primary and secondary qualities; there is current among them the notion of a correspondence of mental contents to material things and the assertion of a causal connection between them. Accordingly, as one would expect, they insist, for the most part,[1] upon the principle that all knowledge is either given in sense or derived from sense-perception, and consciousness itself (where it is at all admitted) they reduce to trains of particulars, while they regard physical objects as groups ('classes' or 'families') of similar particulars. Finally, they believe in the existence of two kinds of knowledge: *a posteriori*, or empirical knowledge about matters of facts, consisting of synthetic propositions, and *a priori* knowledge (logic and mathematics) involving only analytic propositions and asserting nothing but tautologies. In fact, modern empiricism is an almost unqualified return to the fundamental conceptions of pre-Kantian thought (Russell, indeed, is reputed to have said that the philosophy of Kant was a disaster), and the question arises how those who have made this return have been able to dispose of the criticisms of the earlier empiricism, both explicit and implied, in the formidable body of philosophy which has intervened.

IV. THE 'REFUTATION' OF IDEALISM

10. There are three principal ways in which modern empiricists deal with the post-Kantian tradition:

(1) Some members of the school have made direct attempts to refute

[1] The exceptions to this rule which some of them admit are curious, and, in certain cases, they would, if pressed, have disastrous consequences for the theory. I shall deal with them in the sequel as occasion arises.

arguments which they consider fundamental to 'idealism', with which they identify any philosophy showing affinity to Kant or Hegel. But the positions which are attacked are almost invariably not those which their opponents have actually maintained and in many cases are what they emphatically reject. Consequently the criticisms are irrelevant to the main issue and display a lack of understanding hardly to be credited in otherwise competent philosophers. Nevertheless, this failure of comprehension has an explanation. It is not by any conscious intellectual act of the scientist that the presuppositions of science are changed. On the contrary, as Collingwood has pointed out,[1] we are not ordinarily conscious of our absolute presuppositions at all; and though the basal assumptions of science have changed since the 17th century, the majority of scientists were not aware of it in the opening decades of the 20th, and even now comparatively few of them have come to appreciate the fact. The leading and most influential among contemporary empiricist philosophers, moreover, began their careers as physicists and mathematicians in the early years of the present century, and they became imbued from the beginning with ideas which scientists still acknowledged, at a time when they had not yet realized how far the progress of science itself had rendered them untenable. These ideas were still those of the 17th century; for physics, even at the beginning of the 20th, had not been much influenced by the new cosmological conceptions which had begun to emerge in geology and biology some fifty years earlier. In fact, it was not until the last decade of the 19th century that the new physics, which was so radically to alter the presuppositions of science and to modify the Newtonian conception of nature, began to arise. So deep a hold did the 17th-century preconceptions seem to gain upon the minds of those philosophers who acquired their early training as physicists, that every theory with which they have come into contact has, in their eyes, become coloured by those preconceptions and has been interpreted in terms of them. In the case of theories which have sprung from the sort of intellectual revolution embodied in the work of Hegel, such interpretation is, of course, sheer misinterpretation, and it is easily understandable how writers, whose thought is as thoroughly permeated by the presuppositions of Renaissance science as is that of the modern empiricist, could totally fail to comprehend the teaching of those who had appreciated the effects of the Critical Philosophy and the developments which Hegel had subsequently initiated.[2]

[1] *Metaphysics*, pp. 43 and 48 n.
[2] Perhaps the most outstanding illustration of such failure of comprehension is to be found in Russell's account of the philosophies of Kant and Hegel in his *History*

266

Some examples of arguments purporting to refute 'idealism' I have already examined in connection with the philosophy of Berkeley, but something must be added here about their bearing upon the work of later writers. The type of philosophy which the empiricist opposes is, he believes, one which attempts to reduce all things to mental events. But to attribute this attempt to thinkers like Hegel, Green or Bradley is even more gross an error than to attribute it to Berkeley. Hegel's polemic against subjectivism is one of the outstanding features of his philosophy and the essence of his whole teaching is that 'it is to be regarded as the highest purpose of Philosophy to reconcile conscious reason with the reason in being, with actuality'.[1] And as for those who have been reputed his followers, they have been, perhaps, the most emphatic and outspoken of writers against the very 'mentalism' which Professor Broad, for instance, attributes to them. To demonstrate this in detail would require a multiplication of citations which is warranted neither by the space at my disposal nor on the ground that the examples would be unfamiliar. I shall therefore confine myself to three, the last of which, if somewhat lengthy, has the merit that it speaks for at least five of the writers who have expounded the kind of idealism against which the empiricist criticism is directed.

T. H. Green's theory of the relation of mind to nature is set out in the opening chapters of the *Prolegomena to Ethics* in which he protests at length against the reduction either of nature or of consciousness to a series of mental events. He asserts, it is true, that both nature and our consciousness of it are the expression of what he calls a spiritual principle, but he rejects uncompromisingly 'the absurdity that nature comes into existence in the process by which this person or that begins to think'.[2]

'There are difficulties enough, no doubt,' he writes, 'in the way of accepting such a form of "idealism", but they need not be aggravated by misunderstanding. It is simply misunderstood if it is taken to imply either the reduction of facts to feelings—impressions and ideas, in Hume's terminology—or the obliteration of the distinction between illusion and reality.'[3]

'It is our cognisance of the successiveness or transitoriness of feelings', he continues, 'that makes us object intuitively to any idealism which is understood to imply an identification of the realities of the world with the

of Western Philosophy, Bk. III, chs. xx and xxii. It is significant that such names as F. H. Bradley and T. H. Green appear in this work only in passing references, and that the work of Whitehead (apart from his collaboration with the author in *Principia Mathematica*) is not mentioned.

[1] *Enc.* 6.   [2] *Op. cit.* Bk. I, ch. i, § 36.   [3] *Ibid.* § 37.

feelings of men. Facts, we are sure, are in some way permanent. They are not "like the bubble on the fountain", a moment here, then "gone, and for ever". But if they were feelings as we feel them, they would be so. They would not be "stubborn things"; for as each was felt it would be done with. They would not form a world to which we have to adapt ourselves; for in order to make a world they must coexist, which feelings, as we feel them, do not. But the idealism which interprets facts as relations, and can only understand relations as constituted by a single spiritual principle, is chargeable with no such outrage on common sense. On the contrary, its very basis is the consciousness of objectivity. Its whole aim is to articulate coherently the conviction of there being a world of abiding realities other than, and determining, the endless flow of our feelings....'[1]

In like manner, Joachim, in *The Nature of Truth*, writes as follows:

'Subjective Idealism has rightly fallen into discredit. It will not stand as a theory of Reality; and it affords no foundation for a sane theory of knowledge or of conduct. It fails when it takes the consistent form of Solipsism; and it fails equally when it assumes the half-hearted form of a spiritual pluralism. Neither I myself and my psychical states, nor an assemblage of finite selves each wrapped up in his own ideas, can constitute the ultimate reality. And the failure of Subjective Idealism is in no way lessened by the introduction of an infinite mind and its psychical states *besides* the finite self or selves. It is indeed "a short way with Idealists" to identify them with the advocates of this type of theory: and if the identification were established, Idealism would be finally refuted. But the point at issue is whether this identification is sound or not: and I am contending that it is not.'[2]

In a footnote commenting on Moore's *Refutation of Idealism*, he says: 'Even if Mr. Moore really had reduced all Idealism to Subjective Idealism his "refutation" is far from convincing; but it will be time enough for Idealists to meet Mr. Moore's "refutation" when the reduction has been made'.

But Bosanquet's assessment of Moore's *Refutation* [3] is still more apt for my purpose, and I hope, therefore, that the length of the quotation may be tolerated.

'I take as a notable illustration Dr. Moore's well-known "Refutation of Idealism". This, as I read it, is to be welcomed from the standpoint of speculative philosophy in two respects at least: (i) The implication, as I understand it, on the first half-page, that the Idealist is in the wrong if he maintains that particular things in space are in themselves altogether

---

[1] *Ibid.*   [2] *Op. cit.* (Oxford, 1906), pp. 61-2.
[3] *The Meeting of Extremes in Contemporary Philosophy*, pp. 3 ff.

different from what they look like to us (except in the sense of the strictly continuous and additional determinations proffered by physical science). Here I take Dr. Moore to be with Plato and Hegel, and, to go to their minor successors, with T. H. Green and, say, Nettleship. It is hardly fair to attempt to answer for a living writer, but I should have thought Mr. Bradley would condemn any departure from this attitude as a misuse and misconception of the doctrine of "relativity" in its older sense. "If the reader believes that a steam-engine, after it is made, is nothing but a state of the mind of the person or persons who made it, or who are looking at it, we do not hold what we feel tempted to call such a silly doctrine; and would point out to those who do hold it that, at all events, the engine is a very different state of mind, after it is made, to what it was before." And in the footnote, "We may remark that the ordinary 'philosophical' person, who talks about 'relativity' [in the older sense, of course], does not seem to know what he is saying. He will tell you that 'all' (or 'all we know and can know'—there is no practical difference between that and 'all') is relative to consciousness—not giving you to understand that he means thereby any consciousness besides his own, and ready, I should imagine, with his grin at the notion of a mind which is anything more than the mind of this or that man; and then, it may be, a few pages farther on or farther back, will talk to you of the state of the earth before man existed on it. But we wish to know what in the world it all means, and would suggest, as a method of clearing the matter, the two questions—(1) Is my consciousness something that goes and is beyond myself; and if so, in what sense? and (2) Had I a father? What do I mean by that, and how do I reconcile my assertion of it with my answer to question (1)?" [1] The tone of this passage is what strikes me as so suggestive. Obviously it never occurred to the writer that the chair would be more spiritual if it were not a chair. Certainly for myself, if an idealist were to tell me that a chair is really not what we commonly take it to be, but something altogether different (unless he meant "a dance of electrons" or the like), I should be tempted to reply in language below the dignity of controversy. The position in question—Hegel's and Green's—is, I should say, that a chair is a chair right enough; that is, that what an upholsterer or anyone in a drawing-room would tell you about it is quite a true description. But when you come to ask further questions, there is much more to be said, and these questions the upholsterer has never raised, and, as such, can never raise. Here the physicist's standpoint may fairly be used as an illustration. It is ridiculous to say that it contradicts what the chairmaker says, any more than an economist's view of a sovereign contradicts a metallurgist's. Take Professor Whitehead's "Concept of Nature" with its account of the situation of an object. Does it mean that I am wrong in thinking that I am

[1] Quoted from *Ethical Studies* (2nd ed., pp. 66 f.).

sitting on my chair? Of course, if Dr. Moore's implication is the opposite —viz., that in maintaining the spirituality of the universe, the idealist both does *and must* maintain that we are wholly wrong in our common notion of a chair, then I must think that he has misunderstood the facts necessary to idealism, and so far has failed to bring assistance to speculative philosophy.'

In the face of statements such as these only a thinker interpreting everything he read in terms of the 17th-century dualism could attribute to Hegel and Bradley and philosophers of like mind the view 'that material characteristics are delusive *appearances* of certain mental characteristics', as does Professor Broad under the heading of 'Reductive Mentalism'.[1]

The same error is committed by Moore and is reiterated in several of his writings by Bertrand Russell. There is, in fact, no valid refutation of the main position of Hegelian Idealism (calling it that for lack of a better name) to be found in the works of contemporary empiricists, and the only adverse criticism worthy of serious consideration is what the Hegelians themselves have offered, for they have not been insensible of shortcomings which they have been unable to rectify in their own teachings. Such criticisms as are put forward by empiricist opponents are all vitiated by the same fault: that they depend on an interpretation circumscribed by the presuppositions of the 17th century which the very theories they are attacking have rendered obsolete. To mention only one other such criticism, it is clearly inept to castigate the philosophy of the classical tradition, as Russell, Ayer and others do, for its alleged belief in the omnipotence of *a priori* reasoning;[2] for the pre-Kantian separation between *a priori* and *a posteriori* knowledge is one of the doctrines which the theory criticized rejects. The rejoinder that a view need not be accepted as true merely because it has been held by thinkers of a certain school would, of course, be just; but it is not permissible to reject a doctrine on the strength of criticisms arising out of principles which that doctrine professes to have refuted, unless and until the principles involved can be re-established on a basis which both allows for and is unassailable by the kind of refutation which has earlier been claimed.

11. (2) A second expedient frequently adopted by empiricists for disposing of inconvenient doctrines is to pass them over as out-dated.

---

[1] *Mind and Its Place in Nature* (London, 1925), p. 624.
[2] Cf. Russell, *Our Knowledge of the External World*, pp. 15-21, and Ayer in *Polemic* (no. 7), 'The Claims of Philosophy'.

Russell, thirty-five years ago, said that the classical tradition was a decaying force and that it had 'failed to adapt itself to the temper of the age'.[1] Since then his followers have for the most part simply taken for granted the obsolescence of theories which they disliked or failed to understand. A philosophy, it has been said,[2] is never refuted, it is simply abandoned, and one is put in mind of Locke's remark, more trenchant today in reverse, about 'those who judge of men's heads as they do their perukes, by the fashion'. But if it were permissible simply to abandon a philosophical theory for lack of sympathy with it, we may with as little ceremony set aside empiricism as empiricists have set aside Hegelianism: for not only are the metaphysical presuppositions implied in empiricism three centuries behind the times, but also, if the temper of the age is to be judged by the deliverances of contemporary science, there is (as I hope to show later) every reason for regarding modern empiricism as thoroughly discordant with them.

The supersession of one philosophical system by another is never an arbitrary matter, and if a theory is rightly to be abandoned it must be because by development of what it implied a new and more adequate theory has been developed, the superiority of which constitutes the criticism of its predecessor. But modern empiricism has not developed by any such process. It has come into being partly through misconception of the direction in which modern thought has been developing, and partly it is a relic or hang-over from the 19th-century inebriation with the success of physical science proceeding on the presuppositions laid down at the Renaissance.[3]

12. (3) The third method, by which empiricists have avoided the incidence of criticism from those whom they oppose, has been to reject theories inimical to their own on the ground of a metaphysic dogmatically stated or uncritically assumed. Examples of this have already been noticed in Chapter I. First it is assumed that reality is much what it was taken to be by 17th-century science—a physical complex to which a certain ideal counterpart (called knowledge or science) corresponds. The status of this counterpart is then held to depend upon its (gratuitously assumed) correspondence with the physical complex,

---

[1] *Loc. cit.*   [2] I think by Whitehead.
[3] Cf. Whitehead, *Science and the Modern World*, p. 126: 'The convergent effect of the new power for scientific advance . . . transformed the middle period of the [19th] century into an orgy of scientific triumph. Clear-sighted men, of the sort who are so clearly wrong, now proclaimed that the secrets of the physical universe were finally disclosed. If only you ignored everything which refused to come into line, your powers of explanation were unlimited.'

which is supposed to constitute 'fact' and to be revealed to the mind in sense-perception. The field of such correspondence is arbitrarily restricted to the natural sciences and all other forms of speculation are rejected as meaningless. That the statement of such a doctrine is illegitimate according to its own teaching is ignored by those who are frank enough to state it. By others it is tacitly assumed without acknowledgement, while the conclusion from it is dogmatically asserted and is used to dispense with the need for self-examination and to debar criticism by opponents.

V. HISTORY REPEATS ITSELF

13. It is not to be imagined, however, that the history of empiricism is discontinuous and that between Hume and (say) Russell there were no philosophers who carried on the tradition. The empirical attitude was at no period totally superseded by post-Kantian idealism. The English Utilitarians and the Scottish philosophers of 'common sense' persisted in views similar to those of the earlier empiricists, and in America the later 19th century produced Charles Sanders Peirce and William James. But whatever the importance of these thinkers may be, I propose to ignore them, for while they provide no evidence against the thesis that I wish to maintain, it can be more effectively supported by reference to contemporary writers. My purpose here is no more than to point out certain general tendencies of development in contemporary empiricism by reference to a few writers whose work I take to exemplify the tendencies described, to show that they revert to 17th-century presuppositions, and to criticize the solutions they offer of the problem of knowledge.

14. It seems to me that in modern empiricism three phases can be distinguished and that they correspond broadly to the three phases of 17th-18th century empiricism represented by Locke, Berkeley and Hume. The first is marked by the conception which Whitehead has termed 'vacuous actuality'. It is typified by the doctrine that knowing makes no difference to the known, a doctrine which attempts to envisage a reality the existence and nature of which is independent of and unaffected by mind, even when it becomes the object of knowledge. The second phase is continuous with the first, accepting its primary assumptions but paying more attention to the subjective side of the relation between material things and the knowing mind. Stress is laid upon the sensible character of the material world and the attempt is

made to explain in detail how the knowledge of the external world can be constructed from the data of sense. The third phase is one in which every element in knowledge is repudiated which is not in principle 'verifiable' by the occurrence of actual or possible sense-experience, with an increasing tendency to reduce the activity of thought to speech behaviour and to conceive philosophy as an empirical science of the use of signs, which has been named 'semiotic'. This final phase is not openly and professedly sceptical in an absolute sense, but it implies an absolute scepticism and disguises it only by the elaboration of new and, as I shall contend, spurious sciences.

The conceptions of nature and mind and of the relation between them which typify each of these three forms of modern empiricism are, I have suggested, respectively akin to those of Locke, Berkeley and Hume, but, of course, what was impossible for Locke is possible for the modern empiricist—he can borrow also from Berkeley and Hume and elements of all three are to be found in each of the contemporary forms of the doctrine. Also, the modern theories are complicated and, as it were, sophisticated, by intricacies derived from the modern sciences of physics and psychology. Nevertheless, the affinity to the earlier empiricists is clearly recognizable and I shall draw the parallel as I proceed with the exposition. The ultimate philosophical consequences of the doctrines are, moreover, no less devastating than those of the Humian scepticism.

Chapter XIV

MODERN EMPIRICISM:
THE FIRST PHASE (RUSSELL)

*

1. I SHALL take as representative of the first phase of modern empiricism the sort of position set out by Bertrand Russell, the extraordinary similarity of which to that maintained by Locke I shall try to illustrate as I proceed. But I shall not be able to do justice to the whole of Russell's philosophy. He is one of the more prolific of modern writers and he has not been afraid of changing his mind when the arguments of his colleagues convinced him that he was wrong or when his own thought led him to new conclusions. Space, however, will not permit me to trace the development of his thought in detail, but, numerous though his corrections of his own teaching have been, they have mainly concerned matters of detail and the general character of his main position has been sustained with little alteration throughout a long and eminent career of writing, teaching and discussion. Nor will it be possible for me to discuss every aspect of his theories, and I shall limit myself to the examination of what seem to me to be his main metaphysical and epistemological contentions, neglecting, for the most part, the considerable mass of writing which he has produced on mathematical logic.

I. THE ANALYSIS OF MIND INTO PARTICULARS

2. For Russell, in certain moods, the world is a vast assemblage of finite entities, displaying neither obvious system nor necessary unity, among which minds hold a status differing only in degree (and that but slightly) from the rest. In order to discover how he explains the acquisition by minds of their knowledge of this world, I shall begin with a brief summary of the analysis of mind which he gives in his book of that name. There he strikes the keynote of his theory of mind in the following statement: 'I believe that sensations (including images) supply all the "stuff" of the mind, and that everything else can be analysed into groups of sensations related in various ways, or characteristics of sensations or of groups of sensations'.[1] Here we have the raw material of knowledge, and also, it will presently appear, the point of contact between the mind and the external world. 'Sensations', Russell says,

[1] *Analysis of Mind* (London, 1933), p. 69.

'are obviously the source of our knowledge of the world, including our own body',[1] and we are told that in sensation there is no distinction between mental content and object but that 'what you see or hear is actually part of the physical world'.[2]

The nature of this contact between the mind and the world will be considered later; here we may observe that Russell does not exclude from the raw material of knowledge the deliverances of 'the inner sense'. In an earlier work [3] he distinguishes 'knowledge by acquaintance' from what he calls 'knowledge by description'. The first is the knowledge of things and the second of truths; but it appears almost at once that by 'things' Russell does not mean physical entities; he means sense-data. 'We shall say that we have *acquaintance*', he says,[4] 'with anything of which we are directly aware, without the intermediary of any process of inference or knowledge of truths. Thus in the presence of my table I am acquainted with the sense-data that make up the appearance of my table—its colour, shape, hardness, smoothness, etc.' Knowledge by acquaintance, therefore, is what is afforded by sensation; but Russell also includes in it acquaintance by introspection,[5] which, a few pages further on, is called in so many words, acquaintance with the data of the inner sense. All our knowledge, he says, both of things and of truths rests upon acquaintance as its foundation; thus for Russell, as for Locke, the materials of all knowledge are comprised in what is derived from inner and outer sensation and it is certainly no misrepresentation to say that sensations, in Russell's view, supply the whole furniture of the mind. They are the first beginnings of knowledge and put the mind into immediate contact with external objects. They are one source of what Russell calls elsewhere our 'hard data' concerning which real doubt would be pathological.[6] To this elemental stuff of mind Russell reduces all feeling, pleasure, pain discomfort, desire, belief and thought; and, though we have no direct concern with it here, his account of desire and its connection with discomfort is so reminiscent of Locke that I cannot, in passing, forbear to draw attention to the similarity.[7]

The 'stuff' of mind, however, is said to include images, and these

---

[1] *Ibid.* p. 141.   [2] *Ibid.* p. 19.

[3] *Problems of Philosophy*, ch. v.

[4] *Ibid.* p. 73 (Eighteenth Impression, 1945). Cf. Locke, *Essay concerning Human Understanding*, II, i, 3.

[5] *Ibid.* p. 76.

[6] *Our Knowledge of the External World*, p. 78.

[7] *Vide Analysis of Mind*, Lect. III, and cf. *Essay concerning Human Understanding*, II, xxi, 31 ff.

Russell does not distinguish sharply from sensations, for he admits that every criterion of distinction but one is liable to exception: images, he says, differ from sensations only in their causes and effects. Sensations are caused by stimuli external to the nervous system; they 'come through the sense-organs'; but images are 'occasioned, through association, by a sensation or another image', by mnemic causation.[1] Images, however, are allowed to be (though without very strong conviction) 'copies' of sensations, from which fact 'their mnemic character is evident'.[2]

3. The connection by mnemic causation of sensations and images one with another is the source of their acquisition of meaning, which, when it characterizes certain vocally produced sounds, or written marks, constitutes them words. Not only words, however, have meaning; gestures or pictures may serve a similar purpose and, besides these, images themselves are said to have meaning. When this is the case, that which has meaning is said to be the sign or symbol of that which it means and is connected with it by mnemic causation. Accordingly, a word or other sign may give rise to behaviour appropriate to a certain object or situation without the intervention of any other medium, or it may call up an image. In the first case the meaning of the symbol is the object or situation to which the behaviour stimulated is appropriate; and in the second, it is the prototype of the image. As images are 'copies' of sensations, one would assume that their prototypes are sensations and this is suggested by Russell's explanation of the vagueness of their meaning. 'There is not one definite prototype', he says, 'but a number, none of which is copied exactly.'[3] But the same passage also suggests that the prototype is the physical thing or occurrence sensed—'a memory-image of a particular occurrence, when accompanied by a memory-belief, may be said to mean the occurrence of which it is an image'.[4] Yet strictly, I suppose, we should hold that the occurrence of which it is the image can only be a sensation, as that is the only source of our experience of any physical object or event; and, though Russell is never explicit on the point, this view seems to follow from what he says further about meaning. For, ultimately, meaning turns out to be one or both of two things: (a) that to which the sign has similar mnemic effects, and (b) that which (in the case of an image) it resembles (or, in the case of a word, which the image called up resembles). Now, Russell maintains that there is no ground for admitting

---

[1] *Analysis of Mind*, pp. 149-50.
[2] *Ibid.* p. 80.   [3] *Ibid.* p. 207.   [4] *Ibid.*

mnemic causation in physics,[1] and consequently in the case of the first alternative the meaning of the sign must be something mental; and, as the mnemic character of images is said to be evident from the fact that they are copies of sensations, one would expect the meaning to be a sensation in the second case also, when it is the prototype of an image. We are told, however, that the occurrence of a sensation or image does not itself constitute knowledge[2] and this must apply even to the occurrence of images which are mnemically caused by signs. More than the mere possession of meaning, therefore, is required if sensations and images are to give us knowledge of the external world. That, Russell tells us, results from correlation of our sensations with those of others; but before we turn to his account of the manner of this correlation, we must consider the nature of belief, for, clearly, it is only through the medium of beliefs that any such correlation can give us knowledge.

4. Russell analyses belief into (i) a feeling or complex of sensations demanding analysis, and (ii) a mental content in the form of a proposition which is connected by a specific relation to the feeling.[3] As a vehicle of knowledge what interests us primarily about belief is its propositional character; for it is on account of this that, as Russell puts it, it is characterized by truth or falsehood. The proposition may consist wholly of images or wholly of words,[4] or it may consist of a mixture of these with or without sensations. Russell gives an account only of the first two alternatives. In each case it is in virtue of their having meaning that the images or words enter into the content of the belief, and what they mean is one or a number of sensations which either they resemble or which have similar mnemic effects. How is this meaning connected with their characteristic of being either true or false?

Truth and falsity, we discover, does not depend on anything intrinsic to the belief;[5] in fact, it does not depend upon anything mental at all. 'What makes a belief true or false', says Russell, 'I call a "fact". The particular fact that makes a given belief true or false I call its "objective", and the relation of the belief to its objective I call the "reference" or the "objective reference" of the belief. Thus, if I believe that Columbus crossed the Atlantic in 1492, the "objective" of my belief is Columbus's actual voyage, and the "reference" of my belief is the relation between my belief and the voyage—that relation, namely, in

[1] *Ibid.* p. 88. He does allow that it may be physiological, but it would be difficult to maintain that the meaning of a sign was no more than a modification of the brain.
[2] *Ibid.* p. 109.   [3] *Ibid.* p. 251.
[4] *Ibid.* p. 239. Cf. Locke's distinction between mental and verbal propositions, *Essay*, IV, v, 5.   [5] *Analysis of Mind*, p. 232.

virtue of which the voyage makes my belief true (or, in another case, false).'[1] The 'reference' is apparently nothing which I do or make, for the fact is something beyond my control and the relation 'lies outside the belief'.

II. FACTS AND PROPOSITIONS

5. In the second of his Lowell Lectures, Russell gives an account of the world of fact [2] which it may be well to notice at this point. There we are told that 'the existing world consists of many things with many qualities and relations', but that it is not simply a collection of things, but of things-having-qualities and things-in-relation. A 'fact', therefore, is not just a thing, but is a qualitied thing or a thing in relation to another thing. Such a fact, if it cannot be analysed into other facts, but only into things, qualities and relations, is called 'atomic', and it may be constituted either by one thing and one or more of its qualities, or by two or more things in relation (the number of terms depending on the kind of relation involved). These atomic facts may combine to form a larger complex, and it matters little whether we call the larger complex one fact or more, so long as we realize that it can be analysed into its atomic constituents.

Facts are said to be 'objective' and to be independent of our thought; but, corresponding to any fact, there is an assertion which involves thought and which may be either true or false. This assertion, expressed in a form of words, is called a proposition and, when it corresponds to an atomic fact, it is an atomic proposition. Such atomic propositions may be combined by means of certain conjunctions to form 'molecular' propositions, but the truth or falsity of these does not necessarily depend on that of the constituent atomic propositions. Accordingly, complications arise in the way in which propositions correspond to facts, and although truth and falsity depend on such correspondence, it is not a simple and straightforward matter; for not only is there complication in the case of molecular propositions (for instance, hypotheticals), but also in the case of any false proposition, as there is no fact to which it directly corresponds; for if there were it would be true. I shall return to this point later, and shall investigate first the relation of the proposition to the mind, as a step towards understanding the place of the mind in the world of fact as above described.

6. We have seen already that the assertion of a proposition involves thought, and Russell tells us in *The Analysis of Mind* that propositions

---

[1] *Analysis of Mind*, p. 232.   [2] *Our Knowledge of the External World*, pp. 60 ff.

are the contents of actual and possible beliefs [1] and that believing 'seems the most "mental" thing we do, the thing most remote from what is done by mere matter'.[2] Believing he admits as an act of mind (an element which in other forms of thought he denies [3]) because, he says, believing is 'an experienced feeling'. He also tells us that 'what I believe is something now in my mind' and that this is not the 'object-ive' of the belief (which is a fact in the external world and may be an event that took place centuries ago) [4] but a proposition. If it is expressed in words, it is the same thing, he says, or nearly the same (though he does not make the qualification more explicit) as what is called a pro-position in logic; but it may also take the form of images, or of sensa-tions mixed with images or words, though it cannot consist of sensations alone. On closer scrutiny, all of these constituents of the proposition believed turn out to be mental in character. Words, we are told in an earlier lecture,[5] are sensible signs or symbols intended to call up 'ideas' which are their meanings, and even Russell admits that meaning is the distinguishing feature of words.[6] The content of belief, then, the most mental thing we do, is something expressed either in words, which are words only in virtue of the fact that they call up 'ideas', or in images or in a mixture of these with sensations, and accordingly it would seem to be something essentially mental.

7. Elsewhere, however, Russell denies that the proposition, taken as that which may be either true or false, is mental,[7] and distinguishes it from judgement, belief, assertion and the like, as the *object* which is judged, believed or asserted; but he does not identify this with the fact, which is the 'objective' of a belief, and even suggests that it has a sort of existence, or subsistence, apart from either the fact or the mind. Just what sort of existence this is Russell himself does not seem clearly to know and never fully explains. At times he seems to incline towards the view that the proposition and the fact are, after all, the same thing. 'A proposition', he writes,[8] '. . . does not itself contain words: it con-tains the entities indicated by the words'; and these entities are not (apparently) 'ideas' called up by the words (*i.e.* their meanings), for 'meaning, in the sense which words have meaning, is irrelevant to logic'. 'The entities indicated by the words' must in that case be actual

---

[1] *Op. cit.* p. 241.   [2] *Ibid.* p. 231.
[3] Cf. *ibid.* pp. 17 ff.   [4] *Ibid.* pp. 233 f.
[5] Lect. X, p. 191.   [6] *Ibid.* p. 189.
[7] *Principles of Mathematics* (Cambridge, 1903), I, p. ix, and 'Meinong's Theory of Complexes and Assumptions' in *Mind*, XIII (1904).
[8] *Principles of Mathematics*, § 51.

existing things in the world of 'fact'; and this indeed seems to be Russell's intention, if we judge by what he says in the same passage about concepts having meaning 'in a non-psychological sense'. But if the propositions are to be identified with the fact at all, it can be only true propositions which are so identified. False propositions, as we have already observed, correspond to no fact. Thus, unless we postulate for them some other extra-mental objective, a false belief becomes a belief in *nothing*.[1] For the same reason Russell hesitates to identify the false proposition with the mental constituent in belief, for to do so would necessitate its exclusion altogether from the sphere of logical investigation as a purely psychological phenomenon. Consequently, he decides finally in favour of propositions subsisting apart from either facts or minds. Yet 'finally' is hardly the word, for in *The Analysis of Mind* he abandons the notion of extra-mentally subsisting false propositions, and with it, so far as one can gather, the whole doctrine of propositions-in-themselves. The doctrine, in any case, is one of which it is difficult to make sense, and, if admitted, would force us to postulate at least three spheres of reality: physical existence, logical subsistence and mental existence, which Russell shows little inclination to do. It is in fact the product of abstraction; at best a provisional abstraction made for the special purposes and convenience of the logician, and at worst a vicious abstraction reached first by separating the mental content which is believed (or judged, etc.) from the objective fact with which in some way it is held to correspond, and then by distinguishing the mental event, alleged as the subject-matter of psychology, from its alleged 'object' as the subject-matter of logic. The doctrine is thus itself the fruit of that separation between the subjective and objective elements in knowledge[2] which is characteristic of all empiricism; and whether we attempt to find a place for it in Russell's philosophy, therefore, or whether we omit it as something about which he is never consistent or decided, it will make no difference to the view, which I am concerned to maintain, that modern empiricism, in general, and Russell's theories, in particular, are founded on the 17th-century presupposition of a dualism between thought and things and are, therefore, a repetition in modern form of a philosophical position which has long since become obsolete.

Neglecting the peculiar notion of self-subsisting propositions, then, we find Russell maintaining the existence, independently of our thought, of a world of facts, and, corresponding to certain facts, pro-

---

[1] *Mind, loc. cit.* pp. 218-19.
[2] Cf. Joachim, *Logical Studies*, pp. 241-60, especially 251 f.

positions made up of mental entities. Such propositions, associated with the appropriate feelings, are constituents in mental events such as believing, supposing and so forth; and these events are, of course, also facts, but they are mental facts and their exact relation to physical facts has still to be elucidated.

III. FACTS AND BELIEFS

8. The nature of this relation Russell explains in a subsequent chapter of *The Analysis of Mind*.[1] The objective reference he there re-defines as a function of the meanings of the words of the proposition and by this he means that if the meaning of the proposition 'points towards' the fact the objective reference is such as to make the belief true. If it 'points away from' the fact, it is such as to make it false. The relation of the proposition to the fact is, thus, either that of 'pointing towards' or that of 'pointing away from'. Russell admits that these phrases are metaphorical, but he elucidates them further by saying that, in very simple cases, 'pointing towards' is actual resemblance between the proposition and the fact.[2] And the example he gives is that of a memory belief in which the proposition consists of images of a room with the window to the left of the door. If, in fact, the window is to the left of the door in the actual room, the belief is true, and, presumably, the image proposition points towards the fact. If the actual window is to the right of the door, the opposite is the case. In more difficult and complicated instances, where the relation cannot be one of resemblance, it is not easy to see how we can explain the relation of pointing towards or away from, and Russell's use of this terminology has been criticized as no more than *se payer de mots*.[3] Perhaps for this reason he has now abandoned it and returned to the sort of language which he used in *Problems of Philosophy* and to resemblance as the relation between the true belief and its objective. In the earlier work he wrote 'a belief is true when there is a corresponding fact, and is false when there is no corresponding fact';[4] and in his most recent treatment of the matter[5] he writes: 'Every belief which is not merely an impulse to action is in the nature of a picture, combined with a yes-feeling or a no-feeling; in the case of a yes-feeling it is "true" if there is a fact having to the picture the kind of similarity that a prototype has to an image; in the case of a

---

[1] Pp. 271 ff.   [2] *Ibid*. p. 273.
[3] *Vide* H. W. B. Joseph in *Mind*, XXXVII, p. 22.
[4] *Problems of Philosophy*, p. 202.
[5] *Human Knowledge* (London, 1948), p. 170.

K*

no-feeling it is "true" if there is no such fact. A belief which is not true is called "false".'

9. The position is, then, that in a true belief we have a complex of mental elements (the proposition and its meaning ultimately resoluble into images and sensations) corresponding to or resembling a factual complex, and in a false belief a complex of mental elements to which no factual complex corresponds. The proposition, it will be remembered, is composed of signs (or may as a whole be taken as a sign) and the meaning of the signs consists of 'ideas' which they call up (images the prototypes of which have similar mnemic effects). Let us compare all this with what we found in Locke: 'Truth, then, seems to me, in the proper import of the word, to signify nothing but the *joining or separating of signs, as the Things signified by them do agree or disagree one with another*. The joining or separating of signs here meant, is what by another name we call *proposition*. So that truth properly belongs only to propositions; whereof there are two sorts, viz. mental and verbal; as there are two sorts of signs commonly made use of, viz. ideas and words . . .',[1] '. . . yet it may not be amiss here again to consider, that though our words signify nothing but our ideas, yet being designed by them to signify things, the truth they contain when put into propositions will be only verbal when they stand for ideas in the mind that have not an agreement with the reality of things'.[2]

So far, what we have is a representative theory of knowledge with its inevitable correspondence theory of truth, and we are faced by all the difficulties inherent in such a position. Belief being what I hold (or feel) to be true, the best of our knowledge is but belief, and the theory must stand or fall with our ability to show how we can come to know the criterion of truth—the fact which must correspond with the content of our belief. Russell, at this point, must answer the question which demolished the theory of Locke: How can we know whether and when our beliefs correspond to the facts, or that there are any facts to which they may correspond?

Locke attempted to answer the question by resort to 'that perception and consciousness we have of the actual entrance of ideas' from particular external objects, and Russell's answer, though more complicated, is of a similar nature. We find it in his account of that contact, mentioned above, between the mind and the world of physical facts which is made in sensation, and the theory which he develops is critical for the whole of his philosophical position, a fact of which Russell

[1] *Essay concerning Human Understanding*, IV, v, 2.   [2] *Ibid.* 8.

himself seems to be aware, for he repeats it in several of his writings,[1] though with slightly differing terminology. The doctrine may be called the theory of perspectives and it is the basis of that view of reality which Russell calls Neutral Monism.[2]

IV. PERSPECTIVES

10. The source of all our knowledge of the world is for Russell (as we saw above) sensation, which gives us what he calls our 'hard data'. By this is meant that what is given in sense is something the existence of which, while the experience lasts, cannot be doubted. At any one time, the whole of what is given in sense constitutes the sum of the percipient's hard data, and any portion of it which can be singled out by attention Russell calls a sense-datum.[3] He refuses, however, to distinguish between a sense-datum and a sensation (though he admits that at one time he thought it necessary to do so) as he holds that the occurrence of a sense-datum and the sensing of it are one and the same thing.[4] Apart from 'the general truths of logic' (which Russell includes also among our hard data) sensations, or sense-data, are the only absolutely indubitable experiences we have, and if we are to acquire knowledge of the world of external fact at all, it must be, therefore, by their means. The problem, as Russell himself states it, is 'Can the existence of anything other than our own hard data be inferred from these data?'[5] and in order to understand how such inference may be made Russell thinks it necessary to assume as an hypothesis that 'each mind looks out upon the world . . . from a point of view peculiar to itself'.[6] Each then perceives a view of the world which differs from that perceived by every other, for each depends upon the particular point of view from which the world is surveyed. From points where there are no percipients, however, it may be assumed that there nevertheless exist views of the world which would be perceived if the points were occupied by minds; and though a view, as perceived from a point by a mind, would not be exactly the same as an unperceived view from the same point, because it would be conditioned by sense-organs, nerves

---

[1] Vide *Our Knowledge of the External World*, Lect. III; *Mysticism and Logic*, ch. viii; *Analysis of Mind*, Lects. V and VII.

[2] *Analysis of Matter*, ch. xxxvii.

[3] Vide *Mysticism and Logic* (London, 1919), p. 147.

[4] Vide *Analysis of Mind*, pp. 141 f., and *Our Knowledge of the External World*, p. 83.

[5] *Our Knowledge of the External World*, p. 90.

[6] *Ibid.* p. 94. Russell expounds the theory by reference to visual data only, and it is not easy to see how it could be maintained in all respects with reference to some of the other senses.

and a brain, yet it is reasonable to suppose that some aspect of the world does exist at that point even when no mind is located there.

It must be observed, before we proceed, that the existence of sense-organs, nerves and brain conditioning our hard data is not given directly in those data themselves. But if we are assuming the existence of a world, as an hypothesis, I suppose we may treat these items as part of our initial assumption. We shall, however, have to be very wary of the use made of assumptions of this kind if the whole question at issue is not surreptitiously to be begged.

Views of the world from different points Russell calls 'perspectives', and those which are perceived by minds he calls 'private worlds'. Corresponding to these, the sensed constituents of private worlds are sense-data, and the particular objects which would be sensed in a perspective if it were occupied by a mind are called '*sensibilia*'.[1]

11. By the comparison of private worlds it is possible to correlate the sense-data occurring in them by means of their partial resemblances. If they are nearly similar we say that the perspectives to which they belong are near to one another in space. But this is not the perceived space of any private world. It is the space constituted by the mutual relations of perspectives and it cannot be perceived by any one. It is, in fine, the space of the physical world in which each perspective counts as one point, and Russell calls it 'perspective space'. In this physical space we can imagine perspectives falling between any two private worlds whose nearness we have determined by comparison of their sense-data, and so the relations between perspectives can be rendered continuous.

12. Sense-data correlated in neighbouring private worlds, along with the *sensibilia* assumed to occur in perspectives continuous with them, can be collected together into systems, and these systems constitute what we ordinarily call 'things', while the sense-data and *sensibilia* constituting them are their appearances or aspects from various points of view. The aspects, Russell tells us, are all real, but the thing is 'merely a logical construction'.

Here we have something very like Locke's complex ideas of substances; and, as a 'thing' is only a logical construction, the 'ideal' elements of which, we are told,[2] we cannot know to exist (apart from some *a priori* law), and as we are told also [3] that we may not infer the

---

[1] Cf. *Mysticism and Logic*, pp. 148 ff.
[2] *Our Knowledge of the External World*, p. 117.   [3] *Analysis of Mind*, p. 98.

existence of something that, by its very nature, can never be observed, we come very close, likewise, to Locke's idea of pure substance in general as that unknowable something which we commonly (but somewhat childishly) suppose to support the appearances which go together to constitute one thing.[1]

13. By selecting certain aspects of a given thing in different private worlds, such that they have a certain mutual similarity (all the visual appearances, for instance, of a penny which are circular in shape), and by arranging them in continuous order according to their differences in some other respect (*e.g.* continuous increase in size, in the case of the penny), we construct a series of perspectives which describes a straight line in physical space somewhere along which the thing may be taken to be. If we repeat this process with another series of aspects of the same thing, we can locate it exactly at the point (or perspective) where the two lines intersect; and those aspects which (in the case of visual sense-data) are largest are said to be nearest to the place where the thing is. We can thus correlate the place where a private world is in physical or perspective space with the places where things are and where their various aspects appear.

14. Two places are consequently associated with every aspect: that *from* which it appears and that *at* which the thing is to which the aspect belongs. These Russell calls respectively the 'passive' and the 'active' places of each appearance. And we can classify aspects in two ways: according as we group those of one thing appearing in different perspectives, or as we group those of different things appearing in one perspective. The former is appropriate to physics and the latter to psychology. Further, adopting the first method of grouping, we may say that the aspects or appearances of a thing spread outwards from the place where the thing is, and as they recede from it they change according to ascertainable laws and in consequence of the presence of other things. Thus the appearance of a thing from a point at some distance away from the place where the thing is will depend in part upon what exists in the intervening medium. In the case of human perception, the intervening medium contains sense-organs, nerves and a brain located in the immediate vicinity of the perspective occupied by

---

[1] Cf. *ibid.* p. 101: '... the different particulars that belong to one physical object are to be collected together by continuity and inherent laws of correlation, not by their supposed causal connection with an unknown assumed existent called a piece of matter, which would be a mere unnecessary, metaphysical thing-in-itself'.

the private world of the percipient. These, persumably, are located by methods similar to those already described, though it could hardly be by the percipient between whom and the thing perceived they constitute part of the intervening medium. In this fashion Russell locates the private world of a percipient inside the percipient's head.

The doctrine of primary and secondary qualities follows naturally from this conception of an intervening medium between the active and the passive places of an appearance and the inclusion in the medium of the human nervous system. Russell sets out the doctrine, in effect, in *The Problems of Philosophy* (chapter iii), where he writes:

'To begin with it is plain that the colour we see depends only upon the nature of the light waves that strike the eye and is therefore modified by the medium intervening between us and the object, as well as by the manner in which light is reflected from the object in the direction of the eye. The intervening air alters colours unless it is perfectly clear, and any strong reflection will alter them completely. Thus the colour we see is a result of the ray as it reaches the eye, and not simply a property of the object from which the ray comes. Hence, also, provided certain rays reach the eye, we shall see a certain colour, whether the object from which the waves start has any colour or not. Thus it is quite gratuitous to suppose that physical objects have colours, and therefore there is no justification for making such a supposition. Exactly similar arguments will apply to other sense-data.'[1]

A correspondence between the spatio-temporal characteristics of physical objects and those of our sense-data, however, can, he thinks, be established.[2]

15. The matter of a thing is now defined as the limit of its appearances as their distance from the thing diminishes,[3] and physical things are defined as those series of appearances whose matter obeys the laws of physics.[4] It does not appear to trouble Russell that the laws of physics cannot be discovered until the things which obey them have been distinguished.

V. CAUSAL THEORY OF PERCEPTION

16. On the basis of this elaborate hypothetical construction, Russell maintains a causal theory of perception. The aspects of a thing, as we saw, radiate from the place where the thing is, and their changes are

---

[1] *Op. cit.* p. 35. [2] Cf. *ibid.* pp. 48 ff.
[3] *Vide Mysticism and Logic*, p. 165.
[4] *Op. cit.* p. 173. Cf. *Our Knowledge of the External World*, pp. 115 f.

determined by laws, which in the last resort are causal laws.[1] Those which are actually perceived are sense-data, and those which are not are *sensibilia*; but both alike, Russell maintains, are physical entities. 'If—*per impossibile*—there were a complete human body with no mind inside it, all those *sensibilia* would exist, in relation to that body, which would be sense-data if there were a mind in the body. What the mind adds to *sensibilia*, in fact, is *merely* awareness: everything else is physical or physiological.'[2] The awareness added by the mind turns the *sensibile* into a sensation of which the sense-datum is the 'external object'.[3] But, in *The Analysis of Mind*, the distinction between sense-datum and sensation is denied. Thus the mind in becoming aware of the sense-datum becomes aware of something which is physical and is physically caused.[4] How the awareness is caused, however, or what the exact connection is between the mind, which 'adds' the awareness, and the *sensibilia* to which it is added, are questions which Russell never sees fit to raise.

17. In fact, nowhere in Russell's philosophy does one find any very clear conception of the nature of the mind; one rather gets the impression that his constant endeavour is to eliminate it from the world altogether. The nearest he comes to a definition of it is to say that 'subjectivity' is an essential element in its definition, though not by itself sufficient.[5] Particulars which are the appearances of different things from a given place, or perspective, form a 'bundle', which, taken through a period of time, is called a 'biography'. Such particulars are (as we have seen) the effects of the things of which they are the appearances; and one characteristic of the biography is thus passivity. Russell calls the place at which the perspective is located the 'passive' place of the appearances, as opposed to the 'active' places where the things are which appear. This passivity is, for him, the same thing as 'subjectivity' and it is, therefore, characteristic, not only of minds, but also of physical things like cameras and dictaphones, in fact, we should imagine, of anything which is subject to effects from causes external to itself. How it helps us, therefore, to define mind is not easy to see; but

[1] Even the perspectival appearances of things are ultimately dependent on the physical properties of space-time and the way in which they determine the behaviour of light waves.

[2] *Mysticism and Logic*, p. 150.

[3] *Ibid.* p. 152.

[4] In *The Analysis of Matter* (ch. xxxvii, pp. 382 ff.) Russell asserts that what is perceived is actually one's own brain, where the percepts are finally located. Cf. also *Our Knowledge of the External World*, p. 129.

[5] *Analysis of Mind*, p. 296.

it does lead us to the notion that reality is entirely made up of particulars of the same kind (or wholly the same) as sensations, which, if collected together in one way, constitute physical things, and if collected together in another, constitute minds. This is the doctrine of Neutral Monism.

18. How does this theory help us to solve the problem from which we set out of providing a means of knowing the relationship between the content of a belief and the facts which make it true or false? The meaning of the proposition which forms the content of the belief was, we found, reducible to sensations, and these now turn out to be physical components of the external world. Though they give us this direct contact with externality, however, the relation of resemblance to the facts seems to have disappeared altogether. For no sensation, which is an appearance of some thing, can be said to resemble the thing, which is the group (or bundle) of its appearances—how does a cornstalk resemble a sheaf, or an onion a string of onions? Yet without this resemblance between the sensation and the thing, the correspondence between a true proposition and the facts must either be given up or radically reinterpreted. The example of the belief in Columbus's voyage across the Atlantic is rather too complicated to afford us much enlightenment, but the example of the memory-belief that the window in a room is to the left of the door is simpler. Here, however, the only resemblance we can presume is that between the images and the sensations actually acquired when we originally perceived the room; but between these and the objective, which is to render the belief true or false, the relation is something quite different.

19. And if we say that the sensation corresponds to the thing, what exactly can we mean by that? Is it that the *sensibilia* in the brain form a sort of picture or model of the external world? But all that we ever become aware of are these *sensibilia* in the brain. How then can we compare them with the supposed original of the picture in order to know that the correspondence exists? Or is the phrase 'correspond to' to be understood as synonymous with 'caused by', so that a sensation corresponds to that by which it is caused? But, if so, we are still in no better position, for the awareness of the sense-datum does not in itself reveal its cause which is not contained in the *sensibile*. The cause, in fact, has simply been assumed as part of the elaborate hypothesis of perspectives on which the theory is founded.

VI. FAILURE OF THE PERSPECTIVE HYPOTHESIS

20. Russell's initial assumption, in fact, does not in the least enable us to understand how it is possible to infer from our own hard data the existence of anything else. Even on the assumption of perspectives, so long as each percipient is confined to his own data, it would be impossible to achieve that correlation and grouping of particulars which is necessary for the construction and location of physical things. No perspective, we are explicitly told, and no appearance is shared by two percipients. There is therefore no means of correlating the appearances which occur in any one perspective with those which occur in any other. The means on which Russell relies for such correlation are the movement (presumably) of the percipient and the acceptance of the testimony of others; but, on his hypothesis, neither of these is admissible. It must be remembered that the existence of things is not initially to be assumed, nor of anything which cannot be observed, but that everything is to be constructed from hard data, including the existence and situation of the percipient's body. What, then, is constituted by the movement of the percipient? It can be no more than a change in the appearances which he perceives, and this cannot be interpreted in terms of movement in space without the assumption of the existence of things and their spatial relations which have yet to be constructed by the correlation of data. Further, in what space is the percipient supposed to move? Clearly it cannot be his own *private* space; and physical space, which is perceived by no one, is the product of the logical construction which depends for its possibility upon the movement of the percipient. The very most to which a percipient could infer from changes in his data is that his perspective has altered, and he has no means whatsoever of determining the spatial relation of the new perspective to the old.

21. Similar difficulties beset the acceptance of the testimony of others. First, the existence of the bodies of other people cannot initially be assumed; they and their positions in space, including their spatial relation to the percipient making the correlations, must all be constructed from that percipient's hard data. Testimony can only be given through the medium of visual and auditory sense-data of the bodies of those testifying; and though we may admit the sense-data, we may not, at this stage, interpret them as belonging to human bodies or other external things, or as evidence of the experience of other minds. The

correlation of data in different perspectives, therefore, depends for its possibility on the knowledge of those objects which is only accessible as a result of that correlation. But, let us waive this objection and assume some quasi-telepathic means of communication between percipients. Even so, how are they to determine which data in one private space correspond with which in another? What could lead me to correlate a bright trapeziform patch on the left side of my visual field with a brown rectangular patch in the centre of yours? (unless, of course, I assume illegitimately that I am seeing the shiny top of a polished table from an angle and that you are looking directly down upon it, so that to you it does not shine). Even if we could so arrange it, as Russell requires, that our data were closely similar, in shape, in colour and in their mutual disposition in the visual field, we get no clue either to our own mutual positions in unperceived space or to our positions relative to the objects perceived in each private space.[1] Nor does it help to define 'nearness' in terms of similarity, for we cannot decide in terms of our own perceived space either the nature or the direction of a movement defined in terms of the divergence of our data.

22. The introduction of other senses than sight serves only to complicate the matter without facilitating that correlation of data which is the *sine qua non* of the construction of an external world. For Russell holds that each sense has a separate space of its own [2] and that the correlation of one with another is in itself a difficult matter. When, for instance, I touch a penny at the same time as I see it, my sensation of touch has no sort of similarity with my visual sensation. It is, moreover, a mistake to imagine that the shape of the object can be directly felt, as it can be directly seen, for our determination of shapes by touch is largely a matter of inference based partly upon our localization of tactual and kinaesthetic sensations in the body (not itself a matter of direct feeling) and partly upon prior experience in which the shape of the object touched is already known by other means. Consequently, there is no direct way of knowing from the actual sensations received that the penny touched is the same thing as the penny seen. If we are to take Russell's theory seriously, we must hold that the two *sensibilia*, as they occur in the brain, are totally separate and distinct, and that sensation itself gives us no means of relating them to each other. Though I may see the penny in my hand at the same time as I experi-

---

[1] Cf. '. . . the space of one man's objects and the space of another man's objects have no place in common'. (*Mysticism and Logic*, p. 138.)

[2] *Our Knowledge of the External World*, p. 86, and *Problems of Philosophy*, p. 48.

ence the tactual sensation, this does not give me the information I require, until the existence and relation to me of that external object which is my hand has been determined by a correlation of sense-data, for which the correlation of touch-space and sight-space is a prior condition. *A fortiori*, therefore, no help can be derived from enlisting the other senses to correlate our data with those of other percipients, and the attempt to conclude to the existence of other minds from comparison of what we see and hear of other bodies with our own direct experience [1] is a venture fraught with the utmost difficulty and hazard, and capable, in the end, of apparent success only by the use of circular reasoning.

23. Let us assume, however, that these difficulties in the way of correlating data have been so far overcome as to enable us to determine which appearances go together to form a particular thing; still, the method which Russell describes of placing it in physical space could not give the desired result. We are required to arrange in ascending order of magnitude a set of appearances, no two of which are ever simultaneously perceived by the same percipient. Possibly, with the help of memory, a series of appearances differing only by constantly increasing magnitude could be experienced. This series, which is purely temporal and no two members of which co-exist, is to be regarded as a line in physical space. If we can now discover another similar series of appearances different in shape from those of the first set but belonging to the same object, these are to constitute another line in physical space. We are now to decide where the two lines intersect, and obviously there is no possible means of doing so. Two intersecting lines have a common point; but the two series of appearances above described have no members in common whatsoever. Nor could we succeed better if we assumed that each separate appearance in either series was perceived by a separate percipient and that these percipients, *per impossibile*, could compare notes; for their comparison would reveal only difference in the size of their experienced appearances but not any positional facts. Such comparison, be it noted, would be *per impossibile*, because the sizes of objects can never be compared without a common standard of measurement, and no such standard is available as between the sense-data perceived by different percipients.

24. The truth is that Russell first assumes the existence and position of things in physical space, including human organisms inhabited by

---

[1] Cf. Russell's arguments in *Analysis of Matter*, ch. xx, and pp. 48-9 above.

minds; he imagines the lines joining percipients with the things, and their intersection at the place where the things exist, and then, in imagination, he arranges his sense-data along these lines. But none of this elaborate construction could be made without the initial assumption and solely from the hard data of one or of any number of percipient minds. Nor has Russell shown that it is possible, from our own hard data, to infer the existence of anything else, unless that existence and its relation to our data are, in the first place, assumed. This method of demonstrating that our knowledge of an external world is derived from our sense-data is, therefore, an immense indulgence in *petitio principii*.

25. It might be urged in Russell's defence that the theory of perspectives is not claimed as something known to be true but is intended only as an hypothesis, against which there is no good evidence, and which renders the occurrence of our sense-data intelligible and our inference from them to the existence of an external world plausible. But this last is exactly what it fails to do. For, if our sense-data were produced in the manner which Russell supposes, they would give us no information about their sources, no means of communication with the experience of other percipients and no access to the *sensibilia* in perspectives other than those which formed our own private world (if, indeed, 'world' were a word that could appropriately be applied). Consequently, no sort of inference from hard data to the existence of anything other than those data would be at all possible, let alone plausible, on the suggested hypothesis.

But our experience *is* the experience of a common world—a world of things other than our own sensations, including other persons with whom we are able to communicate and who profess to experience the world much as we ourselves do. If after philosophical reflection we adopt a theory that this experience is not what it seems, that it is purely 'private' and that the existence of a world such as it presents to us has still to be proved (however readily we tend to assume it), such a theory must still explain the appearance. This is precisely what Russell cannot do. He fails to explain not only how a 'private' world is taken to be public, but also how from hard data alone even a private experience of a world could be constructed. The evidence against his hypothesis, therefore, is the manifest character of our experience itself, and if that is not to be regarded as sufficient it is difficult to understand what evidence could ever be admitted as relevant. In short, the hypothesis so little renders intelligible our experience of a world in which we are ourselves finite members that its results could lead only to its rejection.

26. If human minds were what they are assumed to be according to the theory of perspectives, the conception of the world which it envisages would be possible only for some god-like intelligence which had access to the views contained in all private worlds and to the *sensibilia* present in every perspective. These it would be able to compare and to correlate, as no finite percipient could do, and to relate them in one spatio-temporal system. If the theory were true, then, Russell, in propounding it, would by implication be claiming to experience a supernatural revelation of the nature of reality like that which he himself has maintained is characteristic of mysticism.[1]

VII. ASSESSMENT OF RUSSELL'S THEORY

27. The failure of the perspective theory brings with it the most devastating consequences for Russell's whole system. For this hypothesis was intended to bridge the gap between physical reality, conceived as existing devoid of mind and independent of being known, and knowledge, conceived as a mental content to which the facts externally correspond. But no bridge has been built, and knowledge if it can exist at all remains a mystery while the physical world continues in the splendid isolation of its independence of mind. Yet it is itself the zeal for a reality uncontaminated with mind which forces us into the impasse. So long as we insist that things are what they are independent of our knowing and that knowledge makes no difference to the known, so long shall we be forced to assert that knowledge is the result of an external relation between the mind and the world, a relation of which *ex hypothesi* we can never know more than one of the terms (knowledge of necessity being confined to the mind). Consequently, we shall be forced in the end to admit that between our knowing and the world of things there is a great gulf fixed and we shall be deprived of all pretext for asserting the relation in which knowledge is supposed to consist.

Only the passion for this doctrine could lead empiricists like Russell to espouse, with so little compunction, the absurdities arising from the postulation of entities which are objects of thought for no mind, and the subsequent description of the manner of their existence and interrelation. In this way we are asked to conceive 'perspectives' which are not experienced by any mind (regardless of the etymology of the word),

---

[1] *Mysticism and Logic*, ch. i.

and then to determine how they may be related mutually and to those actually perceived—a task which we can accomplish only if we (in imagination) place ourselves in the assumed perspectives as well as at some ideal point from which their mutual relations in 'perspective space' become evident. Similarly we have the absurdity of unsensed *sensibilia*, which are stated to be physical entities and are also said to resemble (presumably in quality) data which are sensed, while we are told that apart from our sensing we have no reason to assume that the qualities (*e.g.* colour) we experience exist in the physical world. And finally we are asked to believe that the *sensibilia* which we do sense are located in our own brains so that, in seeing trees and hills and earth and heaven, what I am actually perceiving is (apparently in some illusory form) simply my own grey matter, while the objects and events of which these percepts somehow inform me are things altogether separate from and independent of my perceiving.

28. But if this zeal for a physical reality independent of the mind is given up, we can find in a theory such as Russell's a great deal of illumination. He describes to us a physical world every detail of which is constituted by its relation to a percipient either actual or imaginary and the entire constitution of which is made to depend on the correlation of sense-data as perceived by minds and on the systematization of perspectives in a manner possible only for an intelligent consciousness. It is only the manner in which the world is perceived which makes it an intelligible interrelated system, and one, moreover, not only of entities each and all of which are constituents of minds, but also of individual things most intimately interrelated; so that it would be true to say that each of them was constituted by its relations to all the rest, that every part was a microcosm of the whole and that to know any part completely would be to know the whole—or alternatively, that unless and until one did know the whole one could not know any part completely. The doctrine is closely akin to that maintained by Whitehead which we shall be studying in a later chapter and it is one exceedingly like that advocated by the Hegelians and Absolute Idealists, on whom Russell loses no opportunity to pour scorn.

Accordingly, though his theory, taken in one way, leaves the physical world for ever inaccessible to our minds and confines each mind to the appearances of its own private world, yet, taken in another way, its effect is to introduce mind into every particle of the physical world. But Russell would undoubtedly repudiate the latter interpretation, for it would involve the abandonment of the empirical point of view. Yet it is just that interpretation according to which most value could be derived from Russell's thought; and it is just that empirical attitude which brings about its failure and puts a philosophy that is reputed to be (and in some respects genuinely is) so characteristically modern some three centuries behind the times.

VIII. COMPARISON WITH LOCKE

29. For the failure of the theory is once again the result of the contradiction involved in the 17th-century presuppositions, which I pointed out in connection with the philosophy of Locke. If mind and physical nature are to be held apart, knowledge of the latter by the former becomes impossible; for neither can it be generated in the mind alone, nor can it be imparted causally by transmission of effects from the outer world through the animal organism to the mind assumed to be embodied in it. So the similarity, in its main tenets, of Russell's philosophy to the position set forth by Locke is borne out by the similarity of its results. Briefly we may outline the parallelism as follows:

(i) Locke begins from simple ideas of sensation and reflection, and so does Russell. For Locke the first of these are caused by the transmission of insensible particles from bodies through the nerves and animal spirits to the brain. Russell holds that the bodies are themselves groups of particulars similar in character to sensations (but lacking the element of awareness), but what such unsensed *sensibilia* really are remains obscure in the extreme. Strictly we cannot regard them as waves in the ether or streams of electrons or any other such physical entity; for these, Russell would maintain, are constructions from sense-data actually sensed and *sensibilia* merely postulated 'on principles of continuity'.[1] But if he had adhered consistently to this position, Russell should have abjured the causal theory of perception upon which he unfailingly insists, and should have abandoned the doctrine of physical things uncontaminated by mind. As it is, he leaves us with a causal account of sensation entirely similar to that of Locke, a notion of waves propagated from physical sources, entering the body by way of the sense-organs, transmitting impulses through the nervous system to the brain (Russell, of course, has no need of the 'animal spirits') and producing there *sensibilia*—entities to which the mind but adds awareness to convert them into sensations.[2]

[1] Cf. *Our Knowledge of the External World*, p. 117.
[2] Cf. *Problems of Philosophy*, p. 55, cited above; *Mysticism and Logic*, p. 150; *Analysis of Matter*, p. 216; and *Our Knowledge of the External World*, p. 129.

(ii) To simple ideas of sensation and reflection Locke traces back 'our whole stock of ideas', and Russell from our 'hard data' professes to derive all our knowledge of the external world.

(iii) The theory of primary and secondary qualities is common to both thinkers, and (iv) Locke's complex ideas of substances find a counterpart in Russell's logical constructions of physical things.

(v) Similarly, to Locke's doctrine of our confused idea of substance in general, as an unknown something supporting qualities which go constantly together, corresponds Russell's rejection of an 'unknown assumed existent' which is the cause of our data and the nucleus of the group of *sensibilia* which is the physical thing—the inconsistency with a causal theory of perception is the same in both cases.

(vi) The theory of knowledge as the correspondence between our ideas and the facts is common to both, along with similarity of doctrines about language and the nature of propositions; and in the end the doctrines of both come to grief in the attempt to find a satisfactory criterion for the discrimination of truth from error.

30. (vii) Both philosophers, consequently, are landed in a position where they are logically committed to a subjectivism which they abhor and which leads their successors to develop a subjectivist theory. Berkeley does this with almost complete consistency but the thinkers who belong to the second phase of modern empiricism hark back to the all too attractive realism which demands a self-existent reality. They do so, however, only by means of a *volte-face* which on their principles they are hard put to excuse. The Berkeleyan tendency in Russell's teaching is apparent in his theory of physical objects as classes of sense-data. For once the contradictory notions of independently existing unsensed *sensibilia* and our ability to know them are given up, Russell's 'logical constructions' become wholly ideal, as is clear from his account of physical entities given in Lecture IV of *Our Knowledge of the External World*:

'. . . Let us recall the hypothetical Leibnizian universe of Lecture III. In that universe, we had a number of perspectives, two of which never had any entity in common but often contained entities which could be sufficiently correlated as belonging to the same thing. We will call one of these an "actual" private world when there is an actual spectator to which it appears, and "ideal" when it is merely constructed on principles of continuity. A physical thing consists, at each instant, of the whole set of its aspects at that instant in all the different worlds; thus a momentary state of the thing is a whole set of aspects. An "ideal" appearance will be an aspect merely calculated, but not actually perceived by any spectator. An "ideal" state of a thing will be a state at a moment when all its appearances are ideal. An ideal thing will be one whose states at all times are ideal. Ideal appearances, states, and things, since they are calculated, must be functions of actual appearances, states, and things; in fact, ultimately they must be functions of actual appearances. Thus it is unnecessary, for the enunciation of the laws of physics, to assign any reality to ideal elements: it is enough to accept them as logical constructions, provided we have means of knowing how to determine when they become actual. This, in fact, we have with some degree of approximation; the starry heaven, for instance, becomes actual whenever we choose to look at it.'[1]

[1] *Op. cit.* p. 117.

Chapter XV

MODERN EMPIRICISM: THE SECOND PHASE
(SENSE-DATA THEORIES)

I. MOORE, BROAD AND PRICE

1. THE philosophy of Berkeley in the 18th century marked a development distinct from that of Locke, and while it accepted the main features of Locke's teaching, it presented also a definite criticism of his realistic prejudices. The second phase in modern empiricism is less clearly marked. Much more is accepted from Russell than Berkeley accepted from Locke and the criticism of the Russellian position is not usually made explicit. In fact, at the cost of some inconsistency, similar conclusions to those of Russell are striven after, and it is rather the method of reaching them that is modified than the conclusions themselves. Russell, like Locke, assumes external physical things in causal relations to minds and then tries (unsuccessfully) to show how knowledge of the physical world can be educed from sensations. His efforts to justify his initial hypothesis from the evidence of experienced sense-data are never particularly convincing. But the philosophers of the second phase are much more careful to avoid question-begging assumptions (though they also fail in the end), and make the most determined efforts to construct a physical world from sense-data with the help of an absolute minimum of non-sensuous auxiliaries. Consequently, their theories have a kinship with Berkeley's though they are not in all respects similar. They purport, like his, to construct a physical world entirely subjectively and from wholly subjective materials. But in Kant's theory, also, we find this sort of construction, which, as contrasted with the independent reality of things-in-themselves, is always purely subjective. For this reason Hegel classed Kant as an empiricist, and, so far as this classification is just, one might well say that the theories of the second phase of modern empiricism are Kantian, particularly as they are prepared to admit in perceptual knowledge certain *a priori* categories without which the experience of objects could not be derived from sensuous material. But whereas Kant's philosophy contained the seeds of a development in which the Renaissance presuppositions were entirely superseded, contemporary empiricists, including those I am next to discuss, persist in the attempt to return to the assumption of a self-existent material world uncontaminated by mind.

2. The presupposition of empiricism being the separate and independent existence of the physical world, the acquisition of knowledge by the mind must, as I have said, be somehow accounted for by its reception of sensible data from the outer world. The nature of perception, therefore, becomes of central importance to the empiricist. It is, as it were, the gateway of the mind, the portal through which knowledge comes in, and the manner of its entrance and the tractability of the materials which are admitted are matters upon which the whole character of our knowledge and the veracity of its representation of the external world must, for the empiricist, depend. It is therefore natural that the attention of those who belong to the second phase of modern empiricism should be largely devoted to the subject of perception, and particularly to what they hold to be the perceptual basis of scientific theory. Consequently, they begin by defining what they consider to be the primitive elements in our knowledge. As empiricists generally do, they take these to be the data provided by sense and they set themselves to describe the manner in which, from the data received in this way, we arrive at our notions of material things and our judgements that we are at particular times perceiving them. For this reason I shall call the theory of the second phase the theory of sense-data, and though that name might also appropriately have been used to describe much that is to be found in Russell, he had far greater propensities to break through the veil of sense and describe in quasi-scientific manner the mystic revelation of what lies beyond.

The chief representatives of this second phase of modern empiricism are Professors G. E. Moore, C. D. Broad and H. H. Price. I shall, in the main, confine my attention to the last named, as he gives the clearest, most complete and most self-consistent statement of the doctrine. Broad is perhaps the nearest to Russell and his thought has the same kind of scientific background, but he emphasizes rather less the doctrine (which he nevertheless holds [1]) that judgements as 'psychological attitudes' are about propositions which correspond to (or accord with) existent facts, and he has spent much time and trouble on elaborating a theory of perception purporting to show that our knowledge of the world of material objects can be built up out of sense-data (or 'sensa' as he calls them). Moore's statement of a similar theory (in which he calls sense-data 'sensibles') is brief and somewhat fragmentary; but Price has put the whole doctrine together in a continuous and very carefully developed exposition, arguing persuasively both in favour of what he

---

[1] *Vide The Mind and its Place in Nature*, p. 292, and *Scientific Thought* (London, 1923), pp. 70-1.

considers sound and against what he thinks must be rejected in alternative theories of perception.

3. Certain characteristics common to the theories of all three of these thinkers are continuous with elements in Russell's thought. First, they take over from Russell the notion of sense-data as the primitive elements in perceptual knowledge, though they do not, with him, deny the existence of an act of mind into relation with which the datum enters in sensation. Moore explicitly analyses sensation into 'object' and 'consciousness' and speaks of an 'act of direct apprehension',[1] and a similar view is implied in the treatment of the subject by the other two.

Secondly, with Russell also, they hold the view that the data of sense may exist without being sensed. But whereas Russell assumes outright that unsensed *sensibilia* exist and builds his theory on that assumption (though he asserts that the assumption cannot be proved certainly to be true), these thinkers simply allow that the assumption may be true, but do not rely on it for the construction of their theories.

Thirdly, just as Russell 'constructs' material things out of sense-data, so do these three thinkers. But Russell asserts that sense-data are physical entities, and these thinkers are not prepared to go so far. Price and Moore hold that sense-data are not phases in any substance at all, that they do not occupy physical space,[2] but that physical entities cannot in the end be defined without reference to sensibles,[3] and Broad, though on the whole non-committal, is at least not prepared to deny that sensa may be qualitatively mind-dependent and admits that the arguments in favour of their being 'mental' are by no means lacking in plausibility.[4]

4. So much similarity the second phase of modern empiricism has with the first, but with respect to two of its most characteristic features it differs from the sort of doctrine propounded by Russell. The first is the attitude adopted to the causal theory of perception. Broad very strongly inclines towards it and in consequence is prepared to accept a version of the doctrine of primary and secondary qualities. But, though much of his exposition seems to assume a causal theory, he never finally commits himself to it in any way which is either definite or

[1] *Philosophical Studies*, p. 175. Cf. Broad, *Scientific Thought*, p. 264.
[2] Price, *Perception* (London, 1932), pp. 130 and 136; Moore, *Philosophical Studies*, p. 195.
[3] Price, *op. cit.* p. 137; Moore, *op. cit.* pp. 188 ff.
[4] *Scientific Thought*, p. 266.

intelligible.[1] Price, whom I take to be the thinker most representative of the second phase, rejects the causal theory in any form comparable to that admitted by Russell or Locke though he does hanker after a modification of it which is hardly consistent with his main teaching.[2]

The second, and the most characteristic of all features of this phase of empiricism, is agnosticism with regard to the existence of the external world. Russell, it is true, sometimes speaks as if the existence of the physical world were something we could at best presume, but, in the main, he contends for our knowledge of it as a reality. Thinkers of the second phase leave it as wholly conjectural (or, as Kant might have called it, problematical). Moore states that, on the view which he holds to be the only true interpretation of perceptual judgements, assertions that physical things exist will be true only in an 'outrageously Pickwickian sense', and that the belief in their existence in any non-Pickwickian sense (however strong our inclination to it) may be mere prejudice.[3] The view is almost exactly summed up in the following passage from Broad's *Scientific Thought*:

'There are groupings among my own sensa and correlations between my sensa and those of others which fit in extremely well with the belief in a physical world of which all the sensa are so many appearances. It might be held that this at least forms the basis of a logical argument in inverse probability, to show that the belief in the physical world is highly probable. But the snag here is that all such arguments only serve to multiply the antecedent probability of a proposition, and, unless we have reason to suppose that this probability starts with a finite magnitude, they lead us nowhere. Now, although I do not know of any reason antecedently against the existence of a physical world, I also know of no antecedent reason for it. So its antecedent probability seems quite indeterminate, unless we are prepared to hold that the fact that everybody does in practice believe it, is a ground for ascribing a finite antecedent probability to it. It seems to me that the belief that there is a physical world is logically in much the same position as those assumptions about the constitution of the existent on which all inductive proofs of special laws of nature rest. If these assumptions start with a finite antecedent probability, their success justifies us in ascribing a high final probability to them. But do they have a finite antecedent probability? We can say of them, as of the belief in a physical world, that we all do believe them in practice, that there is no positive reason against them, and that we cannot get on without assuming

---

[1] His conclusion to the discussion of the matter in ch. xiii of *Scientific Thought* amounts to little more than that, though sense-data may have physical causes, the manner of their causation is well-nigh unintelligible.
[2] Cf. *Perception*, chs. iv and x.   [3] *Op. cit.* pp. 190-1.

them. But, having said so much, we shall do wisely to change the subject and talk about the weather.'[1]

What Price says upon the subject amounts to much the same thing. He holds that we may reach a degree of assurance of the existence of a material thing that is as near to certainty as is ever possible in the knowledge of matters of fact, where absolute certainty cannot be expected.[2] But we do so by the accretion of corroborative perceptual evidence, and this, if taken along with what he says about coherent systems of propositions, should bring us to the same conclusion as Broad has stated in the passage quoted. For Price says that mutual corroboration, by a set of propositions one of another, only strengthens their probability if at least one of the propositions can be shown by independent evidence to be true,[3] and in the case of perception such independent evidence is obviously unobtainable.

Having listed these general characteristics of the second phase of contemporary empiricism, I shall proceed to summarize the theory of sense-perception which is typical of it, for it is on perception that our knowledge of the material world is held ultimately to depend, and once we understand its nature and the manner in which it gives rise to our belief in the existence of material things, we shall be well on the way to the solution of our main problem. How far, then, do empiricists of the second phase help us?

I shall base my summary of their view on Price's very thorough and careful exposition of it in what is, to date, his most considerable work.

II. PERCEPTION

5. In describing the structure of our perceptual knowledge we are to begin from that in perception the existence of which is insusceptible of doubt. This is what is 'given', but data may be of more than one sort and we must distinguish between the intuitive apprehension of particular existents and the intuitive apprehension of 'facts'. This distinction originates from Russell, who defined facts as existents having certain qualities and as standing in certain relations. They are complexes of existents and qualities, or existents in relation, and the apprehension of such a complex is, in most cases (though not all, for we may be acquainted with the shade, shape and size of a colour-patch), knowledge by description; but the direct intuitive apprehension of a particular existent is knowledge by acquaintance. As Price puts it:

---

[1] *Op. cit.* pp. 268-9.   [2] *Perception*, p. 203.   [3] *Ibid.* pp. 182-3.

'The first is apprehension *that*, the second is apprehension *of*'. Now that with which we are directly acquainted in any perception is the present occurrence in it of the sensuous element: in visual perception, the colour-patches of definite shapes and sizes; in auditory perception, noises; in tactual perception, 'premencies', and so forth. These sensuous elements are the data of sense and by their means all our beliefs about the material world are acquired. Empirical science cannot discredit the deliverances of the senses, for upon them all empirical science ultimately rests.

The naïve realism of common sense, which takes the sense-datum to be literally part of the surface of a material thing actually present to the senses, is rejected on the strength of the argument from illusion (despite objections to the usual manner of stating it and shortcomings which it is held to display even when clearly stated). The causal theory, according to which the sense-datum is held to be the effect of a material thing and so to indicate the presence of its cause, is rejected likewise; but, curiously enough, the reason given is not the obvious one that the theory asserts a connection between two terms one of which is unknown and unknowable, whereas causal connections can be established only between terms both of which fall within experience. It is that we all believe in the existence of material things to which we take our sense-data to belong and never go about trying to prove it by doubtful causal arguments. True though this may be, it is surely the doubtfulness of the argument which is relevant to the refutation of the theory and not what we happen, without argument, to believe. If we all happened to believe 'instinctively' in solipsism, that surely would not be a cogent argument against a causal theory of perception. But it is also satisfactorily demonstrated that the arguments by which the causal theory is supported *are* unsound, inasmuch as they presuppose the existence of things (as causes for sense-data) the proof of which is supposed to depend on the causal inference from sense-data. This, in effect, is the objection I have myself brought against Russell's version of the theory in the last chapter.

6. Our natural propensity to take it for granted that there is a material thing present to us to which a sense-datum that we now experience belongs is made the foundation stone of the theory of perception to be developed. The primary element in perception is called 'perceptual acceptance' and is just this taking for granted of the presence of a perceived material thing on the strength of the *prima facie* evidence provided by the sense-datum. The acceptance includes not

only the bare existence of the material thing but also the presumption that it has a surface confronting us of a certain kind, the nature of which depends in the main on that of the present sense-datum. We take for granted, likewise, that it has a back and side surfaces and an inside, all of which (so far as they are not included in the present data) are specifiable as a result of further perceptual acts. What is taken for granted, then, is the truth of a set of propositions evidence for which is as yet lacking.

Such perceptual acceptance is quite unquestioning and non-inferential. Intellectual acts and acquired dispositions may condition it, but they are not conscious elements in it inasmuch as we do not make the inferences or even, properly speaking, remember them in the act of perceiving. That is pseudo-intuitive, as if we intuited the actual presence of the material thing, whereas all we really do intuit is the sense-datum—the rest is simply accepted or taken for granted without evidence. In fact, in the act of perceiving, we do not even distinguish the datum from the material thing the existence of which is presumed on the strength of it. Such acceptance is an innate disposition of the mind, but of course it does not constitute knowledge and provides no proof of what is taken for granted. But it does require that the notion of material-thinghood should be *a priori* in experience—something contributed by the mind to experience *ab initio* and not derived by generalization from the observation of sense-data. This is asserted quite definitely both by Broad and by Price.[1]

7. Despite this 'primitive credulity', however, we do distinguish between correct and illusory perception and we do acquire convictions that in most cases what we perceive are actual existents in the material world, though in some cases we are mistaken. On what are such judgements based and how are they justified? It is by progressive confirmation (or failure of confirmation) in successive perceptual acts of what is initially accepted, by making more definite what in the original perception was indefinite and by progressive specification of what was hitherto unspecified. In successive perceptual acts more sense-data are obtained which overlap or are partly identical with those previously sensed and which can thus be fitted together in a definite way so as to specify those parts of the material thing which were not included in the original sense-datum and the existence and specifiability of which were initially taken for granted. Further, that we may be sure it is the same thing to which, in each case, the further specifications belong, the

[1] Broad, *Mind and its Place in Nature*, p. 217; Price, *Perception*, pp. 102 and 168-9.

successive sense-data must specify different surfaces which fit together to form a single three-dimensional solid.

Each successive perceptual act might have been, like the first, a mere acceptance, but in its special relations to the first and to the whole set which specify the material thing perceived, as well as to the total act of mind involved in the process, each is a further stage in a progressive confirmation of what was originally taken for granted. But the specification can never be completed and the confirmation can never be absolute. It can lead up to the perceptual confidence which is characteristic of our daily lives and further, if we persist with the process, to adequate assurance. But it can never give us knowledge, in the strict sense of the word; that is, absolutely certain knowledge.

8. What is immediately remarkable about this description of the process of confirming the original acceptance is its similarity to the theory maintained by Joachim, Bosanquet and Bradley of the systematic, or coherent, character of our experience. Price, however, points out that a coherent system of propositions such as emerges from the process of perceptual confirmation can enhance the probability of what was initially taken for granted only if there is independent evidence for the truth of at least one of them, and in this instance they all seem to be on the same level of probability and, outside the system, we seem to have no evidence for any of them. How then is the conviction (which we do undoubtedly reach) of the existence of the material thing perceived ever justifiable? Price is hard put to answer this question. He says that the existence of a particular visual or tactual sense-datum is *prima facie* evidence for that of the material thing to which the sense-datum belongs, and this he calls the Principle of Confirmability (meaning that unless this is so no confirmation of our original acceptance would ever be possible [1]). It is, he says, an *a priori* principle and is not based on observation, for it is itself necessary in order that observation should be possible. Moreover, it is not right, he maintains, to assert that each successive act of perception of the confirmation series *is* on the same level with every other, for after the first none is, in fact, *mere* acceptance (though any might have been had it been isolated) because each fulfils, to a further extent than the last, the requirements of the Principle of Confirmability.[2]

If I have understood him aright, then, Price himself does in the end adopt a coherence theory, at least of perceptual assurance, for the only evidence for the fact of which we are assured is contained in the system

[1] *Op. cit.* p. 185.   [2] *Ibid.* p. 188.

of confirmatory perceptions, and our only reason for taking any one of them as contributory evidence at all is the *a priori* principle of confirmability, *i.e.* that, if it is confirmed by other acts of perception, it may rank as evidence (which might just as well have been called the principle of coherence). Price insists that we cannot go beyond perception for our assurance of the existence of material things. Perceptual assurance is an ultimate form of consciousness (he says), autonomous and self-correcting, which can neither be overthrown nor justified by any other form of consciousness.[1]

9. The specification of the material thing is next given in terms of the interrelation of sense-data. The successive perceptual acts, which confirm the first acceptance of the existence and general character of the material thing perceived, build up a systematically interrelated set of sense-data which Price calls a 'family'. Among these, certain visual and tactual data are said to be spatially constructible; that is, they can be fitted together to form a three-dimensional solid, which constitutes the 'nucleus' of the family. On this nuclear solid there converge series of sense-data, each of which consists of progressively less constructible and less differentiated data. The most constructible and differentiated datum in such a series is called the 'standard' datum, and it is the standard data of all the converging series that form the nuclear solid. It may, therefore, as well be called the 'standard solid' of the family, while the series as they diverge from the nucleus consist (in the case of vision) of such data as perspectival and other distortions, and are therefore called distortion series. The more specific detail a datum contains, the 'better' it is held to be, but an exception to all this is made in the case of microscopical visual data, which contain a high degree of specific detail but are not constructible. These form a distortion series of a special kind and converge on a standard datum which is constructible though less differentiated.

The process leading to perceptual assurance is, accordingly, one which tends to discover whether the sense-data concerned belong to a family of this kind, and, if they do, what the nature of the nuclear solid might be. Hallucinatory data are those which we take to belong to a family, the membership of which, however, the confirmatory process fails to establish. An illusory datum is one which does belong to a family, but which we take at first to have a status other than that which it actually has. In most cases it belongs to a distortion series and is taken to be one of the standard data. A mirror-image is curiously

[1] *Op. cit.* pp. 192 f.

intermediate between illusory and non-illusory data, for mirror-images form among themselves unfinished or incomplete series with no nuclear solid. They are said to simulate a family without being one.

10. The sizes and positions of things can now be determined, but these spatial relations apply only to nuclear solids and not to whole families. Size can be determined only relatively and is assessed by comparing the nuclear data under the same conditions and at the same visual depth. Position is determined by comparing different sense-fields which, for this purpose, must partially overlap and must be continuous with one another in time and in quality. Then, by observation of pairs of sense-data occurring in succession such that (i) in each the two members sensibly adjoin each other, (ii) in each the two members face in sensibly different directions, (iii) two pairs have a member in common and (iv) in each pair one member is sensibly to the right of (or above) the other, we may proceed by 'the method of progressive adjunction' to determine the relative positions not only of nuclear data but also of standard solids.

These positions are in physical space—'the space of standard solids' —but the sense-data which constitute the solids cannot be said to be in physical space (and even less so can those belonging to distortion series), because sense-data are not solids but are at most 'extents', or 'expanses', which do not occupy space, though they do sometimes coincide with the surface of a material thing. Position in space is thus a collective characteristic and, extraordinarily enough, the collections which have it are collections of elements themselves having no position.

The point of view of the percipient is defined (i) with reference to a single sense-field, as approximately that point where a visual sense-datum in the centre of the field of vision is at minimal visual depth; and (ii) with reference to standard solids in standard space, by taking as this determining sense-datum one which is nuclear to a standard solid and fixing the position of the solid to which it belongs. Changing one's view-point is, then, to experience a series of sense-fields in each of which the central sense-datum of minimal depth is a constituent of a standard solid with a different position in standard space from that to which the corresponding sense-datum in the previous sense-field belonged.

It is to be observed at once, and it is admitted by Price,[1] that a family of sense-data can only be discovered by a process of synthesis involving successive changes of view-point on the part of the percipient. The view-point must thus be changed before it is possible to determine

[1] *Ibid.* p. 266.

the constituents and positions of standard solids and therefore prior to the determination of the percipient's own point of view. This requirement, however, is not held to upset the theory, because, presumably, it is assumed that constructible data can be obtained and fitted together without the necessity of knowing from what point of view they are obtained. But we shall see later that this cannot be maintained, for unless the view-point is determinate, the spatial relations of the sense-data cannot be known. Consequently, this difficulty about determining the view-point of the percipient infects the obtainability of data and in the end it is the rock on which the theory is wrecked.

11. The synthetic process by which families of sense-data become known is called by Price 'syngnosis'.[1] It is the knowing of a family as a whole, though its parts can be experienced only in succession. The unsensed data of a family are said to be alternatively 'obtainable' at any one time, so that there is a sense in which they are all simultaneously possible; and as there can be a succession of sets of 'equipossible' data constituting one family, the family may be said to endure or 'to prolong itself' in time.

III. REALISTIC HANKERINGS

12. A material thing is not held to be simply identical with a family of sense-data nor even with its nuclear solid, although many characteristics commonly attributed to material things belong to families of data. One such characteristic, however, does not: namely, causal efficacy. In order to possess this a material thing must 'physically occupy' the space contained by the nuclear solid. Such physical occupancy, with the consequent manifestation of causal characteristics, can be directly observed in the way in which one family affects the manner of prolongation of others, and the causal characteristics may be manifested though none of the data belonging to any of the families concerned are actually sensed during the process (e.g. when butter placed near a fire melts in the absence of observers). Accordingly, Price concludes, the family is not the subject of causal characteristics, 'for how can actual and manifest characteristics be said to characterize something at a time when the alleged *characterizandum* is but a system of potentialities?'[2] The physical occupant must, therefore, be something other than the data sensed and must have intrinsic qualities by virtue of which the causal relations observed are manifested. But these qualities cannot themselves be observed and what they are we have no

[1] *Op. cit.* p. 287.   [2] *Ibid.* p. 291.

means of knowing.[1] The physical occupant and the family together constitute the complete thing and, strictly speaking, it is only between complete things that causal relations hold.

It should follow that the causal properties can only be inferred; for we observe only the way in which families prolong themselves in time, and from uniform concomitances in their changes we conclude to their causal relations one with another. But Price holds that the possession by a material thing of causal characteristics is part of what we originally accept in perception[2] and that it becomes confirmed in the course of the further specification process by observation of the way in which other families alter their manner of self-prolongation in the vicinity of the thing in question.[3] It would seem, then, that the notion of causation as manifested in concomitant variation is 'categorial' or *a priori* along with that of material-thinghood.

13. Price goes on from this doctrine of physical occupancy to maintain that the physical occupant is believed to be, and in one sense at least almost certainly is, the 'vertical' cause of the sense-data of the family whose nuclear solid it occupies. But this is not causation proper, for that holds only between 'complete things', and sense-data are not constituents of the world of complete things, while physical occupants alone are not complete entities. Sense-data are events, but they happen nowhere and to nothing. They are therefore not events in the natural world but events 'of a different order'.[4] Though the physical occupant is thus the 'source' or remote cause of the confamiliar sense-data, this is not an instance of natural causation. The knowledge of this vertical causation is not regarded as necessary to perceptual assurance and is acquired in the first instance by observations of the behaviour of organisms other than one's own and its correlation with other material things. The evidence thus acquired is augmented by comparison of the deliverances of the different senses in one's own experience, and, finally, by a sort of argument from analogy with observed cases of horizontal causation, we arrive at the conclusion that our sense-data have vertical causes in the material things to which they belong.

14. Apart from the doctrines of physical occupancy and of vertical causation of sense-data, Price admits that the theory he is presenting is similar to that of Phenomenalism, for which, in all his references to

---

[1] *Ibid.* p. 294. [2] *Ibid.* pp. 286, 293 and 310.
[3] *Ibid.* p. 310. [4] *Ibid.* p. 319.

and discussions of it, he shows great respect. He rejects it in the end only because he holds that causal properties, which are manifested even when no sense-data are actualized, cannot belong to mere families of equipossible sense-data, which need not be actualized at all and never are all actualized at once (unless, of course, we postulate, as Price does not, the existence of an omnisentient God). If the sense-data of families could all be actualized at once, presumably this difficulty would disappear and we could dispense with physical occupants and vertical causation. The difference between Berkeley's position and Price's, in the main essentials, therefore, lies only in the part played by God in Berkeley's system; and the substitution for this of physical occupants and vertical causation is (I shall argue) a reversion to Locke and an inconsistency in the theory. Of course, there is much more in Price's account of perception than is to be found in Berkeley and much of it is an elaboration of elements imported from Kant. But if we are to adhere strictly to our starting-point from indubitable sense-data and to construct the world out of them with the help only of principles or categories taken to be *a priori* and innate in the mind, we can never arrive at all at physical occupancy and will find ourselves in some difficulty also about the publicity of the material world.

15. The argument for the existence of physical occupants in material things springs from the contention that what is a system of largely (and sometimes wholly) potential entities cannot exercise causal properties. For they are manifested at many times and places where no sense-data are actualized. But what are these causal properties and how are they *manifested*? They are nothing more nor less than uniform concomitances of change in the temporal prolongation of families. Whenever the nuclear solid of a family which belongs to a red-hot coal is brought near to that of a lump of butter or a piece of paper, certain changes regularly take place in the manner of self-prolongation of the butter-family and the paper-family. Though these changes may occur even in the absence of observers when none of the sense-data belonging to the families concerned are actualized, no different principle is involved in that than in the fact of confamiliarity itself. Sense-data are held to be confamiliar, not because they are simultaneously actualized, but because relations between them, which can themselves be sensed (*e.g.* spatial continuity and constructibility), enable us to systematize (or 'syngnose') them according to the category of material-thinghood. These systematic relations are both spatial and temporal. The syngnosis of the family includes both, and the way in which it prolongs

itself in time is part of the way in which it is constructed. But its self-prolongation is already the manifestation of immanent causation, and transeunt causation is no more than the relation between the immanent causal properties of different families established by observation of concomitant changes in their mode of self-prolongation. All the relations between sense-data which make the necessary syntheses possible must, directly or indirectly, be sense-given. If they are not, no causal properties can ever be *manifested*. Such as are assumed to be exercised unobserved are assumed on the same principle as non-actualized sense-data in a family are assumed to be 'obtainable'. In fact, what we mean by saying (*e.g.*) that the butter melted in our absence is that certain sense-data would have been actualized had we been present. We may conclude, therefore, that there is as little need to postulate a physical occupant to support causal characteristics as to support the syngnosis of confamiliar sense-data. All we need is the *a priori* category of causation to assist us in our synthesis.

Had Price argued in this way he would have likened the physical occupant rather to the Kantian category of substance (the permanent underlying causal change) than (as he does) to the *Ding-an-sich*;[1] and the fact that for him its intrinsic properties are unknowable indicates his return at this point to the Lockian position. For Locke too maintained that the intrinsic properties of substances are unknowable. And if physical occupancy is required to support causal characteristics, it should equally be necessary to support confamiliarity, so that we should have to postulate with Locke an unknowable somewhat to support the qualities that go constantly together in a material thing. Price's doctrine of confamiliarity, however, is not Lockian; it is Berkeleyan (with a dash of Kant), and his doctrine of physical occupancy is inconsistent with his main position.

For the same reason the notion of the vertical causation of sense-data is a retrograde step. Clearly, if physical occupants are to be abandoned, so must vertical causation, and the description of the way in which we come to know of it reveals itself as inadequate.[2] The observation of concomitance between the occurrence of a datum (say a green light) and certain behaviour on the part of others is no more evidence for the causation of their sense-data than it is for my own. For what I assume to be cause and effect in either case are not the sense-data *I sense* but the families to which I take them to belong. Once the distinction between particular data and families is recognized, and as soon as the spatial relation of the latter to one's own body is determined (taking one's own

---

[1] *Vide Perception*, p. 296.   [2] *Vide ibid.* pp. 311-13.

body as another family of sense-data), the presumption of a causal connection between the two is a simple matter and is commonly made. But the apprehension and syngnosis of the sense-data is a prior necessity to the presumption of this causal connection and the data by themselves can never rank as the effect. We may assume or even establish a causal connection between material things and physiological processes in our bodies, but all this *presupposes* the apprehension of the sense-data and is based upon it, and it cannot establish *their* causes. For the sense-data are particular members of the families the syngnosis of which (along with their self-prolongation) is necessary to the establishment of the causal connection. To take Price's example of seeing the approaching cricket-ball before feeling its impact on the body: the visual sense-data belong to the cricket-ball-family along with the pressure (and should we include also the organic?) sense-data of its impact; but the latter form part also of the somatic family which constitutes the body. They are, as it were, the point of coalescence between the two families which reveals their contact. But the impact of the cricket-ball can no more be regarded as the *cause* of the somatic data than can the somatic data be regarded as the cause of the impact. They *are* the impact.

The other examples which Price gives amount only to evidence that certain visual data are obtainable in conjunction with (or in the absence of) certain others, not that they are caused by anything other than themselves. That they could be caused by the family which they help to constitute is impossible, as he himself affirms.

IV. DEFECTS OF THE THEORY

16. Once we give up the doctrine of vertical causation, however, and realize that physical occupancy and horizontal causation are no more than aspects of the category of material-thinghood according to which we synthesize our sense-data, we are left with a totally subjective world. Price himself maintains that we accept, along with the other characteristics of material-thinghood, its causal efficacy in our first perceptual act. If so, the notion must be innate and *a priori*. But sense-data, we have been told, are private to the percipient, and though the material thing is taken to be public to many observers, this is part of an *a priori* conception which is innate in the percipient's mind. The actual occurrence of other percipients' data can be known, if at all, only indirectly and they cannot (as we shall presently see) contribute to the syngnosis of a family by any one mind. Perceptual acceptance is a

subjective propensity of the mind and the whole process of construction and synthesis by which it is confirmed is subjective, proceeding on the *a priori* principle of confirmability and seeking no support beyond the limits of actually sensed data. Our belief in the existence of an external world, accordingly, begins from a gratuitous acceptance and is generated by a purely subjective process out of purely subjective materials. It has no 'justification' apart from this private synthesis of private data, which are, in fact, the only existents available to constitute a world of any sort.

17. But, taken as a form of phenomenalism, the theory will not withstand critical examination. It would not, of course, be pure phenomenalism, because it requires the existence in some sense of 'obtainable' sense-data which are not and may never be sensed—though we may well wonder what sort of reality such potential sense-data might have. If, as I have argued in an earlier chapter, the existence of unsensed *sensibilia* is logically impossible, the conditions on which sense-data were said to be obtainable could only be expressed in terms of sense-data already obtained and of changes in the percipient's point of view. But the mutual relations of sense-data which make them constructible into complete solids (apart from their intrinsic characteristics) are spatial relations of a very definite kind, and if those data now unsensed are held to be so related to those which are now sensed, the condition of their obtainability must be the adoption of the determinate point of view by the percipient which those spatial relations require. And if we are to know how to construct the solid which these data are to form we must know how the successive points of view from which they are obtainable are mutually related. For example, if the sense-data of the under side of the table (which I do not now sense) are to be suitably related to those of the upper surface (which I do now sense), the condition of their being obtained is that I should move to a view-point determinately related to that which I now occupy, and unless I know exactly the movement required, I cannot tell how the data fit together, nor would they strictly be obtainable except by the merest chance. But we have seen that the determination of the view-point which I now occupy or any which I may subsequently adopt is possible only after the syngnosis of families, though that is possible only so far as sense-data are constructible into nuclear solids. Accordingly syngnosis requires one or other of three conditions none of which are permissible: (i) either sense-data must exist unsensed, and that is a contradiction in terms; or (ii) they must be obtainable from definitely determinable

view-points, and that is a *hysteron proteron*; or (iii) they must all be simultaneously sensed, but omnisentience is the prerogative of God alone.

The simultaneous sensing of co-existent data by different percipients, though assumed by Price, cannot help us, for syngnosis requires that all the data in their mutual relations should be known by a single mind, and the difficulty of establishing the mutual relations of data perceived by different minds purely by means of description we saw in our discussion of Russell's theory. A percipient could only determine the relations of other percipients' data to his own from their description of them, if he had already constructed for himself a systematic world of material objects to which the described data could be referred.[1] But this construction involves syngnosis and that, we can now see, would be impossible for the isolated percipient, because the occurrence of private sense-data is not such as to provide the required conditions.

Consequently, we are again confronted by the obstacle set in the path of all empiricism by the fact which Hume discovered—Hume, whose awful warning Price would not heed—that mere particulars cannot be synthesized and cannot give us an external world. And sense-data are mere fleeting particulars, coming and going in endless procession; nor will they tarry to be syngnosed.

18. More than all this, however, the very existence of sense-data has been challenged and arguments against it have been put forward which have not been refuted.[2] The belief in data, as Joachim has shown, springs from a confusion between the formal immediacy which belongs to every experience, perceptual, conceptual, inferential or intuitive, and the material immediacy which is supposed to give, at a stroke, acquaintance with some actuality in its completeness. That perception does not give us the second of these is clear from Price's own account of it. That pure sensation (or sensing) does not give it either is clear from the fact that no such mental process can be isolated. The sensuous elements (or 'moments') in our consciousness are not separable from the cognitions to which they belong, and those cognitions (or apprehensions) are always of objects, never of pure sense. An object, more-

---

[1] Cf. Price's example, *Perception*, p. 274: 'Thus if I see the inside of the door while you see the outside, I can know that your sense-datum is the sort of one that I should be sensing, if my point of view differed in an assignable way from what it now is. And you can know the same about mine.' All this presupposes a fully constructed system of objects and positions.

[2] *Vide* Joachim, *Logical Studies*, II (especially § 9), to which I am heavily indebted for much that follows.

over, however simple or rudimentary, is cognized only as something discriminated and distinguished within a presented manifold. What have been called sensa are objects, and so far as we are aware of them at all, they are always cognized as something presented, that is, as something discriminated out of and distinguished from the felt background of sensuous presentation. The product of such discrimination and distinction, however, is not seized in one undifferentiated flash of intuitive enlightenment, but requires for its apprehension some sort of discursive activity. The apprehension of every object, however primitive, is, in short, always a form of syngnosis, and none is ever simply given. The indubitable element in a perceptual act is not any simply given datum but the whole perceptual experience, which, like every other experience, is formally immediate. We cannot doubt that we have it, or that as we have it so it is. What we certainly can doubt, however, is that it contains an isolable core of sensation.

No doubt there are levels of experience, such for instance as the first moments of waking from deep sleep or the effects of an anaesthetic, at which we are aware only vaguely of sensuous qualities which are not referred to material things. We see colours or flashes of light, hear noises and feel vague unidentified discomforts. But we can be aware of these at all only so far as they are cognized (even if a moment later they may be forgotten or transformed), and cognition requires that they should be distinguished as this colour, that flash, such-and-such a noise, and so forth. Thought must already be at work in them to bring them to consciousness at all, identifying them and marking off their differences one from another. We may therefore agree with Price so far as to admit that when I see a tomato I cannot doubt that I am experiencing visually something round, red and bulgy which I take to be a tomato; but in doing so I am judging, not merely sensing. Even if I were aware only of a floating patch of colour, I should have to be aware of a shape, involving determinate spatial relations, and colour contrast, marking out the patch from its background: differences in brightness and quality, none of which could be cognized without an activity of distinction and identification which is discursive and is not covered by any mere sense-acceptance. In full waking consciousness, as Price himself admits, the alleged datum is always instinctively taken to be part of the surface of a further specifiable solid, and such taking-to-be is itself a highly discursive act. In other words, what we apprehend in every perceptual act is some object, material or otherwise, and never a mere sense-datum. The perceptual act is always a judgement, what Joachim calls an analytic-synthetic discursus, and less than this, some intuitive acceptance of a bare particular involving no sort of judgement or discursus at all, is not to be found in our experience. Even writers such as Price, Broad and Moore arrive at the notion of pure sensing only by a process of analysis of the perceptual act—a process which is through and through discursive—and no flash of intuition ever gives us anything like the sensing which they seek. And when they have analysed it out, what have they but the product of abstraction, of which they have as little right to say that it is a constituent of our experience as they would have to say that geometrical points are the constituents of a brick-bat.

19. In Price's refutation of arguments against the existence of sense-data,[1] he tacitly assumes, throughout, the position which he ought to prove. If it is said that the most rudimentary experience we ever have is already interpretative, he replies that the datum is then presupposed as that which has been interpreted. But why should it be always assumed that the experience *must* consist of (i) a datum plus (ii) the interpretation of it? This is just what the opponent of sense-data is denying. He maintains that the experience is an analytic-synthetic discursus in which all the elements (or 'moments') are equally fundamental and mutually elucidatory. If it is said that every perception is coloured and conditioned to an indefinite extent by past experience, Price replies that we must then have received other data in the past. But that is to assume what has yet to be proved. All that his opponent has alleged is that we have had other *experiences* in the past some of which were perceptual. If it be urged that whatever we cognize is already the work of thought, Price replies that thought must have had something to work on and that its work does not transform its object but only changes the thinker's attitude towards it or clarifies his state of mind with respect to it. But this again is to assume that there is and must be a given element before thought can go to work, and Price has done nothing to show that this must be the case. What necessity forces us to assert the existence of a datum? Why is it not possible that thought should create its own object, as life creates its own organism, and by its own inherent processes develop and elaborate it? At least, if it is alleged that this is not the case, some evidence ought to be produced to the contrary and not merely the gratuitous (if insistent) assumption that knowledge must and can only begin from a datum given by sense. And how is it possible, further, that changes of mental attitude and clarification of mental confusion should leave the object with which the mind is

[1] *Perception*, pp. 5-19.

concerned unaltered? If my perception is confused so that I doubt what it is I see, the object must at best be something indeterminate; and if the perception becomes clarified and my doubt dispelled (whatever the process) the object must of necessity have changed. This must be the case if by 'object' we are to understand that which is immediately present to consciousness, which any alleged datum certainly must be. The belief that the object remains unchanged throughout the process of clarification is due to an ambiguity in the common use of the word 'object', which applies it to an assumed external and independent existent taken to be the correlative of what is experienced at any stage of the process, and applies it also to that which is directly experienced. In the first sense, however, the 'object' can never be a datum. Yet it is probably this former application that is in Price's mind when he asserts that the activity of thought does not transform its object, for the assumption of an independently existing external world is characteristic of all empiricism (even when it is unacknowledged and when the results of the empirical theory conflict with it), and it is (paradoxically) this assumption that leads to the insistence upon sense-given data as the first beginnings of knowledge.

V. POSITIVE CONTRIBUTION

20. None of this adverse criticism, however, amounts to a denial of the very substantial contribution to the theory of knowledge made by philosophers like Broad and Price. There is no need to reject the assertion that sensuous elements can be distinguished within our experience which correspond to what they have called sense-data, though they are not data received passively and swallowed whole. They are elements in which thought has already been at work making them what we apprehend them to be. And it is only if and because thought is already at work in them in this way that the sort of construction and synthesis described by these writers becomes intelligibly possible. It is only because of the pattern of spatial and other relations distinguished and united in any visually or tactually experienced expanse that it is constructible with others into a solid having determinate qualities. It is only a discursive activity of the mind, distinguishing and relating the variegations of a sense-field, that enables us to relate solids one to another in space. And it is only due to a similar discursive activity of thought that we become aware of the time relations implied in the successive changes of sensuous experience which constitute for us the self-prolongation of material things.

What is, in fact, chiefly remarkable about the positive doctrines of philosophers of the sense-datum theory, is their likeness to those which they believe themselves to be opposing. What, for instance, is a family of sense-data as Price describes it but an example of what others have called a concrete universal? Price is always asserting that perception is of wholes and he even maintains that wholes can be directly sensed. Sense-data, he says, are not momentary; they may be patterned and may include spatial interrelatedness. He constantly speaks of sense-given relations. Data must then be already relata in relation, already syntheta in synthesis, already wholes; and the apprehension of them as such, whether we call it sensing or something different, can hardly be other than an analytic-synthetic discursus. Furthermore, syngnosis is not a process of pure perception, still less of pure sensing; it is a process involving *a priori* conceptions (the postulation of which is itself a departure from die-hard empiricism), and it is difficult to describe it otherwise than as a process of thought, even if it is not one of formal inference. But the insistence upon wholeness and system, as the essence at once of experience and of the real, is the hall-mark of all those theories which have benefited from the lesson taught by Kant that knowledge is at once both *a priori* and *a posteriori*, at once both perceiving and conceiving, at once both objective and subjective; and from that other lesson also, taught by Plato, that everything which comes to be comes to be as a whole.

Chapter XVI

MODERN EMPIRICISM: THE THIRD PHASE
(LOGICAL POSITIVISM)

I. THE BOURNE OF EMPIRICISM

1. THE third phase of modern empiricism does little more than draw the conclusions implicit in the first two phases, as might with equal justice have been said of the philosophy of Hume, who merely forced to their logical conclusion in scepticism the arguments developed by Berkeley and Locke. Most of the writers whose work belongs to this last phase of contemporary empiricism openly claim to be presenting a position similar in essentials to Hume's, and the main doctrines of Professor A. J. Ayer, their most important representative in English, show the influence of Hume to so marked a degree that even a casual reader could hardly fail to notice it. It is, I think, justifiable to apply the name Logical Positivism to theories displaying the characteristics which I regard as typical of this phase of empiricism, though not all the authors of those theories would accept it, for the disagreements between them that lead some to reject the title which others assume do not affect their most characteristic doctrines and the general spirit and attitude distinguishing their thought are sufficiently alike in all of them to mark them as a single group. Briefly, these characteristic doctrines are the assertion of the meaninglessness of metaphysics and the claim to demonstrate conclusively by logical analysis the purely empirical reference of all significant propositions.[1]

2. As the logical positivists develop the consequences involved in the position to which the radical empiricist is committed, I shall begin my discussion of their work with a brief recapitulation of that position and an outline of the consequences that emerge from it. The empiricist begins from the assumption of an independently existing world of reality which is revealed to the mind through sense-perception and holds that the primary elements of empirical knowledge are, therefore, sense-data. These are the prototypes of images and the elements constituting the meanings of words and propositions. The truth or falsity of propositions is held to consist in their agreement with the facts, but the only facts with which we are directly acquainted turn out to be the

[1] Cf. J. R. Weinberg, *An Examination of Logical Positivism* (London, 1936), p. 1.

occurrence of sense-data, and accordingly only this can be the ultimate test of truth for factual propositions. No proposition, therefore, which cannot in principle be verified by comparison with relevant sense-data can be a factual proposition and if its purport is factual it must be meaningless. It follows that all talk of unsensed *sensibilia* is inadmissible and the empiricist is committed to unqualified phenomenalism.

The occurrence of sense-data is wholly contingent and between them there are no necessary connections. All general statements about them are therefore the result of inductive generalization depending on the principle that what has frequently occurred in the past is likely to occur again. No justification for this principle is, however, possible on empirical grounds, so that one has to accept it gratuitously, and the adherents of empiricist views often maintain that to do otherwise would be 'unreasonable'.[1] It follows also that inductive generalization, to which category all general propositions having factual reference belong, can be taken only in extension, for they arise out of, and their truth depends on, the enumeration of particular cases, and such meaning as they have can always be analysed into statements about particulars.

3. Certain conclusions follow concerning the nature of reasoning and logic:

(i) There can be no deduction of facts one from another and all reasoning about factual matters concerns the verification of hypotheses, which is never complete and never more than probable in a greater or lesser degree. This is the case because complete verification would require complete enumeration of instances, and even in the special cases where that is possible, the fact that all the instances have been inspected is itself an empirical hypothesis requiring verification.

(ii) Inference will always be either (a) a matter of class inclusion, where the class-concepts are taken only in extension[2] or (b) the analysis of the definitions of terms.[3] In both cases the cogency of the

---

[1] Cf. Price, 'The permanent significance of Hume's philosophy', in *Philosophy*, XV, no. 57, and Ayer, *Foundations of Empirical Knowledge* (London, 1940), pp. 190-1. Russell maintains that the principle of induction is 'an *a priori* logical law' (*Our Knowledge of the External World*, p. 225). This is, of course, a departure from strict empiricism and in the last chapter of *Human Knowledge* Russell frankly admits that the problem is insoluble for strict empiricism. Nevertheless, he persists that it is the least inadequate theory of knowledge.

[2] Cf. Russell's 'principle of abstraction', *Our Knowledge of the External World*, p. 51, and the discussion of Classes in ch. vi of *Principles of Mathematics*.

[3] Cf. Hobbes, *Leviathan*, ch. v: 'Reason . . . is nothing but reckoning, that is adding and subtracting of the consequences of general names agreed upon for the marking and signifying of our thoughts'; and Ayer, *Language, Truth and Logic*:

reasoning—its necessity—arises from the purely formal characteristics of the propositions concerned and not at all from their matter or content, for that is factual and between facts there can be no necessary connections.

(iii) Consequently, in logic, we can omit all reference to the factual content of propositions—we must, in fact, do so—and can represent it symbolically simply by variables. The logical connections between propositions will then be evident purely from their form. They will depend solely upon the nature and use of the logical constants involved. But logical constants do not stand for anything in the real world and are simply part of the linguistic apparatus by means of which we express propositions. The results of inference, therefore, depend ultimately (a) on the definitions of general terms (the names of classes), (b) on the way in which we define the logical constants and (c) on the rules we adopt for their use.

(iv) As all propositions are taken in extension and logical deduction is concerned purely with formal analysis, all logical propositions are tautologies. The only statements that can be *a priori* and necessary are such tautologies and they give no information about the world but are merely analyses of the definitions of those terms which make up the linguistic apparatus necessary to represent the world to ourselves and to one another.

(v) But language is a matter of convention, and in the main of arbitrary convention, so we arrive finally at the paradoxical conclusion that the results of deductive reasoning, proceeding by necessary logical steps, depend ultimately upon arbitrary linguistic convention.

There are thus, for the empiricist, two kinds of knowledge, (a) factual or empirical knowledge depending on the correspondence between factual statements and experienced data, and (b) *a priori* knowledge, which is certain but is entirely empty of factual content, consisting of tautologous analyses of linguistic forms. In neither of these is there room for metaphysics, which professes to deal with the nature of reality, but the propositions of which cannot be compared with any experienced facts and are in principle unverifiable. All verifiable factual propositions fall within the province of the natural sciences and those of metaphysics are (in the logical sense of the word) meaningless. Logic, on the other hand, as the analysis of linguistic forms, is able to clarify the terminology of science and this is regarded as its most important, if not its whole, function.

'. . . the propositions of philosophy . . . express definitions, or the formal consequences of definitions' (p. 57).

This is the position, stated in bare outline, which is developed by the Logical Positivists, their principal aims, as announced by the members of the Vienna Circle, being 'first to provide a secure foundation for the sciences, and second to demonstrate the meaninglessness of all metaphysics'.[1] As I shall contend immediately, the repudiation of metaphysics does not prevent the logical positivist from making metaphysical presuppositions and unless he did so the denial of metaphysics would have no foundation. Moreover, these presuppositions are still those of the Renaissance, a symptom of which is the belief that genuine knowledge is all derived from empirical data and that it is exhausted by the natural sciences.

II. UNDERLYING METAPHYSIC

4. The metaphysical foundations of logical positivism are actually stated by Wittgenstein in the *Tractatus Logico-Philosophicus* and they are, for the most part, adopted from Russell. Wittgenstein's statement is unfortunately obscured by a number of inconsistencies as well as by the use of familiar terms in unexplained technical senses, which puzzle the reader and mar the exposition, but it is not my intention to dwell upon these defects, for the doctrine, taken as it stands and judged by its own criteria, can readily be shown to destroy itself.

The world, Wittgenstein tells us, is everything that is the case, that is the totality of facts, and can be analysed into atomic facts (*Sachverhalte*) which are mutually independent and each of which can either be or not be the case without affecting any of the others. Consequently they cannot be inferred one from another. These atomic facts are constituted by things or objects [2] which are absolutely simple and are arranged or patterned in the fact in a structure or configuration. An atomic fact is thus a combination of objects. The structure, we are told, forms the fact,[3] but we are also told that the form is the possibility of structure [4] and that the fixed form of the world consists of objects; [5] nevertheless, Wittgenstein seems on the whole to mean structure when he speaks of form and that is how I interpret the term.

In the thing the possibility of occurrence in atomic facts is said to be prejudged, so that if I know an object I also know all the possibilities of

[1] Weinberg, *loc. cit.*

[2] Wittgenstein seems to use '*Ding*' and '*Gegenstand*' synonymously (see *Tractatus*, 2·01, 2·011-2, 2·0121-3, *et seq.*). He speaks of the thing as a constituent of fact and of the object as known or thought of, but if he intends any distinction of meaning between them he does not make it clear.

[3] *Tractatus*, 2·0272.   [4] *Ibid.* 2·033.   [5] *Ibid.* 2·023.

its occurrence in atomic facts and, if all objects are given, all possible atomic facts are given. This would seem to imply a world of objects constituted by their mutual relations, and so a coherence theory of knowledge, for if the sort of implication exists between facts and objects that Wittgenstein asserts, facts cannot be atomic and independent as he alleges and they must be inferrible from the nature of the objects and so one from another. Similarly, if, as he states, the possibility of its occurrence in atomic facts is prejudged and is the form of the object,[1] the object cannot be simple but must be what it is in virtue of the way in which it is combined with other objects in the atomic facts and must therefore display an internal complexity. These contradictory implications are, however, disregarded by Wittgenstein and I shall pass them over without further comment.

We picture the facts to ourselves and the pictures are said to be models of reality. They represent the facts by virtue of a common structure or form which is the same in the picture as in the fact, the elements of the picture corresponding to the objects combined in the fact. The structure, or connection of the elements in the picture, is called its form of representation and is the possibility that the things to which those elements correspond are similarly combined in the fact. Thus the picture has in common with what it represents its form of representation. In order to represent reality at all, a picture must have in common with reality the logical form (or, as Wittgenstein explains, the form of reality). This seems not to be identical with the form of representation, but the difference is never explained. It does, however, seem clear that every picture, whatever its form of representation, must also have a logical form and, accordingly, every picture is *also* a logical picture (*i.e.* one in which the form is the logical form of the fact represented).

Such a logical picture, Wittgenstein says, is the thought of the fact pictured and he apparently equates thinking with imagining, for he says: '"An atomic fact is thinkable"—means: we can imagine it'.[2] If the thought is expressed by means of a perceptible sign it is a proposition and the sign is a 'projection' of the possible state of affairs pictured in the thought. This I take to be Wittgenstein's meaning, for he says that the method of projection of the possible state of affairs is the thinking of the sense of the proposition, and this is what the picture expressed by the proposition represents. If this sense agrees with reality the picture is true; if it does not it is false. To discover whether a thought or proposition is true, therefore, we must compare what it represents (its sense) with the facts as they really are.

Both the picture and the propositional sign are facts in their own right, and the first represents, and the second is a projection, solely in virtue of their form or structure. But the picture cannot *represent* its form, it simply shows it forth. Similarly, the proposition cannot represent the logical form, but the logical form 'mirrors itself' in the proposition. In short, that by virtue of which thoughts and propositions picture or represent the reality cannot itself be pictured or represented. It cannot therefore be the subject (or, in the technical language of modern mathematical logic, the argument) of a proposition. It follows that the sense of every proposition must be factual, for we are told that every statement about complexes can be analysed into a statement about their constituent parts. The constituent parts will thus be elementary propositions representing atomic facts, and the elements (names) in these propositions stand, and can only stand, for things. They may be combined in ways which correspond to no actual combination of real objects (*e.g.* when the proposition is false), but unless they represent real things they can have no meaning and the proposition in which they occur can have no sense. A proposition, therefore, presents the existence and non-existence of facts, and cannot present anything else. This being so, every proposition falls within the sphere of the natural sciences, the totality of which is the totality of true propositions; and metaphysical propositions are senseless. Philosophy, not being a natural science, must confine itself to the logical clarification of thoughts and is an activity, not a theory. There are no philosophical propositions.

5. The doctrine is patently self-destructive. It is itself a theory and does not belong to any natural science—a metaphysical theory standing in evidence against what it maintains. This has been already observed in Chapter I; but we must notice here that the contradiction involved is the age-old contradiction of Empiricism inherent in the teachings both of Russell and of Locke. The critical question is: How do we determine whether or not a proposition is true? We have been told that its truth consists in the agreement of its sense with the fact. But to be known (or thought) the fact must be pictured, and the picture is expressed as a proposition with the pictured fact as its sense. The demand that we should compare the sense of the proposition with the fact is therefore nonsensical, for the sense of the proposition *is* the fact, as we picture it. We cannot compare the fact as we picture it with the fact as it is in itself,

because it is known to us only as we picture it. The criterion of truth which is offered to us, therefore, is beyond our reach. Wittgenstein himself declares that the proposition does not contain its sense but only its form,[1] and we are told, also, that the form mirrors itself in the proposition but is not expressed by it. All that the proposition contains, then, is the possibility of expressing a sense. All that our thought can contain, therefore, is the possibility of picturing the fact, but that there is a fact corresponding to it, it can never reveal. If, however, we cannot know that there is a fact corresponding to the picture, we cannot know that our thought is a picture of anything, for to represent something is to have an original, and that which has no original, whatever it may be, is no picture. And even if there is an original, so long as it is not known to exist, that which represents it cannot be recognized as a picture. It follows that the whole of Wittgenstein's theory of the world, of thought and of propositions must, by its own criterion of truth, be unknowable.

Further, the picture is said to represent the reality by virtue of the fact that it has in common with the fact a certain form; thus the agreement of the fact with the picture is revealed by comparison of their structures. But the form cannot be represented in the picture nor expressed by a proposition; in other words, it can neither be thought nor stated. It cannot, therefore, be sensibly stated that a fact has such-and-such a form nor that a particular proposition mirrors that form. Consequently they cannot be formally compared and we can never know whether a proposition agrees with the fact, *i.e.* whether it is true. But if this is so, we cannot say of propositions in general that they are true when they agree with the facts. Wittgenstein maintains that the verb of the proposition is not 'is true' or 'is false',[2] for to say that p is true is no more than to assert p. But the mere assertion of p does not make it true. What is supposed to make it true is agreement with the fact, but that cannot sensibly be asserted. Accordingly, the inexpressibility of form in propositions makes the whole theory of truth which Wittgenstein offers inexpressible—yet he has not scrupled to express it.[3]

6. A possible counter to these criticisms might be that they hold good only because they presume atomic facts to be somehow outside of experience, whereas this is what the positivist especially wishes to deny. Atomic facts are intended to be the facts of experience—sense-given data—which we know by direct acquaintance. Agreement between such

---

[1] *Tractatus*, 3·13.   [2] *Ibid.* 4·063.
[3] Cf. Weinberg, *op. cit.* p. 196.

facts, it might be maintained, and what is presented in propositions can be seen by inspection, and no difficulty arises in consequence of the inexpressibility of the relation.

This argument, however, even if it were sound, would be no valid defence of Wittgenstein, for he maintains that 'the limits of my language are the limits of my world',[1] and what cannot be expressed, therefore, cannot be experienced. But the argument is not sound. If elementary propositions express experience they should be able to express the experience we have on inspection of the agreement or disagreement between sense-given data and the propositions which picture them. But what could such inspection possibly reveal? The inspection of sense-given data is simply the sensing of them, and the proposition in its symbolic reference (as distinct from the propositional sign) is not another datum to be sensed. We cannot therefore compare the two by inspection. The proposition cannot be inspected at all, it can only be asserted (or denied). Thus the identity of form between the proposition and the fact is not sensible. The proposition is a projection of the fact, as it were on to another plane, and can be compared with it only as a different stage or level in the process of giving expression to direct experience. Agreement between them is either a meaningless phrase, or, if it refers only to the projective relation, nothing which could possibly be seen by inspection; for the projection is not a datum.

7. The failure of Wittgenstein's theory of truth has been pointed out in a different way by Weinberg, who shows that the exclusively empirical content of elementary propositions is proved by Wittgenstein by means of a circular argument.[2] The gist of Weinberg's reasoning is this: In order to prove that all propositions are analysable into elementary propositions, the existence of logical simples must be demonstrated and Wittgenstein seeks to do this by the assertion that elementary propositions are pictures of reality. His argument is: 'If the world had no substance (*i.e.* simple objects) then whether a proposition has sense would depend on whether another proposition was true. It would then be impossible to form a picture of the world true or false' (*Tractatus*, 2·0211-2). This is paraphrased by Weinberg as an apagogic argument running: 'If the world does not consist of simple objects then: any proposition has sense implies another proposition is true; this, in turn, implies that there are not pictures of the facts. Hence if the world does not consist of simple objects there is no connection between discourse and reality.' He then states the argument in its direct form thus: 'If

---

[1] *Tractatus*, 5·6.   [2] *Vide An Examination of Logical Positivism*, pp. 48-56.

there are pictures of facts then some propositions have sense without being truth-functions of other propositions; thus the existence of propositions with independent senses implies the existence of simple objects'. When so stated the circularity of the argument is immediately apparent, for the existence of propositions with independent sense is what should follow from the establishment of the existence of simple objects, it is what has to be proved, and it cannot be used to prove the existence of simples. In effect, what Wittgenstein has done is to assume that the only possible connection between discourse and reality is the representative relation and then to argue that if this were not so there could be no connection between discourse and reality. The exclusively empirical reference of elementary propositions is not proved by the argument because it is already assumed in the assertion that they are pictures of the facts.

Weinberg concludes that the existence of simple objects cannot be demonstrated and that the ultimate reference of significant discourse to empirical facts cannot be supported by what he calls 'Wittgenstein's logical atomism'. In short, the empirical reference of elementary propositions is implicit in the metaphysical dogma that thought corresponds to facts and apart from that it cannot be maintained. This is of the utmost importance because the repudiation of metaphysics follows from the contention that the ultimate reference of all significant discourse is empirical, and we now see that the contention itself presupposes a metaphysic. The great value of Wittgenstein's work is that he has shown this to be the case and his conclusion to the *Tractatus* is perfectly sound: that on the principles he has enunciated his own propositions are senseless and must be rejected; for the metaphysical basis of positivism is, as we have seen, false and self-destructive. One cannot therefore proceed, as Wittgenstein himself and other positivists attempt to do, as if it were true. If one does, the alleged elimination of metaphysics amounts to no more than the refusal to criticize the presuppositions of one's own theory. This is the error committed by those who paraphrase Wittgenstein's doctrine, that every proposition is reducible to elementary propositions which directly picture atomic facts, into the principle of verification, which states that the meaning of a proposition is the method of its verification, and who make this the basis of their theory of knowledge, asserting with Wittgenstein that all the propositions of metaphysics are senseless and that those of logic are permissible only because they are tautologous and assert nothing. For, so far from ridding themselves in this way of metaphysics, they are committed by implication to the metaphysical doctrine set out by

Wittgenstein. The verification principle itself is, after all, neither a tautology nor empirically verifiable, and should therefore be devoid of sense.

III. THE VERIFICATION PRINCIPLE

8. Let us, however, provisionally accept the position adopted by those who, like Carnap and Ayer, assert that only such propositions as can be empirically verified are significant (apart from such as are purely analytic and so have no factual content) and let us develop its consequences. It must at once be admitted that this statement of the position is not strictly accurate. A non-significant proposition is strictly a contradiction in terms, but sentences which are grammatically correct may, it is held, express nothing significant and so no proposition. Even so, we must take the word 'significant' in a purely logical sense, for such sentences may arouse feelings or have imaginative associations, which in a psychological sense might be called their 'meanings'. What is meant by calling them non-significant is, therefore, simply that they do not convey any information about reality despite the fact that they are not *a priori* (or analytic) propositions and are not translatable into such analytic propositions. Ayer proposes the use of the word 'sentence' for any grammatically sensible form of words, and the word 'statement' for what a sentence expresses, whether it is literally significant or not. 'Proposition' is then to be reserved for such statements as are literally significant, and literal significance is to be conditional upon empirical verifiability for all synthetic propositions.[1]

9. Some positivists (*e.g.* Moritz Schlick) originally insisted upon conclusive verification as the condition of significance, but others (notably Carnap and Ayer) consider this to be an impossible requirement in the vast majority of cases and are therefore prepared to accept as significant statements which can in principle be rendered more probable by empirical observation. Actual verification has never been insisted upon, for there are statements which cannot in fact be verified, owing to practical difficulties which in some cases may even be insuperable, but which are in principle verifiable (in the 'weaker' sense): that is to say, it would be possible to state the kind of empirical observations which would render them probable if they could be made. What is meant by verification in this connection has been precisely set down by Ayer as follows: 'A statement is directly verifiable if it is either itself an observation-statement, or is such that in conjunction with one

[1] *Vide Language, Truth and Logic*, 2nd ed., pp. 8 f.

or more observation-statements it entails at least one observation-statement which is not deducible from these other premises alone; and . . . a statement is indirectly verifiable if it satisfies the following conditions: first, that in conjunction with certain other premises it entails one or more directly verifiable statements which are not deducible from these other premises alone; and secondly, that these other premises do not include any statement that is not either analytic, or directly verifiable, or capable of being independently established as indirectly verifiable.'[1]

It is clear from this definition that, strictly speaking, the only verifiable statements are observation-statements, for no statement is verifiable unless, directly or indirectly, with or without other premises, it entails an observation-statement. It will, therefore, repay us to consider just what the character of such statements is taken to be.

10. The phrase 'experiential proposition' was earlier used by Ayer to designate what he now proposes to call an observation-statement, and it is clear from what he says in various contexts[2] that by 'an observation' he means the occurrence of a sense-content. That, again, is used to refer to 'the immediate data not merely of "outer" but also of "introspective" sensation'.[3] As an observation-statement is defined as a statement which records an actual or possible observation,[4] it follows that it records the actual or possible[5] occurrence of immediate data of sense. The same result is obtained by examining at least one of Carnap's statements of the verification principle; for he says that a proposition is directly verified if it is about a present perception and if that perception is actually occurring at the time, and that no proposition can be indirectly verified unless one which is directly verifiable can be deduced from it together with other already verified propositions.[6]

The insistence on the verification principle, therefore, is simply a repetition of the old empiricist doctrine that all genuine knowledge of the world is derived from sense-data, and it is evidence of the persistence of the metaphysical presuppositions of the Renaissance. It implies and is implied in the profession of complete phenomenalism, and this is admitted by Ayer and developed in his published works.

[1] *Ibid.* p. 13.
[2] Cf. *ibid.* pp. 31, 53, 58 f., 63 ff., 123, etc.
[3] *Ibid.* p. 53.   [4] *Ibid.* p. 11.
[5] The inclusion of 'possible' is, however, unmeaning. One cannot record a *possible* occurrence. Moreover, it will presently appear that observation-sentences are the same as 'protocol-sentences', and these are said to be indubitable or 'incorrigible'. They cannot, therefore, be either false or hypothetical. (See *Foundations of Empirical Knowledge*, pp. 78-90.)   [6] *Philosophy and Logical Syntax*, pp. 10-11.

329

NATURE, MIND AND MODERN SCIENCE

Material objects are said to be logical constructions out of sense-contents and are built up much in the same way as is described by Russell and Price but with this difference, that they are not assumed to exist unperceived and logical construction is taken to mean no more than that statements about material objects can be analysed (or translated) into equivalent (or equipollent) statements about sense-contents. One's own mind and those of other persons are constructed in an exactly similar manner, so that the entire world of physical and mental entities is no more than a complicated system of logical construction in accordance with the rules of linguistic transformation of observation-statements into statements about objects of various kinds. The only actual facts there are are those of immediate sense-experience and not even the experience of thinking is admitted as a fact (apart from the occurrence of the 'immediate data of introspective sensation'), what is normally called thought being explained away in terms of behaviour.[1]

The kinship of this doctrine with that of Hume is so obvious that space need not be wasted in drawing a detailed parallel and I shall confine my attention in the sequel to demonstrating that its results are at least as disastrous as those of Hume's theory. First, I shall examine the view of empirical knowledge that is being advocated and I shall argue that the verification upon which it is held to depend for its validity is, according to the requirements of the theory itself, in every case impossible. Secondly, I shall consider the relation between empirical knowledge and *a priori* reasoning or logic and shall try to show that the conception of logic advocated is such that it completely undermines factual knowledge and dissolves away its own cogency.

11. (i) According to the theory under examination there are two kinds of empirical proposition. First, there are those which are expressed in observation-sentences. They are purely ostensive and the words used in them are intended simply to designate the sense-data actually sensed at the time and to indicate nothing further at all. These propositions could never be doubtful or false, as no experience beyond what they record could be relevant to them, and sentences which express them are called 'basic' or 'protocol' sentences. Secondly, there are empirical hypotheses which include (a) propositions describing sense-data, classifying them and asserting relations between them; (b) propositions asserting the existence or interrelation of material things, and (c) empirical generalizations.

[1] Cf. Ayer, *Thinking and Meaning* (London, 1947). A similar position is developed by Carnap in *Der logische Aufbau der Welt*.

In his first statement of the doctrine Ayer denied that there could be ostensive propositions, because the notion implies that there could be sentences consisting of purely demonstrative symbols. But purely demonstrative symbols would be merely ejaculatory and so could not express a proposition at all.[1] He is now prepared to admit them on condition that the words used do no more than designate the sense-datum actually occurring,[2] but this, he admits,[3] 'does not serve to convey any information either to any other person or indeed to oneself'. Why he should subsequently have made this concession is difficult to see, because, if the words of a sentence are used simply to designate a sense-datum actually occurring at the time, they are on a par with an exclamation such as one might emit on feeling the prick of a pin, and no such exclamation constitutes a proposition for there is nothing which it asserts. As soon as the words of a sentence are understood to convey anything, as soon as they are taken to do more than designate the present sense-datum, the sentence, as Ayer himself maintains, ceases to be 'basic'; for any statement describing a sense-datum or assigning it to a particular time necessarily goes beyond what is immediately given and so becomes an empirical hypothesis. If, however, there can be no ostensive or 'basic' sentences, there can be no observation-sentences and no other kind of statement can therefore sensibly be said to entail an observation-statement in any circumstances, and, if that is the case, no statement can ever be verifiable either directly or indirectly.

Let us, however, assume that there could be basic propositions which record the present occurrence of sense-data. Though no such proposition could be false or doubtful, it is plain that it could only be true and could only be verified in the moment at which it was asserted; for such a proposition cannot assert of the future and at any moment after its assertion it will have ceased to apply. Further, it is obvious that it could not be asserted or verified by any person other than the one enjoying the experience which the proposition records. Though it could not properly be doubted, neither could it properly be known or understood by any but the person who made the assertion; for no report of the experience of sense-data, which could be intelligible to others, is expressible in protocol sentences. In these circumstances, empirical hypotheses could not be reduced to basic propositions and could not be verified by their means, and we should be committed to an ultimate solipsism in which the very word 'verification' would lose its meaning.

[1] *Language, Truth and Logic*, p. 91.
[2] Cf. *Foundations*, pp. 81 ff.   [3] *Language*, etc., p. 10.

An empirical hypothesis expressed by a proposition which describes a sense-datum inevitably refers to other data which have similar qualities to the one described. That one cannot describe without classifying has been clearly shown by Ayer in the following passage: 'Let us suppose that I assert the proposition "This is white", and my words are taken to refer, not as they normally would, to some material thing, but to a sense-content. Then what I am saying about this sense-content is that it is an element in the class of sense-contents which constitute "white" for me; or in other words that it is similar in colour to certain other sense-contents, namely those which I should call, or actually have called, white. And I think I am saying also that it corresponds in some fashion to the sense-contents which go to constitute "white" for other people. . . .'[1] Even so simple a proposition as 'This is white' is seen to imply the relations between other sense-contents both of my own and of other persons such as are involved in classification, and it might with justice be maintained that it implied a great deal more as well. But the sense-data recorded by purely ostensive propositions are at most the bare terms of possible relations, and there is nothing in the stark record of the occurrence of any one of them to suggest in the very least that these relations exist or what they might be. Any one or any number of basic propositions would, therefore, leave us completely in the dark about the relations (if there are such) which might exist between the experiences that they record. No empirical hypothesis of the first kind could, for this reason, ever be reduced to or translated into basic propositions.

Nevertheless, it might be held that it is sufficient for its significance that an empirical hypothesis should entail one or more basic propositions; and in the example given above, and in all similar examples, the sort of relations implied between the sense-data entail at least the existence of those sense-data. But what the empirical hypothesis asserts *over and above* the bare existence of the sense-data is what has to be verified, and this is just what never can be verified by basic propositions. Accordingly, just that in the empirical proposition which we should normally call its main significance, would be altogether non-significant if the verification principle as defined were strictly applied.

Material-object-propositions are still less capable of verification in the manner required by logical positivism, for they imply systematically related groups of sense-data obtainable under certain definite conditions. Each is resoluble not only into propositions asserting relations between sense-data, but also into a set of hypothetical propositions

[1] *Language*, etc., p. 92.

stating the conditions of obtainability of the sense-data out of which the material thing is constructed. Now it is quite obvious that no ostensive proposition can give the slightest intimation of the conditions on which the sense-datum, the occurrence of which it records, can or does exist, nor could such information be derived from any number of ostensive propositions. It follows that no hypothetical proposition can ever be reduced to basic propositions and *a fortiori* that no material-object-proposition can be verified by their means. The proof of the existence of a material thing is always a complex process, as became apparent in our discussion of Price's theory. The attainment of perceptual assurance is never simply a matter of sensing, but depends on the acquisition of a systematic body of evidence.[1] It is consequently quite impossible to verify material-object-propositions by reducing them to basic propositions as the positivist theory demands.

Having reached this point—*cadit quaestio.* If hypothetical propositions are incapable of verification in the manner required all empirical hypotheses are, in the nature of the case, ruled out of court. As for empirical generalizations, they are not only notoriously hypothetical, but their verification always involves that of numerous material-object-propositions and statements asserting the interrelation and assuming the classification of sense-contents. Their chances of retaining any sort of significance in the positivistic sense of the word are consequently non-existent and the whole body of empirical knowledge, including the much-respected natural sciences, is revealed as a vast babble of meaningless verbiage.

Though we are entitled at this stage to draw this conclusion, there are yet further considerations which impress upon us the destitution of the logical positivist theory of knowledge, and of these not the least damaging is that concerned with the nature of prediction. We are told that the function of an empirical hypothesis is to enable us to anticipate experience,[2] and that 'if an observation to which a given proposition is relevant conforms to our expectations, the truth of that proposition is confirmed'. Verification, in fact, always involves prediction, for if the observation which is supposed to confirm an hypothesis had occurred in the past, another observation would be needed to confirm the fact that the first one had actually taken place, and this second observation could take the form only of reference to some kind of record of the earlier occurrence—a reference which must be made subsequently to the propounding of the hypothesis. In other words, verification is

---

[1] Cf. my discussion, 'Mr. Ryle and the Ontological Argument', in *Mind*, XLV, no. 180.   [2] Ayer, *Language*, etc., p. 99.

always the occurrence of an observation predicted by the hypothesis verified. A prediction, however, is always an assertion that a certain event will occur at a certain (future) time and place on the fulfilment of certain specified conditions; but basic propositions are no more than the records of present occurrences, which are said to be 'present' only because they are simultaneous with the assertion that they are occurring, not because any time relation with other events is implied. Strictly speaking, we should not even call them 'present' occurrences. But what is predicted is always an event, and an event is never simple but is always a nexus of spatio-temporal relations. The fulfilment of a prediction, therefore, always requires the establishment of a systematic interconnection of occurrence such as could never be expressed in a protocol sentence or in any number of them. No basic proposition, therefore, can fulfil a prediction, for it cannot inform us of the occurrence of an event; it cannot tell us whether the experience it records is related in time and space and conditioned as the prediction required. Even if it were maintained that each of the events to which the one predicted must be related could severally be recorded in a basic proposition, another proposition, which would not be basic and would not record an observation, would be needed to inform us of their mutual relations. No observation, which is no more than a bare observation of a sense-content, can ever fulfil a prediction; and if the function of an empirical hypothesis is to anticipate experience, the success with which it is performed can never be discovered by purely empirical means. But these are the only means provided by the logical positivists. If we cannot verify our propositions by reducing them to observation-sentences we cannot verify them at all. And this is not simply because 'strong', or conclusive, verification is never attainable (the number of observations necessary being always infinite), but because however few or however many are considered sufficient, none of them can give the requisite information for the confirmation or rejection of any empirical hypothesis whatsoever. The mistake lies in the conception offered of verification and it can be corrected only at the cost of abandoning the empirical principle.

The validity of this criticism against the views of Professor Ayer may, however, be doubted, whatever is the case with other logical positivists, for Ayer's admission of the existence of protocol-sentences and ostensive propositions has always been rather grudging and is heavily qualified. At first he emphatically denied their existence, declaring that it was not a logical possibility for a sentence to consist of purely demonstrative symbols and be at the same time intelligible. Now that he has modified this opinion he still contends that basic propositions do not convey any information either to other persons or to oneself. Is it even plausible to suggest that he believes such propositions to be the essential and ultimately the only source of the verification of empirical hypotheses? For my own part, I suspect that he does not, but it is difficult to discover what alternative he has in mind. He does say that for a statement to be a genuine empirical proposition some possible sense-experience must be relevant to the determination of its truth or falsehood, and that, I presume, means that if the sense-experience were actual it would contribute significantly to that determination. But just how much or how little is meant by a 'sense-experience' is not divulged. He does say also—and that immediately after he has emphatically rejected the existence of ostensive propositions—that 'empirical propositions are one and all hypotheses, which may be confirmed or discredited in actual sense-experience'. But if the statements which are alleged to register actual sense-experiences are held to be either unintelligible or uninformative, what use can be made of them and how can the sense-experience be made relevant to the hypotheses to be tested? On the other hand, if we are to understand by 'sense-experience' something other than is registered by a basic proposition, we are given no indication of the meaning of the phrase. From the account which Ayer gives of the character of empirical knowledge in Chapter V of *Language, Truth and Logic*, one would almost suspect that he wished to advocate a coherence theory of truth, if he had not elsewhere so decidedly rejected the conception. But no adherent of the coherence theory could accept the account there given, for it provides no stable criterion even of probability, and though it enjoins as the one indispensable requirement that we should not simultaneously maintain incompatible hypotheses, we are left to choose at will, if observed facts conflict with an hypothesis, between ignoring them, or explaining them away, or abandoning one or more of the subsidiary hypotheses always involved in the assertion of any one, or modifying our accepted theories about the world. We are recommended to take the course which will render our hypotheses more fruitful as a means of anticipating experience, but, as we have seen, the criterion for judging their efficiency in that respect is doubtful in the extreme.

We can only conclude that, unless we are to depart from the fundamental tenets of logical positivism, the source of verification which the theory offers is one which reduces the realm of significant discourse to the enunciation of propositions which register immediate sense-given experience; and such propositions, we have seen reason to hold, cannot be intelligibly expressed. The nemesis of empiricism, which was visited upon Hume, has again descended upon us. Sense-data are particulars, and left in their bare particularity they cannot cohere; but every proposition asserts a universal, and neither can a pure particular be intelligibly affirmed nor can it conceivably be the test of truth of universal judgements.

12. Quite apart from the bankruptcy of the verification principle, however, the view that the only significant propositions are those the truth of which can be attested by actual or possible sense-experience is no more nor less than complete solipsism. For sense-experience is private, and if the sense of a proposition is confined to its empirical reference and its meaning to the method of its verification, it can be significant only for him who has the experience by which it is verified and its sense cannot be communicated to others. This feature of the positivist position has been admitted by Wittgenstein [1] and is discussed at length by Weinberg.[2] Both Ayer and Carnap make some attempt to escape it, but neither is successful.

Weinberg makes the position clear by pointing out that in Wittgenstein's theory all propositions are truth-functions of elementary propositions, to which, therefore, all important problems of structure and meaning pertain. An elementary proposition, however, is a structure composed entirely of names picturing the immediate combination of objects in an atomic fact; it can, accordingly, be understood only if the meanings of the names are known. But, as they are logically proper names they are indefinable and so their meanings cannot be communicated either by definition or by demonstrative gesture. The way in which the names occur in the proposition mirrors the structure of the fact, and structure is not expressible by language. Accordingly, neither the names nor the structure can be defined or explained in any way, and as their sole function is to picture the facts, which are facts of immediate experience, communication of the sense of elementary propositions (and so of all others) is an impossibility. The meaning of signs, therefore, can be understood only by the person using them, for symbolic reference is only to direct experience and a sign used by one person signifies something that no other person can directly experience. It can therefore be interpreted by others only in terms of their own perception of the behaviour of the user. Thus, Wittgenstein and Ayer argue that

[1] *Tractatus*, 5·62 *et seq.*
[2] *Examination of Logical Positivism*, chs. vii and viii.

'A says (knows, believes, thinks, etc.) p' is not a truth-function of p but the statement of a fact about A's behaviour (or his dispositions to use signs on the appropriate occasions).[1] If this were so, language could not be a means of communication and would become the medium of expression of a purely private experience that could not be the experience of a common or objective world. It is plain that such a doctrine can give no account of our membership of the world which we know in science, for not only does science become something entirely subjective (the antithesis of what we normally understand by the scientific knowledge of objective fact) but, as will presently appear, the knowing mind could only be a member of the experienced world by forfeiting the knowledge of that world and becoming a mere logical construction within the linguistic system by which the facts of sense-experience are expressed.

Carnap attempts to avoid the solipsism implied in Wittgenstein's position by rejecting atomic facts and regarding experience as a given totality which forms the basis of a system of concepts (or 'objects') derived from it by abstraction.[2] These concepts are derived from elementary experience by the formation of logical constructions, the principle of which is the linguistic definition enabling sentences containing the name of the concept to be replaced, without alteration of truth or meaning, by others containing only the names of the concepts from which the first is constructed. In this way the world is built up in three stages: (a) the construction of the private psychical realm (the self), (b) the construction of the world of physical things and (c) the psychical realm of other persons.

It is not necessary to go into the details of the process of construction. It will be sufficient to observe that physical objects are first constructed out of visual sense-contents, 'my body' and 'other persons' bodies' among them. An 'expressive relation' is then assumed between psychical processes and bodily movements, facial expressions, utterances and the like; and also a 'psycho-physical relation' connecting psychical processes with corresponding processes in the physical organism. The use of a sign by some other person to designate an object is then interpreted as the co-ordination of that person's behaviour in

---

[1] *Vide* Ayer, *Thinking and Meaning*, pp. 16 ff., and Wittgenstein, *Tractatus*, 5·542: 'But it is clear that "A believes that p", "A thinks p", "A says p", are of the form "'p' says p'". The implication is that A does not think at all, and indeed to say that he does would be meaningless for the positivist in any other than a behaviouristic sense.

[2] *Vide Der logische Aufbau der Welt* (Berlin, 1928), p. 92. The similarity to Bradley's doctrine will be immediately apparent. See above, p. 258.

M

using the sign with the occurrence of the object. All this, as Weinberg points out,[1] is a logical construction within one experience (presumably 'mine'), so that sentences used by other persons are never *symbols* but only *facts*—instances of behaviour. The correlation of these facts with other facts, *i.e.* those of psychical occurrences in 'the mind' of the person speaking, is again purely a matter of logical construction, in which a great deal seems to be taken for granted. What does seem clear is that the elementary experience of another person is never, and on this theory never can be, communicated, if it can be said at all to exist.

Using the same methods of construction, Carnap asserts that it is possible to construct the world of another person and to determine what, in that world, constitute the objects correlative to the objects in 'my' world, and then, by means of this correlation, to construct an 'intersubjective' world, which is the world of science. In this way solipsism is thought to have been overcome.

But solipsism is far from having been overcome. In the first place the argument is circular, for the physical world of objects has to be constructed as a prior condition of the construction of the worlds of other persons and must be assumed in the correlation of them with 'mine'. The allegedly 'intersubjective' world is therefore no more intersubjective than the world originally constructed from 'my' private experience. But worse than this, 'my' self, and so presumably also 'my' private experience, is no more than a construction out of the total mass of elementary experience that constitutes the world. What then does the constructing? Are we not here in imminent danger of having to postulate an Absolute Mind, or a transcendent God, or some other awful metaphysical entity, the affirmation of whose existence could never be verified?

Ayer's effort to escape what he calls 'the egocentric predicament' succeeds no better. He criticizes Carnap for saying (in *The Unity of Science*) that the protocol languages of different persons, each referring to the content of the experience of a separate person, are not intercommunicable either with one another or with the physical language, 'for the realms of experience of two persons do not overlap'. This, Ayer maintains, is a mistake, because it does not follow, from the fact that the two realms of experience do not overlap, that a protocol-sentence used by one person cannot occur in the language used by another.[2] Nor, he says, does it follow from the reference of sentences of protocol languages to private experience that the languages themselves are private. Protocol-sentences, Ayer maintains, can be, and are,

[1] *Op. cit.* p. 219.   [2] *Foundations of Empirical Knowledge*, p. 150.

perfectly well expressed in a language which is common to a number of people.

The mistake, however, lies rather with Ayer than with Carnap, for a sentence may be regarded either as a symbol or as a sign. As a sign it is merely a fact to be observed; but as a symbol it has meaning, and its meaning is, according to the positivist theory, the method of its verification. That, again, by Ayer's own argument, involves its reduction to basic propositions directly expressing sense-experiences. As a symbol therefore, it can be significant only as referring to private experience and its significance cannot be communicated. Its common use as a sign is irrelevant to this fact and means no more than that 'I' observe other people to use the same sign as 'I' do in correlation with the occurrence of certain objects which 'I' have constructed within 'my' experience.

The privacy of sense-data Ayer holds to be largely a matter of linguistic convention, inasmuch as 'we have resolved not to attach any meaning to the statement that different observers sense the same sense-datum',[1] and he suggests conditions under which we might be inclined to alter the convention which we now normally adopt.[2] Further, he regards the fact that a particular experience is 'mine' rather than somebody else's as a purely contingent matter. Where selves are no more than logical constructions and where there is no necessary connection between sense-data, this is a very natural opinion to hold. Whatever I sense, therefore, might have been experienced by another person and *vice versa* and the verifiability of basic propositions would then involve nothing different in principle from that of propositions about the past.[3] But what all this overlooks is that 'my' self as well as other selves *are* nothing but logical constructions (according to the theory) and that logical constructions are only operations upon language according to certain rules of formation and transformation of sentences; so that what is contingent is only the way in which the constructions are applied to the facts concerned. Those facts are and can but be facts of sense-experience which is undeniably 'private' in a way which cannot be accounted for in terms of logical constructions nor explained away by their means. All that Ayer is doing is turning in circles within the enclosure of his own sense-data, and that he is to some extent aware of the fact is indicated by his admission [4] that the argument he has used here 'is very dubious'.

Logical positivism is inescapably committed to solipsism, and that it is, as Weinberg says, a solipsism without a subject is nothing

---

[1] *Ibid.* p. 153; *vide* also pp. 138 ff.   [2] *Ibid.* pp. 141 f.
[3] *Ibid.* pp. 167 f.   [4] *Vide Language, Truth and Logic*, pp. 19-20.

remarkable; for no solipsism can admit a subject as opposed to an object if only because the existence of the object is denied and its correlative must go with it. Solipsism, furthermore, goes hand in hand with phenomenalism, and once thorough-going phenomenalism is professed, all talk of verification must be given up. For phenomenalism there can be no distinction between appearance and reality and so none between falsity and truth, and once that distinction has disappeared, to speak of verification is to use words without meaning. Ayer contends that the distinction depends on the predictive reliability of the judgements we make about sense-data. But, apart from the difficulties in the way of prediction which have already been observed to beset this theory, if sense-data are supposed not to be inferrible one from another, any successful prediction must be purely accidental. To appeal to the principle of induction will not help, for if there is no necessary connection between one empirical fact and another, to judge of the future in the light of the past is an entirely arbitrary procedure. Consequently, we are left without a criterion of truth, and the very word 'verification' loses its meaning.

13. (ii) The conception of logic canvassed by logical positivists, so far from mitigating the difficulty, only plunges the doctrine deeper into scepticism. Logic is conceived as a purely formal discipline concerned with the syntax of the language in which propositions are expressed. Being formal, no reference whatever is made in it to the meanings of the symbols used, and the sole purpose of the science is to define classes of symbols and logical terms, to set out an axiom-system and to formulate rules for the formation and transformation of sentences in the language concerned. As no reference is made to the meanings of the symbols, it is maintained (in Carnap's words) 'that we have in every respect complete liberty with regard to the forms of language; that both the forms of construction for sentences and the rules of transformation ... may be chosen quite arbitrarily'.[1] What forms we adopt and what meanings we give to our symbols may be determined purely according to their convenience for practical purposes, but that is not a matter of logic; it is a matter of practical policy. In logic there is no such thing as 'correctness' (except, we may presume, within the scope of the axiom-system and the rules arbitrarily laid down). The striving after 'correctness', says Carnap, is an impediment which has now been overcome, 'and before us lies the boundless ocean of unlimited possibilities'.[2]

It follows that there are no necessary propositions in logic any more

---

[1] *Logical Syntax of Language*, p. xv.   [2] *Loc. cit.*

than there are in the empirical realm, or rather that such necessity as exists is purely provisional and is limited to a syntactical system which is itself arbitrary. The source of this internal necessity is, moreover, no more than tautology and every necessary proposition is exclusively analytic, asserting nothing, but merely repeating in different forms the same syntactical formulation. According to Ayer, all we are doing in enunciating an analytic proposition is 'calling attention to the implications of a certain linguistic usage' (though the word 'implications' must surely be misplaced, for all we should be doing is restating the linguistic usage in another way). Logical propositions are, therefore, necessary because they say nothing, and the necessity they contain is not a connection between contents or concepts but only the necessity that two equivalent terms asserted one of another should constitute a repetition. It does not derive, therefore, from the axioms or the rules of the system but is a matter of self-evidence. 'Every logical proposition', writes Ayer, 'is valid in its own right. Its validity does not depend on its being incorporated in a system, and deduced from certain propositions which are taken to be self-evident.'[1]

The effect of a strict application of this notion of logic to the logical-positivistic doctrine as a whole is most deleterious. It is vaguely felt by its authors and begins to be evident in their view that the choice of protocol-sentences in a linguistic system is arbitrary. This being so, the reduction of an empirical hypothesis to elementary propositions—the whole method of its verification—is arbitrary likewise, and to make a proposition verifiable all that we need do is to choose our linguistic system in such a way that it can be reduced to elementary propositions. There is nothing in the nature of the case to prevent our constructing a 'transcendental' language in which this sort of verification would be possible for metaphysical propositions—in which the elementary propositions were all non-empirical. But this possibility has not been developed by logical positivist writers. Nor is its development necessary in order to show that if verification is to be a significant term we need some better conception of logic than they provide.

If the only necessity ever contemplated is the self-evidence of a tautology, the necessity by which we observe the syntactical rules arbitrarily adopted is excluded. This is not simply because the rules adopted are arbitrary, but because the statement of a rule of procedure is not a tautology. Consider, for example, this passage from *The Logical Syntax of Language* (I have substituted Latin for Gothic lettering for typographical simplicity); 'S_3 is called directly derivable from

---

[1] *Language*, etc., p. 81.

S_1, or from S_1 and S_2, when one of the following conditions is fulfilled:

1. S_3 has the form $S_1\left(\dfrac{z}{Z}\right)$.

2. (a) S_3 is obtained from S_1 by replacing a partial sentence (proper or improper) of the form $S_4 \vee S_5$ by $\sim S_4 \supset S_5$, or conversely; (b) likewise with the forms $S_4.S_5$ and $\sim (\sim S_4 \vee \sim S_5)$; (c) likewise with the forms $S_4 \equiv S_5$ and $(S_4 \supset S_5).(S_5 \supset S_4) \ldots$'[1] Taken as a single statement, this is an hypothetical proposition of the form, If p then q (or, q on the conditions x, y, etc.). It is a syntactical proposition and therefore not an empirical hypothesis; but it is not a tautology (although the conditions of derivability quoted are such that to be derivable one from another two sentences have to be synonymous). But the statement that S_3 may be derived from S_1 if they are synonymous is not itself tautologous. For if it be held to be a definition of synonymity (a determination to use 'synonymous' in a certain way) it cannot, at the same time, be a definition of derivability; and if it be a definition of derivability, it cannot be one of synonymity. And even if it is taken to be no more than the assertion that derivability and synonymity are the same thing, it is still a synthetic proposition. But if that is so it cannot be necessary, and as a transformation rule it cannot hold universally even in the syntactical system to which it applies. In fact, the very interconnection of parts that gives the word 'system' its meaning disappears.

But if formation and transformation rules are not universally valid within the language to which they belong, and if there is no internal necessity binding together the elements of a syntactical system, the whole edifice of logic immediately disintegrates and it is even doubtful whether the barest tautologies would be assertable—for even the assertion that A is A presupposes some rule prescribing the conditions of identity. And if logical necessity fails us, the processes of empirical verification are paralysed because they are processes of reasoning and involve logical principles. We cannot tell, for instance, what is entailed by an empirical hypothesis unless we can rely on some rules of inference (or transformation rules), and if such rules are not universally valid even in the language used they are useless for our purpose. Further, empirical proof (or verification) takes the form: If p, then x will be experienced. That is the form of an hypothetical proposition and it involves some sort of logical nexus, even if it is only one which arises from the manner in which language is used.

Finally, then, the positivistic principle that all significance is derived from empirical reference, which is only the empirical principle pressed

[1] *Op. cit.* p. 32.

to its uttermost extremity, destroys all knowledge; for by reducing logical propositions to tautologies and emptying them of significance it undermines the very empirical reference which is the only acknowledged criterion of truth upon which its advocates rely.

IV. PSEUDO-SCIENCES?

14. The attempt to erect new sciences of language on so hollow a foundation is hardly likely to produce anything genuinely scientific, and though the sciences collectively known as Semiotic appear at the present time to flourish in some quarters, many of their pronouncements provoke the judgement that they are pseudo-sciences. I am not prepared dogmatically to assert that a genuine science of the use of signs by human and other animals is not a possibility, or even that it may not be profitable. Much of it, I should imagine, would fall within the legitimate province of psychology, and perhaps a special branch of pictography might be included within it. I should also be disinclined to deny that much valuable work has been done, and that more may still be done, by philologists and etymologists on the clarification and exact determination of the meanings of words. There may be a real and important field of study forming the province of a genuine science of semantics and it is far from my intention (and it would be an impertinence for me to attempt) to attack the results of researches which may have been conducted within that field. But the sciences which go by the name of semiotic in certain contemporary philosophical circles are quite different, and though space will not here permit of a thorough analysis of them, a few examples of their manner of procedure and of the kind of results they have produced will be sufficient to show whether they may be expected to fulfil the requirements of genuinely scientific investigation.

In order to judge the value of a science some yard-stick is required by which to measure its integrity, and though the detailed requirements of genuine science could not be set out without a complete methodological account of the nature of science, certain obvious minima can be stated which would generally be admitted. Of these Collingwood has suggested three:[1] (i) a genuine science does not pursue red herrings; that is, it does not, under the pretence of discussing one topic, discuss something entirely different (especially, I should add, if the topic of which it is supposed to be treating is fundamental to its subject-matter); (ii) it does not contradict itself by pronouncing as

[1] *Metaphysics*, p. 122.

the fruits of scientific research two propositions which cancel each other out; (iii) it does not indulge in plagiarism by presenting as discoveries of its own what are in fact matters of common knowledge. I should include under this third requirement the avoidance of platitudes wrapped up in complicated technical jargon and the pontifical pronouncement of empty tautologies. Besides these three marks of a genuine science suggested by Collingwood, I should be inclined to add a fourth: the avoidance of the use of elaborate technical devices in order to produce futile results.

15. Semiotic is divided by its professors into three branches: syntactics, the formal science of the structure of language, which includes all that has hitherto passed by the name of symbolic logic; semantics, the study of the relation between signs and the objects which they designate; and pragmatics, which is concerned with the relation of signs to their users and interpreters. As examples of pragmatical investigations, Carnap gives: 'a physiological analysis of the processes in the speaking organs and in the nervous system connected with speaking activities; a psychological analysis of the relations between speaking behaviour and other behaviour; a psychological study of the different connotations of one and the same word for different individuals; ethnological and sociological studies of the speaking habits and their differences in different tribes, different age groups, social strata; a study of the procedures applied by scientists in recording the results of experiments, etc.'[1] The systematic development of this third branch of semiotic has not yet been seriously attempted, but it is pretty plain from the examples offered by Carnap of the topics which would fall within its sphere that it would be little more than a hodge-podge of results taken from other sciences. I shall therefore confine myself to discussion of the other two, and it is not difficult to cull examples from syntactics and semantics exemplifying failure to satisfy all four of the suggested tests for genuine scientific pronouncement.

16. (1) *Syntactics*. I am not competent to judge whether symbolic logic may be regarded as a genuine and valuable branch of mathematics, but its claim to afford a theory of logic certainly cannot be substantiated. Despite controversy it would be generally admitted that the central and most important topic of logic is the nature of inference —the principle according to which a conclusion may be educed from premises—and what has rightly been called 'the nerve of inference' is

[1] *Introduction to Semantics* (Harvard University Press, 1946), p. 10.

implication. The acid test of the genuinely scientific character of a logical theory should thus be its treatment of implication. That the various accounts of implication provided by symbolic logic do not even touch the principle which actually operates in ordinary scientific and common-sense thought, has been very ably demonstrated by Blanshard [1]—so ably, in fact, that one feels tempted to quote at length his thorough and close-knit reasoning in order to show that what in symbolic logic purports to be a theory of implication—one of the most important, if not quite the most important topic with which the science is concerned—is no more than the pursuit of a red herring. I shall, however, content myself with a summary of Blanshard's conclusions.

It is clear from his reasoning that all three forms of implication which appear in symbolic logic, material, formal and strict, come to the same thing in the end: namely, a relation between two propositions (or propositional functions) such that (i) they both happen to be true, or (ii) they both happen to be false, or (iii) the first happens to be false while the second is true (in the case of strict implication 'self-consistent' and 'non-self-consistent' are substituted for 'true' and 'false'). It is a relation that involves no necessity, for the logic is extensional, and if we are precise we must deny that it is a relation at all. Blanshard admits the relation of likeness in the first two cases and that of unlikeness in the third, but in so doing he concedes too much, for the likeness and unlikeness are not between the propositions themselves but between the value judgements we pass upon them. There is no relation between petty larceny and adultery, not even that of likeness, which makes them both morally reprehensible; similarly, there is no relation between propositions which makes them coincidentally true or false. But even if we allow the relation of coincidence, the definition of implication in symbolic logic makes it, not that, but a *disjunction* of cases in which different (alleged) relations hold. To treat a disjunction of heterogeneous relationships between propositions as if it were one particular kind of relation is hardly the mark of scientific procedure; but what is more important is that implication as here defined cannot be the principle which enables us to infer the truth of a proposition from our knowledge of the truth of another, because unless and until we know whether both of the propositions are true or false we cannot tell if the so-called relation of implication holds. We can never know that q follows from p, unless we know the cases in which q is true, which means that we could never *infer* the truth of q from that of p without

---

[1] *Vide* Brand Blanshard, *The Nature of Thought* (London, 1939), ch. xxix. Cf. H. W. B. Joseph in *Mind*, XLI, XLII and XLIII.

petitio principii. The implication of symbolic logic, accordingly, is not the implication in which the genuine logician is interested, and if the theory offered is supposed to be one of genuine implication it is an imposture.

One example will suffice to show that symbolic logic claims without turning a hair the proof, by scientific methods, of both of two contradictory propositions. In Lewis and Langford's text-book of the science we find the theorem:[1]

$$\sim(p \circ p) \prec \sim(p \circ q),$$

i.e. a proposition which is not consistent with itself is not consistent with any proposition. But a few pages further on we find this theorem used to prove the following:[2]

$$\sim \diamond p . \prec . p \prec q,$$

i.e. a proposition which is self-contradictory or impossible strictly implies any proposition. It is, however, a blatant contradiction that a proposition should imply that with which it is inconsistent and the two theorems are in violent conflict. The first is plausible but the second is a desperate paradox. Yet not only does the symbolic logician claim to prove each of them by strict scientific demonstration, but he does not scruple to use one as a means to the proof of the other.

The enunciation of tautologies and platitudes in technical jargon so complicated as to be almost unintelligible is to be found in almost every section of Carnap's *Logical Syntax of Language*. One example of this has already been quoted from the statement of rules for inference in Language I. These rules state the conditions on which a sentence is said to be directly derivable from other sentences (S_3 from S_1 or from S_1 and S_2) and Rule 3 gives one of these conditions as 'S_2 has the form $S_1 \supset S_3$'. (Again I have replaced Gothic by Latin lettering.) But $S_1 \supset S_3$ means no more than that S_3 is derivable from S_1, so that this rule is the barest of tautologies. And the rest are hardly less platitudinous, for, as every careful reader will observe, they amount only to the assertion that S_3 is derivable from S_1 if it means the same as S_1.

One more example may be permitted from the same source:[3]

'The *regressive definition* of an $fu_1{}^n$ has the form: (a) $fu_1{}^n$ (nu, $\mathfrak{z}_2$, . . . $\mathfrak{z}n$) = $\mathfrak{Z}_1$; (b) $fu_1{}^n$ ($\mathfrak{z}_1{}'$, $\mathfrak{z}_2$, . . . $\mathfrak{z}n$) = $\mathfrak{Z}_2$. In $\mathfrak{Z}_2$, $fu_1{}^n$ is always followed by the argument-expression $\mathfrak{z}_1$, $\mathfrak{z}_2$ . . . $\mathfrak{z}n$, the variables of which are not bound. *Example*: Def. 3 for "prod", p. 59 [1. prod $(0, y) = 0$; 2. prod $(x', y) =$ sum (prod $(x, y), y)$]; the first equation

[1] Lewis and Langford, *Symbolic Logic*, p. 167, Theorem 19.1.
[2] *Ibid.* p. 174, Theorem 19.74.   [3] *Op. cit.* p. 24.

serves for the transformation of $\mathfrak{fu}_1$ (nu, 3); the second equation refers $\mathfrak{fu}_1$ (3₃', 3₄) back to $\mathfrak{fu}_1$ (3₃, 3₄) so that, for example, in "prod (6, y)", by using the second equation six times and the first equation once, "prod" may be eliminated.'

All this tells us is that the 'regressive definition' of a functor is one which employs two equations, the first displaying the result of the operation with the functor upon nought, and the second the result of its operation on any other number in terms of its predecessor, so that it can be discovered by regression. The example shows that we can in this way define 'product' by displaying the facts (a) that $0 \times y = 0$ and (b) that (for instance) $6 \times y = y + y + y + y + y + y$, the suggested method being as follows:

$$\begin{aligned} 6y &= 5y + y \\ &= 4y + y + y \\ &= 3y + y + y + y \\ &= 2y + y + y + y + y \\ &= y + y + y + y + y + y. \end{aligned}$$

Parturiunt montes—from the prodigious effervescence of symbols issues the kind of definition of an arithmetical operation which might be appropriate in the kindergarten.

The employment of elaborate technical procedures in order to produce futile results is exemplified by the use made of Poretsky's Law to show that from any premise or set of premises 'an infinite number' of valid conclusions may be drawn.[1] The law states:

$a = 0$ is equivalent to $t = a - t + - at$;
$a = b$ is equivalent to $t = (a - b + - ab) - t + (ab + - a - b)t$.

As an example, the following premises are taken:

All men (a) are mortal (b): $a - b = 0$
All men (a) are fallible (c): $a - c = 0$.

The combined premises, $a - b + a - c = 0$ are equivalent to

$$t = (a - b + a - c) - t + - (a - b + a - c)t.$$

Choosing b for t, we get the result:

$$\begin{aligned} b &= (a - b + a - c) - b + - (a - b + a - c)b \\ &= a - b + a - b - c + (- a + b)(- a + c)b \\ &= a - b + (- a + - ab + - ac + bc)b \\ &= a - b + - ab + bc, \end{aligned}$$

[1] *Vide* Lewis and Langford, *Symbolic Logic*, pp. 70 ff.

which gives the impressive conclusion, 'The mortal beings are those who are men but not mortal, or mortal but not men or fallible mortals' It is admitted by the symbolist that the implication that there are men who are not mortal is false, but this is discounted on the ground that the class of immortal men is taken to be 'empty', so that its addition to others makes no difference. It is not, however, stated whether this also excuses the flat contradiction of the suggestion that some mortal beings are not mortal. It is admitted also (and we may readily agree) that to add an empty class in this way is no more than a logical 'joke' and that the final result is useless, but for this fact we are to console ourselves with the authors' questionable testimony that it is logically valid.

By substituting *bc* for *t* and making a similar algebraical calculation we achieve the result 'All those who are either men but not mortal or men but not fallible are fallible mortals', and we must suppress our astonishment when we are told that this blatant self-contradiction is only another way of saying that all men are fallible and all men are mortal. Having done so, however, we shall observe that that is what we knew to begin with.

Substitution of *a* for *t* gives the less surprising but not more informative conclusion that 'All men are fallible mortals', and, as the authors of the work quoted remark, 'we seem not to have had much luck in drawing from our premises conclusions which are both important and other than obvious' (I should have said 'either . . . or'). But as we are entitled to substitute for *t* anything we please, it is quite probable that some of the infinite number of conclusions we could draw would be not a little exciting.

(2) *Semantics*. The special subject-matter of semantics is the relation of signs to their *designata*; and, as truth is held to consist in the agreement of a proposition with the fact it pictures, the relation of the signs by which the proposition is expressed (*i.e.* the sentence) to the objects for which they stand should be of great moment for the discovery of the conditions on which sentences can express true propositions. 'A *semantical system*', says Carnap, 'is a system of rules which state *truth-conditions* for the sentences of an object language and thereby determine the meaning of these sentences.'[1] This is a matter of no mean importance, and if we find that the account given by the semanticist of truth-conditions is lacking in significance, our suspicion that the science is not genuine will be confirmed.

We learn from Carnap that 'to assert that a sentence is true means

[1] *Introduction to Semantics*, p. 22.

the same as to assert the sentence itself'.[1] He gives us, also, an example of the construction of a semantical system in which individual constants are symbolized by 'in$_1$', 'in$_2$', 'in$_3$', etc. (he uses Gothic symbols to indicate object-language) and predicates by 'pr$_1$', 'pr$_2$', etc.

in$_1$ designates Chicago.

in$_2$ designates New York.

in$_3$ designates Carmel.

pr$_1$ designates the property of being large.

pr$_2$ designates the property of having a harbour.

Truth-conditions are then stated as follows:

pr$_1$(in$_1$) is true if and only if Chicago is large.

pr$_1$(in$_2$) is true if and only if New York is large.

pr$_1$(in$_3$) is true if and only if Carmel is large.

pr$_2$(in$_1$) is true if and only if Chicago has a harbour . . .

and so on.

To say 'pr$_1$(in$_1$) is true', however, means the same as to assert 'pr$_1$(in$_1$)', and that again means (or 'designates') 'Chicago is large'. The truth condition for pr$_1$(in$_1$) in consequence is: 'Chicago is large if and only if Chicago is large', and that is the emptiest of tautologies. We find, then, that the only help we can derive from semantics in discovering the conditions on which sentences express true propositions is no help at all, for we are not advanced one step by being told that a sentence is true if and only if it is true. If this is what is meant in semantics by conditions of truth, it is not what is normally meant by ordinary scientists and laymen, nor is it anything in the least significant. Accordingly, semantics, in pretending to discuss truth-conditions, is trailing a large and very artificial red herring across the main road of its province of investigation.

Further, the pseudo-scientific character of the proceeding is characteristically displayed when the poverty of this supposed concept of truth is camouflaged under the following network of technicalities: '$\mathfrak{A}_i$ is true in $S_2 =_{Df} (\exists x)(\exists y)(\exists z)(\exists F)[\mathfrak{A}_i$ consists of x, $\mathfrak{a}_6$ y, $\mathfrak{a}_7$ in this order and $x \epsilon \mathfrak{R}_2$ and $y \epsilon \mathfrak{R}_1$ and $[(y = \mathfrak{a}_1$ and $z =$ Chicago) or $(y = \mathfrak{a}_2$ and $z =$ New York) or $(y = \mathfrak{a}_3$ and $z =$ Carmel)$]$ and $[(x = \mathfrak{a}_4$ and $F =$ the property of being large) or $(x = \mathfrak{a}_5$ and $F =$ the property of having a harbour)$]$ and $F(z)]$'.

It might be objected by the semanticist that this criticism is unfair because it fails to observe the distinction between object-language and meta-language. In the examples given above, sentences of the form 'pr$_I$(in$_I$)', etc. are sentences in the object-language, ' "pr$_I$(in$_I$)" is true' and the like are sentences in the meta-language, while 'Chicago is large' is simply the statement of a fact. Hence, what the truth-condition tells us is that the sentence in the object-language is true if (and only if) it corresponds with the fact to which it refers. But this truth-condition is still spurious, for the reference of the sentence is contained in what the proposition asserts. 'Chicago is large' attributes largeness to Chicago: it asserts the largeness of Chicago to be a fact. It cannot help us to discover whether or not this is true to be told that it is true only if the fact asserted is a fact.

Moreover, the distinction between object- and meta-languages is itself pseudo-scientific, representing either no real distinction or quite a different one from that supposed. It springs, like so much else in semiotic, from the metaphysical doctrine that propositions picture facts and are projected as sentences. That further projections should be made of these would seem, therefore, not to be impossible, and of these again, and so on *ad libitum*. But even the assumed metaphysic should lead one to suspect an error, for in all these projections of projections the *sense* of the sentences is always the same, and that, we must never forget, is all that language of any sort can ever express. It should never be possible, therefore, to construct a language about another language, but only to construct an alternative language about the facts. And when we seek to discover from the writings of the semanticists what the meta-language in any instance is, we find either that it is another language on the same level as the object-language (*e.g.* German in a treatise about English), or a mere transliteration of the symbols of the supposed object-language into symbols of a different character (Gothic into Latin), or else it involves no more than the enclosure of the words and sentences of the object-language in a set of quotation marks. C. W. Morris makes this perfectly clear when he writes:[1] 'A sign combination such as " "Fido" designates A" is an instance of a sentence in the language of semantics. Here " "Fido" " denotes "Fido" (*i.e.* the sign or the sign vehicle and not a non-linguistic object), while "A" is an indexical sign of some object (it might be the word "that" used in connection with some directive gesture). " "Fido" " is thus a term in the meta-language denoting the sign "Fido" in the object language; "A" is a term in the thing-language denoting a thing.' But, as the object-language is the same as the thing-language 'Fido' and 'A' are identical—the sentence in the

[1] *Foundations of a Theory of Signs* (Chicago, 1938), p. 22.

meta-language could have been written: ''Fido' designates Fido'. Accordingly, the distinction between meta-language and object-language is no distinction; unless it is one of subject-matter—that of the meta-language being linguistic and that of the object-language not.

But to mistake a distinction of one sort for one of quite another sort is by no means scientific, and when the substitution is used to create the impression that trivial and rather silly tautologies convey important information, it is the undoubted mark of a pseudo-science. It is indeed remarkable that philosophers usually so ready to protest against the invention of bogus entities should have gone to such lengths to give to airy nothing a local habitation and a name.

17. I think I may claim to have made my point sufficiently clear without giving further examples, and I have already been occupied long enough with logical positivism. I have tried to show that in order to maintain the meaninglessness of metaphysics it must itself rest upon a metaphysic, and a metaphysic that is, moreover, vicious; that in limiting the significance of language to its empirical reference it has undermined all knowledge, whether factual or *a priori*, by insisting on a test of empirical truth which is inapplicable and by reducing to arbitrary convention the canons of right reason; that it is confined to a solipsistic phenomenalism in which the knowing self, the objective world and the minds of other persons are all spirited away in a mist of linguistic equivalences going by the name of logical construction, so that we are left only with a subjectless stream of sense-experience and a web of linguistic conventions, established and accepted by one cannot say whom; for minds are themselves but the product of logical construction, which is dependent on these very conventions, and thinking no more than the 'behaviour' of yet other such logical constructions. In the epistemological wilderness thus created the pseudo-sciences of semiotic are the mirages, beguiling the traveller with the specious appearance of knowledge, and abandoning him to intellectual inanity.

All this is the final fruit of an empiricism which has reverted out of due season to the metaphysical presuppositions of Renaissance science and has so monopolized the fora of contemporary philosophical discussion that it still remains what Collingwood held it to be, the undischarged bankrupt of modern philosophy.

Section C
Contemporary Science and Philosophy

Chapter XVII

MODERN SCIENCE

I. SCIENTIFIC VERIFICATION

1. IT is commonly claimed for empiricism that it is a scientific philosophy in harmony with the scientific temper of the modern age. It will be my object in this chapter to show that this is far from being the case.

Since the time of Plato it has been recognized that the business of the scientist is to formulate hypotheses which will 'save the appearances'. It is what he observes that prompts the hypothesis as a means of rendering those observations intelligible and the test of the hypothesis, whatever else it may include, certainly does require that it should be consistent with the observed facts. It is, however, important to understand just what sort of facts are needed for scientific verification, and it is very easy to show that they are not bare sense-data nor anything the occurrence of which could be recorded in 'protocol' sentences.

Let us consider what J. B. Conant calls a 'case history' in 'the tactics and strategy of science'.[1] I shall choose an example which is comparatively simple and as favourable as any to the positivist interpretation—that of the overthrow by Lavoisier of the phlogiston theory of combustion.[2] The hypothesis current in the 18th century to explain the observed facts of combustion was that a fluid substance, phlogiston, was contained in inflammable materials and was given off during combustion. Thus the formation of an oxide (known as a calx) by heating a metal was thought to be due to the emission of phlogiston, and the re-formation of the metal, by heating the calx with charcoal, to the combination of the calx with the phlogiston given off by the burning charcoal. It was found that the calx was invariably heavier than the metal and so phlogiston was said to be 'naturally light' (like Aristotle's fire). Lavoisier disproved all this by means of his classic experiments

---

[1] Vide On Understanding Science (Oxford, 1947).
[2] Vide ibid. pp. 74-97.

with mercury. By heating a quantity of the metal of definite weight in a retort, the outlet of which led into a vessel containing air and inverted over water, he found that, as the mercury was calcined, the volume of air in the vessel decreased a measurable amount and the weight of the calx exceeded that of the metal. He then reversed the process by heating the calx in a crucible enclosed in a vessel similarly inverted over water and found that the volume of air in the vessel increased by the same amount as, in the former experiment, it had decreased, and the weight of the re-formed metal was the same as it had been originally.

These experiments proved that the increase in weight could be correlated with the absorption of a gas, afterwards identified as oxygen (Priestley's 'dephlogisticated air'), and the loss of weight in the reverse process with the emission of this same gas. The hypothesis of phlogiston was thus disproved.

2. What exactly is the evidence relevant to the establishment of the theory of oxidization? In Lavoisier's experiments it consists of the facts: (i) that the volume of air in the enclosed vessel first decreases as the mercury calcines, (ii) then that it increases as the calx is reconverted into metal; (iii) that these changes are the same in quantity; (iv) that they correlate with the observed changes in weight. None of these 'facts' are, of course, the bare occurrence of sense-data. But are they even perceived as such? No doubt the movement of the water-levels inside and outside of the enclosed vessel is perceived. But it is not barely sensed. What is sensed is interpreted as such movement. Further, what is sensed?—certain colours and lines, shall we say, interpreted as marks on a measuring scale, coinciding with others, interpreted as the level of the water, and so forth. If any of these can be recorded in protocol sentences, they do not in the least, as so recorded, give us what we want. The perception of coincidence between certain marks and other marks, apart from its being itself an interpretation, does not amount to a measurement or a pointer-reading. That implies a whole system of interpretations, involving the interpretation of some sensuous apprehensions as the perception of a measuring instrument, the interpretation again of the behaviour of the measuring instrument in terms of scales and units of measurement, and of yet other sensuous apprehensions as the behaviour of the liquids and other bodies which are being measured.

Even so, the observation of pointer-readings, or coincidences between liquid-levels, and marks on a scale, is not, by itself, relevant as evidence for a theory unless it is interpreted in terms of an arrangement of objects and events which gives it significance as the measurement of just what is needed. In the example under consideration, the position of the water-levels on the scale has no relevance at all except as an indication of the volume of air enclosed in the vessel. It is such an indication only for a mind which comprehends the whole system of facts involved in the experiment, and it can be accepted as evidence only on certain quite definite (but unstated) assumptions which are not specifically observed (*e.g.* that the water itself does not emit gas, that the vessel is not porous, and so on). Again the *correlation* of the changes in weight with those in volume cannot be observed at all, it can only be inferred, and in more complicated scientific experiments such correlations would have to be calculated. The greater part of the evidence in most modern experiments consists in the results of calculation which could never be given directly in sense-perception. Einstein's special theory of relativity, for instance, was established partly by the exact calculation it made possible of the aberrations in the movement of Mercury. The facts had been observed long before, but, apart from these calculations, they established nothing (except the difficulty of accounting for Mercury's behaviour on Newtonian principles).

This all goes to show that any attempt to reduce scientific evidence to bare sense-data would deprive it of everything that makes it scientifically relevant—namely, its interpretation in terms of a developed body of systematic knowledge, apart from which no purely sensuous apprehension can have any scientific value or significance.

Scientific verification, in short, is not, as it is so frequently misunderstood to be, comparison of the theory with the observed facts. The observation of a fact is itself an interpretation involving theory, and the scientist's purpose is the development of that interpretation, its adjustment and correction to render it coherent whenever some elements in it collide with others, and its integration into a single systematic body of scientific knowledge. This is quite clearly shown in the example taken. The evidence is itself the result of considerable interpretation and inference, and it is only by systematic correlation of the facts observed that the theory emerges:

The volume of air in the enclosed vessel decreases during calcination (interpretation of the perception of changes in the water levels); the weight of the calx is found to be to a definite extent in excess of that of the metal (inference from the perception of the behaviour of a balance on various occasions). If the increase in weight is due to the fixation of oxygen, that could be derived only from the air in the vessel (another inference depending on the system of objects and events involved in the experiment); the volume of air would accordingly decrease (further inference) . . . and so forth.

3. Scientists have long believed in the fallacy that their method was to compare theory with observation and to make the first correspond with the second; but in so doing they have been misled by preconceptions about the relation of mind to nature to which their practice has never conformed. 'A scientist commonly professes to base his beliefs on observation, not theories', writes Sir Arthur Eddington, '. . . I have never come across anyone who carries this profession into practice—certainly not the hard-headed experimentalist. . . . Observation is not sufficient. We do not believe our eyes unless we are first convinced that what they appear to tell us is credible.'[1]

Empiricism is the philosophical doctrine which arose out of those same preconceptions and the claim that it is adapted to the temper of a scientific age is therefore unfounded. When the nature of scientific verification is properly understood, it becomes clear that the teachings of the empiricists are altogether discordant with the practice of scientists, not only in the modern era but in any age; and what the above description of scientific procedure indicates is that a much better account of scientific method is given by those philosophical theories which adopt coherence as their criterion of truth. For the work of the scientist is always the building of a system in the light of which the facts, unintelligible in isolation, become explicable. Coherence as the test of truth is much more definitely one of the presuppositions of contemporary science, which have so far changed from those of the 17th century that today the vogue of empiricism is a curious anachronism. Both the procedure and the theories of science today require a philosophical interpretation the general character of which is not empiricist but Hegelian. In order to support this thesis it will be necessary to glance at the history of scientific progress from the beginning of the last century, and this, as has been maintained above, was largely dominated by the conception of evolution.

II. BIOLOGICAL CONCEPTIONS

4. The effect of the theory of evolution upon the outlook of the 19th century was not the immediate abandonment of the Renaissance dualism. It is true that, with the development of biology, the notion of

[1] *The Expanding Universe* (Cambridge, 1933), p. 17.

life came to form a bridge between those of matter and mind, but the question still remained whether matter would use this bridge to invade the province of mind, or mind to invade that of matter. At first the former alternative seemed more probable, for according to the Darwinian doctrine, evolution of living forms was due to natural selection, which was largely a matter of accidental material conditioning. As a vastly greater number of off-spring is produced in every species than can ever hope to survive, the animal, it was held, is always involved in a struggle against natural enemies and physical forces which threaten its existence, and variations from the average type which favour the individual's survival in this struggle naturally tend to persist and to be passed on to the progeny of the successful creature. These variations accumulate and so gradually modify the race to produce a new species. The variations were regarded as purely accidental and the conditions of the environment which made them favourable to survival fortuitous, so that natural selection was materially determined. Even the element of striving involved in the struggle for existence was largely a matter of stronger forces overcoming and eliminating weaker. It was a physical impossibility for all the offspring of any creature to survive,[1] and which individuals would be actually selected was determined by the degree of physical 'adaptation' to the environment which they happened to possess. If all material systems could be mechanically explained (as had been believed for the past two centuries), natural selection was no contradiction of mechanical principles.[2]

By this process of selection Darwin held that different species might be differentiated from a common stock and, if the principle were generalized, it would follow that all living forms might have a common progenitor. The evolution of species with superior intelligence, therefore, could be accounted for by mechanical means, intelligence being simply a property of considerable survival value. But if this were so, intelligence would have to be the result of an accumulation of small

---

[1] Cf. E. W. MacBride in *Evolution in the Light of Modern Knowledge* (London, 1932), p. 215: 'The common thrush begins to produce eggs when it is one year old and its average length of life is about ten years. Every year a pair of thrushes will rear two broods, each consisting of about four nestlings. Starting from the off-spring of a single pair we find that if all survived and mated, at the end of the tenth year, that is at the completion of the life cycle of the parents, they would have produced a population of $19\frac{1}{2}$ millions. These in another ten years would grow to nearly 200 billions, and at the end of thirty years to about 1200 trillions. There would not be room for more than $\frac{1}{150000}$ part of such an army of thrushes on the entire surface of the earth even if all stood side by side touching each other.'

[2] For the sense of 'mechanical' see below, p. 376.

physical variations from a character which was non-intelligent, and indeed the materialists of the time sought to maintain that the difference between mechanical, living and conscious entities was no more than a degree of complication.

Moreover, co-temporary scientists did not hesitate to extend the conception of evolution to make the process continuous from the physical to the animate realm, and T. H. Huxley felt confident in writing: 'It is no less certain that the existing world lay potentially in the cosmic vapour and that a sufficient intelligence could, from a knowledge of the properties of the molecules of that vapour, have predicted, say, the state of the fauna of Britain in 1869'. The fauna of Britain, presumably, included man, and if the 'sufficient intelligence' were of the same kind as (though of course much more highly developed than) Huxley's own, the same principle of evolution should account also for it. The complication involved did not seem to trouble Huxley. Thus, if the theory of evolution (at any rate in its Darwinian form) had served to bridge the chasm between matter and mind, it had seemingly done so by reducing mind to a complicated material system, and so, in effect, by eliminating it altogether. This was the root cause of the violent controversies of the day between the evolutionists and the leaders of religious thought.

5. I am not concerned to follow the fortunes of Darwin's theories nor to record in detail how many of the assumptions he made have since been disproved. Subsequent experiment[1] brought evidence to light more favourable to Lamarck's contention that evolution resulted from the effort of the animal to adjust itself to changes in its environment and the consequent alteration of its habits. On the other hand, doubts about the survival value and heritability of small accidental variations were resolved by the results of Mendel's experiments (rediscovered in 1900 by de Vries, Correns and Tschermak) and the work of Bateson and others, which established the occurrence of mutations. But the whole doctrine of natural selection raised questions concerning the nature of inheritance and the biological processes which it involves. Not only was the inheritance of acquired characters in question but also the source of variations and the manner of their heritability. In the consequent course of development of the science of genetics facts were

[1] Kammerer's experiments with salamanders and Alytes (which provided much valuable evidence, despite the discovery that some had been tampered with); Durkhem's experiments with the pupae of white butterflies, and Pavlov's on the learning capacity of white mice.

357

disclosed which led biologists to the conclusion that the processes of life could not be completely explained physico-chemically.

It is not, of course, to be denied that biological processes have—in fact, must have—a physico-chemical basis. Because the substances in which they take place are all chemical substances, every biological process must also be a chemical process and must be chemically explicable. This is why the work of the bio-chemist is indispensable. But when the chemical explanation has been given, and however complete it may be, the changes which occur in living organisms remain radically different from those which occur in inorganic matter, in that they are subservient to biological ends and are mutually adapted to produce organic wholes.[1] This teleological character of biological functioning has been more and more obviously revealed as biological discovery has progressed, and clearly it cannot be explained in physico-chemical terms, so long as such explanation is assumed to exclude the notion of final causality.

The first result of this consideration was the doctrine of vitalism. It was not universally accepted by biologists and a new debate arose between vitalists and mechanists. But the facts on which the vitalistic doctrine rested could not be denied and the arguments by which it was supported have never been demolished, so that it would be fair to say that at the beginning of the 20th century the vitalist attitude in biology had triumphed and that it formed a definite step in the advancement of scientific thought. As I shall presently show, however, subsequent developments in physics have so completely undermined the mechanistic hypothesis that the issue between that and vitalism is no longer a live one.

6. In his theory of the germ-plasm, Weismann alleged that in the nucleus of the germ cell there was a minute, multiplex mosaic structure, one copy at least of which is passed on in inheritance while another is disintegrated in the process of ontogenesis and directs the development of the new organism, each element of the mosaic producing a special feature or organ. This doctrine (as Driesch points out[2]) is a variant of the old theory of 'evolutio' current in the early 18th century and opposed to the notion of epigenesis. It seemed to derive support from experiments performed by Wilhelm Roux on the egg of a frog in which, by killing one of the daughter cells after the first

---

[1] Cf. L. von Bertalanffy, *Modern Theories of Development* (Oxford, 1933), p. 8.
[2] *Vide The Science and Philosophy of the Organism*, I, Gifford Lectures, 1907 (London, 1908), p. 54.

cleavage, he succeeded in rearing a half embryo. It seems also to gain support from more recent work which has led to the correlation of inherited characters with chromosomes in the nucleus of the fertilized ovum and has located mendelian units in segments of the chromosome fibre, known as genes. The correlation of a heritable characteristic with a gene, however, reliable though the experiments are which lead to it, does not in the least explain how this microscopic portion of the cell nucleus can produce the characteristic as it is manifested in the developed organism, and the mystery is still further deepened by a mass of experimental evidence adduced by Driesch.

Driesch repeated Roux's experiment on the egg of the common sea-urchin (*Echinus*) and obtained an exactly contrary result. He was also able subsequently to explain the divergence from his own result of Roux's experiment on the frog's egg. In fact, a repetition of Roux's frog experiment under slightly different conditions produced not half an embryo but a complete organism.[1] And that was the result obtained by Driesch in his own work with sea-urchins. He found that one daughter cell, after the first cleavage, continued to develop, preserving the half formation in the first stages, but at a later stage producing a complete but diminutive 'blastula' and finally a complete pluteus larva half the normal size. He found, further, that the blastula could be cut in the plane of its polar axis, at any angle, into portions of any size and, provided that each was more than one quarter of the whole, it would produce a complete organism. A similar result was achieved by bisecting the developing organism in a still later phase, known as the 'gastrula' (so long as both ectoderm and endoderm were present in each section). Operations giving rise to restoration phenomena in the hydroid polyps (*Tubularia*) and the ascidian *Clavellina* displayed a similar tendency of the whole to reassert itself in the dissevered part and led Driesch to formulate his theory of 'harmonious' and 'complex equipotential systems'.[2]

An organic system is called harmonious when the development of each of its parts fits in with that of all the rest to form a complete organic whole. The 'prospective value' of each part is what it actually becomes in the process of morphogenesis. Its 'prospective potency' is what it is capable of becoming. Driesch's experiments prove that prospective potency is far wider than prospective value. For instance,

---

[1] *Vide* Driesch, Gifford Lectures, I, pp. 66-7.

[2] It is impossible to reproduce here the wealth of experimental material used by Driesch to establish his conclusions and I have mentioned only the more compelling examples.

every daughter cell formed by the division of the original egg-cell—
every 'blastomere' (as it is called)—up to a certain stage of ontogenesis,
is capable of becoming either the whole or any part of the complete
organism. The same is true of any vertical segment (greater than one
quarter) of the blastula. In fact, the prospective potency of any suitably
selected fraction ($\frac{1}{2}$, $\frac{3}{4}$, $\frac{3}{8}$, $\frac{5}{8}$, etc.) of the system is the same, though,
taken as a part of the entire system, its prospective value is different
from and complementary to every other part.[1] The system is therefore
called 'equipotential'. In cases where each portion is equally capable
of producing a similar complex structure, the system is called a complex
equipotential system; and some systems are, of course, both complex
and harmonious. Examples of complex equipotential systems given by
Driesch are: the cambium of Phanerogams (the hollow tube running
throughout the stem from any cell of which either branch or root may
be formed as required); the line of consecutive possible cross-sections
of a limb or organ from which regeneration can take place (e.g. in the
regeneration of the leg of a newt); the branchial apparatus of the ascidian Clavellina (all or part of which is capable of regenerating the whole
organism), and the system of propagation cells in the sexual organs.

The application of the notion of an equipotential system, however,
to certain phases of development requires some qualification in view
of the fact (recognized by Driesch) that there is a certain polarity and
bilaterality establishing gradients in the protoplasm of the cell and so
predetermining the development of some of its parts. This bilaterality
was found to be the explanation of the result of Roux's experiment; and
the polarity makes it impossible to obtain results similar to those of
Driesch if the egg of Echinus is cut in the horizontal plane after the
third cleavage (into eight blastomeres). The upper cells are now found
to have different potencies from the lower. When Driesch distorted the
egg by pressing it between glass plates so that all the blastomeres took
up positions in the horizontal plane, this difference was eliminated. The
polarity of the cytoplasm, accordingly, seems to be dependent, at
least in part, upon gravity.

The egg, after a certain stage of its segmentation, would seem not
to be a strictly equipotential system; but this, as we shall see, is a general
characteristic of living development, which is a process of specific
differentiation. What is important here is not that this process is, after
a certain stage, irreversible, but that it is always the differentiation of a
whole into an organically integrated system of parts, and that the
differentiated system is never completely present (in miniature)

[1] *Op. cit.* p. 80.

ab initio. What we begin from is an equipotential system and in many respects it remains so throughout the first few stages of the development.

Driesch argues that no mechanical explanation is at all possible of systems of this kind. It is impossible that any sort of mechanism can be present in an egg-cell such that any part or proportion of it (exceeding a certain minimum) could indifferently perform the specific function of any other part, or group of parts, or of the whole. Mechanism is thus banished from morphogenesis. In like manner, because the ovary is the outcome of hundreds upon hundreds of cell-divisions of a very few cells (themselves traceable to the division of only one) and every egg-cell is generated by this ovary by means of similar cell-division, mechanism must be banished also from the process of reproduction, and so from the explanation of heredity. What sort of machine, Driesch asks, could be so divided and redivided, and yet give rise in the end to a mechanism for reproducing the whole set of characters of which it is itself only a relatively small part?

7. The conclusion at which Driesch arrives, therefore, is that physico-chemical principles do not account in full for the phenomena of life. He maintains, further, that living processes must be regulated by something immaterial and to this something he gives the name Entelechy. It is what he calls a 'unifying cause' because it so regulates the activity of the living matter as to produce a whole or unity. The matter, he holds, is used by entelechy, the influence of which is non-energetic (so that physical laws like the conservation of energy are not violated) and consists simply in the suspension of certain potentialities in the material parts, or in their release, to fulfil the requirements of the coherent pattern. Accordingly, individuality, for Driesch, depends upon wholeness, and though he is unable to provide conclusive evidence to support his view, he is inclined to believe that phylogenetic development is also determined by entelechy and that, therefore, could we but discover it, there should be a principle of wholeness in phylogenesis as well. He suspects, further, and for similar reasons, that there may be a teleological principle at work in human history.

Just what entelechy is, however, remains a mystery and it is equally mysterious how it can suspend or release now these potentialities and now those in the same material units in differing sets of circumstances. In the case of the regeneration of an entire ascidian from the branchial apparatus (or even from part of it) of *Clavellina*, it must not merely restrain or release potentialities, but must abolish actualities already realized and re-establish potencies already relinquished. For the truncated organ loses its structure and *de*generates to a condition corresponding to an earlier phase of ontogenesis and then proceeds afresh to regenerate the complete animal. From all this it would seem as if entelechy were nothing less than a thinking mind, yet one which must be lodged both in the organism as a whole and in any of its separated parts. It seems, in short, to be little more than a name for the inexplicable.

Even if his theoretical conclusions are scouted as over-speculative, however, Driesch's work has established once and for all the inadequacy in biology of mechanistic interpretations. He has shown conclusively that neither morphogenesis nor heredity can be completely explained in terms of physics and chemistry, and accordingly that the evolution of living species cannot be viewed as a purely mechanical process. The evolution of minds in living organisms does not, as seemed at first, enable us to reduce consciousness to a mechanical process.

Nevertheless, conclusive as Driesch's demonstrations seem to be, his theory has not met either biological or philosophical requirements. His experimental work has been shown by later research to be insufficient to prove his hypothesis. The phenomena of super-regeneration (*e.g.* the regeneration of superfluous legs and tails in certain Amphibia as a result of experimental interference) have been adduced by Roux to refute the theory that development is guided by a purposive agency. These phenomena do not enable us to dispense altogether with teleology, for even super-regeneration is teleological in detail, but they do suggest that development cannot be attributed to a quasi-intelligent entelechy always directing the process to a typical end-result. The assumption of equi-final regulation producing typical end-results from atypical beginnings has also been disproved by Boveri, Schaxel and Hörstadius[1] by experiments on the eggs of *Strongylocentrotus*, *Echinus* and some Asterids, which proved that they cannot be regarded in an unqualified sense as equipotential systems. What these experiments go to show, however, is not that development is mechanically determined, but only that the purposive and teleological character of biological processes is not properly explicable by means of Driesch's assumption of entelechy. Along with the results of other experimental work, they point to the existence of 'immanent forces of the living system'[2] which are adequate to account for the persistent tendency of the process to result in wholes of specific kinds. The indication is that the 'unifying cause', though it must indeed be

---

[1] *Vide* Bertalanffy, *Modern Theories of Development*, pp. 79-83.   [2] *Ibid.* p. 84.

presumed if the phenomena are to be at all satisfactorily described, is immanent in the organism itself and is not a mysterious immaterial entity inexplicably regulating processes which would otherwise be purely mechanical.

L. von Bertalanffy points out that to postulate an entelechy is to remove all possibility of biological explanation of the phenomena, for the processes are in themselves admittedly physico-chemical and entelechy is a metaphysical conception presenting the biologist with a problem beyond the scope of his science.[1] But we may go further and assert that even metaphysically, as has already been noticed, entelechy in no way helps to make the character of living processes intelligible. The value of Driesch's work is to have shown the impossibility of explaining, or even properly of describing, biological facts apart from the recognition that the organism is a special kind of whole and that all its processes are processes at once of differentiation and of integration on successive levels of increasing complexity of organization. The ascription of this organic process of unification through differentiation to the agency of a mysterious immaterial entity makes it no more intelligible either biologically or philosophically.

8. More recent attempts to counter vitalism by the revival of some form of mechanism have, however, not met with success. These attempts are convincingly disposed of by Bertalanffy in the work already cited,[2] and only the briefest reference to them is possible here. Apart from their failure to account for precisely that which is typically characteristic of the living organism—its organization—such theories almost invariably assume tacitly a non-mechanical and non-physico-chemical principle in their own attempts at explanation. The notion of a machine is itself 'crypto-teleological', for every machine is a systematic arrangement of parts, each designed to fulfil a definite function (as is the whole), and it presupposes a designer with a purpose. If this is not assumed, mechanisms themselves become inexplicable. 'Locomotives and watches do not grow of themselves in nature; is this, then, the case with the endlessly more complicated organic machines?' asks Bertalanffy.[3] Goldschmidt's theory of chemo-differentiation,[4] similarly, tacitly assumes a systematic totality by which this differentiation is governed and which (in incredibly complicated ways) it always

[1] *Ibid.* pp. 43-6. [2] Pp. 28-43 and Part II, chs. iv and vi-vii.
[3] *Ibid.* p. 37.
[4] Goldschmidt, *Physiological Theory of Inheritance*; *vide* Bertalanffy, *op. cit.* ch. vi.

subserves and reproduces. Neither the existence nor the persistence of this totality is explained by chemo-differentiation—by the stratification of organ-forming substances or the competing catalytic agency of the genes. No purely chemical explanation is given to account for the order and precision with which the differentiation takes place so that each reaction shall occur precisely when it is required to supply a recognizable biological need.

But apart from their inevitable presuppositions contradicting the mechanist assumption, these theories are not supported by the facts. No machine theory can account for the equipotential systems, the existence of which (even though not to the full extent which he assumed) Driesch's work certainly established, and the theory of chemo-differentiation is defeated by that 'morphaesthesia' of the organism to which Noll drew attention and which Driesch further emphasized. The growth of a mushroom into a definite and typical shape takes place in the absence of any chemo-differentiation, as does the establishment of the arrangement and the precise shapes of the bones in the skeletons of vertebrates.[1]

Of course, the actual processes involved are physico-chemical, but the regulation of development to produce wholes, even when the normal process is obstructed and diverted, cannot be wholly explained by physico-chemical causes. It is true that the polarity of a magnet (which, by division, produces more magnets) or the arrangement of molecules in certain crystals, might be given as 'mechanical' analogues to the cytoplasm in the egg. Nor is it necessary to deny that there may be (in fact, if we take the principle of evolution seriously we must assert that there is) continuity between inorganic and organic processes. But what Driesch's arguments and the results of much reliable experimental work go to show is that between inorganic and living processes there is a difference of degree of integration and organization which marks them as belonging to altogether different levels of natural functioning. The polarity of a magnet is simply repetitive. It is an aggregate of polarized atoms. The self-adjustment of a crystal is geometrical and it too is an aggregate—of symmetrically arranged molecules. But the polarity of protoplasm and the regulation of ontogenesis is not a matter of simple aggregation or repetition; it results in the organization and integration of parts, specifically widely different, so that they are mutually complementary and co-operative in the functioning of an organic totality.

[1] *Vide* Bertalanffy, *op. cit.* p. 95, and Driesch, Gifford Lectures, I, pp. 136 f. and 157 f.

9. Accordingly, the explanation of biological phenomena is today considered to be accomplished best by what Bertalanffy calls 'organismic' or 'system theories', which recognize and insist upon the organic character of living things. All the typical processes and properties of life are seen to be dependent, not simply on the chemical constitution of living matter, but upon the organization both of material parts and of the processes of change which go on within the organism. Explanation cannot, therefore, proceed by mere analysis of the organism or of its processes into supposedly simple parts. What especially escapes any such analysis is the property of 'regulation' which so eminently belongs to living activity. This can be explained only in terms of a system organized hierarchically, governing and controlling its subordinate parts and processes so as systematically to generate, maintain and reproduce itself.[1]

'Organismic' biology rejects both (a) views which require the mechanistic assumption of elemental parts and processes (isolable by physico-chemical analysis) merely added together or superimposed to produce the observed organic phenomena, and (b) views which imply the no less mechanistic assumption of such elementary physico-chemical parts and processes, coupled with the further assumption of a mysterious entelechy to guide and regulate them in the production of wholes inexplicable on physico-chemical principles. In opposition to these views it holds that the organism is alive and displays the properties of life by virtue of its organized and systematic character in every phase, and that the forces regulating its activity are immanent in it. Moreover, it recognizes that system and organization are not peculiar to the biological field. In the physical and chemical spheres forms of wholeness are also to be found; but the differences in the realm of life are mainly two: first, the wholes are of a higher order both of articulation and of integration, and, secondly, they are *developing* wholes, which are not only organized totalities at any one moment, but become more highly differentiated and integrated on successively higher levels of integration, so that their past history determines their present nature and functioning.[2] This development is itself regulated by the totality of which it is the product and the producer, and itself constitutes a typical coherent temporal whole.

10. The 'organismic' type of theory is supported by the work of such thinkers in Germany as Schaxel, Gurwitz and Spemann and is consonant also with the position maintained by English biologists as different

---

[1] Cf. Bertalanffy, *op. cit.* p. 49.   [2] *Ibid.* pp. 173-6.

in philosophical outlook as J. S. Haldane, J. H. Woodger and Joseph Needham, who all reject vitalism and all agree that the typical phenomena of life appear only at higher levels of organization than the physico-chemical. On the basis of physiological observation and experiment Haldane maintains the thesis that biology must proceed upon axioms of its own as a science independent of physics and chemistry. 'When we interpret biologically any observation we had previously tried to interpret in physical or chemical terms', he writes, 'we have radically transformed our mode of perception . . . from the standpoint of biology, physically interpreted phenomena become mere imperfectly perceived phenomena, awaiting further interpretation and perception.'[1] The fundamental assumption must be the unity of the life of the organism, and in studying this it is not, in his opinion, possible to separate the living organism from its environment, either in observation or in thought. Haldane illustrates, in his description of the process of breathing, the intricate way in which the physiological processes in the living body are mutually co-ordinated to maintain the general condition of normality. As one process is abnormally increased or diminished, so others are adjusted to compensate it and restore the normal equilibrium. Thus the carbon-dioxide pressure in the lungs is maintained at an almost constant level, despite external and internal changes, by regulation of the rate of breathing by the central nervous system. Oxygen pressure is similarly regulated, but this time by the rate of the blood circulation. These and many other processes are not only adjusted to one another but also to alterations in the physical circumstances as well as to the changing activities of the animal. Consequently, organization is seen to be the special characteristic of life. It 'is not something external to organized material, but is absolutely identical with the material, so that both the material and its organization are nothing but manifestations of the organization. It is life and not matter that we have before us.'[2]

Needham rejects the suggestion that organization is something axiomatic and so inscrutable. He asserts that the organizing relations are analysable into others obtaining at lower levels of order. But he says, 'the living differs from the dead in degree and not in kind because it is on a higher plane of complexity of organization, but it would also be correct to say that it differs in kind since the laws of this higher organization only operate there'.[3]

[1] *The Philosophical Basis of Biology* (London, 1931), p. 32.
[2] *Organism and Environment* (Yale University Press, New Haven, 1917), p. 104. Presumably this means 'not merely matter', for Haldane admits the material basis of life.　　　[3] *Time the Refreshing River* (London, 1944), pp. 242-3.

Haldane goes even further. He asserts that the organism and its environment cannot be separated but form a continuous organic whole. He shows, by reference to physiological examples, how the 'structure' of the parts of an organism is only apparently distinguishable from their functioning, becoming modified as function is modified so as to maintain a constancy of specific activity in changes of environment. But this specific persistence of life cannot, he maintains, be accounted for so long as the organism is regarded 'as a mere labile structure which determines, and is at the same time determined by, its environment'.[1] Both internal and external environment are regulated by the functioning of the organism, as its activity is in turn regulated by environmental conditions, so that function, structure, internal and external environment are all organically interdependent and indisseverably linked in one organic process. Phenomena of adaptation, of recovery and restitution of tissues, of vicarious functioning of organs when one is damaged or destroyed, of memory, of habit-forming and of heredity convince Haldane that 'it is literally true of life, and no mere metaphor, that the whole is in each of the parts, and each moment of the past in each moment of the present'. 'Organic wholeness', he continues, 'covers both space and time, and in the light of biological fact absolute space and time, and self-existent matter and energy are but abstractions from, or partial aspects of, reality.'[2] This conclusion, he says, is as true to the facts of biology as the conservation of mass and energy are for the physicist. Consequently life, for him, is 'Nature expressing herself as a characteristic whole which has no spatial bounds'.[3] This position is reminiscent both of Aristotle and of Hegel and, as I shall show presently, it supports in various ways the contention made in an earlier chapter about the presuppositions of modern science.

Though Needham does not agree with all of this, he also asserts the identity of structure with function, as well as the wholeness of nature, advocating 'the acceptance of the existence of diverse levels of complexity and organization, and the interpretation of them as successive stages of a world process the nature of which is synthetic or dialectical'.[4]

The astonishing interplay of the life of an organism with its so-called 'environment', both living and non-living, is again displayed in the life-cycles of parasitic animalcules which depend for their existence

[1] *Organism and Environment*, p. 93.
[2] *Ibid.* p. 99.
[3] *The Philosophical Basis of Biology*, p. 74.
[4] Cf. *Time the Refreshing River*, pp. 122-3, and *Order and Life* (Cambridge, 1936), p. 6.

on the hospitality of at least two quite different hosts. The liver-fluke spends part of its existence in the internals of a water-snail and part in the body of a bird or mammal. The malaria plasmodium, which requires both mosquito and man, at different stages of its development, to sustain its life, is one of a vast number of similar parasites. Often the transition from one host to the other depends on 'external' factors which seem altogether fortuitous and are yet as essential to the realization of the complete pattern of the creature's life as are the processes internal to its own organization. In the life of these organisms natural phenomena are so interlocked that we cannot delimit the system upon which they depend, and in the last resort we are compelled to regard all nature as one single web of interconnected entities and events.

Modern biology, therefore, cannot but assume that nature is a single system of cohering parts and an absolutist philosophy is entirely in harmony with its findings. This holism of nature is, moreover, repeated in the life of every individual organism and manifests itself even in the distinct processes of its living activity. In the development of the complex anatomy of the animal from the relatively simple and almost structureless egg-cell, the direction and governance of the totality which is being developed is apparent throughout. The form of the whole is the key to every process, and it is this that constantly reasserts itself if the natural course of that process is disturbed. But the form of the whole—the systematic totality—is precisely what has been called the concrete universal, and it is this universal which is manifesting itself in, presiding over and directing the living activity in every case. It is this universal that should be substituted for Driesch's entelechy. That, as we saw, was supposed to suspend some of the potentialities of the living cells and release others so that their respective developments should be complementary; but in some circumstances it does so in one way and in others in another, and in yet other circumstances it may reverse its action and revive potentialities already passed over, cancelling those which have already been realized. The essential fact, however, is that all these variations result in the same organic totality—the same universal—and it is precisely to this that the whole process of development is directed at every stage. No better example of this direction of the process by the universal need be given than the way in which the skeleton of the pluteus larva of *Echinus* is formed. It is described by Driesch as follows:

'About thirty of the mesenchyme cells are occupied in the formation of the skeleton substance on each side of the larva. They wander through the interior space of the gastrula—which at this stage is not filled with sea water but with a sort of gelatinous material—and wander in such a manner that they always come to the right places, where a part of the skeleton is to be formed; they form it by a process of secretion, quite unknown in detail; one of them forms one part, one the other, but what they form altogether is one whole.'[1]

11. Furthermore, the process of development is demonstrably dialectical in character. It begins from a relatively undifferentiated unity (the cell) which differentiates itself into a relatively disunited manifold (the segmented daughter cells), and this, as the process continues, is reintegrated into an organic totality in which both the unity of the first stage and the variety of the second are preserved and reconciled. These phases, mutually distinct and opposite, yet definite stages in a continuous process of progressive revelation of the whole, are even more arrestingly displayed in the embryonic development of vertebrate animals. The earlier stages of their development give no clue to the nature of its conclusion. There is nothing in the fertilized ovum to indicate the species of individual which will emerge, and in the first stages of its development the embryo of one species is indistinguishable from that of another, and even from species of different genera. Von Baer, referring to specimens of embryos which he had forgotten to label, wrote: 'I am quite unable to say to which class they belong. They may be lizards, or small birds, or very young mammals, so complete is the similarity in the mode of formation . . . of all these animals.'[2] What is it that determines the embryo to become an organism of this or of that species, the same as its parents and bearing an individual resemblance to them? The mystery is not altogether removed, but it is perhaps rendered less obscure if we regard the universal which determines the individual character of the organism—the whole which is in becoming—as immanent throughout and in each phase.

'The first stage of development is the establishment of a *direction* for the future embryo', writes the biologist;[3] 'when an artist is about to draw a complicated picture he roughs it in, very faintly, in pencil, to decide where the main masses and lines will lie. So with the egg. The first thing it has to do is to make up its mind, so to speak, which part of it will be right and left, front and back.' 'The artist', 'its mind' which the egg must 'make up'—what do these metaphors represent? Can we

[1] Gifford Lectures, I, p. 42.
[2] Quoted by Wells and Huxley in *The Science of Life* (London, 1938), p. 367. The whole section is relevant.
[3] Wells and Huxley, *op. cit.* p. 579.

give any better answer than that they stand for the universal differen-
tiating itself in and through its particular manifestations? The orientation of the egg (by whatever physico-chemical means it is achieved)
is the first realization of the complex whole which it is about to
become.

And how does the development proceed? At first there is simply a
multiplication of cells by segmentation with no more internal organization than the preliminary orientation already described and a certain
gradation of activity corresponding to the varying distribution of the
yolk. In the earliest stage the egg behaves as a whole and its material is
entirely plastic. If divided in half, each half will organize itself into a
new whole and produce a complete animal, all the cells being indifferently material for the potential development of any of the several
organs of the developing creature. Later differentiation takes place and
the cells form groups corresponding to the different parts of the body.
Specialization now occurs in an irreversible process, so that the cells in
each group will produce their appropriate organ and that organ only.
The character of this specialization appears to be determined by
chemical activity in the dorsal side of the egg (what will eventually
become the back of the embryo), but beyond this there seems to be
little mutual co-ordination of the parts, which develop well-nigh
independently.[1] The occurrence of these distinct phases has been
established by ingenious grafting experiments in which cells from
different embryos have been interchanged at various stages of their
development. Cells transplanted in the earlier stage develop in accordance with their position in the new host, becoming skin or limb or
organ as their new environment requires. Cells from the same relative
position in the original embryo, transplanted at a later stage, develop
according to their differentiation in their original position and quite
irrespective of their surroundings in the new host. The process is
summed up in the following passage:

'Thus the acquisition of complexity, that greatest marvel of development, is bound up with a narrowing down of the possibilities open to
each region. The same group of cells which, when the limb-bud is well
grown, can do nothing but turn into a finger-tip, a little earlier could have
turned into palm or wrist, but not into upper-arm. Twenty-four hours
earlier, again, they could have been turned into any part of a fore-limb,
but not into anything else but a fore-limb. But in the earliest stages of all

---

[1] Certain chains of inductions have been observed, in which the development of
one organ stimulates that of another. But there is, so to speak, no central direction in
this phase.

they could have been switched over to becoming any organ whatsoever, from liver to eye, from brain to bladder.'[1]

In the second phase of development, therefore, the embryo becomes a kind of 'mosaic of chemically independent parts',[2] each developing without reference to the others, but always maintaining among themselves the general pattern prescribed by the anatomy which is being developed (the universal).

A third phase supervenes in which the mosaics are reintegrated and co-ordinated, now by the flow of blood and lymph throughout the body and the activity of a common nervous system which eventually subjects the entire organism to the control of the brain. The activity of the hormones is also brought into play regulating the processes of growth and development, and the organs proceed to function each in the service of the whole. A totality is thus created to which every part is completely organic.

The process is essentially dialectical in character. First, there is the vague undifferentiated potentiality; next, a differentiation so specialized that there is scarcely any connection between the parts (apart from their spatial pattern conforming to the structure of the body which is in the making); finally, there is an integration of specialized parts so linked as to serve the common life and welfare of a thoroughly organic whole. Throughout the process the guiding and presiding influence of this whole which finally emerges is apparent. It is specified both in the phases of the development and as those phases. The first is its unity undifferentiated, and it is maintained in the final form, not only as the interdependence of its parts, but also as represented in each individual cell. The second is its diversity disunited, and it is preserved in the complex variety of the organs. The last phase is the explicit unity in diversity, the mature living and organized whole which is at once the goal of the development, that which has all along been developing and the totality in which every phase of the process is sublated.

But the universal is not only the guiding and presiding influence throughout the process, it is also the dynamic which impels it to proceed. The uniform potentiality of the fertilized ovum is, as such and without further explication, meaningless and futile. It is what it is only in the light of what it is not yet, and its differentiation is necessary to its own significant existence. It can continue to be only if (to use a Hegelian phrase) it 'goes over into its other'—the mosaic of separately developing organs, within each of which again the same process is

[1] Wells and Huxley, *op. cit.* p. 585.   [2] *Ibid.* p. 586.

repeated.[1] This mosaic, however, is itself a worthless collection of parts except as the preliminary stage to the integration of the organism. It survives only by re-establishing the unity which was present, though without diversity, in the earlier stage. The final synthesis is the reconciliation of both moments in the emergence of the complete animal—the totality or universal which has been immanent in every phase, the influence directing the course of the process and the cause, both efficient and final, which has impelled each phase to become its successor.

12. Embryology, however, is one of the sources of evidence for the theory of the evolution of living species from a common stock. Taken along with the evidence supplied by palaeontology, genetics and biogeography, it has been sufficient to establish the hypothesis as a definite tenet of modern scientific thought which requires us to regard the whole of animate nature as a process of development. The entire system of orders, phyla, genera and species of living things is to be linked in a single process. This whole process, moreover, at any rate if we attend to aspects of it which Bergson has emphasized, displays dialectical characteristics similar to those already noticed in individual morphology. Living things have evolved in three main directions, two of which are directly connected with one another and depend for their existence upon the third: it is as if the stream of development bifurcated and then one of the branches again divided. All life depends upon the possibility of fixing and storing chemical substances from the earth and atmosphere, and to the perfection of the methods of doing so the evolution of plant life has been almost exclusively directed. This has imposed upon plants the necessity of leading a fixed and immobile existence. Animal life, on the other hand, has developed in the direction of activity and the perfection of the means of locomotion and perception, depending upon the vegetable organisms (or other animals), which serve it as food, for the absorption of the chemical substances necessary to sustain its life. Within the animal kingdom, again, the lower species (especially invertebrates) have highly developed instincts, tending to stereotyped action exactly suited to specific purposes, but the higher species show greater capacity to adapt and adjust their activity to changing circumstances by the use of intelligence.

These different levels of life display opposite yet obviously complementary characteristics. The lower functions are maintained and used to subserve the higher, and at each stage the living activity is

[1] *Vide* Wells and Huxley, *op. cit.* pp. 584-5.

directed to the perfection of a total pattern of life. It is not possible here, as it is in individual morphology, to demonstrate by direct reference to the biological facts the immanence of the end in every lower phase. But if the process is to be continuous that must be presumed. Ontogenesis, in which this immanence can be observed, is, after all, only a stage in phylogenesis. It is through the processes of heredity that the species evolves, and the embryonic development is part of the process by which the species is reproduced. If one accepts the hypothesis of continuous evolution, therefore, one must presuppose that what emerges at the end has been present all along, immanent, implicit and self-evolving throughout the process.

But what is it that emerges at the end? A species capable of intelligent behaviour—the intelligent activity of a mind.

Now what has been insisted upon throughout the discussion of biological discovery and theory has been the persistent manifestation of wholeness in the phenomena of life; and the kind of whole concerned has been such as to exemplify the notion of the concrete universal. But it was maintained above that the one really adequate exemplification of the universal was the activity of an intelligent and self-conscious mind. It now transpires that just this activity is the end-product of the entire evolutionary process, within the detail of which we were able to recognize the self-development and self-specification of the universal exemplified as a living organism. The activity of thought, it was maintained by Bosanquet, is no more nor less than the self-development of its object, or, in other words, the self-specification of the concrete universal,[1] and if a process of just this sort can be detected in living activity, and if it is just this process in consciousness which is regarded as the final outcome of evolution, we do seem very strongly impelled to the conclusion that what is immanent in every phase of the development is mind. Surely it is something very like this that is implied by Driesch's doctrine of entelechy—the 'unifying cause' which he finds operative in every manifestation of life, and the operation of which has an uncanny similarity to the operation of a thinking mind.

13. The underlying presuppositions of modern biology turn out, accordingly, to be those which I have predicted.

(i) Its discoveries make it necessary to regard nature as one system from which the separation of any distinguishable parts can be only provisional. The life of the organism has no set bounds and there is

[1] *Vide The Nature of Mind*, pp. 70 ff. and 156 *ad fin.*, and *Implication and Linear Inference, passim.*

no sharp frontier between animate and inanimate nature. So much, however, might equally have been maintained by the Renaissance scientist with his view of nature as a vast machine, but the modern biologist departs from this view in his second main assumption.

(ii) For modern biology this whole of nature is a continuous process of evolution in which the character of any phase is determined by what it is in process of becoming. The conception is teleological and, in consequence, the notions of efficient and final causation tend to overlap as they did in the philosophy of Aristotle.

(iii) Once this is admitted, it follows that the ultimate principle of interpretation is a standard of value. The very vocabulary of the theory of evolution gives evidence of this implication, for it makes 'fitness', 'survival value' and 'adaptation to environment' serving the ends and purposes of life the criteria which determine the course and direction of change. All biological interpretation is given in terms of function, which alone enables the biologist to explain the structure of the organism. This is a persistent and universal assumption in the science, even 'vestigial remnants' being explained in terms of ends which they served in the past but which have since ceased to be of value.

(iv) Another necessary presupposition in which any attempt to explain biological phenomena is involved is that the mainspring of every living process is a 'unifying cause' and that organic processes are the activity of a principle of wholeness which, in its manner of operation, is extraordinarily like a mind. The continuity in evolution between life and mind, as it is eventually manifested in the highest species, makes it impossible for the biologist to separate them rigidly from each other, and this presumption of continuity of development leads to the idea (never, of course, explicit in the biologist's thought) that mind is immanent throughout the process.

(v) In that case, the objects which the biologist studies, if he did but realize it, are the phases of the development of his own mentality and we are on the way to the identification of subject and object. That identification, as we saw in the philosophy of Hegel, only becomes fully explicit when the human mind recognizes itself as the world come to consciousness.

14. The trend of development in biological theory beyond the position of vitalism is to be welcomed by the philosopher, for vitalism in itself was not sufficient to dispose of the Renaissance dualism; life had been more or less assimilated to mind, but matter remained unassimilable. No theory of non-spatial and immaterial entelechy 'acting "into"

space'[1] can bridge the fatal gap and, in consequence, new philosophical attempts to do so were called forth. These took two main forms: the vitalist philosophy of Bergson, which attempted to remove the dualism by explaining away matter as a by-product of life; and the theories of emergent evolution, which united the scale of natural forms by postulating a new and inexplicable kind of relationship, called 'emergence', between the various levels of existence.

A critical examination of these doctrines must be deferred to the next chapter, but whatever may be their merits or demerits, their main historical importance lies in their recognition of the change which had taken place in the presuppositions of natural science. Their exponents realized that teleology, banished from nature in 17th-century thought, had now been reintroduced and that final causes of some kind must be presumed. Though science had not yet found evidence of continuity between the provinces of physics and biology which would have justified the extension of the process of evolution back into the inanimate world, this continuity was already being assumed, and it is reflected in the philosophies of emergent evolution. The implication of holism in evolution is also, to a very large extent, recognized in philosophies of this type (though it is rejected by Bergson), but that recognition is limited in a way which renders the theories of emergence philosophically unsatisfactory and inadequate as statements of modern scientific presuppositions. Similarly, the implied immanence of mind in nature is overlooked and the consequent need to identify subject and object in knowledge. To develop these implications to the full is a philosophical task which, although it is fulfilled in much greater measure in the work of Whitehead, still remains to be completed, and the need for persisting in it has been emphasized by the recent revelation of similar implications in the findings of contemporary physics.

III. THE REVOLUTION IN PHYSICS

15. In the classical physics of the 17th and 18th centuries a mechanical system was one consisting of solid particles of matter moving in a fixed frame of space and time as the result of the push and pull of forces of specifiable kinds. The forces were dependent on the disposition and movement of the particles, which were thought to act upon one another either by impact or, at a distance, by gravitation.[2] What

[1] Cf. Driesch, *The Problem of Individuality* (London, 1914), p. 73. It is to be observed that Driesch openly adopts a dualistic metaphysic (*ibid.* ch. iv).

[2] Cf. Jeans, *Physics and Philosophy* (Cambridge, 1943), pp. 108 ff., and H. Margenau, *The Nature of Physical Reality* (New York, 1950), p. 35.

gravitation was and how it acted nobody sought to explain. It was simply evident that all bodies did exert a mutual force of attraction, for the determination of which Newton had given the mathematical equation. The conception of nature as a mechanical system such as this was the basis of Laplace's claim that an infinitely industrious mathematician, who knew the exact position and velocity of every particle in the universe at its creation, would be able to calculate its precise state in the minutest detail at any instant of its future history. My use of the word 'mechanism' and its derivatives is intended always to refer to this classical 17th-century conception.

The phenomena of heat and electricity, however, were not easy to explain in these terms and at first gave rise to the hypothesis of imponderable fluids. Later it was found that electric and magnetic forces conformed to an inverse-square law of the same type as the law of gravitation and it was hoped that a similar account of them might be given. This, however, proved impossible, for whereas gravitation apparently acted instantaneously, the transmission of electro-magnetic force through space was found to take time. Moreover, an electric charge, though it exerts a simple and single force while at rest, exerts also magnetic forces as soon as it moves, and similarly a magnet in motion gives rise to an electrical force. The equations expressing the laws governing these complicated matters were found to be of the same general form as those expressive of wave-motion in a liquid and there arose, in consequence, the hypothesis of the electro-magnetic wave. But a wave, according to the classical conception, requires a medium in which the undulation takes place, and so an ether was postulated, ubiquitous in space, through which electro-magnetic waves could be transmitted.

This idea of waves in an ether was still entirely consonant with the classical mechanics and, as Jeans points out,[1] the state of a system of moving particles acting one upon another by gravitation, by impact, electrically and magnetically could still be completely described by equations which conformed to the simple canonical type of Newtonian mechanics.

16. Nevertheless, field physics which developed in the 19th century was already moving away from the classical conceptions. It laid emphasis not so much on the charged particle from which, as it were, the field emanates, but rather upon the structure of the field which could be completely determined by means of Maxwell's equations.

[1] *Vide Physics and Philosophy*, pp. 115 f.

Moreover, the field extends throughout space and time and its structure in any portion of space and at any time could be calculated. The exact location of the charged particle, accordingly, is not restricted to a particular point, for the particle exists, as it were in varying degrees, wherever its effects can be detected or calculated. A definite sense, therefore, begins to attach to the notion that a particle is ubiquitous and has no *simple* location.

With the advent of the Theory of Relativity, moreover, simple location goes by the board. The Michelson-Morley experiment finally disposed of the ether and Einstein's theory disposed of much more. Absolute space and time had also to go, as well as the concept of force. The Theory of Relativity welds space and time into one four-dimensional continuum into which matter introduces a curvature, and motion occurs only along lines determined by this curvature in space-time. No forces, in consequence, need be postulated to explain the movement of macroscopic bodies, which in all cases may be considered simply as following a geodesic.[1] Further, with the abolition of absolute space and absolute time, absolute motion is also dispensed with. Whether a body moves or is at rest is entirely relative to the frame of reference adopted, and as no particular frame takes precedence over any other, every body is at one and the same time at rest and in motion, with various velocities according to the innumerable alternative frames of reference which can be chosen. Accordingly, not only have we to dispense with forces, but even the wave-picture of the fields irradiating from a charged particle will vary according to the frame of reference, for it varies with the state of motion or rest of the particle and with its velocity. No classical mechanical representation is therefore possible of any system of bodies moving under the influence of alleged forces, and the actual pattern of physical events in any system can be expressed only in mathematical formulae. It is, in fact, impossible to say without qualification that this pattern is precisely so-and-so. It is indefinitely various according to the different frames of reference relative to any one of which it may be interpreted. And, though the alterations of the state of affairs as we transfer it from one frame to another can be mathematically specified, the actual selection of the frame of reference is subjective and depends upon the arbitrary choice of the observer.

The Newtonian picture can thus be at best only a limited and partial aspect of any set of physical events, and the basis of Laplace's claim, if it has not already disappeared, has become infinitely more complicated.

---

[1] The movement of protons and electrons demands still other principles of interpretation and the relativity theory has not yet been successfully applied to it.

Moreover, the Theory of Relativity has dispensed with the last vestige of simple location of events in space and time. Simultaneity of distant occurrences is a conception meaningless in modern physics. The clocks by which it could be measured must first be synchronized, and this could be done only by the correlation of instants at different places by light or radio signals. But such signals travel at a finite velocity for which allowance must be made, and that velocity cannot be measured except by means of distant clocks already synchronized.[1] Simultaneity accordingly becomes a relative term, and of two events, A and B, which are simultaneous for one observer, A will precede B, and B will precede A, if measured by reference to frames travelling at different velocities relative to the first. Moreover, the difference will vary with the velocities. The placing of events in a time series can therefore never be final and absolute, for though one region of the space-time continuum will represent the absolute past for all co-temporary observers and another the absolute future, the actual placing of events in the time series will depend on the reading of simultaneity peculiar to each frame of reference.

Similarly, the position of a particle in space cannot be specified simply. The curvature of space varies not only according to the presence or absence of matter but also according to the velocity with which it moves. But this velocity is relative and differs with the frame of reference. Accordingly, space must be variously distorted with reference to various frames and the position of any point will differ in each case.[2] But if we cannot specify simply (or absolutely) where a particle is nor how fast it is moving nor when an event occurs, and if we cannot postulate forces dependent on the positions of particles and their movement, we can form no absolute picture of the events which occur but can describe them only relatively to specific observers. Accordingly, if any absolute account of the real is possible at all it can be expressed *only* mathematically by means of tensors.

The position of the traditional mechanist cannot, therefore, be maintained on the basis of modern science and, with the addition of the Quantum Theory to that of Relativity, it ceases to have any meaning at all. But before I go to that, I shall pause to consider briefly the implications of what has been stated so far.

17. Relativity has combined space and time into a single continuum, and it is a continuum which does not extend indefinitely in opposite

[1] Cf. Eddington, *Philosophy of Physical Science* (Cambridge, 1939), pp. 38 f.
[2] *Vide* Eddington, *The Nature of the Physical World*, pp. 12 ff.

directions. Recent astronomical observations have led scientists to conclude that it curves in upon itself and closes up, so that it is finite in extent. Different conceptions of this closed universe have been suggested. According to Einstein's, the space component is spherical and the time component cylindrical; according to de Sitter's, space-time as a whole is spherical, the movement of time slowing down as we proceed from a point taken as centre to the outermost limit. There time, as observed from the centre, stands still.[1] It has, so to speak, come to an end, so that we might say that all time is enclosed within the 'hypersphere' of the complete universe. This hypersphere is said to be finite but unbounded, but it could as well be described as infinite, if that is taken to mean not endless but self-complete.

Moreover, the state of any physical system within this spatio-temporally closed universe is dependent on its relation to every other. In every physical system, what and where the particular elements are and what they do depend on their relation to the frame of reference adopted. Mathematical transformations enable us to relate the description of events relative to one frame to their description relative to another, and the tensor calculus correlates all frames. The entire universe, accordingly, forms one coherent system, each part of which is what it is in virtue of its relations to every other,[2] and the mathematical formulae which give us the key to these interrelations are the principles of systematization which enable us to 'read off' the state of affairs in one part from our knowledge of the state of affairs in another. Such a system is exactly what Bosanquet called a concrete universal, and the Theory of Relativity manifestly supports the view that the nature of the physical world can only be understood if interpreted in terms of this principle.

In stating this position I have purposely tried to avoid as much as possible the use of the word 'observer' and I have substituted for it the phrase 'frame of reference' in order to reduce to the minimum the element of subjectivity involved in the determination of physical fact. That element, however, cannot be excluded and, however we try to express the facts, it remains an ever-present and inescapable factor. For the very meaning of the phrase 'frame of reference' includes an act of thought—that of referring—and, as was stated above, the choice of any particular frame is an arbitrary one. The physical system con-

[1] *Vide* Dampier, *History of Science* (Cambridge, 1946), p. 444, and Margenau, *The Nature of Physical Reality*, pp. 163-4. The curvature of space is altered by the presence of matter so that the 'spherical shape' of the universe is liable to be variously distorted (*vide* Eddington, *The Expanding Universe*, p. 34).

[2] Cf. Whitehead, *Concept of Nature* (Cambridge, 1930), pp. 141 f.

tains no inherent reference to any particular frame, and such reference as can be made is made only by the thinking scientist in his interpretation of the facts. What the facts are, however, is not distinguishable from their interpretation. The facts cannot be divorced from the frame of reference; they vary with it, so that it is impossible to separate the object described from the act of reference (or thought) by which it is determined. Subject and object, therefore, are inseparable in modern physics; they are but distinguishable moments both indispensable to the constitution of the facts.

Philipp Frank's attempt to avoid this conclusion[1] by substituting the instrument of measurement for the observer is unavailing.[2] 'It is asserted', says Frank, 'only that in accordance with the motion of the measuring instrument, the results of the measurement will be different.' But what determines the motion of the measuring instrument? It cannot be absolute and will vary according to the frame of reference, nor is it specified in the pointer-reading which the instrument provides. In fact, 'the measurement' is not the pointer-reading itself but depends upon the equation into which the reading is incorporated. If this were not so, the Lorentz transformations would be valueless for the determination of physical facts. But the selection of a frame of reference is arbitrary and the act of reference is an act of thought, and it is upon this selection and this act that the results of the measurement depend. Accordingly, the contamination of the physical world by the knowing mind cannot be escaped by the substitution on which Frank insists. It does not, however, follow that all physics is *purely* subjective (as even some physicists tend to argue), unless thought is taken to be a purely subjective phenomenon, which is exactly what it cannot be because it is always and only the determination of an object.

Two of the presuppositions which have been listed above as characteristic of modern science are necessitated by the Theory of Relativity: (i) that the universe is a coherent and systematic whole and (ii) that the knowing mind and its object are inseparably united. I shall return to these two principles anon, after I have shown that they are still further implicated by the Quantum Theory and the system of wave mechanics.

18. Of the traditional mechanical picture of physical facts all that seems to have been left by the Theory of Relativity is the presence of

---

[1] *Vide Between Physics and Philosophy* (Harvard, 1941), pp. 111-13.
[2] It is to be noticed that both Eddington and Planck include the observer in the category of measuring instrument. *Vide* Eddington, *The Nature of the Physical World*, pp. 10-11, 17, etc., and Planck, *The Philosophy of Physics* (London, 1936), p. 104.

matter. Force has gone; simple location has gone; absolute motion has gone; but what still remains are bodies moving through space-time. The Special Theory of Relativity, however, brought Einstein to the conclusion that mass and energy were not essentially different; that energy is equivalent to mass and mass represents energy, and that there is a simple quantitative relation between them. This identification of mass with energy leads us to suspect that matter may be resoluble into something more ultimate, and this is just what recent developments in physics have established.

According to the classical conception, matter was ultimately composed of minute, hard, solid and (mysteriously) elastic atoms. But later work both in chemistry and in physics revealed the fact that these atoms were complex in structure and consisted of still more minute electrically charged particles. At first the atom was represented as a kind of microscopic solar system in which one group of particles formed a nucleus with a predominantly positive charge, and another group with negative charges revolved round the nucleus like infinitesimal planets. The positively charged particles are protons and are relatively heavy, while the mass of the negatively charged electrons is all but negligible. Here, then, we have charged particles in motion, and the laws of electro-magnetism should apply. On the contrary, however, this view of the atom and the behaviour of its parts seemed to involve a direct contradiction of all the principles of classical mechanics; it had, therefore, to be abandoned and new explanations were in demand.[1]

Field physics had resulted in the conception of an electro-magnetic field as a system of waves, the structure of which was determinable by Maxwell's equations, but the mechanical interpretation of these waves by means of an ether broke down and the physical property of transmitting waves had to be imputed to space itself. The field (or fields), however, are not the same in relation to every frame of reference and the differences are calculated with the help of the Lorentz transformations. It follows that neither the field nor the waves are anything real in themselves, but are simply the pictorial way in which we try to represent to ourselves whatever it is that answers to the mathematical formulae enabling the physicist to determine the structural relations of the phenomena.

Investigations both into the nature of electro-magnetic waves and into that of elementary particles of matter (electrons) have, in recent years, revealed a somewhat embarrassing similarity between them. Experiments have shown (a) that electro-magnetic waves behave in

[1] Cf. Jeans, *Physics and Philosophy*, pp. 123 f.

certain respects like a shower of particles (which have come to be called 'photons') and that there is a minimum quantum of action, no fraction of which can occur in nature, and (b) that in certain circumstances electrons display the characteristics of waves of very short wave-length. The distinction between energy and the ultimate constituents of matter has, in consequence, broken down. The Quantum Theory has led to the conception of radiation as granular—or atomized—and of the electron as a 'wave-packet', and some disconcerting corollaries ensue.

First, waves continuously spread. A single photon emitted from a source of radiation will be continuously attenuated. It would seem, therefore, that the whole of its energy could never again be concentrated on one point. On the other hand, the expulsion of an electron from a film of potassium in a photo-electric cell requires at least a quantum of energy. It is known that light from a distant star produces this photo-electric effect, and also that it cannot be due to an accumulation of doses of energy each less than a quantum. Thus a single quantum of energy must somehow travel through space from one point to another as a compact unit. All the experimental evidence, however, supports the view that radiation traverses space *only* in the form of waves. What then happens to the photon between its emission from the source and its impact upon the film in the photo-electric cell? Secondly, if electrons are wave-packets these will spread, so that a packet now identified as a particle will at any future moment have more or less dissipated. This is confirmed in experiment by the failure of physicists in their attempts to determine both the position and the velocity of the particle at the same time. If the packet is very small, the velocity, which is dependent upon the wave-length, is proportionately indeterminate; if, on the other hand, it has spread to any great extent so that the wave-length can be ascertained and the velocity determined, to the same extent the position has become indefinite and cannot be precisely assigned. Yet electrons emitted from a known source seem to arrive at a determinate destination. How have they traversed the intervening space? The answer may be that they have not![1]

In any case it is known that there is no medium which undulates and what the wave-picture directly represents is not actual reality. The conclusion, in fact, which physicists have reached is that the waves represent only probabilities—the probability, for instance, that the photon will fall at a particular point on the film, or that the velocity, or the position, of an electron has a particular determinate value—and

[1] Cf. Jeans, *Physics and Philosophy*, pp. 166 ff., and Eddington, *The Nature of the Physical World*, pp. 211-25.

these probabilities they represent exactly. In short, there are no waves of any material sort at all in nature, but only in our physico-mathematical calculations.

To deal with this situation the physicist has devised calculi, of which the most advanced is Dirac's quantum mechanics, enabling him to state accurately the correlation between the observable events. The sort of theoretical conception which has arisen in consequence is one of an unobservable substratum of reality revealing itself at isolated points as observable phenomena, but between the substratum and the phenomena there is no necessary uniformity of co-ordination, at least so far as we can ascertain. The phenomena are measurable and provide pointer-readings in numerical form, but the substratum cannot be expressed in terms of number. Dirac represents it by what he calls 'q-numbers', *i.e.* symbols of which no numerical interpretation can be given. But, in the calculus he evolves, to use Eddington's phrase, 'numbers are *exuded* from the symbols', so that using the q-numbers p and q, we discover that

$$qp - pq = \mathrm{i}h/2\pi,$$

where h is Planck's constant, and the right-hand side of the equation is numerical. Eddington sums up the position thus: 'The idea is that in digging deeper and deeper into that which lies at the base of physical phenomena we must be prepared to come to entities which, like many things in our conscious experience, are not measurable by numbers in any way; and further, it suggests how exact science, that is to say the science of phenomena correlated to measure-numbers, can be founded on such a basis'.[1]

What now has become of matter, the last surviving remnant of the classical mechanics? It has been resolved away into waves and the waves into mathematical formulae. Sir James Jeans concludes from this that reality must be mental in its ultimate nature, because pure mathematics is a purely mental activity.[2] One should not quarrel with a great scientist if when he indulges in philosophical speculation he uses the wrong technical terms. What Jeans intends is right enough, but he has expressed it somewhat inaccurately, and as so many contemporary philosophers fall into the same kind of error he is hardly to be blamed. We should not agree that mathematics is no more than a 'mental' activity, if that means (as it usually does) a psychical process confined to a singular consciousness. For mathematics is essentially

---

[1] *The Nature of the Physical World*, p. 209.
[2] Cf. *The Mysterious Universe*, p. 173; *Physics and Philosophy*, pp. 203 f.

an objective discipline, in the sense that its methods of reasoning, its deductions and conclusions, are rigorous and must be the same for all minds. But certainly mathematics is an activity of thought and one in which the identity of thought with its object is most apparent and unquestionable. The conclusion to which Jeans draws our attention, therefore, is that the reality which the physicist investigates has turned out to be of the same essential nature as the activity of thought in which subject and object are one, and this the Theory of Relativity had already given us grounds to believe.

Frank's objection to this view[1]—that it might equally well have been derived from Newtonian and Galilean physics which also expressed its laws in mathematical form—this objection falls beside the point. The mathematical formulae of Newton were used to apply to a model involving solid particles with presumed forces acting between them in an absolute frame of space and time. The mathematics of the modern physicist cannot possibly be so applied. Nor can it apply to waves in a material ether, nor to anything that can remotely be described as material. To what then does it apply? Frank maintains that it is simply a form of tautologous statement giving simple expression to laws of nature and that such laws are no more than summary statements of observations or pointer-readings.[2] That the laws of nature propounded by the physicist and discovered with so much labour are mere tautologies is hardly credible, whether or not they are mathematically expressed. That mathematics is a system of pure tautologies is in any case certainly untrue,[3] and if the laws of nature summarize intelligibly the results of observation they cannot be tautologous. But the important question is: What has been observed? or What do the pointer-readings indicate? If, as Frank seems inclined to believe, the answer is, 'Nothing but sense-data', we must give up all belief in an external world, as Berkeley did, and we shall find ourselves ultimately committed to solipsism and worse. But the modern physicist can give no answer to the question—except the one to which Frank so rootedly objects.

19. The task of exact science Eddington describes as the establishment of numerical connections between pointer-readings. What lies behind these pointer-readings it cannot determine. It can tell us only that whatever it is, it is nothing 'physical', 'material' or 'mechanical'

---

[1] *Vide op. cit.* pp. 114 ff.   [2] Cf. *ibid.* p. 113 and pp. 121-2.
[3] *Vide* G. J. Whitrow, 'On the Synthetic Aspect of Mathematics' in *Philosophy*, XXV, no. 95 (October 1950).

in the old sense of these words. 'The physical atom', says Eddington, 'is, like everything else in physics, a schedule of pointer-readings. The schedule is, we agree, attached to some unknown background. Why not then attach it to something of a spiritual nature of which the prominent characteristic is *thought*?'[1]

The physicist as such can give no reason for or against accepting this suggestion. His concern is not with the 'unknown background' but only with the phenomena. In consequence we find an epistemological interpretation of physics evolved by the physicists themselves which is pronouncedly Kantian in its character. Jeans expresses the view as follows: 'We may picture the world of reality as a deep-flowing stream; the world of appearance is its surface, below which we cannot see. Events deep down in the stream throw up bubbles and eddies on to the surface of the stream. These are the transfers of energy and radiation of our common life, which affect our senses and so activate our minds; below these lie deep waters which we can know only by inference.'[2] But this assumption of what goes on below the surface is quite unwarranted by the findings of physical science, for Jeans himself has written some few pages back: 'Causality disappears from the events themselves to reappear in our knowledge of events. But, since we can never pass behind our knowledge of events to the events themselves, we can never know whether causality governs the events or not.'[3] Here again Jeans is using terms loosely. The phrase 'knowledge of events' should be corrected to read 'knowledge of phenomena', for the events themselves are unknowable, and then the Kantian character of the view becomes manifest. The pictures we form to represent the discoveries of physics, he says, are not pictures of the real but only analogies to aid our imagination; they take us only to the doorstep of the mansion of reality, not into its halls and corridors.

Eddington propounds a doctrine which is professedly Kantian.[4] In *The Nature of the Physical World* he had shown that physics deals only with pointer-readings and defines its concepts only in terms of experimental procedures of measurement; its reasoning is circular and its results determined by the concepts so defined.[5] Theoretical physics, therefore, depends upon the means of observation and interpretation at our disposal and these, he says, are our sensory and intellectual equipment. As these are 'subjective', so are the theoretical conclusions

[1] *Nat. of the Phys. World*, p. 259.
[2] *Physics and Philosophy*, p. 193.   [3] *Ibid.* p. 173.
[4] *Vide The Philosophy of Physical Science*, pp. 188 f.
[5] Cf. *Nat. of the Phys. World*, pp. 260-5.

of physics. This is the position developed in *The Philosophy of Physical Science* where Eddington maintains that all fundamental physical concepts are epistemological, by which he means that they are supplied by the intellect, and that in discovering them the scientist is merely deriving from nature what he has already put into nature [1] by his use of the conceptual scheme of interpretation which is the only one at his disposal. It is the only one because it is derivative from the character of the 'sensory and intellectual equipment which is our means of acquiring observational knowledge'. Accordingly, Eddington holds that it is 'subjective' and that all physical knowledge is 'subjectively selected'. The general character of its results is determined by its fundamental concepts, as the size of fish caught in a net is determined by the size of the mesh. The laws of physics are thus subjective in origin. But the reality which they seek to determine is not subjective, and, for all that physics can say, it is determined by other, non-physical, laws which may well be the laws of life and consciousness. [2] 'The universe' about which scientists maintain we can discover nothing *a priori* is not, says Eddington, 'the physical universe'. That is circularly defined as the world described by physical knowledge. [3] The *objective* universe is not touched by physics, and its laws, when discovered, need not turn out to be physical laws. Some of them may indeed have already been discovered as the laws of biology and psychology. 'The pure objective sources of the objective element in our observational knowledge have already been named; they are life, consciousness and spirit.' [4]

The main features of Kant's philosophy are here. Our (physical) knowledge is confined to phenomena which are created by the imposition *a priori* of intellectual concepts (or categories) upon observational material. They are not ultimately real, for ultimate reality lies beyond our science and is for it an unknowable thing-in-itself. But when we step outside the limits of our science, we do *think* the thing-in-itself and we conceive it to be of the nature of a mind. But whereas for Kant to think is not to know, for Eddington the 'objectively real' may be known (for all the physicist can tell) in the sciences of biology and psychology.

20. In dealing with the theory of Kant in Chapter IX above, however, I argued that it did quite definitely involve a coherence view of

[1] Cf. *Nat. of the Phys. World*, p. 244; *Space, Time and Gravitation*, p. 200.
[2] Cf. *Philos. of Phys. Sc.* pp. 179-84.
[3] *Op. cit.* p. 3.
[4] *Op. cit.* pp. 68 f.

knowledge and that, so far at least as the world of our experience is concerned, it established the identity of subject and object. By adopting a Kantian position, therefore, the modern physicist necessarily presupposes both of these tenets. The further assertion that the underlying reality which is manifesting itself in physical phenomena is spiritual, we may leave aside for the moment as the private speculation of two philosophically minded physicists, not necessarily endorsed by their scientific colleagues. It is a metaphysical doctrine to which they incline, but before I consider it I wish to display the implied presumptions of the physical theories themselves. These seem unquestionably to include: (i) the conception of the universe as a complete, self-contained and closed system (which is consonant with the philosophical doctrine of absolutism), and the consequent conception of scientific knowledge about it as a coherent whole;[1] and (ii) the recognition that subject and object are united in physical knowledge, and that between the knowing mind and the known phenomenon there can be no absolute separation.

None of the objections which have been brought against this view have been well founded. I have not thought it necessary to deal at length with the criticisms of Jeans and Eddington by Dr. Joad[2] and the late Professor Stebbing,[3] for what the main gist of their criticism amounts to is that these two scientists have abandoned the presuppositions of 17th-century science and have 'confused' the knowing mind with the object known, or have overlooked the distinction between theory and fact, as well as the necessary derivation of all physical knowledge from the data of sense. But this sort of criticism only reveals the extent to which the critic is oblivious of the changes which the presuppositions of science have undergone in the last hundred years and is hardly valid against attempts to give expression to those very changes. For the rest, both Joad and Stebbing (the former with more moderation and less aggressiveness) have exploited rather too easily the ignorance of technical philosophy confessed by the scientists, which makes many of their statements and arguments fair game for any trained philosopher.

On the other hand, the necessity in modern physics of the two

---

[1] Cf. in particular, Eddington, *The Expanding Universe* (Cambridge, 1944), pp. 104 f.: 'As in the closed universe described in Ch. II, where the galaxies form a system having no centre and no outside, so the conceptions of physics link into a system with no boundary; our goal is not to reach an ultimate conception but to complete the full circle of relationship'.

[2] *Philosophical Aspects of Modern Science*, chs. i and ii.

[3] *Philosophy and the Physicists*.

presumptions stated above is attested by other scientists besides Eddington and Jeans. The concept of a closed space is now an established geometrical conception of which Sir Edmund Whittaker writes: 'The space of non-Euclidean geometry of positive curvature is *finite*, that is, it contains only a definite number of cubic miles, but it has no *boundary* or *frontier*. This distinction between finiteness and boundedness is obvious to a mathematician, but seems to be very difficult for everybody else.'[1] Is it not, however, an admirable example of what Hegel called 'the true infinite'; and might it not well be regarded as a provisional characterization of the Absolute? But it is not merely from the curvature of space that the wholeness of the system results—in fact, spatio-temporal relations may be only a summarized form of interlocking relations of other kinds. The introduction of curvature into space enabled Einstein to give an interpretation of gravitation and other field phenomena which according to the Euclidean conception could not be interpreted without contradiction.[2] The wholeness of the physical universe is indeed already adumbrated in the conception of fields; for the field suffuses the whole of space and time and so must affect physical conditions everywhere and always, and the equation which gives the key to its entire structure is thus a principle of unity embracing the entire physical system. The field, moreover, is the continuation (so to speak) of the charged particle from which it emanates, and as it affects all other particles, every physical entity is inseparably interlocked with every other. In contemporary quantum physics this pervasion of space by every particle is even more complete, for mass has been equated with energy and energy with frequency, making it impossible to determine the last as a quantity localized in space (as energy is not a local quantity) but only by taking into consideration the physical system as a whole to which reference is being

---

[1] *From Euclid to Eddington* (Cambridge, 1949), p. 188.

[2] This fact and others like it are frequently overlooked by critics of the coherence theory of truth seeking to show that a system may be coherent and yet false. Euclidean geometry is often given as an example of such a system. *In abstraction* it is, of course, true that any geometrical system is self-consistent; but the admission that it is taken in abstraction is *ipso facto* a limit upon its truth. As soon as we seek to bring it into concrete relation with the requirements of physics, contradictions appear. As a representation of physical space (one degree less abstract than geometrical space) Euclidean geometry breaks down just because it leads to the kind of contradictions which the Relativity Theory was devised to remove. 'The Theory of Relativity', writes Planck, 'has proved to be the completion and culmination of the structure of classical physics . . . one of the most important steps towards conferring unity and completeness. . . . The Principle of Relativity has advanced the classical physical theory to its highest stage of completeness. . . .' *The Universe in the Light of Modern Physics* (London, 1931), pp. 17-20.

made. Accordingly, Max Planck writes [1] that we must no longer regard causation as a relation between localized events. In order to obtain an adequate version of the laws of motion we must regard the physical system *as a whole* and each individual particle as, in a certain sense, existing in every part of space occupied by the system. Elsewhere he tells us that the lesson of the Quantum Theory is that we cannot discover the laws of the physical universe by dividing it into parts and studying each part separately, but only by fixing our attention on the whole system and the interconnection of its parts.[2]

Planck also supports the notion that subject and object have become inseparable for science. 'In principle', he writes, 'a physical event is inseparable from the measuring instrument or the sense-organ that perceives it; and similarly a science cannot be separated in principle from the investigators who pursue it.'[3]

Eddington's introduction into physics of 'epistemological principles' corresponds very largely to the method Planck describes as the construction of a 'world image', which, he says, contains no observable magnitudes but only symbols having exact mathematical relationships, some of which have no meaning as applied to the world of sense.[4] This world image is a purely theoretical construction, yet it is the specific object of the physicist's study. As Eddington says, 'Physical knowledge (as accepted and formulated today) has the form of a description of a world. We *define* the physical universe as the world so described.' Likewise, the ideal experiment,[5] the use of which Planck defends as a method of physical inquiry, implies that the intellectual activity of the theoretical physicist is one with the object of his study. Whether or not this reduces him to an 'armchair physicist' the results of his lucubrations are indispensable to the experimentalist.

21. Modern physical science, therefore, necessarily presupposes a coherent and systematic world, as well as the identification of subject and object in knowledge, in a way which could not have been tolerated by the scientist of the 17th century. The position which has resulted so far has been Kantian rather than Hegelian, but Kant's error was to impose the limits of physical science upon all human knowledge and

[1] *The Universe in the Light of Modern Physics*, pp. 23-6.
[2] *The Philosophy of Physics* (London, 1936), p. 33.
[3] *Ibid*. p. 104.
[4] *Vide ibid*. pp. 51 f.
[5] *Ibid*. pp. 27 f. He even goes so far as to recommend the conception of an 'ideal intellect' and the solution of problems by consideration of the way in which it would view physical events. (*Vide op. cit.* p. 71.)

this error is not repeated by the modern physicist. The *Ding an sich*, the modern physicist is prepared to believe, may reveal itself in other branches of natural science. He has passed beyond the standpoint of 'the understanding' and recognized the object of his science as a mere phenomenon. The noumenon of which it is the appearance, though unknowable by physical science, is not held to be unknowable altogether. The very recognition of the inseparability of subject and object in physical knowledge gives some clue to its essential nature, and the sciences of biology and psychology, he thinks, dealing with nature at higher levels than physics, may prove to be channels of approach to the knowledge of the ultimately real. Max Planck, indeed, seems to think that some progress in that direction is possible by pure reflection upon physics itself, which would constitute an advance beyond the viewpoint of the understanding into the province of reason.[1] The modern physicist, in consequence, does not rest finally within Kantian limits but is prepared to contemplate a more thorough-going absolutism. 'Modern physics', says Jeans, 'is not altogether antagonistic to an objective idealism like that of Hegel.'[2]

But in one respect at least it has gone beyond Hegel; for Hegel restricted natural science to the level of the understanding, and by recognizing the inseparability of subject and object the modern physicist has adopted what, according to Hegel, is the attitude of speculative reason. Moreover, the researches of physics have reached a point where the work of observation and experiment can make no good progress without the more speculative theories of the 'scientific epistemologist'. This is Eddington's strong conviction and it is supported by the views of Planck. The scientist, in short, in order to progress, must also philosophize and the two species of knowledge, science and philosophy, reveal the hall-mark of the philosophical universal—they overlap. Modern philosophy, accordingly, must take account of this overlap and propound a theory of nature and mind in conformity with it.

We have been brought to the conclusion that what we have hitherto thought of as matter (alien to mind) is essentially an activity of some-

[1] *Vide Where is Science Going?* (London, 1933), p. 96: 'But when we are faced with the indivisible quantum of action, the limit is laid with mathematical accuracy, beyond which the most delicate physical measurement is unable to give a satisfactory answer to questions connected with the individual behaviour of the more minute processes. The result is that the problem of these infinitesimal processes has no longer a meaning for purely physical research. Here we come to the point where such problems have to be dealt with by the speculative reason. And it is in this abstract way that they must be taken into account in our attempt to complete the physicist's picture of the universe and thus bring us nearer to the discovery of external reality itself.'

[2] *Physics and Philosophy*, p. 204.

thing beyond the reach of physics, an activity which manifests itself as physical phenomena and which some philosophically inclined physicists suggest may be of the same kind as the activity of thought. At any rate, both the activity of thought and that which underlies the physical phenomena can be expressed as mathematics. The classical mechanics has disappeared and the case of the old philosophical materialist has dissolved away. Mechanism in biology now, if it means no more than the hope of interpreting biological facts in terms of physics and chemistry, holds no terrors for the vitalist; for chemistry and physics give only statistical laws governing the manifestation as material phenomena of something unknown to physics, and what the vitalist claims for biology is something exactly similar—viz. that it formulates the laws according to which something immaterial, called life, manifests itself in a material medium. Ultimately for the physicist matter is resolved into energy and energy into some substrate activity which, in Jeans' analogy, 'throws up bubbles' that we can perceive. For the vitalist life is the manifestation in the living organism of an entelechy or life-force. The more philosophical physicists suggest that, for all their science can tell, the behaviour of electrons and protons may be governed by an activity of precisely the same kind.

22. Schroedinger has suggested that the gene is a molecule and the chromosome fibre an aperiodic crystal. Might it not be that this substrate activity, represented in Dirac's quantum mechanics by q-numbers, when it determines the behaviour of electrons and protons so that they form atoms in the molecules of a periodic crystal, manifests itself as inorganic matter obeying the laws of physics; but when it determines them so that they form atoms in the molecules of an aperiodic crystal, manifests itself as living matter obeying the laws of biology? Haldane claimed that the axioms of biology were *sui generis* and could not be assimilated to those of physics, but Schroedinger maintains that the physical laws governing the behaviour of an aperiodic crystal (living matter) have yet to be discovered. 'We must be prepared', he says, 'to find a new type of physical law prevailing in it.'[1] When this new type of law is discovered may it not turn out to be the very type of biological law that Haldane contemplates? If so, the continuity between physics and biology will have been established, not at the expense of biology nor of the concept of organism, but because of the introduction of the conception of organism into physics itself. There is no longer a conflict between 'mechanism' and 'vitalism', and

[1] *What is Life?*, p. 81.

the consequent possibility of viewing the whole of nature as one continuous process of development reinforces the absolutist presupposition of contemporary science and points to a philosophical interpretation of the Hegelian type, in which the antithesis of empirical realism and subjective idealism has been overcome and must be regarded as a thing of the past.

Chapter XVIII

PHILOSOPHIES OF EVOLUTION

I. BERGSON

1. IN one respect the most typically modern philosophy is that of Henri Bergson, the philosopher of evolution *par excellence*. For him it is the very essence of reality to which the keywords are time, change, movement, process, creation and evolution. Everything else is to be accounted for in terms of these ideas—or rather there *is* nothing else, for everything else is an illusion. No other philosopher has been so absolute and extreme in his reduction of all reality to the moving, creating process of life—*l'élan vital*.

Bergson strives to give expression to a conception of nature exactly opposite to that which 'the new science' of the 17th century had created. He is radically opposed to all notions of mechanism, automatism, determinism and materialism, which threaten the freedom of life and seek to deny its creative spontaneity. His whole philosophy is an attempt to vindicate this freedom and creative advance against the deterministic claims of mechanical and physical science. He maintains that the difficulties which philosophers had experienced in their attempts to relate matter to life and determined causation to free action were due to their taking as real the physical view of the world, and especially of time, whereas, he maintained, it is not real, but is only a special kind of appearance. The only thing which is real, he says, is life, and the distinguishing characteristic of life is free, indeterminate action as opposed to the apparently determined behaviour of mere matter.

2. We come to think that life may be determined because we misunderstand the nature of real time, and this also makes us believe in the determination of matter; then we extend our notions of time and matter to life. Real time (*durée*) is, according to Bergson, the continuous flow of conscious experience, in which the past persists into and 'interpenetrates' the present and the future. What I experience now is what it is, because of what I experienced before. My consciousness at any moment is shot through and through with past experience and future expectations. For consciousness, time is indivisible into past, present and future; indivisible into instants. It is a continuous flow in

393

which the past is carried on into the future and grows like a fugue. Consequently, nothing in this flow of conscious time is ever exactly repeated; for if something recurs similar to what had occurred before, it is changed by the fact that it has a different past.

If we understand this, we can understand how living behaviour is free, creative and undetermined. Here also experience modifies action and no exactly similar action is ever repeated because the second occurrence is modified by the fact that the first had taken place. Consequently, exact prediction of living activity is impossible. We cannot calculate mathematically what it will be because until it has happened we do not possess all the terms of the necessary equation. It is not the result of a set of predetermined conditions, it creates its own conditions in the course of its activity.

Material action, on the other hand, is held to be predictable, because it depends on causes which recur exactly and because we assume the laws of conservation of energy and matter. In such cases 'all is given' (*tout est donné*) and all we have to do (if we know enough of what is given) is to calculate, in order to discover future events. Time as the physicist takes it makes no difference to things, and change results only from spatial rearrangement. In life and consciousness, on the other hand, time makes all the difference, for life and consciousness are perpetually changing and for them time and change are identical.

The physicist thinks of time as a line, as a series of events lying one beside the other—on the analogy of space—in fact he calls it a fourth dimension. But such a procedure Bergson repudiates as the 'spatialization' of time, which falsifies its real character. Real time is altogether antithetical to space and *durée* cannot be conceived on any spatial analogy.

Why then do we normally agree with the physicist in his conception of time and matter? Because, says Bergson, our intellect, which is a product of the life-force, was evolved for a special purpose—namely to help us in action. We can act most efficiently only when we deal with a world cut up into unchanging, instantaneous chunks. To act upon something constantly in motion is like trying to keep one's hold upon Proteus, the Old Man of the Sea, and we must arrest the flow at convenient moments. We thus take momentary cross-sections of the stream of time for practical purposes and then reconstruct its course by stringing together our artificial sections to form a picture of the world as the physicist conceives it—a world of dead matter spread out in space and behaving according to mechanical laws. Its behaviour seems to be of this mechanical kind because the changes which seem to occur in it are simply the result of putting together the instantaneous snap-shots which the intellect successively takes, as the appearance of movement in the cinema is generated by a rapid succession of 'stills'. But this appearance of motion is not real motion, which cannot be cut up into sections and then strung together again; it is only an appear-ance, a sort of useful illusion produced by the intellect. The real world is a constant continuous flow of change which the intellect cannot grasp, and, so far as it can be known at all, it can be known only through intuition—the direct feeling or experience of one's own ever-flowing life. The world of physics—the material world—is thus a distorted appearance and the only reality is the moving, living life-force, con-stantly pushing on to create new and unpredictable forms. It is sheer movement, sheer activity, sheer tension.

The underlying reason for this elevation of life at the expense of all else is Bergson's determination to resolve the dualism still dogging the heels of philosophy after the scientific triumph of vitalism. The 17th-century dichotomy between mind and nature had become a dichotomy within nature between life and matter, and as life manifests itself in material organisms, the dualism can be overcome only if either life is derivative from matter, or matter can somehow be derived from life. Biological evidence convinced Bergson that the former could not be true and he set himself, therefore, to propound a theory embodying the latter hypothesis. In doing so, however, he tacitly accepted the Renaissance dualism, if only to react against it, and his reaction is not a resolution of the antithesis so much as the annihilation of one of the opposites.[1]

3. In his zeal to get rid of matter, Bergson first attempts to explain it away as a product of the analysing intellect cutting its cross-sections out of what is really an indivisible flux in which past, present and future inseparably interpenetrate. The intellect, however, is an instrument developed by the evolving species to increase its capacity for action; and so matter, as a product of the intellect, is itself a product of life instrumental to the evolutionary purposes of the life-force.

The idealistic affinities of this theory are easily recognizable. To make matter a cross-section produced by the intellect from something indivisibly continuous is not so very different from making it an 'ideal construction' or an abstraction from a total experience and is strongly reminiscent of Bradley; but this must not mislead us, for Bergson

---

[1] As Collingwood has made clear, Bergson's philosophy is no more than the obverse of the old 18th-century materialism. *Vide Idea of Nature*, pp. 138 f.

rejects idealism as well as realism. Also, the view of the intellect as that which separates out and cuts off artificial segments of a reality which these segments by themselves misrepresent, is reminiscent of the abstract understanding in Hegel's doctrine. But Bergson does not subordinate this abstract, intellectual view of the world to a transcendent reason, but to an all-producing life-force, adequately known only through intuition which is logically inferior to the intellect, though metaphysically more reliable.

Bergson rejects both idealism and realism because he maintains that in action the organism is aware of an opposing reality which it does not create and which it can control only by learning the independent nature and the laws governing the independent behaviour of things apart from its own activity. Science, in short, as a more accurate development of the common-sense view of things, is necessary to successful action, and science must treat its objects as independent of mind. On the other hand, every attempt to explain consciousness in terms of physical and physiological facts is bound to break down and leave us with a system of material interactions, plus an epiphenomenal consciousness. 'All realism', says Bergson, 'is bound to make perception an accident, and consequently a mystery.' For idealism, on the other hand, science will become an accident and its success a mystery.[1]

But if the action of the organism presupposes an independent world of reality against which to act, and if matter is no more than an intellectual abstraction, what is the independent reality against which *l'élan vital* (expressing itself through the organism) reacts? At first one is inclined to think that the reality which the intellect dissects is the living process of evolution, enduring (not merely occurring) in time, so that *durée* is its very essence. But this cannot be the reality against which the organism exerts itself in action, for life is said to be continuous in all organisms and Bergson does not explain how it can come into conflict with itself. Moreover, the life-force is not a material or mechanical force, it is an immaterial activity. In what then does it manifest itself? Clearly, unless the argument is hopelessly circular, it cannot manifest itself in a product of the intellect which it has itself developed as an instrument of action in a material world so created. Accordingly, Bergson has a second theory of the origin of matter. For reasons which he does not reveal, the life-force in certain (unspecified) circumstances weakens in tension—its tension, he says, becomes relaxed. He calls this relaxation 'de-tension' and its effect, he maintains, is to create the appearance of space (or extension) and of dead

[1] Cf. *Matter and Memory* (London, 1919), p. 16.

matter spread about in it. This appearance is analogous to that which occurs when a fast train passes a slower one and the slow one appears to be stationary, or even to be moving backwards. So the detended life-force appears to the intenser and more active life to be static and dead—*i.e.* it looks like dead matter.

Matter is therefore the slough of life falling back upon it like the cinders of spent rockets. The movement of the life-force, says Bergson, 'is like the fiery path of a rocket through the black cinders of spent rockets that are falling dead'. Matter is what life throws off and leaves behind in its progress—and this accumulates and (so to speak) dams up the life stream; it hems it in, pushes it aside, drives it into channels ('canalizes' it) and may stop it altogether at some points or turn it aside or back. The only point where this seems not to have happened is where man has emerged, for he still progresses where other living species seem to have reached the limit of their development.

Matter, we now see, is not a mere illusion or intellectual distortion of the real. It is an actual by-product of the life-force—it is the life-force, as it were, in reverse, and presumably our inability to realize this is due to our intellectual distortion of reality.

4. This is a brief and admittedly inadequate outline of the philosophy of Bergson, and when we come to assess its value, we are faced with a difficult task, for most of Bergson's constructive philosophy is expressed in metaphor, and when we press the metaphors and try to gain a precise understanding of their meaning, that meaning eludes us. Metaphors, when pressed, almost invariably lead to contradictions and that is exactly what we find when we try to make sense of what Bergson has written. How are we to conceive, for instance, a life-force which is at once a force and yet not material, and which presses on against—nothing? What sort of manifestation could such a force have, in its original form? What is the source and the nature of the 'tension' in *l'élan vital*? Tension implies an opposition of forces, a pulling in different directions. How is this idea applicable to the onward surge of life? Again, how can this onward impetus become relaxed and throw off spent bits of itself—an immaterial 'force', generating matter by relaxing itself—and for what conceivable reason would it do this? Further, Bergson alleges that the mechanical appearance of the material world is a creation of the intellect for practical purposes. But if this is a false appearance of the real, how can it be useful for practical purposes? Do we act only in a dream-world of artificially produced illusions? If so, how can our actions be creative or have any effect at all upon what

is real or actual? But on the other hand, if matter is the relaxed life-force falling back upon its more vigorous activity, the material world must in reality be much as we conceive it in physical science and our intellect need not be impugned as a source of illusion.

These contradictions and difficulties result from Bergson's refusal to admit the most necessary of all the implications of evolution—namely, its relativity to a completion—an end which sublates and consummates the entire process. He asserts instead that the tendency of time and change, and consequently of life, is always novelty and indetermination. 'The impetus of life ... consists in a need of creation ... it seizes upon matter, which is necessity itself, and strives to introduce into it the largest possible amount of indetermination and liberty.'[1] This negative conception of freedom is for him the ideal. Consequently he has no way of deciding the direction of evolution, and so no ground for asserting that the process is one of evolution at all, as opposed to a process of simple change. It is an onward movement towards no assignable or conceivable end.

But Bergson's steady refusal to see the process of evolution as a whole is only a facet of his constant opposition to mechanism and determination in which *tout est donné*—his opposition to the Renaissance conception of nature. It is this that marks his philosophy as typically modern, but also it is this that brings his system toppling to the ground. He opposes the Renaissance mechanism simply by annihilating matter and so has left the life-force no medium in which to realize its activity. What is required is not simply to deny one pole of the opposition but to give a new account of both, which will effect their reconciliation.

So, far from having succeeded in rendering intelligible the mind's knowledge of nature, he has in effect rendered it impossible. Nature for him is life, and mind and matter are its secondary products. But what mind knows as nature is not the life-force which produced the intellect, but the intellect's own misconception of the products of *l'élan vital*. And the mind which life produces is not that by which reality is known, but a subordinate instrument of life's activity. We are thus abandoned on the horns of a dilemma. Either Bergson's theory itself is a misrepresentation due to over-intellectualization, in which case we may reject it together with the limitation it imposes on our thought, or else the nature of reality is after all knowable by the intellect, in which case it cannot be such as Bergson would have us believe.

Are we then to reject Bergson's theory as barren? On the contrary,

[1] *Creative Evolution*, p. 265.

he has in many important ways given expression to the modern idea by showing that the ultimate substance of the real is an activity which is better likened to life than to inert matter. He repudiates the mechanism of the earlier epoch which modern science has outgrown, and he has seen that the problems centring in the problem of knowledge can find a solution only if we take seriously the notion of evolution and think of reality as a continuous process in which the phases interpenetrate and the past is incapsulated in the present.

II. THE THEORY OF EMERGENCE

5. Dualisms in philosophy are never entirely spurious and there is always some foundation in the nature of things to justify them. They cannot therefore be removed by the annihilation of one of the terms or by its simple absorption into the other. If the dualism is to be resolved at all, justice must be done to both terms and both must be referred to something more fundamental than either. The theory of emergent evolution is therefore an improvement upon Bergson's monism of life, because it does treat seriously, not only time and life, but also space and matter. But the majority of its exponents fail in the end because they cannot quite relinquish the presuppositions of Renaissance science. The most authoritative expositors of the doctrine, Lloyd Morgan and Samuel Alexander, quite openly espouse the empirical view-point and the advantage gained by the evolutionary idea is lost as a result of the attempt to couple it with an epistemology based upon the very conception of nature which emergent evolution had come to replace. Alexander resolutely sets his face against the union of subject and object in knowledge and desires 'to order man and mind to their proper place among a world of finite things'.[1] He assumes throughout that minds are finite entities separate from and externally related to their objects—at best 'the most gifted members known to us in a democracy of things'.[2] And just for this reason his theory of emergence fails in the end to save his theory of knowledge, which succumbs to criticism the same in principle as that which proved fatal to Locke's.

As a result of this empirical attitude Alexander, like so many other empiricists, tends to renounce the claim to logical cogency for his theory, asserting that philosophy (like science) is purely descriptive of the real. It does not and ought not to attempt to 'preside over its creation'. It cannot argue deductively from first principles to the

---

[1] *Vide Proceedings of the British Academy*, 1913–14, p. 279.
[2] *Space, Time and Deity*, I, p. 6.

nature of the actual world from no one factor of which can any other be logically deduced. The facts must be simply accepted, as they are found, 'with natural piety'. The reasons which might justify such an attitude are not those which Alexander gives. It is not because philosophy is purely descriptive that it cannot deduce reality *a priori*—on the contrary, purely descriptive it can never be—but because *a priori* deduction, so far as it is possible at all, belongs to the most abstract of the sciences, and philosophy seeks to understand the concrete nature of the real. Its method, therefore, is both deductive and inductive at once—a method in which these two classes of reasoning overlap.

But empiricism is only the debit side of the account of emergent evolution. On its credit side it gives us a view of nature as an evolutionary process and if we concentrate primarily on the doctrine of emergence and develop from that the theory of mind and knowledge which it warrants—a theory untainted by empiricism—we arrive at a result very different from and much more satisfactory than any reached by its official exponents.

6. As Alexander's monumental work is the most imposing statement of the theory, I shall, in the main, confine my attention to his version, according to which the 'stuff' or matrix of reality is pure space and time united into a single continuum: space-time or motion. His account of what he calls 'the empirical nature' of space and time is somewhat complicated and obscure and it need not detain us here. It will be sufficient to say that it leads to a theory of time as a movement discriminating points in the extendedness of space. Space, says Alexander, is full of time and is variegated by motion. Just what this means is difficult to follow, as it is held to be true independently of objects situated and moving in space, or of events occurring in time, or even of minds making distinctions within space and time *in abstracto*. But I shall not here enter into the discussion of these difficulties. Despite valiant efforts to avoid it, moreover, Alexander is forced in the end to adopt the more common conception of time as duration, in which all space co-exists at every instant and so cannot be variegated by time's movement. This is apparent in the simile by which he illustrates his theory. He compares space-time to a volume of gas [1] in which the molecules are dashing about in all directions. These molecules are the instants of time which are constantly and continuously being redistributed among the points of space. But this results in a kaleidoscopic

[1] *S.T.D.* I, pp. 63 f.

succession of patterns in space-time (what he calls configurations of motion) and it involves the presumption of a time series in which each instant is represented by a new pattern and not by a single molecule. Every point in space must then be present at every instant. This contradiction in Alexander's theory of space-time is not unconnected with the flaw which eventually destroys his theory of knowledge. But let us pass first to the doctrine of emergence.

7. Some of the configurations of space-time carry (in a manner soon to be investigated) the qualities by which we recognize them as separate existents. These existents are what Alexander calls 'complexes of motion', and the qualities which distinguish and characterize them are, at least *prima facie*, contingent to the nature of space-time and they are, therefore, called 'empirical qualities'. But all things being, as it were, pieces of space-time, there are certain features which are all-pervasive throughout reality—the features of space-time itself which Alexander differentiates into various categories, but of which no detailed discussion is called for here.

If pure space-time itself may be said to possess a characteristic at all analogous to quality it is what Alexander calls 'the spatio-temporal quality of motion'.[1] But time as the dynamic principle in space-time is the source of new configurations of motion, and as a new complex arises it possesses, 'as a matter of observed empirical fact', a new emergent quality. We cannot say *why* this should happen; it is simply a fact of experience and must be accepted 'with natural piety'.

We have been told that new complexes of motion arise in space-time, which in virtue of their special pattern carry an emergent quality. But we must not imagine that the new quality is, in any sense, added to space-time, *ab extra*. When the appropriate configuration arises it *is* the quality, just as radiation of a certain frequency is the quality of colour.

The term 'quality' is used, in this connection, in a very wide sense. It means any empirical qualification of space-time or of any level of qualified existence which may have emerged up to the point in question, and correlative to this use of 'quality' the term 'matter' also acquires an extended meaning. In ordinary speech, 'matter' is that which has physical properties, such as cohesion, resiliency, fluidity, etc., and 'quality' means, in general, the way in which such matter affects our senses. By 'qualities' we usually mean colours, sounds, smells and so forth—though, of course, in everyday speech the word has other and more divergent senses besides. But for Alexander

[1] *Ibid.* II, p. 45.

'materiality' itself is a quality—that which emerges in certain configurations of space-time (unless indeed there be an intermediary level of emergence between space-time and matter—such as energy). This is the narrower meaning which he attaches to the term. In the wider sense not only what we generally call matter, but higher emergents such as living organisms may be regarded as the 'matter' of still higher 'qualities'—*e.g.* consciousness. In short, Alexander's use of these terms is parallel to Aristotle's use of 'matter' and 'form'.

8. At this stage two points need elucidation. First, we must know more fully what we mean by an emergent and if, in any sense, emergence is to be viewed as development and not simply change. Secondly, if emergence is not mere change, can we say anything about the reason of its occurrence or is it simply a fact to be accepted?

(a) With regard to the first of these points we find that though the emergence of qualities is due, in the last resort, to nothing more than a change of spatio-temporal configurations, the qualities themselves do not form a bare series of changes. There certainly is an aspect of mere alteration evident in the world, for entities do change their qualities in a way which does not involve emergence. But a new emergent quality is not merely a change of form in the material basis in which it inheres. Matter is not simply a different pattern in space-time, it is a special kind of pattern. It arises, it is true, as the result of a change, but it gives us something new and something more than is to be found in pure space and time. What we get from the mere change of relations between point-instants is no more than a variety of geometrical figures—mere potential shapes of the bodies which emerge later. More than this may, of course, be involved in levels of emergence (if there are any) below matter and certain varieties of movement may take the form of energy, which, Alexander says, may be an emergent between space-time and matter. But when we do get a real emergent it is something of an entirely new order of being. Among the different patterns of motion which arise in the course of time some appear which are not mere shapes. The constellation of motions produced in them involves an absolutely new feature of existence—a new quality.

Just as the meaning of a sentence is more than the simple sum of the words which go to make it, or as certain harmonies in music produce something above and beyond the sum of the separate effects of the component sounds, so an emergent quality cannot be reached by mere computation of the elements which are combined in it. Certain syntheses produce new *wholes* which are in a special sense individual and coherent, so that the whole is more than the sum of the parts and bears a character which the separate factors in isolation or in haphazard juxtaposition do not presage. This new character is the emergent.

Lloyd Morgan contrasts 'emergents' with what he calls 'resultants'.[1] What can be produced by mere mathematical combination and permutation within any one type of existence is a resultant: *e.g.* the geometrical figures mentioned above are of this class, and when a number of forces are acting at a point along different lines, a 'resultant' force may be found equivalent to their combined effect. But an emergent is like a new chemical compound, the properties of which are not the mere resultant of the combination of its elements. It is something in a more special sense new.

This being the nature of an emergent, it is easy to see that a range of gradations will arise of which each presupposes all that have gone before. Particular configurations of motion give rise to matter; special combinations of matter carry definite qualities (which, for minds, become sensa); further syntheses of these according to the proper pattern produce a material substance with the emergent quality of life and eventually the appropriate constellations of living functions are 'qualitied' with consciousness. The final emergent is deity, the quality of mind in the highest forms of its spiritual activity.

So far, therefore, as each emergent quality involves all those that have gone before but is not involved in them, each emergent is more complex than, and is an advance upon, those preceding it. In this sense the gamut of emergents does constitute a development, though we may well ask whether that word does not imply something more than has so far been described. In a true development not only is the prior involved in the posterior, but the posterior is also potential in the prior; otherwise the later has not really developed out of the earlier but has been merely superimposed upon it or built up out of it as a house is built of bricks. Without this *mutual* implication between the members of a series we have only accretion or a sort of geometrical progression and nothing that can properly be called development.

There is, however, a vague suggestion of 'something more' even in Alexander's theory which I shall indicate in discussing the next point to be explained.

(b) The question may be asked whether the occurrence of a new configuration bearing an emergent quality is to be regarded as purely contingent. If this were so, the series of emergents would consist of a number of successive accidents. Or, on the contrary, is there, perhaps,

[1] *Emergent Evolution*, ch. i, § 1.

some real principle of progress which runs through the whole development urging it on from one stage to the next?

What Alexander says in the earlier part of *Space, Time and Deity* would suggest that the former is the case. I have already quoted his statement that a new emergent quality is 'a matter of observed empirical fact' and have noticed his doctrine of 'natural piety'. Yet in the last book of the same work he reverts to the notion of time as the principle of movement and says: 'Now since time is the principle of growth and time is infinite, the internal development of the world, which before was described in its simplest terms as the redistribution of moments of time among points of space, cannot be regarded as ceasing with the emergence of those finite configurations of space-time which carry the empirical quality of mind. . . . *There is a nisus in space-time which, as it has borne its creatures forward through matter and life to mind, will bear them forward to some higher level of existence.*'[1]

The notion of time as a mere continuous succession is hardly adequate to meet the needs of such a theory. A *nisus* is more than a succession; it is a force or an urge and it implies direction of some sort. Perhaps there is some premonition of this in Alexander's insistence on the unidirectional movement of time.[2] But even so, the metaphor of movement through space is not adequate to express the nature of a *nisus* which involves a compelling principle, forcing on its subject from one form to the next. This point needs further development and it is left by Alexander veiled in obscurity. He does indeed suggest that a kind of natural selection determines the sequence of configurations. 'I dare to ask', he writes, '. . . whether . . . nature or Space-Time did not try various complexes of simple motions and out of the chaos of motion preserve certain types.'[3] But why should some complexes be preserved in preference to others? Trying, preferring and selecting imply the activity of a developed mind with a conscious purpose, an idea that Alexander would violently have rejected; yet we are given no clue to any different interpretation of the matter. The suggestion of a *nisus* is perhaps the most significant feature of Alexander's theory and it would be quite the most fruitful if its implications were developed to the full. But it is never followed up, for it would have committed him to more than he would ever willingly have accepted.

Yet without some principle of development we shall find that the whole system breaks down, for apart from the *nisus* the whole universe,

---

[1] *Space, Time and Deity*, II, p. 346. (My italics.)
[2] *Ibid.* I, p. 51.
[3] *Ibid.* II, p. 55.

on Alexander's theory, can be no more than a series of accidental complications of point-instants of which we can give no explanation. We know only that they do happen in the order described. The connection between consecutive complexes in this series is provided solely by the continuity of time and this is insufficient to account for emergence. We have a bare succession of patterns in space, each different from the last but, so far as the theory provides, nothing in the nature of any one pattern to determine the variation to follow. There is no mutual implication between them, and without mutual implication there can be no real continuity between events, yet any legitimate or intelligible notion of a *nisus* in a temporal succession of events involves the potentiality in the earlier phases of what is later to emerge. It is the doctrine of 'natural piety' that obscures this point and hides from Alexander the defect of his own theory. His principle is really no proper explanation of the appearances. In fact, he disclaims all ability to give a reason why any emergence should occur and consequently the full significance of the term is never brought out. It remains a mere name for an inexplicable relation between the different evolutionary levels. Accordingly, the development is broken up; each emergent quality comes apart from the matter in which it arises and, as the relation between them is inexplicable, the entire system falls loose at the joints.

III. EMERGENT MIND

9. But this ataxia is not endemic in the theory of emergence itself. It is an infection inoculated into it by the empiricism of its exponents and directly connected with the view that the objects of knowledge are external to mind. This view dictates the treatment of mind as an adjectival attachment to a finite material entity and so blinds the theorist to the organic relation between the material counterpart and its surroundings. If we follow out the consequences of the emergence theory uninfluenced by empirical prejudices, we can find reason to hope for a more successful account of mind and knowledge than either 'idealism' or 'realism' provides. If mind is emergent from a whole or totality of which the parts are themselves wholes of less concrete kinds, and if such wholes are not mere aggregates but are (each in its appropriate degree) really organic, then every level prior to mind is indispensably involved in the emergence of consciousness. Consciousness, in fact, is just that quality of wholeness which is achieved at the level subsequent to life, and the factors which go to make up the whole are the lower phases of emergence. Mind is a totality of living and material

parts raised, so to speak, to a higher power of wholeness than either matter or life. But it is quite ridiculous to suggest (as Alexander does) that for that reason consciousness is separate from its objects. The organic wholeness that produces the quality of life is just that which combines the material elements of the organism, not only with one another, but also with the so-called environment, in such a way that no sharp separation between them is possible. If mind is then a higher power of organic wholeness this union of self and other, of subject and object must, at the mental level, be even more complete. Accordingly, knowledge can now be accounted for as the coming to consciousness through the living organism of all the lower phases—of the whole evolutionary process which is nature—a coming to consciousness that is itself a higher phase of wholeness than what is qualitied by mere life. Mind, therefore, is nature come aware of itself as a whole.

The apparently obvious objection to this view is that the organism is a small part of the physical world and that the quality of life arises only in it and not in the physical world as a whole. Similarly consciousness is the quality which supervenes upon a particular constellation of vital processes and upon that alone, not upon the system of the universe as such. Alexander develops his theory on just these lines leading, as we shall see, to the view that consciousness arises as a result of the simple relation of compresence between the qualitied organism and other things. But this is to ignore altogether the holistic element of the doctrine, without which the entire theory of emergence would collapse.[1] The new qualities are said to emerge only on the formation of configurations of more organic wholeness than the earlier ones, and whatever we may think or say of the purely physical level of reality we must admit that the sort of organic wholeness involved in life is not a mere pattern of physico-chemical action within the physical limits of the organism. No pattern of physico-chemical reactions within those limits is possible at all except in reaction with things and events beyond those limits. And this reaction is not mechanical, in the sense of being simply repetitive, it is differentiated in a way which makes each variation relevant to a definite set of purposes. The only feasible interpretation of the phenomena of life must be teleological, and that involves a pattern or whole of things and events uniting the activity of the organism—the interplay of functions within it—and the 'external' circumstances in relation to which those functions operate. A living creature is, therefore, not just a complicated piece of matter which

[1] This aspect of the theory is brought out much more adequately by Smuts in *Holism and Evolution*.

behaves in a distinctive way. It is the focus of a systematic interplay of functions in which all parts of the organic and inorganic world are, in varying degrees, involved.[1] We saw that this was true even in the inorganic sphere, where every particle and every field of radiant energy pervades the entire physical universe. At the level of life the organic and teleological character of the interplay of functions is raised to an even higher power. The organism *is* the universe made more intimately one. To raise this to a higher power still is to bring it to consciousness, and the finiteness of the mind in which it occurs is measured only by the degree of its failure to achieve coherence or concreteness in its experience.

The theory of knowledge which should follow from that of emergent evolution, therefore, should naturally be Hegelian in type. In fact, Bradley's doctrine, could it have been grafted upon Alexander's, would have been much nearer the truth than either by itself; but Alexander reacted so violently against Bradley (under whose influence his early philosophical training had taken place) that he did not realize how far in the theory of emergence he has supplied the deficiences of Bradley's metaphysic. Instead, he hammered a defunct empiricism on top of the doctrine of emergent evolution, smothering its vitality, and, with the belief in natural piety, shattering the continuity of the evolutionary process.

10. In his anxiety to keep the mind finite Alexander identifies it completely with the neural processes whose special configuration is the basis of the emergent quality of consciousness. This in itself would be unobjectionable if he did justice to the nature of the organic totality presupposed by the existence of those neural processes. But this he fails to do, for he insists simply that a mind, like any other entity in the democracy of things, is a piece of matter qualitied in a certain way, the material element in its lowest terms being just a complex of point-instants in space-time, and the quality being emergent from the specific empirical variation of pattern involved.

The special features of mind are entirely dependent on the peculiar nature of its emergent quality but, as Alexander is at great pains to show, there are analogues, at all levels of existence, to the various mental activities involved in knowing. Not only is it the case that mind has in common with other existents the relation between its matter and its emergent quality, but also its activity is simply a special variation of a universal fact. All things, we are told, are compresent in space-time,

[1] *Vide* Smuts, *Holism and Evolution* (London, 1927), pp. 115-21.

and everything behaves in the presence of other things in accordance with its specific nature—that is, in accordance with the nature bestowed upon it by its special emergent quality. 'The plant lives, grows and breathes, and twines around a stick. The material body resists, or falls, or sounds when struck, or emits light when touched by the sun. The mind knows.'[1] Knowledge is simply the product of the mind's activity in compresence with other finite entities, in accordance with its own emergent quality of consciousness.

This quality of consciousness is such that when the mind is compresent with another entity it 'enjoys' an experience. The enjoyment is an awareness of the other entity as an object and is called the 'act' of mind, but the object is not enjoyed. We enjoy only the experience or act of awareness and what is meant when we say that we are aware of an object is that we 'contemplate' it. Nevertheless, without contemplation of an object there can be no enjoyment.[2] The contemplation of the object, therefore, is no more than the occasion for the mind's enjoyment of itself in experiencing.

The point which is emphasized most strongly is that the object is entirely non-mental. It is quite wrong, according to Alexander, to call it a mental—or an ideal—content. The mind does not contain the object in any sense at all but is characterized only by the quality of consciousness which it enjoys in the contemplation of objects. On the other hand, the mind does not and cannot contemplate itself; it can never become its own object, and knows itself only in enjoyment.[3] The possibility of introspection is held not to be inconsistent with this fact, for introspection is the direct description of our enjoyment and does not require that the mind should become an object to itself. Furthermore, in experiencing objects the mind does not receive the quality of the object (*e.g.* such quality as colour or sound) but enjoys only its own quality of 'mentalness'.[4] Objects excite neural processes which differ with the variety of categorial features of the respective objects, and these processes are enjoyed as consciousness.[5] The mental quality is thus the same for *all* objects—only the categorial features of the neural processes vary. How we are to square this view with the theory that the emergent quality depends upon the specific constellation of the 'material' factor (which, presumably, may be resolved finally into

[1] *S.T.D.* II, p. 81.
[2] *Vide ibid.* I, p. 25: 'No action of the mind is possible without its object any more than a plant can breathe without air'.
[3] *Ibid.* I, pp. 17 f.
[4] *Ibid.* II, pp. 82 and 90.
[5] Cf. *ibid.* I, pp. 101 ff.

spatio-temporal determinations) is difficult to explain. But, for the moment, we may pass this point by.

The view of knowing which results from this theory, its author admits, is very nearly akin to E. B. Holt's so-called 'search-light view'. In fact Alexander confesses himself much inclined at times to adopt Holt's position, but he is deterred from doing so by consideration of one point on which he feels it to be inadequate. The view is that consciousness is merely that selected cross-section of reality to which the mind (or, perhaps, the organism as a whole) makes specific responses (e.g. the turning of a plant towards the light). Consciousness is then not 'in the mind' at all but, as Alexander says, 'out there', and it consists in the illumination (so to speak) of a certain section of reality as if by a search-light, resulting from the selection of that part of reality by the mind for specific response. Alexander's only objection to this view is that it does not account for the element of ownership in consciousness. When I see a fire it is, in a sense, *my* fire. We cannot say that the total cross-section of reality to which response is made includes the relation between me and the object for that would be 'to import into the cross-section itself the theory that seeing happens when there is a cross-section containing colour and there is a neural response outside that cross-section'.[1] Accordingly, to account for the essentially personal element in consciousness, Alexander feels constrained to postulate a quality in the subject himself. This is 'enjoyment' of which the so-called cross-section is but the contemplated object. ' Consciousness ', he says, following Santayana, 'is the search-light itself.' Nevertheless, as regards the objective aspect of knowledge, the search-light view provides a useful metaphor appropriate to Alexander's theory. It stresses the point that he makes the object entirely extra-mental. It cannot be claimed that in knowledge it is possessed by the mind (for all that has been said of the fire being 'my fire'), for what the mind possesses is only a quality, differences in which, if they can be produced at all, are somehow to be only categorial differences and not differences of quality.

The reference to 'my fire' is indeed puzzling, for though Alexander's theory does provide a subjective element in knowing, it gives no grounds for any claim by the subject to possess the *object*. It is not 'my fire' but, at best, 'my enjoyment of the fire' which I experience and it is even doubtful how far the last three words of this phrase are at all legitimate.

[1] *Ibid.* II, p. 112.

o*

IV. ALEXANDER'S THEORY OF KNOWLEDGE

11. The remarkable feature of this doctrine is the thoroughness with which the object of consciousness is externalized. Not even secondary qualities are to be mind-dependent. Nature is, therefore, not simply a physical system with mathematical properties, as it was for Galileo, Newton and Descartes. It comprises also the imponderable and immeasurable qualities of colour, sound, fragrance and savour and even the quality of life itself. The conception of nature which Alexander suggests is far richer than was possible for any Renaissance thinker. But when we look to find, as we should expect, a correspondingly richer view of mind, we find it whittled away to a bare unvariegated quality of consciousness 'enjoying' only itself in the contemplation of objects; a doctrine which either makes knowledge inexplicable or itself absurd.

Instead of using the conception of emergence to explain how the lower phases in the process of evolution come to consciousness as mind, Alexander explains only how finite pieces of matter become qualitied with consciousness—a quality which, by itself, in no way renders intelligible the cognizance of objects in the sense required by the problem to be solved. In the first place, the quality of consciousness is not coextensive with space-time as is the quality of motion; for mind emerges only where special constellations of vital processes occur in particular portions of space-time. These constellations—at least so far as the human mind is concerned—are not of infinite extent; yet the province of knowledge is the whole universe and this has somehow to be correlated with consciousness.

12. But a second and more important difficulty is that consciousness is apparently a single quality (that which is enjoyed by mind) and is uniform in all experience. This seems clearly to follow from the relation between 'enjoyment' and 'contemplation'. But the exact meanings to be attached to these words in Alexander's theory are by no means clear. Some guidance as to their use, however, may be had from his discussion of mental space.[1] I shall neglect the discussion of mental time as the distinction between this and physical time is too subtle and difficult to make it a good illustration of the distinction between the two factors in knowledge. We are told that mental space is 'the space in which the mind experiences itself as living or which it enjoys'.[2] And we find as the

[1] S.T.D. I, p. 16.   [2] Ibid. I, p. 93.

discussion proceeds that it is not, as we may have thought, the whole system of space-relations which we experience as the extended world, but is simply the neural tracts which carry the 'quality' of consciousness. The objective system is what we contemplate, not what we enjoy. Now, what is meant by saying that we enjoy the space occupied by the conscious part of our nervous system? Alexander says that we experience 'streaks and shoots of consciousness [1] and cites Tennyson's words about a great thought's 'striking along the brain' which, he thinks, should be taken literally. But does anybody really experience such 'shoots and streaks'? The nearest I can find in my consciousness to these phenomena are the well-known cases of localization of sensations. But Alexander does not admit these as cases of enjoyment,[2] though he asserts that localization is possible only through correlating the enjoyed space with that of the contemplated object. He distinguishes between 'the contemplated sensa . . . belonging to the body' and 'the movements of consciousness itself'. Our localized sensa, then, are, *qua* localized, contemplated, and what the enjoyed space may be it is difficult to imagine. Moreover, there are many acts of consciousness (like the thought of an abstract mathematical principle) which are not accompanied by any sense of locality at all, yet on Alexander's theory they should be enjoyed in mental space. 'I feel myself', he says, 'somewhere in my body or more particularly in my head.' [3] If this means that we are consciously aware of our minds as so located, it is surely untrue. We may come to learn by experiment on other people or on animals that certain events in consciousness are accompanied by certain neural processes which may be definitely located in the physical organism, and we may or may not conclude from this fact that the consciousness actually takes place there. But this conclusion can never be derived directly from the consciousness itself. In fact, Alexander himself declares, in another place: 'Immediate acquaintance with our past and future tells us nothing about neural processes',[4] but if this is so, what we 'enjoy' would seem to be what we are never conscious of at all, and that surely cannot be his intention.

But supposing we admit that there is some obscure kind of consciousness, accompanying our apprehension of objects, which we may call enjoyment. It is obvious that for the purpose of cognition it is quite otiose. Everything definite in our knowledge is contemplated except the bare fact of our own subjectivity which is enjoyed as a vague consciousness without any really describable content. The varieties

---

[1] *Ibid.* I, p. 98.
[2] *Ibid.* I, pp. 101-2.
[3] *Loc. cit.*
[4] *Ibid.* I, p. 133. See also Intro. (p. 22).

and differences which make up 'the great life and spectacle of the universe' are not reflected in it but are external to it and are only contemplated by it. Yet all this varied detail is the subject-matter of knowledge (as is indicated by the fact that Alexander himself is able to describe it in his own theory). It is true, therefore, to say that this subject-matter of knowledge has not, on the theory we are discussing, 'come to consciousness' at all; it does not enter into consciousness, as such, but remains external. All that can be said to have come to consciousness is the actual complex of vital functions in which this specific quality has emerged and, even so, it has not come to consciousness in the sense that it is cognized by the mind as an object. It has merely become conscious. Emergence, therefore, as Alexander conceives it, cannot explain how the mind comes into possession of the objective world in the sense that it is conscious *of it*, and not (in some mysterious way) just simply conscious.

We are now in a dilemma. If the meaning of 'contemplation' is to include the notion that the mind assimilates the sensible and intelligible nature of its objects, we must include contemplation in consciousness. The mind will then become coextensive with the known universe and its distinct existence will disappear—at least, it will no longer be one finite entity among a multitude of others. For, according to Alexander, the real things are cognized directly in contemplation and there can be no 'ideas' to represent them in the mind.[1] In short, the whole position would be an impossible contradiction on his theory. We should have to include the whole world of objects in space-time within the 'quality' emergent in one finite entity.

The only other alternative, however, is to exclude contemplation from consciousness in which case the word ceases to convey its common meaning. When we talk of contemplating an object, we ordinarily mean that we appreciate in idea the *nature* of an object which is before us and *the fact that* it is present to us. We do not suggest that the object is in any sense excluded from consciousness, but rather the opposite. But if we confine consciousness to a merely subjective mental quality, we can mean by contemplation only the bare fact that something (we can hardly call it 'an object') is before us. We shall have no right to assume that this something figures in consciousness at all. 'Contemplation' then becomes simply another word for 'compresence' and we are back again at the search-light view of consciousness. Everything that is intelligible in experience has now been excluded from mind. Knowledge, so far as the word has meaning, is the external world and does

[1] *S.T.D.* I, p. 16.

not belong to the mind at all. What belongs to the mind is only enjoyment—an undifferentiated, unintelligible quality which, whatever else it may be, is not knowledge. But this position Alexander himself admits to be untenable. It does not explain what we really do experience—the assimilation by our minds of the sensible and intelligible nature of the world so that it can enter into all our behaviour and mould it to conform to our environment.

13. It may, however, be objected that another interpretation of Alexander's theory is possible. 'You have made', his defender might say, 'an artificial separation between contemplation and enjoyment and have turned a distinction into a cleavage. The two are only two aspects of the same thing—namely, consciousness—to which both belong. Enjoyment is the act of contemplating and contemplation as an act of mind does belong to consciousness. Only the object which is contemplated in the enjoyed act is external to the mind.'

Certainly, there is much in Alexander's theory which suggests some such interpretation. But closer inspection reveals it to be no more tenable and far less consistent with a realist and objectivist outlook than the one already criticized.

To interpret the theory in this second fashion we must show that in some manner the distinctions and differentiations which are synthesized in the known system of the world are conveyed into the enjoyed consciousness of mind. The mental 'quality' will no longer be regarded as blankly uniform throughout experience but as differentiated into infinite variations corresponding to the varieties of shape, quality and character of its objects.[1] How this is possible, chapters v and vi in Book III of *Space, Time and Deity* might be taken to explain. There we learn that the variations in the mental quality are due to the categorial differences in the neural processes which carry the quality, and these again are due to the types of motion involved in the reality of the objects. We need not go into the detailed description of the processes but, taking it for granted that they do occur and are effective in producing the desired result, let us examine the consequences.

We now have a world of objects external to mind and a variegated subjective quality of consciousness correlated with it. How the variations in consciousness are to be regarded Alexander does not state. Apparently the mind is somehow capable of apprehending from them directly the nature of the objects from which they arise. If so, we cannot escape some form of correspondence theory of knowledge which

[1] Cf. *ibid.* I, p. 26.

will be, in consequence, unavoidably subjectivist. For we have, on the one hand, the consciousness enjoyed and, on the other, the things of the external world which are contemplated, and we claim that because the latter are, in some way, the cause of the former our knowledge is of the real world. Yet we never can make the claim consistently with our theory, for the mind's experience is confined to what it enjoys; hence it cannot possibly know the objects of the world as external nor how its own consciousness is related to them, and the very existence of the theory is our best guarantee of its falsity.

Our conclusion, therefore, must be that on the principles Alexander lays down there are but two courses open to him. If he insists on keeping the things of the world entirely external to mind, he must abandon all hope of knowledge or any consciousness *of objects*. If, on the other hand, he attempts to explain knowledge in terms of 'enjoyment', he cannot, in any sense, postulate the existence of an external world.

14. Nevertheless the suggestion of union between subject and object effected by making enjoyment and contemplation simply two aspects of a single fact is significant and is of the utmost value. If the act of mind in cognizance is taken to embrace both these aspects, the quality of consciousness may be regarded as just that which emerges upon the totality which is subject and object in one—the organism aware of itself in organic relation to the world. If, like Spinoza, we regard consciousness as the 'idea of the body' (the 'enjoyment' of themselves by the vital processes) and remember that the vital processes are the ways in which the body reacts to and registers its surroundings, then we must assert that what is 'enjoyed' in consciousness is *the world*—the united whole which comprises both organism and environment.

It is, therefore, only if we interpret Alexander's doctrine, as he himself desired, as a form of realism (or empiricism) that it breaks down so hopelessly. If, on the other hand, it is taken as a genuine attempt to unfold the implications of the idea of evolution, and the theory of knowledge which results is interpreted in the light of that idea, we get something much more satisfactory, albeit rather more Hegelian in aspect. In fact, the theory of knowledge to which both Alexander and Lloyd Morgan adhere has really nothing whatever to do with the conception of emergent evolution. It is simply the old doctrine of empiricism superimposed upon the theory of emergence which must be considerably strained and distorted to hold it. It is in the notion of evolution that the positive value of their philosophy lies and if that notion is clarified and freed from empiricist entanglements, we get a doctrine both characteristically modern and far in advance of other contemporary theories. To such a doctrine A. N. Whitehead's 'philosophy of organism' takes us nine-tenths of the way.

Chapter XIX

THE PHILOSOPHY OF ORGANISM

I. WHITEHEAD'S VACILLATION

1. THE philosophy of A. N. Whitehead is difficult and obscurely written and it is expounded in technical language so unusual as greatly to increase its difficulty. Whitehead's writings vary enormously in merit. Some of them contain the most important and valuable philosophical thought of the age, while others consist of little more than *obiter dicta*, neither profound nor always accurate. His great work, *Process and Reality*, is in parts obscure to the point of unintelligibility; its material is ill-arranged and unco-ordinated; yet it is the exposition of the most truly advanced of all modern philosophy. His main contribution seems to have been made, as it were, absent-mindedly and his estimate of his own work is often as erroneous as his estimate of the thought of others. For instance, writing of *Process and Reality*, he admits close affiliation with Bradley and Bergson but professes to disagree with them so far as they suggest that the temporal world is an illusion.[1] Neither of them, however, makes this suggestion. Bradley expressly denies that 'appearance' is mere illusion and Bergson's main thesis is that time is real, though he asserts that our physical conception of it is a distortion. Whitehead then goes on to state as his own a view what is in essentials Bergsonian and is little at variance with Bradley, and elsewhere he expounds a theory, not unlike Leibniz', which makes space and time an abstraction from the concrete process of reality—a doctrine with affinity to Bradley's and not incompatible with Bergson's account of the spatialization of time by the intellect. 'Bradley', says Whitehead, 'gets into a muddle because he accepts language which is developed from another point of view.'[2] This is not an apt description of Bradley's thought, but if it is intended to draw attention to the defect in his philosophy which I have pointed out on p. 257 above, I agree with it—yet one cannot be sure that Whitehead means anything like this. He confesses complete ignorance of Hegel's writings, yet often permits himself to criticize Hegel in ways which are obviously the result of this ignorance. Nevertheless, his own philosophy is, in its general character, Hegelian and he has far more in common with the

[1] *Essays in Science and Philosophy* (London, 1948), p. 88.
[2] *Ibid.* p. 89.

so-called 'objective idealists'[1] than with the empiricists in whose company he began his philosophical career. The influence of empiricism, however, is never entirely absent from his thought and he frequently asserts that the work of Hegel and his followers constitutes a digression in the history of philosophy. Yet we may compare Whitehead's aversion to 'any view which reduces science to a mere subjective day-dream with a taste for the day-dream of publication'[2] with Hegel's sarcastic reference in the first preface of *Die Wissenschaft der Logik*, to the Kantian tradition 'that the Understanding may not go beyond experience; otherwise the faculty of knowledge becomes theoretical reason which produces for itself nothing but phantasms (*Hirngespinnste*)'. Hegel is objecting here to the reduction rather of speculative philosophy than of science to 'a mere subjective day-dream', but the spirit of the objection is the same as Whitehead's. We may notice also Professor Emmet's allegation that Whitehead claims to have returned to a position similar to that of Plato and Aristotle, in holding that there is a λόγος in the nature of things which is identical with the principle of reason in our minds.[3] About the reason in the nature of things, Hegel was most emphatic and he also considered himself to be adopting the outlook of the Ancients. It is not Hegel and the idealists that have digressed from the main direction of philosophical development, but rather Russell and the empiricists; and Whitehead, in parting company with them, has indeed returned to the central line of advance and has placed himself in the van.

Whitehead's failure to appreciate his own position is due to his anxiety to deny what he thinks is the typical idealistic doctrine 'that cognitive mentality is in some way inextricably concerned in every detail' of reality.[4] Here we see the traces of empiricism in his thought, for the empiricist is pathologically anxious to avoid contamination of the real with mind. But Whitehead himself, as we shall see, does find mind inextricably concerned in every detail of the real, and if by 'cognitive mentality' he means only 'explicit consciousness', then it is surely too obvious to require stress that it is not so concerned, and no 'objective idealist' has ever maintained that it was.

The presuppositions of Renaissance science die hard. Even in this most modern of all philosophies their effects linger, and empiricist

---

[1] Cf. Bosanquet, *Contemporary Philosophy*, pp. 12 ff., 17 ff., and Dorothy Emmet, *Whitehead's Philosophy of Organism* (London, 1932), p. 34, where the theory of 'misplaced concreteness' is compared with Joachim's theory of error.
[2] Emmet, *Whitehead's Philosophy of Organism*, p. 45, and *Process and Reality*, p. 468.   [3] *Vide* Emmet, *op. cit.* p. 46.
[4] *Science and the Modern World*, p. 112.

prejudices divert the mind of its author from the course which he sets himself and produce conflicts in his thought. Such conflict is apparent in the very first chapter of *The Concept of Nature*, where, as if in deference to 17th-century ideas, he declares that 'nature is closed to mind', and then immediately launches an attack on the notion of matter which completely undermines the Renaissance conception of nature. He introduces at once the modern view that the real 'substance' of the world is composed of events, and follows with a masterly criticism of views which assert the 'bifurcation' of nature into what is supposed to be mind-dependent and what is not, maintaining that 'science is not discussing the causes of knowledge, but the coherence of knowledge'[1] and that the object of the sort of metaphysics most needful is 'to exhibit in its utmost completeness our conception of reality'.[2] Despite his occasional wobblings towards empiricism, Whitehead's deepest conviction is in the coherence and the wholeness of the universe, as well as in the creativeness of its perpetual process. His rejection of 'bifurcation' is just the abandonment of that doctrine of primary and secondary qualities which springs directly from the separation of nature from mind and is incompatible with the conception of nature that he proceeds to establish—a conception of nature as one whole in which 'matter' and 'mind' are inseparable aspects of even the most rudimentary elements.

II. CREATIVITY OR PROCESS

2. The shortcomings of Alexander's theory of emergence, we have found, are (a) that it provides no adequate principle of development which ensures that the mind which eventually emerges is the real fruition of factors implicit in lower nature and (b) that as a result of this, consciousness is a supervenient quality, which makes its appearance within the confines of some limited entity with a structure of a certain degree of complexity, and which can accordingly make no contact with the rest of reality lying beyond and external to that entity. These two defects Whitehead does much to remedy. In the first place, though he strongly maintains that consciousness appears only as a late stage of development and declares that the prior stages are independent of it, some important characteristics of mind are declared to be present from the outset. Whitehead's great advance on so many of his predecessors is his repudiation of what he calls 'vacuous actuality'—that is, actuality 'void of subjective experience'. In every actual entity, he asserts,

[1] *The Concept of Nature* (Cambridge, 1930), p. 41.   [2] *Ibid.* p. 32.

there is a mental as well as a physical 'pole', and consciousness is a high phase of development of the former which occurs under special conditions. Here, then, we have a real evolution of mind, present *ab initio*, from some primitive form to the highly developed consciousness capable of reflective speculation. In the second place, Whitehead improves on Alexander by declaring that the objects of consciousness actually do enter into the 'real internal constitution' of the experiencer. They do not remain merely external to be contemplated from without, for the experient subject is entirely constituted by the way in which it feels its world.[1] And this after all, if it can be maintained, is what we are seeking; for it gives at once an individual entity, which is distinctive yet capable of grasping within its own being, not only the knowledge of a world in which it is one individual member, but also of its own place in and relation to that world.

3. Whitehead sees the ultimate basis of all reality as an activity of creation and he calls it 'creativity' or 'process'. There can thus be no question of the difficulty besetting him, which beset Alexander, of rendering intelligible the *nisus* and the continuity of development. For Whitehead the essence of reality is 'a creative advance into novelty'. What is not process is nothing, and every entity is an 'event' or an 'occasion', an atomic element of the fundamental process which constitutes 'the passage of nature'. These occasions or 'actual entities' (as they are also called) have something in common with Russell's 'perspectives' and also with Alexander's point-instants, for each is a pattern of aspects—a 'concrescence of prehensions'—of all other entities in the universe. But they are not completely devoid of size, like mathematical points; each endures through a minute portion of time and occupies a volume or quantum of space. Whitehead therefore compares them to cells rather than to point-instants and they form the basis of what he calls 'the epochal theory of time' in which instants, like points, are abstractions from events.

4. The precise nature of process can be understood only after the notion of 'prehension' has been explained. In *Science and the Modern World* we read that 'nature is a process of expansive development necessarily transitional from prehension to prehension'[2] and immediately prior to this Whitehead has explained the term by reference to a passage in Bacon where the word 'perception' is used of inanimate bodies to mean 'taking account of the essential character of the thing

---

[1] *Vide* Emmet, *op. cit.* p. 48.   [2] *Op. cit.* p. 90.

perceived'. In this sense, Whitehead maintains, all things have 'perception', but as that word suggests cognitive apprehension he proposes to use instead the term 'prehension' to denote 'uncognitive apprehension'.[1] But the phrase 'taking account of' is to be very liberally interpreted. It is used not merely in the sense in which a billiard ball might be said to 'take account of' a blow from the cue by rolling away, or a mirror to 'take account of' the light by reflecting it back; but in a sense which includes much more than what might be classed as reaction to a stimulus. Even relations in space are to be described in terms of prehensions. Every volume in space has an 'aspect' from every other, we are told, and it is what and where it is because these aspects are what and where they are. Its position, in short, is the system of its relations to all other parts of space and is constituted by the various aspects of the other parts from it. These aspects are called the modes in which the other parts of space enter into the constitution of the volume under consideration. Accordingly, 'every volume mirrors in itself every other volume in space' and, by the same reasoning, the same is held to be true of time.[2]

It seems then that every way of taking account of other entities, from the mere fact of being in spatio-temporal relation, to such complex reactions as human perception, is covered by the term 'prehension', and the important point is that what is prehended enters into the composition or (as it is called in *Process and Reality*) 'the real internal constitution' of the prehending subject. It follows accordingly that, in various ways, all things in the universe are prehended by every entity, or putting it in another way, the whole universe enters into and constitutes each individual entity. An individual now is not a mere piece of an all-pervading 'stuff' (as in Alexander's theory) but is the universe in microcosm. At the same time each entity, by its prehensions of all others, binds the multiplicity of existents into one coherent and self-constituting whole.

We have now the basal conception of Whitehead's theory and shall be able to understand the more important of his terms.

The universe is, for him, a continuous process of creation consisting at every phase (in every 'event' or 'actual entity') of the grasping into unity (the 'prehension') of the whole. This he expresses by saying that 'creativity' is the 'substrate process' of 'prehensive activity'. 'It is that ultimate principle by which the many, which are the universe disjunctively, become the one actual occasion, which is the universe

---

[1] Cf. Leibniz' use of 'perception' and 'apperception'.
[2] *Vide Science and the Modern World*, pp. 81 f.

conjunctively.'[1] Each actual occasion is a 'concrescence of prehensions' of all others and is an atomic 'actual entity'. The universe, in short, is a complete and absolutely organic system of interlocked existents, and implicitly we have a combination of the views of Leibniz and Spinoza in which the principle of the concrete universal is obviously entailed.

5. If the above account of process were taken as complete we might be inclined to think that the term was a misnomer. We have been describing a system of mutually determining entities constituting one another by their mutual relations. Why should we regard this as a process rather than as a fixed structure? Presumably the element of time enters into the system; mutual relations change; the prehension of A by B may take the form of the effect of a prior cause and we need not necessarily think of the whole system on the analogy of the system of spatial relations. Even so, however, 'the principle by which the many become one' is indifferent to *how* they become one. To it lapse of time is irrelevant and there seems no reason to represent it specially as process. Moreover, as every 'occasion' prehends and is constituted by every other in time (just as every volume in space prehends all others), the whole of time is 'mirrored' in each occasion and the aspect of lapse or flowing is lost in a view *sub specie aeternitatis*.

But here we must beware of misunderstanding. Whitehead is as anxious as Bergson or Alexander to maintain that the essential nature of reality is fluent—'a creative advance into novelty'. 'Creativity', he declares, 'is the principle of novelty.'[2] Yet, on the other hand, he does not hold a view of time similar to that of Bergson or of Alexander. The ultimate reality for Whitehead is process and we find that process is not necessarily (perhaps not at all) temporal. It is a principle of concrescence and in each concrescence the whole of the universe, including all time and all space, is involved. The spatio-temporal scheme (what he calls 'the extensive continuum') is a type of order arrived at by an artificial division of the concrete unity of the real by reference to arbitrarily chosen co-ordinates ('co-ordinate division of the concrete'), but the phases of concrescence are not temporal.[3] Whitehead's doctrine of time and space is, in fact, very similar to that of Leibniz. 'Space and time', he says, 'are simply abstractions from the totality of prehensive unifications as mutually patterned in each other.'[4] The interlocking

[1] *Process and Reality*, p. 28.   [2] *Ibid.*
[3] *Vide ibid.* p. 401: 'This genetic passage from phase to phase is not in physical time'.   [4] *Science and the Modern World*, p. 89.

entities are mutually constituted by internal relations, and these relations can be construed serially in various ways. As Kant showed, our awareness of objects comes to us through successive presentations and the objects themselves are constituted by the way in which these '*Vorstellungen*' are synthesized. Whitehead approaches the matter from the other side. The objects are the synthetic wholes which we cut up, as it were, into sections along more or less arbitrarily chosen lines and the result is the spatio-temporal scheme. 'The "extensive" scheme is nothing else than the generic morphology of the internal relations which bind the actual occasions into a nexus, and which bind the prehensions of any one actual occasion into a unity, co-ordinately divisible.'[1] Accordingly, process (like the dialectical movement of Hegel) is prior to space and time and we must seek an interpretation of the phrase 'creative advance into novelty' other than temporal advance. This other interpretation is the activity of concrescence and is something which is accomplished on the initiative, so to speak, of the actual entity itself.

6. The parallel with Hegel hardly needs pointing out. For him the dialectical process also is one of 'concrescence', for each phase is more concrete than the last, a more adequate expression of what is ultimately and finally concrete. At first, Whitehead's process of concrescence might seem to be different—it seems to be a combination or integration of separate aspects, whereas for Hegel each phase is a reinterpretation of the last as an identification of opposites. Certainly, Whitehead's process and Hegel's dialectic are not in all points the same; but we shall see presently that the activity of prehension is one of interpreting the prior phase of the process, and that the stages of Whitehead's concrescence do constitute a triad not altogether unlike a dialectical triad. The correspondence of Whitehead's actual entity with Bosanquet's concrete universal is even more marked, and the connection between this and the dialectic has already been noted.[2] But of all past philosophers, the one of whom Whitehead's thought is most reminiscent is Leibniz, whose monad is clearly a concrete of perceptions of all other monads, just as Whitehead's actual entity is a concrescence of all other actual entities.

III. THE 'MENTAL POLE'

7. What is the motive force or dynamic of this 'activity of prehension'? Just as we asked ourselves in connection with the theory of

---

[1] *Process and Reality*, p. 408.
[2] Cf. pp. 233 ff. above and Bosanquet, *Implication and Linear Inference*, ch. v.

emergence what brought the new qualities into being, so we must ask here for what reason the various aspects of things should be gathered together into concrescences. It is obviously impossible for all physical things literally to 'rush together' (a phrase which I think Whitehead actually uses) and constitute new entities, for all things in the universe do not *physically* congregate in each. One is naturally tempted to conclude, therefore, that the concrescence is an *ideal* unity. Is it not the mind which sees the whole in every part and which can find its object intelligible only by so doing? What we mean by saying that A, B and C enter into the constitution of D is that D only is what it is because of the relevance to it of A, B and C. This is what Whitehead means when he says that D prehends A, B and C. But the word 'relevance' implies thought, and it is clear that bare, dead, 'non-mental' material can be relevant to anything only for a mind; that entities, if they could be barely and purely material without relation to a mind, could not possibly enter into one another, constitute one another and be transfused into one another, while still remaining separate and distinct material things. Accordingly, either the whole scheme of interrelated actual entities must be the object of one mind: the content of one experience, as Bradley would probably have said, or else each entity must itself be a mind of some sort with an experience of its own nature as constituted by its place in and relation to its world. Whitehead recognizes this necessity and, avoiding subjectivism of the Bradleian type, he adopts the latter position. He asserts that there is no 'vacuous actuality' but that every entity has a 'mental pole' to which the main work of concrescence is to be attributed.

8. The activity of prehension involves three factors: (i) the prehending subject, or as Whitehead puts it, 'the occasion of experience within which the prehension is a detail of activity';[1] (ii) the entity prehended, which is the object of prehension and is called the datum, and (iii) the 'subjective form', or affective tone, which, we are told, determines the *effectiveness* of the prehension in the occasion of experience.[2] It is this effectiveness which is of importance in determining the nature of the advance into novelty and that invites further investigation. But before I proceed to that, something must be said about the second of the above factors—about the 'givenness' of the object of prehension.

Here we have another trace of the influence upon Whitehead of empiricism and it is underlined by what he writes in *Adventures of Ideas* about the primacy of sense-perception in knowledge and the

[1] *Adventures of Ideas*, ch. xi, § iv. [2] *Ibid.*

nature of percepta.[1] But he transforms the empirical doctrine into something very different from empiricism proper, and it soon transpires that what is 'given' is by no means a passive datum (passivity he constantly rejects) in *pari materia* with the prehending subject, but is *the prior phase of the process of creativity*. What the entity prehends is what Whitehead calls its 'settled world' of 'stubborn irreducible fact' and this consists of actual entities in which the process of prehension has been completed, has reached 'satisfaction' and 'decision' (both technical terms, the meaning of which will shortly appear). They then pass into the real internal constitution of a new entity as the objects or data of its prehensions and constitute its physical pole. 'Two conditions', says Whitehead, 'must be fulfilled in order that an entity may function as an object in a process of experiencing: (1) the entity must be *antecedent*, and (2) the entity must be experienced in virtue of its antecedence; it must be *given*.'[2] An occasion (or entity) 'perishes into the status of an object'.[3] It is clear, therefore, and will become clearer as we proceed, that what is prehended is the prior phase of the process which passes over into the new prehending entity as the succeeding phase.

9. Turning next to the third factor in prehension—its subjective form—we find that this is what supplies the motive power of the process. The phrase 'subjective form' is used to cover all forms of emotion as well as everything which is usually meant by 'secondary qualities'; but, in its most general use, it means emotional qualification or affective tone, and it is for this reason that Whitehead declares all actuality to involve emotion. Further, he tells us that consciousness 'is a special element in the subjective forms of some feelings'[4] so that cognition and emotion have a definite interconnection. The subjective form of a prehension, however, is not determined (or at any rate not entirely) by what is prehended. It is the relation of the 'datum' to all others as prehended by the subject and literally the effort of the subject to co-ordinate, organize and unite its data into an organic totality: in short it is the *nisus* to the whole that ultimately gives each prehension its emotional tone or 'value'. The teleological character of the whole process is therefore evident. In Whitehead's own words: 'A reference to the complete actuality is required to give the reason why such a prehension is what it is in respect to its subjective form. This subjective

---

[1] *Vide* ch. xi, § vii *et seq.*: '. . . all percepta are bare sensa, in patterned connections given in the immediate present'. [2] *Ibid.* ch. xi, § ix.
[3] *Ibid.* § v. [4] *Process and Reality*, p. 72; cf. *Adventures of Ideas*, ch. xi, § ii.

form is determined by the subjective aim at further integration, so as to obtain the "satisfaction" of the completed subject. In other words, final causation and atomism are interconnected philosophical principles.'[1]

We have here the answer to the question about the dynamic of process. It is the subjective aim at further integration which supplies the motive force, and it is designated 'appetition'. Here lies the originative character of the actual entity and here the opportunity for the production of 'novelty'—new modes of concrescence. This integrative activity of the entity is the chief manifestation of creativity, which, in the light of what is said of the subjective aim, appears as the energizing force by which the entity moulds a multitude of 'given' prehensions into a coherent system. For Whitehead, as for Hegel and Bosanquet, the dynamic of process is a *nisus* to organic wholeness, and this is an appetitive urge which, if successful, brings satisfaction. Final causation, as he says, is an essential principle in his system and the nature of things is determined by their value.

But, as Hegel insisted, appetition and value cannot be divorced from thought and Whitehead also identifies them, though not in so many words and in spite of apparent denials. Appetition he defines as 'the conceptual valuation of an immediate physical feeling combined with an urge towards the realization of the datum conceptually prehended', and again as 'immediate matter of fact including in itself a principle of unrest, involving realization of what is not and may be'[2], and it is given as an alternative name for 'conceptual prehension'.[3] This is the important point, for a conceptual prehension is the prehension of an 'eternal object' and is the special differentia of the 'mental pole' of an actual entity, with which the dynamic of process is thus definitely connected. Eternal objects are Whitehead's second order of reals and their nature and status must be explained before further progress is possible.

IV. ETERNAL OBJECTS

10. To the nature of eternal objects we already have a clue in the statement that appetition involves 'the realization of what is not and may be'. Eternal objects are defined as 'pure potentials for the specific determination of fact, or forms of definiteness'.[4] They are also referred to as potentialities of definiteness,[5] and indeed potentiality is the key-word to the understanding of them. They are, in one sense, specially

---

[1] *Process and Reality*, pp. 25-6.   [2] *Ibid*. p. 43.
[3] *Ibid*. p. 45.   [4] *Ibid*. p. 29.   [5] *Ibid*. p. 54 and *passim*.

concerned with what is *not* actual, although, in another sense, with what is (for they have 'ingredience' into actual entities). But as so ingredient they are prehensions which are concrete factors in the constitution of the actual entity, and, though they are said to find realization in actuality, *qua* eternal they are not actual. This statement is, I think, justified by suggestions and implications which constantly recur in Whitehead's writings, although he is never quite clear on the point.

11. From much that he writes the eternal objects seem to be precisely the same as the old abstract universals of the understanding which are always dogging the heels of empiricism, and, however else he may conceive them, one cannot help feeling that his notion of eternal objects is never quite free from confusion with that of the abstract universal. He allows such general qualities as colours and shapes, which are always the same wherever they are met, to rank as eternal objects, and he does say quite definitely that they are abstract, adding: 'by "abstract" I mean that what an eternal object is in itself—that is to say, its essence—is comprehensible without reference to some one particular occasion of experience'.[1] Such, he also admits, have in the past been called universals though he prefers to call them 'eternal objects'. They are the predicates of propositions in which the actual occasion to which they belong is the subject. But what Whitehead writes in the same context makes the flat identification of eternal objects with abstract universals unsatisfactory. For he stresses the point that those qualities which are not predicable of the subject are also relevant to it. 'An event is decisive', he says, 'in proportion to the importance (for it) of its untrue propositions: their relevance to the event cannot be dissociated from what the event is in itself by way of achievement.' And this is nothing less than a statement of the doctrine of significant negation which underlies Hegel's principle of the identity of opposites. Eternal objects, therefore, both are systematically related among themselves and systematically determine the character of actual entities. As potentialities of definiteness they seem to be principles of systematization (which is much more than the abstract identity of a colour or shape in each instance of its realization).

12. But from the account already given of the process of mutual prehension by actual entities, one would think that the 'definiteness' and systematic interconnection of elements in the constitution of each

[1] *Vide Science and the Modern World*, p. 197; also, pp. 107 and 196.

was fully determined by the prehension of its 'settled world' of 'stubborn fact'. But, from the purely physical interrelations, which (at times) Whitehead seems to envisage as such prehensive activity, the 'secondary qualities' are excluded, and not only must room be found for them but also some source in the universe of reality from which they can derive. Colours and sounds and all general qualities of things are, at least *prima facie*, not entities constituted by relations to one another of such things as chairs, trees and stones (though these, strictly speaking, are not what Whitehead means by actual entities). Red is the same wherever and whenever we find it; so is the pitch of a tone. How are such things to be accounted for in a theory which delineates reality as a process of concrescence of mutual prehensions by actual entities? In other words, what sort of reality have universals? The eternal objects are Whitehead's answer to this question. He compares them to Plato's forms and they are in some respects similar also to Leibniz' 'eternal truths'. But whereas for Plato the forms possess a reality superior to perishing particulars of everyday experience, for Whitehead the actual entities seem to be more fully real and the eternal objects only to achieve realization by 'ingression' into actual entities.

Whitehead, however, had committed himself from the outset to the assertion that what other philosophers would have called universals are real, by insisting on what he calls the 'ontological principle'. This is variously stated but in effect it lays down that nothing can exist except actual entities or what can be traced to an actual entity. 'Nothing', he says, 'floats into the world from nowhere', and the universals must, therefore, have some actual origin. They are abstractions from the actual entities in which they are exemplified but, *qua* abstractions, what sort of existence do they enjoy? Whitehead cannot say that they are 'ideas', for that would mean that they can only exist where there is 'cognitive mentality', and cognitive mentality occurs only within a late phase of concrescence. To call eternal objects ideas, therefore, would imply that they did not exist below the level of cognitive mind. But then no entities which were below that level of development could be characterized by any 'forms of definiteness'. There could be no 'conceptual prehensions' and so no 'subjective form' where there was no consciousness. This would be quite contrary to the position which Whitehead is maintaining, for he is very definite in his assertion of the possibility of conceptual feelings in what he calls the lower phases of concrescence and (as we have noticed above) he holds consciousness to be only 'a special element in the subjective forms of some feelings'. But the eternal objects, even though they are abstractions from the actual entities in the passage of nature, cannot be originally derived from that source because, until they have had ingression into these entities, the character of the entities themselves is not definite and they are not complete realities. The eternal objects are the sources of novelty in the creative process and cannot, therefore, be mere abstractions from reals that are already formed and decided.

Accordingly, we must have some actual entity which will, so to speak, store up for us the 'ideas' or 'universals' or 'eternal objects' and have them ready at all times for ingression into the process of the actual world. This entity, in the Philosophy of Organism, is God, who is the arrangement of all eternal objects according to a principle of order (the first and most comprehensive of all such principles) such that every eternal object has a definite grade of relevance to each actual occasion. This system of eternal objects is called the 'Primordial Nature of God' and is prior to all things except creativity itself, for without it no sort of limitation is imposed on the absolute potentiality of process and there is no definiteness anywhere. But we are not to regard God, in an unqualified sense, as the creator of the universe, or as the ultimate source of all reality. He is held to be simply the first and most general limitation upon the completely undetermined possibility inherent in pure creativity.[1] God's Primordial Nature is described as 'the first created fact' and is the condition of there being any determinate entities. In this sense only is He the creator of all finite things.[2]

13. The conception is a difficult one, especially in its reference to potentiality, for we are first led to think that process or creativity is the basis of actuality and 'hard fact', as opposed to the pure potentiality of eternal objects, and are then told that the Primordial Nature of God, which is a system of eternal objects, is the first limitation on the pure potentiality of creativity. This strange oscillation may, however, be explained by Whitehead's distinction of two kinds of potentiality: '(a) the "general" potentiality, which is the bundle of possibilities, mutually consistent or alternative, provided by the multiplicity of eternal objects, and (b) the "real" potentiality, which is conditioned by the data provided by the actual world'.[3] The latter is the potentiality of creativity, the former of eternal objects. The pure potentiality which God's Primordial Nature limits, therefore, is presumably 'real'

[1] *Vide Science and the Modern World*, p. 221, and Emmet, *Whitehead's Philosophy of Organism*, p. 264: 'So God "does not create the world" for the actualities of the world are themselves processes of self-creation'.

[2] *Process and Reality*, p. 317.

[3] *Ibid.* p. 90; *vide* also *Adventures of Ideas*, ch. xi, § x.

potentiality, where 'the data provided by the actual world' are completely vague, indeterminate, chaotic and disorderly so that (as we commonly say) anything might happen. The first step towards reducing this chaos to order is then the imposition upon it of the system of quasi-ideal principles which is the Primordial Nature of God.

But the distinction between 'general' and 'real' potentiality does not altogether remove the difficulty. In the light of the theory of prehensions and the 'Ontological Principle' it appears at first as if the relativity of each actual entity to all actual entities was absolute and complete. If there is nothing besides this relationship of each to all others which contribute to the real internal constitution of an entity, its 'definiteness' must be dependent on these relationships alone and they must supply all the conditions governing possibilities. In this case 'real' potentiality would be the only kind of potentiality conceivable. Nothing besides other actual entities could have ingression into the constitution of any one occasion and there would be no room for eternal objects. But this interpretation is mistaken. Whitehead contends that the distinctive character of the entity is not so determined; it is not merely its relations to and its position among its fellows that makes it what it is; these are simply the materials out of which it creates itself. The manner in which the prehensions of the universe are integrated depends on the subjective aim of the entity which determines the subjective form of each prehension. Its total character is therefore determined *a fronte* by final causation and not entirely *a tergo* by efficient. Now the subjective aim involves conceptual prehensions (prehensions of eternal objects) and the 'decision' (or determination) of the entity involves something very like choice between alternatively possible forms of definiteness.

It can hardly be doubted, therefore, that by 'real' potentiality Whitehead means what the given settled world has in it to become (it is 'given' and 'settled' only as a datum for further concrescence). Its potentiality is its capacity to create new entities.[1] But this cannot derive simply from the prehension of entities in the immediate past. There is in every such prehension a subjective aim at *further* integration — something beyond what has so far been achieved. This something beyond involves a self-transcendence by the actual entity which can hardly be otherwise described than, in the Hegelian phrase, as a going over into its other—a self-expansion to a whole so far only partially realized. For Whitehead, this self-transcendence is achieved by the prehension of eternal objects as systematized in God's Primordial

[1] Cf. *Adventures of Ideas, loc. cit.*, and ch. xii, § iii.

Nature; and such prehension is conceptual prehension belonging to the mental pole of the actual entity. We may say, therefore, that real potentiality is the efficient causation of the given, while general potentiality is the final causality of God exercised through the prehension by actual entities of eternal objects and manifesting itself as appetition in occasions of experience. But in the given nature of the settled world itself there must be and is the potentiality of further integration. Its real potentiality is nothing more nor less than its potency of producing that which the conceptual prehensions of the mental pole in every entity make actual.[1] The two sorts of potentiality cannot be divorced and, as we shall have further reason to assert at a later stage, the Primordial Nature of God seems not unlike the Hegelian logic—a system of concepts or categories defining the stages of the process of becoming in the actual world. Hegel himself said: 'It is the mind of God before the creation of Nature and Finite Spirit'.

To put the matter in another way, the actualities of the world are not static but are phases in a creative process the activity of which is progressive organization or integration. They are constituted by their mutual interrelation, but the character of each entity is determined by the degree in which its relations to the rest can be grasped and systematized in organic activity. This again depends upon the qualification of the system by principles of order involving the interpretative activity of thought, which, though it becomes conscious only at a high level of development, is present throughout the process being essentially one of continuous self-interpretation. The degree (or form) of definiteness (or organization) of any entity depends upon the stage it has reached in this process, and the principles of interpretation (*Denkbestimmungen*) which are exemplified by each stage are thus the determinants of definiteness. These are Whitehead's eternal objects: the interpretative principles of the process of the real. The whole system of these principles in their relevance to every actual entity (that is, to the stage represented by each in the process of self-integration) will be a system of categories in progressive sequence like the sequence of the Hegelian dialectic; and this system of eternal objects is for Whitehead the Primordial Nature of God.

V. THE PHASES OF CONCRESCENCE

14. According to Whitehead, there are three main phases in the process of concrescence:

[1] Cf. *Adventures of Ideas, loc. cit.*

(a) The given settled world of 'decided' actual entities supplies the data for all physical prehensions and these are gathered into the entity which is coming to be, to constitute its physical pole. This is the first phase of concrescence and is called the 'responsive' or 'conformal' phase because of the continuity of subjective form between the entity which is perishing into objectivity and that in which it is being prehended. The objective entity already involves eternal objects which are ingredient in it, and these are now passed on and are prehended in the object by the newly emerging entity.[1]

(b) There supervenes upon this a second phase of concrescence called the 'supplemental' phase,[2] which, so far as can be gathered from Whitehead's very technical and often obscure exposition, seems to be one of interpretation.[3] It is here especially that conceptual prehensions play their part, though it must not be forgotten that eternal objects make their entry also in the earlier phase in the way which has been explained above. In the data of sense and in immediate feeling, thought has already been at work, but the supplemental phase provides the first opportunity for 'origination' on the part of the subject. No complete account is given of the way in which this interpretation of physical prehensions is carried out, but what are called 'symbolic reference' and 'propositional feelings'[4] apparently occur at this level and these can hardly be anything but interpretative.[5] In fact, Whitehead's account of symbolic reference reminds one strongly of Bradley's ideal construction.

(c) The final phase of concrescence is that in which 'satisfaction' is achieved. Each entity, urged on by the subjective aim at further integration, eventually reaches a 'decision' or 'satisfaction' which consists in 'the evaporation of all indetermination'.[6] At this point it passes out of existence as an experient subject and is 'objectified' in the new actual occasions which subsequently arise. It thus becomes an 'objectively

---

[1] Cf. *Process and Reality*, p. 36 (the fourth 'Categoreal Obligation') and Pt. III, ch. iii; also *Adventures of Ideas*, ch. xi, § xiv.

[2] *Vide Process and Reality*, Part II, ch. vii, § iv.

[3] Cf. *ibid*. p. 241: 'The responsive phase absorbs these data as material for a subjective unity of feeling: the supplemental stage heightens the relevance of the colour-sensa, and supplements the geometrical relationships of the past by picking out the contemporary region of the stone to be the contemporary representative of the efficacious historic routes'. This activity is plainly interpretative. Cf. also *Adventures of Ideas*, ch. xi, § xii.

[4] *Vide Process and Reality*, Pt. II, chs. viii and ix and Pt. III, ch. iv.

[5] Cf. *ibid*. p. 242: 'What is directly perceived [*i.e.* in the perception of a stone], certainly and without shadow of doubt, is a grey region of the presented locus. Any further interpretation, instinctive or by intellectual judgment, must be put down to symbolic reference.'

[6] *Ibid*. pp. 61 and 301; and cf. *Adventures of Ideas*, ch. xi, § v.

immortal' 'superject', and it is the complex superjective data prehended in this way by the entities which follow that form the settled world for the primary phase of concrescence in them.

15. These three phases occur, we must assume, in the concrescence of every actual entity; yet it cannot be maintained that all entities reach the same degree of integration. They differ, we are told, in the degree of 'intensity' of their experience; and if they did not, all would achieve consciousness, which Whitehead emphatically denies. Some entities are satisfied with little more than conformation and transmission, while others do not reach decision until they have reached no less than conscious, philosophic knowledge (which, presumably, must be included in the 'late phase'). What exactly determines the degree of wholeness which will satisfy in any particular case Whitehead does not explain. We can hardly say that it depends upon the complexity of the inherited data, for it is difficult to understand how the inheritance of any one differs from the rest, as each prehends the entire universe. The difference could be explained only perspectively by some theory of differing points of view, and it is to this notion that Whitehead resorts. But the position does not escape the difficulties into which Leibniz fell and we are left to wonder how, if the whole process of concrescence does not occur in every occasion, it can be built up by the transition from one occasion to the next.

16. It is clear, nevertheless, that what Whitehead conceives is a development consisting of progressive integration in increasingly organic wholes, the three main stages of which are not unlike an Hegelian triad. It is also clear that the motive force of this process is the 'appetition' of the entity, creating a new whole by evaluation of the parts on principles of interpretation (eternal objects), the prehension of which is conceptual (even though not always conscious)—in short, the dynamic of the process is ultimately the activity of thought, unconscious for the most part, but at a certain stage and in favourable circumstances, rising to the level of consciousness.

VI. THE SOLUTION OF PROBLEMS

17. In all this, despite a great deal of obscurity shrouding his theory of body-mind relation as well as his theory of knowledge, Whitehead has provided the means of solving the problem from which we set out. For the kernel of that problem is the relation of subject to object, and

Whitehead's theory of prehension makes that intelligible by constituting the subject out of its relations to its objects. The subject is the comprehension of the world and passes on its concrescence of the universe of objects to its successor in the constant flux of passing events. As Whitehead puts it: 'The objects are the factors in experience which function so as to express that that occasion originates by including a transcendent universe of other things'.[1] Accordingly, as the concrescence grows by transmission from one occasion to another and as these occasions (or entities) are grouped in various patterns, some arise whose inheritance of prehensions is so complex and so highly integrated as to issue in consciousness. And because of the principle of creativity (which, it is now apparent, is that of the concrete universal), this consciousness is of the world which constitutes the actual entity and of which the entity is one product and one elementary part.

18. To develop a satisfactory theory of the body-mind relationship from this should not be impossible, but, as stated by Whitehead, it is exceedingly complex and difficult to follow. There is much in common, here again, between Whitehead's doctrine and Leibniz'. In each actual entity the body-mind relation is represented by its bi-polar structure; and in that immensely complicated net-work of 'loci' of events which constitutes the animal (or human) body, there is always a dominant 'occasion of experience' which inherits, co-ordinates, comprehends and interprets the experience of all the others. 'The human body', writes Whitehead, 'is indubitably a complex of occasions which are part of spatial nature. It is a set of occasions miraculously co-ordinated so as to pour its inheritance into various regions within the brain. There is thus every reason to believe that our sense of unity with the body has the same original as our sense of unity with our immediate past of personal experience.'[2] In other words, the experience of the dominant entity, as passed on from one occasion to the next in its own stream of existence, is the same as that passed on to it from the occasions which constitute its body. Its physical pole and its prehension of the occasions which make up the animal body are one and the same thing (prehensions of the rest of the universe being passed on through these occasions); and in prehending these it is prehending the 'superject' which is the immediately previous occasion of its own experience.

The manner of this transmission of experience, however, is elaborated by Whitehead in an extremely difficult theory, full of obscure technicalities, of the way in which prehensions are 'transmuted' when

[1] *Adventures of Ideas*, ch. xi, § xi.   [2] *Ibid.* ch. xi, § xxii.

passed from one entity to the next. The upshot is a doctrine which often smacks dangerously of representationalism. But this, perhaps, we may be allowed to discount as simply another trace of empiricism still lingering in his mind, and to judge the theory on the means already provided for the solution of the problem of relating the mind to the body.

19. It is not, however, so easy to overlook his leanings towards the correspondence theory in his explicit theory of judgement—though he claims that it is as much a coherence theory as one of correspondence. He sometimes seems to forget that the 'given' element in knowledge is already a product of concrescence involving conceptual prehensions, and consequently gets into difficulties in explaining how it is further interpreted. Instead of being a natural continuance of the process, interpretation appears as something superimposed upon a passively received material, and a separation results, which cannot subsequently be bridged, between data already determined and 'originative' interpretation.

A judgement, according to Whitehead's account of it,[1] is a very complex matter. First there is a physical prehension of a nexus. From that, or from some other physical prehension, there is derived a conceptual prehension according either to the fourth or to the fifth 'categoreal obligation'. If the conceptual prehension is derived according to the fourth (the 'category of conceptual valuation'), its 'datum is the eternal object determinant of the definiteness of the actual entity ...physically felt'. If it is derived according to the 'category of conceptual reversion' (the fifth categoreal obligation), the datum of the conceptual feeling will be, at least partially, different from the eternal object which determines the physical datum. The physical feeling is then integrated with the conceptual feeling in the form of a 'propositional feeling'. This, however, is not a judgement and is not necessarily even conscious. He calls it 'a lure for feeling'. The propositional feeling is now integrated in a 'comparative feeling' with the original physical prehension and only then do we get conscious judgement. If there is identity of pattern between the predicate of the proposition and the nexus (which is at once its logical subject and the datum of the physical feeling), then the judgement takes the form of affirmation; but if the pattern of one of these is incompatible with that of the other, the judgement takes the form of negation; if they are different but compatible, there is suspended judgement.[2] Further, we are told that

[1] *Vide Process and Reality*, Part III, chs. iv and v.   [2] *Ibid.* p. 382.

434

'"truth" is the absence of incompatibility or of any "material contrast" in the patterns of the nexus and of the proposition in their generic contrast', and that if the patterns are not identical 'then the proposition in some sense, important or unimportant, is not felt as true'.[1]

The patterns are, I suppose, eternal objects, for the predicate of the proposition is an eternal object and presumably the pattern of the nexus is its form of definiteness. But I cannot venture to commit myself as to the exact meaning of these statements, nor to explain how, on Whitehead's theory, an untrue proposition could ever be affirmed or a true one ever rejected in error. Taking the theory as it stands let us see what follows from it.

To say the least, this account seems to make the activity of judgement a little unnecessary. If the physical prehension is sufficiently definite to provide the datum also of the conceptual prehension in the propositional feeling, we already know all about it and the judgement adds nothing, either by way of elucidation or of interpretation. I see a green tree (*i.e.* I have a prehension of 'green tree'); what then do I gain by thinking of greenness, formulating *in abstracto* the proposition 'the tree is green' and then (referring again to the actual sensory experience) judging 'the tree is green'? Surely the entire process is involved in the first activity of feeling.

It may be objected that my example begins with a conscious act, whereas Whitehead makes it quite clear that consciousness does not arise until the comparative feeling involved in judgement is reached. The physical prehension is and the propositional feeling may be subconscious, and accordingly it would be quite correct to say that any conscious act may involve judgement, even on Whitehead's theory. But how then can we ever consciously know whether our judgement is or is not true, on what grounds can we affirm or deny, or how can we ever come to know that judgement comes about in the way which Whitehead alleges? If we test the judgement by comparing its predicate with the actual physical feeling of its logical subject, and if the physical feeling is not consciously experienced, we never have in consciousness the criterion of truth. And, even if the comparison could somehow be made unconsciously, we could never know that the process had taken place unless the whole of it could be raised to the conscious level.

The difficulty of the position, however, is somewhat mitigated by Whitehead's assertion that 'whenever there is consciousness there is some element of recollection. It recalls earlier phases from the dim recesses of the unconscious . . . in a wider sense consciousness

[1] *Ibid.* p. 384.

enlightens experience which precedes it, and could be without it if considered as a mere datum.'[1] This may be taken to mean that the datum or object is the prior phase of the process; but even so, the 'recollection' must be cognized if it is to be a subject of comparison with something else, and to be cognized it would, on Whitehead's theory, have to be a 'comparative feeling' already. To raise a physical prehension to the level of consciousness requires a process in which it must be compared *as a mere datum* with a propositional feeling, and *as a mere datum*, we are given to understand, it is not consciously apprehended. Yet if we understand consciousness to 'enlighten' the lower phases of experience in the sense that it is the interpretation or explication of what in the lower phase is implicit, at least the first part of Whitehead's statement may be accepted. But if this is the case it is extremely doubtful whether anything can ever be 'considered as a *mere* datum'. Whitehead himself agrees that it cannot, and the lapse into empiricism apparent here is largely counteracted by what he says elsewhere.[2]

VII. DUALISMS AND THEIR RESOLUTION

20. We may now review the Philosophy of Organism as an interpretation of the presuppositions of contemporary scientific thought. It presents nature as a perpetual creative process involving the mutual integration of its elementary parts into a single, coherent, organic whole which is immanent in each part and in every phase of the process. Further, every atomic entity in this process is beminded, and the creative advance is effected by an activity which is essentially that of mind—the conceptual prehension of eternal objects. This activity is one of explication or interpretation and it is identified with evaluation; for Whitehead constantly refers to eternal objects as principles of 'conceptual valuation' and their interpretative function is plain, not only from the part they play in judgement, but also from their determination of the emotional tone of experience by establishing the 'relevance' of the object. This identification of value with interpretation is the more significant because the principles concerned are regarded as the forms of definiteness of what constitute stubborn fact, and the distinction between fact and value thus becomes purely relative.

The mind is no more than the concrescence, the integration or

[1] *Process and Reality*, p. 342.
[2] Cf. *Adventures of Ideas*, ch. xi, §§ ix and x.

wholeness, the 'definiteness', of the entity which serves as its body (its physical pole), and consciousness is a high degree of such integration. Its objects are earlier phases of itself—of that same process by which it comes to be and is brought to the organic level at which consciousness emerges. Body and mind, object and subject, once again reveal themselves to be related as prior and posterior phases in a process of development, and knowledge is the sublation in experience of the process which has brought itself to consciousness through that development.

21. Furthermore, the determination of relevance involves the interrelation among themselves of eternal objects and the whole system of these principles is therefore implied in the creative process which is the world of nature. This system, however, is God in His primordial character, and God is therefore immanent in nature. The process, moreover, is a constant and progressive realization of definiteness and the urge to further integration can be satisfied only when all indefiniteness and indetermination (all vagueness, confusion and obscurity) has been eliminated. The forms of definiteness, again, are the eternal objects and their actualization in the process of nature is, therefore, the actualization of the nature of God. Apart from such actualization, eternal objects remain 'abstract', but when they have been prehended into the concrete actuality and are completely realized in the natural process, the Primordial Nature of God will have become one with the natural world. This ultimate realization Whitehead calls the 'Consequent Nature of God'. The prehension of God's Primordial Nature by actual entities is, on the other side, God's prehension of the process of nature, and this converts His Primordial Nature into His Consequent Nature.[1] Accordingly, God like all other entities is both physical and mental, and Whitehead explicitly tells us that in His Consequent Nature God is conscious.[2]

God, therefore, is not merely a transcendent system of abstract concepts, but is immanent and self-realizing in the creative process of the actual world—He is 'the principle of concretion'. As the determinant of definiteness, He is logically prior to all actuality; but as the ideal of attainment, He finds an ever-increasing fulness of realization in the continuous process of development in the universe.

22. Like Absolute Mind in the philosophy of Hegel, Whitehead's 'Consequent Nature of God' is the supreme reconciliation of the

[1] Cf. *Process and Reality*, pp. 42 and 488 ff.   [2] *Ibid.*

opposition between nature and mind; and the universe for him, as it is for Hegel, is in every aspect an identification of opposite concepts:

'The Universe is dual because, in the fullest sense, it is both transient and eternal. The Universe is dual because each final actuality is both physical and mental. The Universe is dual because each actuality requires abstract character. The Universe is dual because each occasion unites its formal immediacy with objective otherness. The Universe is *many* because it is wholly and completely to be analysed into many final actualities—or in Cartesian language, into many *res verae*. The Universe is *one* because of the universal immanence. There is thus a dualism in this contrast between unity and multiplicity. Throughout the Universe there reigns the union of opposites which is the ground of dualism.' [1]

[1] *Adventures of Ideas*, ch. xi, § xxiii.

Chapter XX

THE ROAD AHEAD

*

1. IN the foregoing chapters I have attempted to display the history of philosophy as what Collingwood declared it to be: 'a single sustained attempt to solve a single permanent problem'. The problem is that of understanding the place in and relation to the known world of the knowing mind. It has proved most nearly soluble in the light of principles presupposed in the modern conception of nature, but all the great philosophers of the past have made their contributions to the solution, and these very presuppositions of modern science, when stated in philosophical form, can be suitably couched at times in the language of one great philosopher and at times in the language of another. In the main we have discovered some truth in every opinion, for even the views of the empiricists, when we attend to the constructive side of their theories, show some affinity to and convergence with those of their philosophical opponents, displaying the universal tendency of a philosophical species to overlap with others.

I. EVOLUTION

2. The problem which has been my primary concern, however, has proved tractable only by the help of some form of the conception of evolution, which is the prevailing idea in modern scientific thought, and once the implications of this conception are fully grasped, it is possible to gain some intelligible notion of the place of the human mind in the world of nature.

An evolutionary process is one of becoming; one throughout which something is coming into being which is, nevertheless, all along in some way present. It is a process in which what is manifested in the earlier phases continuously becomes what emerges in the end. But what emerges in the end is not something sheerly different from the earlier phases, it is a more adequate realization of that which they too represented in a less adequate form. It is this 'something' which is evolving throughout the process. It is this 'something' which supplies the element of continuity, and this 'something' which unites the series of changes into a single process. Whatever this is, it is not wholly to be identified with any of the evolutionary phases, yet as the development proceeds it becomes progressively more true to say of the latest phase that it *is* what is being evolved and has all along been evolving; and a final phase which would end the development and enable us to say that whatever was evolving had completely come into being, would give us the complete answer to the question what the 'something' is. All earlier phases give us this answer only in greater or lesser degree. But that there is a final phase in which the process ends and is consummated is a necessary presupposition, for without it the whole conception of evolution would collapse. A series of changes without recognizable direction is no evolution, and without a goal of development no direction would be discernible.

The final phase, therefore, must be what unites the process, and accordingly it cannot be a mere phase, for it is not separable from the earlier phases and, in some way, must comprehend the process as a whole. It must be in every phase, for it is the realization of what is potential in each phase; and every phase must be in it, for every phase is an indispensable step to the realization of the end—not as a catalyst is indispensable to a chemical process, though it is no part of the final product, but as youth is indispensable to manhood, or memory to perception, so that what comes before is incorporated in what follows. The end must be the comprehension of the entire process and the process the unfolding of the end.

The paradox involved is apparent, for the end could not be final if it were not other than any prior phase and yet the process is not a development unless every phase is the end-in-becoming. Evolution, consequently, presents us with a standing contradiction which nevertheless is real. How can it be made intelligible? At the level of what Hegel called the understanding, or what Collingwood called the unphilosophical level, development or becoming is simply unintelligible, for at this level entities are held apart and distinguished in mutual exclusion so that 'a thing is what it is and not another thing'. At the level of reason—the philosophical level—this distinction is seen to rest upon an underlying identity and the particular things to be the differentiations of a concrete universal. As Collingwood has it, the specifications of the philosophical universal overlap. They constitute in consequence a series (and not a congeries) of distincta, a scale of forms, each of which is a degree of realization of the universal essence as well as a distinct exemplification of it. Being distincts, the forms in such a scale will necessarily have an aspect of mutual opposition; for, *qua* distinct, they are mutually exclusive. Yet, being gradations in a scale, they overlap and the opposition between them is reconciled in the overlap because

of the common universal they embody. Further, because of the overlap, any one of them contains all its predecessors repeated, as it were,
at a higher level, yet supplemented and transformed by synthesis with
their opposites. The process is thus a dialectical process in which the
lower phases are preserved sublated in the higher and the higher are
implicit in the lower. Accordingly, the universal has no sort of reality
apart from its specification. It is at once the entire scale and the final
phase—its consummation; and this is paradoxical only so long as we
try to conceive the process in material or mechanical terms as something
self-external. In terms of self-consciousness it is both natural and
necessary, for it is of the essence of conscious experience to be the
consummation of the process which has gone to produce it, and at the
same time to be the totality of the process. My 'experience' is my
conscious past sublated in my present state of mind, and my past
history as a consciousness is 'the course of my experience'. Here there
is no equivocation in the use of the word, for what we mean by
'experience' in either case is precisely the same.

An important corollary must be noticed here. The series must, as
Collingwood maintains,[1] begin with a minimum realization of that
which is about to evolve. Its initial term must have the value unity and
cannot be zero. Likewise, the series cannot go on to infinity (in the
mathematical sense), for there must be a definite finality about its
ultimate attainment. It would seem to follow that the process cannot be
wholly in time, if time is to be regarded as an infinite succession—
though it might be, if time, as in some modern cosmologies, is held to
be, like space, wholly contained within a 'finite' universe which is
nevertheless a complete whole in itself. This last suggestion, however,
is inadmissible, for even the de Sitter universe falls far short of absolute
completeness. At best it is a physical universe exemplifying the universal at a lower level of integration than that of life and mind. To be
complete it must come to consciousness, and at the stage of the evolutionary process where that occurs the development becomes logically
independent of time as the reflective interpretation of the temporal
series. It may still, as consciousness, require a temporal psychological
process, but it is not to be identified with this. The subjective succession, as we have seen, must not be confused with the objective totality
which is cognized by its means.[2] We may, accordingly, think of the
process of development as temporal so far as physical and animate
nature are concerned, but as transcending time at the point where the
development passes over from life to consciousness. If we think of it in

[1] *Philosophical Method*, pp. 82 ff. and 89 f.   [2] Cf. above, pp. 191, 193 and 249 f.

441

this way we can more successfully cope with the difficulty of reconciling the two necessary aspects of the final phase (or end): that it must be both immanent in the process and transcendent beyond it; it must at the same time sum up and comprehend the entire series of developing forms and constitute one of them, the last. These conditions are satisfied by self-conscious thought, which can grasp the logical unity of the complete scale of forms in a timeless analytical-synthetic discursus, and also operates as the activity of human minds which are temporal products of natural evolution.

But as conscious intelligence is admittedly the product of biological evolution, it must then be this which is immanent throughout nature, which is throughout being unfolded or evolved and which unifies the process.

3. The concrete universal finds adequate expression only in and as a conscious mind, and it is not fully expressed even in every form of consciousness. Our finite minds fall notoriously short of what is required; but they themselves develop; our knowledge grows and advances and with it our practical capacities are augmented. Even though the history of recent times gives little encouragement, we may hope, also, that conditions may be restored in which moral advancement, not altogether imperceptible in the past, may yet continue. Such development of human mentality, like all other development, is directed towards a perfection which would crown the entire process. Perfection is necessarily implied in the conception of development, both as its end and as immanent in all its phases. Consequently, the complete manifestation of the universal in a perfect mind is the inescapable presupposition of all science and all thought based upon the concept of evolution. An absolute mind must be implicit in every phase of the process, and that alone is what makes any phase (as a phase of the whole) intelligible. This Absolute is, accordingly, the ultimate criterion of intelligibility and truth, as it is also the ultimate standard of value and perfection. Here we have the real foundation of the Ontological Argument;[1] for the existence of God is presupposed as the ultimate criterion of all proof, as well as the ultimate source of all existence. It is an absolute presupposition of modern science.

II. THE PHILOSOPHICAL TASK

4. The future course of philosophical research must accordingly be to work out in detail the implications of this idea at the various stages

---

[1] *Vide* my discussion in *Mind*, XLV, no. 180, p. 478.

of the developmental process. I have tried to show that contemporary science has provided some evidence of the immanence of mind in natural phenomena, but much remains to be done in the way of philosophical interpretation of the results of scientific research to display the activity of thought in the various departments of its subject-matter. If this activity of thought is recognized as an objective synthetic-analytic activity, operating on the dialectical principles already outlined, and is not imagined to be a merely subjective process confined to the more specially developed operations of the human mind, it is very probable that much valuable material will be found in the deliverances of contemporary science, philosophical analysis of which will reveal just such an activity manifesting itself in the natural processes that the sciences study.

(i) Modern theories of space-time based upon the principle of relativity already give indications that physical space-time is entirely the product of an analytical-synthetic discursus. Alexander set out a doctrine of space-time (not wholly unrelated to contemporary theories of relativity) which when purged of empiricist importations leads to just such a conclusion. The essential point of his analysis is that both space and time are essentially unities in and through difference, and for that reason he finds it necessary to unite them into a single continuum.[1] More recent mathematical and physical research has provided further material and much remains to be done by way of working out its metaphysical implications.

(ii) Scientific theories of energy and matter, particularly the Quantum Theory, also point to a philosophical interpretation such as I am suggesting. Here we must notice the continuity established by contemporary physical concepts between space-time and matter. Particles which are the elementary constituents of matter have come more and more to be regarded as modifications of space-time itself. With the disappearance of the ether from physics, waves and fields have come to be regarded as modifications in the curvature of space, and matter itself, as we have seen, has been resolved into waves. There is every reason to believe, therefore, that the discursive activity manifesting itself as a system of spatio-temporal relations will be manifested likewise in energy and matter. It is true that the waves into which matter has been resolved are ultimately to be interpreted (at all events at the present stage of physical theory) as probability waves; but the statement of chances relevant to any particular phenomenon is not wholly unconnected with the particular type of curvature in space which the

[1] Cf. *Space, Time and Deity*, I, pp. 45 ff.

description of the phenomenon involves. The philosophical implications of all this have to be worked out, and Whitehead has led the way to the development of the kind of theory which would probably result. His principle of creativity is a principle of concrescence, and the process in which it results is one effected, in the main, by 'conceptual prehensions'. It is essentially the binding of a many into a one—an analytic-synthetic discursus—and the conception is the product of direct reflection upon the discoveries of modern physics.

(iii) The science of biology in all its branches affords a vast field for the application of the same idea. The material brought forward in Chapter XVII of this study is but a small fraction of what could be found. Bergson here has set the course and Driesch, Roux, Schaxel, Gurwitz and Spemann have provided a mass of material, but this has to be brought under a single principle of interpretation which would establish the continuity of biology with physics on the one hand and psychology on the other. The only principle likely to do this without distorting the facts in any of these fields is that of the concrete universal, which is also the principle of thought.

(iv) That psychological processes are manifestations of mind it is mere perversity to deny. But that they express, at characteristic levels, the activity of thought is by no means always self-evident. But the conformity of the psychologist's attitude to the prevailing conception of nature is illustrated by the fact that his dominant interest, nowadays, lies in the fact (which he recognizes and asserts) that living behaviour is *motivated*, and his predominant problem is to discover and explain the source of its 'drives'. The notions of teleology and purpose thus pervade psychological thinking and have done so since the early years of the century, when William McDougall established the view that living behaviour, the proper subject of psychological study, is distinguished by its recognizably purposive character. The same principle was assumed by Freud and his followers, as is evident from their use of the word 'libido' as the name for the primary psychological urge. But any attempt to dissociate purpose from thought is bound to stultify itself. It is sometimes alleged that animal 'drives' may be wholly accounted for in terms of the chemical action of the hormones on the central nervous system. But not only is it impossible fully to explain the physiological processes themselves as chemical action, it is clear also that no living behaviour, in its purposive aspect, can be divorced from the cognition of objects. It is never mere reaction to bare stimuli, but always the reaction to perception, and enough has been said of perception above to establish that, without the co-ordination and interpretation of 'data', no such thing ever occurs. But this co-ordination and interpretation is the typical analytic-synthetic activity of thought, and it is therefore at the root of all psychological phenomena.

The work of the Gestalt school of psychologists reinforces this opinion. For they insist that we can only understand psychological phenomena as involving the apprehension of patterned wholes and the manifestation of such wholes in the behaviour of the organism. The principle of the concrete universal is here again asserting itself and it is clear that a field of great promise is provided by the work of these psychologists for philosophical interpretation of the sort I am suggesting.

Consequently, a new philosophy of nature as the self-manifestation of the concrete universal (and, therefore, of mind) worked out in detail on the basis of scientific discovery, must be one of the tasks of future speculation. The new philosophy of mind will be continuous with it. Their newness, however, will be only relative for they will be outgrowths from the past and their tenets will be traceable to earlier thinkers. Only in this way is reliable philosophy developed and the craze to produce something new and strange results always in the appearance of something superficial and unsound. Leaving aside Aristotle and Hegel, Bergson, Alexander and Whitehead have all helped to point the way for further advance in the philosophy of nature, and Collingwood (fragmentary though much of his work on the subject remains) points the way for the future philosophy of history as that of the self-knowledge and self-development of mind.

5. It is the earlier phases of the process of evolution that we identify as nature and study through the natural sciences (though we also acknowledge a sense in which nature embraces the whole of the process). But at the stage where mind emerges as human personality capable of consciously organizing a life lived in co-operation with other persons, the continuation of the process becomes history—the process in which the human mind develops itself by its own conscious effort. It is not, of course, conscious at every stage, of the general trend of its own development, and becomes so in proportion to the degree of its self-consciousness and the extent of its reflection upon its own progress. Yet it is only by men's conscious aiming at ends which are known and desired that the course of human history is directed, even though the ends pursued are not always (in fact, are seldom) the actual result of the actions they prompt. The study of history is the study of *res gestae*;[1] the

---

[1] *Vide* Collingwood, *The Idea of History*, p. 9.

study of men's choices as they combine to constitute the organization of their social life and to facilitate the growing awareness of human nature and the world in which it is set. The mind of man expresses itself in social organization, in the production of wealth, the invention of economic and political forms of order, in the study of the sciences and the practice of the arts, in religion and in reflection upon his experience in all these fields. The course of its development, as displayed in every aspect of its activity, is the course of history. Accordingly, Collingwood sets us on the right path when he defines the study of history as the self-knowledge of mind,[1] and his statement that 'no one can answer the question what nature is unless he knows what history is'[2] is significant in the light of that definition. For history is not merely the chronicle of political events, but is the study of the self-development of thought and action, moral and political, artistic and religious, scientific and philosophical; and until one has grasped this, has recognized the direction in which the development proceeds and discerns the conclusions towards which it tends, one does not realize that nature too is the self-development of mind at a lower level of evolution, and one cannot answer the question which the philosophy of nature poses.

The understanding of the trend and character of this development, particularly with respect to scientific and philosophical thought, has been my object in the preceding pages—to trace its course and determine its direction and, by doing so, to arrive at a concept of nature which makes its relation to our minds intelligible and explains the apparent paradox of human knowledge.

A new philosophy of history is required of the sort suggested by Collingwood, which will be continuous with the philosophy of nature. The old denomination of the natural sciences as 'natural history' bears witness to the continuity between them and the sciences of human affairs, and Collingwood's identification of history as 'the science of human nature'[3] is the converse of the same fact. It is really all nature: physical, animal and human. It is all one continuous process of development, in and through which the basal activity which is the 'substance' of the real—the activity of thought—comes to consciousness of itself in and as a mind, makes its own history and reflects upon itself and the process of its own development, and by so doing makes still further progress towards the completion of the development in the infinite spiritual consummation which is God.

[1] *Vide Autobiography*, ch. x, and *Idea of History*, pp. 217 ff.
[2] *Idea of Nature*, p. 177.
[3] *Vide Idea of History*, pp. 205 ff.

III. THE PLACE OF THE HUMAN MIND

6. In the view of the world which would emerge in this philosophical scheme, the mind of man would be regarded, not as some sort of attenuated image or shade inhabiting his body, nor as a kind of ideal *camera obscura* in his head through which passes the 'magic shadow-show' of an external world, but as a phase in the process of evolution, implied in and presupposing all the lower phases and holding them within itself so that they constitute its nature. It is the fruition of their development. This being so, the lower phases cannot be argued away in Berkeleyan fashion, nor can they be denied existence in their own right, except so far as the claim to such existence is intended to cut them off from their dependence each upon its place in and integral membership of the whole process. The demands of the old-fashioned realism may thus be met. On the other hand, the emergence of mind at a late stage in the process is evidence that mind must be in some manner present from the first. It must be immanent, or implicit, in that from which it emerges. There can, therefore, be nothing in nature which is wholly devoid of mind. In fact, we have found that the presupposition of contemporary science is that the fundamental character of reality is an activity essentially of the nature of thought. The main requirement of the objective idealisms which followed Hegel in the late 19th century is, accordingly, also met.

7. The content of our experience, 'the world in the mind', is the world of reality. It contains the evidence which reveals at once the nature of itself and of the mind that knows it. As analysed by science and interpreted by philosophy, it proves to be a world of graded forms —not separate but linked in a continuous process of evolution—of which each is a fuller realization than its predecessor of a totality towards which the whole process moves, and the *nisus* towards which is the dynamic of the process. The nature of this totality is adequately presented by nothing less than conscious experience, which is a late phase in the process and is therefore implicit in all the lower forms. Though the consciousness of the finite human mind, which is so emergent, is not the finally adequate expression of the totality (but only the late phase), yet, as human consciousness is emergent in the process, it is potential in every earlier phase. Therefore the very existence of our consciousness, which (as Descartes discovered) cannot be denied, is evidence of the existence of all the lower phases of evolution which

are indispensable to its emergence. *Cogito ergo sum*, I may argue; but equally, *Cogito ergo res omnes sunt*. For the end of a development without its process is as unthinkable as is the process without the emergent realization of the end.

The world and the mind each guarantees the reality of the other. The mind is the possession of a finite creature in the world, because it realizes itself in and through the evolutionary process of the world. The world is in the mind as the object of its knowledge, because its knowledge is the world come to consciousness of itself, through that same process, in and as the mind. The process of coming to consciousness is the process of nature, which is sublated in that late phase, the consciousness of nature; and that again is the self-consciousness both of nature and of mind. The mind, therefore, is aware of the relation between itself and its object.

8. With the answer to this central question of the relation between the mind and its object, the allied problems resolve themselves. The human body is no mere piece of matter, it is a highly developed organism at a high level of evolution, not only with parts organically related to one another, but also organically related to other organisms and to inorganic nature. It presupposes numerous lower stages of development in the animal kingdom, all of which are organic and many of which (if not all) have reached so high a degree of organism as to have developed consciousness—which is no more than that high degree of 'integration' in which the whole becomes aware of itself. Consciousness is not a new entity, it is (as Alexander held) a new quality—one of wholeness or integrity—characteristic of a high degree of organic unity-in-difference. The relation of the mind to the body is thus that of successive phases in the development, the mind being the 'further integration' of the body. At the stage of development reached by *homo sapiens* it achieves self-awareness and claims the distinction of rationality. But this self-awareness is *ipso facto* an awareness of the world. Its immediate object is its prior phase: that is, the organic functioning of the body in sensation and feeling interpreted as the perception of an external world.

9. But this world, as we saw when discussing Hegel, is one which includes other conscious organisms and the individual's consciousness is developed from its earliest phases in community and mutual intercourse with them. Its awareness of other minds is but part of its awareness of its world and of itself (its body) as a part of the world, and

it presents no separate problem. The evidence of other minds is of the same order as that of any other fact in the world, and, when once the nature of our knowledge of the world is grasped and the relation between subject and object has been established, it can be accepted on equal terms with the evidence for any other established fact. It is the manner of functioning and the behaviour of other organisms, in every aspect; neural reaction, overt activity, facial expression, exclamation and speech are all direct evidence, according to the degree of their mutual integration, of the consciousness of others. The psychologist by studying behaviour cannot exclude the study of consciousness. He is studying all the evidence we have for its existence.

This conclusion is broadly the same as that reached by Professor Gilbert Ryle in his book *The Concept of Mind*,[1] but, as must be obvious, I come to it as a result of very different reasoning. Modern empiricism has reduced all theory to linguistics, and when one examines the way in which we speak of things one discovers incidentally something of the nature of the things themselves; but that is not the same as understanding them or evolving a proper theory about them. Professor Ryle analyses the way in which we use words and phrases referred to mental activities and states and so, incidentally, he reveals the sort of thing a mind does and is. He protests against the Cartesian dualism because he can interpret all words and phrases referring to the mind in terms of behaviour and dispositions to behave, recommending, in effect, that the concepts of mind should be dispensed with altogether. For the mind we must substitute a complicated set of dispositions describable in the main by means of hypothetical propositions. But is it not clear that hypothetical propositions have sense only in reference to some systematic structure of facts and that dispositions to behave in certain ways adjustable to differing circumstances (dispositions described so aptly by Ryle [2]) are no less than concrete universals? Each instance of behaviour is a particular instance adequately explained only by reference to a systematic context which gives its precise character to the disposition. It is a disposition to behave differently in different circumstances, but always in a characteristic way—cautiously, or placidly, or clumsily or intelligently, as the case may be. And what makes it possible to characterize each disposition precisely is just the conformity of the behaviour on each occasion to a general rule determining its type.[3] The behaviour, moreover, is such as could be possible only for a person aware of the situation in which he was acting. A

[1] London, 1949.   [2] *Op. cit.* pp. 42 ff., 71 f., 118, etc.
[3] Cf. Ryle, *op. cit.* pp. 120 ff.

system of such dispositions so complex and highly integrated as Ryle describes is a concrete universal at a very high level of concrescence— a level impossible of attainment without self-awareness. It is, in short, a mind as I have defined it. Few, however, are more likely to be shocked by my reasons for agreement with Professor Ryle than he himself; but his protest against the 17th-century dichotomy is none the less to be welcomed, because, though the view against which he argues has been obsolete for the last 100 years, it is still believed by many and continues to be the unrelinquished presupposition of modern empiricism.

IV. SCIENCE, PHILOSOPHY AND RELIGION

10. In viewing nature as the process of self-evolution of mind, we reaffirm the position which has already appeared at several points in the history of philosophy. Aristotle's interpretation of the universe is of this kind. God, as the form of forms, is the culmination of a scale in which each step is related to the preceding as form to matter (though this relation tends to break down in the case of God Himself, jeopardizing the whole system). Spinoza held nature to be a system of modes of varying degrees of perfection serially approximating to the perfection of God or Substance. Leibniz regarded reality as an infinite series of monads of increasing clarity of perception, culminating in God as the Monad of monads; and, finally Hegel's philosophy is the *locus classicus* of the conception of reality as a dialectical process in which the Absolute Mind defines, manifests and develops itself as a series of natural, psychological, moral and philosophical categories. Alexander and Whitehead belong to this same tradition, though Whitehead maintains greater consistency in developing the ideas of process and organism than does Alexander in developing that of emergent evolution.

Completely freed from empiricist prejudices, the conception of nature presupposed by contemporary science is akin to these. It returns, in some measure, to that of the Greeks, but it is not identical with theirs. Nature is not regarded hylozoically as a vast living animal, nor is it thought of as a set of intelligible forms imposed upon an unintelligible matter. It is not merely 'saturated and permeated' by mind; it *is* mind in its various forms of self-manifestation. But this does not mean that somehow everything firm and solid, everything concrete and rich in content, has been resolved away into *Hirngespinnste*. Mind is no longer conceived as something ghostly and attenuated. 'The ghost in the machine' is an exploded conception characteristic only of the 17th and 18th centuries. But we cannot simply deny the existence of the machine and espouse the ghost, any more than we can merely deny the existence of the ghost and deify the machine. Nature is neither machine nor ghost nor both in juxtaposition. Mind is now conceived as a concrete self-developing whole—its entire being and essence is the activity of self-development, the archetypal form of which is the activity of thought. Such a totality displays itself as a scale of forms, sections of which at appropriate levels are what we distinguish as 'physico-chemical activity', 'living activity' and 'mental activity', but nature, proper, comprises the entire gamut. For it is impossible to divide rigidly any section of it from any other; and though we habitually (and arbitrarily) apply the term to the lower phases more especially, nevertheless our recognition of its wider significance appears in the quasi-metaphorical personification of nature by both scientists and poets when they speak of 'Nature's purposes', 'Nature's experiments' and the like.

11. The philosophy of nature is thus part of the area of overlap between science and philosophy as species of knowledge. Modern science has progressed beyond the empirical attitude and tends to become philosophical. Meanwhile modern philosophy has more and more become allied to the sciences and our foremost philosophers are eminent scientific figures. This is no new situation in the history of thought, for in the past it has been the exception rather than the rule if science and philosophy have not gone hand in hand. But the movement begun at the Renaissance, in reaction against the theological tyranny of the Middle Ages, to split off the sciences as disciplines independent of philosophy, has now come full circle, and science, in the course of its own independent investigations, has come to adopt a philosophical position which is at the same time integral to the body of scientific theory. The philosophy of science is a speculation undertaken by professional scientists as belonging to their own special field.

12. Similarly, the 19th-century conflict between science and religion has passed away, except for vestigial concepts both in science and in religion handed down from the era of matter-mind dichotomy. In the process of evolution which is nature, the crown of the completed series of forms is God; and because, as such, He is the realization of a transcendent perfection, we tend in common parlance to speak of Him as apart from, beyond and above nature—and so, in certain moods to deny His existence altogether. But this, as has been shown, is to break

the undivided and indivisible chain of the series and to render nature as unintelligible and meaningless as the God which the atheist rejects. The same tendency, owing to the divine character of the higher activities of mind, leads to a denial by some of the objectivity (*i.e.* the reality) of values and even of the existence of thinking itself. But though God transcends the process of development—as must be the case if He is its fulfilment—He is also necessarily immanent in and throughout the process—or else it could not be a process of development at all. Consequently, the existence of God is the absolute and most indispensable presupposition of science, and so far from there being an alienation of science from religion in the modern era, there is and can only be the closest *rapprochement* between them if both scientific and religious concepts are rightly interpreted. Such alienation as there has been was due to the influence of empiricism, which created for itself a nature vacuously actual and banished from its purview the mind as a ghost in which only the superstitious could believe. God had then to be imagined as the Supreme Ghost and all things religious as ghostly— and therefore non-existent. But empiricism, though it persists, is a relic of the past without scientific basis, and has itself proved to be, in this age of evolution, relativity and quanta, an outworn and outmoded superstition.

INDEX

Alcmaion of Croton, 79
Alexander, S., 104, 247, 399-415, 418-421, 443, 445, 448, 450
Anaxagoras, 67, 78, 82-4
Anaximander, 69, 71, 80, 112
Anaximenes, 69-71, 75
Aquinas, St. Thomas, 117
Aristotle, 56-7, 63-4, 66-7, 73, 75-6, 78, 80-1, 83-4, 87-8, 97, 99-112, 117-18, 185, 204-5, 212, 220, 222, 228, 235, 247, 265, 352, 367, 374, 402, 417, 445, 450; *De Anima*, 64, 67, 99, 102-5, 108-109, 247; *De Interpretatione*, 104; *Metaphysics*, 63, 78, 81, 103, 109; *Nicomachean Ethics*, 108
Augustine, 113
Ayer, A. J., 5, 7, 25-8, 167, 247, 270, 319-20, 328-41

Bacon, F., 117, 419
Baer, K. E. von, 369
Bailey, C., 82
Bateson, W., 357
Beattie, J., 187
Bergson, H., 372, 375, 393-9, 416, 421, 444-5
Berkeley, G., 117-18, 132-3, 138, 140-163, 165-8, 176, 179, 200, 265, 267, 272-3, 296, 298, 310-11, 319, 384, 447
Bertalanffy, L. von, 358, 362-5
Blanshard, B., 345
Bode, B. H., 248, 250
Bosanquet, B., 32, 196, 233-4, 247, 256, 264, 268-70, 305, 373, 379, 417, 422, 425
Boveri, T., 362
Boyce Gibson, A., 117
Bradley, F. H., 196, 233, 250, 256-64, 267, 269-70, 305, 337, 395, 407, 416, 423, 431
Broad, C. D., 143, 267, 270, 298-302, 304, 316-17
Burnet, J., 66, 71, 73, 75-7, 79, 83, 86, 94, 98
Bywater, I., 71

Carnap, R., Carnapians, 17-26, 28-9, 328-30, 336-42, 344-9
Collingwood, R. G., 5, 29-42, 44, 56-7, 59, 63, 65, 67, 70, 75, 84, 91, 97-8, 111, 132, 189, 208, 222, 231, 247, 255, 266, 343-4, 351, 395, 439-41, 445-6; *Autobiography*, 5, 29-32, 39-40, 446; *Essay on Metaphysics*, 5, 30-1, 34-8,

41, 266, 343; *Essay on Philosophical Method*, 35-42, 222, 441; *Idea of History*, 35, 445-6; *Idea of Nature*, 44, 56, 59, 63, 65, 75, 91, 98, 132, 247, 395, 446
Conant, J. B., 352
Copernicus, N., 44; Kant's 'Copernican Revolution', 187-8, 199
Correns, C., 357
Cratylus, 87
Croce, B., 241, 243

Dampier, W. C., 379
Darwin, C., 203, 356-7
Democritus, 66, 78, 82, 86, 118
Descartes, R., 86, 117, 119-26, 135-6, 140-1, 149-50, 159, 196, 218, 410, 438, 447, 449; *Discourse on Method*, 121; *Meditations*, 121, 136, 159; *Principles of Philosophy*, 121
de Sitter, W., 379, 441
de Vries, H., 357
Diels, H., 71-83
Diogenes of Apollonia, 70
Dirac, P. A. M., 383, 391
Driesch, H., 358-64, 368-9, 373, 375, 444
Durkheim, 357

Eddington, A. S., 355, 378-80, 382-90
Einstein, A., 354, 377, 379, 381, 388
Emmet, D. M., 417, 419, 428
Empedocles, 78-82
Epicurus, 118
Euclid, 388

Farrell, B. A., 18
Frank, P., 380, 384
Freeman, K., 73
Freud, S., 444

Galileo (Galileo Galilei), 113, 123, 132, 384, 410
Gassendi, P., 119, 121
Gentile, G., 241
Glanvil, J., 118, 125
Goldschmidt, R. B., 363
Gorgias, 85
Green, T. H., 267, 269
Gurwitz, A., 365, 444

Haldane, J. S., 366-7, 391
Hallett, H. F., 211
Hegel, G. W. F., Hegelians, 34, 38, 101, 188, 196, 207, 228-56, 263-4, 266-7,

269-71, 294, 298, 355, 367, 371, 374, 388-90, 392, 396, 407, 414, 416-17, 422, 425-6, 429-30, 432, 437-8, 440, 445, 447-8, 450; *Encyclopädie*, 230-2, 235, 237-8, 240-1, 243-51; *Geschichte der Philosophie*, 232; *Phänomenologie des Geistes*, 251, 253; *Wissenschaft der Logik*, 236-8, 417

Heraclitus, Heracliteans, 71-3, 80, 87-8, 112

Hesiod, 80

Hobbes, T., 117-19, 257, 320

Holt, E. B., 409

Homer, 66, 80

Hörstadius, S., 362

Hume, D., 16, 113, 117-18, 132, 138, 143, 154-6, 158-60, 163-81, 187, 189, 198, 200, 265, 267, 272-3, 314, 319-20, 330, 336

Huxley, J. S., *see* Wells (H. G. and G. P.)

Huxley, T. H., 357

Jaeger, W., 66, 70, 72, 81

James, W., 272

Jeans, J. H., 45, 375-6, 381-5, 387-8, 390-1

Jerome, 113

Joachim, H. H., 45, 47, 94-5, 134, 136, 139, 213, 215, 217, 250, 263, 268, 280, 305, 314, 417

Joad, C. E. M., 387

Johnson, S., 141

Joseph, H. W. B., 219, 281, 345

Kammerer, P., 357

Kant, I., 16, 37, 138, 171, 179, 185, 187-200, 203-4, 207, 218, 230, 232-3, 249-250, 256, 262, 265-6, 270, 298, 301, 310-11, 318, 385-7, 389-90, 417, 422

Kemp Smith, N., 187

Knox, T. M., 35

Lamarck (J. B. de Monet), 357

Langford, C. H., *see* Lewis, C. I.

Laplace, P. S., 203, 376-7

Lavoisier, A., 352-3

Lazerowitz, M., 10

Leibniz, G. W., 207-8, 218-29, 253, 296, 416, 420-2, 427, 432-3, 450; *Discours de métaphysique*, 225-6; *Epistola ad Bierlingium*, 223; *Lettres à Arnaud*, 219, 222-3; *Monadologie*, 220, 222-6; *Nouveaux Essais*, 227; *Système nouveau de la nature*, 219; *Théodicée*, 218

Leucippus, 78, 82

Lewis, C. I., and Langford, C. H., 346-7

Lindsay, A. D., 188

Lloyd Morgan, C., 399, 403, 414

Locke, J., 47, 117-18, 120, 123, 125-45, 149, 152-3, 160, 164-8, 172, 187, 199-200, 265, 271-5, 277, 282, 284-5, 295-298, 301, 310-11, 319, 324, 399

Lorentz, H. A., 380-1

MacBride, E. W., 356

McDougall, W., 444

Maier, H., 86

Malcolm, N., 10, 15-16

Margenau, H., 375, 379

Maxwell, J. Clerk, 376, 381

Mendel, G., 357

Michelson, A. A., 377

Moore, G. E., 142-3, 149-54, 268-70, 298-302, 316

Morley, E. W., 377

Morris, C. W., 28, 350

Mure, G. R. G., 88, 95, 103-6, 108, 110, 190, 236-7, 250

Needham, J., 366-7

Nettleship, R. L., 269

Newton, I., 58, 118, 266, 376-7, 384, 410

Noll, 364

Olympiodorus, 71

Orphicism, 66, 68, 73-4, 80, 86

Parmenides, 76-8, 82, 111-12

Paul, G. A., 11

Pavlov, I. P., 357

Peirce, C. S., 272

Philolaus, 75

Planck, M., 380, 383, 388-90

Plato, 29, 36, 66, 73, 76, 80, 84-101, 107, 110-13, 185, 204, 228, 269, 318, 352, 417, 427; *Apology*, 86; *Laws*, 87, 99; *Meno*, 90, 93, 95; *Parmenides*, 96-8; *Phaedo*, 87, 89-90, 94, 98; *Phaedrus*, 87, 90, 93-4, 99; *Philebus*, 87; *Republic*, 36, 89-90, 93, 95-6, 101; *Sophist*, 87, 96, 99-101; *Theaetetus*, 29, 85, 90-1, 93; *Timaeus*, 89-92, 94, 99

Preller, L., *see* Ritter, H.

Price, H. H., 143, 154-60, 164, 166, 170-171, 174, 177-80, 298-302, 304-18, 320, 330, 333

Priestley, J., 353

Protagoras, 85

Pythagoras, Pythagoreans, 68, 71, 73-76, 88, 99

Raven, C. E., 113

Reyburn, H. A., 236

Ritter, H., and Preller, L., 79
Rohde, E., 66, 68, 74
Ross, W. D., 108-10
Roux, W., 358-60, 362, 444
Russell, B., 23, 28, 48, 138, 142-9, 265-266, 270-2, 274-303, 314, 320, 322, 324, 330, 417, 419; *Analysis of Matter*, 48, 283, 287, 291, 295; *Analysis of Mind*, 145, 274-81, 283-5, 287; *History of Western Philosophy*, 138, 142-5, 147-8, 266; *Human Knowledge: its Scope and Limits*, 281, 320; *Mysticism and Logic*, 283-4, 286-7, 290, 293, 295; *Our Knowledge of the External World*, 146, 270, 275, 278, 283-4, 286-287, 290, 295-7, 320; *Principles of Mathematics*, 279, 320; *Problems of Philosophy*, 275, 281, 286-7, 290, 295; Whitehead and Russell, *Principia Mathematica*, 266 n.
Ryle, G., 247, 449-50

Santayana, G., 409
Schaxel, J., 362, 365, 444
Schelling, F. W. J., 244-5
Schlick, M., 328
Schroedinger, E., 13, 391
Sextus Empiricus, 71, 85
Sinclair, W. A., 45
Smuts, J. C., 406-7
Socrates, 75, 84, 86-8, 90-1, 95, 98-9
Sophists, 85-6
Spemann, H., 365, 444
Spinoza, B. de, 53, 95, 117, 122, 125, 207-18, 220-2, 226, 228-9, 235, 247, 249, 260, 414, 421, 450
Stebbing, L. S., 45, 387

Taylor, A. E., 99
Tennyson, A., 411
Tertullian, 113
Thales, 69
Theophrastus, 79
Tschermak, L., 357

Vaihinger, H., 187
Vienna Circle, 8, 322

Weinberg, J. R., 319, 322, 325-7, 336, 338-9
Weismann, A., 358
Weldon, T. D., 4
Wells (H. G. and G. P.) and Huxley, J. S., 369-72
Whitehead, A. N., 217, 229, 243, 247, 253, 255, 263, 267, 269, 271-2, 294, 375, 379, 415-38, 444-5, 450; *Adventures of Ideas*, 423-4, 428-31, 433; *Concept of Nature*, 269, 379, 418; *Essays in Science and Philosophy*, 416; *Process and Reality*, 416-17, 420-2, 424-5, 428, 431, 434-7; *Science and the Modern World*, 255, 263, 271, 417, 419-21, 426, 428; Whitehead and Russell, *Principia Mathematica*, 266 n.
Whitrow, G. J., 384
Whittaker, E., 388
Willey, B., 4
Wisdom, J., 9-18, 25
Wittgenstein, L., Wittgensteinists, 6-18, 322-8, 336-7
Woodger, J. H., 366

Zeno of Elea, 85, 146